Check Out More Titles From HardPress Classics Series In this collection we are offering thousands of classic and hard to find books. This series spans a vast array of subjects – so you are bound to find something of interest to enjoy reading and learning about.

Subjects:
Architecture
Art
Biography & Autobiography
Body, Mind &Spirit
Children & Young Adult
Dramas
Education
Fiction
History
Language Arts & Disciplines
Law
Literary Collections
Music
Poetry
Psychology
Science
…and many more.

Visit us at www.hardpress.net

# Navy And Army Illustrated, Volume 5

## Anonymous

# Navy & Army Illustrated

A Magazine
Descriptive and Illustrative of Everyday Life in the
Defensive Services of the British Empire.

EDITED BY

Commander CHARLES N. ROBINSON, R.N.

## VOL. V.

LONDON:
Published by HUDSON & KEARNS,
83—87, SOUTHWARK STREET, LONDON, S.E.,
— AND BY —
GEORGE NEWNES, LIMITED,
7—12, SOUTHAMPTON STREET, STRAND, W.C.

PRINTED BY HUDSON & KEARNS, LONDON, S E.

# INDEX.

# THE
# NAVY & ARMY
## ILLUSTRATED.

Vol. V.—No. 49]  FRIDAY, OCTOBER 29th, 1897.

Photo. RUSSELL & SONS, Baker Street,

## ADMIRAL SIR WALTER HUNT GRUBBE, K.C.B.

THE late president of the Royal Naval College at Greenwich has seen active service in, perhaps, as varied a degree as any flag officer in Her Majesty's Fleet. Beginning with seven years off the West Coast of Africa, between 1854 and 1861, where he was repeatedly engaged with various enemies, and won his promotion to commander, Captain Hunt Grubbe, after a second spell on the same station, had a third experience of the West Coast in connection with the Ashanti War, where he commanded the Naval Brigade on shore in all the fighting, from Lord Wolseley's landing to the capture of Coomassie. In 1878 he was captain of the "Devastation," during Sir Geoffrey Hornby's memorable command of the Mediterranean Fleet, and after that succeeded the Duke of Edinburgh in the "Sultan." At the bombardment of Alexandria, as senior captain, the attack on the Northern Forts was entrusted to him. From 1885 to 1888 Sir Walter Hunt Grubbe was commander-in-chief on the Cape station, and from 1888 to 1891 he held control at our Western Naval Arsenal as Admiral Superintendent of Devonport Dockyard. He was president of the Royal Naval College, Greenwich, from 1894 until a few weeks ago. Sir Walter was awarded the C.B. for the Ashanti War, and his K.C.B. for the bombardment of Alexandria.

# NAVAL ARTIFICERS AT WORK.

THESE four pictures give some idea of the diversity of trades on board a man-of-war, though they by no means include all, for there are armourers, plumbers, and tinsmiths, in addition to those represented here, to say nothing of tailors and shoemakers.

The blacksmith's forge is set up in some convenient corner, there being as a rule no specially allotted position for it, unless in a vessel intended to be used chiefly as a workshop. In older times it was often "dumped" down on a few loose iron plates just forward of the boom-boats, and there one might see the sparks flying merrily in somewhat dangerous proximity to the foot of the mainsail, while the ship had a steady heel of some fifteen degrees, with an occasional lee lurch. But the blacksmith was not troubled by these small details; he pitched his tent in accordance with the commanding officer's orders, and if the forge "fetched away" or the mainsail caught fire it was not his look-out. There is some very small object under operation in the picture of the "Edinburgh's" forge, and the huge sledge wielded by the assistant seems more likely to effect complete annihilation than any useful purpose. There are, however, delicate gradations of force attainable even with a sledge hammer, and no doubt blacksmiths' mates, like the executioners in one of the "Bab Ballads," "vary very much in touch." Moreover, if their "touch" does not exactly suit the ideas of the head-blacksmith, he has a free, rough and ready, but extremely forcible method of expressing his views, so as to leave no possible room for doubt as to his opinion of his assistant's qualifications

The blacksmith may be called upon at any moment to do either a very rough or a very delicate piece of work. Like everyone else on board a man-of-war, he is supposed to be ready for any emergency, and a broken chain—which is very pretty smith's work—is as likely to be sent up to him as a crowbar that wants straightening. "Take it up to the blacksmith, and tell him to look sharp," says the autocratic commanding officer; and sharp he has to be, and is usually also skilful and efficient.

*Photo. R. ELLIS, Malta.*    *Copyright.—H. & K.*

*The Blacksmiths of the "Astræa."*

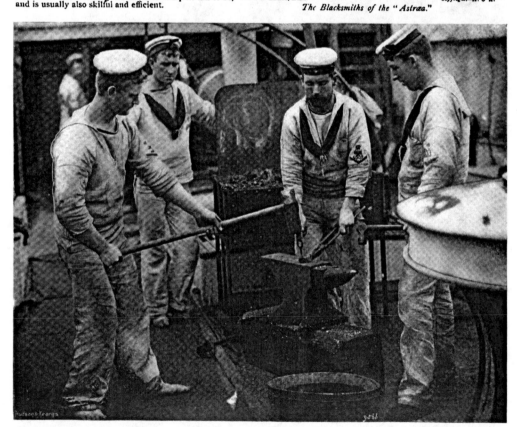

*Photo. F. G. O. S. GREGORY & CO., Naval Opticians, 51, Strand.*    *Copyright.—HUDSON & KEARNS*

*WORKING AT THE FORGE ON BOARD THE "EDINBURGH."*

The Naval electricians, who are getting the electric light ready, form an interesting group. They are manipulating some insulated wire, and joining up some of the familiar little globes which imprison the incandescent carbon. A rough wooden box of implements stands handily on top of a reel of wire, and one of the men is carefully scraping the exposed ends of the copper wires to make a clean junction.

A high standard of skill is exacted nowadays from those who qualify in this department, and the torpedo and gunnery lieutenants must keep themselves up to date in the complicated and ever-increasing inventions and improvements in the adaptation of electricity to the purposes of man, warlike or otherwise.

Then, again, we have the carpenters at work on board the "Edinburgh." The carpenter, like the blacksmith, has often

### ELECTRICAL ARTIFICERS AT WORK.

Obviously, it is not for the display of the white and blinding glare of the searchlight that they are so busily preparing; these little glass globes are used for ordinary purposes of illumination between decks, and also for an extraordinary display on the occasion of some festivity, such as a dance or a Jubilee celebration. It may safely be conjectured that our electricians here are preparing for some such occasion, and that the mellow glow of the little incandescent lamps will presently show up some loyal or patriotic device, or illuminate a gay scene of revelry, to the seductive strains of the band

to set up his establishment in some odd corner, as the near presence of a gun and some coils of rope testifies in this instance. Nor are they merely workers in wood. A modern shipwright must, if he would attain to any distinction in his craft, be a "wood and iron" man, and understand thoroughly the complicated construction of the "skin," the "double bottoms," the "sluices," and other paraphernalia of his ship. Many of them are extremely proficient in joiner's work, besides the heavier and less ornamental tasks of ship and boat repairs, etc. Probably the modern ship's carpenter would look down a good deal upon his brother of the old school, who often combined a considerable amount of manual skill with a grotesque ignorance of the fundamental laws of mechanics. An old carpenter's mate was one day fashioning a globular head to an upright timber for the side-ladder, when an officer good-humouredly rallied him on its not being strictly spherical. "No, sir," he replied, with an air of profound sagacity, "no man can make anything exactly round." "What, not a billiard ball?" "No, sir, of course not; if it was really round it would never stop rolling!"

Photo. F. G. O. S. GREGORY & CO., Naval Opticians, 51, Strand.          Copyright.—HUDSON & KEARNS.

THE CARPENTERS OF THE "EDINBURGH."

# FORECASTING A SHIP'S SPEED.

HOW to overcome, or at least how best to reduce to a minimum, the resistance that the passage through water of a shaped body such as the hull of a steam-ship encounters, has long been a serious problem of the first importance to ship designers. It is not yet solved, though by persistent experiment and scientific investigation a knowledge has been attained of the natural laws that govern the problem. The main causes of the resistance have been proved to be two—the

Photo. J. KING SALTER.          Sheerness.

*Bow Wave of a First-Class Cruiser at Full Speed.*

friction set up by the immersed surface in motion, and the formation and maintenance of waves, fresh series of waves being continually formed by the body in motion, which require a continuous expenditure of energy to overcome their action. As the speed of a ship accelerates, the friction and resistance mount up at an enormously increasing rate, as all who have seen the differences in volume of bow waves raised by ships when going at different speeds cannot help having remarked. In the case of the battle-ships and cruisers of the Royal Navy—and, indeed, nowadays, of all large steam vessels—special experiments are always made before launching.

The system adopted in England is that of the late Mr. William Froude, F.R.S., LL.D., who first showed how it is possible, when the wave-making resistance of a ship is known at a certain speed, to find the resistance of a ship of similar model. The problem had, however, compelled attention as long ago as the time of the famous engineer, Scott Russell; but it was by the late Dr. Froude and his experiments in a tank constructed at Torquay that the problem was first satisfactorily solved. Dr. Froude's work is at the present time being continued for the Admiralty under the direction of his son, Mr. R. E. Froude, F.R.S., a special tank 400-ft. long, at Haslar Gun-boat Yard, being the Government place of experiment. The models used are ordinarily 12-ft. long, and perfectly ship-shape below water, representing the forms of actually existing ships or of designs under consideration. Experiments with each model are made at varying speeds, a special dynamometer recording the resistances encountered with marvellous accuracy. From the various speeds and resistances so obtained a curve is constructed, and the full expression of the relation between the two is given between the limits of speed in regard to which information is required. Having gained the information for the model, it is calculated to the actual ship required on the acknowledged principle that the speeds of ship and model are related to one another as the square root of the lengths of the model and

From a Photo.                                    By a Naval Officer
*The " Repulse"—Wave Going In.*

From a Photo.                                    By a Naval Officer
*The " Repulse."—Wave Coming Out.*

proposed vessel, while the wave-making resistance varies as the displacement of the two varies. Our illustrations show the bow waves in two cases in connection with the first-class battle-ship "Repulse," and also in the case of one of our newest first-class cruisers.

# THE CYCLIST IN THE NAVY.

NO ONE, perhaps, has taken more kindly to the bicycle in its recent and improved form than he whose lot it is to serve afloat on board a ship of the Royal Navy. Indeed, it would be hard to name another modern invention of its kind that is more heartily and thoroughly appreciated, owing to the possibilities that it affords for obtaining health and recreation, both of mind and body, at a reasonable cost and at all times and places whenever a ship is in port, with the result that there is probably not a single ship on any station that does not possess its quota of cyclists of all ranks and ratings. To the officer his cycle affords a handy and ever ready means, in all places where there is a passable road or even bridle path, of getting good shooting or fishing at considerable

Photo. CRIPP.          *Cycle Racing at Whale Island—Just Before the Start.*          Southsea.

Photo. CRIPP.          *Cycle Racing at Whale Island—The Start.*          Southsea.

distances inland from whatever port his ship may be lying in. To other members of a ship's company the cycle affords an inexpensive and handy means of obtaining recreation, of enjoying themselves completely and healthily, and of seeing out-of-the-way nooks and corners in foreign parts, such as Jack's predecessors of the good old times could never have dreamed of visiting.

Of course, too, in the ever-present event in a man-of-war on a distant station of Naval brigade work on shore being required, the riders of cycles would always be available, according to their numbers, for making themselves generally useful, and playing, according to circumstances, very much the same parts that our military cyclist organisations, existing in the regiments of the regular Army and of the

Photo. CRIBB.          *Southsea.*

*The Champion Cyclist of the Navy.*

volunteers, would be called upon to perform in war. No Naval brigade of the future, it is safe to say, will find itself destitute of cyclists to act as scouts, or as orderlies to keep up communication whenever the services of these may be required.

There is another side, though, on which something has to be said about the Naval cyclist, and this is in regard to the opportunities for sport, after the manner and in the form delineated in our photographs, which the cycle affords to the sailor. In days to come it will probably be impossible to hold a fleet or squadron athletic sports meeting or gymkhana anywhere in which bicycle races do not find a prominent place on the programme or card of events. On many stations, as a fact, such a state of things is already the rule, the cycling "events" on these occasions being ordinarily conducted and carried out under the auspices and general direction of a Naval cyclist club, an institution frequently to be found at our Naval headquarters.

The photographs which we reproduce here were specially taken at the cycle races which formed a prominent and very popular feature of the sports at Whale Island, Portsmouth Harbour, held in the second week of September of the present year. Two of the photographs show cycle races being started: one, as a snap-shot taken just a few seconds previous to the competitors' start off, the second as a snap-shot taken at the actual moment of the firing of the signal pistol. The portrait given by itself is that of a notable Naval cyclist, Chief Petty Officer Duguid, captain of the "Vernon" Cyclist Club, kept up by men under instruction at the Portsmouth Torpedo Depôt School. He also holds the cyclist championship of the Royal Navy.

Chief Petty Officer Duguid at the Whale Island sports on September 9th won both the One Mile and the Five Mile Race, open to the whole Navy, and also at the same meeting the Three Mile Club Race open to his own club. He started from scratch each time. Chief Petty Officer Duguid was among the first of those seamen who took up cycling in the Navy. He captained the first Naval cyclist club organised in England, the "Mersey's" Cycling Club at Harwich, at which place, last year, he carried off the Army and Navy prize in the One Mile Race.

## How We Protect Our Deep Sea Fisheries.

AMONG other work performed by the Navy which the public knows little about, is the protection of our sea fisheries.

Amongst the thousands who indulge in the homely bloater or tasty kipper for breakfast, few of them know the amount of trouble that is taken, or money expended, in protecting the interests of the men who catch the fish from the poaching incursions of our various neighbours. Our coast is far better for trawling than theirs, consequently, while we are troubled with visits from them, our boats seldom go over to their coast. These visits have to be prevented, and we have gun-boats and cutters all round the coasts to prevent poaching.

If caught within our limits the offender is made a prize of, and towed into Folkestone, or some other port, where he is tried, and, if convicted, his fish and trawl are confiscated, he is heavily fined, and departs a sadder but wiser man.

A writer thus describes a cruise on board one of the gun-boats employed on fishery-protection duties off the S.E. coast, between Shoreham and the South Foreland:—The work on this division is carried out by a gun-boat and a cutter, each taking a week alternately. The duty consists in seeing that all fishing boats carry their proper lights, and numbers on their bows and sails; that the trawlers

Photo. WEST & SON.          *Southsea.*

*A GUN-BOAT ON FISHERIES PROTECTION DUTY.*

do not interfere with the drift-net boats, nor attempt to trawl within two miles of them or within one mile of the coast; and that all Johnnie Crapauds coming within the three-mile limit are overhauled and run in. Many an exciting chase takes place.

We weighed usually about eight p.m., and started for the fishing grounds, generally round Dungeness, or in Rye Bay, or off Beachy Head, keeping under the lee of Dungeness so as not to be seen, going eight knots. As we got up close, the officer of the watch would ask down the voice-tube to the engine-room, "Can you go sixteen, for a chase?" The answer came, "Twenty, if you want it, sir." Then we make out a boat; at her we go full speed; stop when close up to her. She is not fishing.

Night after night this goes on, until our week's end. On this last night our "sub," a smart boy, has the middle watch, and makes a neat capture. We leave Dover at eight p.m., and go for the "Ness" about ten knots, steam ready for twenty. Up to midnight no poacher is to be seen. We are not expected to-night—it is the cutter's week to patrol, and the fishermen know it, but we have an extra night unknown to them. Our "sub" is on deck now, and has sighted a Frenchman trawling, and makes up his mind to catch him. "Stop," goes the telegraph. "Out bow lights; search-light ready." "Quartermaster, call the captain, and tell him I'm going to board a Frenchman." "Sea-boat's crew, man your boat." When all are ready, "Full speed ahead," and you feel the little craft jump forward at about twenty knots. Our "sub" takes the wheel himself, and in a very short time is close alongside the boat. "Full speed astern." Down goes the boat, in jumps the "sub," and before Froggy has time to slip his trawl, he is caught red-handed one and a-half miles from the "Ness." The "sub" hails the captain from the prize. "Fix her carefully by cross-bearings, sir." The Frenchman practises a favourite little ruse. He was trawling, but he shifts his trawl-rope to his bows, and looks as if he was innocently riding at anchor. This ruse he endeavours to

*From a Photo.*                    *By a Naval Officer.*

*One of the Watch.*

follow up, when our "sub" asks, "Why are you fishing in our waters?" He replies, with an innocent smile, "Me no fish! Me anchi-or!" "Anchi-or be d——d," says the "sub." "Your anchi-or catch fish!" The Frenchman sees the game is up, and smilingly says, "Why you come, and not the cutter?" The reply is, "Heave in your trawl." Up comes the trawl over his bows, with a few fish inside, and a big stone which the Frenchman shows, saying, "Me drag two hours for dis." Our "sub" airs his French, and says, "*Très jolie,* have a cigarette." The skipper laughs and heaves the rock overboard, and they smoke the cigarette of peace.

In the meantime those on board the gun-boat have not been idle, for they have the captured vessel in tow. We arrive off Folkestone and send our prize into harbour. At eleven a.m. the captain and "sub" proceed to the police-court with the French skipper. Caught red-handed and well inside the limit, he pleads poverty, and that he did not know he was so close. He is convicted, and fined £10, or three months' detention.

My friends, the crews of the fishery-protection fleet, sometimes have exciting work, but as a rule their luck is very like that of the proverbial fisherman.

*From a Photo.*                    *By a Naval Officer.*

*A Prize.*

*Photo, WEST & SON.*                    *Sculkies.*

*THE FLAG-SHIP OF THE FISHERIES PROTECTION SQUADRON.*

### A SEAMAN BUGLER.

NAVAL buglers are taught in the training-ships, and there is usually no lack of candidates for the acquirement of the art. Bugling, like many other accomplishments, looks very easy when we see a skilled performer producing loud clear notes and reeling off the various calls with tuneful precision; but there is a certain knack about it which everyone does not easily acquire, and, as with the cornet and other brass instruments, it requires an adaptable mouth to attain any great proficiency. Sometimes a skilled bugler's lips go wrong, and in sounding some familiar call he produces some fearful and wonderful notes, which excite the derision of his shipmates, who tenderly enquire whether there is not a cockroach in the bugle, this being a traditional excuse supposed to be handed down in the Service from some ingenious bugler of bygone days, who invariably excused himself on this plea—a very plausible one in some old wooden ship in the tropics, where one would have been pretty safe in assuming the presence of cockroaches in anything, from the bugle to the captain's pudding. Judging by the purple hue and painful contortions of visage often noticeable in the young bugler when blowing a long call, it must be rather hard work, though some make much "heavier weather" of it than others. The lad represented in the picture is a fine specimen of his class. No doubt he is a very efficient performer, and a slight frown, together with the necessary compression of the lips, are the only distortions his countenance suffers. Of the value of the bugler there can be no doubt; he is in request at all hours, afloat and on shore.

THE NAVY & ARMY ILLUSTRATED. NOTES & QUERIES. SERVICE AFLOAT & ASHORE

For continuity of Naval service, and high honour gained thereby, in one family, that sprung from Alexander Hood, Squire of Mosterton, in Dorsetshire, stands out unique. His eldest son had three grandchildren. The elder, Arthur, was lost in a hurricane in the West Indies. The second, Alexander, died in the moment of victory, when in command of the "Mars," 74, when that ship captured "L'Hercule," 74, after a brilliant engagement. The third, Samuel, by a series of magnificent services, earned a baronetcy, which was inherited by his nephew, Alexander, a son of the "Mars" hero. This nephew left two sons, the elder being the father of the present Baronet, the younger the present Lord Hood of Avalon, raised to the peerage for his own Naval services. The second son of the squire had two children, who both earned well-deserved Naval peerages—Samuel, Viscount Hood, and Alexander, Viscount Bridport. Both titles still illustre the peerage, and to-day to the latter is added one of Nelson's honours, the Dukedom of Bronté, the present Lord Bridport inheriting that title from his mother, the only child left by William, the brother and successor of the great hero.

* * * *

" K. H."—The dynamite gun you refer to is mounted so as to completely command the bay and harbour of New York. Judging by the results of recent experiments, it is not at all improbable that when this new type of ordnance reaches greater perfection, it will find a more universal adoption. In the practice carried out some months ago, the gun was loaded with a 350-lb. projectile containing 500 lb. of nitro-gelatine, which on striking the water, at a distance of 2,100 yards from the gun, exploded, raising an immense column of water, the shock of the explosion making itself felt so far off as thirty miles. The agent employed for projecting the shells is compressed air, conveyed to the gun through pipes from a power-house concealed below ground a mile or so inland. A remarkable feature in these experiments is that, with rapid firing, the gun becomes cooler instead of hotter, owing to the vacuum formed immediately following upon discharge. The interval elapsing between each round, during this rapid firing, was only ten seconds.

* * * *

A correspondent writes:—"A few days ago, turning over an old volume of Commonwealth State Papers, I came across the following. It is the blank form of a captain's commission under Blake, and was the form apparently issued in 1649, on the Navy being reorganised and placed under the three generals at sea—Popham, Blake, and Deane:—

"'By the Comrs. for Ordering and Mannaging the Affaires of the Admiraltie and Navy.

"'Ordered

"'That Captaine . . . . be and is hereby constituted and appointed Commander of the . . . And the said Captaine . . . . is hereby authorized and enjoined forthwith to make his repaire on board the said . . . . and to take the care and command of the same as Captaine for this next . . . . Expedition. And therein to performe the duty and trust of his place with all faithfullness, circumspection, and dilligence; And the severall and respective Officers and company belonging to the said . . . . are hereby required and strictly charged to observe and obey his Commands and Orders as their Captaine. And the said Captaine . . . . is likewise hereby required punctually to observe and follow the Instructions given him herewith and such further Orders and Instructions as he shall from tyme to tyme receive from ourselves, the Generalls or Superior Officers of the Fleet, according to the discepline of Warre for the service of this Commonwealth; And this shall warrant his soe doing.

"'Given under our hands and Seals at Whitehall this——'"

" D. E. T."asks: "Would you kindly let me know the name of the first embodied regiment in the British Army?" The Royal Scots (Lothian Regiment) claim this distinction, being, they affirm, descended from a body of Scots in the service of Gustavus Adolphus, King of Sweden. The King, we read, in 1613 enrolled two companies of these Scottish warriors under his banner, some being drawn from their native land and others from the Netherlands, where they had been in the service of the States-General of the United Provinces. The first colonel of the regiment was one Sir John Hepburn, or Hebrun, a Scotsman of great valour, who saw much service under Gustavus, and later in the French Service. When Charles II. had disbanded the Army of the Commonwealth, he received this regiment, then "Douglas' Regiment," into his service, 1661. The Coldstream Guards likewise claim the distinction, having been in the British Service as early as 1650, and which he took with him from Coldstream in 1660, when he marched to London. The Coldstream Guards were (unlike the other regiments of the Commonwealth Army) never disbanded.

* * * *

Students of old Navy Lists, which are very interesting reading, embodying, as they do, many names which, in the person of descendants, are handed down from generation to generation, must have often noticed the huge batches of flag officers with seniority of the same date, and this at a time when drastic schemes of Naval retirement were not in vogue. Captain Mahan, in his recent exhaustive and most interesting " Life of Nelson," solves the enigma. Promotion to flag rank being then, as now, a question of seniority, " the practical difficulty," he says, " of getting at a captain of conspicuous ability was met by one of those clumsy, yet adequate, expedients by which the practical English mind contrives to reconcile respect for precedent with the demands of emergency. There being no legal limit to the number of admirals, a promotion was in such a case made of all captains down to and including the one wanted, and Lord St. Vincent, one of the most thorough-going of Naval statesmen, is credited with the declaration that he would promote a hundred down the list of captains, if necessary, to reach the one demanded by the needs of the country." The system, however effective as regards the favoured individual, cannot have been an unmixed blessing to the senior officers promoted, who necessarily remained, often for the rest of their career, as unemployed flag officers, instead of sharing in the chances of glory, to say nothing of emoluments and prize money which would have fallen to their lot as captains.

* * * *

In every battalion, regiment, corps, and department of the Army good clerks are greatly in demand. This applies specially to the Army Service Corps and Army Ordnance Corps, where the openings are more numerous and the chances of promotion better. In the cavalry, infantry, and artillery a clerk can find scope for his pen in the orderly-room or quartermaster's stores. In the former case a man may reasonably hope in time to become orderly-room sergeant, if he be steady and well up in his work. The only extra qualification for this is the possession of a 1st class certificate of education. To become a " military staff clerk" the following qualifications are required of a candidate:—He must not be below the rank of corporal or bombardier, and his service must not be less than three years; his character must be thoroughly satisfactory, and he must possess a 1st class certificate of education. A shorthand writer is usually given the preference. The Army Pay Corps offers also employment to suitable non-commissioned officers, but the vacancies are greatly sought after. It would be impossible here to state the pay that can be earned by clerks in every capacity; suffice it to say that it is in all cases good.

* * * *

" J. K."—Your ship draws a foot more water aft than forward, and you want to reduce her draught by six inches, so that she can enter the Suez Canal. The simplest plan is to place the ship on an even keel, as the change of trim will bring about the reduction of draught. The necessary shifting of weights can be calculated nearly by dividing the displacement tonnage by twelve, which gives roughly the "moment" to change trim one inch, i.e., half-an-inch at either end. In long fine ships this will give rather too small a figure; in short broad ships rather too large. Take the " Rodney," of 10,300 tons, as an example. Dividing by twelve gives 858 foot-tons—this being a broad ship, say 800—and the moment required to change trim twelve inches will be 9,600 foot-tons. One hundred and seventy-two of her heavy projectiles will weigh just ninety six tons. Move these forward through a distance of 100-ft., or half the number 200-ft., and you will be very near the mark.

MANY queries have been put to me regarding the Chitral medal. Strictly speaking, there is no such medal. Last year it was decided to issue a new medal for general service on the Indian Frontier, to be known as the India 1895 medal, the first operations for which it was to be awarded being the Chitral Campaign. The design of this medal is the figure of an English infantry soldier standing beside a Bengal cavalry trooper. The ribbon is dark green and red in alternate stripes. This medal replaced that which is known as the India medal No. 2, which did duty for so many expeditions, including the Persian and Burmese Wars, and which was hung by a ribbon in scarlet and dark blue stripes. India medal No. 1 was first granted in 1851 to the surviving officers and men of the numerous engagements in India between 1799 and 1826. Its ribbon was pale blue.

* * * *

"Is there not," writes a correspondent, "some curious story in our Naval annals attaching to the name of the new battle-ship about to be built, the 'Vengeance'?" There is, and it attaches specially to the first bearer of the name, a French twenty-eight-gun privateer of the Seven Years' War, which was captured by us in 1758 and taken into the British Navy under her original name. The story is told in connection with a celebrated battle that the "Vengeance" had in the West Indies in December, 1757, with the British privateer "Terrible," a twenty-six-gun ship, which, according to legend, had been equipped at Execution Dock, with, for officers, Captain Death, Lieutenant Devil, and Surgeon Ghost—so at least it is recorded in the old ballad of "Captain Death." The fate of the "Terrible" in her fight with the "Vengeance" no doubt gained additional point from the names of the three officers. The "Terrible" was taken after fighting until, the story goes, out of her crew of 200 only twenty-six were left alive, all wounded. The "Vengeance" lost 240 out of her crew of 360. She was able at the last to close and board the "Terrible," both ships crawling off into a French port, barely able to keep afloat.

* * * *

HERE is the story of the fight as told in another of the numerous ballads on the battle printed in England during 1758—an extract from the ballad called "The Terrible Privateer":—

> We had not long been on the sea
> Before a Frenchman we did see.
> He was well rigg'd and came from France,
> Her name was called the bold "Vengeance."
>
> We crowded all the Sail we could,
> Our thundering Cannons fire we would
> Many a gallant Sailor fell
> On board the Ship call'd the "Terrible"
>
> Powder and ball did fly so fast—
> Four hours and a-half this fight did last.
> But a sad misfortune us befel
> On board the Ship called the "Terrible."
>
> We boldly gave them gun for gun
> Till the blood out of our scuppers di 1 run,
> Our Captain and our men being sla n,
> We could no longer the fight maintain.
>
> To board us then they did begin,
> And stripp'd us naked to the skin,
> And put us all in the hold together,
> Where twenty-seven poor souls were smother'd.

* * * *

"L. F."—The Order of St. Michael and St. George was instituted in 1818. The Victorian Order, instituted last year, is hardly on a par with the others, as it is a family Order, the management of which the Queen retains in her own hands. But when we add to the list the Distinguished Service Order, the Royal Red Cross, and the Crown of India (for ladies), all created within the last few years, it will be seen how greatly Her Majesty has extended the possibilities of reward.

* * * *

OUR readers who, for some months past, have been following the adventures of Mervyn Crespin and the beautiful Juana Belmonte in "Across the Salt Seas" (and, judging from the marks of approval which we and the author have had spontaneously testified to us, the number of those readers must be legion) will be glad to hear that a new novel in volume form, from the pen of Mr. Bloundelle-Burton, is now to be obtained at all libraries. This is his romance, "The Clash of Arms," just published by Methuen and Co., which has been running in the *People*, and is of thrilling interest, the period chosen being the romantic one of Turenne's war in the Palatinate. Beyond putting our readers in possession of this fact, we will not divulge any more of the story, since they will, undoubtedly, take immediate steps to secure it for themselves and to peruse the remarkable adventures of the hero, a Cavalier soldier, in a gloomy château in the heart of the Vosges Mountains. Marlborough, who, in "Across the Salt Seas," appears at almost the summit of his fame, is here presented at the beginning of his career, and as the colonel of "The Royal English Regiment" in the service of Louis XIV.

THE EDITOR.

## A STORY OF BADAJOS.

### By GODFREY MERRY.

IT is now about twenty years since visitors to the Tower of London were sometimes shown the objects of interest within its walls by a warder who had seen service during the Peninsular War. There may, however, be those who, like the writer, remember a dapper little man who used to walk somewhat lame, in consequence of a wound he had received in one of his legs at the storming of Badajos. The old rifleman (for such he had been) could sometimes be induced to fight his battles over again, and his story of Badajos used to run somewhat as follows:—

"I had volunteered for the forlorn-hope at Rodrigo, and, having escaped without a scratch, I was determined to try my luck at Badajos, so I again volunteered when it was decided to storm that town. A forlorn-hope is the advanced party of a body of troops detailed for storming a fortified place, and, as a consequence, comes in for most of the hard knocks, although in the old days its survivors used to have the first pick of anything worth having when they once got inside, which was, I fancy, the reason why there was never a dearth of men willing to come forward for this dangerous duty. The French used to call them *les enfants perdus*. This particular assault was one of the toughest contests that British troops have ever been engaged in, compared to which the battle of Waterloo itself afterwards appeared to me to be more like a field day in Hyde Park.

"Having received a double allowance of grog, we fell in at about eight o'clock in the evening of the 6th of April, 1812. The stormers were composed of men from the different regiments of the light division. One of our sergeants, coming up, informed the officer in command that a ladder party was wanted. 'Take the right files from the leading sections,' was the prompt order. No sooner said than done. I and my front rank man were immediately tapped on the shoulder for the ladder party. I then gave up all hope of ever seeing the next day. At Rodrigo we had fatigue parties for the ladders, but now the case was altered, for, besides having much longer ladders, we had to carry grass-bags—long sacks about six feet by three, filled with grass or hay, and so stuffed as to enable a party, in case the ladders could not be fixed in time, by pitching them into the trenches, to descend with comparative safety.

"The word was now given to the ladder party to advance, so away we started in the direction of the town, the rifles, as usual, keeping in front. So far things had gone well enough, but now our troubles were to begin, for, having to pass rather near to some earthworks on our left, we were seen by a French sentry, who challenged. This was followed by a shot from the fort, and another from the walls of the town. Then a fire-ball was thrown out, which cast a bright red glare of light around us, and instantly we were saluted with a volley of grape-shot, canister, and small arms, the combination being poured in among us as we stood on the glacis at a distance of about thirty yards from the walls. As may be supposed, we did not stand there long. Three of the men carrying the ladder with me were shot dead at once, and its weight falling upon me, I fell backwards with the grass-bag on my chest. The remainder of the stormers rushed on, regardless of my cries or those of the wounded men around me, for now that we were discovered, the safest thing to do was to make for the breach as soon as possible. Many in passing were shot, and fell upon me, so that, what with the other encumbrances with which I was entangled, I was well-nigh suffocated. At length, after a strong effort, I managed to extricate myself, and, drawing my bayonet, rushed towards the breach. There I found some men putting a ladder down the ditch, and, not daring to pause, fresh lights being still thrown from the town, I slid down the ladder; but, before I could recover my footing, was knocked down again by the bodies of men who were shot in attempting the descent. However, I again succeeded in getting clear of the dead men, and rushed forward; but before I knew where I was, I found myself up to my neck in water. Being a strong swimmer, I struck out for the breach, in doing which I lost my bayonet. Without rifle or any other weapon, I succeeded in clambering up a part of the breach and came to a *cheval de frise*, consisting of a piece of heavy timber studded with sword blades, turning on an axis; but, just before reaching it, I was struck on the chest, whether by a grenade or stone or by the butt-end of some Frenchman's musket, I can't say, but down

I went, senseless. I could not have remained long in this plight, for when my senses had in some measure returned, I could see our fellows still rushing forward, each seeming to share a fate more deadly than my own. The fire continued in one horrible and incessant roar, as if the mouth of hell itself had opened to vomit forth destruction upon all of us, and this was rendered still more appalling by the fearful shouts of the combatants and cries of the wounded that mingled with the uproar.

"I now, strange to say, began to feel as if my arms and legs were entire, for at such moments a man, I believe, is not aware of his wounds. I had lost all the frenzy of the courage that first possessed me, and actually felt all weakness and prostration of spirit, while I endeavoured, among the dead bodies around me, to screen myself from the bullets of the enemy. While I lay in this position, the fire still continued blazing over me in all its horrors, accompanied by screams, groans, and yells, and the crashing of falling stones and timber. For the first time for many years, I believe, I uttered something like a prayer.

"After this sort of thing had continued for some time, I heard cheering, which I knew to proceed from within the town. I can hardly describe the effect this shout of our men had upon myself. My spirits seemed to return at once, and I wanted to be up and doing again; but the moment I attempted to move, I found I could not do so. I had been wounded. At what time I know not, but a musket-ball had passed through the lower part of my right leg, and two others had gone through my cap. At the moment of this discovery I saw two or three men coming towards me, and I was glad to find they belonged to my regiment. One of them, being in my own company, exclaimed, 'What! is that you, Ned? We thought all you ladder chaps were done for.' He then assisted me to rise.

"We walked in the direction of the town, although I found that, even with the help of my comrade, moving was a difficult matter for me. I felt drops of blood trickling down my face, and discovered that one of the balls in passing through my cap had somewhat torn my scalp. In this crippled condition, leaning upon my comrade, and using his rifle as a crutch, I entered the town that had been so gloriously won. We still, however, heard occasional firing and cheering from one end of the town, and imagined the fight was not over, although, as we soon afterwards learnt, the chief part of the French had retired to the citadel, where they surrendered on the following morning, and were marched out prisoners of war.

"We had just turned the corner of a street, when we observed some men, whom we could see were wearing French uniforms. The moment they saw us they all disappeared, with the exception of one man, who seemed disposed to level his musket at us. So, without waiting results, my comrade rushed at him and wrested the firelock from his grasp. I suppose I was angry and irritated by the smarting of my wounds, but suddenly a desire for revenge took possession of me, and I said, 'O'Brien, let me have the satisfaction of shooting this scoundrel; he may be the man who has brought me to this state.' I took my comrade's rifle and presented it at the man's chest, with the full intention of shooting him through the body, but, when I was about to press the trigger, the Frenchman dropped on his knees and begged for mercy. The rifle fell from my hands, and I was glad that I had not committed an act, in a moment of irritation, for which I should never have forgiven myself afterwards. We made the man our own particular prisoner, and a very useful, worthy fellow he was.

"We looked anxiously around for a house where we could obtain some refreshment, and, if truth must be told, a little money at the same time, for, wounded as I was, I had made up my mind not to be a loser by the transaction. At

the first house we knocked at no notice was taken of the summons, so we fired a rifle into the keyhole, which sent the door flying open. This, indeed, was our usual method of forcing locks. We entered the house, and found a young Spanish woman crying bitterly and praying for mercy.

"As the house looked poor, we quitted it in quest of a better, proceeding in the direction of the market-place. It was a dark night, and the confusion and uproar that prevailed in the town I can never forget. There were drunken soldiers, in quest of more liquor, who made the night hideous with their oaths and shouts, the reports of firearms and smashing in of doors, together with the appalling shrieks of helpless women, which might have induced anyone to have believed himself in the regions of the damned.

"We entered a house which was occupied by some men of the 3rd Division. One of them, seeing that I was wounded, struck off the neck of a bottle of wine with his bayonet, and presented some of it to me, which relieved me for a time from the faintness I had previously felt. I had not been long seated at the fire, which was blazing up the chimney, fed by mahogany chairs broken up for the purpose, when I heard screams for mercy from an adjoining room. On hobbling in, I found an old man, the proprietor of the house, on his knees, imploring mercy of a soldier who had levelled his musket at him. I, with difficulty, prevented the man from shooting him, as he complained that the Spaniard would not give up his money. I told the wretched landlord, in Spanish, as well as I could, that he would only save his life by surrendering his cash. Upon this he brought out, with trembling hands, a large bag of dollars from under the mattress of the bed. These, by common consent, were immediately divided among us. The whole treasure, to the amount of about 100 or 150 dollars, enveloped in an old nightcap, was emptied and divided into small heaps on the table, according to the number of men present, and called out the same as messes in a barrack-room. I must confess that I participated in the plunder, and received about 26 dollars for my share.

"The victors, who had by this time got tolerably drunk, next proceeded to ransack the house. Without dwelling on the frightful scene that followed, I may say that our men, more infuriated by drink than before, again seized on the old man and insisted on a fresh supply of liquor, and his protestations that he possessed no more were as vain as were all attempts to restrain them from ill-using him.

"It is to be lamented that the memory of an old soldier should be disturbed by such painful reflections as the foregoing scenes must give rise to; but it is to be considered that men who besiege a town in the face of such dangers generally become desperate from their own privations and sufferings, and when once they set foot within its walls—flushed by victory, hurried on by the desire for liquor, and maddened by drink—they stop at nothing. They are literally mad, and hardly conscious of what they do in such a state of excitement. I do not state this in justification, I only remark what I have observed human nature to be on these occasions.

"Next morning, in the streets, I saw the Duke of Wellington giving directions about the erection of gallows for the punishment of men found guilty of plundering or of such atrocities as had been enacted over-night. But he was surrounded by a crowd of drunken British soldiers, who, holding up bottles with the necks knocked off, containing wine or spirits, cried out to him, 'Nosey, old boy! will you drink? The town's our own! Hurrah!' A little further on I found two carts standing each on end, and a pole was placed across between them. On each were suspended two halters; but I never heard that anyone was hanged."

The hero of the foregoing story lived till a ripe old age within the walls of the Tower, and when the end came the ruling passion was strong in death, for the last words he was heard to utter were, "Rodrigo and Badajos!"

# THE SOUTH POLE
## BY ADMIRAL SIR VESEY HAMILTON G.C.B

"Drifting towards the pack"

THE safe return of Nansen from his most adventurous and successful Arctic Expedition, in which he has beaten all previous records by a very large margin, has stimulated the public thirst that has been gradually increasing for a more extensive knowledge of the Antarctic regions than we at present possess.

Owing to the expansion of our Australasian Colonies it is of far greater importance that the veil of ignorance still hanging over the South polar world should be removed than it was nearly sixty years ago, when the celebrated expedition, under that experienced and scientific Polar navigator, the late Sir James Ross, the discoverer, in 1831 or 1832, of the North Magnetic Pole, was despatched on its Antarctic voyage.

A brief notice of the earlier attempts at Southern discovery may not be uninteresting, as to them we owe the discovery of Australasia.

The ancients had mathematically proved the earth to be round, and, to balance the quantity of Northern land, supposed there must be, as a counter-poise, a vast Southern continent. Therefore, after Columbus's discovery of the Western Continent had roused the civilised world to the importance of geographical research, the quest for this "Terra Australis incognita" served to stimulate Southern discovery as that for the N.W. passage had done Northwards; and, at the close of the sixteenth and commencement of the seventeenth centuries, led to many valuable discoveries by the Spaniards and Dutch. The former navigators discovered the South Sea Islands—now named Solomon Islands—Marquesas, New Hebrides and other parts of New Guinea, Cape Yorke, and the islands off the north part of Australia—Torres Straits being named after the Spanish commander of the expedition of 1606. Australia was also discovered in the same year by the Dutch, from whom its name of New Holland is derived. The Chinese, probably, knew already of its existence. Its coasts were gradually explored during the next century. Tasmania was discovered in 1642 by Tasman, who named it after Van Dieman, the Governor-General of Dutch India. One cape in New Zealand, also discovered by Tasman, is named Maria Van Dieman, after his lady love.

In 1798 Bass, the surgeon of Flinders' Expedition, sailed through the strait now called by his name, thereby proving the separation of Tasmania from New Holland.

In 1772 Captain Cook was sent out by England "to put an end to all diversity of opinion about the curious and important question which had long engaged the attention of the learned men and maritime Powers of Europe" as to "whether the unexplored part of the Southern hemisphere be only an immense mass of water, or contain another continent." Having ascertained that Australia was of continental dimensions, not extending very far towards the South, he pushed on towards the Southern Pole, and was the first voyager to cross the Antarctic circle. which he passed in three separate years—

1773-4-5—in long. 40E., between 100 and 110 W., and again between 135 and 148 W. The highest latitude he attained was 71S. in 107W. On each occasion his Southern progress was arrested by close fields of ice. He sums up: "I have now made the circuit of the Southern Ocean in a high latitude, and traversed it in such a manner as to leave not the least room for the possibility of there being a continent, unless near the Pole and out of reach of navigation."

Thus he carried out his instructions, but adds: "That there may be a large tract of land near the Pole I will not deny, on the contrary, I am of opinion there is. The excessive cold, many ice islands, and vast floats of ice, all tend to prove there must be land towards the South."

Cook saw no land south of Sandwich Land, lat. 59S., long. 70W., which he called the "Southern Thule," and of which, as of South Georgia, he gives a most gloomy account, both being deficient in fauna and flora. The means he took to preserve the health of his crew succeeded admirably, only one man dying during the three years' absence from England. For his success he was posted, made a F.R.S., and received the Copleian Gold Medal, and is most certainly the father of modern Naval sanitation. Cook was, however, mistaken in supposing his discovery was the Southern Thule. Dirk Cherrits, in 1599, had discovered the land, now known as the South Shetlands, in 64S. and 60W., about 600 miles due south of the Falkland Islands. The next voyager to cross the Antarctic circle was Bellinghausen, a Russian, who, in 1821, discovered Alexander Island, in 68S. 72W.; and Petra Island, in 68S. 91W. He sailed through several degrees of longitude, just to the southward of the Antarctic circle, but made no other land discovery.

In 1823 Weddel, an enterprising captain of a sealing vessel, whose narrative is very interesting, attained the latitude of 74N., in long. 35W., with a sea of clear ice; but as his object was sealing, and not discovery, it was inconsistent with his duty to his owners to proceed further South. Another sealing captain, Biscoe, in the employ of Enderby and Co., discovered Enderby and Kemp Islands, on the Antarctic circle, between the meridian of 45 and 60 E. In 1839 Captain Balleny, also engaged in a sealing expedition, discovered Sabrina Land and Balleny Island, a little to the northward of the Antarctic circle, in 120E. longitude.

In 1840 a French Naval Expedition, under Dumont D'Urville, discovered and coasted Adelié and Claire Land, between 140 and 130 E. In the same year Captain Wilkes, commanding a large expedition fitted out by the United States Government, extended these discoveries on the same parallel.

Now we come to the only expedition which, consisting of H.M.S. "Erebus" and "Terror," has ever been properly equipped for Antarctic exploration. It was fitted out in 1839 under command of Sir James Ross, who had accompanied Parry in all his Arctic voyages.

He also was with his uncle, Captain Sir John Ross, in the "Victory," 1830-34, when Sir James, who was a skilled magnetic observer, planted the British flag on the North Magnetic Pole of the earth. The principal object of the voyage was for magnetic observations and the hope of planting our flag on the South Magnetic Pole. Hobart Town was left November 20th, 1840, and the Antarctic circle crossed January 1st, 1841, in 171E.

The heavy ice pack was soon after met with, and on the 10th was cleared in 70S. 174E., magnetic dip. 85, and a course was shaped for the magnetic pole, but soon afterwards an insuperable obstacle was discovered. High land, rising into lofty peaks, was directly in their way. The highest, 10,000 feet high, was named Mount Sabine. This discovery wrested from the Russians the record they had held for 20 years by Bellinghausen's discovery of Alexander and Petra Islands in lat. 69S. Favoured by fine weather, a landing was effected on a small island, named Possession Isle, in lat. 72S. long. 171E., the English flag planted on it, and the health of Her Majesty and Prince Consort drank. Very stormy weather for some days prevented much progress, but by perseverance Weddel's record of 73S. was beaten, and on January 25th they were in 75S., 170E., dip. of the needle 88°. "Two of the mountains of this magnificent range, named Melborne and Monteagle, were here seen to great advantage; the immense crater of the former and more pointed summit of the latter rose high above the contiguous mountains, forming two of the many remarkable objects of this most wonderful and magnificent mass of volcanic land."

Franklin Island, named after Sir John, in 76S., 168E., dip. 88.24", was landed on.

On the 28th of January, 1841, four years after Her Majesty's accession, Mount Erebus, an active volcano, was discovered emitting flame and smoke in great profusion. It is 12,400 feet high, and near it is an extinct volcano 10,900 feet in height, named after the other ship, Mount Terror. The most southern land discovered in lat. 79S. was named after Sir Edward Parry. Thus about 500 miles of a magnificent range of mountains, extending from

"A Providential Escape"

71S. to 79S. and named Victoria Land, was discovered.

The next great discovery was more interesting. It was the great southern ice barrier, extending in lat. 78S. in an east direction from Mount Erebus for 450 miles. It was a perpendicular cliff of ice varying from 150 to 200 feet above sea level, and appeared to be perfectly flat and level at the top, and without any fissure or promontories on its even seaward face. Nothing was seen beyond it, so if attached to land it must be low land. A sounding of 330 fathoms was obtained within a quarter of a mile of the foot of the ice cliff; it must have therefore exceeded a thousand feet in thickness. The highest latitude attained by the ship was 78.4" S. in 165E. Gigantic icicles depended from projecting points of the cliff, proving it sometimes thawed, which otherwise would not have been supposed, for the temperature at noon was 18° below freezing point in the corresponding month to our August, and young ice was forming rapidly, a proof of the approach of winter.

After persevering for some time unsuccessfully in attempting to turn the eastern portion of the continent, and so attain the magnetic pole or a nearer approach to it, or to find suitable winter quarters, a northern course was shaped, and the accuracy of Balleny and Biscoe's discoveries, mentioned previously, confirmed. Hobart Town was arrived at on the 6th April, more perils and dangers having been encountered than befel any other expedition. On one occasion a heavy swell was driving them down on a pack in which 84 large icebergs and many smaller ones were counted, and no opening discernible, "the waves breaking violently against them,

dashing huge masses of pack ice against the precipitous faces of the bergs. . . . Sublime as such a scene must have appeared under different circumstances, to us it was awful, if not appalling." For eight hours they were helplessly becalmed, drifting towards the pack. The sea was too heavy to attempt towing with boats. "We were now within half-a-mile of the bergs. The roar of the surf and the crashing of the ice fell on the ear with fearful distinctness, whilst the frequently averted eye as immediately returned to contemplate the awful destruction that threatened in one short hour to close the world and all its hopes, joys, and sorrows upon us for ever. We called on the Lord and He heard us, a gentle air filled our sails, gradually freshening, and we were saved."

This is only one out of many narrow escapes during the voyage—from most of which steam have saved them.

In 1842 both ships were nearly destroyed by contact with heavy masses of ice in a gale of wind in the pack, the rudders were carried away, and much damage sustained, owing to a heavy sea penetrating very much further into the pack than is generally the case; and on clearing the pack, which had occupied fifty-six days to get through, instead of four as in the previous year, part of the "Erebus's" sternpost was broken, and the ship much strained. Owing to this loss of time, only a few more miles of the Barrier were traced, and only six miles higher latitude was reached than in the last year; and the rapid approach of winter compelled a return to the North. The Falkland Islands, where they wintered, were arrived at on April 6th, the two ships having had a narrow escape from destruction by a collision in a heavy gale at midnight.

The "Erebus" was an hour alongside a berg, and had to set the mainsail flat aback in a heavy gale to make a stern board, washing away gig, quarter-boats, etc., the lower yardarms scraping against the sides of the berg, from which only a strong undertow kept the ship off. This was as narrow and Providential an escape as the eight hours' drift towards almost inevitable destruction previously mentioned.

The Falkland Isles were left on the 4th of September, 1842, in search of more Antarctic adventures. But after taking magnetic observations off Cape Horn and the South Shetland Island, an impenetrable pack in lat. 65 to 63S., long. 55 to 20 W., prevented any progress to the south. On February 4th, the pack with which they had been fruitlessly contending for six weeks was cleared, and on the 14th, Weddel's track was crossed in 65W.; but where he found a clear sea, they met a dense, impenetrable pack. Such are the vicissitudes of ice navigation. On March 1st the Antarctic circle was crossed in 12W., only three days earlier than it had been crossed in former seasons. The highest latitude attained was 71.30S.; in longitude 14.29W.

The homeward voyage was made without any event of importance. The line of no dip was crossed in 13S. 28W. The ships were paid off at Woolwich on September 23rd, 1843. For his discoveries Sir James Ross received the Founder's Medal of the Royal Geographical Society of London, and the Gold Medal of the Royal Geographical Society of Paris.

Since this voyage the Antarctic regions have been recently visited by English and Norwegian sealers, but no discoveries have been made of any importance.

With regard to the future, I consider an Antarctic expedition a certainty, for after a careful analysis of the various Polar expeditions I have come to the conclusion that while steam has only increased the power of Arctic navigation from twenty-five to fifty per cent., and decreased its risk to about the same amount, in Antarctic exploration the risk is less by about seventy-five per cent., and the range doubled, if not trebled, by the use of steam. Moreover, bergs, instead of being the danger they formerly were, may be utilised by a steam-ship, as was done by Sir George Nares in the "Challenger."

ACROSS THE SALT SEAS

A ROMANCE OF WAR AND ADVENTURE
By JOHN BLOUNDELLE-BURTON
AUTHOR OF
"IN THE DAY OF ADVERSITY", "DENOUNCED!",
"THE HISPANIOLA PLATE" ETC.

### SYNOPSIS OF PREVIOUS CHAPTERS.

The hero, Mervyn Crespin, who was lately lying in the prison of Lugo under sentence of death, found himself there in consequence of a hazardous ride which he set out upon from Vigo (of which town he has taken part in the capture), with the intention of joining the English forces under the command of Marlborough in Flanders. He had originally been despatched by the Earl on a mission to the British Fleet, which was expected to be at Cadiz (but which, he found, had left for England), as the bearer of important information, to the effect that some Spanish galleons from the West Indies had altered their destination and, instead of going to Cadiz as they intended, had, on hearing that the English Fleet was in the neighbourhood, proceeded to Vigo. On his way to the former place he encounters a man whose name is supposed to be Carstairs, and whom he and the master of the ship regard as a pirate. Meanwhile, he by chance falls in with the English Fleet proceeding home, is enabled to convey the information he carries to Sir George Rooke, and goes with it to Vigo. After the battle, which is fully described, he is sent to board one of the captured galleons, and here he encounters a young Spanish gentleman, as he supposes, who has been a passenger in the ship, as well as a monk named Father Jaime. Eventually, he sets out for Flanders on the above-mentioned perilous ride, the young Spaniard, who has conceived a warm friendship for him, insisting upon being his companion, to which he reluctantly consents. They encounter on their way a series of stirring adventures, culminating in a fight with the Spanish police near Lugo, and, though entering that town in safety, are followed and arrested. Father Jaime has, however, joined them and rendered great assistance in the combat, he appearing no longer as a monk (which he acknowledges himself not to be), but as a traveller, himself on the road to Lugo. As they are endeavouring, however, to escape capture, they overhear a conversation between Jaime and the man Carstairs, who has also arrived here in search of some property which he expected to come in the galleons, and from it they learn that Jaime, far from being a monk, is no less a person than the renowned Gramont—a pirate loathed in the Indies, but supposed to be long since drowned. Señor Belmonte, the young Spaniard, who has confided to the Englishman that he does not know who his father was, except that he was enormously rich, also discovers now to his horror that Gramont is the man. This, however, is not the only discovery made. As the young Spaniard reels against Crespin on gleaning that intelligence, Crespin, in his turn, is astonished to find that his companion is a woman and not a man, who has travelled to Europe disguised thus in her hopes of finding Carstairs, whose right name is Eaton, and of punishing him for having robbed her, and also because the galleons would not take women as passengers. All are arrested and imprisoned, Gramont and Crespin being sentenced to death, while Juana, which is the name of the Spanish lady, is protected by the Alcáide of the city, who has fallen in love with her striking beauty. He, however, agrees that her father shall be allowed to escape provided she leaves Spain with him; and, in her misery and despair over that father's crimes, she consents. Crespin regrets his fate the more because he has learned from Juana that her instantaneous love for him at first sight was the principal thing which prompted her to insist on accompanying him in all his dangers. Also, he knows now how fondly he has come to love her. He has, however, been able to himself escape in the manner recently described, and to follow Juana until he comes up with her in company with the Alcáide. How he made that escape, and how he and Gramont have once more met, has also been shown in the chapters preceding the present instalment, which deals with the last parting between her and her father, and also describes how they set forth in their endeavour to proceed either to England or Holland.

### CHAPTER XXX. *(continued)*.

AGAIN Gramont paused—again he pointed at the coming dayspring outside. Hurriedly he went on:

"I saved her. Twenty of us—that vile Eaton was one!—passed through the garden at midnight—up those stairs—killing three blacks who opposed us" (even as he spoke, I remembered Eaton's ravings in "La Mouche Noire" as to the dead men glaring down into the passage; knew now what his frenzied mind had been thinking upon!)—"bore her away. Enough! Three months later we were married in Jamaica."

He rose as though to go forth and seek his horse, determined to make his way on in spite of the snow that lay upon the ground in masses—because, as I have ever since thought, he had sworn to undergo his self-imposed expiation of never gazing more upon his child's face!—then paused, and spoke once more:

"She died," and now his voice was broken, trembled, "in giving birth to her who is above; died when I had grown rich again—so rich that when I sailed for France, my pardon assured, my commission as *Lieutenant du Roi* to Louis in my possession, I left her with Eaton, not even then believing how deep a villain he was—thinking, too, that I should soon return. Left with him, also, a fortune for her. What happened to her and that fortune you have learnt. Yet, something else you have to learn. Her mother's name had been Belmonte, and, when Juana fled from Eaton, driven to do so by his cruelty, she, knowing this, found means to communicate with an old comrade of mine, by then turned priest and settled at the other end of the island—at Montego. Now, see, how things fall out; how, even to one belonging to me, God is good. 'Twas in '86 I sailed for France, my commission in my cabin—nailed in my pride to a bulkhead—when, alas! unhappy man as I was, I encountered a great ship—a treasure-ship, as I believed, sailing under Spanish colours. And—and—the Devil was still strong in me—still strong the hatred of Spain —the greed and lust of plunder. God help me! God help and pardon me!" and, as he spoke, he beat his breast and paced the dreary room, now all lit up by the daylight from without. Even as I write I see and remember him, as I see and remember so many other things that happened in those times.

"We boarded her," he continued a moment later. "We took her treasure—she was full of it—yet, even as we did so, I knew that I was lost for ever in this world, all chance of redemption gone—my hopes of better things passed away for ever, too. For she was sailing under false colours—she was a French ship, was one of Louis' own, and, seeing that we ourselves carried the Spanish flag, the better to escape the ships of war of Spain that were all about, had herself run them up. And we could not slay them and scuttle the ship—we had passed our word for their safety—moreover, if we would have done so, 'twas doubtful if we should have succeeded. There were women on board, and, though they fought but half-heartedly to guard the treasure that was their King's, they would have fought to the death for those. Therefore, we emptied the vessel of all that it had—we left them their lives—let them go free."

"But why—why?" I asked, still not comprehending how this last attack upon another ship—and that but one of many stretching over long years!—should be so fateful to him. "Why not still go on to France, commence a new life under better surroundings?"

"Why!" he repeated. "Why! Alas! you do not understand. I, a commissioned officer of the French King, had made war on his ships, taken his goods—also," and he drew a long breath now, "also, there were those on board who knew and recognised me—we had met before—knew I was Gramont. That was enough. There was no return to France for me—or, if once there, nothing but the block or the wheel."

"God pity you!" I gasped. "To have thrown all chance away thus. Thus!"

He seemed not to heed my words of sympathy, wrung from me by my swift comprehension of all he had lost; instead, he stood there before me almost like those who are turned to stone, making no movement. Only, speaking as one speaks who recounts a doom that has fallen on him, like one also who tells how hope and he have parted for ever on wide diverging roads.

"There were others besides myself," he continued, "who had ruined all by this act of madness, others of my own land who had gained their pardon and lost it now for ever, flung away all hopes of another life, of happier days to come, for the dross that we apportioned between ourselves, though, in our frenzy, we almost cast it into the sea. As for my share, though 'twas another fortune, I would not touch a pistole, but sent it instead to the priest I have spoken of, sent it by a sure hand, and bade him keep it for my child, add it to that which Eaton held for her. Told him, too, to guard it well, since neither he nor she would ever see me more!"

"And after? After?" I asked.

"Afterwards—we disbanded, parted. I went my way, they theirs. Earned my living hardly, yet honestly, in Hispaniola—should never have left the island had I not discovered that Eaton, who even then sometimes passed under the name of Carstairs—that was his *honest* name!—and who had long since disappeared from my knowledge, was having a large amount of goods and merchandise shipped under that name in the fleet of galleons about to sail as soon as possible. And then—then—knowing how he had treated the child I left in his care—the child of my dead and lost love—I swore to sail in those galleons, to find him—to avenge——" He paused, exclaiming, "Hark! What is that?"

Above—I heard it as soon as he!—there was a footfall on the floor. We knew that Juana was moving, had arisen.

"Go to her," he said, and I thought that his voice was changed—was still more broken. "Go. It may be she needs something. Go."

"Is this our last farewell? Surely we shall meet again."

"Go. And—and—tell her—her father—— Nay—tell her nothing. Go."

O'ermastered by his words, by, I think, too, the misery of the man who had been my companion through the dreary night—my heart wrung with sorrow for him who stood there so mournful a figure—I went, obeying his behest.

But, ere I did so, and before I opened the door that gave on the stairs leading to her room, I took his hand, I whispered:

"It *is* our last farewell. Yet—oh! pause and think—she is your child. Have you no word—no last word of love nor plea for pardon—to send?"

For a moment his lips quivered, his breast heaved, and he turned towards the other and outer door, so that I thought he meant to depart without further sign. But, some impulse stirring in his heart, he moved back again to where I stood; murmuring, I heard him say:

"In all the world she has none other but you. Remember that. Farewell for ever. And—in days to come—teach her not to hate—my memory. Farewell."

Then, his hand on the latch of the outer door, he pointed to the other and the stairs beyond it.

"You are better I said."

While I, stealing up them, knew that neither his child nor I would ever see him more, and, so knowing, prayed that God would at last bring ease and comfort to the erring man.

As I neared the door of the room in which she had slept, she opened it and came forth upon the bare landing—pale, as I saw in the light of the now fully broken day, but with much of the fever gone. Also with, upon her face, that smile which has ever made a summer in my heart. Both then and now.

"You are better?" I said, folding her to me. "Better? Have slept well? Is it not so?" But, even as I spoke, I led her back to the room whence she had come. She must not descend *yet*! "You have not stirred all through the night, I know."

"I dreamed," she said, "that you came to me, bade me farewell for ever. Yet that passed, and again I dreamed that we should never part more. Therefore I was happy, even in my sleep." Then broke off to say: "Hark! They are stirring in the house. Are the horses being prepared? I hear one shaking its bridle. Can any go forth to-day?" and she moved towards the window.

"Juana," I said, again leading her back, although imperceptibly, to the middle of the room, "do not go to the window. The cold is intense—stay here by my side."

Not guessing my reason—since it was impossible she should understand what was happening below!—I led her back. Led her back so that she should not see one come forth from the stable whom she deemed dead and destroyed—so that she should not be blasted by the sight of her father passing away in actual life from her for ever. Next, I sat down by her side and led the conversation to our future—to how we should get away from here to England and to safety. Also I told her not to bewail, as she did again and again, my failure to proceed further on my journey to Flanders and the army; demonstrated to her that at least there had been no failure in the mission I had undertaken. That my secret service had been carried out, and well carried out, too, and, consequently, my return mattered not very much with regard to a week or month. The allies, I said, could fight and win their battles well enough without my aid, as I doubted not they were doing by now, while—for the rest—had I not done my share both here and in Spain? Proved, too—speaking a little self-vauntingly, perhaps, by reason of my intense desire to soothe and cheer her, and testify that she, at least, had been no barrier in my path of glory—that I also, though far away from my comrades, had stood in the shadow of Death, had been face to face with the grim monster equally with those who braved the bayonets, the muskets, and the cannon of Louis' armies.

But all the time I spoke to her my apprehension was very great, my nerves strung to their bitterest endurance, my fear terrible that she would hear the man below go forth;

that she might move to the window and see him—and, thus seeing, be stricken by the sight.

For I knew that he was moving now, that he was passing away for ever from this gloomy spot which held the one thing in all the world that was his and linked him to the wife he had loved so dear; knew that, friendless and alone, he was about to set forth into a dreary solitude which held no home for him nor creature to love him in his old age.

I heard, too, the bridle jangling again; upon the rough boards of the stable beneath the windows of the fonda, I detected the dead, dull thump of a horse's hoofs; I knew that the animal was moving—that Gramont was setting out upon his journey of darkness and despair.

"You are sad, Mervan," she said, her cheek against mine, while her voice murmured in my ear, "Your words are brave, yet all else belies them."

"It is not for myself," I answered, "not for myself."

The starry eyes gazed into mine, the long slim hand rested on my shoulder.

"For whom?" she whispered. "For whom? For him? My father?"

I bowed my head—from my lips no words seemed able to come—yet said at last:

"For him. Your father." Then, for a moment, we sat there together saying nothing.

But soon she spoke again.

"My thoughts of him are those of pity only, now," she murmured once more. "Pity deep as a woman's heart can feel. And—and—my love—remember, I never knew who my father was until that scene in the inn at Lugo—thought always his, our, name was, in truth, Belmonte. The secret was well kept—by Eaton, for his own ends, doubtless; by my father's friend, the priest, who had once been as he was, for past friendship's sake. If I judged him harshly, a life spent in pity for his memory shall make atonement."

As she said these words, while I kissed and tried to comfort her, she rose from where we were sitting and went again to the window, I not endeavouring to prevent her now, feeling sure that he was gone. For all had become very still, there was no longer any sound in the stable nor upon the snow, which, I had seen as the day broke, had frozen and lay hard as iron on the ground beneath it.

Yet. something there was, I knew, that fascinated her as she gazed out upon the open; something which—as she turned round her face to me—I saw had startled, terrified her! For, pale as she had been since we had met again here, and with all the rich colouring that I loved so much gone from her cheeks, she was even whiter, paler now, than I had ever known her—in her eyes, too, a stare of astonishment, nay, terror.

"Mervan!" she panted, catching her breath, her hand upon her heart. "Mervan. Look, oh! look," and she pointed through the window.

"See," she gasped, "see. The form of one whom I deemed dead—or is he in truth dead, and is that his spectre vanishing into the dark wood beyond?—see, the black horse; the one which he bestrode upon that night—oh! Mervan—Mervan—Mervan—why has his spirit returned to earth? Will it haunt me for ever? For ever punish me because of my shame of him?"

While, as I saw the horseman's figure disappear now—and for all time!—into the darkness of the pine forest, she lay trembling and weeping in my arms. To calm which sorrow, and also bring ease to her troubled heart, I told her all.

## CHAPTER XXXI.

### ALWAYS TOGETHER NOW.

The frost held beneath a piercing East wind which blew across the mountains that separated Portugal from Leon, so that now the snow was as hard as any road, and there was no longer any reason to delay our setting forth. More especially so was this the case because my beloved appeared now to have entirely recovered from the fever into which she had been thrown by the events of the past weeks.

"I am ready, Mervan," she said to me the next day, "ready to depart, to leave behind for ever these lands—which I hope never to see again—to dwell always in your own country and near you."

Wherefore I considered in my mind what was best now to be done. That we were safe here in Portugal we knew very well—only it was not in Portugal that we desired to remain, but rather to escape from it. To cross the seas as soon as might be—to reach England or Holland. Yet how to do that we had now to consider.

I have said we were safe here, and of this safety we had sure proof not many hours after her unhappy father had departed on his unknown journey; a journey that led I knew not where, no more than I knew what would be the end of it.

And this proof was that, in the afternoon of that day, the landlord of the inn came running into us as fast as he could scamper across the already frozen snow; his face twitching with excitement, his voice shaking, too, from the same cause.

"Holy Virgin!" he exclaimed, while he gesticulated like a madman, his wife doing the same thing by his side, "who and what have I sheltered here in my house? Pirates and *filibusteros*, gaol breakers and murderers, women whose vows are made and broken day by day. 'Tis mercy we are not all stabbed to the death in our beds." And again he grimaced and shook and spluttered.

"You are as like," I said, sternly, with a tap to my sword hilt, "to be stabbed to the death now, and at once, if you explain not this intrusion and your words, fellow."

For he had roused my ire by bursting in on Juana and me in the manner he had done, and by frightening her, as I perceived by the way she clung to me. "Answer at once, what mean you?"

"There are at the frontier," he said, speaking now more calmly, also more respectfully, as he noted my attitude, while his wife ceased her clamour, too, "some half-dozen Spaniards from Lugo all demanding where you—and—and—the wo—the lady are; also one they call their *Alcaïde*, as well as one whom they say is a hundred-fold assassin. Likewise, they affirm they will have you back to Lugo."

"Will they! Well, we will see for that. Meanwhile, what say the frontier men on this side, here in Portugal?"

"They dispute. They refuse. They say 'tis whispered o'er all our land that the King has joined with the English brigands——"

"Fellow, remember." And again I threatened him.

"With the English nation against Spain and France. It may be so or not, I do not know. Yet I think you will be spared to—to—slay——"

Again he halted in his speech, reading danger in my glance, while I, turning to Juana, bade her keep calm and await my return from the border, to which I meant to proceed to see what was a-happening.

At first she would not hear of my doing this; she threw herself upon my neck, she besought me by our newly-born love, by all our hopes of happiness in days to come, not to go near those men. Reminded me, too, that even now we were free to escape, to seize upon the horses, push on further into Portugal and to safety. Also she pleaded with me to remember that, if aught happened to me, if I was taken again and carried back to Spain, all hope would indeed be gone, no more escape possible. Wept, too, most piteously, and besought me to recollect that should such as this befall, she would indeed be alone in the world, and must die.

Yet I was firm; forced myself to be so. Bade her, in my turn, remember that I was a soldier, that soldiers could not skulk and run away whether them was aught to fear or not. "For," I said, whispering also many other words of love and comfort in her ear, "it may well be true that the King has joined with us. For months it has been looked for, expected. And if 'tis not even so, these people hate Spain and all in it with a deep hatred. The Spaniards cannot harm us, certainly no half-dozen can. 'Twould take more than that. Let me go, sweetheart."

So, gently, I disengaged her arms from my neck, and went away amidst her prayers and supplications for my safety; amidst also the mutterings of the landlord to the effect that the English seemed to fear neither devil nor man.

'Twas not many moments to the border 'twixt the two countries, and I soon was there—seeing, however, as I hurried towards it, to the priming of my pistols, and that my sword was loose enough in its scabbard for easy drawing forth—and there I perceived that a harangue was going on between the Spanish and Portuguese frontiermen, while, on the side of the former, were also the half-dozen other Spaniards of whom the innkeeper had spoken. Amongst them I recognised two or three of those who had captured us in the inn garden at Lugo.

"Ha!" one of these called out as I approached. "Ha! See, there is one, the second of the brigands, though not the worst. Assassin," he shrieked at me, "we must have you back to Lugo."

"Best take me then," I replied, as I drew close up. "Yet 'twill cost you dear," while, as I spoke, I whipped my sword from out its scabbard.

There was to be neither fight nor attempt at capturing me, however—in truth, as you have now to see, my weapon had done its last work in either Spain or Portugal!—since the men on this side meant not that the Spaniards should have their way.

"Back, I tell you," shouted the Portuguese chief, "or advance at your peril. We are at war, 'tis known over all our land, the English are our allies. You have come on a bootless errand."

*(To be continued).*

*Photo* **MAULL & FOX.**                                                                                              *Piccadilly.*

### GENERAL SIR WILLIAM LOCKHART, K.C.B., K.C.S.I.

NO better choice could have been made for the post of Commander-in-Chief in India than that of Sir William Lockhart, whose name as the officer in command of the punitive expedition against the Afridis is in everyone's mouth just now. In this last special service, of course, Sir William was only performing the duties of the general officer commanding on the N.W. Frontier. In addition to having been in charge on the disaffected border for some years, Sir William Lockhart has had as extended an experience of Indian frontier warfare as any man living. He served on the staff in the Black Mountain Expedition of 1864, while in the Afghan War of 1879-80 he was actively employed as road commandant in the Khyber Pass (the scene of the recent operations), and later on the staff of Lord Roberts, in the fighting round Cabul. Subsequently he saw a great deal of frontier fighting in N.W. India. Sir William Lockhart's frontier medal bears six clasps. He entered the Army in 1858, and in addition to the frontier services spoken of, has seen fighting in Bhotan, in Abyssinia, and in Acheen.

# Old Battlefields: Crecy and Agincourt.

ABOUT seventeen miles from Boulogne, on the main line to Paris, is the old town of Montreuil, which makes a good centre from which to visit the battlefields of Crecy and Agincourt. Situated as it was in the district of Ponthieu—the marriage portion of Margaret, wife of Edward I.—Montreuil belonged by right to Edward III., but its inhabitants would not acknowledge him as their ruler, and *une compagnie bourgeoise* from the town assisted in the attempt to prevent Edward from crossing the Somme by the ford of Blanq Taque on the 25th of August, 1346, the eve of Crecy. Crecy-en-Ponthieu, as it was called, is a desolate little village on the Maie. One hundred and twenty feet above this stream is a small plateau. Here on a mound, of about 30-yds. in diameter, are to be seen the foundations of an old stone windmill. This, according to tradition, was the very mill by which Edward stood surveying the progress of the fight, and commanding the third division, which he held in reserve on the right rear. The actual battlefield is a slope

*Crecy: Monument Erected at the Spot where the King of Bohemia was Killed.*

now called La Vallée des Clercs, measuring little more than a mile in breadth and two miles in length, stretching from the mill eastwards to Fontaine village, and to the high road from Abbeville through Hesdin to the north. Edward's first division under the Black Prince lay in advance of the third, with its right towards the Maie, the archers in front, and—according to Villani—between the archers were placed "bombards that threw small iron balls that frightened or killed the horses." The second division was to the left of this line. The French arrived by the Marcheville and Fontaine road, "in no regular order but one after the other as seemed good to themselves," confident in victory. In advancing to the attack the Genoese archers were in front, Philip, with men-at-arms, in the rear. The stone cross shown in the photograph stands midway between the positions of those two lines. It was erected to mark the spot where fell the blind King of Bohemia with so many of his knights.

From Crecy to Agincourt is a long distance in point of

*Photos. CURZON, ROBEY, & CO.*

*THE WALLS OF MONTREUIL.*

*Oxford Street, W.*

time, but they are less than thirty miles apart. Agincourt should be reached from Blangy-sur-Ternoise, a little village lying in a valley. From here one can follow the road by which Henry and his gallant army marched to the scene of their glorious victory. The road runs for a mile up a gentle slope, then slightly down again for half a mile till a plateau is reached, from the edge of which can be surveyed a tract running between the villages of Maisoncelle and Tramecourt, past Agincourt to Canlers and Ruisseauville. Here in the open Henry spent the night before the battle. The French bivouacked in the plain beyond Agincourt, having no thought of defeat, and

Photo. *CURZON, ROBEY & CO.*  Oxford Street, W.

*Agincourt: The Burial-place of 10,000 French Warriors.*

too careless to occupy the woods and village for defence. The distance separating the woods of Agincourt and Tramecourt is about 1000-yds. Dawn saw the French drawn up in lines across this narrow part, their one object to block the issue of the English. Henry ranged his army so as to form one solid phalanx, his rear covered by Maisoncelle village, flanks resting on the woods, while small detachments of archers were sent into Agincourt and Tramecourt, and from these points of vantage commenced the attack, pouring their arrows on to the enemy's lines. The French, maddened with rage, rushed forward, and were so jammed between the woods,

"that when they had nearly met, they were so pressed by each other that they could not lift their arms to attack their enemies except some that were in front, until the mingled mass of dead and wounded exceeded the height of a man.".

To the right of the photograph can be seen a grassy enclosure 30-yds. square, which marks the burial-place of 10,000 of the French. This small cemetery, standing at the end of the Tramecourt wood, was fenced in at the time of the battle, and a chapel was built in its midst. Fencing and chapel were swept away in the Revolution. The fences are now restored, and a crucifix stands on the site of the chapel.

# OUR INDIAN FRONTIER.

SADDA, in the valley of the Kurram River, a tributary of the Indus, is the site of the camp occupied by the

expeditionary force in 1892, and of an existing permanent one. In one illustration its four fighting towers are shown, these

*THE TURI LEVY—RAISED IN THE KURRAM VALLEY.*

being practically of the same character as the towers found in all the frontier villages, and excellently adapted for the predatory warfare carried on amongst the hill tribes. They were of sun-dried mud bricks, with a projecting roof-top, and with a parapet upon the summit.

One of the native mills is also shown, built over a stream running into the Kurram River.

The history of the Kurram Valley has been for nearly twenty years associated with British expeditions. When we had to send a division up it in 1878, *en route* to Cabul, the Turis, its inhabitants, were at loggerheads with the Ameer, and hence they were regarded as friendly to the British advance. Moreover, the attack on the Peiwar Kotal, which is at the head of the valley, turned out to be a success for our arms, so that any wavering feeling which they entertained towards our troops was overawed by this result, and they never ventured to interfere with our line of march.

General Roberts, in return for this forbearance, made them British subjects, and built himself a bungalow and orchard at Shalazan, a village situated much further up the Kurram Valley, at an altitude of 10,000-ft.,

*Water Mill, Sadda—Small Stream Running into Kurram River.*

at the foot of the Peiwar Kotal Pass, a photograph of which is here presented. This place is still actually the property of Sir Frederick Roberts. He also promised protection to the Turis from their enemies.

In 1892, however, a large "jirgah" of Turis came in to Kohat to see the political officer. They pointed out that the "British subject" business did not pay, and that, as they did not get any help from the Government, they were going to submit to the Ameer, and pay taxes to him. The Ameer had not liked to touch them himself, but he had employed parties of outlaws and refugees from India to harry them. This was executed with great success, and as nearly all their able-bodied men were by this time either killed or wounded, and most of their crops were gone, the "jirgah" appealed for help. This was afforded. A body of troops was sent up to disperse the Ameer's emissaries, together with a political officer and ten lakhs of rupees. The commandant of the outlaws took the rupees, gleefully promised amendment, and went his way. A camp was formed at Sadda, and the political officer began settling the country in the customary manner. The method employed was to surround a village with troops, institute a big dinner, make presents of Birmingham knives and watches, and from this moment the villagers were our devoted slaves for ever. The construction of roads was then started, the natives being employed in this work. The best fighting men of the Turis, and some of the neighbouring tribes, were then enlisted into a frontier militia force, with two British officers, a smart uniform, and Snider rifles, the pay being better than that of a Sepoy of the regular army. Another of our photographs shows the Turi levy as they appeared before and after enlistment.

In 1893, the expeditionary force was broken up, and a permanent garrison was left in the Kurram Valley, consisting of one regiment of native infantry, two guns, two squadrons of cavalry, and the Turi militia. Chikai, the recent commandant of "outlaws," enlisted many of his jailbirds in the militia, and his nephew was made a native officer. This is a condensed story of events in the valley up to the present time. The views up the Kurram are, of course, superb. Our illustration of Shalazan shows the snowy ranges in the vicinity of the Peiwar Kotal. The photographs were taken by Mr. A. Gore.

On the 16th of last month, the camp at Sadda was made the object of a desperate night assault by 2,000 tribesmen, who approached the position down deep and tortuous gullies or nullahs, which enabled them to get close to the parapets on three sides without being perceived. They maintained the assault for several hours, but retired discomfited between one and two in the morning. Sadda is on the left bank of the Kurram River, about midway between Fort Kurram and Thull. The Tochi River joins the Kurram lower down.

*Sadda—Showing Four Tower Forts, now Destroyed.*

*Shalazan—With Peiwar Kotal at Back*

## THE 16th (QUEEN'S LANCERS).

THE 16th (Queen's Lancers) were raised as light horse during the Seven Years' War. They first saw service at Belle Isle, in the Bay of Biscay. The regiment was reviewed by George III. in 1766, who shortly afterwards gave it the title of the "Queen's," and ordered it to wear a scarlet uniform faced with blue. The title it still retains, and the uniform, though of different pattern, at the present day combines the two colours mentioned. The 16th served in America, 1776, and were present at the battles of White Plains and Brandywine. In 1793-94 they fought under the Duke of York in Flanders. As part of the Light Division in the Peninsula, 1809, the regiment was present at all the principal battles and engagements. It fought at Quatre Bras and Waterloo, and the following year was designated as "the 16th (Queen's) Light Dragoons (Lancers)." As such it fought at Bhurtpore, in India, 1825, and at Ghuzni in the first Afghan War. It acquitted itself gallantly at Maharajpore, and in the Sikh War at Sobraon. The uniform is scarlet with plastron or front and facings of blue. The plume is black. The 16th are alone among Lancers in wearing a scarlet uniform.

# AUTUMN MANOEUVRES IN FRANCE.

THE photographs reproduced here were taken during the late manœuvres in the north of France, and give one a very fair idea of Tommy Atkins's *confrères* hard at work.

The first is an artillery forage waggon with two spare gun wheels attached. It is early morning, and the men, no doubt, feel grateful for the bright warm sun as it breaks through the mists gathered by the yesterday's rain. The column is halted close up to the off side of the old paved road, so as not to impede the march of any other troops which may come along. Their guns have left the gun-park but a short time previously, and they are waiting for them to gain the regulation distance ahead before moving off.

Boys are no longer enlisted in the French Army as drummers or musicians, and no wonder, for they could not carry the big packs borne by the stalwart fellows in the third picture. They are "marching at ease," with their drums carried in

*Drummers and Buglers.*

commissioned officer of the guard. The man in the centre with his hands in his pockets is a quartermaster-sergeant, distinguishable by the silver braid on his arms above the elbow. On the right hand are several officers wearing field-service caps very similar to our own. The officer with the light-coloured cap

*Artillery Forage Waggon.*

front, as there is no room for them behind, and they look cheery enough, although they have been marching in pouring rain for hours. Some of the knowing ones have fixed a handkerchief on to their *képis*, or tied it round their throats to keep the rain from running down their necks. Round the outside of the knapsack is strapped a section of a *tente-abri*, which, when put together, is big enough to shelter a couple of men. The drummer in the foreground has his left shoulder strap rolled up tight, so as to form a rest for his rifle (when carried).

The next picture shows a village guard-room—perhaps it is the local police station turned for the nonce into a guard-room. The party on duty belong to the 5th Dragoons. On the left is the sentry, and just coming out of the door is the non-

*Guard, 5th Dragoons.*

is a light cavalry man—*chasseur-à-cheval*—and is, perhaps, discussing some knotty point about his men's billets, for the 3rd Chasseurs are also quartered in the village. It was here in Bucquoy that many of our own troops were quartered during their return march to the coast after the cessation of hostilities in 1816. Who knows but that the ghost of many a gallant trooper of the 10th Hussars occasionally pays a visit to his old haunts!

Here we see a couple of *chasseurs-à-cheval*. The one on horseback wearing a tunic is a non-com., for we can just catch a glimpse of the silver chevron low down on his bridle arm. He seems to be giving some instruction to the trooper in the stable jacket standing by his horse's head; perhaps it is about their new billets—or have they lost their way? Very likely the latter, for maps are tricky things!

The soldier just getting into the ambulance waggon, depicted on the opposite page, no doubt thanks his stars that he is in a big town with quarters in barracks and is not billeted on some poor old peasant chap, where, though he may get a pretty good shake-down on clean straw, shopping would be out of the question. How a French soldier ever manages to find cash for shopping at all is a puzzle. Look at the rate of his daily pay: Sergeant-major, 2s. 2d.; sergeant drummer, 1s. 3d.; colour-sergeant, 1s.; sergeant, 9d.; corporal and bandsman of ten years' (!) service, 4½d.; drummer, pioneer, and bandsman, 3d.; private, 27 centimes (rather more than 2½d.).

*Chasseurs-à-Cheval.*

Below are two officers' servants. The one on the right with his master's boots belongs to the *Chasseurs d'Afrique*, as we can see by the fez he is wearing—*chechia* the French call it. No doubt his master has some staff appointment, and that is how this sturdy little trooper has wandered thus far from Algiers, or Constantine, or Oran. Presently he will swagger into the town with his broad red cummerbund wrapped round him and make all such common-place soldiers as linesmen green with envy. The soldier servant talking to him is a *chasseur-à-cheval*, and seems to have some "funny story" on tap.

Then we have two cuirassiers. They have just returned from a long and hard day's manœuvring, and yet find time to stop and crack a joke. The one on the left is just taking his saddle and kit off to his billet. He has taken his cuirass off, and we can see the little canvas waistcoat which the French men-in-armour wear underneath their cuirass to save their tunics. His comrade—such is the force of habit—has not yet bothered to get rid of his armour, but has just popped on a field-service cap. Notice his cartridge pouch on a belt round his waist outside the cuirass, with the water-bottle hanging on his left side.

The soldier in another photograph stooping down has just grubbed a little hole in the ground for a fireplace  Beside him, stuck in the ground, is the little entrenching spade which he has used for the purpose. A few twigs carried on the outside of his knapsack and perhaps a handful of straw from his capacious breeches pocket will soon produce a merry crack-

*Ambulance Waggon and Driver of Military Train.*

*Chasseur-à-Cheval and Chasseur d'Afrique.*

ling little fire. Whilst he is adjusting his pan to the fire-place, another man goes with his canvas bucket to the farmhouse hard by to get some water, whilst a third gets out the coffee mill and grinds enough for his squad (eight

men). When, oh! when, shall we be as practical as the French? There cannot be a doubt that it is this practice of taking the midday coffee which enables the little *pioupiou* to do the work he does. Hot coffee to the soldier is like gruel to the tired hunter. But with our present wretched system of "tactical exercises"—as Sir William Butler rightly calls them—we cannot realise the importance of such a system. Have we forgotten the morning of the battle of the Alma, when we agreed with the French to attack at 5.30 a.m.? On that morning, when at nine o'clock our army, encumbered with its baggage train, was still *crawling* into position, the French, in desperation, piled arms and had their coffee. Only at eleven o'clock were we ready. Another little dodge tried by one or two companies at these manœuvres was to put

*Infantry of the Line Cooking Coffee (54th Regiment).*

a few raw potatoes and a pot of lard in the men's haversacks, so that after the coffee they could have a savoury mess of fried potatoes. I believe this novel addition to their fare was much appreciated by the men.

Over page is shown an artillery trumpeter. The comrade at his horse's head is armed with a revolver, the strap round the waist preventing the weapon from flopping about when he is mounted. All Frenchmen are born trumpeters; their *fanfars*, as they call their cavalry trumpeters, are really excellent. Why is it, we wonder? Perhaps talkativeness and "trumpeting" are first cousins. We all remember Cæsar's epigrammatic description of the Gauls—*Gens loquax et pugnax.*

In another picture we see the head of a regiment on the march. The men are "pioneers," but only one of them has grown a beard—the corporal on the left. Alas, in these degenerate days of short-service armies, the old-fashioned pioneer, with beard reaching down to his chest, has all but disappeared, and the French saying, "*barbu comme un sapeur,*" is but a memory of the past. Behind the pioneers come the

*Cuirassiers.*

regimental cyclists, ready to dart off with a message at a nod from the colonel or adjutant. What should we do without cyclists nowadays? and yet for long the army was fearfully prejudiced against cycling. Why, it would make our ancestors turn in their graves could they see the field officer of the day at Aldershot visiting the various guards on a bicycle!

The two *chasseurs* are waiting just outside a big farm building whilst the quartermaster-sergeant of the regiment is busy at work on doors and windows with his chalk marking off quarters for men and horses. They belong to the "enemy," as can be seen by the white cap covering the shako of the trooper on the left. He wears the carbine slung on his back, like all the rest of the cavalry, except the cuirassiers, who wear theirs in a bucket, like our own cavalry. The horse on the right is evidently quite sick of the whole business, and is, no doubt,

*Chasseurs-à-Cheval (White Cap, Enemy).*

pioneers—crossed axes—whilst underneath is what looks like the badge of a trumpeter; but this is not so, it is a marksman's badge, given for good shooting. The men's swords are quite straight, being only used for pointing—never for cutting—and are much longer than our own cavalry swords. It is curious that between dragoons and *chasseurs* there is no love lost. The *chasseur* looks down on the

*Infantry of the Line on the March.*

saying to himself, "What tomfoolery all this is, bucketing us about like this from morning to night; why on earth they want to go tearing about all over the country, instead of having a nice quiet parade on our own 'dust-hole,' is more than I can say; and don't they pack us tight at night! It really is infamous—worse than cab-horses. That a well-bred horse like me should be treated thus is outrageous."

Here is a party of dragoons doing escort to a general officer. The wind has blown the horse-hair "tail" (mane, as the French call it) to one side, so that the man's helmet looks rather like a fireman's. However, it is a smart, soldierly headgear, and has not the straight-pointed peak sitting on top of the nose which our "heavies" have the pleasure of wearing. Just included in the picture on the left is a non-commissioned officer, wearing on his arm the badge of all

*Trumpeter of Artillery.*

dragoon with supreme contempt, as on some hybrid animal, neither fish, flesh, fowl, nor good red-herring, considering that a light horseman is the only cavalry soldier in the world fit to do anything. Yet the *real* heavies—the cuirassiers—are very popular with *chasseurs* and hussars. They are familiarly known throughout the army as "the big brothers" (*les gros frères*). The hussar will tell you that in a regiment of dragoons each man has to be helped into his saddle by his neighbour, and the last man to mount gets up by the aid of a heap of stones. Such are some of the curiosities of *esprit de corps*. This joke, quaint as it may seem, has some foundation in fact, for we were told by an officer that at the military school of St. Cyr (corresponding to our Sandhurst) the cadets are *taught* to mount in this manner, that is to say, each cadet holds his next-door neighbour's stirrup, the idea being that by this means the saddle is not pulled over when the rider mounts, and a frequent source of sore backs is thus prevented. The Frenchman seems to take his three years' soldiering very good-humouredly, but the majority, we fancy, are not sorry when it is done. Over and over again we have heard people who had men billeted on them ask their guest the question, "Are you of the class?" (*êtes vous de la classe?*), which meant, Is your time nearly up; do you belong to the class about to be dismissed? Each man serving for three years, there are three classes of men in the ranks—men with one, two, and nearly three years' service. Three years—not very long in which to make a soldier, perhaps some will say. Well, it may be so, but yet, look at our guardsmen! Many of them enlist for only three years, and are they the worse for that? "Length of service is nothing—*leadership* everything."

*Dragoons—Escort of a General Officer.*

# THE
# NAVY & ARMY
## ILLUSTRATED.

Vol. V.—No. 50.]  FRIDAY, NOVEMBER 12th, 1897.

Photo. *ELLIOTT & FRY, Baker Street.*

### REAR-ADMIRAL HILARY GUSTAVUS ANDOE, C.B.

CHATHAM DOCKYARD is fortunate in possessing for its Admiral Superintendent an officer of such ability and energy as Rear-Admiral Andoe, the officer who has held the charge of our great eastern Naval Arsenal for the past two years—since September, 1895. Afloat, Rear-Admiral Andoe has seen a variety of service, beginning with the Baltic campaign in the Russian War of 1855, in which he distinguished himself as a Naval cadet. After that he saw service for four years on the East Coast of Africa, being actively employed in the suppression of the slave trade. During the Transvaal War of 1881, Captain Andoe, as he then was, acted as principal transport officer in Natal, and he again acted as principal transport officer in the Red Sea during the Soudan campaign at Suakin in 1884. For his services at Suakin he was mentioned in despatches and granted the C.B., the campaign further adding a clasp to Captain Andoe's Egyptian medal, granted for service, as captain of the "Orontes," during the campaign against Arabi in 1882. Rear-Admiral Andoe wears also the bronze medal of the Royal Humane Society, won by him when a lieutenant for assisting to save the life of a boy. He entered the Royal Navy in March, 1855, and obtained his flag on New Year's Day, 1894.

# THREE NAVAL NOTABILITIES.

STAFF-CAPTAIN SIR WILLIAM BURGESS GOLD-SMITH is the hero of an incident of unique interest. The occasion was on Tuesday, August 31st last, when Her Majesty the Queen conferred on him the honour of knighthood on board the Royal yacht "Alberta." Her Majesty was on her way from Osborne to Gosport to proceed to Balmoral, and had just made her passage across the Solent. As the "Alberta" came alongside at Gosport, the Queen sent for Staff-Captain Goldsmith—who had commanded the "Alberta" ever since 1883, and being about to retire from the Navy under the Age Clause, after forty-five years' service, had now escorted Her Majesty across for the last time—and on the quarter-deck of her yacht knighted him. Sir William Goldsmith, who is the son of a Naval officer, the late Commander Charles Goldsmith, R.N., entered the Royal Navy in 1852, and in his earlier days saw much active service. He acted as staff-commander of the "Serapis" during the Prince of Wales's visit to India. Sir William traces his descent from the same family to which the celebrated Oliver Goldsmith belonged, and is Sergeant-at-Arms in the Queen's Household.

*Photo. HOLLOWAY.*          *Cheltenham.*

**Commander PERCY CULLEN, R.N.R.**

*Photo. KIRK.*          *Cowes.*

**Captain Sir W. GOLDSMITH, R.N.**

Captain Robert Stevenson Dalton Cumming, R.N., is the officer who commands the King of Siam's Royal yacht, and brought His Majesty, King Chulalongkorn, from Bangkok to Europe. He is an officer of Her Majesty's Navy, and until recently was in charge of the Queensferry training-ship "Caledonia." He entered the Royal Navy in 1866, and became captain in January last. Captain Cumming wears the Egyptian medal and Khedive's bronze star, for services rendered as a lieutenant in the Suakin campaign of 1884-85.

Commander Percy Cullen's name has come prominently before the public of late in connection with the Naval and Military operations of the British Central African Protectorate round Lake Nyasa, the great inland sea of the continent of Africa, south of the Equator. He was appointed in April, 1895, commander in charge of the Naval gun-boat flotilla of the British Protectorate, and has done notable work with the force under his orders, both in the way of transport service and surveying, and of assisting the troops of the Protectorate before the enemy on shore. Commander Cullen is a lieutenant in the Royal Naval Reserve, with seniority dating from February, 1896.

*Photo. SPEAIGHT.*          *Regent Street.*

**Captain ROBERT CUMMING, R.N.**

Photo. R. ELLIS, Malta.

Copyright.—HUDSON & KEARNS.

*WARD-ROOM AND OFFICERS' BERTHS, H.M.S. "BRUISER."*

THE above illustration gives a view of the ward-room of a "destroyer" seen from the after end. On each side are the officers' bunks, with drawers underneath; at the foremost end is a stove, for cold weather, and a small library; overhead may be seen the cutlasses, all the arms being kept aft by the officers' quarters. The vessel is lighted electrically when steam is up, but the lamp has to be used otherwise. The whole place, where three officers live entirely, is hardly larger than the ordinary cabin of a commander in a battle-ship, yet the contrast of this ward-room to the life on deck in these vessels, which are so very exposed, makes it not uncomfortable to young fellows who are keen on their work and do not mind roughing it. From the thinness of the plating the cabins alter their temperature very quickly to hot or cold, being very hot in hot weather and *vice versâ*. Needless to say, the exceedingly lively motion of these small craft, owing to the great speed they go at, is enough to upset any but the most seasoned salts.

# Naval Force of the British Central African Protectorate.

*Commander Cullen, Lieutenant Phillips, and Messrs. Brighton, Savage, and Nixon (Warrant Officers).*

THE accompanying illustrations serve to show the Naval Forces of the British Central African Protectorate. This part of the British Empire includes Lake Nyasa, one of the great inland seas of Africa, which covers an area of about 14,000 square miles, and is known as the Lake of Storms, from the violent gales which obtain during the greater part of the year. The sea which gets up during these gales is very nasty, short, hollow, curling, and very dangerous to small craft.

*Naval Depôt, Fort Johnston.*

The three gun-boats we illustrate were sent out in 1892, but not completed till 1893, when Admiral Sir F. Bedford visited Fort Johnston to see them launched. They were under the command of Commander C. Hope Robertson, R.N., C.M.G., and took part in the various campaigns against the slave-raiding chiefs on the lake shore.

In April, 1895, the Government of the Protectorate took them over from the Admiralty, and a Colonial Naval Force was

*"Pioneer" and "Dove."*

organised. Lieutenant Percy Cullen, R.N.R., was selected for command with rank of Commander, the other officers being Lieutenants E. L. Rhoades and W. B. Phillips, R.N.R., and subsequently Lieutenant S. F. Sheppard, R.N.R. Since that time the boats have been employed in surveying and transport service, and the officers and men landed with the field guns in the various operations which took place in 1895 and finished with the complete destruction of the Arab power in December of that year, Mlozi, the Arab Sultan of the Northern Nyasa District, being captured and executed after being tried and found guilty of many crimes and atrocities.

The Naval Brigade on this occasion did good service with their guns under Commander Cullen and his officers, the entire operations being under the command of Major C. A. Edwards, 35th Sikhs, an officer of great promise and ability, who, for his services, received his brevet lieutenant-colonelcy, but who, unfortunately, succumbed to an attack of fever in May this year.

Commander Cullen is at present at home supervising the construction of a new gun-boat which he has designed to meet all the requirements of the services which she will have to render, combining light draught, great carrying capacity, handiness, and sea worthiness. During his absence Lieutenant Rhoades is in command, and is doing very useful work in completing a new chart of Lake Nyasa, and Lieutenant Phillips is adding to it a survey of the Upper Shiré River.

In addition to the ordinary duties required of the officers of the gun-boats, those of brick making and house building have been undertaken. Dwelling houses for themselves and men, stores, and an engineering workshop have been built at Fort Johnston, and a steel lighter, 56-ft. by 13-ft., draught 14-in., sent out in plates, was built by the engineer and gun-boats' crews in twenty-one working days.

*"Adventure."*

It is a great drawback there being no railway communication as yet between the lake and the coast, the cataracts and rapids on the Upper Shiré compelling all material to be carried overland from Katungas on the Lower Shiré to Mpwinhi or Liwondi on the Upper river; and the task of transporting the steamer which is being constructed and of building her at Fort Johnston, with the very limited means available, both of money and skilled labour, will be no light one, and a very creditable achievement to the Naval Department of the Protectorate

*Native Sailors at 7-pr. Field Gun Drill.*

The new gun-boat will be a very great acquisition to Lake Nyasa, and no doubt in a few years' time the other great lakes, viz., Tanganyika and Victoria Nyanza, will also have British gun-boats patrolling them. The scheme which was published in the *Army and Navy Gazette* some few weeks ago, concerning the formation of an African Naval Service somewhat on the lines of the Australian Navies, would then be partly accomplished, it only remaining for the Colonies having a coast-line to join hands with the Central African organisation and make one service of it.

*Crew of "Adventure"*

P. & co NOTMAN STUDIO.     Halifax.

THE COMPANY OF THE "CRESCENT" AT HALIFAX, NOVA SCOTIA.

THESE are the officers and men who served in the first-class cruiser "Crescent" during that ship's recent commission as flag-ship on the North America and West Indies station. All ranks and ratings are shown, there being upwards of 600 portraits in the photograph, from Admiral Sir James Erskine—who is shown in the second row from the front, in the right centre of the photograph—down to the youngest boy on board. The admiral is seated next to an officer wearing aiguillettes—Flag-Captain Powell, C.B.—and immediately behind two officers in the front row wearing aiguillettes, and each with a dog—Flag-Lieutenant Halsey, and the admiral's secretary, Mr. Krabbé. The "Crescent" was commissioned for the North America and West Indies station, as flag-ship, on March 12th, 1895. On Vice-Admiral Erskine attaining the rank of admiral in the spring of the present year, and having consequently to vacate his command, the Admiralty arranged to replace the "Crescent" by the battle-ship "Renown." The "Renown," flying the flag of Sir James's successor, Vice-Admiral Sir John Fisher, relieved the "Crescent" at Halifax, N.S., a few weeks ago, shortly before which event our photograph was taken. On her relief, the "Crescent" at once returned home and paid off at Portsmouth.

THESE two pictures represent very different phases of life on board a modern man-of-war. Saturday night is the traditional time among sailors for recalling the tender associations connected with "sweethearts and wives," and Dibdin, the popular sea-poet, has more than one song devoted to the subject. No doubt Jack would be supremely happy if the rules of the Service permitted the actual presence of the special object of his devotion; but, failing this, he wisely refrains from giving way to vain regrets and joins with his shipmates in gay and harmless convivialities, all the musical talent available being enlisted for the occasion. In this instance it is represented by several banjoes, two fiddles, and a cornet—a very pleasing combination—and, in default of the more entrancing charms of the fairer sex, some of the men select their chums as partners in the dance, while others form a good-humoured but critical audience.

Sunday morning brings a striking change of scene, though the same portion of the deck is represented. Everyone, from the captain downwards, is present at morning prayers,

Photo. GREGORY.　　　　*Saturday Night Festivities.*　　　　Copyright.—H. & K.

Photo. GREGORY.　　　　*Sunday Morning Devotions.*　　　　Copyright.—H. & K.

and stands bareheaded while the chaplain, duly attired in canonicals, reads the service, the marines alone remaining covered, in accordance with military etiquette, which ordains that a soldier appearing otherwise on parade is guilty of a breach of decorum A more elaborate preparation is made, when circumstances permit, for service on Sunday, the carpenters and others being called upon to "rig church," a somewhat grotesque phrase in the ears of a landsman, but conveying a perfectly intelligible signification to those concerned. Stools are placed for the men and chairs for the officers, and the service is enlivened by hymns, etc., in which the bluejackets join very heartily, to the accompaniment of a harmonium, or some selected band instruments. In each picture the long muzzle of one of the big turret guns serves to remind one of the actual *raison d'être* of the huge vessel, to which both Saturday revels and Sunday devotions must give place, should occasion arise.

## Scenes and Life in the Austrian Navy.

Photo. Alois Beer.　　　　*The "Ferdinand Max."*　　　　Klagenfurt.

THESE pages have already illustrated some features of the Austrian Navy. The Imperial Fleet, alone among the Navies of Europe, holds the inspiring tradition of a great Naval engagement, in which it was victorious under modern conditions. Since the great day of Lissa, in 1866, Austria has made but slow progress in Naval matters. Yet her Fleet presents abundant objects and scenes of interest, from which we have selected some to-day. Four of the illustrations depict life on board a war-ship still engaged in active service, although she bore her part at Lissa more than thirty years ago, being then fresh from the builders' hands. This is the armoured frigate "Habsburg," of 5,140 tons, which, with the "Kaiser," is the last wooden ship to which Austria has attached fighting value; and she is even now being relegated to the picturesque category of the old vessels which have done their work and go to sea no more.

Her character is admirably seen in the pictures. A lieutenant, accompanied by the master-at-arms and a ship's corporal, is making his periodical round, and inspecting the clothes which a party of men have brought on deck. This duty over, one of them finds himself a tub and a bucket, and sits down, at the ship's side, to write a letter home. Here is the romance of the sea. The good fellow has dear ones at home on shore, and you may see, though he has something to say, and, perhaps, tender thoughts to express, that the words come slowly at his bidding. He is not one of those who, in another picture, are ranged as defaulters before an inspecting officer. Insubordination and a prone-

*Inspecting a Seaman's Kit.*

ness to be lazy are the faults of these, and, while the officer deals with their cases successively, the master-at-arms looks on with stern and reproving face. Another picture taken on board the "Habsburg" shows a number of bluejackets manning the wheel and awaiting the word of command. Here the

*To the Dear Ones at Home.*

character of the ship is particularly well seen. The steering apparatus is unlike that found in modern ships, and the high poop, mast, and standing rigging mark the obsolete character of the old "Habsburg."

Very different in character is the armoured cruiser—or, as she is called in the Austrian Navy, "ram-cruiser"— "Kaiserin Elizabeth." She is such a vessel as we should rank in our own Navy as a second-class cruiser, and she belongs to a small class of swift and powerful vessels that Austria is adding to her Fleet. She was launched at Pola in 1890, and we here see her engaged in her trials, and steaming at twenty knots' speed. Her engines are of 9,000 horse-power, and she attained 18·6 knots with natural draught, and twenty knots with forced draught, this being one knot in excess of the estimate. The ship displaces 4,064 tons, being slightly

Photos. ALOIS BEER.    Klagenfurt.

*THE RAM-CRUISER "KAISERIN ELIZABETH."*

larger than the sister cruiser, "Kaiser Franz Joseph." She is 321-ft. 6-in. long, with 46-ft. 7-in. beam, and is protected by a steel deck of 2½-in., and has 3½-in. of steel on her turrets.

She carries, as may be seen in the picture, a 9·4-in. Krupp gun in a barbette turret forward and another aft, and there are, in addition, six 6-in. guns mounted in sponsons on each side, of which the one amidships is high above the water-line. The quick-firing armament consists of eleven guns of smaller calibre, and there are five torpedo tubes.

In another picture we have representatives of a smaller class of war-ship. Here are a brace of torpedo-boats engaged in operations at high speed, one presenting to the spectator her broadside, showing well the great wave from the bows, which is still better seen in the swirling water cut through by

*Steering Wheel of the "Habsburg."*

*Dealing with the Defaulters.*

the stem of the other, as she steams straight towards the spectator. The Austrian flotilla has been built chiefly at Poplar, Chiswick, Elbing, and Trieste.

The first picture is of a truly famous ship which, having

done splendid service, is now being used as a tender to the gunnery ship. As we may see, the "Erzherzog Ferdinand Max" has been roofed in, and otherwise altered and fitted for her present duties. She has been supplied with certain modern guns and a modern fighting top, and many alterations have been made internally to accommodate the large number of men who are always on board. But in 1866 the "Ferdinand Max" was quite new, her guns being still at Krupp's works at Essen, her internal fitting not begun, and her masts not yet on board. She was hastened forward, however, to fly the flag of Admiral Tegettoff, with Baron Daublebsky von Sterneck, now the highly-respected chief of the Austrian Navy, whose Service jubilee was quite lately celebrated with great enthusiasm, as his flag-captain. When the Italian squadron was sighted at seven o'clock on the morning of the memorable 20th of July, 1866, it was in the mind of Captain von Sterneck to use the full power of his ship as a ram. The opportunity presently came, and he bore straight down upon the frigate "Re d'Italia," from which Persano, the Italian admiral, had removed his flag to the "Affondatore" earlier in the day. The unfortunate vessel, which was under command of Captain Faa di Bruno, and carried 600 men, was struck almost amidships, with terrible effect. Von Sterneck immediately went full speed astern, while the "Red'Italia," heeling first to starboard and then to port, rapidly filled, and sank with her colours flying.

It was a terrible catastrophe for Italy, and the most remarkable episode in a very remarkable battle.

The "Ferdinand Max" is thus a notable veteran of a great engagement, and our picture of her, adapted to her modern and useful service, is appropriately selected as one of our illustrations of the Austrian Navy.

*Photo. Alois Beer*          *Austrian Torpedo-Boats.*          *Klagenfurt.*

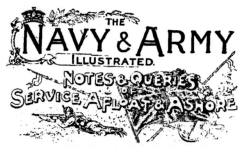

THE NAVY & ARMY ILLUSTRATED. NOTES & QUERIES OF SERVICE AFLOAT & ASHORE

A CORRESPONDENT, who describes himself as "Enthusiast," asks me to enlighten a friend with whom he has been holding an argument. The subject of their discussion was the relative importance and precedence of the two Services. "Enthusiast" was well-founded in the belief that, as a maritime nation with great possessions and a world-wide trade to protect, the Navy should deservedly rank first in national importance. He did not wish to depreciate the Army, but evidently felt that, without the Navy, the Army would be absolutely powerless. His friend put forward an extraordinary argument. He was prepared to allow a certain amount of precedence upon minor occasions, but was very decisively of opinion that the Army must rank first, on the ground that, while the Navy has "done nothing of importance" since the "Crimean War," the Army has constantly been employed all over the world, winning for itself fresh laurels year by year. He went further, and said that, in the event of European war, the struggle would be decided in places where the Navy would be of quite secondary importance.

* * * *

WE have often heard such arguments before. But within recent years there has arisen in the public mind a more just appreciation of the duties of the Fleet and the Army, and we suspect that "Enthusiast's" friend, whom we may call "Rip Van Winkle," has not "been in the movement." His very allusion to the "Crimean War" shows that he has never looked upon the events of that time as a *Russian* war. He is not aware that the presence of our ships in the Baltic, though their work disappointed those who had expected of them what they were never intended to perform, was sufficient to detain many thousands of soldiers in Northern Russia, who else would have been concentrated where they might have dealt with the Army very effectively. We should recommend "Rip Van Winkle" to read our Jubilee Number, especially its article upon the "Influence of Sea Power" during the Queen's reign. He will there learn that the Navy has been ubiquitous, and that its influence has been of extraordinary advantage to the State. Wherever, indeed, our power has been exerted, it has been exerted through the agency of the Fleet. Is it not a fact that, during the fighting in China and in the Indian Mutiny, as in all the subsequent operations of our troops, we have been absolute masters of the sea? It is an elementary principle of strategy that communications must be protected, and, because the Fleet has been sufficient, ours have never been attacked. In other words, the Navy has been enabled us to use military force wherever the need has arisen. But this is not all. The Navy has been engaged in every part of the world in checking the slave trade, crushing piracy, and protecting the rights of our countrymen where they have been assailed. It has never been found wanting when British subjects have been wronged or their goods or occupations destroyed. It has sent detachments ashore in nearly all our military operations, and has alone, in malarious climates, punished the natives of Africa for their outrages. It lately exerted our power in Nicaragua, it protected our interests at Zanzibar, and it has made manifest our purpose in Delagoa Bay. In short, we may say, for "Rip Van Winkle's" instruction, that the functions of the Navy and the Army are distinct, but that Naval force is the precedent condition of military operations. It is the Navy that protects us from invasion, and invasion can never happen until Englishmen forget that the Navy ranks first, indeed, in national importance.

* * * *

THE French have decided to hold a grand Naval and Military Exhibition in the year 1900, or, as they call it, "An International Exposition of the Armies of Land and Sea." None but French architects are invited to send in plans and proposals for the building, and all such are to be deposited not later than the 13th November, 1897. It is to be erected on the Quay d'Orsay, between the bridges of Alma and Jena, and will be about 380 yards in length, consisting of a ground floor and upper story, which, together, will afford a space of over 15,000 square yards. Guns, carriages, balloons, war-pigeons, electric apparatus, etc., will be collected, and the various metals and other materials used by the Naval and Military Services will be shown in different stages of production. The administrative Services will likewise be represented, and the soldier's every-day life in peace and war will be illustrated, including the sports in which he is most interested. Our neighbours are just the people to excel in a demonstration of this kind, and the building on which they are about to decide will, doubtless, be worthy of the object in view.

* * * *

A CORRESPONDENT asks me where he can find details of the movements of British war-ships, their description and classes, etc., employed during the American War of Independence—1775-82. There is no one book in which these details are to be found with any approach to accuracy. In the Appendices to "Schomberg's Naval Chronology," published in 1804, and to "Beatson's Naval and Military Memoirs," published in 1802, much useful information from the annual returns of ships and squadrons on the North America station is to be gleaned, but the only really trustworthy method of getting at the facts is to search among the admirals' and captains' letters, preserved among the Admiralty documents in the Record Office, Chancery Lane. There the courteous superintendent of the search-room is always ready to assist, and his acquaintance with the Naval documents in his care is very extensive. From the Record Office papers the correspondent will be able to learn, also, details of the squadron blockading Boston in August, 1774, to which, a manuscript private letter he refers to, alludes.

* * * *

"E. A." asks : "When an officer (a captain) commanding a detachment in column of route is marching it to a field or other specified point, which is the position of the commanding officer, and which that of the adjutant? Who is entitled to command the detachment—the commanding officer or the adjutant?" The usual position of the commanding officer is at the head of the column, that of the adjutant in rear of the column ; but it is obvious that both must often change their positions in the execution of their duty. The third question is somewhat paradoxical—the commanding officer must, of course, command ; but "E. A.'s" difficulty is evidently to decide who the commanding officer is, viz., whether the adjutant or the captain referred to. An adjutant of volunteers holding Army rank not below that of captain ranks regimentally as senior captain, and would therefore command any captain on parade. If the adjutant should hold the Army rank of lieutenant he is appointed to serve as a captain in the volunteer corps of which he is adjutant, and ranks among the captains according to the dates of their appointments. No adjutant of a volunteer infantry battalion is below the rank of captain, but lieutenants of the Royal Artillery are appointed adjutants of artillery volunteers.

* * * *

HUMANITARIANS of the present day would be rather startled by some of the punishments inflicted in the Navy, and Army also, in times gone by. The "Calendar of Domestic State Papers," in the time of Charles II., for instance, records the following exemplary punishment awarded to Robert Johnes, boatswain of the "Francis," for embezzling a hawser and other stores. He was ordered to be rowed from Chatham Dockyard to one of H.M. ships "with the usual ceremony of a drum beating at the head of the boat, his crime written in capital letters and fixed on his head, breast, and back ; to stand an hour on the gunwale of the ship with a rope from the yardarm round his neck, and then to have fifteen strokes on his naked back ; to have the like punishment at Woolwich and Deptford ; to be dismissed his ship, and rendered incapable of ever bearing any office in any of H.M. ships."

* * * *

ONE of the finest episodes of the Great War was the capture of "L'Hercule," 74, by the "Mars," 74, fought in one hour in the dusk of a spring evening. The ships were so close that the guns on the lower deck could not be run out, but had to be fired inboard. Twice were "L'Hercule's" boarders repulsed with terrible slaughter. In all she lost 290 killed and wounded, out of a crew of 680, while the "Mars," which carried 634, had ninety casualties. So terrific was the fire of the "Mars," that to repair "L'Hercule"—a brand-new ship, only twenty-four hours out of port on her first cruise—was estimated at £12,500. Twenty minutes after the action commenced Captain Hood was shot in the femoral artery, and only lived long enough to know the victory was won. No sadder or more glorious sight was seen during the long war than the "Mars," with her flag at half-mast and the body of her dead captain in the after cabin, towing the shattered "L'Hercule" into Plymouth Harbour on the morning of the 27th April, 1798.

ACCORDING to latest returns, the number of battle-ships in the British Navy available on the active list and in case of war is fifty-seven. They are distributed into twenty-nine first-class, seven second, and twenty-one third. Our coast defence ships—old armoured ships of small size—are returned at fourteen. Our cruisers number: armoured, nine; first-class, thirteen; second and third classes, fifty-nine—making a total of eighty-one. Light craft, classed as "look-out ships," number nineteen; torpedo gun-boats, thirty-four; torpedo-boat destroyers, ninety. The whole make up a total of 295 vessels of war, in addition to our torpedo-boat flotilla of between 160 and 170 of all classes—sea-going, first, second, and third classes, and vedettes.

* * * *

A CORRESPONDENT asks why in our Army major-generals rank below lieutenant-generals, when the rank of major is senior to that of lieutenant. The answer is perhaps sufficiently interesting to be given here. The institution of the ranks dates from Cromwell's time, when three grades of generals were regularly set on foot for the Commonwealth Army, under the titles of—the first and senior—the captain-general; the second, the lieutenant-general; and the third, the sergeant-major-general. In James II.'s reign these posts, which had temporarily disappeared at the Restoration, were all revived: the first under the abbreviated title of "general"; the second, in its original form exactly, as "lieutenant-general"; the third, under the abbreviated form of "major-general." This later form of nomenclature has remained ever since, and that is how in the British military establishment the rank of major-general comes to be junior to that of lieutenant-general.

* * * *

OF the many vicissitudes which attend the career of Her Majesty's ships few, probably, have been greater than those of the "Royal Escape," a name which has disappeared from the list of the Royal Navy for many a year. Originally named the "Surprise," she, being then a coal brig, commanded by Nicholas Tattersal, had the honour of conveying Charles II., after the disastrous battle of Worcester, across the Channel from Shoreham, or, as some accounts state, Brighton to Fécamp, Tattersal, thanks to a lucky change of wind, managing to put in a subsequent appearance at Poole with sufficient rapidity to enable him to establish an *alibi*, and thereby escape the unpleasant consequences of his loyalty and daring. At the Restoration he, as a delicate reminder of his services, brought her up the Thames, enlarged

and ornamented, and moored her opposite Whitehall, with the result that she was taken into the Royal Navy as a fifth-rate, Tattersal being given command of her, with reversion of the emoluments of the captaincy to his son. In the Navy List of 1684 she is described as an unarmed smack of 34 tons, with a complement of ten men. After the death of Charles II. she remained in inglorious inactivity at Deptford, until broken up in 1791.

* * * *

FEW of the great composers have so particularly identified themselves with the military prowess and fortunes of their country, through their musical scores, as has the veteran Verdi, whose eighty-fourth birthday has recently been celebrated. In Mr. F. J. Crowest's singularly interesting and masterly work on "Verdi: Man and Musician" (J. Milne), just published, we find the composer of *Aida*, etc., in the character of quite a political fomenter. Mr. Crowest writes:— "Thus was Verdi, the musician and patriot, entwined inseparably round the hearts of his countrymen, to the lasting advantage of both, at a time when Italy stood in great need of the support and succour of all her sons. In the eyes of Verdi the national liberty was a thing to be accomplished, and if he did not shoulder the rifle in the struggles of 1859 and 1860, which, beginning with the freeing of Lombardy, ended in a free and united Italy, the clarion sounded was so certain that no one would mistake its intent. Directly he began to sing, the inflammatory ring of his music arrested and stirred the Venetians. Rossini may well have dubbed Verdi '*le musicien qui a un casque*' (the musician with a helmet). The first signs were detected in *Nabucco*, then in *I Lombardi*, and with *Ernani* there was a further outburst of the musical liberator's mind. The highest pitch of enthusiasm followed his ardent strains, and scarcely a performance of the *Ernani* went by without political demonstration. *Attila* fired a further desire for liberty. The feelings of the Venetians—still clamouring for independence —when they heard the air, '*Cara patria, già madre e regina,*' knew no bounds, and for a while the performance could not proceed. At the verse, '*Avrai tu L'universo vesti L'Italia me!*' the whole audience, seized with frenzy, shouted with one voice, '*A noi! L'Italia a noi!*' Then when Palma, the Spanish tenor, sang his air, '*La patria tradita,*' in *Macbeth*, the people were so reminded of the foreign despotism they were suffering from that they became uproarious, and the Austrian Grenadiers had to be called in. *La Battaglia di Legnano* was purposely pitched in an aggressive key."

THE EDITOR.

# THE 1st BATTALION GORDON HIGHLANDERS.

THE 75th became, under the Territorial Scheme of 1881, the 1st Battalion of the Gordon Highlanders. The new scheme was by no means popular, and one is not surprised at the way in which the old numbers were treated. Both the

92nd (2nd Battalion) and the 75th buried them with military honours at Malta. Henceforth the 75th were to distinguish themselves as an integral part of the "Gay Gordons" (the 92nd). The battalion sailed the following year for Egypt, and after

*Photo. T. WINTER.*          *THE OFFICERS OF THE 1st BATTALION.*          *Murros.*

having been under fire at Damanhour, moved forward to join the Highland Brigade at Kassassin. It took its place between the "Forty-twa" and the Cameron Highlanders (the old 79th) at Tel-el-Kebir, and well maintained the traditions of the tartan, donned for the first time the year before.

After that famous charge, the 75th went to Tantah, and afterwards were stationed at Cairo.

At Trinkitat, in the Eastern Soudan, the battalion was part of Buller's Brigade. As was to have been expected, the 75th there won fresh laurels At El Teb, where they stormed the guns of the enemy, and at Tamaï they well deserved the official praise of Sir Gerald Graham, who referred to their bravery in flattering terms.

The battalion returned to Malta in 1885, where the bronzed warriors called forth the admiration of all who saw them.

From Malta the 75th proceeded to Ceylon, and then to India. They rendered a good account of themselves when fighting in the Malakand Pass last year, and fresh accounts have lately reached us of their gallantry on the frontier. The storming of Chagra Kotal must always be remembered as one of the most creditable performances of the British Army.

## THE SIGNALLERS.

After the British force had scaled the greater part of the cliff, several attempts were made to carry the position by the Ghoorkas and the Derbyshire and Dorsetshire Regiments, but without success. Then the Gordon Highlanders were chosen to assail the enemy.

"The General says the position must be taken at all costs. The Gordon Highlanders will take it," were the words of Colonel Mathias. This was enough. The 75th moved forward to the skirl of the pipes, than which there is no more inspiriting instrument, and, after encountering a heavy shower of lead, succeeded in capturing the heights.

Well did they deserve the cheers of their comrades in arms as they returned victorious from the charge, and well do they deserve the thanks of all loyal British subjects. There were many instances of individual heroism. One especially deserves to be recorded here.

It is related that one of the pipers, as he marched forward playing his pipes, was shot through both ankles, and fell. This, however, had little effect on the brave fellow, who continued to play as he fell, among a shower of bullets, until the position was won.

A photograph of the battalion appeared in No. 46, along with many more photographs of regiments engaged on the frontier.

THE PIPERS.

Photo: T. WINTER.    THE SERGEANTS OF THE 1st BATTALION.

# THE ROYAL MILITARY COLLEGE, SANDHURST.

### By LIEUTENANT-COLONEL JOHN GRAHAM.

*SANDHURST CADETS OF* 1812.

"WHAT to do with our boys" is a problem which people have got somewhat tired of trying to solve The fact is that, if the boys can do nothing for themselves, nothing can be done for them in these days; and this is beginning to be comprehended both by fathers and sons. It was very different between forty and fifty years ago, when boys were admitted to Sandhurst between the ages of thirteen and fifteen, on the nomination of the Commander-in-Chief, after passing a merely qualifying examination. Ready money and a good position can even now accomplish much, but they cannot obtain a passport for Sandhurst—that must be agonised for in a competitive trial, which only the fittest survive. The consequence is that nowadays the cadets of the Royal Military College have more than average ability, have been carefully educated before entering, and are fitted to ensure more and more the efficiency of the commissioned ranks of the cavalry and infantry.

The Royal Military College was founded at the close of last century, but its infancy was passed at Great Marlow. In 1809, Lewis Theophilus Peithmann, a professor in the Great Marlow institution, published a pamphlet to defend it against an attack which had been made on it, seemingly, in a spirit of pure mischief. The *naïveté* with which he does battle for the site of his college is in marked contrast to what we have come to know as the spirit of latter-day writing. The professor said: "Here the young mind is inspired with those ideas of romantic beauty which a hilly country like Buckinghamshire must naturally excite. . . . Here, on the verdant banks of Father Thames, the young soldier contemplates his future destiny. His mind, pure like the air he breathes, is free from vice and corruption, which so often undermine the morals of the young soldier in large and populous towns." I trust that the enthusiastic professor was subsequently as ready to stand up for the salubrity and beauty of Sandhurst, with its pine woods and sandy soil, as ever he had been for the advantages of Great Marlow. This was probably the case, for in another place he referred to the present college in the following terms: "It must be known to all our readers that the House of Commons has given its liberal support to the new military college which will soon be erected at Blackwater, and which, in magnificence and in the excellence of its plan, will surpass any military establishment in Europe." Before taking leave of Professor Peithmann, it may be interesting to observe that, had he lived till now, he would have been quite in accord with the decision by which attention will henceforth be paid to French and German. He remarks: "If French is absolutely necessary for a British officer, the German language is still more so: for Germany

has perpetually been the theatre of war, the rendezvous of all European nations, and the school for soldiers."

It is amusing to look back and observe that authors took the trouble, or thought it worth while, to write books in defence of the Royal Military College of their day. In 1849, just forty years after the publication of Professor Peithmann's work, there appeared a "Complete Guide to the Royal Military College, Sandhurst. With a Reply to the Aspersions on the Cadets contained in the *Quarterly Review*. By an Experienced Officer."

In 1858 competitive examinations began to be introduced. About the same time the applicants for admission to Sandhurst were required to be older, and their period of residence was reduced. In 1871, the entrance of officers into the Army by purchase was abolished, and in 1875 the present system of competition was established.

It may be said that since that time there has been no royal road into and through the college except for Queen's cadets. These young gentlemen are admitted after passing a qualifying examination, and they are maintained during their period of residence without any payment of fees. But these advantages have been won for them by their fathers, and long may the State show this generosity and gratitude. These cadets are the sons of officers in the Army, Navy, or Marines, ' who have fallen in action or died of wounds received in action, or of disease contracted on service abroad, and who have left their families in reduced circumstances."

The annual payment for the son of a private gentleman is £150, but the sons of officers are admitted on greatly reduced terms, in accordance with a scale which is regulated by the rank and services of their fathers. Cadets receive pay at the rate of 3s. a day to cover messing and other expenses; but, with the exception of Queen's and Indian cadets, they have to pay, on first joining, a sum of £25 for uniform, books, and other items.

The office of president is filled by the Commander-in-Chief; the governor and commandant is a major-general; and the assistant-commandant and secretary is a lieutenant-colonel. There are also a quarter-master, riding-master, surgeon, assistant surgeon, and chaplain. The instructional duties are performed by a professor of fortification, with seven instructors; a professor of military topography, with eight instructors; and a professor of tactics, military administration, and law, with six instructors.

The governor has the power of rustication, but must report each case to the Commander-in-Chief, and in serious cases, cadets may, on the governor's report to the Commander-in-Chief, have their names removed from the list of candidates for the Army. Cadets salute their officers, professors, and instructors, whether in uniform or not, and all other officers if in uniform. For purposes of superintendence and drill, they are distributed in companies of a manageable strength, each company being under the charge of an officer selected by the governor from the staff of instructors. It is by a wise exercise of the power of selection that order and discipline are best maintained. So much depends on the personality of the individual in dealing with young gentlemen of that age, that where one man would cause discontent or insubordination, another, not a whit less strict, would make everything go comfortably. This is especially the case when the cadets are not at study or drill. It is then that the tact and influence of the officer come to his aid in preventing all "underground" business, without his appearing to be on the look-out for it.

Officers commanding companies live in their company quarters, mess with the cadets of their company, and are responsible for them in every respect. They are assisted by under officers and corporals selected from the cadets and by Army non-commissioned officers. The cadets are organised in six companies for parade, messing, and quarters, and in three educational divisions, comprising classes of various sizes. The institution is regulated on a military basis, an officer of the day and a corporal of the day being detailed for college duty, as well as an orderly corporal for the week, in each company. Cadets are always in uniform, except when on leave, or when specially exempt.

It may be well to state in a word or two the subjects in which instruction is given preparatory to entrance. These are mathematics, Latin, French, German, English composition and geometrical drawing, Greek, English history, chemistry, physics, physiography and geology, geography and freehand drawing. Considerable latitude is allowed to candidates in the selection of their subjects.

I believe that there is great unanimity among the highest authorities on the desirability of adding French and German to the Sandhurst syllabus, as the acquaintance made with these languages at school is likely to die out if not continuously cultivated.

Enough has probably been said to furnish the reader with a general idea of the Royal Military College, and of the gentlemen cadets attending it; and when it is added that the normal number under instruction is 360, the national importance of keeping the institution up to the highest possible standard will be realised.

*Sandhurst Cadets of 1886.*

The care of the riding-school horses, and the duties entailed by the practical work of the cadets, require the constant presence of a large number of soldiers, who, with indoor servants and others, bring the number of subordinates up to about 200. Nor is it probable that there would be any advantage in attempting to reduce that number. The paramount object of the authorities is to facilitate the instruction, and to have everything done in a thorough and perfect manner.

This brings me to an important part of my subject, namely, the Board of Visitors. It is composed of experienced and distinguished men, mostly general officers, who are appointed by the Secretary of State for War, and annually make an independent inspection of Sandhurst and Woolwich, afterwards sending to him their report on the state of both institutions. There is not the slightest doubt that the Visitors have done very great service to the Army and the country, by the wise recommendations which they have made from year to year, and the present efficiency of both the college and the academy is in a large degree due to them. For instance, it was in consequence of their recommendation that unnecessary expenses were reduced at Sandhurst, the financial arrangements placed on a more satisfactory footing, and the accounts regularly and officially audited. They likewise brought about a reduction in the cost of the cadets' uniform, a revision of the time table, the assimilation of the vacations at Sandhurst and Woolwich, which has just come into force, and many other most desirable reforms.

However capable a governor may be, and however well his officers and instructors may do their duty, he cannot fail to have his hands strengthened by the visits of so influential and independent a body. The Visitors have the best possible opportunities of comparing our two great military schools. They come to them with a fresh eye, and can see, far better than those on the spot, whether in any department there is a tendency to fall short of the proper standard.

The Visitors undoubtedly know their own mind, and if what they suggest one year is not carried out before their next visit, the fact is stated in their report and the suggestion repeated. This is sometimes done three years in succession. There is, therefore, no possibility of quietly shelving their recommendations.

It may not be known by the general public that the contemplated addition of French and German to the Sandhurst course, which has caused a rush of linguistic professors to the War Office, is the direct outcome of a report by the Visitors. In their report for 1895, the following passage occurs: "The recommendation that the study of French and German should be encouraged by allowing cadets to take up one or other of these languages, as a voluntary subject, has not been attended to. The Board again call attention to this subject, and now recommend that French or German, at the option of the cadet, should form part of the obligatory course of study at the college, in which proper instruction should be provided at the cost of the State." This recommendation, after the lapse of another year, was still under contemplation, as appears from the following passage in the Visitors' report for 1896:—"The Board were glad to learn that French or German is likely to form part of the obligatory course of study."

An eminently practical piece of advice given by the Board of Visitors in 1896 was that more attention should be paid to riding. There is a general feeling among those who are interested in military education that the Visitors have not been a day too soon in pointing out this weak spot in our system. They say: "A riding class was seen, and from the performances of the cadets, the Board are disposed to recommend that riding lessons should commence at an earlier period of the course. This is especially desirable, as the majority of the cadets have little or no experience in riding before entrance. It would be preferable if attention to this exercise could be encouraged before the entrance examination, but having regard to the difficulties of imposing any compulsion in this respect, the Board confine themselves to the above recommendation." The difficulty of making equitation an obligatory subject of examination before entrance should surely not be too great to be overcome by the military authorities. Indeed, some of the more enlightened and far-seeing military tutors are systematically encouraging the attendance of their pupils at military riding schools, and it would be no more than fair that marks should be given for proficiency in a subject so essential to the education of an officer.

In the report for 1895 it is stated that, although the Sandhurst college and the Woolwich academy are both maintained for the education of young gentlemen of about the same age for the Army, the standing orders of the two places "differ widely in several essential points." "The Board recommend that they be revised, and made to agree as much as possible." The last recommendation has been adopted, and the present year will see a more uniform and more effective system in force. Several faulty arrangements in both places will be abolished, and the reforms thus introduced will place our military educational establishments on a more satisfactory footing. For this result we shall be indebted in a great degree to the Board of Visitors.

ACROSS THE SALT SEAS

A ROMANCE OF WAR AND ADVENTURE
BY JOHN BLOUNDELLE-BURTON
AUTHOR OF
"IN THE DAY OF ADVERSITY" "DENOUNCED!"
"THE HISPANIOLA PLATE" ETC.

### SYNOPSIS OF PREVIOUS CHAPTERS.

The hero, Mervyn Crespin, who was lately lying in the prison of Lugo under sentence of death, found himself there in consequence of a hazardous ride which he set out upon from Vigo (of which town he has taken part in the capture), with the intention of joining the English forces under the command of Marlborough in Flanders. He had originally been despatched by the Earl on a mission to the British Fleet, which was expected to be at Cadiz (but which, he found, had left for England), as the bearer of important information, to the effect that some Spanish galleons from the West Indies had altered their destination and, instead of going to Cadiz as they intended, had, on hearing that the English Fleet was in the neighbourhood, proceeded to Vigo. On his way to the former place he encounters a man whose name is supposed to be Carstairs, and whom he and the master of the ship regard as a pirate. Meanwhile, he by chance falls in with the English Fleet proceeding home, is enabled to convey the information he carries to Sir George Rooke, and goes with it to Vigo. After the battle, which is fully described, he is sent to board one of the captured galleons, and here he encounters a young Spanish gentleman, as he supposes, who has been a passenger in the ship, as well as a monk named Father Jaime. Eventually, he sets out for Flanders on the above-mentioned perilous ride, the young Spaniard, who has conceived a warm friendship for him, insisting upon being his companion, to which he reluctantly consents. They encounter on their way a series of stirring adventures, culminating in a fight with the Spanish police near Lugo, and, though entering that town in safety, are followed and arrested. Father Jaime has, however, joined them and rendered great assistance in the combat, he appearing no longer as a monk (which he acknowledges himself not to be), but as a traveller, himself on the road to Lugo. As they are endeavouring, however, to escape capture, they overhear a conversation between Jaime and the man Carstairs, who has also arrived here in search of some property which he expected to come in the galleons, and from it they learn that Jaime, far from being a monk, is no less a person than the renowned Gramont—a pirate loathed in the Indies, but supposed to be long since drowned. Señor Belmonte, the young Spaniard, who has confided to the Englishman that he does not know who his father was, except that he was enormously rich, also discovers now to his horror that Gramont is the man. This, however, is not the only discovery made. As the young Spaniard reels against Crespin on gleaning that intelligence, Crespin, in his turn, is astonished to find that his companion is a woman and not a man, who has travelled to Europe disguised thus in her hopes of finding Carstairs, whose right name is Eaton, and of punishing him for having robbed her, and also because the galleons would not take women as passengers. All are arrested and imprisoned, Gramont and Crespin being sentenced to death, while Juana, which is the name of the Spanish lady, is protected by the Alcalde of the city, who has fallen in love with her striking beauty. He, however, agrees that her father shall be allowed to escape provided she leaves Spain with him; and, in her misery and despair over that father's crimes, she consents. Crespin regrets his fate the more because he has learned from Juana that her instantaneous love for him at first sight was the principal thing which prompted her to insist on accompanying him in all his dangers. Also, he knows now how fondly he has come to love her. He has, however, been able to himself escape in the manner recently described, and to follow Juana until he comes up with her in company with the Alcalde. How he made that escape, and how he and Gramont have once more met, has also been shown in the chapters preceding the present instalment, which, with the next, brings the narrative to an end.

### CHAPTER XXXI. *(continued).*

NOW this, as I learnt later, was not the case in absolute fact, since Portugal joined not with us till the next spring had come; yet it served very well for my purpose. For these Spaniards did, doubtless, think that they would have got me—and, I suppose, Juana, too—bloodlessly, and have been able to hale us back to Lugo and its accursed *brásero*; but now they found out their mistake. They would have to fight to get me, and, as I think they feared my sword as much as the four or five others of my new found Portuguese friends, they very wisely desisted from any attempt. Wherefore, after many angry words exchanged on both sides, in which I took no part,

I went back to the inn, feeling sure that, since I should never venture into Spain again, I was free of its clutches.

\* \* \* \* \* \*

Once more, a few hours later, my girl and I were on the road as travelling companions, only now we were lovers instead of friends, and the companionship was, by God's mercy, to be for the length of our lives. And sweet it was to me, beyond all thought, to have her by my side, to hear her soft voice in my ears, and to listen to the words of love that fell from her lips. Sweet, too, to me to make reply to them.

For one thing, also, I was devoutly grateful—namely, that I had not hesitated to tell her that her father still lived, that he had yet, by Heaven's grace, many years before him in which to expiate his past; that he had escaped the awful end to which he had been doomed, and which, during some few hours, she imagined he had suffered. Devoutly grateful that I had done this because, now, the sorrow which she felt for the erring man was chastened by the knowledge that it was not too late for him to repent and obtain pardon, and that his death, whatever it might be, could scarce be one of such horror as that from which he had escaped.

After some consideration I had decided that 'twould be best we should make our way to Oporto, where I thought 'twas very like we might find some ship for either England or Holland—perhaps, also, since the trade of that town with our country is of such extreme importance, some vessel of war acting as convoy for the merchants. Moreover, the distance was not great in so small a land as this, and, by the chart I carried, seemed not to be more than thirty or forty leagues, though, to compass them, we should have to pass over mountains more than once. Yet the horses were fresh—I rode now my own, on which Gramont had come and had then exchanged for the black one on which I had escaped, it having been prepared for him ere I took his place; the snow was hard as iron; it was not much to do. And, much or little, it had to be done.

And so we progressed, passing through Mirandella and Murça, striking at last a broad high road that ran straight for Oporto, scaling mountains sometimes, plunging sometimes into deep valleys and crossing streams over shaking wooden bridges that, by their appearance, seemed scarce strong enough to bear a child, yet over which we passed in safety. And, though neither she nor I spoke our thoughts, I think—I know—that the same idea was ever present to her mind as to mine, the idea that we might ere long come upon some sign of her father. For, now and again, as she peered down upon the white track we followed, losing more than once the road, yet finding it again ere long, she would rein in the jennet and look at the tracks frozen in the snow, then shake her head mournfully as we went on once more.

But of Gramont we saw no sign—nor ever saw him again in this world. Going on and on, however, we drew near to, as I judged, the coast, still climbing the mountains and still passing at other times through the valleys, over all of which there lay the vast white pall, burying everything beneath it.

We heard, also, the great river, which is called the Douro, rolling and humming and swirling beneath the roof of frozen snow which, in some places, stretched across it from bank to bank. In some places, too, where the road we traversed approached nearer to the stream, we saw it cleaving its way through banks so narrowed by their coatings of ice that it o'erleapt and foamed above the sides, while, with a loud swish, such as a huge tide makes upon a shingly beach, its waters spread out with a hissing splash from their eddies and swept over the borders on either side. Yet, because the way this river rushed was likewise our way to peace and happiness—the road towards the great sea we hoped so soon to traverse—we regarded it with interest.

"See," I said to Juana, as now we rode close to it, so that at this time our horses' feet were laved by its overflow, "see how it bears down with it great trees from far inland—from where we have come. Also other things—the wooden roof of some peasant's hut, some household goods, too. I fear it has swept over the country, has burst in places from its narrow frost-bound sides."

'Twas true. Such must have happened, for, even as I spoke, there went by the body of a horse—the creature's sides all torn and lacerated, doubtless by some narrow passage in which the spears of ice would be as sharp as swords' points; then, next—oh! piteous sight!—a little dead babe rolled over and over, as the waves bore it along in their swift flight.

"Look! look!" she murmured, pointing forward to where the river broadened, and out into the breadth of which there projected a spur, or tongue, of land. "Look! that catches much of what comes down—see! the dead horse's progress is stopped upon it—and, Mervan, the little babe is also rolled on to that slip of land; also there are many other things besides. More bodies of both men and animals."

There were, in solemn truth. As we rode nearer to that little jutting promontory, we saw that much of what the Douro had brought down was stopped by it; upon the frozen tongue of protruding land were mixed many things in confusion—the dead horse and another which had preceded it, some poor sheep, a dog, the little babe which had just passed before our eyes, and two or three dead men. Some on their backs, their arms extended on that frozen refuge—one on his face.

Also I saw that she knew, too. Neither scarlet coat nor battered weapon were strange to her.

"I will descend," I said, speaking in a low voice, such as those assume who stand in presence of the dead. "I will descend and make sure," whereon she bowed her head in reply, making no demur. At that moment she, perhaps, thought it best to be certain that he who had sought her soul's degradation would never traffic with another woman's honour.

But as I went down, on foot now, to that tongue of land on which the drowned reposed, I had another reason, besides this one of assuring ourselves that the body was that of her tempter, the *Alcáide.* I desired to discover if 'twas by the river alone that he had come to his death, borne down and into it by some streamlet nearer the Spanish border, and not by the avenging weapon of the man who said that I should never have spared him, have never let him quit my side with life. For they might have met, I knew—the one who went first might have been belated on his road—snowbound; the second might have overtaken him, his vengeance have been swift and sure.

Stepping across the bodies of the drowned animals, avoiding those of the peasants, and putting gently aside that of the little babe, I reached him, recognising as I did so the coal-black hair flecked and streaked with grey, the rings upon the hands stretched out, backs upwards. Then I turned him over, seeing that the face was torn and cut by the jagged ice through which he had been hurried, also bruised and discoloured. But in all the body no sign of rapier wound, nor pistol shot, nor of avenging finger marks upon the throat.

So I went back to her and took my reins from her hands, and once more we set out upon our way.

"The Battle was Won!"

Mostly they were peasants—their garb told that, also their rough, coarse hands, which showed black against the leper whiteness of the ice and snow beneath them. But he who lay upon his face was none such; his scarlet coat, guarded with galloon, had never graced a peasant's back, no more than any peasant had worn that sword (with, now, both blade and scabbard broken) that was by his side.

And, halting upon the little ridge which made the summit of that promontory—gazing down upon that man, I knew as well as though I could see his down-turned face whose body it was stretched out there upon its icy bier.

But the dark, lustrous eyes, as they gazed into mine, asked a silent and unworded question—so that I guessed my thoughts had been in her mind, too—and when I answered with an equal a silence, I knew that I had brought comfort to her heart.

## CHAPTER XXXII.

### "MALBROUCK S'EN VA-T'EN-GUERRE."

More than a year had passed since my love and I reached England in safety, since she became my wife—nay! a year and a-half. And still we were parted once more. She at home in my father's house with the little child which had come to bless our union, I in Bavaria, and once more with the regiment. A captain now, yet with my colonelcy assured; the reward promised me by the Earls of Athlone and Marlborough earned. Only—should I ever live to enjoy it! That was the question which I asked myself to-night, a question similar to that which thousands were asking themselves on this night. How many of us would be alive in another twenty-four hours?

For it was the night of Tuesday, the 12th of August, in the year of our Lord 1704. On the morrow we knew that there would be fought a battle which must decide—perhaps for ever—the fate of England and France, of Louis and of Anne—of, in sober truth, all Europe.

We lay outside and around the village which we have come to speak of as Blenheim, though some there are who call it Plintheim, while the French name it Hochstett; a little, unclean village whose name is destined, I love to think, to go down the years to all posterity; to be mentioned with pride and with a warm, fierce glow at the heart by all who are Englishmen; to be commemorated in unborn days by that great noble palace now a-building near Oxford for my Lord Duke of Marlborough—the victor-in-chief of this great struggle. Well enough did that young student, whom I have since met and conversed with, Mr. Joseph Addison, send forth from his humble chambers in the Haymarket—though now he is rising fast to great riches and honours—those noble and inspiriting lines in which he speaks of His Grace, at the end of his poem, as one who upon that memorable day—

"Pleased the Almighty's orders to perform,
Rides in the whirlwind and directs the storm."

For so it was with His Grace of Marlborough, as you—if still willing to follow the narrative told by one more used to the blade than the pen—shall see.

By rapid and forced marches (the Duke having obtained secret intelligence of the French intentions), we had come to the neighbourhood of this place, situated upon the banks of the Danube, we crossing the Maas, or, as the French list to call it, the Meuse, at Maestricht; then on to the Rhine, and meeting the enemy for the first time at Schullenberg, near Donawert. And we beat them, too, as we did at Rain and Aicha; we ravaged the Palatinate as years before Turenne had done, and as Tilly had done still earlier; then went on again, learning that Vendôme was blocked up in the Tyrol. On and on, now joining forces with Prince Eugene, until at last we stood upon the spot where all our efforts were to be crowned with either eternal glory or a defeat which could scarcely ever be repaired. The French were stronger than we were by four thousand men, also they were almost all of that nation, the Bavarians being but one-fifth part of the whole; while, for us, we were indeed a motley crowd, consisting of English, Dutch, Prussians, Danes, Hessians, Wirtembergers, and Hanoverians—yet we feared nothing! For Marlborough was the head of all, while, next to him, or rather in noble rivalry to him, came that other greatest soldier of Europe, Eugene of Savoy. Against such as these, not even the Marshals, Tallard and Marsin, aided by the Bavarian Prince, Maximilian, could, we trusted, succeed. Yet, nevertheless, we knew that the task before us was no easy one, nor any child's play. We had to win to-morrow, or to hide our heads for ever. To be swept from off the Continent of Europe back to our own little island, and with no further hopes left than the utilising for our benefit of our American and West Indian colonies—to sink into a fifth-rate Power. We! who had dominated Europe for centuries, who had given laws to the whole world, who had crushed beneath our heel all who had dared to cross our path and to oppose us!

It could not be, we told each other. Nay! we swore it should not be. Not while there ran one drop of our island blood within our veins, not while the memory of our fathers' past deeds of conquest held its sway.

France had never beaten us yet. She should not do so on the morrow.

Her great army, the army of her great tyrant king, was massed around Blenheim and the neighbouring village of Oberglau, Tallard having the Danube behind him and Blenheim to his front, the latter being garrisoned by numerous battalions and squadrons of native French troops. Also Oberglau was occupied by more battalions, including three corps of Irish veterans—men who had mostly followed the Stuart king into exile, and who had sworn to slay Marlborough on that day or take him prisoner—because he had deserted the last of those Stuarts. Yet we, too, had sworn our oaths and made our vows—if the blades of our English dragoons could fall more heavily upon any one set of men than upon another, if the bayonets of our English foot could pierce deeper than elsewhere, they should do so with those who, our own kith

and kin, were on the morrow to support the Frenchmen against us.

Further on, in front of the village of Lutzingen, was the left wing of the enemy—in full face of the dreaded Eugene!—an enormous phalanx. In all, this great army numbered sixty thousand men, and, though the disposition of their forces made them weak in their centre, their position was a strong one. Also they had not neglected the strengthening of the villages at the extremities of their line, and had not only thrown up entrenchments and barricades all around on which they had placed heavy cannon, but had, likewise, dragged out the villagers' furniture—their beds and cabinets and household things—and used them for the purpose, as well as their carts and other goods.

And since they were upon a slope, the whole of the plain by which we must advance was covered by their guns.

Yet, if God were with us, we meant so to advance, to possess ourselves of those villages, and to hurl into the Danube some thousands of those Frenchmen who now awaited our attack.

It was from our camp, at a little place called Munster, on the river's bank, that we set forth at dawn of this August day, leaving all our tents standing, yet not before we had commended ourselves to the God of Battles, Divine Service being performed shortly after midnight at the head of every squadron and regiment in our army. Also, the Duke did previously receive the Holy Sacrament with great fervour and solemnity. And at about six of the clock we were in view of the enemy, who—as has so often happened when we have been a-fighting of the French—seemed not at all to have expected us. What did they think we were a-doing? Perhaps they were deceived by a rumour which had been industriously circulated that we were retiring on Nordlingen—though they must have forgotten our character, I have often thought, if they supposed we had rushed thus far into the bowels of Europe, only to retire when once we had come up with them! Nevertheless, and however this may be, they knew now (and well they knew it) that we were upon them, and they began firing off guns and putting themselves into some sort of order to give us a reception, which they did with their cannon. Yet we took little or no harm from this. All the same, the battle had begun!

Now, there were two little rivulets as well as a morass 'twixt the French and us, which we had to get over or around somehow, also there were two mills placed on to the banks of these rivulets, and, being full of Frenchmen, they served as a defence against our passage as well as redoubts for the village of Blenheim, and these obstacles teased us much. For, while we were endeavouring to bridge these little rivers—which at last we did, establishing five pontoons, over which the forces under the Duke passed, while those under the Prince went round by a great *détour*—the enemy were pouring their cannon shot into our ranks, so that already we were suffering severely. Yet, by one o'clock in the day the whole of our army was advancing towards the enemy.

And soon we were in the thick of the *mêlée*. It was to be death or victory now.

It seemed at first as though the latter alone could be our portion.

As we advanced towards Blenheim itself—the gallant Lord Cutts commanding the division, and General Rowe leading the first line—a terrible fire was opened by the enemy, but not until our troops came within thirty yards of the palisades which they had set up all around the place. Yet the latter commander would give no order to fire; under a murderous discharge which mowed down officers and men, that gallant band held on until those palisades were reached. Then, and not till then, and only as Rowe struck the pales with the blade of his sword, was the command given, as well as one to force an entrance at the point of the bayonet.

It was a grand spectacle—yet, we feared, a hopeless one. Also, it looked already as if our chance was gone. Those accursed piles of stakes had been well planted, neither bayonet nor sword could break them down—nay! not even men's strength; they would not yield. The soldiers fought with them with their bare hands, as though they were living things, pulling, wrenching, striving; their weapons thrown away—or, where swords, held in their teeth. And all the while through the opening of the stakes were coming hail-storms of bullets, great flecks of flames which blinded men and singed their wigs and eyebrows, with bayonets darting out that spitted their faces and ripped them open. And Rowe fell writhing at his followers' feet; his lieutenant-colonel and major, endeavouring to drag him off, were shot down, and fell dead a-top of him; some French gendarmes charged, and, amidst the curses of Rowe's men, seized the colours of his regiment. Yet, soon, some Hessians who advanced had gotten them back—that disgrace was spared!

*(To be concluded in our next).*

*Photo. JULES DAVID.*                                                                 *Paris.*

*Lieut.-Gen. Sir C. J. EAST, K.C.B., Governor and Commandant, R.M. College, Sandhurst.*

LIEUTENANT-GENERAL SIR CECIL JAMES EAST entered the Army in 1854, served with the 82nd Regiment in the Crimea from the end of September, 1855, and was present at the siege and fall of Sebastopol (medal with clasp and Turkish medal), also in the Indian Campaign in 1857, and was severely wounded at Cawnpore on the 26th November (medal). General East graduated at the Staff College in 1862, and served as assistant-quartermaster-general with the Chittagong column of the Lushai Expeditionary Force in 1871-72 (mentioned in despatches, received the thanks of the Governor-General in Council, medal with clasp, and brevet of major). His next war service was in the latter part of the Zulu War of 1879, as deputy adjutant and quartermaster-general. He was present in the engagement at Ulundi (mentioned in despatches, brevet of colonel, medal with clasp); served with the Burmese Expedition in 1886-89, in command of the 1st Brigade after the capture of Mandalay (mentioned in despatches, C.B., and two clasps). General East was appointed to his present position in December, 1893, being then a major-general. He is universally respected, and has done much to sustain the high reputation of the Sandhurst College as a place of military education.

# The Royal Military College, Sandhurst.

*The Royal Military College, Sandhurst.*

*The Boathouse.*

THE grand frontage of the college, and, indeed, all the permanent buildings connected with it, are highly creditable to the foresight and public spirit of its founders. The first picture on this page conveys some idea of the extent of ground occupied by the main building. In addition to the offices of the governor, of the assistant commandant, of the officer of the staff, and the other rooms necessary to the business of a large institution, there are situated here the "halls of study." Therein the 360 gentlemen cadets receive instruction in fortification, military topography, tactics, military administration, and military law, the educational duties being carried out by three professors and twenty-one instructors. The educational staff is composed of officers, a large proportion of whom are graduates of the Staff College, and all of whom receive their appointments by virtue of their eminent fitness for the duties involved.

The lake is not only an interesting feature of the scene, but offers the advantages of boating and swimming, without which no military college should be considered fully equipped. In continental armies the practice of swimming has of late been much encouraged among the men, in order to facilitate the crossing of rivers by men and horses in a body. The British Army should not be left behind in such an acquirement; it is therefore gratifying to read, in the last report of the Board of Visitors, the following recommendation with regard to the college at Sandhurst:— "The provision of a covered swimming bath would be highly desirable when funds permit, and the Board consider that every cadet should pass a qualifying examination in swimming, both at Sandhurst and Woolwich."

The wisdom of the recommendation is undeniable, because in this exercise, as in every other, the officers should be the leaders and superiors of the rank and file.

*Photos. W. SHAW*     *Camberley.*

*THE COLLEGE, FROM ACROSS THE LAKE.*

*Photo. W. SHAW.*

*Cambeley.*

## THE COLLEGE THROUGH THE TREES.

THE picture above shows the college through "the loopholes of retreat," and suggests pleasant and picturesque surroundings of wood and water. It has been said that an institution of this kind should be placed in the midst of attractive scenery. This produces a certain, if almost imperceptible, effect on the minds of the young, and enhances the affectionate remembrance with which, in after life, they look back on their Alma Mater. Not only from a sentimental, but from a hygienic point of view, the Sandhurst site, as may be gathered from its name, is a well-chosen one. The dry soil, the extensive pine woods of the neighbourhood, and the ample scope within the grounds, furnish all the external conditions requisite for the maintenance of robust health. Such a place cannot but be pronounced admirably fitted for its purpose, and among the many thousands of cavalry and infantry officers to whom it has proved a home between their boyhood and manhood, few have not remembered it with feelings of kindness and regret.

*Governor, Professors. and Officers.*

*Non-Commissioned Staff.*

THE governor, assistant commandant and secretary, chaplain, staff officers, professors and instructors are represented in the first group on this page. The next group consists of the sergeant-majors and sergeants who carry out the non-commissioned duties pertaining to the supervision of subordinates, and assistance in the outdoor instruction of the cadets. These duties are sufficiently onerous, as there are about 200 soldiers employed in various departments of the institution.

The third picture shows the cadets and their officers saluting, as a battalion in line at open order. The infantry drill undergone by the cadets has a most salutary effect, and it may be taken as a general rule that the manner in which any corps of military students parades for inspection and marches past is a tolerably fair index of its application to study, as well as of its discipline. Infantry drill, properly conducted, is no waste of time, even in establishments where book-work is of paramount moment. It changes the current of thought, quickens and sharpens mind and body, and increases the value of the whole man. It brings the body into such subjection to the will that its obedience thereto is prompt and effective. But one of its greatest benefits is that it aids and promotes good order and discipline, making its influence felt in study, in outside work, and in all the intercourse between the cadet and his authorities. It establishes that feeling of subordination which is indispensable in a soldier.

Photos. JULES DAVE.          *THE BATTALION IN REVIEW ORDER.*          Paris.

*A TRESTLE BRIDGE.*

*Photos. JULES DAVID.*                                                      *Paris.*

*A LIMBER LADDER BRIDGE.*

THE bridging operations represented above form part of the course of instruction in field fortification. The public generally understand by fortifications, permanent works, such as fortresses and coast batteries. These buildings are entrusted to the corps of Royal Engineers. Field fortification, on the other hand, must be known and practised by all arms, as it enables them to throw up hasty defences, and to move across streams and other hindrances that they may encounter in the field. Trestles, planks, spars, rope, casks, boats, and, in fact, anything available for the purpose, may be used in the construction of one or another kind of military bridge. The method of construction, the use of materials, and the duties of each member of the party, are taught by an instructor, who sees that the work is practically carried out by the cadets themselves. Experience of soldiers' duties, not only by being drilled as privates in company and battalion, but by performing their manual labour, is one of the best qualifications for command.

Photo. W. SHAW.

*A RIDING SCHOOL PARADE.*

Camberley

Photo. JULES DAVID.

*PUTTING A BUILDING IN A STATE OF DEFENCE.*

Paris.

EQUITATION is a very important feature of the Sandhurst course, and it is one to which greater attention is likely to be paid in the future than has yet been the case. When last the Board of Visitors inspected the college, they were "disposed to recommend that riding lessons should commence at an earlier period of the course. This is especially desirable, as the majority of the cadets have little or no experience in riding before entrance. It would be preferable if attention to this exercise could be encouraged before the entrance examination; but having regard to the difficulties of imposing any compulsion in this respect, the Board confine themselves to the above recommendation." It is undoubted that all candidates for commissions in the Army should be able to ride fairly before their entrance examination, and that they should be proficient in the exercise before being finally passed into the Service. Any officer, even of the infantry, may be called upon to ride, and if he be not master of his horse and of the mounted sword exercise, he is in a helpless and painful position.

*HASTY ENTRENCHMENTS.*

*TOPOGRAPHICAL CLASSES.*

Photos. *JULES DAVID.*                                                                    *Paris.*

*RIFLE RANGE.*

SOME further elements of Sandhurst life are presented on this page. At the top is a working party of cadets engaged, under the superintendence of an instructor, in digging rifle pits and shelter trenches. They are artistically akin to Mr. Ruskin's batch of undergraduates who did navvy work at Hincksey, near Oxford, a number of years ago. The motive idea was that to make a road was quite as æsthetic as to pull an oar, and much more productive. However that may be, there is no doubt that pick and shovel work brings out solid qualities, and teaches officers duly to estimate the efforts of Tommy Atkins in like circumstances. The next picture is composed of two topographical classes equipped for a surveying excursion; and the last shows cadets practising on the rifle range, and thus preparing themselves for the intelligent supervision of men who, if they cannot shoot straight, are worse than useless. When it is added that gymnastics and physical drill are not neglected at Sandhurst, it will be seen that a sensible and robust all-round military training is there provided for the future officers of the British cavalry and infantry.

*EXTERIOR OF CHURCH.*

Photo. *JULES DAVID.*    Paris.

*INTERIOR OF CHURCH.*

NO large place of education is complete without a house of Christian worship, and the devout recognition of the Supreme Being, from whom all power and wisdom are derived. The sanctions supplied by the Christian faith give stability to the moral principles of young men, purify their aims, and elevate their conceptions of duty. It is, therefore, of the utmost moment that at this great college, where young men are prepared by hundreds for positions of influence, and for representing a Christian country in all quarters of the globe, the claims of religion should always be presented with distinctness and simplicity. In fact, simplicity is requisite in all military places of worship. Church of England soldiers are obliged to attend their church, and nothing should be permitted in its service or ornamentation that will offend any section of churchmen.

The Glories & Traditions of the British Army

THE GLOUCESTERSHIRE REGIMENT.
BY CAPT. A. C. LOVETT.

F the final issue of the struggle against the French, William III. realised that success depended on more than English gold, and he consequently increased the standing Army to 83,121 men, adding to it ten new regiments of horse and fifteen of foot.

To raise one of the latter, the King appointed Sir John Gibson as its Colonel —no honorary title, as his duty was to command his corps in the field as well as in quarters; and he was, moreover, commander of one of the companies, drawing pay as such, and claiming as well an ensign of his own.

Regiments at this period took precedence according to the seniority of their respective colonels, and so we find that John Gibson's (28th) comes after Luke Lillingston's (38th), and precedes Thomas Farrington's (29th).

The warrant for the creation of Sir John Gibson's regiment runs as follows:—"Whereas We have directed Three Regiments of Foot to be forthwith Raised under the Command of Coll. John Gibson, Coll. Thomas Farrington, and Coll. William Northcott. We do hereby declare Our Will and Pleasure to be, That for the better and more speedy raising and compleating thereof, the said Regiments shall be allowed as full and compleate, from the Twentyeth day of this instant March, Provided the respective companys do appear in a Condition of service, on or before the Twentyeth day of May next; and with all their Cloathing and accoutrements on or before the First day of June following. And if any Captain or other Officer shall be faulty herein, such Officer or Captain shall Incurr Our highest Displeasure, and shall be immediately cashiered, as also an abatement of Pay made in proportion to the defective Numbers of men, whereof the Pay Master Generall of Our Forces, the Commissary Generall of the Musters, and all the Officers whom it may Concerne are to take due notice, and to Govern themselves accordingly.

"Given at Our Court at Whitehall, this 12th Day of March, 169⅞.

"In the sixth year of Our Reign.'

"By his Ma'ty's Command,

"WILLIAM BLATHWAYTE."

John Gibson's regiment of foot consisted of twelve companies, each sixty men strong, divided into fourteen pikemen and forty-six musketeers, the former selected for strength of build, and carrying a pike, sword, metal helmet, and breastplate. In addition there was a grenadier company, composed of picked men, who were chosen for their height as well as agility, for they carried a ponderous equipment, comprising a fusil with sling, cartridge box, grenade pouch, bayonet and hatchet, and girdle. A "hanger" or basket-hilted, slightly curved sword completed a grenadier's outfit.

The musketeer was simply armed with a matchlock, collar of bandoliers with ball-bag, priming flask, and sword.

The officers of the grenadiers carried fusils; but of the others, the captain bore a pike, the lieutenant a partisan or halberd, and the ensign, when not carrying a colour, had a half-pike.

Such was Gibson's regiment of foot, which did not, however, proceed forthwith into the field and join the King in the Low Countries, but passed the next three years in the West Indies and Newfoundland. Leaving a detachment in the latter country, the greater part of the regiment returned home and was disbanded 16th March, 1698, in consequence of the Treaty of Ryswick, return of peace, and the reduction of the numbers of the Army by 10,000 men. The peace with France lasted but a short period, and in 1702 the regiment—with many others—was brought back into existence, its detachment meanwhile having remained intact in Newfoundland during these four years.

In 1704, under Lieutenant-Colonel Robert Dalziel, the regiment of De Lalo, who had recently purchased Gibson's Colonelcy, was employed in Holland under the Duke of Marlborough, and next year the regiment received its baptism of fire at the retaking of Huy from the French. This town is situated on both sides of the Meuse, and was an important strategical point. De Lalo's men had first to force their way into the town, after which Fort St. Joseph and two other forts were successfully escaladed, and the castle finally surrendered. By the end of the year the French barrier of fortified lines had been turned, and the troops were able to look forward, confident that this advantage would tell in favour of their great leader.

During the winter, John, Viscount Mordaunt, secured the command of the regiment. Marlborough's Army took the field again in May, 1706, and soon commenced their march towards Mierdorp to encounter the enemy, who were found in the very position the Duke was about to occupy at Ramillies. On the 23rd May the British, formed in two lines, advanced to turn the French out of the villages in front. After a fierce fight, lasting three hours and a-half, the victorious cavalry found themselves masters of the height of Ottomond on our left, while the troops who had made the attack on Ramillies, penetrated through the swamp and hurled the enemy out of Offuz. In the midst of this rout the infantry regiments of Churchill and Mordaunt, who, with five squadrons, had hitherto been in the second line, no longer remained idle spectators of the conflict. With that boldness that characterised all the movements of that day, and led by the intrepid Churchill, they forced their way through the morass, and ascending the high ground beyond, they charged and defeated with considerable slaughter those who still formed the enemy's left flank. The French were completely broken, and the fate of the Netherlands was decided. Amongst Marlborough's letters one reads: "Colonel Lalo is acquainted that his officers must conform themselves to other regiments, and use pertuisans as those of the regiment of Welsh Fusileers." Evidently this cumbersome weapon did not find favour with the officers of our regiment.

Early in 1707, Mordaunt's regiment threw in their lot with that unfortunate expedition under the Earl of Galway whose object was to create a diversion against the French and Spanish on behalf of the Archduke Charles of Austria, who was to be placed on the throne of Spain. The force of Dutch, Portuguese, and English landed on the east coast of Spain, and on the 25th of April, 1707, was fought the battle of Almanza. The enemy had assembled together the entire strength of

101 squadrons and fifty-one battalions, and awaited the furious onslaught of the British and their allies, who numbered but two-thirds of their adversaries. Our foot, amongst whom was Mordaunt's, are said to have done wonders, and were victorious in the centre. But at the first shock, the Portuguese cavalry gave way and abandoned the foot, who were forced to beat a retreat. Had the bravery of the English and Dutch been seconded, victory would certainly have inclined to the confederate side. On this occasion, it is curious to find that the English army was commanded by a Frenchman—the Earl of Galway, being son of the Marquis of Ruvigny, a supporter of William III., and the French army was commanded by an Englishman, the Duke of Berwick, son of James II.

After such a disastrous but glorious conflict, it was found necessary to renew Mordaunt's regiment, in order that they should keep the field in the Spanish Peninsula. A correspondent with the army in 1708 thus writes:—"We cannot give yet any certain account of the number of our forces, but those we have are the finest in the world. Such are the regiments of Southwell (6th), commanded by Lieutenant-Colonel Hunt; that of Blood (17th), commanded by Lieutenant-Colonel Bourgnet; and that of Mordaunt (28th), commanded by Colonel Dalziel," a tough old veteran who had made eighteen campaigns under the greatest commanders in Europe. Eleven years of peace gave the 28th time to regain their well-tried strength, which was again to be put to the test in Spain. The town of Vigo was successfully attacked and captured by a force under Viscount Cobham, and the 28th again returned home, to make a stay of no less than twenty-two years in Ireland; but this is nothing to another regiment we read of as having put in seventy-eight years at a stretch in the Emerald Isle.

In 1734, Philip Bragg was appointed seventh Colonel, and he continued in that position for nearly a quarter of a century, so that till this very day the regiment style themselves "Old Bragg's." One had not heard of the age limit in those days, and in the list of officers on the half-pay of the Army for 1740 is to be found the name of Lieutenant Henry Davis of the 28th Regiment, aged 111 years, with half-pay of 2s. 4d. per diem! In truth, one of the King's hard bargains.

About the year 1742 the uniform of "Bragg's" consisted of a red coat, faced, lined and lapelled with white, bound with white like the red waistcoat. The leg was incased in a white gaiter bound with a black garter. The belts and pouches were black. A cocked hat was worn by all except the Grenadier Company, whose mitre-shaped cap added to their stature. The latter bore at the back the number "28," being at this time the only place where the number was shown by all regiments. Bragg's regiment again went over to Flanders in 1743, to take the field under Marshal Wade in the following year against the French, and on the 11th May, 1745, the combined Dutch, Hanoverian, and British forces encountered the French in their entrenched position near Fontenoy. Bragg's were in the right attack of the British, which bore all before them, driving the French out of their

lines of entrenchments back into their camp. Taken in flank, however, by a battery of twenty-five pieces, concealed behind a wood, they were forced to retire. The second assault was as brilliantly executed, but unfruitful of result, and in face of such losses the British Commander slowly retired. At every hundred paces the battalions fronted, but the enemy made no attempt to seriously disturb them, which shows how severely they had been handled. Had we fought solely against men and not against 266 pieces of cannon, the siege of Tournay would undoubtedly have been raised. No colour, standard, or drum was lost; but we took one standard. Bragg's regiment lost one officer and sixteen others killed, while Lord George Sackville and eight other officers were wounded. From Flanders the regiment went for a well-earned rest of twelve years to Ireland.

The year 1758 is an important one in the history of the Gloucestershire Regiment, for it marks the constitution from the second battalion of the "Old Buffs" of the 61st Foot, or "Young Buffs," who became in 1782 the South Gloucestershire, and later, in 1881, the second battalion of the Gloucestershire Regiment.

To meet the threatened absorption of the whole of North America by the French, our armed forces were increased, and

*At Grenade Drill,* 1758.

to the "Buffs" was added, as in the case of many other regiments, a second battalion in 1756, which is therefore the more correct date of the birth of this battalion. It very soon became schooled in the stern lessons of actual warfare, and took part in the capture of the Isle of Aix, off the coast of France; and, again, in 1758, Elliott's (61st) sailed for the West Indies, where they took an active part in the wresting the island of Guadeloupe from the French.

In the meantime the 28th were not leading an idle life, but were busily engaged in ousting the Frenchmen from North America. Louisburg, the capital of the island of Cape Breton, capitulated on the 26th July, 1758, after the besiegers had overcome almost insurmountable difficulties, and endured harassing fatigue. Here Bragg's Grenadiers were incorporated with the famous "Louisburg Grenadiers," who were foremost among the storming party, and afterwards acquitted themselves so brilliantly on the heights of Abraham.

The battle, which resulted in the surrender of Quebec, and decided the fate of Canada, is familiar to the majority of Englishmen; how the immortal Wolfe led his little army by a small path up the steep heights in the face of 12,000 Frenchmen. Forming his force into battle array with the Louisburg Grenadiers and Bragg's (28th) on the right, Wolfe calmly awaited the onslaught of the enemy.

But the French could make no impression on the English line of steel, and when at length the foe were seen to waver, Wolfe led forward the grenadiers, and gave the order for the advance of the entire line. Before this Wolfe had received his third and mortal wound, but would not quit the field. "Support me; let not my brave soldiers see me fall; the day is ours, keep it," he murmured to Lieutenant Brown, of the 28th, who, with Mr. Henderson, a volunteer in his company, and a private soldier carried the dying hero to the rear. "See how they run!" someone cried. "Who run?" asked our hero. "The French; they give way in all directions," was the reply. "Now, God be praised, I die happy," were his last words.

One more glorious event may be added to the deeds of "Bragg's" ere they returned home, and that was the capture of Havannah and its dependencies from the Spanish in August, 1762. The same force also recaptured the island of Martinique about the same time.

*Bragg's Grenadiers at Louisburg,* 1758.

*The 61st Marching Out of Fort St. Philip*, 1782.

On the outbreak of the War of Independence, Bragg's regiment went to America in 1775, and next year, under General Howe, marching from New York, turned the enemy's position at King's Bridge, and moved towards the Americans posted behind the river Brunx, entrenched at the entrances to the White Plains. The banks of this river are swampy, and the waters deep, except at the ford, where the banks are very steep and rocky. The enemy, seeing our columns in motion, despatched 8,000 men out of their lines, and posted them on a steep hill above the ford. It was the special duty of Brigadier Leslie to carry this strongly-held post, and thus to turn the American entrenched camp. The 28th and 35th Regiments, supported by the 5th and 49th Regiments, thereupon rushed forward to the attack. Thick and obscuring clouds rose from bank to bank, from eminence to eminence, as the loud thunder of war burst from ten thousand muskets. In spite of the hail of grape-shot the river was passed, and the foot of the steep hill was reached. Unable to successfully climb the cliff with one hand alone, the flintlock was cast away, and the 28th, drawing their short swords, sprang over the breastworks and cut down those who waited their approach. Justly proud of its conquest, Bragg's regiment made the hills echo to its loud huzzas. The rest of the army that had just witnessed this dangerous and apparently impracticable manœuvre, as well as the terrific onslaught of the 28th, sword in hand, at once nicknamed them the "Slashers," a sobriquet which has remained to them till this day. Soon after this turning movement General Washington evacuated his entrenchments, and abandoning his stores, retired with his army towards Connecticut.

During this period the 61st Foot were reaping fresh laurels in quite a different part of the world. While in garrison with the 51st Foot on the island of Minorca, an overwhelming force of 14,000 French and Spaniards, under the Duc de Crillon, landed there and at once encompassed the little band of Englishmen in the Fort St. Philip. Then began a siege memorable for its display of indomitable British pluck. The garrison held out against fearful odds until 5th February, 1782, when, worn out by the severity of scurvy, they were forced to capitulate. The last few days men could not be found for the several posts and guards, requiring 415 men daily; and on the night before the capitulation only 660 men capable of bearing arms could be mustered. The extent of endurance exhibited by the 61st during this siege has been rarely equalled, and never surpassed. Possibly, a nobler or sadder scene than that of the 5th February, when the little remnant of the garrison of St. Philip, marching with bayonets fixed and colours flying through the Franco-Spanish ranks, has never been witnessed. The little band did not exceed 600 old and decrepit soldiers, weakened by disease and pinched by hunger, who crawled rather than marched through the two long lines of foreign battalions fronting each other. So excessive was the distress written

on the emaciated figures of our men that both the Duc de Crillon and the Baron de Falkenhayn declared that many of the Spanish and French troops shed tears as they gazed on the sorry spectacle. The colours of the 61st passed into the hands of the Spanish, and existed in excellent preservation in the Royal Armoury at Madrid till quite recently, when a fire broke out and destroyed them, together with many other relics.

Minorca, however, again fell into our hands in 1798, when the 28th Regiment strangely enough formed part of the besieging force. But three years previous to this the "Slashers" were found again in their old happy hunting ground of Flanders, under the Duke of York. It was during the retreat on Bremen that Lord Cathcart mentioned in his orders: "Whenever danger is to be apprehended and difficulties to be surmounted, you have the 27th and 28th to call upon."

One of the most daring designs of General Bonaparte had been the seizure of Egypt in 1799, which was to have been the first step to the extension of the French Republic to Syria, Asia Minor, and even to Persia and India. Deserted by Bonaparte, and cut off from France by Nelson's destruction of their fleet in Aboukir Bay, the pick of the French Army, under General Kleber, was to finally succumb to the British expedition under Sir Ralph Abercromby. Landing on the morning of March 8th, 1801, the British force drove the French back on their position in front of Alexandria, where was fought that battle which took Egypt from France, and won such imperishable fame for the gallant "Slashers." The position taken up by the British was along some low sandhills, with its right resting on a Roman ruin close to the sea, and it was on this that the French dealt their main blow. And here were posted the 28th and 58th, supported by the 23rd and 42nd Regiments. The enemy began his assault soon after three in the morning, and, thanks to the gloomy mist of the atmosphere and unequal surface of the ground, was able to penetrate, almost unperceived, the ruins on the right, and to envelop the redoubt occupied by the 28th, who were thus surrounded and cut off from the rest of the army. Colonel Paget, nothing daunted, at once shouted "Rear rank, 28th, right about, fire!" The order was obeyed, and not a man gaveway. The "Slashers," refusing to acknowledge themselves beaten, fought on with true British pluck, and remaining fixed to the platform of the parapet, continued a contest unexampled before this day.

During this attack the French and British exhausted their supply of ammunition, and the former actually pelted stones from the ditch at the 28th, who returned these unusual, yet not altogether harmless, instruments of offence, as a sergeant of the 28th was killed by one breaking through his skull. In commemoration of their cool intrepidity on this ever-famous occasion, the 28th have been granted the singular distinction of wearing the regimental device on the back as well as on the front of their headdress, an honour which has never been conferred on any other regiment of the British Army. Their Colonel, Hon. E. Paget, who was wounded at the head of the regiment, early in the day, received the highest praise. This gallant officer was connected with the "Slashers" for more than half-a-century. The 61st, after a trying voyage of sixteen weeks, labouring against the monsoon, joined Baird's force from the Cape, and although the regiment numbered over 900 men, they landed at Cosseir, on the Red Sea, on the 10th of July, exposed to intense heat, and having one sick man. This was before the days of pith helmets and tropical clothing, yet this gallant battalion reached Kinnch, on the Nile, in eight days with the loss of only one drummer boy, which good fortune is due to the strict orders received by the rear guard not to allow of any man stopping behind.

The 61st were next defending the Neapolitan interests in Italy.

An expedition was organised by Major-General Stuart, to cut off a French Division under Regnier in Calabria, and on the 4th July, 1806, was fought the brilliant and spirited victory of Maida, which was shared in by the 61st flank companies, of which the "Light Bobs" were incorporated together with other light infantry companies to form the light battalion. The action was almost entirely an infantry one, and the light battalion in their onward charge found themselves face to face with the flower of the French infantry, the famous "1er. Leger," a corps that had hitherto proved itself invincible against all comers. The two corps at a distance of a hundred yards fired reciprocally a few rounds, when, as if by mutual agreement, firing ceased, and both battalions marched forward in awful silence. At length bayonet crossed bayonet. At this moment the enemy became terrified, broke, and endeavoured to fly, but too late: they were overtaken with dreadful slaughter. For this never-to-be-forgotten episode the word "Maida" was worn on the appointments of the 61st flank companies till they ceased to exist in 1858. The next year, 1807, it was considered advisable to seize the Danish Fleet, which offered such a temptation to the European Coalition against the very existence of England. Copenhagen was besieged and captured, the 28th Regiment sharing in the hardships of the trenches, and eventually manning and bringing home some of the Danish prizes.

unlucky with his pork, for in the hurry of embarkation piggy was taken on board one ship, and the major on board another."

However, 1809 opened up for our heroes a stupendous volume of brilliant victories fought out in the Peninsula, where the Portuguese and Spaniards, aided by the British, were striving to free themselves from the French yoke. The 61st landed at Lisbon in June, and the month following had the honour of sharing in the battle of Talavera. Forming part of Hill's Division, the regiment aided, by its well-regulated musketry, in repelling Lapisse's final assault on the English centre, and Lieutenant-Colonel Saunders and Major Coglan were rewarded with gold medals. Wellington found it impracticable to work with the Spanish generals, and in spite of his victory was forced to return to Portugal, which next year was invaded by Massena, boasting that he would drive the English into the sea. But on the 27th of September he met with some rough handling at Busaco. Here the 2nd battalion, 28th, and the 61st formed part of the Reserve, and were not seriously engaged; so that, although the medal was awarded them, yet the honour has been withheld from a place on their colours.

The North and South Gloucesters now retired with the rest of the army to the fortified position of Torres Vedras, an insuperable barrier covering Lisbon and defying all efforts to force it on the part of the French Marshal.

The 61st were quartered in the convent of Alenquer, while the 28th found excellent shelter in the village of Bucellas, celebrated for its wine. Almost every other house in the town was a wine-store, and immense vats and tuns, containing many hogsheads each, were to be found even in the rooms occupied by the officers and men—far too great a temptation to put in the way of soldiers, as the following

*The 28th at Alexandria, 1801.—Colonel Paget gave the Simple Order—"Rear Ranks, About—Fire!"*

The memorable retreat from Corunna began on Christmas Day, 1808, and in the post of honour of the rear guard were placed the "Slashers" under Colonel Paget, and the 7th Hussars commanded by his brother, Lord Paget, who were engaged almost daily in checking the pursuit of a confident and untiring enemy. Sir John himself wrote: "The Reserve was commanded by an indefatigable officer (Paget) and the regiments that composed it were admirable." For nearly a fortnight these brave fellows guarded the rear, often passing the night under arms in the snow on the mountain side; yet fewer men fell out of their ranks than in any other division of the army. Every attack was repelled with vigour, and when Moore concentrated his force and offered battle at Lugo, it was refused by Soult, who dared not attack. When at length the French resolved on accepting battle on the heights of Corunna, the 28th again were with the Reserve, and made a vigorous counter attack on the enemy at the moment when the village of Elvina was lost to us for a time. All the attacks of the French were beaten back, and the army embarked without disaster. The immortal Moore fell in the hour of his triumph, and the 28th for the third time found themselves the guard of honour to the illustrious slain, for had not Wolfe and Abercromby received their mortal wounds in the presence of the regiment. An officer wrote: "All our animals were left on the beach at Corunna. I recollect but one exception. The wife of Sergeant Monday, the orderly room clerk, actually carried a lap dog in a basket over her arm throughout the whole of this dreadful retreat, and brought it home to England with her. Major Browne was fortunate enough to get a pig in exchange for a horse. The major was rather

anecdote will prove: "The officers of our light company, having given a wine party to which some brother officers were invited, had found, when too late in the evening, the stock of wine which they had laid in for the occasion to be exhausted; upon which the junior subaltern was requested to proceed with a camp kettle to the vat for a fresh supply, as it was excellent. On turning the cock, and finding no wine to run, the vat was pronounced dry. However, it was determined to make another attempt by letting down the camp kettle by a rope through a trap-door in the top of the vat.

"Still finding it not return replenished, but rather that some obstacle interposed, the officer procured a lamp to examine the interior, when, to his horror, the first object that presented itself was a British drummer in full regimentals, who had been missing for some days, and was supposed to have deserted! 'Drummer's wine' was long a bye-word with us."

Despairing of forcing the English lines, Massena at length evacuated Portugal, our two battalions following up closely in pursuit. The 61st proceeded to the blockade of Almeida, and on the approach of the French to its relief took part in the brilliant affair at Fuentes d'Onor. Almeida soon after succumbed, and Captain Furnace, at the head of the 61st Grenadier Company, was the first to enter the town.

Down south the 2nd battalion 28th, covering Badajos, were fortunate in taking part in that day of rough experiences when Marshal Beresford's marvellous infantry struggled against the elements and masses of French cavalry fought for hours with the bayonet, and at length thrust their enemy across the Albuera.

In the same year the 1st battalion 28th, that had been garrisoning Tariffa, fought at Barossa on the 5th March ; here Colonel Belson distinguished himself by the coolest intrepidity, and caused his battalion to display conspicuous steadiness. The 28th being the left regiment, he moved them up, without firing a shot, close to the French right battalion, which just began to deploy. Colonel Belson then gave orders to fire by platoons from centre to flanks. "Now, lads," he said, "be sure to fire at their legs and spoil their dancing." The "Slashers" obeyed the order with fearful effect, then spurred on by victory, reached the top of the hill whence the Frenchmen had been driven in the greatest confusion. Looking down from the height on the fast disappearing forms of the dismayed and crestfallen foe, our men gave them three parting cheers in true British fashion.

A high tribute of praise was bestowed on the regiment by Sir Thomas Graham, whose gratitude and high approbation for their gallantry was unbounded. And on their return to Gibraltar a few days later, they were fêted by the Governor, who ordered a *feu-de-joie* to be fired by the whole Garrison in honour of the Barossa heroes.

For many years the word "Barossa" was engraved on a scroll beneath the 28th's ancient crest of the King's Cypher worn on the cap.

After the fall of Ciudad Rodrigo and Badajos, where the 61st were present covering the sieges, Wellington pushed forward into Spain and proceeded to reduce the defences of Salamanca. In the assault of the Forts S. Cajetano and La Merced, the 61st displayed great zeal and impetuosity. The light company showed the way in the most gallant style, led by their captain, John Owen, who, while in the act of entering, fell pierced by two bullets and was thrown to the bottom of the ditch. On seeing his captain's misfortune, Private Charles Carr jumped into the ditch under a heavy fire, and helped to carry him to a place of safety. Carr was rewarded by his grateful Commander with an annuity for life for his brave action.

The all-important battle of Salamanca was fought on the 22nd of July, and the prodigies of valour performed by the 61st on that occasion in no small measure contributed to the utter rout of the French.

*Drummer's Wine.*

A very severely contested struggle took place for the possession of the Arapiles Hill—the key of the position—on the British right flank. Our fourth division had lost it to the French, whereupon the 61st and 11th Regiments, forming Hulse's Brigade, were called upon to retake it.

With three ringing cheers they bounded forward, and after firing a volley, made use of their bayonets with so great effect that the tide of battle was turned, the French overpowered, and the Arapiles Hill recaptured. Napier, in his history of the war, wrote: "The struggle was no slight one. The men of General Hulse's Brigade, which was on the left, went down by hundreds, and the 61st and 11th Regiments won their way desperately, and through such a fire as British soldiers only can sustain." The remnant of this noble brigade then reformed and made a second charge against the French, who appeared to assemble from all directions with intent to retake the coveted Arapiles. This second onslaught carried our heroes under the very guns of the enemy, and the safest plan appeared to continue their onward career, so with three loud huzzas the gallant Gloucesters carried the second position. The French gave way now in every direction, yet hanging on to a third height, which the men of the invincible sixth division again mastered. In General Hulse's own words, "Never did British troops acquit themselves in a more gallant style." But at what costly price and precious sacrifice! Three officers and seventy-eight men alone remained of the 61st at the close of the action. Under the colours no less than six reliefs were shot down in their defence.[*]

For many years the men had a song, which ran :

"The 61st and 79th, great numbers they had slain,
They got their jackets dusted well on Salamanca Plain."

Traditions live long in a regiment, for in 1839, when the 61st Depôt Companies were moving from Clonmel to Cork, they met the 79th on the road. Both corps simultaneously broke their ranks to fraternise, and were with great difficulty reformed to continue their march.

Many of the wounded quickly took their places again in the ranks, for we find 200 of the 61st, under Captain Annesley, who was awarded a gold medal for the exploit, storming an outwork at Burgos on 4th October. During the subsequent

* A curious coincidence when one refers to the fight at Dijon in 1871, where the 61st Prussian Regiment likewise lost six reliefs under their regimental colour.

*The Colours of the 61st at Salamanca,* 1812.

retreat from Burgos the 61st lost one man only, which speaks volumes for the perfect discipline of that gallant little corps. "Whenever you find the British Army in retreat," said Soult to his successor, "let them alone; but if you go near them, they will get into their places, and give you such a drubbing as you never had before."

This was Wellington's last retreat, and next year, 1813, he dealt that fatal blow to the French at Vittoria, where both the North as well as the South Gloucesters were present. The war was soon to be carried into the enemy's own country.

While jealously holding the paths crossing the Pyrenees, the enemy tried in vain to bar our further progress; and on the 25th July, at the pass of Maya, he had the audacity to resume the offensive. Strong columns of French suddenly overpowered our advanced picquets, and the brigade of the 50th, 71st, and 92nd, pressed forward to their support; while the 28th hurried up and formed on the right flank of the 92nd, opening at the same time such a series of telling volleys as to nearly annihilate the leading French regiment and check the advance of the remainder. Great was the surprise of the gallant "Slashers" afterwards to discover that the corps they had so roughly handled was the French 28th—the ancient "Regiment du Roi." Major Irving, of our 28th, who was taken prisoner on this occasion, saw the skeleton remnant of the French 28th, consisting of two officers, four non-commissioned officers, and a few men marching through Bayonne on their way to their depôt.

The eagle of this French regiment was brought to England, and was for many years hanging in Whitehall.

The glorious battles of the Pyrenees followed three days after, when our fellows had the honour of first driving the French out of Spain. The conflict was renewed by the enemy on the 30th, when the 61st stormed Sauroren, led by the gallant Coglan, who received the gold medal for the action. The taking of another village—El Ariba—found Lieutenant Anderson and eighteen "Slashers" assisting our friends the Portuguese. Here, the conduct of a very powerful fellow named Tank, of No. 2 company, was most conspicuous. On charging the enemy down the hill, towards the village, they came to a precipice, where Tank's muscular arm rendered good service; he could be plainly seen at work with his musket and bayonet, forking the Frenchmen over it like sheaves of corn tossed from a cart.

The winter was now fast approaching, and all were anxious to change their cheerless quarters on the mountain sides, without a bush or tree as shelter, for the fair plains of France, which the men saw spread at their feet. The attack was soon made, however, on the Nivelle. The river was soon passed, and the 61st were called upon to storm three redoubts on the heights beyond. This task they performed with an impetuosity which the Frenchmen could not withstand, and called forth from Sir Rowland Hill his repeated thanks.

On the night of the 8th of December a bridge of pontoons was placed over the Nive and the 6th Division crossed over, preceded by an advance guard commanded by Captain Greene, 61st, who managed to surprise the French on the opposite bank, which exploit gained for him the gold medal.

The battles of St. Pierre and Orthes followed in quick succession, and at last took place the last event of the war— the struggle around Toulouse on Easter Sunday, 1814.

Before ascending the Plateau de Calvinet the whole division witnessed a singular scene. The light company of the 61st were skirmishing, when a French regiment in close column descended by a road, intending to deploy at the foot of it. A soldier of the 61st advanced and shot the colonel at the head of the column, and the instant he fell the regiment went to the right-about and retired. The 6th Division, while working round the enemy's right, could not but admire the spirited and well-ordered conduct of the 61st, who led the way under incessant showers of grape, cutting down the devoted corps by whole sections, while Soult was perhaps not losing a man, being so safely sheltered from our musketry. On entering the first redoubt their gallant Colonel Coglan was killed on the spot, and found a grave not far from the spot where he and his undaunted little battalion proved so quickly victorious, that scarcely a Frenchman, but

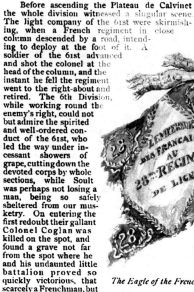

*The Eagle of the French 28th Regt.*

dead or wounded, was to be seen on the ridge by the time the rest of the division reached it. It was the Duke of Wellington's pleasure, however, to have the body disinterred and conveyed to the cathedral at Toulouse in procession, attended by himself and his entire staff to pay the last tribute of respect to departed valour. The 61st continued to press on, and again in the afternoon were hotly engaged in driving the French from their last positions. Captain Charlton, whose wound was dressed on the field, rejoined to lead his regiment in their second attack. After the action the few surviving men were led out of the field by their Adjutant Bace, nineteen other officers having fallen during the day. Its loss exceeded on that day that of any other corps of the Army, and on that account received the sobriquet of the "Flowers of Toulouse."

Not a subaltern left the field without a wound, and the honour of the colours was assigned to sergeants.

Lieutenant-Colonel Oke, Captain Charlton, and Adjutant Bace received gold medals, of which no less than seven had been conferred during the war—a greater number than had been received by any other regiment. No less than twenty-one non-commissioned officers of the 61st had been rewarded with commissions for gallant conduct in the field.

It is supposed that during the Peninsular War the officers of the 61st retained the long-tailed coatee instead of the shorter jacket adopted by the majority, and the nickname

*" The Spirited and Well-Ordered Conduct of the 61st, Who Led the Way, and the Fall of Their Gallant Colonel Coglan."*—NAPIER.

*From a Painting.* By Colonel J. MARSHMAN.

*Quatre Bras, 1815.* "*Bravo 28th! The 28th are still the 28th, and Their Conduct this Day will Never be Forgotten,*" *cried Their Brigadier.*

*From a Painting.* By Colonel J. MARSHMAN.

*Chillianwalla, 1849.* "*Never did Men Deserve Better of Their Country than, During that Mortal Struggle and on that Strange Day of Stern Vicissitudes, did the Gallant 61st.*"—MALLESON.

From an Etching by W. WOOLLER.

THE DEATH OF GENERAL WOLFE.

After B. WEST

of the "Silver-tailed Dandies" was presumably given them on that account.

Napoleon's abdication now put an end to further hostilities, and the event was celebrated with great enthusiasm amongst our men. While quartered in Toulouse the English soldiers were treated with great civility by the inhabitants, and the most gentlemanly conduct was often experienced from the French officers, as the following incident will show :—" Coursing was often indulged in by our fellows, and one day a fine hare was seen in a cornfield between the outposts. A couple of greyhounds were let slip, and after an exciting course the hare was killed in the French lines.

"An officer to whom the hounds belonged, bowing to the French officer, called off the dogs; but the Frenchman politely sent the hare, with a message and his compliments, saying that we required it more than they did."

Our men were much disappointed after the war at not seeing Soult—" Fighting Jack," or the " Duke of Damnation," as they used to call him. He had won the greatest admiration of our men for his plucky resistance.

The escape of Napoleon from Elba reopened hostilities, and took the "Slashers" back to their old haunts in the Low Countries, under the redoubtable Wellington. On the 16th of June, 1815, in Kempt's Brigade, in the tall ryefield at Quatre Bras, as represented in Lady Butler's well-known historical picture, the 28th stood firm in square till after eight o'clock that evening, hurling back in confusion Ney's steel-clad Cuirassiers of terrible memory, and the Polish Lancers—those famous chevau-legers of France.

"Bravo 28th! The 28th are still the 28th, and their conduct this day will never be forgotten!" cried Kempt, their brigadier.

Two days afterwards at Waterloo the gallant Gloucester lads showed themselves invincible against repeated onslaughts of cavalry, and their steadiness called forth the greatest praise from the noble Picton, who was standing in their centre. "Twenty-eighth!" he said, "If I live to see the Prince Regent, I shall lay before him your bravery this day." After the repulse of one of the French divisions, Lieutenant Deans, of the regiment, carried away by wild enthusiasm, dashed after the retreating cavalry. He attacked, sword in hand, every Frenchman that he came across, and had cut down a brace and wounded several, when he was overpowered and taken prisoner; stripped of all his clothing, except his shirt, and severely wounded, he found his way back next day to the regiment.

It was during the charge of the "Greys," the "Slashers" pursuing the enemy, that the "provisional" flag of the 45th French Regiment was captured by Private Whaler of No. 8 company. It was carried hung over the King's colour to Paris afterwards, but was eventually ordered to be sent to headquarters, and never seen again. It will be remembered that the eagle of the 45th was taken by Sergeant Ewart, of the "Greys."

In his Waterloo despatch to Lord Bathurst, Wellington wrote :—" I must particularly mention the 28th, 42nd, 79th, and 92nd Regiments."

Paris was soon in our hands, and on the 24th July, before the allied Sovereigns, the 28th passed with the rest of the Army in review. Our men still wore their tattered uniforms, and mustered four companies only. The Iron Duke drew the attention of the monarch to the 28th's shot-shattered colour poles; one of them was two yards long while the other was only one. Shortly afterwards, when at a field day Wellington was exhibiting the evolutions of the battle of Salamanca, the "Slashers" attracted the special attention of Alexander, Emperor of Russia, who admired particularly their fine grenadier company. He enquiringly drew attention to the brown calf-skin packs then carried by the 28th, and seemed highly amused when Major Cadell told him that they were found in a French store taken in Egypt. Not bad valises those—for they had been in wear fourteen years, and carried through several campaigns.

The first Anniversary of Waterloo was commemorated by the presentation of a magnificent stand of silk colours by the Hon. Sir Edward Paget, Colonel of the 28th, now to be seen preserved at Sandhurst. On this occasion the men drew and kissed their bayonets; the officers did the same with their swords, and both swore to stand to their colours, saluting them, while the band played "God save the King." Sixteen years after, a second pair, generously given by Colonel Paget, were presented by his brother, the Marquis of Anglesea, and these are to be found in the same resting place near to the monument erected to Sir Edward, who had so often led his beloved regiment to battle and to victory.

During the next thirty years the North and South Gloucesters were spending a well-earned period of rest. In 1845, however, the 61st embarked for India, to subsequently take a very prominent share in conquering the Punjab. The "Army of the Punjab," under Lord Gough, took the field at the close of 1848 against the Sikhs, who had declared for war

Perhaps a worthier foe had never been confronted by us in the Far East than these.

After the minor engagements of Ramnugger and Gadoolapore, which secured for us the passage of the river Chenab, Gough at length came on the Sikh Army of 23,000 men, under Shere Singh, near the village of Chillianwalla, where on the 13th of January, 1849, ensued one of the most sanguinary conflicts ever chronicled in the annals of the British Army. Strange to relate, the site of the battle also marks the ancient victory of Alexander the Great over Porus, King of the Central Punjaub, and even to this day it is known by the natives as "the house of slaughter."

Owing to the density of the jungle, touch was lost between the several brigades, which consequently attacked the Sikh position independently. The right brigade of our left division (Campbell's), after carrying every battery opposed to them, fell into an ambuscade, against which their thinned and broken ranks were unable to contend, and here fell 42 officers and 756 others. Our cavalry had likewise failed to make an impression on the hordes of Sikh horse, which, now unopposed and mad with excitement, fitted by equipment and education to act most successfully in jungle, dashed through the gaps and completely enveloped the left brigade. The brigadier ordered the 61st to change front to the rear; but Colonel McLeod gave the simple command, "Right about face," and fired one volley. Then "Front rank, about face!" was the sudden order given, and instantly obeyed. The regiment thus stood back to back for some time, while the seething waves of some 8,000 Gorchurra light horse dashed full on the wall of steel. A most destructive file-firing was opened; riders, cased in heavy armour, fell tumbling from their horses; the horses reared, plunged, and fell on the dismounted riders; steel helmets and chain cuirasses rung against unsheathed sabres, as they fell to the ground; shrieks and groans of men, the neighing of horses, and the discharge of musketry rent the air, as men and horses mixed together as one heap of indiscriminate slaughter. Once clear of these formidable and daring assailants, Colonel McLeod gave the order, "Rear rank, front!" Under the skilful guidance of Sir Colin Campbell the 61st lost not a moment in advancing against the enemy's guns, thirteen of which they captured in their victorious career. The day's contest at a close, Lord Gough, baring his white head, rode up and expressed his heartfelt thanks to the regiment for their gallant conduct; and later on the Duke of Wellington averred that the 61st were instrumental in saving the British Army, and the feat performed by this regiment on that day was pronounced by him to have been one of the most brilliant exploits ever performed by any regiment of the English Army. The crowning victory of Goojerat, and the final surrender of the Sikhs, closed the campaign, and decided the fate of

*28th Drum-Major and Drummer,* 1844.

*The 61st at the Delhi Magazine, 1857. On Arrival Near the Breach, Colonel Deacon gave the Word, " Charge !"*

the Punjab. The regiment lay encamped at Peshawar but a short time. Called upon to share in the Ussefzie expedition, they saw plenty more hard fighting and lost many men.

Next year, under their old leader, Sir Colin, they assisted to force the Kohat Pass. Seven summers later, when the Indian Mutiny cloud burst on us with such violence, found the South Gloucesters at Ferozepore, where the 45th and 57th native regiments were also quartered. On the afternoon of May the 13th, the latter threw off the mask and attempted to rush the Ferozepore magazine, where was stored tons of ammunition and the heavy siege train so indispensable afterwards at Delhi. The light company, 61st, under Major Redmond* and young William Deacon,† however, entered the magazine just in time to save it. The former officer fell, but Deacon took command, and single handed disarmed the native guard on duty there. The 61st now moved off without loss of time to assist at Delhi. It being the middle of the hot season, they used to march throughout each night, halting at 10 in the morning for three or four hours' rest under canvas, and then off again.

The enlivening strains of the incoming Gloucester band on the 1st of July filled the besiegers with renewed energy, and Delhi was invested with undiminished ardour. Two days after saw the 61st hotly engaged, in company with the 9th Lancers, Carabineers, and Guides, in keeping a vastly superior body of mutineers at bay till the arrival of the guns. Fighting was incessant, but on the 25th of August a big action took place at Nuseffghur, when, on account of the inundations, the guns were left behind, and three strong positions had to be carried at the point of the bayonet by the 61st and the 2nd Europeans. Before the word to advance was given, Nicholson thus addressed them :—" Men of the 61st, remember what Sir Colin Campbell said at Chillianwalla, and you have heard that he said the same to his gallant Highland Brigade at the Alma. I have the same request to make of you and the men of the 1st Bengal Fusiliers. Hold your fire until within twenty or thirty yards, then fire and charge, and the serai is yours."‡ The mutineers were utterly discomfited, and their object of cutting off the approaching siege train frustrated. At 9 o'clock next evening the 61st returned to camp, after having marched fifty miles, and stormed three strong positions, with the thermometer at 120 degrees in the shade! The storming of the magazine before daybreak on the 16th of September by the 61st, under Colonel C. Deacon, was one of the last episodes of the siege.

Here Surgeon (afterwards Surgeon-General) Reade, 61st, won the Victoria Cross for being one of the first in at the breach and tending the wounded under fire.

In 1854 Britain roused her soldiers from their peaceful slumbers, and the 28th were amongst the first to embark at

* Now Major-General P. Redmond, C.B., the oldest surviving officer and honorary colonel of the regiment.
† Now a Military Knight of Windsor.
‡ " Forty-one Years in India." Lord Roberts.

Liverpool for the Crimea, under Frank Adams, as brave a colonel as ever drew sword. In Sir Richard England's Division they fought at the Alma, and two days after closed on Sebastopol. On the day of Inkerman, as many of the "Slashers" as could be spared from trench duty were hurried up in support, and took a lion's share in that struggle between 8,000 Englishmen and 60,000 Russians.

The Crimean Campaign at an end, the 28th were hurried out to India, but they found on arrival, to their bitter disappointment, that the Mutiny was quelled. They were partially consoled by joining in the expedition to Ottamundel to exterminate a body of Kattiawar dacoits, who had installed themselves in the holy forts of Beyt and Dwarka. These were stormed, not without sacrifice on the part of the "Slashers."

Yeoman Warder Baker, whose picture is given below, served in the Punjab Campaign, 1848-49, with the expedition to the Kohat Pass, 1850 ; he was sergeant-major of the 61st at the siege and assault of Delhi.

Forty years have now elapsed since the gallant North and South Gloucesters gathered their last laurels on the battlefields of the Far East, and now, united as the Gloucestershire Regiment, we may bid them farewell, confident that the glorious traditions built up by their noble predecessors will be worthily maintained by the present representatives of this famous regiment.

*Yeoman Warder Baker.*

# THE BATTLE HONOURS OF THE BRITISH FLEET.
## The "Royal Sovereign" By Edward Fraser.

*LAUNCHING THE FIRST "ROYAL SOVEREIGN."*

THE name of the "Royal Sovereign" is just as old as the modern Navy of England. We owe the institution of our Navy as a national force, it is commonly accepted, to the first of our Tudor monarchs, Henry VII., and one of the two men-of-war with which King Henry "started" his Fleet, if one may use the phrase, was our first "Sovereign." The date of the event is August, 1488, just 409 years ago, in which month and year our first "Sovereign" was sent afloat from the King's Naval Dock at Hamble, on the Hamble River, Southampton Water—the Portsmouth Dockyard of mediæval times.

For herself, in many ways our first "Sovereign" should be to us a ship of special interest. Timber for timber and plank for plank, the greater part of Henry VII.'s "Sovereign" man-of-war was put together out of the framework of Edward IV.'s old flag-ship, the "Grace Dieu," whose name, taken from the Royal style of our Plantagenet kings in the Norman French of the day, goes back into English history for another two centuries, back, indeed, to the famous flag-ship, "Grace Dieu," of Edward III., the first of the line, on whose quarter-deck the Black Prince himself trod. The same man-of-war that came out of the Naval Dock at Hamble in August, 1488, as our first "Sovereign" went in there in August, 1486, under the name of "Grace Dieu." They took the "Grace Dieu" to pieces, and replaced parts here and there, and then putting her together again, a mitred prelate, with attendant train of priests and choristers, crozier in hand, with candle, book, and bell, and holy water stoup, in the presence of King Henry and his Court, formally renamed the ship the "Sovereign,".blessing the renovated vessel with a'l the imposing religious ceremonial display customary in Catholic England in pre-Reformation times.

Four-and-twenty years passed before the "Sovereign" first fired an angry shot—not, indeed, until after King Henry himself had been laid to rest in the gorgeous chapel in the Abbey at Westminster that bears his name—but the gap is not all a blank. Our Tudor flag-ship, the "Sovereign," was, for one thing, the first man-of-war of the Royal Navy that ever entered a dock at Portsmouth, on the first regular establishment of Portsmouth Dockyard and the completion of the first dock ever made there—May 25th, 1496, is the date

exactly. That in itself is an interesting memory. Another is that the "Sovereign" was the first man-of-war that ever carried heavy guns at sea. The great transition on board ship from a light armament consisting of numerous small pieces—pop-gun weapons, called "serpentines," firing half-pounder "pellettes" of lead, and square "dice shot" of iron, designed solely to scour an enemy's decks and cut his sails and rigging, as the ships, in accordance with the maritime tactics of the Middle Ages, sheered alongside one another in action, to grapple and board—the change from an armament of many small, light guns to an armament of fewer pieces of heavy metal, 18-pounder culverins and 40-pounder "cannon" —designed to shatter or sink a hostile ship or compel surrender from afar—took place in the "Sovereign's" time, and was first made in the English Navy in the "Sovereign" herself. What is more, the successful result of the experiment so made—it was only an experiment at first, of course— determined the adoption of the system on which the whole art and science of modern gunnery is based.*

Two battle-day glimpses of our first "Sovereign" are afforded us. The one is at the great fight off Brest of August 10th, 1512, memorable for the disastrous burning in action of the French and English flag-ships side by side. The "Sovereign," commanded by Sir Charles Brandon as captain, with Sir Henry Guildford in second command on board, at the head of sixty picked Yeomen of the King's Guard, opened the fight. At the head of the five-and-twenty men-of-war that formed the English Fleet she showed the way, steering to close with the French flag-ship, "the great Carrack of Brest," the "Marie de la Cordelière." The "Sovereign," however, just missed getting to close quarters with the French admiral, "by negligence of the master, or else by the smoke of the ordnance," as it was said, and the "Cordelière" passed on, to be run into and grappled by the English flag-ship, the "Regent," and to be involved with her

* In 1488 the "Sovereign" mounted 121 serpentines and "stone gonnes," firing nothing bigger than a half-pounder ball; in 1509 this armament was replaced by twenty-five heavy pieces—"curtalls of brass" (12-pounders), culverins (18-pounders), "heavy yron gonnes" and "falcons" (3-pounders)—the remainder of the serpentines ft on board being reduced to fifty-six pieces, making a total of eighty-one guns in all.

in one common destruction. The "Sovereign" then engaged with broadside fire some of the biggest ships among the French men-of-war, and bore herself, it is admitted on all hands, as befitted her Royal name, but the chroniclers of the battle of Brest of 1512, in the accounts that have come down to our times, do not give details of the part she took.

More memorable for its sad occasion is our next meeting with the "Sovereign" before the enemy—on the day of the galley fight in Conquet Bay in April, 1513—when her admiral, Sir Edward Howard, lost his life. Putting off from his flag-ship in a galley, to attack, in company with a second English galley, six French galleys moored close in shore under the guns of a fort, the gallant Sir Edward stood right in and boarded the French admiral's galley, sword in hand. Seventeen brave fellows had boarded with him, when suddenly, before the others could follow, Howard's galley broke clear and sheered off from alongside, leaving the admiral and his handful of men to fight the whole French ship's crew. They did their best, but in vain. Fighting to the last gasp, the heroic Howard and his men, after disputing every inch of the deck, were by sheer weight of overpowering numbers forced overboard. The admiral himself, conspicuous by his richly gilt breastplate, was the last left of all. As his final act, as he stood at bay on the French galley's gunwale, Howard, it is recorded, "took his chain of gold nobles about his neck and his great gold whistle, the

*Admiral Sir Edward Howard at the Galley Fight in Conquet Bay.*

ensign of his office, and threw them into the sea, to prevent the enemy from possessing the spoils of an English admiral."

Of the "Sovereign" after this we hear but little. Six years later she was reported as nearly worn out and needing large repair, and six years after that, nothing having been done to her meanwhile, another appeal was made to save the "Sovereign," "the form of which ship is so marvellous goodly that great pity were it should die." But in vain, as it would seem. The name of our first "Sovereign" appears no more on the roll of the English Fleet, or again at all except for one

passing mention in an old document of the year 1534. A reference is there made to the granting of Royal letters "for the freighting of the King's ship called the 'Sovereign,'" but what the entry means is unknown. After that, all records, in the State papers or elsewhere, are silent as to the "Sovereign."

Charles the First's "Sovereign of the Seas," perhaps the best known of all our men-of-war of the olden time, takes up the tale — with a gap between of just 100 years. In 1534, as has just been said, we have a last passing glimpse of the old Tudor flag-ship "Sovereign," of Henry VII. In 1634 King Charles I., with his own hand, drafted the dimensions of a second "Sovereign," to whose name, appointed by himself, Charles added later the specially chosen affix "of the Seas." Both ship and name were the King's own idea. Charles had suddenly become awake to a very real danger to England that was then taking shape from a threatened alliance between Holland and France. Ostensibly it was to be an alliance against Spain, with whom the Dutch had for twelve years past been at war, but there was ground for suspicion that a design was on foot to challenge the old English claim to supremacy in the Narrow Seas. King Charles, as one way of meeting the situation, determined to reinforce his Fleet by adding to it a man-of-war the most powerful that the world had yet seen. A three-decker, of over 1,500 tons, to carry 100 guns, was the King's proposal. At the same time, in view of the situation on its political and diplomatic side, the King, by way of rejoinder to the pretensions of Holland and France, specially designed for his great man-of-war the name of the "Sovereign of the Seas."

The leading Naval experts of the day received the King's proposal with objections, on the score of the size of the new ship, in a way that is curiously paralleled by the objections that were raised in 1889 by certain modern experts against the building of our present "Royal Sovereign" and the sister ships of her class. In particular, the Trinity House Brethren, who constituted the Naval Constructor's Department of the day, were startled at the daring of the proposal, as it seemed to them, and made formal remonstrance. So large a ship, the Brethren set forth, in a document still in existence, would be of no use. No port in the kingdom would be able to harbour her. She would have, they said, to lie exposed to tempests; and no anchors or cables would be able to hold her. "The art and wit of man," they proceeded, "cannot build a ship fit for the Service with three tiers of ordnance, and we advise His Majesty to build instead two ships of 400 or 500 tons burthen and forty pieces of ordnance, which shall beat the great ship back and side." We heard eight years ago exactly the same style of arguments about our present "Royal Sovereign." In spite of the Trinity House authorities, however, and "the art and wit of man," King Charles held to his opinion, and the "Sovereign of the Seas" was taken in hand, and, in due course, completed.

The "Sovereign" was begun in January, 1636, on the 16th of the month, when her keel was laid in the presence of King Charles and his Court in the old "mother dock" of England, as it used to be called, the big dock at Woolwich Yard. She was built of picked timber, mostly sent by sea from Northumberland, and finally floated out of dock, again in the presence of King Charles, on October 13th, 1637. All England rang with her praise. She was, said people in England, "the wonder of the age," "the greatest ship our island ever saw."

What the "Sovereign" actually looked like we can see for ourselves in the official model of her, specially made for the King in 1636, and now preserved in the Naval Museum at Greenwich Hospital. Pictures of the ship, also contemporaneous, still exist, and at least one of the special medals struck by order of King Charles, on which is shown the ship as she appeared when sent afloat.

August, 1638, saw the "Sovereign" for the first time at sea, making her trial cruise. There exists to this day a curious memento of the event. The cruise extended from the Downs westward, off the Sussex Coast, and the exact spot at which the "Sovereign"

*The Trial Trip of the "Royal Sovereign" off Eastbourne.*

turned back, after having acquitted herself to the satisfaction of all on board, was just at the edge of the shoal off Eastbourne where the present "Royal Sovereign" lightship has its moorings.

The "Sovereign" underwent her baptism of fire with Blake in the second action of the First Dutch War, the battle fought off the Kentish Knock on September 28th, 1652. Her presence in the fight as the biggest ship the world had ever seen attracted special attention, and letters of officers present at the battle describing the part that the "Sovereign" took are in existence. Writes one officer:—

"Although I know not ship or man-of-war of ours that deserved not his share of honour in this service, yet, when we only think of the execution performed by the 'Sovereign' (which was like a wall of brasse) . . . we may well imagine that the Hollanders have sustained exceeding great losse."

"The 'Sovereign,' that great ship, a delicate frigot (I think the world hath not her like)," says another writer, "did her part; she sailed through and through the Holland Fleet and played hard upon them. And at one time there were about twenty Holland frigots upon her, but, blessed be the Lord, she hath sustained no very great losse, but in some of her tacklings had some shot in her which her great bigness is not much prejudiced with."

"The 'Sovereign' (a frigot which all the world cannot parallel)," says a third writer, "plaied her part. She sail'd through and through the Dutch Fleet and did great execution;

but at last she was surrounded by twenty of the enemies' frigots, who let fly many broadsides at her. Nevertheless, she cut her way quite through them, receiving only a little loss in her tackling and about twenty of her men slain. She hath, at least, 300 shot in her sides, but most of the bullets stuck in her, for very few was of force to enter quite through."

One of the "Sovereign's" broadsides, says a news-letter writer of the time, "shot down the masts of three Hollanders' ships," and another news-letter writer relates that she "sunk one of her opponents alongside, who attempted to board her." Altogether, for our champion English man-of-war of the time, it was a very satisfactory entry on the scene of active warfare.

The enemy, the Dutch, for their part, too, paid particular attention to the big "Sovereign." They gave her, in memory of the devastation she wrought among them in this fight off the Kentish Knock, a nickname by which for many a long year after they remembered the "Sovereign"—the sobriquet of "The Golden Devil." "The Dutch," says Whitelock, in his "Memorials," writing under date October 11th, 1652, "were frighted with the 'Sovereign,' and call her the 'Golden Devil.'" "Golden," of course, was in reference to the "Sovereign's" gorgeously decorated hull; "Devil," because of the hot reception that their own ships received under the fire of the "Sovereign's" guns.

The "Sovereign" had the honour of fighting her second battle also under Blake's orders. It was at the memorable action fought off Lowestoft in June, 1653. Monk and Deane began the fight while Blake and the squadron of the Fleet in his particular charge were completing their fitting for sea in the Thames, but Blake's ships were able to get out of the river in time to take a decisive part in the latter of the two days' fighting. The same officer, Captain Nicholas Read, who had commanded the "Sovereign" so well in the battle off the Kentish Knock, commanded her again in the Lowestoft fight.

The "Sovereign" proved her metal, at the expense of Tromp and his captains, a third time, in the final battle of the war— Monk's great victory off Camperdown on July 31st, 1653. In the long day's mêlée no English ship acquitted herself with more distinction than did the "Sovereign."

The Restoration of May, 1660, gave the "Sovereign" the name by which the Navy has known her ever since—her full name of "Royal Sovereign." Originally called, as we have seen, "Sovereign of the Seas," that somewhat cumbrous appellation had by common consent been laid aside in favour of the shorter, more colloquial form, "Sovereign," by which name the Navy insisted on calling her, in spite of official orders to the contrary. In King Charles's time special directions had been given to employ only the full title. After the Parliamentarian usurpation, official efforts had been made to induce the Navy to know her under the name of the "Commonwealth." But in both cases the sailors of the Fleet would have no other name but that of the "Sovereign," plain and simple. The name "Royal Sovereign" was formally bestowed on the ship by Charles II. at the Restoration, in the first week of June, 1660. On his way to London after his landing at Dover, Charles specially turned aside at Chatham to pay a visit to the great ship in which his father had taken such pride, at that moment lying in ordinary off Upnor, and he then and there, in honour of his restoration, gave the ship the name "Royal Sovereign."

Six years later we meet the "Royal Sovereign" once more on battle day, in perhaps the bloodiest and most desperately fought sea battle the world has ever seen—

*THE DEATH OF SIR WILLIAM REEVES.*

the tremendous " Four Days' Fight," as it is known in history, off the North Foreland, in June, 1666. Monk, Duke of Albemarle, and Prince Rupert, at the head of eighty sail, had been lying at the " Nore " in May, waiting for news of the Dutch Fleet, under De Ruyter, when a report that a French squadron was coming to join the Dutch, drew off Rupert with twenty sail, one of which was the " Sovereign," to meet the French off the Isle of Wight. The news proved false, however, and on reaching Portsmouth Rupert learnt that Albemarle had, in his absence, come into collision with De Ruyter. He headed back, and got as far as Dover, to find Albemarle almost overpowered by De Ruyter's superior force, making a fighting retreat against immense odds to gain the shelter of the Thames. Albemarle had fallen back before De Ruyter close off the North Foreland, when, on the afternoon of Sunday, June 3rd, Rupert rejoined him. With streamers flying, and trumpets and drums sounding defiance, Rupert's squadron pushed in between Albemarle's rear ships and the Dutch van, and compelled De Ruyter to haul off for the time. The next morning the English turned to bay to make one tremendous forlorn-hope effort. Rupert's squadron, in a compact mass, headed the English onset with, as the leaders of all, in the van, the " Sovereign " and the " Victory " —the two going into the fight with the same generous rivalry that at a later day inspired a later " Sovereign " and a later " Victory " within sight of the headland of Trafalgar. Throughout the eight hours, from ten in the morning till six at night, that the desperate battle lasted, the two ships fought within a stone's throw of each other, now hotly engaged broadside to broadside with the enemy, now for dear life's sake thrusting off Dutch fire-ships as they tried to close under cover of the smoke, now relieving one another when hard pressed; so, on that memorable day of June, 1666, began the companionship in arms to which Trafalgar set the seal.

For the gallant bearing of the " Sovereign " on that Monday of June, 1666, and also for the brilliant part that the " Sovereign " took in the second great battle of the year, the famous St. James's Day Fight, July 25th, 1666, Captain John Cox of the " Royal Sovereign " was specially knighted by King Charles in the Presence Chamber at Whitehall. In the St. James's Day Fight the " Royal Sovereign " fought, among others, with De Ruyter's flag-ship, and close to the " Royal Charles," of unfortunate memory, as " second " to the flag-ship of the English Fleet, under the eyes of the Duke of York and Prince Rupert, the joint Commanders-in-Chief.

Next to be recorded on the " Sovereign's " roll of battle honours is the great battle of Solebay, fought on May 28th, 1672, the opening encounter of the Third Dutch War. The actual part that the " Sovereign " took at Solebay is recorded in detail in a rare manuscript still in existence, the journal kept on board ship by her captain, Sir Joseph Jordan. It is too long, unfortunately, for more than a few notes from it to be jotted down here.

The " Sovereign," Captain Jordan tells us, was one of the first ships to get clear, when at four in the morning the Dutch surprised the Duke of York at anchor, and after getting out of the Bay, " led the van, with the starboard tack on board, standing towards Lowestoft, having most of her division in a line about her."

After that, on the battle becoming general, about eight o'clock " there fell in with the 'Sovereign' a rear-admiral with some others (with fire-ships attending), with whom there was a dispute near an hour." " The 'Sovereign,'" after that, " keeping close to the wind, caused, as was presumed, the rear-admiral and the rest to tack, then stretching it out so far that she got the wind of them and all the rest, she maintained a hot dispute against an admiral, vice-admiral, and rear-admiral, and five or six great ships more, with four or five fire-ships (one whereof was the—ex-English—'Merlin' galley). They strove to get the wind, which was not reasonable in our apprehension to give them, for that the 'Sovereign' had not one fire-ship to attend her, which if she had she might have gone closer and done better service. . . .

" About eleven the enemy tacked, and the 'Sovereign' after them, still keeping her wind of them and battering along. About noon we espied ships on fire to leeward of us, not knowing what they were. Two ships we saw sinking, which we judged to be the enemy's.

" About two, afternoon, the 'Sovereign' bore nearer to that party or squadron of the enemy, and continued battering till six at night. Then, perceiving His Royal Highness to leeward of the enemy's van, we endeavoured by all means to join with and assist him. . . . The 'Sovereign' joined with His Royal Highness between eight and nine at night."

There is perhaps less known about the three battles that Prince Rupert fought with De Ruyter, May, June, and July, 1673, than about any other actions in our Naval annals. For one thing, they were drawn fights, and the Navy does not like drawn fights. For another, though full and complete despatches were drawn up and signed by Prince Rupert, it was found convenient to burke them. Evelyn, the Diarist, drew up a complete history of the year's campaign for King Charles, and Pepys tells us that he read it; but Evelyn's manuscript, at the instigation of some high personage in Court circles, was suppressed in circumstances of some mystery. The whole business, indeed, is a State mystery that historians have repeatedly tried, in vain, to solve.

The " Sovereign," however, we know for certain, had her share in all three of the battles. In the first, fought on the anniversary of Solebay, May 28th, 1673, she took part as a private ship, commanded by Captain John Hayward, in the squadron led by the daring Sir Edward Spragge. In the second and third, fought on June 4th and August 11th, she flew Prince Rupert's flag as Commander-in-Chief's ship of the English Fleet. Practically, however, all we know of what took place on board the " Royal Sovereign " in these two fights is that her captain, Sir William Reeves, was killed by

Rupert's side on the quarter-deck of the "Sovereign" during the third and last battle, that of August 11th.

Torrington's battle off Beachy Head, on June 30th, 1690, the tenth action in which, from first to last, the "Royal Sovereign" took part, comes next. Here, flying Torrington's flag, the "Sovereign" was again the ship of the officer in chief command, in which part she, like all her consorts, did her duty to her country, although the circumstances of the fight prevented any opportunity of special distinction coming the "Sovereign's" way. Macaulay's partisan and cruelly false charges against Torrington are absolutely baseless, and have, in our own day, been shown up, and nailed to the counter as historic lies.

We may pass at once to the great event of 1692, the battle of Barfleur-La Hogue, where, flying the flag of Sir Ralph Delaval, Vice-Admiral of the Red, the "Royal Sovereign" had her part in the van of Admiral Russell's own squadron.

It was on the Red Squadron, in particular, that the brunt of the fighting fell on the forenoon of May 19th. Tourville concentrated his attack on the Red Squadron, bringing two-thirds of his whole Fleet to bear on Russell, while the remaining third engaged the attention of the Dutch squadron that formed the van of Russell's Fleet. One-third of the English Fleet, the whole of the Blue Squadron, was out of action all day, out of touch with the main body and to leeward, unable to close with the French until the battle was over.

The "Sovereign's" special antagonist at Barfleur was the flag-ship of the French Vice-Admiral of the White, the Marquis de la Villette. With that ship, "L'Ambitieux," a three-decker like herself, of the same size and mounting, the same number of guns—ninety-six—the "Sovereign" maintained action for some hours, as well as the flat calm and foggy day would allow, engaging, in addition, several other French ships of Villette's squadron, notably "Le Téméraire," "L'Excellent," "L'Illustre," and "L'Intrepid," all ships, by a coincidence, whose names in later wars the fortune of battle transferred to our own Navy List.

Having done enough for honour by nightfall on the 19th, Tourville next day began his running retreat to gain a French port, until, foiled by Russell's close pursuit, the French off Alderney broke up into groups. One, comprising three ships—Tourville's own flag-ship, the famous "Soleil Royale," and the "Admirable" and "Conquerant," also three-deckers—ran for the refuge of Cherbourg Roads. To settle accounts with these, Delaval's squadron was specially told off. How the admiral carried out his orders an extract from the vice-admiral's official letter to the Admiralty, dated "On board the 'Royal Sovereign,' near Cherbourg, May 22nd," in Delaval's own language, shows.

"Finding that some of them endeavoured for the Bay of Cherbourg, I stood in for that place, where I found three three-decked ships of the enemy's. . . . Coming very near, they galled us so extremely, and finding the fire-ships could not get in, I judged it best to retreat without shot, and there anchored, and immediately called all the captains, when it was resolved to attempt them in the morning with all the third and fourth rates and fire-ships. But, after having drawn them into four fathom and a half of water, I found we could not do our business, the water being shoal, upon which I ordered three fire-ships to prepare themselves to attempt the burning them, going myself with all the barges and tenders to take them up if, by the enemy's shot, they should miscarry. Indeed, I may say, and I hope without vanity, the service was warm, yet, God be praised, it was so effectually performed, that, notwithstanding all their shot, both from their ships and forts, two of our fire-ships had good success by burning two of them; the other, by an unfortunate shot, was set on fire, before just going on board the enemy."

Later in 1692, the "Sovereign" flew the flags, in turn, of Admirals Killigrew and the famous Sir Cloudesley Shovell, and in the following year, 1693, that of Vice-Admiral Matthew Aylmer, another officer of high distinction. The "Sovereign" returned at the end of 1695 to lay up at Chatham until the dockyard people could take her in hand for a complete overhaul. It was her "last return from duty." On the night of January 29th, 1696, through the negligence of the ship's cook, who left a naked light unattended below, the "Royal Sovereign" was set on fire and burned to the water's edge.

The successor to the old "Sovereign," appointed at the earliest possible moment, was laid down, as it befel, in the very same dock at Woolwich Yard in which the "Sovereign of the Seas" had been built in 1637. She was launched on July 25th, 1701, St. James's Day—a date already famous in the "Sovereign's" story. The new "Sovereign," a three-decker 100-gun man-of-war, of 1,883 tons, was the largest man-of-war up to that date ever launched in England. She was, like her predecessor, destined to have a long career—the "Royal Sovereign" of 1701 did not pass out of existence until nearly seventy years later—but, otherwise, in her battle record, the second of our "Royal Sovereigns" was the exact opposite of the first. Only once in her long career, in fact

F.om an Engraving.                                After THOMAS BASTON.

THE "ROYAL SOVEREIGN" OF 1701.

was the " Royal Sovereign " of 1701 present at any fighting, and there, moreover, she took but a spectator's part. This was at Vigo Bay in August, 1702, when Rooke made his memorable attack on the Spanish treasure galleons.

The old ship remained afloat until the Peace of Versailles, in 1763, after which the " Royal Sovereign " was paid off for the last time, in 1768 to go alongside the shipbreaker's wharf.

The most distinguished " Royal Sovereign " of all now comes on the scene, the fourth of the line, the "Royal Sovereign" that bore Collingwood's flag at Trafalgar, a 100-gun three-decker of 2,175 tons, launched at Plymouth Dockyard in 1786. Hers is a battle story hardly to be matched by any other British man-of-war. It begins with the " Royal Sovereign " at Lord Howe's famous fight, the great battle that our ancestors of a hundred years were so proud of—"The Glorious First of June." The "Royal Sovereign," on June 1st, 1794, was flag-ship of Admiral of the Blue Thomas Graves, Lord Howe's second in command, and her experiences on the occasion were probably unique. Attacking the French 110-gun-ship " Terrible," flag-ship of the French second in command—against whom the " Royal Sovereign," in her order as fifth in the line of battle, matched herself—the " Sovereign " was overpowering her antagonist after an hour and a quarter's hot fight, when a second French flag-ship, the French Commander-in-Chief's flag-ship, the 120-gun-ship " Montagne," came to the rescue, and, joining in, ranged alongside. The " Montagne," fresh from her opening fight with Howe's flag-ship, the " Queen Charlotte," placed herself on the "Sovereign's" disengaged side. But Graves was ready for her. Fighting both broadsides at once between the two French flag-ships— for the half-mastered " Terrible " promptly took heart of grace and reopened a fierce fire from her three tiers—for a fast forty minutes more the " Sovereign " hotly engaged her two big antagonists, as well as a third French ship, the " Jacobin," a big 80-gun two-decker, that joined in.

*Cornwallis Addressing His Men.*

Three to one though the odds were, the " Sovereign " stood up to her antagonists right gallantly, until, getting the worst of the encounter, first the " Jacobin " retired, and then the two French flag-ships. There is no other case on record in Naval history of a set-to between three flag-ships, and the " Royal Sovereign " well deserved the cheers that every ship in the Fleet gave her after the battle, as did her admiral deserve the peerage that King George bestowed on him.

The " Sovereign " followed the " Montagne " and " Terrible " in their retreat for some distance, but, unable to

*THE FRENCH AND BRITISH SHIPS, JULY 17th, 1795.*

come up with them, and being badly knocked about in hull and aloft, she had to haul up. In killed and wounded her loss was upwards of sixty men wounded (including Admiral Graves, seriously wounded)—a light "butcher's bill," all things considered.

Yet the "Royal Sovereign's" part at the glorious 1st of

brilliant affair known in our Naval annals as "Cornwallis's Retreat."

With a squadron comprising the "Sovereign" as flag-ship, four seventy-fours, the "Mars," "Triumph," "Brunswick," "Bellerophon," and two frigates, Admiral Cornwallis was cruising on detached duty from the Channel Fleet, to the

*THE "ROYAL SOVEREIGN" AT TRAFALGAR.*

June, fine as it was, was bettered twice over on two later days. First on a notable occasion that, for some reason or other, has passed out of the memory of most of us. The "Royal Sovereign," in the year following Lord Howe's victory, distinguished herself, as flag-ship to Vice-Admiral Cornwallis, in a yet higher degree by the part she took in the

southward of Brest, when suddenly, on July 17th, 1795, he found himself in presence of the whole Brest Fleet—thirteen ships of the line, a 120-gun-ship, and twelve seventy-fours, with fourteen frigates. The French came down on Cornwallis in force, making to bar his way homeward and surround him. But they did not know their man. Holding his force well in hand, the British admiral, despite the overwhelming odds, held his own all day, beating every attack of the enemy off, while he retired northwards, two ships in the van, two in the rear, and two in the centre, at his own pace. Every time that the French seemed pressing our rear ships, the "Sovereign" would go about and move down to aid her consorts with her

"Men," said the admiral to his flag-ship's company when he called them to the quarter-deck before the fighting began, "remember that the 'Sovereign's' flag and ensign are never to be struck to an enemy; she goes down with them flying."

At the same time Cornwallis neglected no precaution for

*'TWEEN DECKS IN THE "ROYAL SOVEREIGN," OCTOBER 21st, 1805.*

powerful three tiers of guns, and in each case the attack drew off baulked. Our fellows fought hour after hour, from seven in the morning till six at night, ship cheering ship all the time, the French, for their part, too overawed at Cornwallis's dauntless front to close all through the day. It was sheer calm courage, for Cornwallis well knew his grave peril.

attracting aid from the main Channel Ficet under Lord Bridport, Howe's successor, then expected off the coast. To take advantage of every chance, one of his two frigates, the "Phaeton," was sent ahead early to look out for the main Fleet. The captain of the "Phaeton" had further orders, if no friend should come in sight, to make sham signals later ln the day, as if to an approaching fleet, below the horizon from where the fight was going on. If things came to the worst, Cornwallis hoped, as the admiral himself said to the captain of the "Phaeton," to "humbug those fellows astern." The ruse proved in the end to be needed, and it succeeded to perfection. Late in the afternoon, when it was plain that Cornwallis could not shake the enemy off, the "Phaeton" duly began to signal, first that a fleet was in sight, then, on her own account, as though communicating with distant friends. At the same time she let go topgallant sheets, a signal that a fleet was in sight as well known to the French as to ourselves. By a coincidence, it happened at that moment that the topsails of a number of ships in the far distance came into view from the mastheads of the French Fleet. The strange sails were really only a convoy of merchantmen passing down Channel, but the French could not know that. They believed that Lord Bridport and the whole Channel Fleet were coming up to cut them off, and they forthwith drew off and made sail to seek shelter in Belleisle Roads.

For the splendid conduct of the "Sovereign" and her consorts, the admiral and the captains of the squadron were specially thanked by both Houses of Parliament, and every landsman and ordinary seaman engaged was specially rated "A.B." Of these last, indeed, Cornwallis himself, in his official letter to the Admiralty, said, "Could common prudence have allowed me to let loose their valour, I hardly know what might not have been accomplished by such men." The last survivor of Cornwallis's squadron, one of the midshipmen of the "Royal Sovereign," died as recently as 1869.

In 1797 the "Royal Sovereign," as before with the Channel Fleet, flew the flag of Sir Alan Gardner, captain of the "Duke," in Rodney's "Twelfth of April" battle; in 1803, again with the Channel Fleet, she flew the flag of Sir Henry Harvey, the captain of the "Ramillies" on "The Glorious First of June"; in 1804 she flew the flag of Sir Richard Bickerton, Lord Nelson's second in command in the Mediterranean Fleet, under which officer the "Sovereign" served with Nelson all through the long watching off Toulon.

What splendid service the "Royal Sovereign" rendered on October 21st, 1805, should be familiar to every British man and boy. In the words of Captain Blackwood—written immediately after the battle—"Of the 'Victory' and the 'Royal Sovereign' it is impossible to say which achieved the most." The "Sovereign," which had gone home to refit when Nelson went off across the Atlantic in pursuit of the Franco-Spanish Fleet, rejoined the British Fleet off Cadiz just three weeks before Trafalgar, when Collingwood, who hitherto had had his flag in the "Dreadnought," moved into her. The "Sovereign's" captain at Trafalgar, Collingwood's flag-captain, was, like the admiral, a gallant Northumbrian, Edward Rotheram, the son of a Newcastle doctor, and the bulk of the "Sovereign's" company, it also happened, were sturdy North Country men. "We'll show them, my lads, what Tars of the Tyne can do," Collingwood himself is related to have said to the "Sovereign's" men, when he went round the decks on the morning of Trafalgar.

As pre-arranged by Nelson, the British lee column at Trafalgar, fifteen ships strong, began the action before the weather column, by leading down and breaking the enemy's line near its centre. The manœuvre was begun a few minutes before noon, when, at Collingwood's order, the "Sovereign," with every sail set, stu'ns'ls and all, and every reef shaken out, "like a frigate" dashed forward by herself, ahead of the whole Fleet. Taking on herself the fire of the enemy's whole line, centre and rear, as she advanced, she passed under the stern of the Spanish flag-ship "Santa Ana," a gigantic 112-gun three-decker, more than a mile in front of Collingwood's second astern, the "Belleisle"—"the most remarkable incident of the battle, a feat unparalleled in Naval history," as it has been called. "See," exclaimed Nelson with delight to Captain Hardy, as he watched the "Sovereign's" advance, "how that noble fellow Collingwood carries his ship into action," just at the moment, as it happened, that on the "Royal Sovereign's" quarter-deck Collingwood himself was saying to his captain, "Rotheram, what would not Nelson give to be here?"

The way the "Sovereign" was taken into action, indeed, called forth, as one of the captains of the lee line following Collingwood describes it, "the admiration of the whole Fleet." Another (Tyler of the "Tonnant") declared further, "It so arrested my own attention that I felt for some minutes as if I myself had nothing to do but look on and admire." We know, too, from what French officers at Trafalgar have written, that the confident daring of the "Sovereign's" single-handed advance positively appalled Villeneuve.

*"Rotheram, what would not Nelson give to be here?"*

As the "Sovereign" neared the enemy a French ship, the "Fougeux," ranged up close under the stern of the "Santa Ana," as though to bar the passage through the line to Collingwood. Rotheram noted this, and pointed it out to the admiral. Collingwood replied: "Steer straight for the Frenchman and take his bowsprit." So they closed, and then, driving through the line close under the towering Spanish flag-ship's stern, the "Sovereign" opened the fight with her full broadside trebly shotted. The terrific discharge at one blow disabled fourteen guns and struck down 400 men. "*Il rompait todos,*" in the words of a Spanish officer of the "Santa Ana." Then the "Sovereign" ranged alongside the big Spaniard to leeward to fight the battle out with her chosen opponent, gun-muzzle to gun-muzzle. But, as the event proved, it was not to be with one opponent only. No sooner was the "Sovereign" alongside the "Santa Ana" than four other ships, two French—the "Fougeux" and the "Indomptable," and two Spanish—the "San Leandro" and the "San Justo," closed round and joined in to help the "Santa Ana." So hot a cross fire, indeed, did these four ships keep up on the single British ship in her, at first, unsupported fight, that, in the words of some of those in the "Sovereign," "we could see their shots meeting and smashing together in mid-air round us." It was a battle of the giants, a heroic defiance of heroic odds for nearly twenty minutes, when, after the "Sovereign" had by herself beaten off the "Fougeux," the leading British ships following astern of the "Sovereign" came up and took off her enemies one by one, except, of course, the "Santa Ana." With the Spanish flag-ship the "Sovereign" continued in close encounter, until, after a two hours' ship to ship duel, the "Santa Ana's" colours finally came down. At that moment it was that Collingwood received, by an officer of the "Victory," Hardy's first message—that Lord Nelson had been "dangerously wounded."

The gallant stand the "Santa Ana" made

*THE FIRST ARMOURED TURRET-SHIP IN THE BRITISH NAVY.*

was a disappointment to the "Sovereign's" people. After their terrible raking broadside at the outset they seemed to have so "sickened" the Spaniards, as our fellows expressively put it, that they thought the enemy must surrender at once. The "Sovereign's" gallant fellows, it is on record, actually thought that the "Sovereign" would have the proud distinction of capturing an enemy's flag-ship in the midst of her own fleet before another British ship could get into action. Even Captain Rotheram thought so, and he approached Collingwood with, "I congratulate you, sir; she is slackening her fire, and must soon strike." But the Spaniards were brave men, and recovering after their first scare, they managed to make a far more stubborn defence than seemed possible.

"No ship besides ourselves fired a shot at her," said one of the "Sovereign's" officers afterwards of the "Santa Ana," "and you can have no conception how completely she was ruined." "Her side," wrote Collingwood himself, "was almost entirely beat in." As to what the Spaniards thought of the "Sovereign." Said the senior surviving officer of the "Santa Ana," on going on board the "Sovereign" to hand his sword to Collingwood: "What ship is this to which we have to strike?" He was told. The Spaniard threw his hands up with an ejaculation: "'Royal—Sovereign!' Madre de Dios!" he exclaimed. "She should be called the 'Royal Devil!'"

The "Sovereign" pushed off from her giant prize, which, in Collingwood's own words, "towered over the 'Sovereign' like a castle," to seek another enemy. But the fall of her main and mizen masts, cut through by shot, prevented her taking a further active part until after being taken in tow by the "Euryalus" frigate. The "Sovereign" was able then, during the rest of the action, to employ her broadsides with effect. Her last service was at the very close of the battle, when she formed one of the small group of ships that Hardy summoned round the "Victory" to support the dying chief's flag-ship against a threatened attack on the "Victory" from fresh ships of the French van squadron.

The "Royal Sovereign's" list of casualties, as reckoned up on the morning after Trafalgar, amounted to forty- even killed and ninety-four wounded.

When all was over Collingwood shifted his flag from the "Sovereign" into the "Euryalus," and then the "Sovereign," after weathering the great gale which wrecked the "Santa Ana" and so many more of our Trafalgar prizes, and refitting temporarily at Gibraltar, proceeded home under jury rig.

Collingwood, on being made a peer for Trafalgar, was granted a special additional crest representing the stern of the "Royal Sovereign," with, for heraldic supporters to the Collingwood family arms, representations of two sailors of his heroic flag-ship.

In the course of 1806 the "Sovereign" again went to the Mediterranean as Admiral Edward Thornbrough's flag-ship, returning home, after a commission as guard-ship at Gibraltar, towards the end of 1811. After that she served with the Channel Fleet until the Peace. In 1814 the "Royal Sovereign" took part in the great Naval Review before the Prince Regent, the Czar, and the King of Prussia; and in 1815, for a short while during the "Hundred Days," she was again commissioned—for the last time.*

In 1834, a new "Royal Sovereign" man-of-war was ordered at Portsmouth, but her keel was not laid down until ten years later. This was the "Royal Sovereign" launched in 1857 as a 121-gun-ship, of 3,760 tons, which, between 1862 and 1864, was, under the direction of Captain Cowper Coles, cut down, reconstructed and armoured, and became the first turret-ship ever seen in the British Navy. All her service, however, was as tender to the "Excellent," gunnery ship, at Portsmouth, after filling which *rôle* for some years the "Royal Sovereign" was in 1884 sold out of the Navy. Of this "Royal Sovereign" are still preserved at Portsmouth Dockyard two figure-heads, one that belonged to the ship when a three decker, and, second, the lion figure-head—"the old dog Toby," as it was called—the ship had while a turret ironclad.

Finally, the present magnificent first-class battle-ship, "Royal Sovereign"—the sixth bearer of the name—was laid down at Portsmouth Dockyard in 1889, and named by the Queen herself with State ceremony in the presence of the Prince and Princess of Wales, the Duke of Edinburgh, the Duke of Connaught, and a brilliant assemblage of Naval and Military officers, on February 26th, 1891. The "Royal Sovereign" was the first sent afloat of the eight battle-ships built under the Naval Defence Act of 1889; and as a vessel of 14,150 tons was at the time the largest ship of war ever launched for the Royal Navy. Until the coming of the "Majestic" and her sisters, the "Sovereign" and her group held their pre-eminence. From May, 1892, to December, 1895, the "Royal Sovereign" served as senior flag-ship to the Channel Squadron, flying, meanwhile, the flags of Sir Henry Fairfax, Sir Robert Fitzroy, and Lord Walter Kerr. At the end of 1895, on the "Majestic" joining the Channel Squadron, the "Sovereign" became a private ship. She has recently left the Channel for the Mediterranean.

* From 1804 until comparatively lately there was also a Royal yacht bearing the name of "Royal Sovereign." She played a prominent part in the great Naval Review of 1814 (at which Collingwood's Trafalgar "Royal Sovereign" man-of-war was present, as we have seen), flying the Imperial and Royal Standards of the three great personages in whose honour the parade was held, who also reviewed the Fleet on board her.

*A Casemate in the "Royal Sovereign" of 1891.*

*The next Special Number of this Series will contain the History of the "Britannia," Past and Present.*

# THE
# NAVY & ARMY
## ILLUSTRATED.

VOL. V.—No. 51.]     *FRIDAY, NOVEMBER 26th, 1897.*

### ADMIRAL SIR WILLIAM GARNHAM LUARD, K.C.B.

NELSON'S Hardy, the captain of the "Victory" at Trafalgar, was First Lord of the Admiralty when Sir William Luard entered the Royal Navy in February, 1833. England was at peace with all the world just then; but, as usual with us, it was not for long. The opening up of the Far East to British enterprise was at hand, and in the thirty odd years that the operation took, dating from the time of Sir William Luard's entry into the Navy, he had an active share in what was done. As mate of the "Samarang" he fought in the first China War, being specially promoted lieutenant for his services at the storming of Fort Tycocktow and the forcing of the passage of the Bocca Tigris. Ten years later, when we were opening up Burma to English trade, as commander of the "Serpent" he was specially mentioned in despatches for his services at the capture of Rangoon and the destruction of Kemmendine. Ten years after that again, as captain of the "Conqueror," he superintended the landing of the storming parties in the attack at Simonoseki. In later years Sir William Luard has served as admiral superintendent of Malta Dockyard and as president of the Royal Naval College at Greenwich. He was retired as full admiral in 1885, and was promoted K.C.B. in June last.

# BOATS AT THE BOOM.

*Photo. F. G. O. S. GREGORY & CO., Naval Opticians, 51, Strand.*                    *Copyright.—HUDSON & KEARNS.*

ONCE the anchor is dropped and the welcome signal, "usual leave," runs up from the flag-ship, the ship's boats enter largely into the daily life of both officers and blue-jackets. In our illustration a steam picket-boat, such as is carried by all large craft, is shown at the end of the boom, while inside of her is a large broad-beamed rowing, or sailing, boat. In harbour, the uses to which boats are put are many and various. Liberty men have to be taken ashore and re-embarked again at the time when their brief run on shore has expired. Fresh provisions and necessaries have to be brought on board. A boat has to be run for the postman and the use of officers. It is not entirely, however, for the comfort and pleasure of the ship's crew that the Fleet's boats are so much in evidence in harbour. Sailing and rowing instruction is given almost daily, and "out boats," to row round the Fleet, is a common exercise. Again, the boats will be frequently used for the practising of mine-laying, and the protection of a Fleet at anchorage.

# HOW A SHIP IS COALED.

*Photo. SYMONDS & CO., Portsmouth.*

*On a Battle-ship's Quarter-Deck during Coaling.*

THE operation of coaling is, of course, a matter of vital import-ance on board ship in these days of steam propulsion, but it is, at the same time, to all concerned one of the most trying and unpleasant of duties. That it is done cheerfully and taken as "all in the day's work"-being carried out where several ships are to-gether in a spirit of the keenest rivalry, ship against ship as to which shall be done first and make a record—is another question. Briefly, this is what happens during coaling. The collier comes alongside, and the coal in its hold is placed in sacks by a party of bluejackets from the ship to be coaled, the sacks being then swung on board the battle-ship, where they are placed on barrows, wheeled to the coaling shoots, and emptied into the bunkers, to be finally trimmed and stowed away there in the smallest possible space. That is an outline of the process. In its details, coaling a battle-ship or cruiser involves a great many other things.

The first outward sign, which shows that coaling a war-ship is, to say the least of it, a big business, is the covering up of all the breeches of the guns on board, large and small, the quick-firing guns and machine guns, with tarpaulins. After that comes the closing of all sky-lights and cabin ventilators, and all open spaces—except those required for the actual operation in hand—leading below from the upper deck. Practically the whole ship's company of all ranks and ratings, from quarter-deck officers to boys, take some part in coaling a ship, for which the officers turn out in their oldest and worst clothes. For the men a white coaling dress is provided out of a special allowance, known as the "C.D.B." The work begun, in a very short time the spotless upper deck and upper works of the beautiful man-of-war, whether battle-ship or cruiser, are com-pletely transformed into a scene of grime and discom-fort. The upper deck speedily becomes buried, from bow to stern, beneath a layer of coal dust, which insinuates itself everywhere and lodges itself in every nook and cranny. The bright barrels of the guns become smudged, and the white paint everywhere looks grey. At the same time, down below particles of coal dust manage to find lodgment, floating in between decks and depositing themselves here, there, and everywhere in thinner layers. To remain in the cabins or in the ward-room, should anyone be disposed so to do, is practically to court asphyxia,

*The Coal Coming on Board.*

at the same time that, on the other hand, to be on deck means for everybody, from captain to cabin boy, the prompt under-going of a transformation into the appearance of a coal heaver or of a Moore and Burgess Minstrel. It is difficult to recog-nise the smartest of officers in the dingy persons who are

Photo. SYMONDS & CO..

*HOISTING OUT COAL FROM A COLLIER ALONGSIDE.*

CONVEYING   THE   COAL   SACKS   TO   THE   COALING   SHOOTS.

superintending the coaling parties. All in garb and face look like mourners in sack-cloth and ashes. So the work progresses, the coal coming on board in marvellous rapidity, sack after sack being whipped up over the side in endless succession, as it seems, until the last ton required has been safely received, trundled to the shoot, and stowed away and trimmed in the bunkers.

After that comes the cleaning up both of the men themselves and of the ship, during which latter process, fore and aft, the whole vessel becomes filled with a sound of rushing waters, the upper decks being flooded, while the scuppers run like brooks as the dust and dirt of an hour ago is swept into the sea in rushing torrents of water. The ship is washed and scrubbed throughout from end to end, the barefooted bluejackets working with such will that in a wonderfully short space of time, thanks also to the yards of hose and unlimited water at their disposal, the ship's toilet is speedily completed and the vessel herself restored to her former spotless condition. Then cabins and skylights and ventilators are all thrown open, and fresh air and sweetness and light are let in once more.

Such is the scene at the coaling of a war-ship in the daytime. At night electric lamps fore and aft cast a brilliant light over all, the scene as the work progresses being one that might well have inspired Dante, could he have seen it, to write another canto to his "Inferno." The black night, the clouds of steam and coal dust, the clattering din of the winches, the crowd of dusky figures swarming everywhere as they work at top speed—the scene would make the fortune of an artist to depict.

The operation of coaling, thanks to modern ingenuity, can nowadays be carried on as easily at sea as in harbour, by means of the Temperley transporter, an ingenious mechanical contrivance that is now fitted on board all our

*Photos. SYMONDS & CO., Portsmouth.*

*Weighing  Coal  Sacks  before  Emptying  into  the  Bunkers.*

modern battle-ships and large cruisers. The Temperley transporter consists of a light beam attached to a derrick, along which a carriage travels, with a pulley attached, for the rope carrying the sacks of coal to pass over. By one continuous pull on board the battle-ship the coal sacks are lifted clear up from the hold of the collier, conveyed directly up the side, and run on board on to the deck of the ship taking in coal, where the men receive it and bestow it as already related.

It is to a great extent by means of the Temperley transporter that our ships are able to coal as expeditiously as is done in the Channel and Mediterranean Fleets, where an average of over 120 tons an hour has been passed in the case of several of the larger battle-ships. The differences recorded among ships in commission in their rates of taking in coal are, in fact, the result of differences in the position of the bunkers, making it easy for some ships to coal quickly, while others cannot possibly do so.

Photo. J. KING-SALTER.    *Cleaning Ship after Coaling.*    Sheerness.

## THE CHINA STATION.

*The Naval Commander-in-Chief in China, with His Staff:—The " Centurion," 1897.*

THE story of the China station begins in 1833, when the regular trade with China and the Far East, hitherto carried on exclusively by the East India Company, was thrown open to the British Empire. War with China followed a few years later, owing to the determined efforts of the Chinese to baulk British enterprise and keep out the hated foreigner, and the war resulted in the cession of Hong Kong and the establishment of the Treaty Ports in 1842. Henceforward British men-of-war, up to then but rarely seen in the Yellow Sea, began to show the flag there regularly, the duty being performed by cruisers detached from the regular East Indies Naval station, who used Hong Kong—where a dockyard establishment on a small scale now first began to be organised—as their Naval base. Between 1856 and 1862 came the second war with China, and after that followed the regular organisation of a separate Naval station for the China seas, with a squadron and admiral of its own, distinct from the "East Indies and China station."

Recent events have led to the strengthening of the squadron and the addition of a rear-admiral as second in command, until the China station has become next in importance after the Channel and Mediterranean. Our photograph shows the commander-in-chief in China, Vice-Admiral Sir Alexander Buller, K.C.B., and the officers of his personal staff, on board the flag-ship "Centurion."

# SPORT ON BOARD SHIP.

NO keener sportsmen are to be found in any section of Society than the officers of the Royal Navy. The Channel or Mediterranean Squadrons could any day

*A Game of Hockey on the Upper Deck.*

*Improving Their Shooting.*

turn out a team that at cricket, football, golf, or polo, would be hard to beat. Our illustrations show that even at sea sport can be obtained, and, though carried on under difficulties, it gives exercise and good training to eye and muscle. In one of our illustrations, a game of sling the monkey is shown, which needs no explanation. The wily sub-lieutenant triced in the bight of a rope will not be long before he finds a victim to take his place. In another illustration, hockey, a sport very popular on board, is well depicted. In both these pictures it will be noticed that flannels are worn, and it is interesting as showing the zest and real earnestness with which the games are entered into. A further illustration depicts a rifle match with Morris-tube ammunition—a sport keenly entered into at sea, and one which not only whiles away many an odd hour, but helps to make our seamen the first-class shots that they are. Cricket is also common, and golf is not unknown. A captive ball teed on a coir mat is driven astern, and points allowed for accuracy and direction of drive. Lofting over obstacles —of which there are plenty on board—is good practice for approach shots, and putting over a chalked hole on a rolling deck makes the trickiest of greens.

In one ship there was a combination of cricket, hockey, and football. The game was tip and run, but the batsman might strike the ball as often as he liked—or could. His side could obstruct the fielders and the fielders could obstruct him. The result may be more easily imagined than described, but the game was glorious fun.

*Sling the Monkey.*

# A FAVOURITE NAVAL DISPLAY.

HERE is a scene to which the public of Greater Britain is often treated, on those occasions when the ships of our Fleets and Squadrons all over the world hold their periodical competitions in smartness and agility at Naval displays on shore. The man-of-war's man is an adept at single-stick and sword play. It is one of Jack's favourite recreations on board ship when he takes his pleasure on the upper deck on fine evenings at sea, in the interval between supper and turning in for the night, and forms by no means a bad method of exercise towards developing the men physically, and helping forward their regular training in general activity, strength, and the acquisition of a quick eye, which are so essential for the seaman.

Sword exercise, out of which single-stick practice springs as an adjunct, is, of course, regularly taught in the Navy as a regulation drill, its special *raison d'être* being for use in boat work.

*Single-Stick Play.*

Photo. F. G. O. S. GREGORY & CO., Naval Opticians, 51, Strand.

## A QUIET SMOKE.

MEN ashore, who can practically have recourse to the fragrant weed whenever opportunity offers, know little how a pipe is prized by Jack afloat. Unlike the labourer so often seen repairing the streets of London (smoking the while), he can only light his pipe at certain times and in certain places. Smoking is permitted only on the upper deck. No one on any account is allowed to smoke between decks. On board ship, even more so than in barracks, everything is kept scrupulously clean, and it is not surprising to learn that spitting on the deck or over the side is strictly forbidden. Safety lanterns for lighting pipes are placed in convenient localities. The soldier on board a troop-ship no doubt considers it hard to be deprived of his smoke at table after dinner, but it must be remembered that all these stringent rules on board ship are made in order to minimise the risk of fire. Afloat a fire is a much more serious thing than in barracks, for a ship, unlike a building, cannot be abandoned with ease. The above illustration depicts a bluejacket enjoying a few minutes' ease over a pipe of peace. The expression on his face betokens that feeling of satisfaction begotten only of tobacco.

## THE OFFICER OF THE WATCH.

FROM the moment that one of Her Majesty's ships hoists the pennant on commissioning, until she is paid off, there is never a moment, day or night, that there is not an officer of the watch responsible for her. In harbour, the responsibilities of the officer of the watch are comparatively slight compared to the onerous nature of his duties at sea ; but even then he is, to a great extent, responsible that the routine duties of the ship are properly carried out, and he has to receive all reports and generally supervise. Moreover, he has to keep an eye on all boats leaving or coming to the ship, and it is especially laid down in the regulations that the officer of the watch shall be responsible, as far as possible, that a careful look-out is kept on all boats away from the ship under sail. On this duty the pair depicted in our illustration are probably engaged. The officer with the telescope under his arm is the lieutenant of the watch, while standing by him is the midshipman on duty. At sea, of course, the duties of the officer of the watch are of a very weighty character. His station then is on the bridge, and on him devolves the work of seeing that the ship is steered on her set course, and that she keeps her proper station when in a fleet or squadron ; and no small responsibility is the keeping of accurate station when in a fleet organisation. He also is responsible for seeing that the ship's progress is duly recorded, and all necessary entries made in the deck log ; and although the course steered is by order, and under the direction of the navigating officer, yet the officer of the watch must keep himself fully informed of the position of the ship, and more especially when near land.

In accordance with a promise made some time since, our next number will be devoted to illustrating the Indian Army. It will be the first of a series to be issued at intervals during the next few months devoted to picturing and describing our Indian and Colonial Forces, representatives of which were present at the Jubilee celebration last June. Finding it impossible to deal with all these forces adequately in one number, I have taken the Native Forces of India first, and upwards of 100 illustrations will be found in No. 52, comprehending the Armies of Bombay, Bengal, Madras, and the Punjab, and the Imperial Service Troops. This is the first time that the British public has had an opportunity of obtaining at small cost and under one cover a complete and artistic representation of the soldiers of our great Indian Empire. A concise and interesting description accompanies the pictures. As there is sure to be a large demand for this number, it is well to order it in advance.

\* \* \* \*

THE number following that devoted to the Indian Army will also contain some novel features. In it will be commenced a new serial by that popular author, Major Arthur Griffiths, who contributes a tale of adventure in which we shall accompany an officer of the Military Intelligence Department through a series of stirring scenes and incidents, brought about by his accession to great wealth. In the course of the story we make acquaintance with the internal working of the Intelligence Department, as well as learning something of life in a Service club. I am sure that our readers cannot fail to be interested in a story dealing with so much that is novel, in a style which Major Griffiths has made his own. For the future, also, I shall give in each number, under the title "The Service Bookshelf," a column of crisp and brightly-written reviews of all books which those concerned in Naval and Military matters will like to know about. In addition to books that are purely Naval and Military, I intend to review volumes of travels, good fiction with any Service colour, and works on Imperial politics, biography, sport, athletics, games, etc. I think this feature cannot but add to the value of the paper, and trust it will be appreciated.

\* \* \* \*

A CORRESPONDENT writes: "Will you allow me to point out a slight inaccuracy in your 'Notes and Queries' anent the wearing of sashes, in which it is made to appear that these are not worn by officers of Highland regiments? The officers of Highland regiments wear crimson silk sashes, and very handsome and costly ones they are. They do not wear pouch belts, but from the front they appear to do so, as their sword belt is worn over the shoulder and the dirk belt round the waist. I need hardly say you can do as you like about publishing this; but as one who wore the uniform, every detail of which is dear to my heart, I could not refrain from calling your attention to the mistake."

\* \* \* \*

A NAVAL officer is often applied to with the question, "How am I to get my boy into the Navy?" The regulations for entry had altered but little for several years, but lately there has been a great change, principally in the age for entry to the examination; but it is more the preliminary undertaking of obtaining a nomination about which information is required. A boy cannot present himself for examination without first obtaining a nomination. All nominations are made by the First Lord of the Admiralty, with the following exceptions: A few by members of the Admiralty Board and its secretaries; an admiral appointed to a command is allowed the gift of one nomination, and a captain on his first appointment to the command of a ship, but the latter is only allowed one nomination for the whole time that he holds the rank of captain.

THE boy should be prepared specially for the examination he will be expected to pass, and then an application must be made in good time beforehand for a nomination through one of the sources mentioned. All further information will be supplied on application to the Admiralty. Six or seven nominations for Service cadetships to sons of officers of the Navy and Army and Marines, who have seen distinguished service, been killed in action, or died of wounds, are given annually. Also six nominations are given to sons of gentlemen in the Colonies, on the recommendation of the Secretary of State for the Colonies. A boy before examination in other subjects will have to pass a strict medical examination, and should he possess any physical defect or constitutional weakness, the time would only be wasted in preparing him for the Navy.

\* \* \* \*

"WE will beat them to their own tune," said the gallant Colonel Doyle, laughingly, to his young soldiers of the 14th Regiment, at the attack of Famars. The regiment, composed almost entirely of young lads, finding themselves opposed to the French 14th *de la ligne*, rushed up the heights with such ardour as to lose their formation, when the colonel halted them and reformed the ranks, then ordered the band to play *Ça Ira*, the march of the French regiment, and gave the order for the attack, when they beat their opponents most thoroughly. The regiment play *Ça Ira* as their regimental march to the present day. It is recorded that, in passing through Dartford in 1793, the inhabitants took offence at the democratic tune, and pelted the regiment with stones.

\* \* \* \*

"A. M.," Trinidad.—The mercantile cruisers—such as the "Campania" and "Lucania"—which are fitted with emplacements for the mounting of guns in time of war, are in receipt of an annual subvention and permitted to fly the blue ensign—denoting that they belong to the Naval Reserve. Their *rôle*, in the event of their being employed upon active service, would be of a protective, rather than of an aggressive, character. It is not intended that they should act as "eyes of the Fleet," or in evolutions with groups or squadrons of other war vessels, but that they should be able to defend themselves from predatory attacks, for which service their quick-firing armament and great speed precisely fit them. They would have instructional parties sent on board in time of war from the Naval Reserve headquarters, who, with the assistance of the European portion of the crew, would work the guns.

\* \* \* \*

THE armament for these merchant cruisers is kept at Portsmouth, Devonport, and other places at home; and at Hong Kong, Malta, Bermuda, and other places abroad. It consists of 5-in. breech-loading rifled guns, and 4.7-in. quick-firing guns, together with a proportion of 6-pounder Hotchkiss guns. Eight 5-in. or eight 4.7-in. guns and eight Hotchkiss 6-pounders comprise the armament of such cruisers as the "Campania" or "Lucania." The mounting is of the ordinary pedestal, central-pivoted, description, with a 4-in. shield to protect the gunners at the larger weapons. It is intended eventually to issue only quick-firing guns to these vessels. The ammunition to be carried, therefore, would be a very considerable item. Two thousand rounds of 4.7-in. and 3,200 rounds of 6-pounder Hotchkiss would be the proportion maintained in the magazines. This allows of action being carried on for a lengthened period. The worst feature of these improvised cruisers is the absence of all cover in the conveyance of ammunition to the guns.

\* \* \* \*

"F. S. P." asks: "What is a Vice-Admiral of the Coast?" A Vice-Admiral of the Coast is a judicial and ministerial officer, representing the Lord High Admiral in his *Civil*, as distinguished from his *Naval*, capacity. The office is of great antiquity, but has fallen into some desuetude during the last hundred years. The letters patent of the appointment confer on this officer an Admiralty jurisdiction over the coast of the county for which he is appointed, and over the seashore, public streams, and arms of the sea adjoining, with power to take cognisance within that jurisdiction of all causes, civil and maritime, and of crimes and offences. In time of war he has frequently impressed mariners for the Navy. The sea coast of England and Wales is divided into nineteen circuits or vice-admiralties, many of which are at present vacant. In some Scottish burghs the Provosts are vice-admirals, *ex-officio*, and not by special appointment.

IT is on record that soon after the conclusion of the war in 1748 the Thames watermen were increased by 2,000, while the price of boats was raised by one quarter. Our great Naval sea-ports were then the scenes of riot and drunkenness now undreamed of. Thus, a correspondent writing from Portsmouth, in the year 1748, to a friend in town, says: "The sailors paid off as their ships arrive get mad with drink and commit great violences," adding, "it is well that 300 soldiers are here to protect us." How far off all this seems, now !

\*   \*   \*   \*

"A YOUNG VET." tells me that he is desirous of entering the Army Veterinary Department, and puts some questions as to the qualifications of which candidates should be possessed. I am not surprised that such inquiries are made, because the Veterinary service has of late been more sought after, its officers are well educated and do their duties in a highly creditable manner, and their recognised Army rank is an additional attraction to young men of good family and position, many of whom have elected to serve in this branch. As a rule, candidates must be between twenty-one and twenty-seven years of age, unmarried, and members of the Royal College of Veterinary Surgeons. They must produce certificates of birth or baptism and moral character, and be approved by the Commander-in-Chief, but if they show, during their examination, any deficiency in general education, they are liable to rejection. The examination in professional subjects is both written and practical. The medical examination must prove the conformation, health, hearing, and speech to be good. The teeth must be in good order, and the loss or decay of ten teeth is a disqualification.

\*   \*   \*   \*

### THE LAUNCH OF THE "CANOPUS."

#### 13th October, 1897.

I SAW the silent, dark, expectant crowd,
   That ringed the huge sea-castle, white as snow,
   I heard the merry shipwrights far below
Loosen the blocks with hammers clanging loud ;
And much I marvelled at the mind endowed
   With sure foreknowledge that could shape the prow,
   And weigh it as in balance—wondering how
Man's might should move that hull to ocean bowed.

Then prayer was said, and children sang their praise.
   God the Invisible, who made us kings,
   And moulds the nation's purpose, came more near ;
And without pain or travail down the "ways"
   The ship for Peace went forward with a cheer,
   And all the void was filled with angel wings.

                       H. D. RAWNSLEY.

\*   \*   \*   \*

OWING to a mistake, which we regret, no acknowledgment was made in the double number, "Nelson and Trafalgar," to the Art Union of London, 112, Strand, of their copyright in the engraving of the Death of Nelson, by Maclise, which appears at the top of page 370. I am the more sorry that this should have occurred as the Council of this Society have always been most ready to grant me permission for the reproduction of their work. In No. 49, also, the photograph of Sir W. Hunt Grubbe was wrongly attributed to Messrs. Russell and Sons, of Baker Street, owing to a printer's error. The photograph belongs to Messrs. W. Heath and Co., 24, George Street, Plymouth.

MR. BLOUNDELLE-BURTON'S great following of readers will be delighted to know that, even as "Across the Salt Seas" is at its end in these pages, another highly romantic story of adventure from his pen is now issued in volume form by Methuen and Co. This is a romance entitled "The Clash of Arms," and will sustain his well-acquired reputation for novels full of life and fire, of perilous situations, and of wild dramatic incidents. Space does not allow us to criticise, but only to call attention to this new work of Mr. Burton's, and to remark that those who have perused breathlessly the career of Mervyn Crespin and his sweetheart Juana will do the same with the narrative embodied in "The Clash of Arms," and they will say adieu regretfully to Andrew Vause after they have followed him eagerly through the stormy incidents of the novel. Our only complaint against the author is that he keeps us out of our beds when we ought to be in them, and compels us to read his books when we should be about other work.

                       THE EDITOR.

# FISHING IN THE NAVY.

### By NAUTICUS.

THERE are few of Her Majesty's ships that do not count among their crews a considerable number of enthusiastic fishermen.

This is wisely recognised by the Admiralty, who provide a seining-net for every ship, and allow the boatswain to expend from his stores sufficient cod, mackerel, and whiting line to supply each mess with fishing lines. Hooks are also provided.

These benevolent views, however, are not generally shared by the commanding officers of ships. They—although perhaps disciples of the gentle Izaak themselves—not unnaturally object to the smearing of their vessels' glistening sides consequent upon general fishing.

Hence it comes to pass that fishing from the portholes—the most convenient places—is forbidden, and that much of the good work in this, as in other pursuits, is done by stealth. Many a luckless bluejacket has run himself head first into the black list by incautiously protruding himself from the port when fishing. He felt, perhaps, what he thought was a bite; but found it, to his cost, to be his first luff twigging at the line from a boat.

The impossible places in which a bluejacket will stow himself in order to indulge in a little illicit fishing are surprising. In or under the chains (as the plates are called where the rigging is fastened to the ship's side), under the cover of the quarter-boat, and even perched on the bobstay under the bowsprit—any coign of vantage not readily seen from within is seized upon.

In home harbour ships fishing follows the usual lines. Good sport is generally to be obtained, as the bottom beneath a ship at anchor becomes good feeding ground owing to the number of scraps thrown overboard. Mullet, whiting, conger, and even gulls are caught, the latter by floating a piece of pork astern.

Conger abound in the western ports. At Falmouth, in particular, they are very plentiful, and frequently run to an immense size. The writer well remembers the fright he got from his first catch there, when he was a youngster.

It was on the staging alongside the old "Ganges," training-ship, that the monster was landed one summer night. It opened its mouth as it was hauled out of the water, and barked like a dog. It was about five feet long, and it couldn't be persuaded to die.

The picture of a group of fellow-fishermen following its wrigglings about the upper deck by the light of a purser's lantern, and striking at it, as opportunity offered, with stretchers and belaying pins, is still very vivid.

Another familiar experience of those youthful days was watching, from a stern port, the beautiful grey mullet nibbling round the rudder post, almost within arm's length—so near and yet so far, for we could never catch them. A messmate—an imaginative genius who has since left his bones in the Soudan—would stand by the while and excite our appetites by enlarging on the delicious eating qualities of the mullet. He was well acquainted with them, as the Medway—his native stream—simply swarmed with them. It was, he said, the richest fish in the sea, and would fry in its own fat. The flavour he couldn't describe, to do justice to it. It wasn't exactly like chicken, because there was a sweet smack with it—something like strawberry ice, and yet soft and slippery like a junket. I never eat mullet to this day without thinking of strawberry ice, and recalling the sunlit water in which the silver fish glistened and the black rudder post ran down to endless depths.

Fishing at sea is, of course, limited to whiffing, *i.e.*, fishing on the move, and has to be conducted with a view to keeping clear of the patent log, the lead, etc.

One enthusiastic fisherman the writer recalls—a chaplain—who always had his line overboard. He was very successful, and, on long trips, his contributions to the larder were very welcome. So regular and reliable was he that, when he occasionally failed to provide a fish item to the bill of fare, it came to be regarded as a grievance.

He was had once, though—by the middies, of course. They hooked a *tin* fish to his line while he was at dinner, and passed the word round, so that everybody was there to hear his extempore sermon when the joke unfolded.

Fishing with the rod is to be obtained on most stations,

particularly in the North Pacific, where the rivers swarm with fish. This form of sport is confined to officers, the book of the dry fly being beyond the bluejacket's ken, and the equipment being too cumbersome and expensive.

Fishing for sharks has often been described, oftener, it is to be suspected, than witnessed; for cutting up a shark on a ship's upper deck is a "messy" affair, and on board a man-of-war nothing is so much objected to as a mess. The Indian Ocean is the happy hunting ground of the sharks. They will follow a ship there like a pack of hounds. They are caught with a specially large hook—generally made by the ship's blacksmith—baited with a four-pound piece of salt pork. It is generally understood that salt beef (or salt horse, as it is called) should not be used for this purpose, because of the difficulty in getting the hook to penetrate it. The line is rove through a block at the yardarm, and the bait allowed to trail astern. A shark does not, as a rule, make two bites at a cherry of this description, but swallows it whole; so that the hook obtains a good hold in his interior, and he is hauled, gurgling, up to the yardarm.

The ship's butcher cuts him open, firstly, to make sure that he is dead, and, secondly, out of curiosity to see the contents of his stomach, his omni-voracity being notorious.

A little-known shark is the "hammer-headed" variety, which has a curious projection on each side of its head something like the blade of a propeller. It is smaller than the man-eater, and is sometimes caught from the jib-boom end by getting a running noose over its head.

On foreign stations, more especially in out-of-the-way places, where time runs somewhat slowly, seining is one of the methods of whiling away the Thursday half-holiday (rope-yarn Sunday).

The writer has a pleasant recollection of one of these outings. The scene was one of the land-locked bays in the north of Japan. We left the ship after dinner in a large pinnace, towing a dinghy containing the net and a portable cooking apparatus. Rowing to the nearest beach, we commenced to fish in the following manner. The long net was dropped overboard from the dinghy, in a wide semicircle, and the ends taken to the beach. These were hauled in and walked together at the same time, till at length the bight of the net was landed containing the fish that had been enclosed. This went on all the afternoon, little being caught except the poisonous toad-fish with the curious trick of puffing itself out when scratched. Somebody had plainly brought bad luck to the party, and wishes were loudly expressed that the qualified *Jonas* had stayed on board. We had better luck afterwards, and caught a fair quantity of salmon-peel, some herrings and plaice, and a mullet or two. About five o'clock we piped to tea. Each man had provided himself with "chow" of some sort. Tea was made, and some of the fish fried; and I, for one, made a glorious meal.

We buckled to again in the evening, like giants refreshed. Fires were lighted along the beach to attract the fish, and when darkness fell the scene was most picturesque. The dark water, the darker hills beyond, the phosphorescent flashings round the boats, and the fires and moving lights along the beach, made a striking picture; and when the moon slowly rose and threw her search-light over the hill, all hands stopped to admire.

"The moon behind the hill," said somebody, sentimentally, in the words of a song.

"The hill before the moon," said somebody else.

"The moon be d——d," said another; "what we wants is fish—clap on here."

About nine o'clock we began to tire, and, after three or four "last" shots, packed up and made for "home," shortening the distance and keeping time with the oars by singing choruses. Altogether a most delightful outing.

During a long commission the fish caught in this manner will pay over and over again for the cost of the net, to say nothing of the physical and moral benefit the men derive from the expeditions. This is an instance of a sensible and thoughtful provision by the Admiralty which is quite justified by the results.

It seems ungracious, after this, to find fault; but if their Lordships, the next time the boatswain's stores are being revised, would look into the question of fish-hooks, they would earn the gratitude of Naval fishermen.

The hooks supplied are generally too large. The whiting hooks are quite large enough for mackerel, and are generally so used. For bream, pollack, etc., the mackerel hooks answer very well; it is the smaller fishes that are unprovided for in the sailor's outfit. And, if you think of it, it is an irritating thing to a fisherman to be anchored over a sandbank in which the plaice can be seen packed one above the other, and to know there is not a hook in the ship that he can catch them with. Of course he can easily remedy this by taking some small hooks to sea with him when the ship commissions. But when the British sailor becomes capable of forethought such as this, he will be changed indeed, and not altogether for the better, perhaps.

Another stumbling-block to the Naval fisherman may be mentioned here. This is the depredator who comes in the quiet hours to the mess-shelf and appropriates the fishing lines for his own private use.

The whiting line is of a very convenient size for making "clothes stops"; and the cod line does excellently well for rolling up the tobacco leaf, of which each man gets one pound per month.

In explanation of "clothes stops" it may be mentioned that, with very few exceptions, the whole of a seaman's outfit is regularly washed; and the clothes, when

"About five o'clock we piped to tea"

drying, are tied to the rigging by means of these "stops," each article being fitted with small eyelet holes for the purpose.

The only pardonable use to which the thief can put his messmates' fishing line is to hang himself with it; and he has been known to do even this.

Fishing as practised in troop-ships is worthy of special notice. The state of the average soldier when afloat is but feebly expressed by the proverb, "Like a fish out of water." The horror with which he regards even a short sea trip seems almost ludicrous to a sailor. It is the goal of every soldier's ambition, while making such a trip, to catch a flying fish for stuffing purposes. To this end he snips off pieces from the inside seams of his—or preferably somebody else's—red coat, to bait his hook with. He stretches the potato-net on a hoop taken from the bread "barge," and rigs it out of the port-hole, so that the fish may be caught as they fly past. But his ingenuity is never rewarded, and the rare specimens obtained are usually found in the chains, or on the upper deck, having flown on board unsolicited.

A method of fish-taking probably peculiar to the Navy is by submarine explosions. The shock from a submarine mine or a boom torpedo is sufficient to kill or stun all the fish within a considerable radius; and, after exercising with these destructive forms of modern warfare, large numbers of fish are frequently found floating about in the vicinity.

# Swedish Naval Cadets

### by "Davy Jones"

The Naval College at Skeppsholmen.

IF Sweden does not now occupy such a famed position among the nations of Europe as she did of yore, it is not, as is the case in some other countries, due to physical degeneracy, but it is only the result of an inexorable law which condemns the smaller nations in point of number to occupy a secondary place, whilst the larger ones push their way forward, and eventually succeed in reaching the topmost place. Sad as this may seem, as it is indeed, it only proves that, in spite of our grandiloquent theories and spiritual aspirations, the pound of flesh is of more importance in the life of a nation than almost any other factor, and that to neglect the cultivation of the physical qualities of a people is neither a wise course to pursue, nor the best way of ensuring the greatness of a country.

However, if Sweden now occupies a secondary rank as a European nation, it is otherwise with Sweden considered purely as a maritime Power. Indeed, Sweden, with its small population of five millions of inhabitants, not only possesses a mercantile Navy superior in number and quality to that of many other larger countries, but she is also the proud possessor of a Navy which, though numerically inferior to some others, is, nevertheless, in point of quality and efficiency, among the very best in the world, and well able to hold its own against great odds. The officers who command the Swedish Navy are also among the best specimens that any Navy can offer us, not only from the social point of view, but also from the physical. Indeed, those who have seen Sweden, and who know the Scandinavian populations of Northern Europe, will have no difficulty in realising the fact that no race abounds in finer men and women. Those who have not been fortunate enough to see those amiable Scandinavians can still form an idea of what they are by going across the Channel, and visiting some of the old haunts of the Norsemen, such as the country round Bayeux and Caen, where they will find specimens of manhood and womanhood not to be found among the smaller race of more Southern France.

Those who can afford to pay a visit to Sweden should on no account omit to go to the island of Skeppsholmen, on which have been erected the buildings which constitute the Royal Naval College of Sweden. Their time will not be wasted, for, in addition to seeing the beautiful building in which the Swedish Naval Cadets are instructed in the theoretical portion of their profession, they will also be able to see the naval dockyards close by, and this visit will not be made less pleasant by the courtesy that will be shown to them by all concerned, be they high dockyard officials, naval officers, or ordinary bluejackets.

The Naval College is indeed a splendid structure, and the illustration at the head of this article will, I hope, give an adequate idea of it.

It will be seen that it is a really fine piece of architecture, and that it is rather different from some of the plans that have been submitted to our Admiralty for the future Dartmouth College, plans which if followed will make our English Naval College resemble a country workhouse, or a series of

almshouses. The Swedish Naval College, as I have already said, has been erected on the Skeppsholmen Island, close to the Royal Dockyards. Besides the usual rooms and offices required in such a place, the Naval College contains six spacious class rooms corresponding to the six different sets of cadets of which the entire school is composed. There is also a large and handsome assembly hall used for the daily muster of the cadets, and also on various State occasions. Attached to the college is also a very interesting museum of objects connected with the sea, a laboratory replete with first-rate instruments, and—what is a rarity in a naval school—an excellent observatory.

Near the college is a well-appointed gymnasium, in which the naval cadets are daily exercised for one hour at a time, and in which they are also instructed in the use of the cutlass and other side arms. There is also another building in which they are exercised in the use of firearms. The training a Swedish naval cadet receives is twofold, that is, one part is purely theoretical, and the other practical. The college course opens on the 1st of October in each year, and lasts until the end of April, with a break of about three weeks at Christmas. As I have already said, there are six classes in the college course, and although, as a general rule, a cadet goes through a class in one year, yet there are cases in which a youngster has to re-enter the same class for another year, but in no case can a cadet remain longer than nine years in the college. Now, though this may seem a very long time, we must bear in mind that Swedish cadets frequently enter when they are thirteen years of age, and that at the end of the course they emerge as full-blown sub-lieutenants. No one can enter the college after the age of sixteen has been reached.

Admission to the college is gained after a double examination, the first of which is not unlike the one our own "Britannia" cadets have to pass before joining the training ship, and the other of a very practical character, and designed to test the fitness for sea service of the candidates. To this effect those who have passed the theoretical examination are sent on board one of the training ships of the Royal Navy for a two months' cruise. The naval authorities of Sweden attach the utmost importance to this test, for they hold that the great desideratum is to officer the Navy with men who have a real aptitude for the sea, and they firmly believe that an officer with a modicum of science, but who is a thorough seaman, may render greater services to his country than a man whose brains are replete with mathematical formulas but whose aptitude for sea service is practically nil.

Acting upon this belief, this two months' cruise is the real test, for on it depends the final admission to the college. At the end of the cruise the captain who commands the vessel sends to the Swedish Admiralty a report in which are detailed the following important particulars: Apparent fitness for sea service, conduct, industry, health, general character, etc., etc. To this report are appended the marks obtained at the entrance examination. As a rule not more than a third of the total number of candidates are finally admitted. Those who have been successful enter the college on the subsequent 1st of October, but it will somewhat astonish our readers to learn that the Swedish cadets do not reside within the precincts of the building, but that they board in the town in lodgings that are selected with the utmost care, and which are approved of by the Admiralty. Those who keep those boarding-houses must be persons of unblemished character, and they must submit to their premises being inspected by the officers attached to the Naval College at almost any time. We must remember that a system which, as I have been told, has given excellent results in Sweden, owing chiefly to the home life and home influences the Swedish cadets enjoy, would be impracticable in larger towns, or with a very great number of cadets.

The college is entirely under naval discipline, and is commanded by a captain, assisted by three other naval officers. This captain has under him a staff of eighteen professors or lecturers. The course of studies is so calculated as to facilitate the re-entrance into ordinary scholastic establishments of those who, for some reason or other, may be compelled to discontinue their studies. In order to attain this object a certain parallelism is maintained between the Naval College course, and that of other establishments. The technical subjects are taught, as they should be always and everywhere, by naval officers, and in the case of such special subjects as fortification, an army officer is chosen as instructor. The college possessing the immense advantage of being in close proximity to the dockyards renders possible the study of such subjects as gunnery, torpedo practice, and steam.

The cadets meet every morning at 7.45 a.m., when there is a general muster and inspection, followed by morning prayers. Lessons begin at eight o'clock and last until eleven. From eleven to twelve there is daily instruction in gymnastics, or fencing, except once a week, when this same hour is devoted to infantry drill. The cadets are then free from twelve until half-past one, when lessons are resumed for two hours. Soon after half-past three they go home, where they have to prepare a certain amount of work for the next day. The subjects of instruction are pretty much what they are in most naval training establishments; but the great—I might say the peculiar—feature of the Swedish system is that the utmost importance is attached to all technical subjects, and that, unlike what is often done in other places, the Swedes entrust the teaching of these subjects to those who have a practical acquaintance with them and not to mere theoreticians. They do not admit, for instance, that navigation can be efficiently taught by men who have no experience of the sea, who cannot handle a ship, and who, with all their theory, could not, for the life of them, navigate a vessel across the English Channel in the finest weather. This great feature of the Swedish system receives its sanction during extended cruises at sea. These cruises are always divided into two periods succeeding each other closely. The first cruise takes place in the training ship "Saga," of which we give an illustration. This vessel is a wooden corvette of 1,500 tons burthen, provided with an auxiliary screw, and she is ship-rigged. Her armament consists in one 15-centimetre and six 12-centimetre rifled breech-loading guns, and four machine guns. She has a crew of 260 men, and is usually commanded by the captain in charge of the Naval College, assisted by his own staff of officers.

The cadets join the ship some little time before the departure of the "Saga," in order to take part in the fitting out and rigging of the vessel, the mizzen mast of which is entirely rigged by them under the direction of experienced hands. The "Saga" sails early in May from Karlskrona, and, for a period of three months, she cruises about in the North Atlantic Ocean, visits a few ports on the coasts of England and Spain, and enters the Mediterranean, where she also pays a few visits to some of the western ports of that sea.

Whilst on board the "Saga" the cadets occupy a mess room of their own, and one or two studies near the ward room on the lower deck. The mess expenses of the cadets are defrayed by the Admiralty. The cadets have to do the cleaning of their own mess room. The junior cadets sleep in hammocks, and the seniors have bunks. Their

The "Saga"

work consists in following the usual routine of ship life afloat, except that between the hours of ten and half-past eleven a.m., and three and five p.m., are devoted to some special study.

The cadets who belong to the sixth class, that is, those who are at the top of the school, perform the duties of officer of the watch, under the supervision of the actual officer of the watch. So thorough and so well graduated is the practical training that the cadets almost work the vessel by themselves. Thus some of them have to act as navigating officers, some as captains of the forecastle, others as topmen, look-out men, etc., etc., and when under steam some of them discharge the duties of assistant engineers and engineers, whilst others act as stokers, according to the class they are in, and to the watch or station bills. At general quarters all the 12-centimetre guns are manned by the cadets. In short, it will be readily understood from this that the principle followed is that of making the cadets share in the duties that naturally fall to the lot of a ship's crew, in so far as is expedient.

At the end of this cruise the three classes which are at the head of the college embark, in the early part of August, in a gun-boat, to which is attached a torpedo-boat as tender. The three junior classes which do not take part in this cruise spend two weeks in the dockyard in making themselves familiar with its various parts and practising boat sailing. They then go home on leave until the 1st of October.

Those who have embarked in August for the second cruise devote their time afloat to the study of hydrography, steam, pilotage, and torpedo practice in the inshore waters of the Baltic. With the exception of a few officers, and warrant officers and seamen, both the gun-boat and the torpedo-boat are manned and worked by the cadets during the month this cruise lasts. On the 1st of September the cadets land and go home on leave.

The theoretical examination takes place every year in April before a Board of Examiners appointed by the Admiralty. There is another examination at the end of the instruction cruise, and the marks obtained, both in the college examination, and those won during the cruise, determine the removal of a cadet from a lower class to a higher one.

The captain and officers of the training ships are, *de officio,* the examiners before whom the practical examination has to be undergone at the end of the period of training afloat. Those cadets who during the cruise may have given unmistakable proof of their unfitness for the Service, or whose idleness has been such as to show that they would be but indifferent naval officers, or, again, those who seem unable to follow the course of studies, are discharged from the Service.

Those who have gone through the complete course are further examined, professionally, in the month of October following the second cruise, before a Board of Examiners presided over by two captains.

After this examination, which bears almost entirely on naval matters, the marks obtained at this and previous examinations are added together and determine, for the future, the seniority of the cadets. Those who have passed successfully receive a commission as sub-lieutenant in the Royal Navy, whilst those who have not quite come up to the mark are only entitled to a warrant of sub-lieutenant in the Naval Reserve, or, if they prefer, they may receive a certificate of competency as ship-master in the merchant service.

The discipline is good, but not severe, except in cases when bad characters have to be dealt with. Minor faults are punished by the captain, who deals with the culprit according to his judgment, and whose aim is much more to prevent the recurrence of a breach of discipline than to punish. Admonition or stoppage of leave are the usual punishments awarded. In graver cases temporary exclusion from the college or expulsion may be pronounced by the Admiralty.

Such are the leading features of a system of training which presents so many good points, and so thoroughly instructs the cadets in the duties they will be called upon to perform, that I cannot help thinking that others, who shall be left unmentioned, might with great advantage take a leaf out of the book of our Swedish friends.

## SYNOPSIS OF PREVIOUS CHAPTERS.

The hero, Mervyn Crespin, who was lately lying in the prison of Lugo under sentence of death, found himself there in consequence of a hazardous ride which he set out upon from Vigo (of which town he has taken part in the capture), with the intention of joining the English forces under the command of Marlborough in Flanders. He had originally been despatched by the Earl on a mission to the British Fleet, which was expected to be at Cadiz (but which, he found, had left for England), as the bearer of important information, to the effect that some Spanish galleons from the West Indies had altered their destination and, instead of going to Cadiz as they intended, had, on hearing that the English Fleet was in the neighbourhood, proceeded to Vigo. On his way to the former place he encounters a man whose name is supposed to be Carstairs, and whom he and the master of the ship regard as a pirate. Meanwhile, he by chance falls in with the English Fleet proceeding home, is enabled to convey the information he carries to Sir George Rooke, and goes with it to Vigo. After the battle, which is fully described, he is sent to board one of the captured galleons, and here he encounters a young Spanish gentleman, as he supposes, who has been a passenger in the ship, as well as a monk named Father Jaime. Eventually, he sets out for Flanders on the above-mentioned perilous ride, the young Spaniard, who has conceived a warm friendship for him, insisting upon being his companion, to which he reluctantly consents. They encounter on their way a series of stirring adventures, culminating in a fight with the Spanish police near Lugo, and, though entering that town in safety, are followed and arrested. Father Jaime has, however, joined them and rendered great assistance in the combat, he appearing no longer as a monk (which he acknowledges himself not to be), but as a traveller, himself on the road to Lugo. As they are endeavouring, however, to escape capture, they overhear a conversation between Jaime and the man Carstairs, who has also arrived here in search of some property which he expected to come in the galleons, and from it they learn that Jaime, far from being a monk, is no less a person than the renowned Gramont—a pirate loathed in the Indies, but supposed to be long since drowned. Señor Belmonte, the young Spaniard, who has confided to the Englishman that he does not know who his father was, except that he was enormously rich, also discovers now to his horror that Gramont is the man. This, however, is not the only discovery made. As the young Spaniard reels against Crespin on gleaning that intelligence, Crespin, in his turn, is astonished to find that his companion is a woman and not a man, who has travelled to Europe disguised thus in her hopes of finding Carstairs, whose right name is Eaton, and of punishing him for having robbed her, and also because the galleons would not take women as passengers. All are arrested and imprisoned, Gramont and Crespin being sentenced to death, while Juana, which is the name of the Spanish lady, is protected by the Alcáide of the city, who has fallen in love with her striking beauty. He, however, agrees that her father shall be allowed to escape provided she leaves Spain with him; and, in her misery and despair over that father's crimes, she consents. Crespin regrets his fate the more because he has learned from Juana that her instantaneous love for him at first sight was the principal thing which prompted her to insist on accompanying him in all his dangers. Also, he knows now how fondly he has come to love her. He has, however, been able to himself escape in the manner recently described, and to follow Juana until he comes up with her in company with the Alcáide. How he made that escape, and how he and Gramont have once more met, has also been shown in the chapters preceding the present instalment, which brings the narrative to an end.

## CHAPTER XXXII. *(continued).*

NOW came our turn—the turn of the cavalry. And stirrup to stirrup we rushed down—ay! knee to knee—while, as we did so, we thought at first that we had won. The gendarmes vanished like smoke —I saw one of my own cuirassiers slice a man's head off as a child might slice an apple in twain—I saw another take a second beneath his eyes with his sabre, and the eyeballs of the fellow glint upon the great broad blade as they sprang forth from his head—we drove them back and back; we were winning. Then down upon us came the dragoons of Vassey and Rouen, and those of *Le Regiment de La Reine,* also some of Rohan's *sabreurs,* and they drove *us* back—curse them!—while a scathing, crushing fire took us in the flank and mowed us down as we reeled back to our lines. Battered, decimated, we reeled back, but, thank God, not beaten yet, and ready to re-form and charge again, supported now by all the cavalry and the infantry, under the command of Churchill, His Grace's

brother. Yet, even at this time, those reinforcements could not get up—there was a stream called the Nebel to cross, fascines and planks had to be flung in ere it could be done. But done it was at last—yet only to lead to more rebuffs. No sooner was this cavalry over the river than down upon us came the whole front line of the French horse, their cannon and musketry poured in volley upon volley—we were forced back again. Also, at this time, Prince Holstein was routed, and he himself taken prisoner—the Irish brigade helping to inflict this disaster on us.

Were we beaten? Almost it seemed so. Yet—still there was Marlborough! I see him rise before me now as I saw him then—leading squadrons against those Irish, putting himself at the head of the cavalry again and again—his face calm beneath his hatless head—rallying those who fell back, sending messages to Prince Eugene, who, with the Prussians, was nobly withstanding shock after shock from the French on their side.

And seeing him as I saw him then, in the dim of the approaching summer evening, I did not fear for the result. If we could only last!

Who could have feared who saw what we all saw, hear what we all heard!

The glittering sword drawn forth from its sheath now, the order ringing out in those clear, shrill tones for the trumpets to sound the advance, the handsome form well ahead of his army, leading them on. On, towards where ten thousand French horsemen barred our way, towards where their artillery belched forth death and destruction. Towards the chivalry of France, the flower of the land. For there, as I gathered afterwards from one of the prisoners, flew the banners of France's most highborn and illustrious sons. Banners that centuries before had waved over their ancestors at Crecy and Agincourt, at Ascalon, and outside the walls of Jerusalem—the banderoles of Rohan and of Hautefeuille, of Montpéroux and de Marivaux, of St. Pouange and Valserne, of D'Amigay and Denonville, de Croissi, and many more. Blue, scarlet, and crimson, they glistened in the evening air, their devices of gold and silver shining in our eyes; and against them we advanced. Slowly at first, then at a trot, and then—were driven back once more by the fierce rain of the French artillery. Back sixty paces, but, thank God, no more. For again that clear shrill voice rang out, again the trumpets sounded, again we charged. Up the slope, to the crest of the ridge, to where the ten thousand of France's cavalry stood. Up—up—with no colonel at the head of the Fourth Horse— he was gone for ever, his brain shot through; with the troop next to mine led by an ancient sergeant—the chief now in command of that troop—up, with the gallant grey dragoons of Scotland—the "Scots Regiment of White Horses," as they term themselves—near us, and led by Lord John Hay. Up and towards those glittering banderoles.

Then as we neared them, from all their carbines there came an awful volley, saddles were emptied, the ping of balls rang on gorget and cuirass, horses went down among our ranks with hideous shrieks and piteous yells, those in the rear rode not over the earth, but, instead, over a carpet of dead men and chargers; eyes glared up from white or bloody faces into ours as we passed above; over the rattle of the musketry, the bray of trumpets, the screams and curses of dead and dying, the shrill voice of the great commander pealed, encouraging, directing, applauding.

The smoke cleared away—and this is what we saw. The banderoles of France no longer erect and defiant, but bending down as bends the cornfield 'neath the southern wind, the chivalry of France in full flight, and—woe to France and those who formed that chivalry!—their backs towards us. They *were* in full flight. And we were after them. As slips the torrent from the mountain-side, spreading o'er all the valley underneath, we rushed into the plain 'twixt the two villages, we cut the flying cavalry to pieces, we drove those who still fled into the Danube, where many of them were drowned. The broken mass was driven helter-skelter here and there—where they resisted they were slain in bodies, so that they lay as they had stood once, in ranks, but upon their backs now, and dead. An hour or so later Blenheim was taken, it being by then in flames, and Tallard was a prisoner in the Duke's coach.

The battle was won!

Yet at what a price! On our side we had lost five thousand men under Marlborough, and six thousand under Eugene, amongst them being Brigadier Rowe, the Colonels Dormer, White, and Sir John Sandes; Dalziell, Cornwallis, Festonhaugh, and many others. The French lost thirteen thousand.

Of officers on both sides, the loss was terrible, and when the roll was called that night many of us did weep bitterly to see how our comrades were gone. Nor could I myself help but weep when I found that, of all superior to me in the Fourth Horse, there was not one left alive.

Also, including of myself, there was scarce one still alive who was not wounded.

Yet, thank God, the battle was won; the Lilies lay beneath the maimed paws of the Lion —lay there crushed and ruined.

That day had set the seal of victory and triumph on England's head for ever!

## CHAPTER XXXIII.

### THE END.

The early part of September, 1704, had been stormy and wet and very dismal in London, so that all in the city feared the great spectacle which had been arranged with much pains and forethought for the seventh of that month must be partly spoilt, if not totally so, by the inclemency of the weather. And many there were who, during the night that passed away, and also when the dawn came, rose from their beds to peer out and see what the day promised.

Yet, by great good fortune, none were doomed to disappointment. For from away over the river, down by where the great ships were all a-lying dressed with flags, the sun came up in great magnificence and splendour; the clouds turned from purple to a fair pure daffodil; a sweeter autumn morning none had ever seen nor could hope to see.

And now from very early in that morning the crowds came in from far and wide, from north, and south, and east, and west, from the villages along the river as far away as sylvan Richmond on one side of London or Hampstead on another; while the gentry drove in from their country seats at Clapham or Kensington, and by the road that leads from Fulham. Also those regiments at Hounslow, and the Foot Guards at Kensington, as well as the City Militia from the east side, were all making their way into the town, with drums a-beating and flags streaming out to the fresh morning air, and trumpets braying, while in the City itself my Lord Mayor was getting ready to proceed to Temple Bar, there to receive the Queen and Court. For this day, the seventh of September, had been fixed for the thanksgiving for the victory of Blenheim which the Duke of Marlborough had recently won —the pity only being that, of those who were to take part in the great ceremony, my Lord Duke could not be there, he being still engaged on the Continent.

Nevertheless, from St. James's there set out so great a company for St. Paul's that 'tis never likely anyone then alive could hope to witness a more noble and imposing sight. For there were all the great officers of State, with, amidst them, the Queen in a sumptuous coach drawn by eight horses, Her Majesty being ablaze with jewels. Alone she went in that coach, excepting for one companion, a lady dressed as quietly and simply as could be any lady in the land, there being neither at neck or bosom or throat or in her hair any single trinket to be seen.

Yet, I think, she was that day the proudest woman in all England, not even excepting Great Anna, since she was the wife of the conqueror who had trampled Louis and his armies under foot; was Sarah, Duchess of Marlborough. Could any female heart have desired to be more!

In front of, as well as behind, and on either side of that chariot of State, there rode the Queen's Guards; yet, ahead of those who rode behind—he being nearest to the back of the carriage—was one who yielded to none in thankfulness and gratitude for all which Providence had seen fit to do for him. An officer this, one-handed—his left arm bound up, it having been nearly lopped off at Blenheim by one of the Elector of Bavaria's huge dragoons, whom that officer slew a moment later with his right hand—whose scarf, sword-knot, richly laced scarlet coat, and gold cockade proclaimed him a colonel of horse. Myself.

From where we entered the Strand—by the Cross set up here—we saw that all the shops were boarded up and scaffolded, partly to resist the crowd and partly to furnish benches on which sightseers might sit. On those benches, and also in the shop windows, as well as on the bulks and at the windows of the tradesmen's parlours above, was a noble and splendid company, the ladies of which had all adorned themselves with their choicest dresses and ribbons and laces, the more to do honour to those other two ladies in the great coach. Then, behind, came the Lords of Parliament, and the gentlemen of the Commons, also the Bishops in their wigs and lawn—each and all in coaches drawn by six horses —as well as many others of the nobility; while from the churches all along the route—St. Martin's-in-the-Fields, St. Mary's-in-the-Strand, and St. Clement Danes—the bells clashed and clanged, and inside the organs blew and anthems pealed.

"*Holding up a wee child.*"

At Temple Bar there was a great halt, since the gates were shut, yet opened as the Queen came to them, whereon my Lord Mayor, surrounded by the aldermen and sheriffs, in their red robes and on horses richly caparisoned, received Her Majesty, the former handing to her the sword of the City, which she at once returned. After which we progressed once more towards St. Paul's, where, later, the Dean preached a moving sermon. And now my eyes were fixed and searching for a face—two faces—at a window beyond the Church of St. Dunstan's in Fleet Street—which was all hung with banners and adornments stretched across from side to side— and presently I saw that which I sought for. A lady on a balcony holding up a little wee child in her arms, a lady dark and beautiful and dressed all in her best—her robe a rich brocade, with, at her breast, a knot of ribbons—the colours of the Fourth Horse. The woman who has ever been in my eyes the fairest, most lovely of her sex, my loved and honoured wife. And she stood there seeking for me, leaning over the balcony to wave and kiss her hand; took also our babe's little one in hers and caused her to wave it too.

Riding by, I looked up and saw them, and blessed God.

Blessed God and praised His name because He had seen fit to bring us safe through all the dangers we had encountered together; because He had seen fit to give to me for wife the sweetest woman the world held, and to bring us safe into haven at last.

For that, as well as all else, I blessed and praised His name, even as from roofs of houses and taverns the salvoes roared forth, the bells pealed from the steeples, and we progressed through the City companies ranged 'neath their banners, and between the lines kept by the militia, the Queen bowing from her side of the coach, the great stately Duchess from hers; the people shouting all the time, and crying but two names—"Anne" and "Marlborough"—and women holding up their children so that, in the days to come, when those children were old, they might say they had gazed on the wife of the greatest soldier in the world. And thus, at last, we came to St. Paul's and gave thanksgivings.

\* \* \* \* \*

It was when night had fallen after Blenheim that my Lord Duke sent for me to his room in the inn where he and the Marshal Tallard—who had led the French and been defeated that day, and was now an honoured and well-cared-for prisoner of His Grace—were quartered, and spoke to me as follows:

"Colonel Crespin—for such you will be when the next gazette is published—if it were not that others have a prior claim, it should be you to whom I would confide my message to the Queen and Lords. For," and he smiled sweetly as usual—though, to-night, a little wearily—"I have a recollection of your value as a bearer of despatches. Yet, all the same, you shall go to England. You have a wife and child there, I know." And again he smiled as I bowed before him.

"For which you have to thank me. By St. George! I never thought when I sent you on that journey you were going sweetheart-hunting too."

Whereby you will perceive that His Grace knew very well all that had befallen me two years before, when I set out for Spain to find, if might be, the English Fleet. It would be strange, indeed, if he had not known it, for my story had been told all over the forces from the moment I returned and joined my regiment; nay, more than once I had related it to Marlborough himself.

"I shall not be far behind you," he continued; "the New Year should see me home, too. Yet I have messages for the Queen and my own wife. You shall bear them—it will give you an opportunity of seeing your own wife. She is, I hear, vastly beautiful."

"In my eyes, my Lord Duke, the most beautiful woman in the world."

"That is as it should be. So," he continued, simply, "I think of mine. But, also, you must see the Queen. She has heard of your adventures, wishes she had known you when you were on leave in England. Tell her all—tell her as bravely in words as you can be brave in action—and you will not stop at the command of a regiment of horse. See, also, my wife—her influence is extreme: our enemies say 'tis a bad influence!—yet she will help you."

And I did see the Queen on my arrival in England, also the great Duchess, Sarah, on the night before we went to St. Paul's. After which I wondered no more how everyone loved the former, spoke of her, indeed, as the "Good" Queen—a title, I think, as dear and precious as that of "Great" which Elizabeth had won. She was very ruddy, I noticed when I stood before her, her beautiful, red-brown hair bound most matronly above her brow, while her arms—which were bare—to show, as I have heard, their extreme beauty—were marvellous to behold, as well as her hands. Yet, Queen as she was, and a well-favoured one, too, it was more on the other who stood behind her that my eyes rested. For she was beautiful beyond all I had imagined, so that I wondered not that report said the Duke loved her as fondly as when they were boy and girl together, she only a maid of honour and he an ensign. Yet, also, I thought that beauty marred by an imperious haughtiness which made her seem the Queen and the real Queen her subject.

"So, Colonel Crespin," Her Majesty said to me, "I set eyes on you at last—you of whom I have heard so much. Well, I am vastly proud to know so brave a gentleman. Later, I must also know your wife—whom, I hear, you wooed and won in a strange fashion." Then changing the subject swiftly, while her kindly eyes rested on me, she said: "Your father must be very proud of you."

Not knowing what reply to make to such a compliment, I could but bow, whereon she continued:

"Your arm is bound up, I see—I hear you got the wound at Blenheim. 'Tis very well. In after years it will be as great a distinction to have had that wound as any honours or titles that may come to you. It does not prevent you riding?"

I murmured that it inconvenienced me but very little, whereon Her Majesty said:

"That also is well. To-morrow, I desire you follow behind my coach to St. Paul's. I love my people to see those who have served me faithfully." Whereon with a gracious inclination of her head, accompanied by a sweet smile upon her honest, kindly face, she turned and left the apartment, the Duchess bowing, too, though somewhat more haughtily than the Queen had done. Yet she whispered a word in my ear as she passed out; a word appropriate enough to one as proud as she.

"You have served *him* well," she said. "Those who do that are my friends for ever."

And now the rejoicings for our victory at Blenheim were over—the siege and taking of Gibraltar three weeks before, by my other friend, Sir George Rooke, being not forgotten—the crowds had dispersed, the great banquet to be given by the City was near at hand, and the illuminations of London were beginning.

Yet I had no desire to be feasting in the midst of that great company. Instead I was seated in the room on the balcony of which I had seen my wife that morning, her head upon my shoulder, her lips murmuring words of love inexpressible in my ear.

Words in which, amongst the rest, I caught those that told me how proud she was to have won me from all other women. Proud and happy in knowing that we were each other's for ever in this world.

\* \* \* \* \*

What need to set down more—what more have I to say? Only this. That never would she hear of redeeming any of that second fortune which her unhappy father had left in the custody of the priest in the Indies, who had once been as he himself was; and, consequently, that from the time we became man and wife no further intercourse was ever held between us and those far-off islands from which she came. Nor was that fortune wanted—God has given us good to us; I have prospered exceedingly in my soldier's calling; all is very well.

Of him, Gramont, we have never heard more. Yet that, somewhere, he is, if still alive, expiating his past I have never doubted. The truth was in the man's eyes as he spoke to me on that morning when he went forth broken hearted from the house which held his child; the truth and a firm determination to atone by suffering and hardship for all that he had done. And what stronger or more stern resolve could any sinner have taken than that of his—the determination to tear himself away for ever from the companionship of his newly-found daughter, and to remove thereby from her the shame of his presence?

"Come, Mervan," Juana said to me, as now the autumn evening turned to night, and from every house in Fleet Street the illuminations began to glisten. "Come, you must prepare for the City banquet."

"Nay," I said, "nay. I need no banquets, would prefer to stay here by your side."

"As so I would you should do. Yet, to-night, you must go. I will not have you absent from so great a thing. You!—my hero—my king. And while you are gone I will watch over our child. Or solace myself with this."

Whereon as she spoke, she went over to where the spinet was, and touched a smaller instrument that lay upon it.

The little *viol d'amore*—from which we have never parted and never will.

THE END.

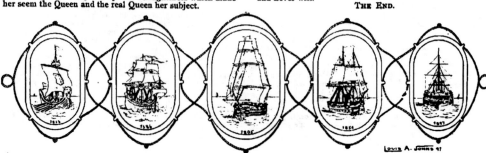

*Photo. DEBENHAM, Ryde.*

### BRIGADIER-GENERAL P. D. JEFFREYS, C.B.

THE name of Brigadier-General P. D. Jeffreys, C.B., has become very familiar to the British public during the past few weeks in connection with the Indian Frontier risings. Being appointed to the command of the 2nd Brigade of the Malakand Field Force, which was despatched in August to restore order in the Swat Valley, General Jeffreys was subsequently entrusted with the task of subduing the Mamunds, a troublesome tribe which on one occasion succeeded in pressing General Jeffreys's force somewhat closely, and which was only reduced to submission after very sharp fighting. General Jeffreys is an old Connaught Ranger, having joined in 1866. His first campaign was the South African War of 1879. In 1886 he accompanied the Burmese Expedition as brigade-major, receiving a brevet lieutenant-colonelcy for his gallant conduct in the capture of the Prince's Camp at Keinmendine. In the Zhob Valley Expedition, Lieutenant-Colonel Jeffreys served as A.A.G., receiving a brevet. In 1894 he was appointed A.A.G. at Indian Army Headquarters.

# CAVALRY AND SAPPERS IN CAMP.

THE Cavalry and Engineer Pioneers' Camp, to which these five photographs have reference, was held this year at Hengistbury Head, near Christchurch, in Hampshire. The encampment included parties from the 15th Hussars, 10th Hussars, 6th Dragoon Guards, and the mounted sappers from Aldershot, and its object was to afford practical instruction in field engineering on a scale impossible without special facilities, both in the way of ground and material. The men worked in small parties, and changed their tasks and positions, in most cases, daily, the result being a most interesting and varied programme, which all concerned seemed to take real pleasure in carrying out with great harmony and vigour. The camp was under the command of Captain Cowie, R.E., and the site, which was admirably adapted for the purpose, was lent by Sir George Meyrick. As a set-off to the latter's liberality, the sappers and cavalrymen encamped accomplished a useful piece of work in throwing a permanent suspension bridge over a channel which had hitherto necessitated a considerable detour. It is worth remarking that the cables of this bridge are formed of old telegraph wires, twenty-one to the cable, other "cast" telegraph stores being freely turned to account for similar engineering purposes by these ingenious military artificers.

Our first illustration shows a party of sappers at work on what would seem to be a particularly difficult task, boat building, namely, with *ex tempore* materials, the latter consisting of a few light ash saplings, twine, and a waggon cover. Craft constructed in this fashion might not, perhaps, be adapted to ocean travel, but would be found extremely useful, if not indispensable, in certain forms of military bridge building. The photograph gives a capital idea of the system pursued, the result being a boat of canvas with wooden ribs, not unlike the Berthon boat when distended for use.

*Improvising a Boat.*

The camp smithy, though unconnected with the special course of instruction for which the camp was instituted, was none the less a most important feature of an assembly in which nearly everyone present was mounted. The arrangements were, it will be noted, of a severely simple, not to say primitive, character, and one would think that the process of shoeing a horse on a rainy day must have been attended with considerable discomfort. In the picture, however, the weather is splendid, and the brawny smith at the forge, whose leather apron contrasts rather quaintly with his cavalry field service cap, is evidently in great good humour.

Swimming horses over a river, as depicted in another photograph, is a branch of cavalry training which until some years ago was greatly neglected. It goes without saying that in many campaigns, especially in the East, unfordable rivers have to be crossed at points where there are no bridges and it is, practically speaking, impossible to construct even a temporary one. Where both men and horses are unaccustomed to the work, the process of crossing even a small stream with the aid of boats may be attended with considerable risk, if not positive disaster, and instances will occur to many minds in which, as in the case of the 10th Hussars in Afghanistan, a number of valuable lives have been lost in this way. Stimulated to some extent by Continental example, our cavalry have of late years made a special effort to perfect themselves in this particular, and in every case where combined cavalry operations are carried out and facilities exist, a feature is made of crossing streams in various styles. The water shown in the illustration is about 200 yards across, and a double system is being adopted, some of the horses being towed across by a boat, while others are about to be swum over independently by their riders. It appears doubtful whether anything like finality has been reached

*Photos. by*     *A Military Officer.*

*The Blacksmith at Work.*

in this matter, as against most present methods there are several strong objections. Independent swimming suits some men and some horses very well, but with others is an exceedingly troublesome and rather dangerous operation. The use of a boat presupposes the existence of the craft in question, which, moreover, must be of fairly substantial construction, and, although Continental cavalry regiments can and do carry boats with them for this special purpose, anything calculated to reduce, however slightly, the mobility of mounted corps is, of course, to be deplored. Probably in time, and by the instrumentality of combined engineer and cavalry corps like the one under notice, a system will be evolved which will make a couple of hundred yards of deep water a not much greater obstacle to a regiment of dragoons, lancers, or hussars, than an equal extent of grassy plain.

*An Equine Swimming Lesson.*

Watering parade in camp does not require any description beyond the pictorial one it receives in the accompanying photograph. There will, however, be many by whom this eminently life-like little group of men and horses will be especially appreciated, if only for the reason that it illustrates just one of those little bits of routine which constitute the "second nature" of the British soldier, and serve to remind the world at large that in military training no detail is considered unworthy of close attention and constant practice.

Even a passing glance at photographs such as these may well give rise to several interesting reflections. Prominent among these, perhaps, will be the thought that, although our magnificent corps of Royal Engineers will always retain its pre-eminence in the matter both of scientific attainments and of their practical application, the remainder of the Army is rapidly and none the less surely "levelling up" to a very high standard of real professional knowledge in other directions than those of mere drill and manœuvre.

Not so many years back the average cavalry regiment took very small heed of anything in the field engineering line, and to ask any sort of trooper to help make a bridge or sink a Norton tube well would have been followed by a stupid stare of mingled astonishment and disgust.

But the military world is spinning "down the ringing grooves of change," and even the smart cavalryman, whose principal work is far remote from anything connected with pick and shovel, must learn nowadays much that a score of years ago he would have regarded with something of disdain.

What is more, there is no question that the average soldier, to whatever branch of the Service he may belong, is genuinely attracted by a really well thought out course of field engineering, notwithstanding the fact that it may mean a very considerable addition to the ordinary day's work.

All of us like to see things growing under our hands, and Thomas Atkins naturally finds bridging and the construction of field defences a welcome change from the apparently inconsequent and futile monotony of repeated drill.

*Watering Horses.*

Photos. by　　　　　*A Flying Bridge.*　　　　　A Military Officer.

# THE MADRAS CAVALRY.

THE Madras Cavalry dates from the year 1780, when four regiments of cavalry were taken over from the Nawab by the Madras Government. The 1st Madras Lancers, originally known as the 5th Light Cavalry, were not raised till 1787. They were present at the action of Bangalore, and afterwards rendered good service at Seringapatam.

During the Burmese War of 1825 a part of the regiment proceeded as far as Ava. The 1st also took part in the Afghan War of 1879-80. The 2nd Madras Lancers distinguished themselves shortly after they were taken over from the Nawab by remaining loyal to their

*Cremating a Horse.*

*Pay Day in Camp.*

*Photos.* BARTON, SON & CO.    *Rifle Practice—Counting Hits.*    *B.ngalore.*

officers while the other regiments joined in a mutiny. After the mutiny of 1784 they became the premier regiment.

The 3rd Light Cavalry was seriously engaged at Coimbatore and Cheyur. It fought also at Bangalore and Seringapatam.

The 4th Light Cavalry, formerly known as Younge's Horse, dates from 1785. In addition to being present at Seringapatam and Mahidpore the 4th gained credit at the famous battle of Assaye.

The accompanying photographs represent scenes in the Madras Cavalry of the present day. Whether his caste be high or low, the native soldier looks forward to "pay day" with quite as much eagerness as his fairer-skinned brother "Tommy," and in the centre illustration one may note the evident eagerness displayed by the Madras troopers as they wait for their names to be called.

When targets are used, such as that depicted in the last picture, the number of hits is counted after each man has fired his allotted rounds before the target is cleaned for the next man. An officer is usually detailed to take charge of the butts, and under his superintendence this operation is carried out. The number of points is then entered in the "butt memo.," as it is called, and signalled to the firing point. In this way the score of each man is checked.

The first illustration represents a charger which has in all likelihood "carried many passengers," but unlike Mark Twain's historical horse, is undergoing the process of cremation instead of "being made into sassengers."

The horse is first skinned and then covered with wood, which two natives are engaged in chopping. A light is set to the funeral pile, and by-and-bye there remain only the ashes of what was once a noble cavalry charger.

## SOLDIERS OF THE GUARDS' BRIGADE.

THE man on the right of his two other comrades is a soldier of the Grenadier Guards. This is recognisable from the grenade on the cap, the red stripe round the bottom of it, and the collar badge—a grenade. Another point worthy of notice is the arrangement of the buttons on the tunic. They are placed at equal intervals down to the belt, and the four buttons on the cuffs are also at equal intervals. The central figure is in the uniform of the Coldstream Guards. The uniform is known from the badge—a garter star—on the collar and cap, and the white stripe round the bottom of the latter. The buttons on the tunic are placed in pairs, with a space between each pair, and there are two pairs of buttons on each cuff—unlike those in the first case, which are placed at equal intervals. The Scots Guardsman is distinguished by the diced border round his cap and the star of the Order of the Thistle above it. The collar badge is a thistle, and the buttons on the tunic are arranged in groups of three. There are three buttons on the cuffs, placed at equal intervals.

# THE ROYAL MALTA REGIMENT OF MILITIA.

*PERMANENT STAFF.*

*SERGEANTS.*

are ten companies in the regiment, one of them being a cadet company. Though essentially a Militia force as regards discipline, pay, etc., the principle of carrying out its drill and training is more to be compared to that of the Volunteer system in England, the regiment being called together for twelve consecutive days' training in the year, in camp or barracks, whilst the remainder, and really the bulk of the drills, each of three hours' duration, are carried out at intervals during eight months in the year, chiefly on Sundays and Festa days, *i.e.*, holidays, in the mornings, as well as on Saturday afternoons, which has proved to be the most suitable arrangement in order to attain the best results as regards attendance and efficiency. Each man is called upon to attend a minimum of fifty drill days during the year, whether partly performed when out for training or not, whilst pay is issued to all ranks for attendances up to a maximum of seventy-two drill days annually. The officers are paid at the same rates as English Militia infantry officers, the non-commissioned officers and men receiving: Sergeants 11d., corporals 10d., and privates 8d., plus a ration allowance of 4d. on each drill day.

When out for the twelve days' training, however, the men receive consolidated pay, amounting, practically, to the above rates increased by one-half, from which a deduction is made for rationing the men, which is managed under regimental arrangements.

The words of command are given in English, the explanation in Maltese—a

THE Royal Malta Regiment of Militia dates back to 1800, when a regiment of Maltese infantry was formed for service against the French, who were besieged in Valetta by the Maltese, assisted by the British, and history tells us that this Maltese regiment fought with great gallantry. It was, however, disbanded in 1802, there being then no further need of its services. But a second battalion of light infantry was raised in 1805, and lasted until 1810. It took part in the battle of Maida and also in the capture of Diamanti, where some thirty-eight merchant vessels and twenty guns were captured from the French.

The present regiment was raised in 1889, and in less than six months had reached its full strength of 1,132 of all ranks, which has, without difficulty, been continuously maintained. There

*Photos. R. ELLIS, Malta.*

*OFFICERS.*

*Copyright -H. & K.*

Photo. R. ELLIS, Malta.

Copyright—HUDSON & KEARNS.

## MALTA REGIMENT ON PARADE.

language somewhat resembling Arabic. In all other respects, this corps is assimilated as far as possible to the Militia infantry in the United Kingdom. The progress made by this corps is certainly marked, and speaks well for the military instincts of the Maltese. New colours were presented to the regiment on 1st January, 1895, in the historic Church of St. John's, in Valetta, the scene presenting an unusually imposing ceremony. The regimental colour is of royal blue, with a white Maltese cross in each corner, and the date MDCCC. under the royal cypher and crown. The permanent staff consists of both English and Maltese, who are either transferred from the regulars, or specially enlisted in the island. They are regularly attested on Army engagements and serve all the year round. The officers consist of an honorary colonel, one lieutenant-colonel, two majors, ten captains, twenty subalterns, a surgeon and chaplain, besides an adjutant and a quartermaster, who, with two exceptions, are Maltese gentlemen. The adjutant, however, is selected from a line regiment, and the honorary colonel is General Sir H. A. SMYTH, K.C.M.G., Royal Artillery, late Governor of Malta. The commanding officer, in the centre of the group, is Lieutenant-Colonel VELLA, well known, especially in Naval circles, as the Civilian Secretary to the Admiral Superintendent at the Malta Dockyard. The above illustration shows the Royal Malta Regiment of Militia on one of its ordinary drill parades. The regiment has now attained a standard of efficiency that would compare favourably with an infantry Militia battalion in the United Kingdom, and will, no doubt, form a useful adjunct to Her Majesty's Colonial Defensive Forces.

# THE ANTRIM ARTILLERY.

THIS fine regiment, the premier brigade of Artillery Militia affiliated to the Southern Division of the Royal Artillery, is not only numerically the strongest, but for efficiency and smartness is not excelled and not often equalled by any other Artillery Militia corps in the United Kingdom. Composed of eight companies, with an enlisted strength closely reaching the authorised establishment, it forms in reality, as it was called by a recent inspecting officer, "one of the finest bodies of men he had ever inspected." Recruited principally from the ship-building yards and peasantry of the North of Ireland, the average height is about 5-ft. 8-in., and the physique of the men is magnificent. Under the command of Colonel E. E. Pottinger, the regiment has gradually, but surely, attained a degree of efficiency and smartness, both in drill and gunnery, which has been acknowledged by the authorities by an extension of Colonel Pottinger's period of command for a further five years. The training of the regiment usually takes place, for the usual twenty-seven days, at Carrickfergus, County Antrim, a town having the unique privilege of being a county in itself, the practice over sea ranges in Belfast Lough being carried out from the historical

*The Battery at Carrickfergus.*

Carrick Castle, famous as the landing-place of King Charles II.

The illustrations are instantaneous photographs taken during the annual practice at a recent training. The top picture, taken just a moment before the gun was fired, will be found to possess a germ of the comic element. The word of command for the group to commence firing has been given by the gun-group commander, the officer on the right of the picture. The lanyard is taut the gun-layer has given the signal, and the gun-captain, who stands to the left rear of the gun, is just giving the word "Fire," and has his mouth wide open for the purpose, when the photograph was snapped at the instant.

The next picture represents a busy scene to be observed almost any and every day during the training on the depository exercise ground, in the garden battery of the old castle. In the foreground a repository squad is standing easy after having dismounted a 64-pounder gun from its carriage. Another squad is moving a 40-pounder R.B.L. gun on a travelling-carriage into position for exercise, and in the middle distance another squad appears to be raising a gun. On the left the adjutant and two officers appear to be detailing the spare numbers to various duties.

The third picture represents a group of the officers of the regiment taken during the training of 1897, and also includes Major-General Geary, C.B., R.A., commanding the Belfast district, and Colonel Hewitt, R.A., commanding Royal and Militia Artillery in that district. The officer sitting on the general's left is Colonel Pottinger, the officer commanding. Major Kursey is seated on the right of the picture. The white fudge in the foreground is meant for Barney, the regimental dog. His active habits have, however, proved too much for both him and the photographer. The regiment possesses an excellent band, and is very popular in the district in which it trains.

*In the Exercise Yard, Carrick Castle.*

From a Photo.     *Colonel Pottinger and Officers, Antrim Militia Artillery.*     By a Military Officer.

# THE NAVY & ARMY

## ILLUSTRATED.

VOL. V.—No. 52 ]    *FRIDAY, DECEMBER 10th, 1897.*

# THE NATIVE ARMY OF INDIA.

*By COMMANDER E. P. STATHAM, R.N.*

*Photo. WINDOW & GROVE, Baker Street.*

*Sir G. S. WHITE, V.C., G.C.I.E., K.C.B., the Commander-in-Chief in India.*

SIR GEORGE WHITE joined the Service as ensign in the 27th Foot, in 1853, when barely eighteen. Ten years later he was promoted captain, exchanging immediately into the Gordon Highlanders. It is with this corps that his career has been most closely connected, and he is now its colonel. For this reason it is a portrait of him taken when in command of the grand old "Ninety-Twa's" that we now present to our readers His Mutiny medal was won in the old 27th, but all the other honours which bedeck his breast were gained in the Gordon Highlanders. As second in command of that regiment he served through the Afghan War of 1879-80, winning the Victoria Cross, a C.B., and his brevet as lieutenant-colonel, to say nothing of frequent mention in despatches. His cross he won by two separate acts of valour. At Charasiah he led two companies of his regiment up a steep mountain-side to attack an enemy strongly posted and eight times superior in force. When his men halted, exhausted, White, seizing a rifle, rushed forward alone, and shot dead the leader of the enemy. Again, at Candahar, White led the final charge, under a heavy fire, riding straight up to the muzzles of the enemy's guns, and himself capturing one. He commanded the Gordons from 1881 to 1885, and since then has seen service in Egypt as assistant adjutant and quartermaster-general in the Nile Expedition. 1884-85; in Burma, in command, from 1885-89; and in command of the Zhob Valley Force in 1890. In 1893 he was made Commander-in-Chief in India, a position he now vacates only to assume that of Quartermaster-General of the Forces, in succession to Sir Evelyn Wood. Like Roberts and Wolseley, he is an Irishman, being the eldest son and heir of the late J. R. White, Esq., D.L., of Whitehall, Ballymena, County Antrim.

# THE ARMY OF BENGAL.

THE magnificent pageant of the 22nd of June, eagerly anticipated, lavishly provided for, splendidly organised, has been relegated by the inexorable hand of Time to its inevitable position among the glories of the past; but it will not be readily forgotten by those who were fortunate enough to be present, and to join in the stupendous

Photo. Gregory.    Copyright.—H. & K.
*Rissaldar-Major Mangal Singh,*
3rd Bengal Cavalry.

Photo. Gregory.    Copyright H. & K.
*Rissaldar-Major Ali Muhammed Khan,*
2nd Bengal Lancers.

Photo. Gregory.    Copyright.—H. & K.
*Rissaldar Kaddam Khan,*
4th Bengal Cavalry.

display of enthusiastic loyalty evoked by the occasion, nor will the future historian fail to find a place for it in his records. The deafening acclamations of the vast multitude which lined the route are still ringing in our ears, as they hailed each section of the endless procession slowly pacing the great thoroughfares, amid scenes of historic interest, military, commercial, and political; loyal subjects of Her Majesty, from every quarter of the globe, ready, if need be, to offer their lives in the defence of her vast empire.

The enthusiasm of Marmion's eager young squire arouses our sympathy, as, gazing at the fair scene spread out before him, he throws up his hand and exclaims:

"Where is the coward that would not dare
To fight for such a land!"

And slow, indeed, must be the pulse and unenviable the state of mind of him who would not experience a keen exhilaration of soul in the contemplation of the huge and prosperous realm thus spread out before him in the persons of its representatives. Where, indeed, is the man who would not risk something, his life if need be, in defence of such an empire and such a Monarch!

Many are the lessons and reflections concerning past, present, and future, which are apt to crowd the mind; but were they to be entered upon here the object of these pages would be defeated. That object is to give some idea of the constitution and strength and honourable records of the Army of India, with

special reference to those members of it who are represented in the illustrations; and, bearing this in mind, let us turn our attention to the men who on this great occasion had the privilege of forming the guard of honour round the Empress-Queen. Who are these men, of swarthy visage and grim soldierly bearing, clad in splendid uniforms, in such close attendance upon the Queen of England? They afford a living proof of the validity of that other title to which she so justly lays claim—Empress of India. They are here to represent the loyal native soldiers of India, who have so frequently and so gallantly fought side by side with their white brothers in arms, and vied with them in deeds of splendid daring. This is no mere figure of speech. The records of India bear ample testimony both to the stubborn courage of bygone generations, who gave us no little trouble ere we conquered them, and to the still greater military capacity and devotion to duty which their descendants have developed under the teaching and example of British officers.

The history of our Native Army is, in fact, the history of British India. In the extension of our influence, during the sway of the East India Company, and the final consolidation of the Empire, native regiments have borne so large a share that it is almost impossible to turn a page without finding some reference to their deeds of arms, in company with British troops, whom however, they usually outnumbered by at least three to one. In the victories of Plassey, Seringapatam, Hyderabad, Bangalore, and Assaye they bore an important part. Clive, Wellesley, Munro, Pollock, Sale, Ellenborough, Napier, Gough, and Roberts have in turn borne testimony to their courage and efficiency. True, there is a sad blot on their scutcheon in 1857; but even the black thunder-

From a Photo    By a Military Officer.
*Troop of Lancers, with Native Officer.*

cloud of the Mutiny is relieved by brilliant flashes—tales of devotion and grand military achievements, in the face of the strongest race prejudices, and temptations of plunder and advancement held out by the rebel leaders, to which they turned a deaf ear, or replied only with the sabre cut and the rifle bullet. It is not intended, however, to enter here upon the history of the Mutiny, except in so far as may be involved in reference to gallant deeds performed by regiments or individuals who are represented, though, perhaps, under different

lieutenant-general, and all under the supreme command of the Commander-in-Chief. This arrangement is, however, of comparatively recent date, having only been finally consummated in 1895, by the abolition of the offices of Commanders-in-Chief of the Madras and Bombay Armies, and the creation of the four Army Corps, as described. The Army Commission, which met in August, 1879, under the presidency of the Hon. Sir Ashley Eden, Lieutenant-Governor of Bengal, was convened for the purpose of

*Photo. Gregor*                                                              *Copyright.—H. & K.*

*RISSALDAR-MAJOR SAYYID ABDUL AZIZ, 5th Bengal Cavalry.*

regimental titles, for the Native Army has been in many respects reorganised since 1857.

The Sepoy Army in the pay of the East India Company had then been in existence for over 100 years, and numbered somewhere about 230,000 men, commanded by British officers, the British troops in India mustering about 45,000 strong. At the present time the British troops number about 72,000, and the Native Army about 140,000 men.

The Army of India is divided into four commands—Bengal, Bombay, Madras, and the Punjab—each held by a

ascertaining how the cost of the Indian Army could be reduced without impairing its efficiency. General Roberts, with characteristic intuition, put his finger at once on the weak spot, and drew up a scheme which was finally, though tardily, adopted, as was the case with almost every suggestion of his, however it may have been scouted at the moment.

The recruiting for the native regiments is necessarily carried out under a very different system from that of our own, and some details will be of interest. To begin with, there is the difficulty in regard to races and creeds, which

*Lieutenant-Colonel J. C. F. Gordon,*
Commanding 6th Bengal Cavalry.

*Rissaldar Neb Ram,*
7th Bengal Cavalry.

though less pressing than in former years, has still to be reckoned with; and in order to minimise it, regiments are constituted on what is known as the "class" system. That is to say, a regiment may be composed entirely of men of the same class, in which case it is known as a "class" regiment; or it may be formed of three or four classes, which are kept together in different companies or squadrons, and this is termed a "class company" or "class squadron" regiment. India is divided into recruiting districts, each in charge of an officer, who only recruits from some particular race. The advantage of this system over that of bygone days is obvious—discipline is more easily maintained, difficulties arising from caste prejudices are reduced to a minimum, *esprit de corps* is fostered, and all goes far more smoothly.

A regiment of native cavalry, with a few exceptions, consists of four squadrons, the total strength usually being as follows: Eight British officers, one medical officer, seventeen native officers, and 608 non-commissioned officers and men. Cavalry is usually organised in a peculiar manner, known as the Silladar system, by which the horses, saddlery, clothing, and arms (except firearms) are the private property of the regiment, provided by a donation on joining, and subscriptions from all ranks, the original donation being refunded when a man is discharged or pensioned. The native regimental ranks are as follows: Rissaldar-major, or chief native officer; rissaldar and rissaidar, half-squadron commanders; wordie-major, or native adjutant; dafadar, or sergeant; lancedafadar, or corporal; and sowar, or trooper.

A battalion of native infantry is composed of two wings and eight companies, the strength being usually as follows: Seven British officers, one medical officer, sixteen native officers, eighty non-commissioned officers, and from 720 to 800 rank and file. The native regimental ranks are as follows: Subadar-major, or chief native officer; subadar, or company commander; jemadar, or subaltern; havildar, or sergeant; naick, or corporal; and sepoy, or private.

A native soldier enlists in the first instance for three years, with the option of claiming his discharge at the expiration of that period, or enlisting for eighteen years more, when he is entitled to a pension. He joins under the express stipulation that he is liable for service in any country, beyond the seas or otherwise.

The extensive subject of the various races and castes cannot be gone into here in other than a somewhat superficial manner, but it is necessary to refer to it briefly, in order to gain some idea of the classes from which our Native Army is mainly recruited.

We have, then, the Brahmins and Rajputs of Northern India; the Jâts and Gujars of the Eastern Punjab and North-East Rajputana; the Sikhs and Dogras of the Punjab proper; the Mahrattas, Mers, Meenas, and Bhils of Western India and Rajputana proper; the Ghoorkas and Garhwalis of the hills; the Tamils and Telegus of Southern India; to say nothing of the Mussulman races, comprising Afghans and Pathans, Baluchis and Brahuis, Punjabi, Hindustani, and Rajput Mussulmans—a sufficiently complex arrangement, which is further complicated by the addition of others from small states, who differ in name only, as a rule, from the inhabitants of the larger territory in which they are located.

The Sikhs and Dogras, Jâts and Rajputs, who are spread over a very large territory, are among the best fighting men in the world; the Brahmins are steady and courageous soldiers; the Afghans and Pathans are wild and undisciplined by nature, and much given to boasting and "swagger," but when once they make up their minds to fight—as they do pretty frequently—they are hard to beat. The Madrasees are not considered such good material as the more hardy and martial men of the North, nor are the Bengalees so well fitted for military service on account of their effeminacy and physical sloth. The little Ghoorkas are among the best-known of our native soldiers. Small of stature, but active as cats, they will go anywhere and do anything; the only difficulty their officers have is in keeping them back and persuading them to shoot at least a few of the enemy before rushing in to bayonet them. The Baluchis and Brahuis are practically identical, and are fine warlike men, but not very easy to enlist, as they have an inherent antipathy to hair-cutting and other small disciplinary details. The Punjabi Mussulmans are good and steady soldiers, but have not the "go" of the fiery Pathans.

Such are the materials of our Native Army. And now it is time to turn our

*Captain C. F. Campbell,*
6th Bengal Cavalry.

*Rissaldar Makbul Khan,*
8th Bengal Cavalry.

*Rissaldar Nadir Khan,*
9th Bengal Lancers.

attention more especially to those portions of it which are represented in these pages. The Army of Bengal claims first notice. Its strength is as follows: Nineteen regiments of cavalry, nine of which are lancers, two mountain batteries, a corps of sappers and miners, and fifty-four infantry and rifle battalions—nearly 57,000 of all arms.

The Bengal Army was more completely re-organised after the Mutiny than that of either of the other Presidencies owing to the fact that disaffection was far more general in its ranks. Up to 1857 it was composed mainly of Brahmins and Rajputs of Oude and the North-West Provinces, and this is believed by some to have contributed largely to the initial success of the Mutiny. The constitution is very different under the present system, and the Bengal Army is one which we may regard with satisfaction. It must not be forgotten, however, that their predecessors, mostly under different titles, rendered good service, and performed acts of valour which are still handed down to the credit of the regiments in their new organisation.

The 2nd Bengal Lancers, of whom a representative will be found on page 94, were formerly the 2nd Irregular Native Cavalry, and date from the beginning of the century. They are a "class squadron" regiment, composed as follows:—One squadron of Sikhs, one of Rajputs, one of Jâts, and one of Hindu Mahomedans. Their uniform is blue, with light blue facings. They bore their part in the capture of Arracan, in Burma, against odds, not only of numbers, but of a deadly malarial climate, by which, before the victorious troops could withdraw, more than half were laid low. In the Punjab Campaign, too, they greatly distinguished themselves, and, under their new title, took part in the Egyptian Expedition, 1882, for which Rissaldar-Major Ali Muhammed Khan wears the Egyptian medal with clasp, and the Khedive's bronze star.

The 3rd Bengal Cavalry, represented on page 94 by Rissaldar-Major Mangal Singh, were formerly the 4th Irregulars, raised in 1814. They are a "class squadron" regiment, consisting of one squadron of Sikhs, one of

Jâts, one of Rangurs, half of Rajputs, and half of Hindu Mahomedans. Their uniform is drab, with blue facings. They had a brilliant record marred by a sad decadence in 1857, when the greater number of them joined the mutineers, and the faithful remnant were disarmed, but afterwards re-enlisted in this or other regiments, in recognition of the heroic efforts they had made to redeem the honour of their corps.

*From a Photo.*                    *By a Military Officer.*
*Native Lancers.*
"Prepare to Mount."

General Sir Hope Grant, in a fierce action outside Delhi on June 17th, 1857, had his horse killed, and was in the utmost peril, surrounded by infuriated rebels. One of his orderlies, a sowar of the 4th Irregulars, who had managed to keep near his chief in the mêlée, rode up, and, dismounting, gave up his horse to the general, and remained by him, actually cutting down more than one man who attempted to attack his officer. This brave man was allowed to retain his horse and his sword. No finer specimen of a soldier could be imagined—native or otherwise. In the Afghan Campaign of 1878-80 the 3rd Bengal formed part of the Cavalry Brigade under General Gough, and took part in some brilliant cavalry engagements about Candahar. It is worthy of note that the 3rd Bengal claims to be the oldest Sikh regiment, having been partly composed of Sikhs when it was first formed in 1814.

The 4th Bengal Cavalry were formerly the 6th Irregulars, and date from the early half of this century. They are a "class squadron" regiment, composed of one squadron of Jâts, one of Sikhs, and two of Hindu Mahomedans. Their uniform is scarlet, with blue facings. They were engaged in the Scinde Campaign, and had some very severe fighting. Colonel Salter, their commandant, was succoured when in considerable danger by a sowar named Mahomed Buckshee, who killed his opponent, and afterwards became a rissaldar. A native officer, named Azim Khan, after fighting most pluckily, was mortally wounded, and Sir Charles Napier dismounted and spoke kindly to him. "General," he replied, "I am easy. I have done my duty. I am a soldier, and cannot die better." With this kind of spirit among them, no wonder the gallant Irregulars carried all before them. The 4th Bengal are

*From a Photo*                    *By a Military Officer.*
*Native Lancers—Drill Order.*

*Photo. Gregory.*                    *Copyright.—H. & K.*
*Rissaldar-Major Khan Bahadur,*
10th Bengal Lancers.

represented on page 94 by Rissaldar Kaddam Khan, who, though he has seen no active service, is highly regarded by his superiors, and has performed good work in the settlement of disputes among the Afridis—rather an onerous task, one would imagine!

The 5th Bengal Cavalry, formerly the 7th Irregulars, are composed as follows: Two squadrons of Hindu Mahomedans,

who was not in favour with the Ameer, and the misfortunes of the uncle were visited on the nephew, so that he was unable to visit his home; but some compensation was allowed him by the Government, and he has been useful in procuring information. He wears the medal for the Afghan War of 1878-80.

The 6th Bengal Cavalry (the Prince of Wales's), formerly

Photo. Gregory.     Copyright.—H. & K.

*RISSALDAR GURDATH SINGH, 12th Bengal Cavalry, and Orderly.*

one of Rajputs, and one of Jâts. They date from 1841, and did good work in the Mooltan Expedition of 1848, and the Bhotan Campaign of 1864-65. Their representative, on page 95, is Rissaldar-Major Sayyid Abdul Aziz, a fine specimen of a native officer. He is the nephew of an Afghan chief,

the 8th Irregulars, date from 1842, and are constituted as follows: One and a-half squadron of Sikhs, a half of Rajputs, a half of Jâts, a half of Hindu Hindus, and one of Hindu Mahomedans. Their uniform is blue, with red facings. They had a brilliant record in their early days, sharing in the victory at Punniar in 1843, and performing valiant exploits at Moodkee, Ferozeshah, and Sobraon. But, alas! the great Mutiny found them faithless, only about twenty standing by their commander, Captain Mackenzie, who, like many other British officers at that time, refused at first to believe that his "children" would turn against their colours. This small band of good soldiers formed the nucleus of the new regiment, which soon established a brilliant reputation, maintained in the latter part of the Mutiny and in the Egyptian Expedition of 1882. Lord Wolseley specially refers to them in his despatches, and five of their troopers, with their commanding officer and Lieutenant Murdoch of the Engineers, performed a smart and brilliant piece of work at Zagazig, by detaining four trains, loaded with the enemy's troops, and on the point of starting. They adopted the practical method of shooting the engine driver of the leading engine, who refused to get down, and kept the whole at bay for half an hour, until the main body arrived. The Prince of Wales is their honorary colonel, and they are represented on page 96 by Lieutenant-Colonel J. C. F. Gordon, their present commandant, and Captain C. F. Campbell. Colonel Gordon entered the Service in 1869, and attained his present rank in 1895. He took part, as deputy assistant quartermaster-general, in the Wuzeeree Expedition, and in the Egyptian Expedition, when he was mentioned in despatches, and wears the Egyptian medal with clasp and the Khedive's bronze star. He had the privilege

From a Photo.                    By a Military Officer.
*Sowar, 14th Bengal Lancers. Review Order.*

forgotten in connection with the Indian Mutiny, and the men he collected round him were animated by the same spirit as their skilful and intrepid commander, whose coolness under fire and keen intuition at critical moments soon became proverbial. Many are the stories told of Hodson and his men in every history of the Mutiny, and they are, probably, familiar to our readers. Whether charging brilliantly against fearful odds, or compelled, as they were before Delhi, to sit still and be shot at to save a position, the same example of dashing attack or of soldierly fortitude was set, the same emulation of their leader's conduct displayed by the men. The occasion of Hodson's death was quite characteristic. He was in the fight at the capture of the Begum Kothi, at Lucknow, though he had, from a military point of view, no business there, and died next day of a wound received there. He has had some detractors, and was probably not more perfect than other men. His conduct, in deliberately shooting the two sons and the grandson of the King of Delhi, has been the subject of controversy among historians.

Photo. Gregory.                    Copyright H. & .
*Rissaldar-Major Sher Singh, 13th Bengal Lancers.*

of commanding the native cavalry officers as guard of honour to the Queen during the Jubilee celebrations. They occupied comfortable quarters in an hotel at Norwood, and were summoned whenever Royalty was present at any function during that time. Colonel Gordon is a fine specimen of a cavalry officer, and evidently inspires respect and goodwill among his following.

The 7th Bengal Cavalry, formerly the 17th Irregulars, date from 1846, and consist of one squadron of Jâts, a half Sikhs, a half Dogras, a half Rajputs, a half Brahmins, and one of Hindu Mahomedans. Their uniform is red, with dark blue facings. They took part in the War of the Punjab, and are represented on page 96 by Rissaldar Neb Ram.

The 8th Bengal Cavalry were formerly the 18th Irregulars, and date from 1846. They are composed of one and a-half squadron of Hindu Mahomedans, a half of Punjabi Mahomedans, a half Sikhs, a half Rajputs, a half Jâts, and a half Hindu Hindus. Their uniform is blue, with scarlet facings. They took part in the last Afghan Campaign, and are represented by Rissaldar Makbul Khan, on page 96.

The 9th and 10th Bengal Lancers have a special degree of interest attached to them, for they were formerly the 1st and 2nd Hodson's Horse. Major Hodson's name will never be

From a Photo.                    By a Military Officer.
*Native Officer, N.C.O., Sowar, and Trumpeter,*
14th Bengal Lancers,

It cannot be discussed here, but it may be remarked that, whether or not it was absolutely necessary, only a man of Hodson's courage and decision could have done it. Lord Roberts, in his 'Forty-one Years in India," disposes of the report which was current at the time, and has gained credit since, that Hodson met his death while looting. As a matter of fact, he must have received his fatal wound almost imme-

*Photo. Gregory.*   *Copyright ·H. & K.*

*Rissaldar-Major Izzat Khan Bahadur, 17th Bengal Cavalry.*

*Photo. Gregory.*   *Copyright.—H. & K.*

*Rissaldar-Major Hukam Singh Bahadur, 16th Bengal Cavalry.*

diately after arriving on the scene of action. So much for Hodson and his Horse; and what about their successors? They have not departed from the high standard set by their founder, but have unflinchingly done their duty when called upon. The 9th did some brilliant work in the latter part of the Egyptian Campaign of 1882, and at Chitral in 1895. The 10th were in the Abyssinian Expedition of 1868,

and the Afghan War of 1878-79, where, on one occasion, led by Captain Strong, they made a brilliant and successful charge on a vastly superior force.

Rissaldar Nadir Khan, whose portrait appears on page 97, was orderly officer to Sir R. Low at Chitral, was mentioned in despatches, and wears the medal and clasp. Rissaldar-Major Khan Bahadur, who represents the 10th, on the same page, has over thirty-seven years' service, and wears the medals for the Kanee Koorum Expedition of 1863, Abyssinia, 1868, and Afghan, 1878-80. He was also with the Zhob Valley Expedition in 1884, is native aide-de-camp to Sir W. Lockhart, and has been granted the 2nd class order of British India. The 9th is composed of one and a-half squadron of Sikhs, one and a-half Punjabi Mahomedans, a half Dogras, and a half Pathans. Uniform blue, with white facings. The 10th consists of one and a-half squadron of Sikhs, one of Dogras, one of Punjabi Mahomedans, and a half of Pathans. Their uniform is blue, with scarlet facings The Duke of Cambridge is honorary colonel of the 10th.

The 11th (Prince of Wales's Own) Bengal Lancers are not represented here by anyone at present serving in the regiment, but they are not passed over, and therefore we give the portrait of a veteran who did good work with them, and whose individual services will be referred to later on. The 11th were formerly the 1st Sikh Cavalry, and were raised in 1857. The regiment is composed as follows. Two squadrons of Sikhs, one of Dogras, a half Punjabi Mahomedans, and a half Pathans. Their uniform is blue, with red facings. They were present at the capture of Lucknow—which is a sufficient guarantee of hard fighting against long odds—and subsequently took part in the Chinese War of 1859-61, where they were known as Probyn's Horse, being commanded by Major Dighton Probyn. He and his men are repeatedly mentioned in despatches for brilliant exploits. On one occasion, when he had only 100 men

*Photo. J. Bliss.*   *Officers, 8th Bengal Infantry.*   *Jubbulpore.*

with him, our position was threatened by large bodies of the enemy, and their cavalry attacked in force. Probyn, with his gallant hundred, went at them with such convincing emphasis that they declined to remain, and fled in confusion. The 11th were also in the Afghan War of 1878-80.

The 12th Bengal Cavalry, formerly the 2nd Sikh Cavalry, were raised in 1857. The regiment is composed of two squadrons of Sikhs, one of Dogras, and one of Punjabi Mahomedans. Their uniform is blue, with blue facings. They were in the Abyssinian Expedition in 1868, and the Afghan War of 1878-80, taking part in the attack on the Peiwar Kotal in December, 1878, than which a more brilliant and skilfully-planned exploit has seldom been performed. In reading Lord Roberts's account of it, one is alternately cast down with fear lest the immense difficulties of the position should prove too much for him, and elated with pride and admiration of the skill of the general and the gallant response of his men. A party of the 12th escorted Sir Louis Cavagnari to the top of the Shutargardan Pass, on his way to Cabul,

*From a Photo.*    *Adjutant and Native Officers, 8th Bengal Infantry.*    *By a Military Officer.*

*Photo. Bourke*    *British Officers, 14th Sikhs.*    *Lahore.*

*From Photos.*    *Native Officers, 14th Sikhs.*    *By a Military Officer*

where he met such a sad fate. Rissaldar Gurdath Singh, whose portrait appears on page 98, was with the 12th through this war, and wears the medal with two clasps.

The 13th (Duke of Connaught's) Bengal Lancers were formerly known as the 4th Sikh Cavalry, and were raised in 1858. They are composed as follows: One and a-half squadron of Sikhs, one of Dogras, one of Punjabi Mahomedans, and a half of Pathans. Their uniform is dark blue, with scarlet facings. They served in the last Afghan War and in the Egyptian Expedition of 1882, where, on one occasion, Major McDonald, with a dozen sowars, made a very important and successful reconnaissance at Tel-el-Kebir; and on another occasion, Colonel Pennington, who commanded, on going out early to post vedettes, found himself in the presence of a strong force of cavalry, with the enemy's main body coming up in rear. He had only thirty men with him, but they were not going to turn tail without giving some sort of an account of themselves. He sent two sowars back at a gallop to warn the camp, and, dismounting the remainder, had a little practice at the enemy from behind a sand ridge, until they were surrounded, when they mounted and charged back to camp, losing only one man. The colonel was a splendid leader, but he must have had good men with him, or he could not have attempted this exploit. Rissaldar-Major Sher Singh, on page 99, was specially transferred from the 9th to the 13th Bengal Lancers, in 1893. In his old regiment he served in the Soudan Campaign of 1885, and wears the medal with two clasps, and the Khedive's bronze star. He has an excellent name with his superiors.

The 14th Bengal Lancers were formerly known as Murray's Jât Horse, having been raised by Captain Murray in 1857. They are a "class" regiment, composed exclusively of Jâts, and have a brilliant record. Their uniform is dark blue, with scarlet facings. At the latter end of the Mutiny they defeated thrice their number of rebel cavalry at Kutchla Gault, and subsequently rendered

*From a Photo.*
*14th SIKHS ON PARADE, FEROZEPORE.*
*By a Military Officer.*

valuable services on the Nepal frontier. They joined the Kuram Field Force under Roberts in 1878, and took part in the fighting in the Kohat Valley. Afterwards, in consequence of the scarcity of transport, they marched many miles on foot, while their horses carried supplies, and then took part in the battle at Charasiah. Some members of this fine lancer regiment are represented on page 99; and very picturesque and workmanlike they are.

The 16th Bengal Cavalry were raised in 1857, disbanded in 1882, and reformed in 1885. They are composed of two squadrons of Sikhs, one of Dogras, and one of Jâts. Their uniform is blue, with blue facings. Their representative, Rissaldar-Major Hukam Singh, on page 100, is a veteran of thirty-three years' service, having joined the 19th Bengal Lancers in 1864, and been subsequently transferred to the 16th. While in the 19th, at the battle of Patkaoshana, 1st July, 1880, he is reported to have charged single-handed five of the enemy who had

*Photo. Herzog & Higgins.*
*Native Cavalryman's Tent.*
*M.h.w.*

surrounded a rissaidar, and killed three of them, rescuing his comrade. Hukam Singh would be a very awkward customer to tackle! He was deservedly awarded the Order of Merit, and has since received the 2nd class order of British India. His son has lately received a direct commission in the 16th, where his military education may safely be entrusted to the gallant rissaldar-major.

The 17th Bengal Cavalry were raised in 1857, disbanded in 1882, and reformed in 1885. They are made up of two squadrons of Punjabi Mahomedans and two of Pathans. Their uniform is blue, with blue facings. They served with the Jowaki Expedition of 1877, and subsequently in the Afghan Cam-

*From a Photo.*
*Tug-of-War, 17th Bengal Infantry*
*By a Military Officer.*

paign, but were not engaged in any of the more familiar actions. Rissaldar-Major Izzat Khan Bahadur, who represents them on page 100, served in Egypt, and wears the medal with clasp, and the Khedive's bronze star. He has done good service in recruiting, having entirely raised one half squadron of Pathans.

This is the last of our representatives of the Bengal Cavalry, and it will be admitted that they give a good account of themselves. It is to be regretted that the 19th Bengal Lancers (formerly Fane's Horse) are not represented, as they had a brilliant name under Captain Fane in China, being repeatedly alluded to in despatches; indeed, the general in command thought it necessary to write a special despatch about this regiment and Probyn's Horse, describing their invaluable services.

The native cavalry of Bengal are not, indeed, to be despised. Of course the men are splendidly led. Native troopers have been heard to say that they will go anywhere for their British officers because they always cry "*Come* on!" not "*Go* on!" This is only another way of saying that the men make splendid material, and the officers know how to use it to the best advantage.

Of the Bengal Infantry there are but few representatives. The British officers of the 8th are seen on page 100, and the adjutant and native officers on page 101. This was formerly the 59th, and was raised in 1815. It is a "class" regiment, consisting entirely of Rajputs, and was engaged at Sobraon, and in the last Afghan Campaign. Their uniform is red, with white facings.

*Physical Drill—17th Bengal Infantry.*

On page 101 will be found groups of the British and native officers of the 14th Bengal Infantry, raised in 1846, and formerly known as the Ferozepore Regiment. They are Sikhs, and have a good record, being among the faithful at Lucknow, and having since seen some hard fighting in Afghanistan. They make a goodly show on parade, page 102, and are indeed a very soldierly and formidable body of men. Their uniform is red, with yellow facings.

The 17th Bengal Infantry, who are to be seen on this and the opposite pages indulging in the tug-of-war and physical drill, were among the first regiments raised after the Mutiny. They are all Hindustani Mahomedans, and fought in the Bhotan Expedition of 1864, the Afghan Campaign, and the Egyptian Expedition, where they had some severe fighting at the battle of Hasheen.

The 45th Bengal Infantry are all Sikhs, were raised in 1856 under the title of Rattray's Sikhs, and were officially added to the Bengal Army in 1864; but they had distinguished themselves long before that. "Behar" and "Defence of Arrah" appear, among other names, on their colours, and tell of a gallant exploit. Arrah is a town in the province of Behar, and Mr. Wake, the Governor, long suspecting mischief, fortified his house so that when the Mutiny broke out, sixteen civilians and fifty of Rattray's Sikhs defended it against thousands of the enemy, until they were relieved by Vincent Eyre, the first relieving party having been annihilated. They served in the Afghan War and Zhob Valley Expedition. Two groups of this fine regiment will be found on page 103. Their uniform is red, with white facings.

*"Ready!"—45th Sikhs.*

*TUG-OF-WAR.—45th SIKHS (BENGAL).*

# THE ARMY OF BOMBAY.

*Photo. Frith.*

*Water Tank, Bombay.*

WHEN Charles II. married Catherine of Braganza, the Isle of Bombay formed part of her dowry, and a rich dowry it was probably held to be, the general idea of India being, as Macaulay says, "a dim notion of endless bazaars, swarming with buyers and sellers, and blazing with cloth of gold, with variegated silks, and with precious stones." All these glories, however, were in India, and not in England; and it does not appear that the Government thought it worth while to assume the responsibility of sending to fetch them. So the Isle of Bombay was, in 1668, rented to the East India Company at the extremely moderate figure, even for those days, of ten pounds in gold per annum, and they proceeded to enter on their tenancy, with the assistance, we are told, of five ships of war.

The Army of Bombay cannot be said to have dated from the period of this tenancy; but in the first half of the eighteenth century there was formed the nucleus of a Native Army, and in 1741 there were about 1,600 native troops employed, and a very nondescript lot they appear to have been. The inevitable march of British influence and organi-

*Photo. Gregory.*　　　*Copyright—H. & K.*

*Rissaldar Jehangir Khan,*
1st Bombay Lancers

tion told rapidly, however, in the latter half of the century, and before its close the Bombay Army numbered some 2,000 cavalry and 28,000 infantry—a larger force, numerically, than that of to-day.

The Native Army of Bombay, as at present constituted, is as follows: Seven regiments of cavalry, three of which are lancers; the Aden troop, of cavalry and "camelry" combined; two mountain batteries of artillery; a corps of sappers and miners; and twenty-six infantry regiments. Total of all arms, about 26,500, or considerably less than half the strength of the Bengal Army. They have a good record, however. Of the cavalry regiments, the 4th have no less than twelve names on their colours, the 3rd eleven, the 5th nine, the 6th seven, and the 1st six. Only the 7th is without active service, having been raised as recently as 1885.

The 1st (Duke of Connaught's) Bombay Lancers were raised in 1817. They are made up of one squadron of Mahrattas, one of Jâts, one of Sikhs, and one of Pathans—about as fine a combination for cavalry as could well be collected. Their uniform is dark green, with scarlet facings. They took part in the Afghan War of 1840-42, and the Sikh Wars of 1845 and following years, in which the splendid fighting qualities of our quondam foes was only an earnest of their value in our service in later years. The fighting in the Sikh War was no child's play, and the 1st Bombay bore their part well, especially at Moultan. During the Mutiny they were in action many times, and were specially referred to by Sir Hugh Rose. They also took part in the Burma War of 1885-87, and were subsequently in the Soudan. On this page will be found the portrait of Rissaldar Jehangir Khan, an officer of twenty-eight years' service. He wears the Burma medal with two clasps, and has also been awarded the Suakin medal, 1896, which was not issued when his picture was taken.

The 3rd (Queen's Own) Bombay Cavalry were raised in 1820, and are composed of one squadron of Jâts, one of Sikhs, one of Kaimkhamis, and one of Rangurs. Their uniform is dark green, with scarlet facings. They are represented on page 105 by Major A. Phayre, who commands them, and was in England with the native cavalry officers this year. He served in the Afghan War of 1878-80, and wears the medal. The 3rd have distinguished themselves in many actions, commencing with the Afghan War of 1842. They were at Hyderabad under Napier, and subsequently in the Persian Campaign, where they took part in the decisive actions at Reshire, Bushire, and Khooshab. At the last named there was some good cavalry work, and a squadron of the 3rd made a very brilliant charge on a body of Persian infantry, who made a determined stand. It was no joke for cavalry, even in those days of smooth-bore muskets, to face a square of infantry with their wits about them, and meaning business; but the 3rd, led by Captain Forbes—only 120 of them—meant business also, and, in spite of a crushing fusillade, drove their charge home. Runjeet Singh, a dafadar, was severely wounded twice during the charge, but he stuck to his saddle and rode it through. He was afterwards given a commission. In the Mutiny and in the Abyssinian Expedition the 3rd are heard of with credit, and their last service was in the Afghan Campaign of 1878-80. They were present at the fatal Maiwand affair, where our brigade, under Brigadier-General Burrows, about 2,500 strong, engaged an Afghan force of some 25,000 Ghazis, and was frightfully cut up. Nearly 1,000 of our officers and men were killed outright, and 175 wounded or missing—significant figures indeed. The remnant retired on Candahar, and Roberts's famous forced march from Cabul to that place followed immediately. The gallant rush of the artillery, by which our guns were saved, and a desperate charge by the 3rd Bombay and other cavalry, when all seemed lost, with other instances of courage and discipline, relieved the dark background of disaster; but it was a terrible day.

The 5th Bombay Cavalry date from 1839, and were formerly known as the Scinde Horse. They consist of two squadrons of Derajat Mahomedans, one of Pathans, and one of Sikhs. Their uniform is dark green, with white facings They were raised by General Jacob, and were at Cutchee, in the Scinde War. Meeanee, Hyderabad, the Punjab, Moultan, Goojerat, all appear on their colours, and testify to many a hard fight, out of which they always came with credit. They went to Persia, and only returned in time to assist in the suppression of the Mutiny. Finally, the many

*Photo. Herzog & Higgins.*     *Mhow.*

*Varieties of Dress—Native Lancers.*

cavalry engagements in the Afghan War of 1878-80 afforded the 5th opportunities of which they were not slow to avail themselves. Rissaldar-Major Mahomed Unar Khan, who represents them on page 106. has over ten years' service, having received a direct commission. He is a man of good family, and has rendered great assistance in recruiting.

The 6th Bombay Cavalry, also raised by General Jacob, and formerly known as Jacob's Horse, date from 1846, and are composed of one squadron of Sikhs, one of Pathans, and two of Derajat Mahomedans. Their uniform is dark green, with yellow facings. They were in the last Afghan War, and acquitted themselves with credit. Rissaldar-Major Faiz Khan, page 107, was formerly in the 3rd Scinde Horse—since disbanded—and fought with them in Afghanistan. He was present at Maiwand and two other actions, and wears the medal with two clasps.

The 7th Bombay Lancers, formerly known as the Belooch Horse, were only formed under their present constitution in 1885. They consist of two squadrons of Derajat Mahomedans, one of Pathans, and one of Sikhs. Their uniform is dark green, with white facings. Rissaldar Mir Haider Shah Khan, whose portrait is given on page 107, has been in the regiment since its re-formation, receiving a direct commission. He was formerly a colonel in Amir Sher Ali Khan's and Sirdar Ayub Khan's territory, and so had not much to learn in the way of soldiering.

*Photo. Herzog & Higgins.*     *Mhow.*

*A Sowar, Native Lancers.*

The Aden Troop of Cavalry date from 1867. having been raised for service in the Aden district. They only number about 100, all told, and forty-five are camel sowars. Their uniform is dark green, with white facings, and a yellow throat plume on the bridle.

Some types of Bombay Lancers are given on pages 106 and 107 The "family group" is an interesting one, showing three generations, all the males of which either have become or are destined to become soldiers. This is quite characteristic of the races from which the native cavalrymen are chiefly drawn.

The Bombay Native Artillery consist of two mountain batteries, Nos. 5 and 6. The complement of each is about 250 all told, including drivers. There are four Royal Artillery officers and three native officers to each battery. On page 109 will be found an illustration of a mountain gun, packed on a mule. These little guns have often considerably astonished the hill tribesmen in our frontier wars. In their mountain fastnesses they were accustomed formerly to reckon themselves secure at least from artillery, to which they have a deep-seated

*Photo. Gregory.*     *Copyright.—H. & K*

*Major A. Phayre,*
*3rd Bombay Cavalry.*

*Photo. Herzog & Higgins.* *Mhow.*

## A FAMILY GROUP, NATIVE LANCERS.—A "Fighting Lot."

*Photo. Gregory.* *Copyright -H. & K*

*Rissaldar-Major Mahomed Unar Khan.*
5th Bombay Cavalry.

and well-founded antipathy; but while they were taking up some strong position, with that intuitive instinct of strategy which some of them possess, an unwelcome visitor in the form of a 7-pounder Shrapnel shell would come singing over their heads, and the next round would plump right into them, to their utter disgust and discomfiture. Often has a flank movement on the heights been covered by the fire of these handy little weapons, which can be brought into position almost anywhere by the sure-footed mules, and have before now crossed snow-covered and precipitous passes many thousands of feet above sea-level.

On page 110 an English officer is seen giving orders to a native gunner, and the kind of country in which these little guns come into action is well represented.

The Native Artillery are combined with the Royal Artillery stationed in India, and are always commanded by R.A. officers. There were, of course, native artillery batteries many years ago in the Bombay Presidency. We hear of them before the middle of the eighteenth century, and the force which acted with Clive in Bengal, in 1757, no doubt included artillery. The Bombay Artillery have a good reputation, and have maintained it well in Afghanistan, the Punjab, the Mutiny, Persia, Abyssinia, and Burma. Their uniform is blue, with red facings, and tan belts.

We are not able to give any representatives of the Bombay Sappers and Miners, but they have a very distinguished record, bearing on their colours no fewer than sixteen names. They muster nearly 1,000 of all ranks, and their uniform is scarlet, with blue facings.

Of the Bombay native infantry regiments, many date back to the latter half of last century, the oldest being the 3rd, raised in 1768. On pages 109 and 110 will be found types of some of these troops, both men and officers. Punjabi Mahomedans are common enough among them, but Sikhs are not often found in the Bombay infantry. The Jâts, Gujars, Mahrattas, and others, however, make good fighting material, though the Bombay Army is not always considered as good as that of Bengal in this respect.

We are not able, unfortunately, to give portraits

*Rissaldar-Major Faiz Khan,*
6th Bombay Cavalry.

of any distinguished British or native officers of the Bombay Infantry, but some account of the more prominent regiments cannot fail to be of interest.

The 1st Bombay Native Infantry (Grenadiers), date from 1788, and are composed of four companies of Mahrattas, two of Bombay Mahomedans, and two of Punjabi Mahomedans. Their uniform is red, with white facings. They took part in the defence of Mangalor, prior to the official date of their formation, and were also at Hyderabad. They were also among those who were so severely handled at Maiwand, under the command of Colonel Anderson, who bravely rallied the remnant of his command again and again, a handful of them being among those who made the last desperate stand.

The 2nd Bombay Infantry (Prince of Wales's Own Grenadiers) are contemporary in origin with the 1st, and consist of four companies of Jâts, two of Gujars, and two of Punjabi Mahomedans. Their uniform is red, with white facings. They were with Sir David Baird in Egypt, and have the Sphinx on their colours. Later they took part in the Mahratta Wars, and behaved with great gallantry at the

*Rissaldar Mir Haider Shah Khan,*
7th Bombay Lancers.

*BOMBAY LANCERS.*

*From a Photo.*                    *By a Military Officer.*

*Punjab Mussulman Native Officer.*

*From a Photo.*                    *By a Military Officer*

*A Sikh Officer.*

battle of Koregaum, on the 1st January, 1818, against overwhelming numbers of warlike Mahrattas, who had long considered themselves invincible. The splendid charge of the 2nd probably turned the tide of battle, and their adjutant, Lieutenant Thomas Pattinson, performed an heroic action. He was struck down mortally wounded, but hearing that one of our guns had been captured, he struggled to his feet, and, seizing a musket, clubbed it and rushed in among the enemy, striking right and left, and calling upon his men to follow him and retake the gun. He was soon down again, but men led in this fashion are not easily repulsed, and the gun was recaptured, the slain lying in heaps. In 1840 we hear of the 2nd again in the Afghan Campaign which ended so disastrously. One of their officers, Lieutenant Walpole Clarke, was greatly distinguished for his zeal and courage, and was appointed to a corps of Scinde Irregular Horse. He met his death fighting against overwhelming numbers of Beloochees, who surprised him while on a foraging expedition with a convoy of camels and some 200 men, nearly all of whom were slain. One would imagine that this was one of those instances in which a little more foresight on the part of those in command might have averted disaster; but risks of this kind are occasionally unavoidable, and the campaign was a difficult and harassing one all through, and was also, politically, a sad mistake from beginning to end.

The 3rd Bombay Light Infantry date from the same year, and are made up of six companies of Mahrattas and two of

*From a Photo.*                    *By a Military Officer.*

*A Sikh Sepoy.*

Bombay Mahomedans. Their uniform is red, with black facings. The first name which appears on their colours is Seedaseer, a very severe fight which took place on the 6th March, 1799, and in which about 2,000 of our troops were surrounded by nearly 12,000 of Tippoo's. The pluck displayed by the Sepoys on this occasion was admirable. They held the enemy at bay until they were reinforced by some British regiments, and Tippoo was beaten with tremendous losses. They were also at Seringapatam, in the Sikh War of 1845, and in Abyssinia.

The 5th Bombay Infantry are of the same age, and are composed of six companies of Mahrattas and two of Bombay Mahomedans. Their uniform is red, with black facings. This regiment early established a good reputation. They were at Kirkee and Seringapatam, and in the Afghan Campaign of 1840-41. When Walpole Clarke, referred to previously, left Kahun on that fatal foraging expedition, Captain Lewis Brown, of the 5th, with a portion of the regiment, was left in charge of the fort. They made a gallant defence, against tremendous odds, for two months, but when the relieving column, under Major Clibborn, was defeated by a great

*Photo. S. Jamsetji.*

*Mhow.*

## TYPES OF NATIVE INFANTRY.

number of Beloochees in the narrow and precipitous Pass of Nuffoosk, Brown was finally forced to capitulate. It is said, however, that the enemy so greatly appreciated the pluck with which he had defended his post, that he was able to obtain very honourable terms, *which were not violated.* This is more or less of a record in itself, in that campaign at any rate, for our opponents were certainly not distinguished by any weakness for giving honourable terms, or for standing by their undertakings. They have, indeed, an unenviable reputation for scheming and general eel-like propensities to this day.

The 13th Bombay Infantry were raised in 1800, and are composed of four companies of Jâts, two of Gujars, and two of Punjabi Mahomedans. Their uniform is red, with yellow facings. As the 1st Battalion of the 7th at Kirkee, they displayed marvellous pluck and rallying powers, and were specially referred to in despatches. They also served well in Central India and in the last Afghan War.

The 14th Bombay Infantry also date from 1800, but they have not been fortunate enough to see service. A group of the British officers appears over page.

The 19th Bombay Infantry must not escape notice, if

*From a Photo.*

*By a Military Officer.*

## MOUNTAIN GUN, BOMBAY NATIVE ARTILLERY.

only to refer to the gallantry of one of their officers, Major S. J. Waudby. On the 16th April, 1880, then holding the appointment of road commandant between Candahar and Quetta, he was at Dubrai, a small commissariat post about fifty miles from Candahar, having with him only two Sepoys of the 19th and three sowars of the Scinde Horse. He heard immediately on his arrival that a strong force of Kakur Pathans—very formidable enemies—were going to attack the post that night, and not placing any confidence in the guard, who were local Pathans, he strengthened his defences as well as he could, and awaited the attack. The guard, as anticipated, deserted him; but he and his faithful five defended the post for three or four hours, killing and wounding over thirty of the enemy; and when at last overpowered, they fell fighting, the bodies of the gallant major and his two faithful Sepoys being found side by side—a "dauntless three," indeed, as those in the "Lays of Ancient Rome."

The 25th Bombay Infantry, formerly the 3rd Battalion of the Bombay Rifle Regiment, were raised in 1820, and consist of four companies of Jâts, two of Rajputs, and two of Punjabi Mohamedans. Their uniform is rifle green. Two officers of this regiment, with a mere handful of men, performed a brilliant exploit at Gwalior on the 19th June, 1858, towards the conclusion of the Mutiny. The town had been recaptured from the rebels by four p.m., but the famous rock citadel, occupied by a small garrison, still held out. The General—Sir Hugh Rose—knowing that it was practically in his hands, allowed his tired soldiers to rest, intending to take it next day. The two subalterns, however, were not as patient as their General. Lieutenant A. Rose had been sent with a guard to take charge of the police station, and he proposed to Lieutenant Waller, who was posted near him, that they should go and take the citadel "off their own bats." Waller, like the renowned Barkis, was "willin'," and so these two adventurous youths, with perhaps fifty men, set off on their errand, accompanied by a blacksmith carrying a heavy hammer, etc. They were seen plainly enough, for it was broad daylight, and had to run the gauntlet of a brisk fire; but they marched steadily up, and having, with the aid of their faithful smith, broken open six gates in succession, found themselves at length face to face with the rebel garrison, who resisted stoutly, but in vain. The little attacking party were not going to be denied after all the trouble they had taken to get in, and they carried out their plan, capturing the citadel. Lieutenant Rose lost his life in the gallant affair which he had initiated.

*From a Photo.*     *By a Military Officer.*
*" Giving Instructions."*
Officer and Gunner, Bombay Native Artillery.

And now, perhaps enough has been said about the Bombay Army to give an idea of the kind of stuff it is composed of. It would be absurd to pretend that every soldier has the makings of a hero about him, in this or any army, but it will be admitted that the record is a creditable one, and that we should not hesitate to entrust important issues to them, when officered by such men—and there are plenty of them—as Rose and Waller, Waudby and Lewis Brown.

*Photo. Herzog & Higgins.*     *Mase.*
*BRITISH OFFICERS, 14th BOMBAY INFANTRY.*

# THE ARMY OF THE PUNJAB.

*FORT AND CITY OF LAHORE, PUNJAB.*

*Rissaldar-Major Kesur Singh,*
5th Punjab Cavalry.

THE Punjab Frontier Force consists of some of the best fighting men in India. They are recruited mainly from the Sikhs, Pathans, Dogras, Ghoorkas, and Punjabi Mahomedans, and it is well that they should be composed of the best and staunchest natives to be found, for they are liable to be called out for active service at any time, to quell the restless and warlike frontier tribes, who, in spite of repeated lessons, seem slow to realise that the British Government intends to have things arranged in its own way on the Indian Frontier.

The Punjab Frontier Force was raised originally in 1849, though some of the regiments bear a prior date, having been incorporated with the force when it was more completely organised. The strength is as follows: Four regiments of cavalry, the Queen's Own Corps of Guides (cavalry and infantry), four mountain batteries, one garrison battery, and eleven battalions of infantry and rifles, bringing up the total to about 13,500 of all arms.

The city of Lahore, which is shown on this page, is the capital of the Punjab, and was the scene, at the outbreak of the Mutiny, of some very prompt and decisive measures, in the face of great difficulties, on the part of Mr. Robert Montgomery, the Judicial Commissioner. The military station was at Mian Mir, about six miles from Lahore, and the fort within the walls of the city was garrisoned by a small force of European and native troops, relieved at regular intervals from Mian Mir, where the native troops outnumbered the British by about four to one. When the tidings of the outbreak at Meerut reached Montgomery, he took measures to ascertain the feeling of the troops at Mian Mir; and, having been informed that they were "up to their necks" in sedition, he determined, with the concurrence of the military commandant, Brigadier Stuart Corbett, to disarm all the native troops. A morning parade was accordingly held for the purpose, and, by most skilful arrangements, the Sepoys found themselves in the unpleasant position of having to choose between obeying the order to "pile arms," or being well-nigh annihilated by the canister and musketry of the British artillery and infantry.

The 1st Punjab Cavalry, though not represented here, cannot be passed over, as they did most valuable work during the Mutiny, and, moreover, they had among their officers a man of heroic type, who stands out in strong relief amid the many brave men who found their opportunity at that time. Lieutenant John Watson, who arrived before Delhi with a troop of his regiment in July, 1857, was not long in convincing both friends and foes that, if his men were few, it nevertheless took a great many to beat them, he being personally equal to a "good few." On one occasion they were engaged with a body of rebel cavalry, who had attacked one of our pickets. The rissaldar in command of them, albeit a mutineer, was a fine specimen of a cavalryman, and a brave man to boot. Him, therefore, by way of encouraging the others, John Watson selected as his opponent, ran him through, and dismounted him. The fellow was still game, however, and others came to his assistance; but Watson managed to hold his own until his men charged and routed the foe, not, however, without receiving several wounds. This splendid officer afterwards received the Victoria Cross, and eventually became Sir John Watson, V.C., K.C.B.

The 2nd Punjab Cavalry have also a very creditable record, and numbered among their officers Captain Samuel Browne, better known in later years as General "Sam"

*From a Photo.*                                        *By a Military Officer.*

*Types of Queen's Own Corps of Guides.*

Browne, who, with only one sowar, attacked a gun at Seerporah, in August, 1858, receiving two severe wounds, one of which cost him his left arm; but he won his V.C.

All the Punjab Cavalry, indeed, have distinguished services; and we are fortunate in being able to give, on page 111, the portrait of a native officer of the 5th, who has on many occasions earned the praise of his superiors. He wears the medal and clasp for the Jowaki Expedition of 1877-78, and the medal with two clasps for Afghanistan, where he was

*Photo. J. W. Caplain.*                              *Jhansi.*

*THE DELHI GATE, AGRA.*

*Photo. F. W. Bremner, Quetta.*

OFFICER, N.C.O.'s, AND TROOPERS, QUEEN'S OWN CORPS OF GUIDES.

Copyright

specially commended for devotion and courage on several occasions, and received the Order of Merit, and a special certificate from Lord Roberts for his work at Sherpur.

We must not devote too much space to the Punjab Cavalry, however, or others who are well worthy of notice will be left out; and the next in order are the Corps of Queen's Own Guides—a very remarkable body of men in more than one respect. In the first place, they are composed of cavalry and infantry—a most uncommon arrangement; and, in the second place, they are among the most distinguished soldiers in the world. Many pages might be filled with accounts of their exploits since their formation in 1846. The men were specially picked to act as "guides" as well as soldiers, and have had a very strong *esprit de corps* from the

mustn't lie here all day. I'll jump on top of that sangar, and they'll all fire at me. Then we'll charge before they reload!" He was as good as his word, jumping up in full view of the enemy, and treating them to some voluble native "Billingsgate." They fell into the trap. All fired, luckily missing the bold Dal Singh, and were instantly rushed, Turner coming up with his men in time to assist in the chase.

Under the command of Captain H. Daly, the Guides marched from Meerut to Delhi, a distance of 750 miles, in the hottest season, in twenty-eight days—twenty-seven miles a day under an Indian sun! When they arrived they were ready for work, and plenty was found for them. It was said that during the siege of Delhi they lost all their officers three times over, either killed or disabled. In a sortie on the 9th

*Photo. F. W. Brunner, Quetta.*                                                    *Copyright.*

OFFICER, N.C.O., AND PRIVATE, 5th GHOORKA RIFLES.

first. In the Khuttuck Campaign of 1852, Captain Turner, with a company of the Guides, was ordered to dislodge some of the enemy from the top of a cliff which could only be approached by a pathway in single file—an awkward position, indeed, but it was tackled by some Ghoorkas, materially assisted by one Dal Singh, a Guide sowar, who, scorning the fact that his long cavalry boots were scarcely suited for cliff climbing, dismounted and strode after them. Presently about five-and-twenty reached the top, and lay flat down; but Dal Singh, on arriving, in spite of his boots, a little later, remarked to Dr. Lyell, who had led the men, "Sahib, we

June, they pursued the flying mutineers right under the walls of Delhi, and exposed themselves to a tremendous fire. Captain Daly and others were wounded, and Lieutenant Quintin Battye, of the cavalry, was mortally wounded, and died next day.

On pages 112 and 113 will be found some illustrations of the native officers and of this distinguished regiment. Their uniform is drab, with red facings. In conclusion, it should be mentioned that, after the fall of Delhi, the Guides were specially mentioned in orders, the troops being paraded in their honour, the following words forming part of the brigadier's eulogium: "Great and important to the British Government have been the services of this gallant body now before you — these gallant Guides, covered with glory."

The view of the Delhi Gate Agra, on page 112, recalls the history of more heroic deeds in the defence of the city and fort for many weeks against the mutineers, and the courage and perseverance of Mr. Colvin. the Governor of the North West Provinces, who died at his post, worn out with the load of responsibility and anxiety he had to bear.

The four regiments of Sikh infantry included in the Punjab Frontier Force all have good records, though no illustrations of them can be given here. The three first regiments served in Afghanistan, and the fourth were at Delhi and Lucknow.

There are five Punjab infantry regiments in the Frontier Force, numbered 1st, 2nd, 4th, 5th, and 6th. The 1st were raised by Captain Coke, in 1849, and early gained a good reputation in the Kohat and other expeditions, being specially referred to in general orders. They were known formerly as Coke's, Rifles, and wear a rifle green uniform, with red piping. A good specimen may be seen on this page, making "a careful shot."

The 2nd Punjab Infantry have greatly distinguished themselves on many occasions, especially during the Mutiny, taking part in the siege and capture of Delhi, and subsequently

*Native Punjabi and Ghoorka Officers.—Full Dress.*    *Jubbulpur.*

marching to Agra, a distance of forty-four miles, in twenty-four hours, and fighting a general action before they tasted food. Colonel Green, in a farewell "order" to his men, says that the only fault he has had to find with officers or men is that they have occasionally been too eager to close with the enemy—not the kind of fault-finding likely to wound their feelings very deeply.

The 5th and 6th Punjab Infantry have also come well to the front. All these regiments, except the 1st, wear a drab uniform, with various facings, and are composed of Sikhs. Dogras, Pathans, and Punjabi Mahomedans. Some types of Punjabi regiments will be found on this and page 116. The

*"A CAREFUL SHOT."—1st PUNJAB RIFLES.*

regiments from which these are selected belong, however, to the Bengal Army.

The 5th Ghoorka (Rifle) Regiment consists of two battalions, one of which dates from 1858, and the other from 1886. They were formerly known as the Hazara Ghoorka Battalion, and have won many distinctions, especially in the last Afghan War, in which they were commanded by Major

*Photo. M. Dadabhoy.*　　　　*Mooltan.*

*Pathan Native Officer,*
19th Punjab Infantry.

Fitzhugh. At the Peiwar Kotal they were in the leading column, and, dashing at the breastwork, engaged in a terrible hand to hand encounter with the enemy. Together with the 72nd Highlanders, they rushed the last position. Major Fitzhugh and Captain Cook were first in, and the latter won the Victoria Cross for his gallantry in rescuing Major Galbraith in a desperate fight. At Charasiah, Cabul, and

*Photo. M. Dadabhoy.*　　　　*Mooltan.*

*Mahomedan Sepoy—Heavy Marching Order,*
19th Punjab Infantry.

Candahar they again came in for great praise, and, together with their "chums," the 72nd and 92nd Highlanders, were specially mentioned in orders. "The very last troops," said General Roberts, "that the Afghans will ever wish to meet in the field are Scottish Highlanders and Ghoorkas." A very pleasing exchange of compliments afterwards took place between the 5th Ghoorkas and the 72nd Highlanders. The Ghoorkas presented the Scotchmen with a shield, "in remembrance of the Afghan Campaign of 1878 to 1880"; and the Highlanders returned the compliment with a handsome silver-mounted drum-major's staff.

The Punjab Frontier Force has, so far, fully justified its formation, and, though numerically the weakest of the Army corps of India, it is in all respects a thoroughly well organised force.

The 24th Baluchistan Infantry, on page 118, belong to the Bombay Army. They served well in Central India and in the Afghan War.

*Photo. J. Bless.*　　　　*Jubbulpore*

*NATIVE PUNJAB OFFICERS.—Undress.*

"ATTENTION!"—OFFICER AND PRIVATES, 24th BALUCHISTAN REGIMENT.

*Photo. F. W. Bremner, Quetta.*    Copyright.

# THE ARMY OF MADRAS.

*From a Photo.*

### TRICHINOPOLY ROCK, MADRAS.

*By a Military Officer.*

THE Madras Army dates back to about 1746. Prior to this date, for pretty nearly a century, the merchants had employed armed men, known as "Topasses" and "Mistices," to protect their factories, but there was no attempt at anything like organisation until the year named. England was then at war with France, and it behoved us to have some kind of army in Madras to protect our interests, which were repeatedly threatened. The troops then raised, if they have any right to the title, were by all accounts a very nondescript lot, con-

† *Photo. Gregory.*            *Copyright.—H. & K.*

*Jemadar Abdul Karim Khan,*
**Viceroy's Body Guard.**

sisting as much of natives of Madagascar, the West Coast of Africa, and elsewhere, as of natives of India. It was not until 1758, however, that the Madras Government began in earnest to get an army together, on anything like an adequate scale; and most of the infantry regiments date from this and the following twenty years or so. The cavalry is of later date, not having been started until 1780.

Prior to that the Company were in the habit of hiring bodies of horse, when necessary, from friendly native princes, or raising irregular cavalry as best they could, these generally proving very apt at foraging and pillaging, but very unwilling to face an enemy. The Madras Army is constituted at present as

follows: Three regiments of lancers, a corps of sappers and miners, and thirty-two infantry regiments, the total strength being over 32,000 of all arms.

There has never been much difficulty in getting the men of the Madras Army to go on foreign service. They are either less home-sick or more curious than the other native armies, and have fought outside their own Presidency from the earliest days, and crossed the sea repeatedly without complaint. Now, of course, as has been pointed out, all our native troops enlist under the stipulation that they are liable to be sent anywhere, but it was a very different thing a century ago.

Another fact worthy of note about this Army is that they remained almost absolutely faithful throughout the Mutiny. There was some uneasiness and a few disturbances here and there, but as a whole they were untouched, and resisted the many inducements held out to them to desert and throw in their lot with the rebels. Some native horse artillery, encamped in the Residency grounds, greatly astonished a body of rebels from the city, who had an idea that these artillerymen would not molest them, and came to attack the Residency; but the gunners opened with grape, which is calculated to damp the ardour of any mob of insurgents, and sent them flying.

The first illustration in connection with the Madras Army is the Rock of Trichinopoly, the scene of some fierce struggles at the time when young Robert Clive was beginning to come forward, most unexpectedly, as a soldier and a leader of soldiers. Dupleix, the French Commandant, had defeated and slain Anaverdy Khan, Governor of the Carnatic, and Mahomed Ali, his son, fled to Trichinopoly with a scanty remnant of the Army. Chunda Sahib, son-in-law of a former Nabob of the Carnatic, assisted by the French, invested Trichinopoly, and the cause of Mahomed Ali, whose claims England supported, shut up as he was at Trichinopoly, appeared hopeless. Then it was that Clive, only twenty-five years old at the time, came forward, and conceived the plan of first capturing Arcot, the capital of the Carnatic, in the hope that this would lead to the raising of the siege at Trichinopoly. With 200 English soldiers and 300 Sepoys, he advanced on Arcot, and the garrison evacuated it in a panic. But Rajah Sahib, son of Chunda Sahib, invested Arcot with a force of 10,000, including some French soldiers. The slender garrison was reduced to 120 Europeans and 200 Sepoys. For fifty days they held out, in spite of the ruinous state of the fortifications and the scarcity of food; and it is on record that the Sepoys came to Clive and represented that they could do very well on the thin gruel strained from the rice, and that the Europeans should have the more substantial part—a touching instance of devotion which has not often been equalled under such circumstances. Hearing that the fierce

Mahrattas were contemplating joining the British, Rajah Sahib stormed Arcot, but his larger force was no match for Clive's military genius and the devotion of his small band. The attack failed utterly, and Clive was left in possession. This was only the beginning of the end. British triumphs followed in rapid succession. Trichinopoly was relieved, and Clive became famous for all time. The story of that period is fascinating, but it is not possible to dwell on it here. It is time to proceed with some account of the various Madras regiments, and the first to claim attention is the 1st Madras Lancers. They were raised in 1787, but only received the appellation of "Lancers" in 1886. Their uniform is French grey, with facings of pale buff, and silver lace—a very tasteful combination, whoever devised it, though it seems rather delicate in tone for service in the field.

Subadar Muhammad Beg, who represents the regiment on page 119, is a great-grandson of Tippoo, ruler of Mysore, who fell fighting against our troops under Wellesley, at Seringapatam, in 1799. He has the Burma medal and clasp. The 1st Lancers have Seringapatam on their colours, though their designation was different in those days—a remarkable example of the turn of Fortune's wheel, and of the transformation which British rule has brought about. They were also in the Afghan War of 1878-79.

The 2nd Madras Lancers were raised earlier as the 3rd Regiment, and served under Captain Stevenson from 1780 to 1784. In the latter year, however, on the final transference of the Madras cavalry regiments to British rule, they mutinied; but Stevenson's showed a better feeling than the others, and became the 1st, and subsequently the 2nd. These changes render the record confusing, unless the whole history be carefully studied.

The uniform is very similar to that of the 1st Lancers. On page 119 will be found a group of the British officers of the 2nd Lancers.

The 3rd Madras Lancers were formed in 1784 by Major Campbell, from the faithful remnants of those which had mutinied. Since then they have rendered a good account of themselves.

Madras has had its artillery, and they rendered very good service up to and including the Mutiny, as in the instance previously alluded to, and in many others; but they were for some reason disbanded soon after, and are no more.

The Madras Sappers and Miners (the Queen's Own) have distinguished themselves in a great number of actions, their colours bearing no fewer than twenty-four names, from Seringapatam in 1799 to the Soudan in 1885. Their uniform is very similar to that of the Royal Engineers, and they are very proud of it. They are said to affect English ways very much, and will smoke a short pipe and have a drink with an English soldier, talking to him very often in his own tongue. After the Egyptian Campaign some of them were in London,

and their cicerone, General Michael, took two of them to Madame Tussaud's where they found, of course, an effigy of Arabi Pacha. The General was conversing and explaining things to them in their own language, but, to the surprise of the bystanders, one of them stepped forward, and, shaking his fist in Arabi's face, exclaimed in excellent English, "Ah, you rascal! What a lot of trouble you have given!"

There is a very strong *esprit de corps* among these men, which renders them most valuable. Their conduct under trying circumstances in the Abyssinian Expedition was favourably remarked upon.

The Madras Infantry, as we have seen, had its origin, officially, in 1758, or thereabouts.

*Subadar Muhammad Beg,*
1st Madras Lancers.

Before that the Sepoys, we are told, had no sort of discipline. They were armed with matchlocks, bows and arrows, spears, swords, bucklers, daggers, or any kind of weapon they could get hold of. They consisted of bodies of various strength, each under the command of its own chief, who received from the Government the pay for all his men, and was supposed to distribute it to them; but the distribution, we may well believe, was relegated in great measure to the regions of supposition.

By the year 1767, however, so much progress had been made that 5,000 of these men, led by English officers, with about 1,000 Europeans, defeated the troops of Hyder

*BRITISH OFFICERS. 2nd MADRAS LANCERS.*

Ali and the Nizam, more than 70,000 strong—a most brilliant feat of arms.

The 1st Madras Infantry and Pioneers date from 1758, and have seven names on their colours, beginning with Seringapatam. They played a good part in many actions, but in 1806 were implicated in the mutiny at Vellore, were partially disbanded, and transformed into the 1st Battalion of the 24th. Under this name, however, they distinguished themselves so greatly at Seetabuldee, in 1817, that, on the petition of the senior native officer, the old number and facings of the 1st Regiment were restored to them in a very complimentary general order; and so they wiped out their bad record, and the name Central India on their colours bears testimony to their loyalty during the Mutiny. They also took part in the last Afghan Campaign, and in 1883 received the name of Pioneers. Some types of this regiment will be found on pages 120 and 121, and also a picture of a Madras Sepoy on sentry, a very formidable-looking customer, challenging some approaching stranger. Their uniform is red, with white facings.

The 3rd Madras Infantry date from 1759, when they were raised as the 4th Battalion. They were in many actions, and

*Photo. H. N. King.*
" *Who Goes There?* "
A Madras Sepoy.

On page 122 will be found a portrait of Subadar Mukhlis Ali Khan, a native officer of the 14th Madras Infantry. This regiment was raised in 1776, and was formerly the 2nd Battalion 6th Regiment.

*Photo. Barton, Son, & Co.*          *Bangalore.*
" *Picking them Off.* "
Madras Light Cavalry.

earned an exceptional distinction by their plucky conduct at Mahidpore, in 1817. It is recorded that they charged up to the muzzles of the enemy's guns without flinching, and in commemoration of their gallantry bear the words " Now or never " after " Mahidpore." Their uniform is red, with green facings.

The 8th, formerly the 9th Battalion, had the honour of being a favourite body with the Duke of Wellington, and often called themselves Wellesley's battalion. After the battle of Assaye, where they suffered considerably, a staff officer found a number of men of this battalion assembled for a funeral, and was informed that they were about to inter five officers and non-commissioned officers of one family. He knew the men well, and was offering his condolences, but they deprecated any such expressions. " These men," they said, " have died in the performance of their duty, and the Government will take care of their children, who will soon supply their places in the ranks." It is not possible to imagine a more patriotic or soldierly spirit.

*Photo. Barton, Son, & Co.*          *Bangalore.*
*Madras Pioneers.*
Full Dress and Field Service Order.

Photo. F. W. Henemar, Quetta.

*MADRAS PIONEERS—FIELD SERVICE ORDER.*

A very brilliant exploit was performed by an officer of this regiment in August, 1780, in the war with Hyder Ali. The troops of our old ally, Mahomed Ali, of Trichinopoly memory, were more than suspected of a treacherous intention of handing over Wandewash to Hyder; and Lieutenant Flint, of the 14th, with one other British officer, and 100 Sepoys, made a night march from Carangoly, arriving in front of Wandewash in the forenoon. Sending in a message to the Khilledar in command, he was warned that if he approached he would be fired upon.

This settled the question of treachery, but did not frighten away Flint and his men. He parleyed with the picket officer sent to stop him, and gradually got nearer, until, by strategy, he obtained the Khilledar's consent to an interview. He found him seated on a carpet within the outer gate, with an armed guard of 130 men. Flint then acknowledged boldly that his story about having a letter was false, but offered to produce the orders of his own Government, issued with Mahomed Ali's concurrence.

The Khilledar told him contemptuously to go back the way he came; but Flint preferred to remain, and seized him, his small guard of four Sepoys, who had been admitted with him, presenting their bayonets at the Khilledar's breast.

A bold action of this kind often pays well. In the confusion which followed, Flint's men got in, and he assumed command of the place—a very pretty episode.

On the next page is an illustration of the colours of the 20th Madras Infantry, formerly the 2nd Battalion 2nd Regiment. They were raised in 1777, and the first name on their colours is Sholinghur, which commemorates their gallantry on September 27th, 1781, when, with another battalion, since disbanded, they received a tremendous charge, made by the pick of Hyder Ali's cavalry, in such steady fashion, and with such a vigorous and deadly fire, that they routed the horsemen, who broke and fled, leaving two standards in our hands, one of which remains with the 20th, who were granted an extra jemadar to carry it, and there it is in the picture.

The other names displayed are Seringapatam, Carnatic, and Mysore.

The 20th bore themselves well on every occasion, but they have no recent triumphs to record.

The square, ready for cavalry, on page 123, comes in appropriately after the colours, and affords some idea of the ugly sort of hedge which cavalrymen have sometimes to face, to say nothing of the hail of bullets usually reserved for a very close range.

*Photo. Del Tufo & Co.*          *Bangalore.*

*Subadar-Major Mukhlis Ali Khan, 14th Madras Infantry.*

The 23rd Madras Light Infantry are well represented on pages 123 and 124. They were raised in 1794, and at one time formed the 1st Battalion 12th Regiment. Their motto is "Now or never"—an inspiriting one at a critical moment.

One can fancy their leaders rallying them with this shout, and that it would take a good deal then to turn them back.

They have on their colours Seringapatam, Nagpore, and Burma, 1885-1887, and have taken part with distinction in other campaigns.

A detachment of 100 men, with two British officers, were engaged in the Irrawaddy and North-East Columns in Burma in 1891, and in the defence of Sadon, where their conduct was very favourably reported upon, and there were several individual acts of bravery in rescuing wounded comrades, one case in particular being rewarded with the Order of British India.

In the last Burma War, shortly after the capture of Mandalay, a number of dacoits were known to have occupied a certain native hut. Now, a dacoit, or armed

*From a Photo.*          *By a Military Officer*

*Native Officers, 20th Madras Infantry.*

robber and highwayman, of Burma is a very unpleasant sort of person. If he catches anyone, he delights in inflicting horrible tortures; and he is not easily caught.

However, a little party, consisting of one non-commissioned officer and eight men of the 23rd, surrounded this hut, and the non-commissioned officer, with one man, broke in the door

They were immediately attacked, but they gave a good account of all the dacoits, who had reason to regret this little afternoon call.

The same non-commissioned officer shortly after rescued Her Majesty's mails, coming at an opportune moment across a postman struggling with four dacoits.

A brilliant record, also, in the history of the 23rd is the gallant defence, in 1803, of the village of Korjet Corygaum, by a small detachment, against some 1,500 Arabs and others. The assailants lost, in killed alone, a number exceeding that of the whole detachment. These brave men and good soldiers received the thanks of General Wellesley in

*"Square, Ready!"—A Warm Welcome for the Cavalry.*

*Colours, 20th Madras Infantry.*

*From Photos.*    *By a Military Officer.*

*British and Native Officers, 23rd Madras Infantry.*

division orders—an honour well merited.

The native staff of the 23rd make a very good group of soldierly-looking men, who, no doubt, take a proper pride in their regiment, which makes a fine show on parade. It is commanded by Lieutenant-Colonel Welch, who has supplied these interesting particulars. It is now time to refer to a somewhat remarkable circumstance in connection with the Madras Infantry regiments.

On consulting the Army List, it will be noticed that the great majority of the thirty-two regiments have red uniforms, with various facings, and are composed of Madras Mahomedans, Tamils, Telegus, and so on, as might be expected, these being the races located in the Presidency; but a closer inspection will reveal the fact that the 10th, 12th, 29th, and four following regiments are quite differently constituted, being composed of Sikhs, Punjabi Mahomedans, Ghoorkas, Dogras, Rajputs, Pathans—warlike races of the north as a rule; also, that their uniform is, in the case of the 10th, dark green, and in the others drab; and that these seven regiments are styled Burma battalions.

Their history is as follows: When Upper Burma was annexed, after the last war, the administration of this large tract of country, equal in area to the whole of France, was a very onerous and harassing task, owing to the universal presence of dacoits, who kept the whole place in a constant state of terrorism.

Lord Roberts, then Commander-in-Chief in India, who went to Burma in November, 1886, conceived the idea of enrolling a strong force of military police, to deal with these dangerous robbers; and as the Burmese

*23rd MADRAS INFANTRY ON PARADE.*

could not be relied upon for this kind of work—being, no doubt, in a deadly "funk" of the dacoits—he proposed to enlist them from among the warlike races of Northern India. This idea was immediately carried out, and with signal success.

A new semi-military force, called "The Upper Burma Military Police," was raised with wonderful celerity, and a battalion of this force was quartered in each of the districts into which the upper province was divided. These battalions were raised in India by officers of the Indian Army specially selected and sent across for the purpose; the military authorities at the various recruiting centres being directed to afford every facility in getting together the men required for the new force.

The new police were brought over as they were enlisted, and soon proved themselves to be admirably suited for the work, as, indeed, might be expected of these types of men, who are not very much, acquainted with the sensation of fear in regard to anyone.

In a marvellously short space of time the country began to get settled.

Dacoits found their business at a discount, and soon acquired a wholesome dread of the big Sikhs and active Ghoorkas, and in no very long time it was realised that so large a force of military police was no longer required.

Then came the question, what was to be done with them?

To disband such a splendid body of picked fighting men seemed utter folly.

It was therefore determined to form ten new regiments, for special service in Burma and her frontiers, and to do away with a corresponding number of Madras regiments. These seven regiments, then, have all been brought into the Madras Army during the past six or seven years, though they bear the numbers of the old Madras regiments. No doubt the remaining three battalions will in due course be transferred. They are splendid regiments, of exceptionally fine physique, and though not quite up to a regiment of long standing in some respects, they will doubtless equal any in shooting and discipline before long. Such is the story of the Burma battalions, and with it must end our account of the Madras Army.

The men of a Burma regiment may be seen on this page, relieving guard.

*Native Staff, 23rd Madras Infantry.*

From Photos          By a Military Officer.

*Burma Regiment.*

# THE IMPERIAL SERVICE CORPS AND IRREGULARS.

TO the uninitiated, the title "Imperial Service Corps" may appear to savour more of regular Imperial troops than of any regiments which could be termed "irregular," and probably there were comparatively few among the vast throng of spectators who viewed the procession on Jubilee Day who would have been able to distinguish between the official status of Sir Pertab Singh and his companions in arms and the native cavalry officers who formed the guard of honour. In one sense, indeed, they may all be justly described as native cavalry officers; but officially they stand on different ground, inasmuch that the officers commanded by Colonel Gordon represented the cavalry regiments regularly enlisted and maintained by the Crown—an essential portion of the Native Army of India—the Imperial Service Corps, on the other hand, being raised and maintained by the rulers of the independent Native States, under the superintendence of British officers, to assist in the maintenance of our Indian Empire when called upon to do so. It will be of considerable interest, no doubt, to many to learn how this arrangement was brought about, and how it seems likely to work, for it is of comparatively recent origin.

When, after the suppression of the Mutiny, India was taken from the control of the Company and made an integral part of the British Empire, the treatment and future status of the native princes were very earnestly considered by the authorities, and in the proclamation announcing the cession of India to the British, it was expressly stated that the Queen had no desire to extend her territorial possessions, and that the estates of native princes—sixty-three in number—would be scrupulously respected. During the State progress made by Lord Canning, the first Viceroy, through India, the native rulers were informed that the right of adopting an heir in default of male issue would be recognised—a very politic move, carried out at the earnest solicitation of Lord Canning, and causing great satisfaction.

The Native States were at the same time given permission to maintain each an army of prescribed strength; but they were and are forbidden to make war upon each other, or to embark upon any enterprise of external aggression. Why, then, these armies? The question has often been asked, and cannot be very satisfactorily answered. Since they were not to fight anyone else, many people have assumed, not without some show of reason, that the armies would be maintained with the principal object of fighting us, should a favourable opportunity present itself. Another point, however, which must not be lost sight of, is the Oriental love of any kind of martial show; and, furthermore, certain portions of these armies, at least, are necessary for the preservation

*Colonel Maharajah Sir Pertab Singh, K.C.S.I.,*
In Uniform of Jhodpur Lancers.

of internal order, insisted upon by the Government as a condition of continued independence.

In the year 1877, during the Viceroyalty of Lord Lytton, the question was first seriously discussed of utilising the armies of the Native States as an auxiliary force for the service of the Empire. Lord Lytton appointed a committee to consider the matter and report upon it; but Lord Roberts, who was a member of the committee, did not at that time see his way to advise the adoption of any such scheme, and many others concurred in his view. It is remarkable that, in the following year, a native of India, of high education, wrote a little book on this subject, which he dedicated to Sir Richard Meade, then Resident in Hyderabad, and in which he advocated far more sweeping measures than were then, or have at any time been, contemplated by Government, by way of utilising these armies.

Nothing more, however, was done in the matter until 1888, the last year of Lord Dufferin's Viceroyalty, when it was brought forward again, and this time, in the light of further experience of the fidelity and fighting qualities of natives during the Afghan Campaigns, and the unmistakable spirit of loyalty evinced by the native rulers when there was danger of war with Russia in 1885, Lord Roberts found himself able to afford the scheme his unqualified support, and this change of views was fully justified by the cordial response of the native chiefs to Lord Dufferin's suggestion.

It must not be imagined, of course, that the whole of the Native States were invited to supply contingents to the Imperial Service Corps: many of them are not capable of doing so. At present twenty-one States have organised, under the superintendence and periodical inspection of duly appointed British officers, bodies of cavalry or infantry, or both, varying in total strength from 150 to 4,200, according to their means. There are sixteen British inspecting officers, of whom Lieutenant-Colonel Howard Melliss is the chief. He came over with the Imperial Service officers for the Jubilee, as did Major F. H. R. Drummond, and Captain F. W. P. Angelo, also inspectors.

The total force of the Imperial Service Corps is at present 19,200—a very small proportion of the combined armies of the native princes, which amount to something like 350,000, but great numbers of these were but recently soldiers only in name, though no doubt they will become very much better in course of time.

This little army is furnished, as has been said, by twenty-one States, of which seventeen were represented in

*Rissaldar-Major Baha-Uddin Khan Sardar Bahadur,*
Central India Horse.

*Commandant Rao Bahadur Thakur Dip Singh,*
Bikanir Camel Corps.

*Sir Pertab Singh, his Nephew, and Major J. G. Turner,*
Viceroy's Body Guard.

England this year, and we are able to give portraits of nearly all these representatives, many of whom are men of good birth and education, and fine specimens of soldiers as well.

The first representative is Colonel Maharajah Sir Pertab Singh, K.C.S.I., commanding the Jhodpur Lancers, whose portrait appears on page 125. Sir Pertab is brother to the Maharajah, and is among the most distinguished of native officers. He is very much liked by Anglo-Indians. He was chiefly instrumental in raising the Jhodpur Lancers, a fine body of horsemen, 1,200 strong. Lord Roberts, while making a tour of inspection, soon after the formation of the Imperial Service Troops, thus gives his impression of this corps: "The cavalry were specially fine. The gallant Rajput horsemen of Jhodpur had always been famous for their chivalrous bravery, unswerving fidelity, and fearless self-devotion in their wars with the Mahrattas and the armies of the Mogul Emperors, and I felt, as the superbly mounted squadrons passed before me, that they had lost none of their characteristics, and that blood and breeding must tell, and would, if put to the test, achieve the same

bred Arab." It is not necessary to add anything to this expression of opinion from so great an expert and so sincere a critic as Lord Roberts. Sir Pertab Singh's lancers have their reputation established, and no doubt will maintain it when occasion arises. On page 126 will be found a group composed of Sir Pertab Singh, his nephew —possibly the lad of nine who led the march-past in 1889, though he looks too old—and Major J. G. Turner, in command of the Viceroy's Body Guard, who came over with them. This corps is composed of about 100 picked sowars, with three native officers, the commandant and adjutant being the only British officers They were raised in 1773, and their principal duty is as indicated by their title. Major Turner, as captain, was in the Chitral Expedition of 1895, first as orderly officer, and afterwards as field intelligence officer. He was mentioned in despatches, and received the brevet rank of major. He wears the medal and clasp.

On this and the two following pages will be found fourteen portraits of Imperial Service officers, and of these—omitting for the moment the two Hyderabad Contingent

*Superintendent Rai Bahadur Jhanpat Rai Bahadur.*
Jeypore Transport Corps.

*Photos. Gregory.*
*Commandant Chatru Singh,*
Bhurtpore Lancers.

results now as of old. There could be but one opinion as to the value of the 'Sirdar' Cavalry, so named after the Maharajah's son and heir, Sirdar Singh, a lad of only nine years old, who led the little army past the saluting flag, mounted on a beautiful thorough-

officers—a few words must be said, though, as their titles are fully given, and but few of them have seen any service in their present positions, there is not very much to say. They are interesting chiefly as the outcome of a recently inaugurated scheme, which

Copyright.—H. & J.
*Rissaldar Abdul Majid Khan,*
Bahawalpore Lancers.

*Rissaldar-Major Husain Khan,*
2nd Lancers, Hyderabad Contingent.

*Rissaldar Thakur Daud Singh,*
Babnaghar Lancers.

*Commandant Abdul Gunny,*
Gwalior Lancers.

may very possibly be largely developed in the future. It will be of interest, no doubt, to note how the numbers are divided among the States. Kashmir takes the lead, with 380 cavalry, 3,600 infantry, and 300 artillery—a considerable force. Rissaldar-Major Sunnyat Singh is a relative of the Maharajah of Kashmir, and some of this corps took part in the Chitral Expedition of 1895.

Patiala comes next, with 600 cavalry and 1,200 infantry. Ulwar makes a good show, with 600 cavalry and 1,000 infantry. Of this corps Lord Roberts remarks : "At Ulwar I found the

600 cavalry and 1,000 infantry (all Rajputs) well advanced in their drill and training. This was evidently owing to the personal interest taken in them by the Maharajah, who seldom allowed a day to pass without visiting the parade grounds."

Gwalior supplies 1,525 cavalry—nearly three regiments, according to the ordinary strength of cavalry regiments in India ; Jhodpur, as already noticed, 1,200 cavalry ; the Jeypore Transport Corps musters 800 strong. This corps has already rendered important service, and the superintendent, with the

*Commandant Nasir Khan,*
Rampur Lancers.

*Commandant Daud Singh,*
Ulwar Lancers.

*Commandant Nand Singh,*
Patiala Lancers.

*Commandant Didar Singh,*
Jind Lancers.

*Commandant Kishan Singh,*
Nabha Lancers.

*Rissaldar-Major Myrab Ali Khan,*
3rd Lancers, Hyderabad Contingent.

very long name, on page 126, is an old and tried warrior, having seen service in many engagements, dating back to before the Mutiny. In his capacity as superintendent of the Jeypore Transport Corps he was at Chitral, where he and his men did well; and he is now, no doubt, at the front with General Lockhart, where his men are again responsible for the transport, and are having a lively time with the Afridis, whose strong point appears to be looting supplies. He has been granted the Order of British India.

Of the remaining corps represented, Bhurtpore has 500 cavalry and 650 infantry; Jind, Nabha, and Kapurthala, 150 cavalry and 600 infantry each; Bahawalpore, 150 cavalry and

420 infantry; Bikanir and Indore, 500 cavalry each; and Rampur, 300 cavalry.

Of the British officers who accompanied them, Major Drummond saw service in the Afghan War of 1878-80. He was twice mentioned in despatches, and wears the medal with clasp. Colonel Melliss served with the Abyssinian Expedition in 1868, was assistant quartermaster-general of the Indian Contingent in Egypt in 1882, where he was mentioned in despatches and received the brevet rank of major, and was also attached to the Burmese Expedition of 1885 as military attaché to the Naval Commander-in-Chief. He wears the medals for all these campaigns, with clasps, besides the 4th

Photos. Gregory

*Rissaldar-Major Sunnyat Singh,*
Kashmir Lancers.

*Commandant Govind Rao Mutka,*
Indore Lancers.

Copyright M-H. & A.

*Rissaldar Hara Singh,*
Kapurthala Lancers.

Photo. F. W. Bremner, Quetta.

NATIVE OFFICER AND NON-COMMISSIONED OFFICER, CENTRAL INDIA HORSE.

Copyright.

class Medjidie and the Khedive's bronze star. Captain Angelo served in the Soudan Campaign of 1885—medal and clasp.

On page 130 will be found two pictures of the Mysore Lancers, who also belong to the Imperial Service Corps, and muster 600 strong. These, with one or two smaller States, contribute each their quota to the Imperial Defence. And now it is time to look at the two portraits on page 127, which represent officers of the Hyderabad Contingent. Many of our readers may not know what the Hyderabad Contingent is, or why it exists. The title seems, to say the least of it, extremely vague; and, indeed, this corps is sufficiently vague in character, being, in fact, " neither fish, flesh, fowl, nor good red herring." It is not a Native Army corps in the same sense as those of Bengal, etc.; it is not an Imperial Service corps; it is not the Army of a Native State in any true sense. However, not to weary the reader any more by what may be called the negative eliminatory process, let us see what it is. We have to go a little way back in the history of India to get at it. As long ago as 1776, a treaty was signed with the Nizam of Hyderabad by which, on certain considerations, a force was to be maintained for the Nizam's service. Then followed many vicissitudes, and the Nizam, chiefly through his own fickleness, entered on troublous times. When he suffered—as he did—for his lack of fidelity, he came back to us and made another treaty; and all this time the contingent was being faithfully maintained by us, though the Nizam's payments were very much in arrears. He was treated, however, with amazing consideration, in spite of repeated acts, or threatened acts, of treachery, and when he joined with us against Tippoo Sahib—after having very nearly joined with him against us—he received a reward very disproportionate to the moderate amount of service he had rendered. Still the payments for the contingent were getting more and more in arrears. Nizam Ali died in 1803, and his son reigned for twenty-six years. Then the latter's son came on, and had a long reign, with more misgovernment and more arrears. At length the Government would stand it no longer, and insisted on the surrender of the province of Berar, to pay for the cost of maintaining the contingent. This was arranged, and the revenue of Berar does pay for the contingent to this day, with something to spare, which, in accordance with the treaty, is paid over to the Nizam, who does not need it in the least. He has at present an immense army of his own, which he could probably increase largely at very short notice; and the Hyderabad Contingent, a relic of the past, remains as a counterpoise to this army, which outnumbers it by at least five to one.

The contingent consists now of four regiments of lancers, four batteries of field artillery, and six regiments of infantry, with a much larger relative number of British officers than

*N.C.O. and Trooper.*
Mysore Lancers.

other native regiments   There are not wanting those who say that the Hyderabad Contingent had far better be abolished, and an equivalent force added to the regular Native Army.

Photos. Barton, Son & Co.                *GUARD TENT—MYSORE LANCERS.*                Bangalore.

THE GUNS AND GUNNERS OF INDORE.

The Officers of the Army of Indore.

From Photos.    Non-Commissioned Officers of Indore.    By a Military Officer.

Possibly there might be some difficulty with the Nizam as to the terms under which Berar was ceded to us, or as to the use of its revenues for other purposes; but treaties are not necessarily intended to be everlasting, and with reference to the Nizam of Hyderabad, or his predecessors, they were made and abrogated very freely for a great number of years.

The two native officers who represent the Hyderabad Contingent on page 127 have both been a long time in the force. Rissaldar-Major Husain Khan, of the 2nd Lancers, has thirty-seven years' service, and comes of a family of soldiers. Rissaldar-Major Myrab Ali Khan has twenty-nine years' service, and was in Afghanistan, for which he wears the medal, and also in the Burmese War of 1886. He is considered a good man, and has carried off honours at friendly competitions in polo, tent-pegging, and shooting.

We now come to another corps, which does not appear in the lists of the four Native Army corps, and so may be termed "irregular." The Central India Horse was raised in 1860 and 1861, for service ordinarily in Central India, but to be available on emergency for general service. It consists of two regiments, composed of Sikhs, Pathans, Rajputs, and Punjabi Mahomedans, each being about 600 strong, with a large staff of British officers. They are represented on pages 125 and 129, and Rissaldar-Major Baha-Uddin Khan Sardar Bahadur is a veteran of long and honourable service, in several different regiments. He began his career in 1851, in the 3rd Punjab Native Infantry, and during the Frontier Wars, from that year to 1856, was in fourteen actions. Then came the Mutiny, when he appears in the 1st Sikh Cavalry, and took part in over thirty actions, including Lucknow, Delhi, and Cawnpore. This

*Photo. Platia Co.*
### PART OF A BULLOCK SIEGE TRAIN.
*Secunderbad.*

is a tolerably good record to start with; but Baha-Uddin Khan had a great many more fights before him. He was in three engagements in the China War, where he was wounded and had his horse killed under him. In the later Afghan Wars he was again to the fore, in the 11th and 12th Bengal Lancers (formerly the Sikh Cavalry), and shared in twenty-five actions, he and his horse being both wounded at Charasiah. On the famous Cabul and Candahar march he rendered valuable service in collecting supplies. He also formed part of Sir Louis Cavagnari's escort, and was entrusted at the time of the fatal attack with a message from Sir Louis to the Ameer—a message which was met by a characteristically evasive reply, amounting practically to a passive acquiescence in the murder of the Envoy and his companions. Though on furlough at the time, he came out to meet Lord Roberts as he approached Cabul, and offered his services, afterwards rendering important assistance in the capture of the murderers. Finally, in the Central India Horse, he greatly distinguished himself in December, 1879, by leading a small party to blow in the door of a fort which was full of the enemy.

The medals which make such a goodly show on this old warrior's breast include the Mutiny, with one clasp, China, with one clasp, Ambeyla, with one clasp, and Afghanistan, with four clasps, besides the Order of Merit, for the gallant action above alluded to, and the 1st class Order of British India. He was also awarded the complimentary title of Sardar Bahadur for his services. He has suffered heavy losses at the hands of his co-religionists on account of his fidelity to the British, for which the Government have partly compensated him, and he has testimonials from Lord Roberts and other distinguished officers, speaking of him in the highest terms. An honourable record, indeed. It seems rather a pity that the crowd on Jubilee Day were not acquainted with the personality and services of this fine old soldier. He would have received a good shout, beyond question.

The officer and non-commissioned officer of the Central India Horse are representatives of a good type of native cavalry. These regiments have on their colours, Afghanistan, 1879-80, and Candahar, 1880. Their uniform is of a workmanlike drab colour, with maroon facings.

On page 131 will be found some illustrations of the Army of Holkar, ruler of Indore. These are not, however, attached to the Imperial Service Corps, in which Indore, as has been stated, is only represented by cavalry. Ho'kar's guns are not exactly up to date, being apparently ancient muzzle-loaders of a very short pattern. The non-commissioned officers are a creditable-looking group, and, no doubt, the officers will endeavour to bring themselves and their men up to a modern standard of efficiency.

On page 132 are some illustrations of Indian heavy artillery, and very remarkable the patient oxen and unwieldy elephants appear in conjunction with their warlike surroundings. One is accustomed from time immemorial to connect the horse with battle scenes, and the gallant and dashing field artillery of the British Army are famous for their rapid movements and skilful handling, the horses appearing to know almost as much about it as the gunners and drivers. The elephant, indeed, is no whit behind the horse in this respect. There appears to be very little which he does not understand, and for the transport of siege trains one cannot imagine a more valuable animal. The gentle ox appears much more out of place, but is, doubtless, of great service in the same line, though it takes a good many of him to make up an elephant.

Here must end our necessarily brief account of Her Majesty's Native Indian Army, which, in conjunction with the Colonial Forces, has been so prominently brought under public notice in England during the present year. The subject is a very large one, and we have been compelled to confine it within bounds by only alluding, in most instances, to those regiments or individuals who are represented in the illustrations.

It is to be hoped, however, that the impetus given to popular interest in our Indian defences by the celebration of the Queen's Jubilee will not soon die out, for it is a question of vital moment that those defences should be as efficient as it is possible to make them, in order to hold and develop the vast Empire added to our realm by the efforts of our forefathers, and consolidated in the reign of Her Majesty Queen Victoria.

### A UNIT OF AN ELEPHANT BATTERY.

# THE
# NAVY & ARMY
## ILLUSTRATED.

Vol. V.—No. 53.]        *FRIDAY, DECEMBER 24th, 1897.*

Photo. W. M. CROCKETT, Plymouth.                                    Copyright.—HUDSON & KEARNS.

*Colonel E. L. ROSE, Commandant, Plymouth Division of Royal Marine Light Infantry.*

COLONEL EDWARD LEE ROSE has served for over thirty-eight years in his distinguished corps. He was born on the 8th December, 1841; entered the Service as second lieutenant 14th April, 1859, and was promoted to first lieutenant 22nd December, 1860; captain, 24th January, 1874, major, 1st July, 1881; lieutenant-colonel, 1st February, 1886; colonel, 1st February, 1890; became second commandant 23rd March, 1892; and was appointed to his present responsible post of commandant 8th September, 1895. The appointment is not one to which an officer rises in his turn by seniority, but is made by selection, and is, of necessity, the last one held before retirement, which may be regarded as fairly earned after over forty years' service. Colonel Rose served in the rank of major with the Marine battalion at the defence of Suakin during the operations in the Eastern Soudan in 1884 and 1885, when the Royal Marines distinguished themselves by their steadiness and efficiency under trying circumstances; he wears the Egyptian medal and the Khedive's bronze star. He is a man of quiet manner and pleasing personality, and commands the confidence and goodwill of his subordinates

# The Plymouth Division of Royal Marines.

*Colonel W. P. Wright (2nd Commandant), and Lieut.-Colonels T. F. Bridge and R. B. Kirchhoffer.*

*The Staff-Sergeants of the Division.*

Photos. W. M. CROCKETT, Plymouth.        Copyright.—HUDSON & KEARNS

## THE OFFICERS OF THE PLYMOUTH DIVISION OF MARINES.

THE first group on this page represents three distinguished officers of the Plymouth Division, the central figure being that of Colonel William Purvis Wright, who entered the Service 31st December, 1852, and was appointed colonel second commandant, 20th November, 1895. On the right is Lieutenant-Colonel Robert Brooke Kirchhoffer, who entered the Service 28th December, 1864. He served as quartermaster of the battalion of Royal Marines sent to South Africa for special service in the Zulu War of 1879, and was also in the Egyptian Campaign of 1882. He wears the Egyptian medal and the Khedive's bronze star. On the left, in profile, is Lieutenant-Colonel Thomas Field Dunscomb Bridge, who entered the Service 26th June, 1866. He served as adjutant with the Marine battalion in the Soudan in 1884 and 1885, capturing a rebel standard at Tulufik on 22nd March, 1885. He wears the Egyptian medal, with clasp for To Frek, and the Khedive's bronze star. In the next group, reckoning from the left, we have Staff-Sergeants Owen, Martin, and McCrae, standing, and Staff-Sergeant Mitchell seated. Sergeant Martin naturally claims attention from his fine display of decorations, which include the Egyptian medal, with clasp for Abu Klea—a memorable engagement—and the Nile, 1884; the Khedive's bronze star; Ashanti medal, with clasp for Witu, 1890; and the long service and good conduct medal. Sergeant Martin may also, without disparagement, be termed a "horse marine," for he served in the mounted infantry and camel corps in Egypt. Sergeants McCrae and Mitchell wear the long service and good conduct medal, a testimonial which is not to be despised. The officers in the lower illustration are grouped round a gun which was captured in the last Burmese War, and was presented to the division by the War Office; the commandant and second commandant stand by either wheel.

THE sergeants' mess numbers some 115 members, of whom over 90 are here represented, the remainder being embarked or absent on detached duties. The commandant and adjutant occupy a central position, immediately in rear of the men who are sitting down. This is an eminently soldier-like group of veterans, in every respect worthy of the high reputation of their corps, and a large sprinkling of war medals bears witness to the part they have borne in active service for their country, some individuals displaying three or four decorations. The dress of the sergeant of the boat's crew presents a curious contrast to that of the remainder, illustrating in a forcible manner the motto "Per mare, per terram."

The entrance hall, or tiled vestibule of the officers' mess, is chiefly remarkable for the interesting collection of trophies of war, referred to elsewhere. On the left are the two brass guns from Japan and the Chinese "jingals," or big wall-muskets. The near trophy on the left includes some of the formidable Japanese swords, with their heavy razor-like blades, and a shield, armour, and arrows from the same country. A South African shield and assegais figure beyond the door, and a grand trophy of various rifles and spears from Egypt and the Soudan adorns the further wall, while overhead hang two star and crescent flags.

The illustration below shows the side of the Barrack Square nearest the main entrance, which is flanked by two turrets, the one carrying a clock and the other a wind indicator, from which one may infer that the Royal Marines preserve on shore a vivid recollection of the interest which the direction of the wind necessarily has for them at sea. On the right the function of "mounting guard" is in process, while on the left the men on turn for embarkation are being mustered and inspected, to see that they are fit and ready in every respect to be marched off.

*Commandant, Adjutant, and Members of Sergeants' Mess.*

*Entrance Hall of Officers' Mess.*

*GUARD MOUNTING and MEN for EMBARKATION MUSTERING for INSPECTION.*

*FIELD TRAINING.—Making a Bridge.*

*CLASS AT FIELD MACHINE GUN.*

*A LECTURE ON FIELD TRAINING.*

THE upper illustration represents a field training class engaged in the task of constructing what is technically known as a "single-lock bridge." This is, of course, an engineering operation, but the Marines appear to have tackled it successfully. The materials are of a rough description, and the rapid construction of such a bridge may obviously be sometimes of the utmost importance. Here, again, is the practical use of machine guns, the deadliest of light modern weapons. The Gardner gun on the left is discharging a stream of fire which would certainly be awkward to face, while on the right is the Maxim gun, being laid for the object; three men in rear are placing the cartridges in the strips of canvas which are used to feed the gun when it discharges a number of rounds automatically. Two recruit officers are included in the class, and have to go through the course in precisely the same manner as the rank and file. The lower picture shows a field training class receiving a lecture from Lieutenant-Colonel Bridge, who stands on the right of the left-hand group. The arrangement of the men in three ranks—standing, kneeling, and sitting—is characteristic of the systematic method adopted; every man can see and hear distinctly, but those in the sitting rank have obviously the best of the bargain. In the background is an exceedingly quiet and inoffensive specimen of a mule—a wooden dummy on which practical instruction is afforded of the operation of loading a live one, which would possibly afford more diversion under the process.

*Photo. W. M. CROCKETT, Plymouth*

COPYRIGHT.—*HUDSON & KEARNS.*

## CONVERGED FIRING.

THIS represents a scene in the battery. The guns have been laid at a certain angle, so as to converge their fire on a point at a given range. The connections are then made with the electrical circuit, and the crews lie down, in order to be in a more favourable position at the moment of the shock of ramming, and one also of greater security from fragments of shells, etc. They have nothing to do with firing the guns, which is effected by the officer in the conning-tower. The sights of the " director " there are aligned to correspond with the guns, and the most auspicious moment is seized to press the firing-key and discharge all the guns simultaneously as the vessel rushes on to ram her opponent. All this is represented in as realistic a manner as is possible in a stationary battery on shore. Looking at the picture it is not difficult to realise the intense suppressed excitement at such a moment in actual warfare, the silence on the gun-deck, the penetration from without and above of various sounds, the increased tension of nerves as the guns are discharged and the shock of impact becomes imminent.

*Knotting and Splicing.*

*" Form the Order of March."*

*Boat's Crew.*

*Orderly Men Taking Dinners.*

Photos. W. M. CROCKETT, Plymouth.                                              Copyright.—HUDSON & KEARNS.

## VARIETIES IN DRESS.

ON this page is represented, in the first picture, a class under instruction in the mysteries of knotting and splicing. They have formed the "clove hitch" in its first stage, and the instructor is pointing out on the board the form it should assume when completed, one of its principal uses being to secure the "ratlines" across the rigging, now perhaps nearly obsolete. The "order of march" and the cook-house call for little remark. In the former the field machine gun's crew are in their places on the drag-ropes for moving the gun, and in the latter an orderly man from each barrack-room attends to take the dinners, arranged in the tins on the table. The boat's crew form a fine group in their semi-aquatic dress. They are under the quarter-master's department, and have various duties afloat in conveying ammunition from the magazine at Bull Point, taking clothing, etc., to men embarked in the harbour, and so on. Two are employed in the steam pinnace, and they have also orderly duties. They are picked men, and make fine oarsmen. Below are represented types in various dress. The two drummers, Sergeant-Major Perry (in line with the doorway), and the two privates on the flanks, are in marching order; the two privates near the flanks in rear are in drill order; while Sergeant-Major Blacker (with his hand on the wheel) and the two sergeants are in undress.

Photo. W. M. CROCKETT, Plymouth.

Copyright—HUDSON & KEARNS.

## THE SQUARE, WITH BATTALION IN MARCHING ORDER.

HERE is represented the Barrack Square, with the battalion paraded in marching order. The buildings along the further side are the men's quarters, and in the distance, rising above the roof, may be seen part of the fine Admiralty schools, attended by the children of the Marines. The barracks were built in 1781, but have since been improved and extended. Previous to that date the Marines were billeted about the Citadel, and probably enjoyed very few of the comforts which they now so fully appreciate in their commodious and well-built barracks. There is ample room in the square to manœuvre a large number of men, and it will be noticed that the body mustered on this occasion occupies but a small portion of the space. The strength present is eighteen officers (exclusive of the colonel commandant and staff officers), one warrant officer, and 271 rank and file. This somewhat meagre display is accounted for by the unusually large number of men embarked at the time, and the absence of a whole company on detached duty; besides, of course, many who are on the strength but are engaged in various necessary duties. The officers stand out in front with their swords at the "carry," the adjutant, Captain Bendyshe, flanking them on the left; the other mounted officers are the Colonel Commandant, Lieutenant-Colonel Kirchhoffer, Major Eagles, and Captain Vincent, staff officer; and the colours—presented to the division in July last by H.R.H. the Duke of Saxe-Coburg—are carried by Lieutenants Rooney and Hood. The average length of service of the men present is about six years, and there are many veterans among them who have seen active service on shore and afloat. On the left flank the band is drawn up; it numbers forty-two, and is under the charge of Mr. F. Winterbottom, who ranks as a warrant officer. The bands of the Royal Marines are famous for their efficiency, and are frequently in request on various festive occasions. In front of the band are the drums and fifes, numbering 34, and composed of buglers ranging from fourteen years old and upwards. They play alternately with the regular band in route marching, marching detachments to and from head-quarters, and "beat off" at sunset and tattoo daily. The principal occasions upon which the battalion is thus paraded in review order or marching order are the visits of the Lords of the Admiralty and the Deputy Adjutant-General of Royal Marines. Their lordships are, no doubt, good judges of general effect, but the Deputy Adjutant-General comes as an expert, and examines everything and everybody with a critical eye. The post is held at present by Lieutenant-General Sir Henry B. Tuson, K.C.B., of the Royal Marine Artillery, an officer of long and distinguished service. The Marines take a just pride in their "turn out" on such occasions, and their precision and steadiness in parade movements, and admirable marching past, are always remarked upon by military critics, sometimes with a note of astonishment; and it is, indeed, somewhat remarkable that men who spend so much of their time exercising their "sea legs" in preserving their balance on the ever-shifting deck, should carry off the palm for efficiency in such pure and simple "soldiering." Such, however, is the fact, and it only goes to show the thoroughness of their training and the practical outcome of their strong *esprit de corps.*

*FIRE BRIGADE AT DRILL.*

*Photos. W. M. CROCKETT, Plymouth.*

*SERGEANTS' MESS-ROOM.*

THE fire engine and fire escape, as will be seen from the dress of the men, are in charge of the boat's crew, who take a proper pride in the smart handling of them. The engine throws a powerful jet, and in the background some men are being "rescued" from a window by means of the fire escape. The little dog which occupies a prominent position on the engine has attached himself, with characteristic canine eccentricity, to this department. He rejoices in the name of "Jack," and evidently considers himself every inch a fireman. The sergeants' mess-room, represented below, is interesting as affording evidence of the advance which has been made of late years in the status of the senior non-commissioned officers, and the accommodation provided for them. The large silver epergne on the table was purchased by the mess, but the remainder are trophies won by members of the corps in rifle and other contests. The small portrait, second from the right in the illustration, is that of Colour-Sergeant Prettyjohn, who was among the early winners of the Victoria Cross in the Crimea, and whose memory is justly held in high esteem by his comrades.

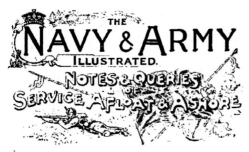

THE NAVY & ARMY ILLUSTRATED. NOTES & QUERIES SERVICE AFLOAT & ASHORE

"G. T." asks: "What are the orders of the Marine sentry on the fore-bridge of a commissioned ship at sea?" and "Is there any difference in the work and duties, ashore and afloat, of the Marine Artillery and Infantry, or are they practically the same?" In a manner the answer to the first question is very simple, because there is no sentry on the fore-bridge when a ship is at sea. Directly a ship gets under way, the fore-bridge sentry takes off his waist-belt, returns his rifle, and is transferred to "sentry over the lifebuoy," where his duties are simply to look out for the case of a man falling overboard, when he should immediately lower a lifebuoy to his assistance. Possibly the query is provoked by our omission in a recent issue, when writing about the lifebuoy, to mention that it is specially placed under the charge of a Marine sentry. The duties of the sentry on the fore-bridge of a man-of-war at anchor are, in addition to routine work: (a) To pay usual compliments to officers passing the ship; (b) To keep off all unauthorised boats from the ship's side, and after dark to challenge all boats passing; (c) To call "All's well" every time the bell is struck after retreat; (d) To fire his rifle at retreat. In sailing ships he unfixes his bayonet when men are at work aloft.

* * * *

On board ship the difference between the work of the *Royal* Marine Artillery and the *Royal* Marine *Light* Infantry is only in degree, not in kind. The Artillery take the most important and most responsible numbers at the guns manned by Marines. The great difference between the two branches of the corps is in their training ashore. The Royal Marine Artillery are selected in the first place for their superior physique, but in the second for their superior intelligence, as evinced by an examination at the end of their first course of gunnery training. The men thus selected for the artillery branch then go through a long and careful course of gunnery, comprising not only the sea service drills, but also field battery and siege and coast defence work, as taught to the Royal Artillery, whom they are thus trained to supplement or replace in land operations. The light infantry, after a course of Naval gunnery, in which it is not obligatory for them to qualify, are prepared for the fight ashore by a course of infantry field training, culminating, perhaps, in a month's manœuvres with the Aldershot Division.

* * * *

Sir Ralph Abercromby, one of those heroes of the British Army whose names should be "freshly remembered," was born in Scotland in 1734, was educated at Rugby School and Edinburgh University, and, when he got his cornetcy in the 3rd Dragoon Guards, was described as being "of prepossessing appearance and with polished manners." In 1758 he went to Germany, and served as A.D.C. to General Sir W. Pitt, after which period he rose steadily through the regimental grades till, in 1773, we find him lieutenant-colonel of his regiment, and, at the same time, serving his country as a Member of Parliament. In 1783 he went on half-pay, and devoted himself to the duties of a country gentleman. He was conscientious and thoughtful, a kind friend to his poorer neighbours, and a warm promoter of education, keeping, withal, his mind and body in a state of perfect training. Such was Major-General Abercromby when, at nearly sixty years of age, he was called to enter on the last and most brilliant epoch of his military career. He eagerly embraced the opportunity of serving in Flanders, and so distinguished himself that he was repeatedly and publicly thanked by the Duke of York. He was in his sixty-sixth year when he took up the military command in the Mediterranean, landed his troops in Egypt in the face of well-posted cavalry, artillery, and infantry, and finally, by his defeat of the French, decided the future of Egypt, and prepared the way for the conclusion of peace. He died of wounds received in that battle, a determined and skilful commander, and a strict disciplinarian, but trusted and loved by his soldiers

My correspondent "F. L."—whom, by the caligraphy, I should take to be of the fair sex—need have no fear. The open throat afforded by the style of clothes our sailors wear is conducive to health rather than otherwise. Most medical men are in agreement as to the hygienic advantages that accrue; and, if statistics prove anything, they show a remarkable absence of pulmonary complaints among bluejackets, notwithstanding that, in all weathers, it is so common a custom among sailors to go barefoot as well as with exposed chests. The wearing of comforters is, indeed, permitted in the Service; but it cannot be said they are held in great favour. Neither are monkey-jackets forbidden; yet, as hindering the free use of limb, the principle aimed at in the seaman's dress, to see them in actual use signifies Arctic temperature.

* * * *

The military forces of New South Wales consist principally of a sort of militia termed the "partially paid forces," horse, foot, and artillery, but there is in addition a permanent force of artillery, garrison and field. Their uniform is similar to the Imperial Artillery, with the exception of the helmet, which has the national badge of N.S.W. in front. Several forts on the coast, and especially at the entrance to Sydney Harbour, are manned by the Garrison Artillery and kept in most excellent and efficient order. The Field Artillery consist of three batteries, A, B, and C, of four guns. The strength of A Battery, which is the only one permanently manned, is twenty-two officers and non-commissioned officers, fifty-five gunners, etc. B and C, which belong to the "partially paid" forces, and are horsed by A Battery when necessary, have each twenty officers and non-commissioned officers, fifty gunners, etc. Nearly all these officers and men are Australian born and trained. Their standard is very high, and they are undoubtedly a splendid corps. Victoria Barracks in Sydney, built originally for the Imperial troops, were some years ago turned over to the Colonial Government, and are now occupied by the Permanent Artillery. This force formed the principal part of the contingent sent to Egypt in 1885. The present arrangement of the Field Artillery was formed under Major-General Hutton, when reconstructing the military forces of the colony. They were then placed under the command of Major H. P. Airey, D.S.O., who went to India for special training with the Royal Horse Artillery.

* * * *

My "specialist" correspondent, who wishes to become a "military mechanist" in the Royal Engineers, should present himself at any recruiting station, and if he passes the medical examination, his name will be submitted to the Deputy-Adjutant-General, R.E. If accepted, he will be sent to Chatham for drill and musketry, and then go through the field works course, or be drafted to the submarine mining companies. In peace and war the Royal Engineers have many duties to perform, including the design, construction, and maintenance of all War Department works, buildings, machinery, and accessories; the preparation of camping grounds; the making of roads, bridges, and canals; the construction and working of railways, telegraphs, balloons, torpedoes, and electric lighting arrangements; the attack and defence of fortresses and positions; and " such other engineer services as may be required." A list of recognised trades is appended to the recruiting regulations, but "men of other trades likely to be useful in the corps" may be accepted under the authority of the Deputy-Adjutant-General. This provides a probable opening for almost every kind of engineer, but it must be remembered that mechanists on probation will be required to come up to a high standard of duty and education. Were it not so, they would be unworthy of the rank and prospects offered to them, and the older soldiers over whose heads they pass would justly feel aggrieved.

* * * *

In reply to "M. P.," I give the following information: The first muster of the Royal Horse Guards (the Blues) took place on 16th February, 1661. Its colonel was Aubrey De Vere, twentieth and last Earl of Oxford, who had previously been colonel of an English regiment in the Dutch Service (now "The Buffs"), to which he had been appointed in 1648. "His Majesty's Own Troop" was commanded by Captain Daniel O'Neale, and the other troops respectively by Sir Francis Wyndham, Lord Hawley, Sir Charles Compton, Sir Edward Bret, Sir Henry Wroth, and Colonel John Fretchville. The captain-lieutenant of the regiment was Thomas Armstrong, afterwards implicated in Monmouth's Rebellion and executed without trial, at Tyburn, in 1684; the cornet (of the regiment), Edward Sheldon, and the quartermaster, William Montgomery. Henry Compton, the cornet of Sir Charles Compton's troop, afterwards took Holy Orders, and became Bishop of London in 1675.

The Editor.

THE astonishing growth of Service literature, and the need of keeping Naval and Military men, and the far larger number of those who possess a keen and abiding interest in the Navy and the Army, abreast of the times, have led to the inclusion in these columns of a "Service Book-shelf." As one passes one's prophetic eye along the books that are to be ranged there, what does one find prepared for the survey? "Oh, for a booke, and a shadie nooke!" cried the old English songster, and here shall presently appear, almost in fleets and battalions, many a "jollie goode booke whereon to looke," we think, when the reading season comes on. Are they merely professional works? By no means. Many touch the history of the Services; not a few are volumes of biography, travel, sport, adventure—all such as concern Service men and their friends; several are works on Imperial politics; a few on equipments, orders, and decorations; others are works of fiction.

The first volume upon which I place my hand is one that will not fail to attract many. It is Mr. David Hannay's "Short History of the Royal Navy" (Methuen, 7s. 6d.), being one of a couple which are to cover that history from 1217, to our own time, I believe. This first volume concludes at the great dividing line of 1688. Here is a book compounded with the skill of a master. It is no dry compilation abounding in classified lists for the student, but a brightly-penned narrative, abounding with interest and with freshness of conception. There was need for such a book, and Mr. Hannay, in his "Rodney" and "Hood's Letters," has shown his full competence for the work. I should have liked to quote many of his spirited stories, but there is no space for that. He passes rapidly up to Tudor times, and gives a vigorous picture of our contest with Spain. He does not magnify our adversaries by any means, and, though full of admiration for the seaman-like qualities of Hawkins and Drake, the unctuous piety of one and very business-like quality of the other do not tempt him to put them upon exalted pedestals. Then Mr. Hannay hastens forward to the Dutch Wars, which he treats in most effective fashion; and I was particularly glad to find him dealing so capably with the little-known events in the Mediterranean. With quite astonishing skill he has contrived to weave in with his narrative a sufficient record of the progress of administration and of the material means prepared for the seaman's hand.

When I had laid Mr. Hannay's volume down, I took up the "English Historical Review" for October (Longmans, 5s.), and found there an article by Mr. E. Armstrong upon the Armada, which, in part, confirms Mr. Hannay's conclusions. It is a most astonishing picture, seen through the spectacles of Venetian ambassadors. Here are the Powers philandering with the Turk, and the Turk, *more suo,* promising much and doing nothing. Philip labours to build up his Fleet; Drake singes his beard; Philip goes at it, toiling and moiling, again; Santa Cruz protests that he cannot work miracles; Sidonia vows that he has no stomach for the task; and Sixtus V. looks on, despising Philip, admiring the earnestness of the Queen, and discerning, too, something more in Drake than Mr. Hannay. "Have you heard," says Sixtus, "how Drake has offered battle to the Armada? With what courage! Do you think he showed any fear? He is a great captain!"

What Mr. Hannay is doing for the Navy, Colonel C. Cooper King has done for our Military forces in the "Story of the British Army" (Methuen, 7s. 6d.). This, too, is a popular work, carrying us from the day when Ethelred fought with the Danes, even to the present time. The Saxon fighting man, the mediæval knight, and the Dugald Dalgettys of the mercenary wars, with the men who "had some conscience in what they did," pass before us in their occupations, achievements, and costumes, these last, by the way, admirably illustrated. Then we have Marlborough and his men, the Peninsular Army, the fighting in the Netherlands, and all that has succeeded, dealt with very satisfactorily. Incidentally a number of ideas are propounded which want of space will not allow me to deal with.

It is well known that most country houses are rich in historic portraits, but it is, perhaps, not so well known that the Director of the National Portrait Gallery is taking steps to induce the possessors of these to catalogue them. A good portrait is a wonderful help to history. When you look at the *debonnaire* face of Charles, the determined features of Cromwell, the resolute and thoughtful face of Nelson, or the strongly-marked features of the Great Duke, you feel that you know the man much better than if he had been merely described to you. Mr. Henry B. Wheatley, who has edited the new edition of Pepys, is a veritable pioneer in his "Historical Portraits" (Bell, 10s. 6d.). His knowledge of the subject is perhaps unrivalled, and, although he is modest enough to say that he has merely scratched the surface, his book is remarkably instructive. When I say that the pictures number nearly seventy, I merely indicate what an excellent treasure-house Mr. Wheatley has provided.

Among the wonders of cheap books made accessible to a wide public, surely nothing can be more attractive than Nansen's "Farthest North" (Newnes), being published in sixpenny parts. The paper, type, and pictures, both plain and coloured, are in every way equal to the original issue.

Other books to be read:—

"History of the Foreign Policy of Great Britain," New Edition, by Montagu Burrows. (Blackwood.)

"Stray Military Papers," by Lieutenant-Colonel H. W. L. Hyme, late R.A. (Longmans.)

"Tactics as Applied to Schemes," by Major J. Sherston, Second Edition. (Thacker.)

"SEARCH-LIGHT."

## The Royal Marine Barracks, Plymouth.

### By Commander E. P. Statham, R.N.

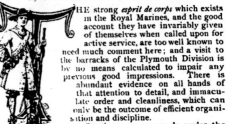

THE strong *esprit de corps* which exists in the Royal Marines, and the good account they have invariably given of themselves when called upon for active service, are too well known to need much comment here; and a visit to the barracks of the Plymouth Division is by no means calculated to impair any previous good impressions. There is abundant evidence on all hands of that attention to detail, and immaculate order and cleanliness, which can only be the outcome of efficient organisation and discipline.

Starting on our rounds under the efficient guidance of the adjutant, Captain R. N. Bendyshe, the first place of which inspection is invited is the sergeants' mess, Sergeant-Major Blacker being summoned to do the honours. The sergeant-major is very proud of the mess, and with good reason, for it is not easy to imagine that it could well be surpassed by any other. The principal room has been recently painted and renovated, and is very lofty, a room above having been thrown in. Round the tastefully-decorated walls appear a number of portraits of officers and men, past and present, and above these the names of various places at which the Marines have been in action; while on a sideboard is displayed a fine array of silver cups, etc., chiefly won in rifle and athletic contests by members of the corps. Another large room opens from the first, in which is a billiard table, various games, etc., and a library.

In the men's recreation-room, which is quite as excellent in its own degree, there are billiard tables, bagatelle boards, books and papers, a roaring fire, and admirable order and cleanliness. Nor is this the only space at their disposal, for there is another large recreation-room adjoining the canteen, which is handy for those who wish to indulge in the cheering cup round the fire; while hard by is a smaller room, set apart for the junior non-commissioned officers, so that every man, when he is advanced even to lance-corporal's rank, finds his position recognised, and adequate provision made for his comfort.

The canteen comes next, divided into "dry" and "wet" departments, the latter, of course, being devoted to the sale of malt liquors, while the former is a remarkable institution, in which can be obtained, at store prices, almost any article one may happen to require, and which must be pretty well appreciated by the men, judging from the fact that the money annually passed through it amounts to some £9,000.

The cook-house, which next claims attention, is commodious, very practical in its arrangements, and, of course, scrupulously clean. On the large ranges and boilers rations can be prepared, if necessary, for some 1,300 men, which represents about the maximum capacity of the barracks.

Near by is the ablution room, provided with ranges of metal basins and water laid on, to which the men have access at all times; and the latrines, a model of cleanliness and efficient sanitation.

The inspection of an orderly and comfortable barrack-room comes next on the programme, in which ten men are accommodated, though there are others which will berth a larger number.

A visit to the officers' mess is naturally a pleasant episode, if only on account of the kind and hospitable welcome accorded; but it is also very interesting, for there are many spoils of war and regimental heirlooms well worthy of notice. The mess-room—an exceptionally fine and lofty room—contains three sets of colours of various dates, the oldest displaying unmistakable evidences of the lapse of time. There is, however, another set, at present at Greenwich, which the Plymouth Division regards with covetous eyes, and which it is not impossible may be handed over to it some day. Here, also, is a large portrait of His Majesty William IV., Lord High Admiral, of which the other divisions have each a copy; and a chair which was used by Napoleon at St. Helena, presented by Lieutenant-Colonel Elliot in 1894. In the small tiled vestibule, lighted overhead, is a trophy of arms from Egypt, comprising rifles of several descriptions, a Soudanese spear or two, by each of which there hangs a tale of personal adventure or prowess; tattered flags, with the star and crescent; two small brass guns, from Simonoseki, in Japan; and two Chinese "jingals," which probably correspond nearly with the "arquebus" of the Middle Ages in Europe—a sort of magnified smooth-bore, very long in the barrel, and throwing a ball of over an inch in diameter. Perhaps the most interesting point about them is that they are breech-loaders; the mechanism, if it is worthy the name, is certainly of the most primitive description, but there is the fact.

In the small ante-room, off the mess-room, is a blue ensign, which was flown by H.M.S. "Tartar" during the attack on Simonoseki, and testifies to the vigour of the Japanese fire by numerous shot-holes. In another room—and also in the sergeants' mess—is a portrait of a former veteran of the corps, General Sir F. Nicolls, K.C.B., known as the "fighting general," and with good reason, for he was in action no fewer than 107 times.

The officers' mess comprises, in addition to the large mess-room, an ante-room, smoking-room, breakfast-room, library, and billiard-room, and very snug quarters they are; but we must reluctantly quit them, for there is plenty more to be seen, and with a view to further investigation we are turned over to Quartermaster William Powell.

Under his guidance the provision-room is first inspected, where the staple commodities of meat and bread are on view, and they are obviously of first-rate quality. The allowance for each man daily is three-quarters of a pound of meat and one pound of bread.

The clothing department is most interesting, for the Royal Marines have their own ideas on the subject, and are quite independent of the Clothing Department at Pimlico except for a few ready-made articles, such as caps, belts, lace, etc. Every man is measured and fitted; and when it comes to the annual renewal every man of the division, in whatever part of the world he may chance to be serving, has his new clothes sent to him in time for issue in April, all made to measure, and altered, when necessary, by measurements sent home.

In the shoemakers' shop some nineteen or twenty men find employment. Boots are made in sixteen sizes, and any man with a peculiar foot is specially measured. Special boots, without projecting nails, are made for sea service, out of consideration for the wooden decks, and

— The Royal Marines at Tofreho.

the moral welfare of the commanding officer on board, who might be tempted to use unparliamentary language otherwise.

The tailors' shop presents a most animated scene. Huge piles of various materials are lying about, and clothing of every description is in process of manufacture. Here, also, is a historical "band-knife," an endless strip of steel, with a keen edge, passing through a slit in the table, and worked rapidly by mechanism. It is said to be the first one ever used, and was devised by the father of a master tailor now working there, and who relates that it was subsequently patented by some-one else—an old story which many inventors could tell.

The quartermaster's department has also charge of the manufacture of certain clothing for the bluejackets, some 500 women being employed at this. Indeed, a separate story might well be written about this department alone; but it is time to pass on, and in doing so, we inspect the wash-house, well fitted up with wooden washing troughs, boilers, and a capital centrifugal wringing machine; the armourers' shop and arm store; an American bowling alley and a shooting gallery; the works department, by which the buildings, etc., are kept in repair without invoking the aid of the Royal Engineers; and a store of complete equipment, rifles, clothing and all, for 800 men, kept always ready in case of emergency.

Bidding adieu to the energetic quartermaster, we are once more taken in hand by the adjutant, and a short walk in the rain brings us to the gun batteries, presided over at present by Captain Crowther, Instructor of Gunnery.

Every officer and recruit has to go through a fifty-three days' course of gunnery, and to renew his knowledge every three years by a twenty-eight days' course. The Instructor of Gunnery has to go through the gunnery lieutenant's course at Greenwich and in the "Excellent," and, moreover, he must obtain a first-class certificate. His appointment extends over five years, and during that time he is responsible for the efficient instruction of recruits and the requalification of others. He is assisted by a staff of sergeant instructors, who are trained in one of the gunnery ships, and must possess the same qualifications as gunnery instructors.

There are two gun batteries, the older one being reserved for guns of more or less obsolete pattern, still in use on board some of the older ships. The Royal Marines are, however, held in too high estimation by the Authorities to admit of their being left to languish with out-of-date appliances and weapons; and the newer and larger battery is of splendid dimensions and equipment. Here are some very much up-to-date breech-loaders, including the formidable 22-ton gun, more than one quick-firing 6-in. gun—a deadly weapon—and a little toy 4-in., quite new. The deadly Maxim gun is not forgotten, every man having to learn how to handle it so as to "squirt" bullets at the foe to the best advantage. Overhead is a conning-tower, with electrical circuit, to illustrate as fully as possible the various conditions under which the men may be called upon to work the guns at sea; and an ammunition-room completes the equipment of this very important and practical department, the gunnery course including also a day at target practice in one of the tenders of the "Cambridge" gunnery ship, and instruction in the knots, etc., in most common use on board ship, together with the mysteries of slinging and lashing up a hammock in a ship-shape fashion.

Truly, no trouble is spared to make the Royal Marine efficient when he goes afloat; but, as is well known, he is frequently called upon to act with force on shore, and his education in this respect is by no means neglected. He has to go through a six weeks' course of field training, during which he is taught how to become a dweller in tents, to construct temporary bridges, throw up intrenchments, and, among other accomplishments, to load a pack-mule.

Musketry is, of course, carried out under a separate instructor; but he is handicapped just now by the admirable qualities of the new rifle, which render the rifle range on Staddon Heights, overlooking the Channel, unsafe for practice.

There are efficient schools for the education of the boys and girls of the men belonging to the division, supported in great measure by the Admiralty, which provides the teachers; but the Education Department also allows a grant under the usual conditions, as is very right and proper.

The Royal Marines, like other people, have their grievances, and one of these at present is that they do not get enough men voted in the Estimates. Formerly a man, after serving afloat, would be in barracks for something like two years before his turn would come on again, but at the present time, owing, no doubt, in part, to the greater number of ships in commission, the intervening time in barracks does not greatly exceed six months as a rule, and is sometimes even less. This year there are 500 more men voted, which, however, only means about 160 to each division; and as it takes fully twelve months to render a man efficient, it will not tell for some time. Valuable as are the services of the Royal Marines afloat, it is obviously undesirable that the latter half of their pregnant and time-honoured motto should be disregarded by permitting the reserve in barracks to fall too low, for there are no better soldiers to be found.

# A CHRISTMAS HUNT ON A CHUR.

## by Colonel F. Pollok.

Horse, man and pig rolled on the ground.

WHEN the great rivers of India subside after their annual freshets, they leave large islands in their beds, which are called lunkahs on the Madras side, but churs in Assam.

The mighty Brahmapootra River is especially rich in these sandy islets, from Doobree downwards. The soil is enriched by the alluvial deposit left behind, and grass, reeds, null, and other jungle get most luxuriant, and harbour in their midst many varieties of wild beasts. The people living on the main banks burn the grass, and as soon as the new appears they take down their cattle to graze, building sheds for their accommodation during the nights. These attract the carnivora, and these, again, British and native sportsmen.

April and May are the favourite months for sport, but one Christmas, whilst constructing the Grand Trunk road, I found the chur near Doobree unusually full of tigers and other game. The rains had ceased early; the river had also subsided earlier than usual; the long grass had been burnt; and the new had grown to some two feet high.

It did not take me long to collect other sportsmen as fond of shooting and hunting as myself. Cooksley dropped down by steamer; Williamson came from Tara, Garrow Hills; and Butter, though no sportsman, was employed on superintending the survey, and joined us for the sake of good-fellowship. The valley of the Brahmapootra, during the cold months, is enveloped, during the nights and mornings, in the densest of fogs, and we hoped by starting early to find the game out in the open. So, on the morning of the 24th December, we sallied forth on elephants at daylight. We four went on well ahead, the beating elephants bringing up the rear at a respectful distance. So heavy was the fog that, although only a few yards apart, we often lost sight of one another.

Our guides took us to about the centre of the chur, where the vegetation was the densest. To get there we had to cross many channels, which were then dry; but which, during the monsoon, were roaring torrents. In the rains all the game, with the exception of a few buffalo, rhinoceros, and pig, migrate to the mainland, returning to the churs again directly the waters subside. With the exception of Butter, who only took my smooth-bore with him, we were all well armed. I had four rifles, Williamson and Cooksley three each.

At this time the dense fog had cleared away, and as we advanced we put up numerous hog; but, as they were in rideable ground, we left them alone, though the Cacharies in camp would have been glad of a little pork to eat.

We then came across a herd of marsh deer. Most of the stags had shed their horns, and were in hiding. One had not lost his yet, and Cooksley wounded him, but he ran on. He had not gone fifty yards when there was a rush, and a tiger rolled him over, and, with the greatest ease, carried him into a patch of long grass close by. The beating elephants were ordered to beat through it from the side opposite, towards us; and as the ground round us was fairly open, we hoped to make the tiger our own before half-an-hour. We took up our positions about twenty yards apart. The patch to be beaten was only about a hundred yards long by some fifty yards broad. As the line advanced we expected that the king of Indian beasts would show himself; but only an old grey boar, with many a grunt, champing his ivories, came out. It was sufficiently astonishing that there should be a boar in such a limited area with a tiger; but when time went by, and the elephants steadily marched along without uttering a single sound of alarm, we did not know what to make of it. The mahouts declared there was nothing there; so we, too, joined the beaters, and carefully retraced our steps. Yet there was not a sign of a tiger being there. We then formed line on the flank, and, with the elephants all but touching, we again advanced, and about the centre of the jungle discovered a deep crevasse, so enveloped in long grass as to be scarcely visible, and generally so narrow that the elephants must either have stepped across it or gone along its edge. We told the jemadar to send a large tusker in, and told the mahout to walk him along its bed. He did not half like the job, but we made him do it, and kept pretty close to him, two on one side and I on the other. Our elephants showed the greatest nonchalance, pulling up succulent roots and grass, and feeding along without a murmur. Generally, when they scent a tiger, there is much trumpeting and striking of the tips of their trunks on the ground; but here there was a tiger, but they did not give tongue.

Suddenly there was a roar. A brindled mass sprang upon the elephant's head, and down the two went. The mahout threw himself off to the right, falling on the green sward; but the elephant and tiger disappeared. Williamson was off his steed in a moment, and, pushing aside the bushes, he too would have fallen, had he not clutched at the nearest bush, which was very thorny, and, with bleeding hands, recovered his footing. "Here is an old bowrie," he called out, and we crowded to the spot. The elephant was crying out blue murder, and, with the aid of our attendants, we cut away the brushwood and then discovered the elephant lying on his back, jammed in the crevasse, which, though at the surface just there about ten feet broad, was at the bottom only about three.

The thing now was how he could be extricated. He made the welkin ring again with his cries, which were echoed by his *confrères* present. What Babel might have been I don't know, but the pandemonium round us was ear-splitting.

Our sport was over for the day. We sent back for men and mamooties to dig a trench to liberate the beast buried alive. Of the tiger and deer there were no signs.

Setting the people to work, we hurried back to camp, had a snack, and then went back to see that there was no shirking on the part of the coolies. But it must have been close on midnight before we managed to dig a trench sufficiently wide to drag out the fallen elephant with the aid of his brethren. We had to work by torchlight, for, as far as I remember, there was no moonlight, or if there was a moon it was invisible through the Scotch mist which set in with the disappearance of the sun. When we got him on his legs we found that he was not much the worse for the accident. The tiger and deer were squashed into pancakes. The basal antler of the deer had made a hole in the tiger's skin, but with that exception it was perfect, and he was probably the first and only tiger ever killed out hunting without man's action having been the cause of death.

On Christmas Day we began operations at six a.m., by which hour we had mounted our steeds and sallied forth to hunt "the boar, the mighty boar." The shikaries led the way right across the chur, and we crossed in a boat to the main bank. Our elephants and horses swam across, the nags being guarded by the pachyderms, for crocodiles of the largest size abounded.

About nine a.m. we took up our positions behind clumps of long grass, and waited. The cry of "soor jatalie" (pigs are on the move) put us on the *qui vive.* The fog had partially cleared away, and we saw not one, but at least half-a-dozen middling-sized boars showing the way to fully twenty sows and many squeakers, whom we allowed to pass. Then there appeared a fine grey boar, and he at once received our attention.

Cooksley was riding Pekoe, a 13-hands pony of mine. I was on Elgin, 12¾ hands. Cooksley was new to the sport; Williamson had had a little experience. At first the boar did not condescend to go faster than at a long, swinging trot, but as we followed him he broke into a mild-looking canter, which took him at a marvellous rate across country, which was undulating as far as we could see.

I kept to Williamson's right, about a stride behind. Elgin was holding his own, and I was in hopes, if the hog jinked, I should be able to cut in. In a hollow I lost sight of the boar, and the next thing I saw was the beast in the air, taking a jump at Williamson's mare. A charging boar is bad enough, but one that jumps or springs at one is the very devil. I saw Williamson job down—he was using a Bengal spear—and the next I saw was horse, man, and pig roll on the ground. I did not slacken speed, but went full pace—more at the dust than at anything I could see. The boar had recovered his feet, and was making for the prostrate steed. Williamson was struggling to his feet. By careful steering I got between the rider and the horse, and met the boar full split. He tried to jump again, but I was on him before he saw me clearly, and my spear went in at the chest and out of the body behind the left shoulder. I had to let go, or the impetus would have floored Elgin. I had no other spear near, and the boar was far from dead. He had fallen, and, in so doing, the shaft had broken off close to the body, and, turning round, the plucky brute seized the bamboo just above the spear head and pulled it out. This gave Williamson time to recover himself, and as the boar rushed at him, he sprang aside and drove his spear well in twice as the beast passed. The unclean monster turned round, and was bearing down upon the dismounted man again, when Cooksley, covered with dirt, and with his clothes more or less torn, appeared on the scene. Pekoe was a mass of dirt, too. It was evident man and horse had come a cropper; but both were full of pluck, and the steed had plenty of go in him. He responded to his rider's call, and went past like the wind. Cooksley gave two jobs, and just escaped

*Suddenly there was a roar, a brindled mass sprang upon the elephant.*

having Pekoe cut. So close were they and the boar that the upward jerk which was meant for the horse's side just grazed and cut the sole of Cooksley's boot as if by a razor; but, in avoiding the collision, the horse caught his foot in a creeper and rolled over. As Cooksley did not rise at once, I rushed up, jumped off, secured the spear, and was back in the saddle just in time to meet our brave antagonist; but his charge was feeble, and with three prods I deprived him of his life. I expected to find Williamson's mare dead, or so injured that she would have to be destroyed; but there she was, about a hundred yards off, cropping at the scanty herbage. Cooksley was all right, with the exception of a bad sprain. The spear had been won by Williamson. When the boar sprang at him, and he had jobbed down, the blade of the spear had furrowed down the back, drawing just enough blood for him to swear by.

After a rest and a libation on the arrival of our syces, we mounted again, and making a circuit round a wet bheel, we soon saw traces of many more pig. We found a good boar, and were riding him in rather high grass when, with a whoop, more of a grunt than a roar, up got a fine tiger.

Seeing Williamson riding him, I called out: "Are you mad? You had better let Mr. Stripes alone." I received the reply: "Gillespie, Outram and others have speared tigers. Why should not we?"

"Don't be silly!" I yelled out. Those were trapped tigers, with all their pluck taken out of them by captivity, but a wild tiger is a different thing."

"Well, go back," said Williamson, "and I will follow him alone."

That I could not permit—it would have been cowardly—so I too followed. But Cooksley, seeing a three-parts grown boar out in the open, had lain in well after him. We were racing along—we could not see a yard ahead—when the tiger sprang across a stream; and the mare, not seeing it, and having the bit between her teeth, went a header. Seeing Butter in my howdah a little way off, I galloped up to him, got a rifle, and, telling him to look after Williamson, I went on as fast as I could, in the hope of getting a shot at the tiger. The ground becoming more favourable, I was able to forge ahead, and got a sight of the quarry, still cantering on, and with the main river not far ahead, so I hurried on; but Elgin was blown, and the tiger disappeared down the bank. I arrived a minute after, but he was swimming strongly; and jumping off and steadying myself, I opened fire. My first two shots missed, but the third struck; and the tiger, with a roar, turned round and deliberately swam back towards me, with a view, I presume, of trying conclusions with me on shore. I fired again hastily, and again I missed. I put my hand into my pockets for more cartridges, and lo! there was not one! "Time to be out of this!" I thought, and was hastening to mount, when I heard a noise in the water, saw a tail cleave the air, and the tiger disappeared! There was no doubt he had been seized by a crocodile. There were many eddies and a good deal of commotion, but nobody ever saw that tiger again.

I was not sorry. I did not anticipate being chased by him with any pleasure, so I hurried back to Williamson to pick up the pieces. It is marvellous the falls one gets out hunting without breaking one's neck. The banks of the nullah where he had been upset were fully ten feet high, and horse and man had fallen right down without a break, and yet were not killed! Williamson had had a bad fall, but no bones were broken. After a brandy and soda, he was glad to get into the howdah with Butter. His mare had badly sprained her shoulder, and had to be led home. My mount was done up, so when Cooksley came up, having killed his boar, we got on to pad elephants, and shot our way back to camp, after about as eventful a day's sport as I ever remember encountering during fifty years' wanderings; and thus ended our "Christmas Hunt on a Chur."

FOREWARNED
a Story
of the
Intelligence
Department

By Major Arthur Griffiths
AUTHOR OF
"The Queen's
Shilling,"
"The Rome
Express,"
"The
Wellington Memorial,"
etc., etc.

"Treasons, stratagems, and spoils."—*Shakespeare*, "Merchant of Venice,"
Act V., Scene I.

## CHAPTER I.

IT was the middle of the night (as I thought) when Savory,
my man, my landlord, valet, and general factotum, came
in and woke me. Someone had called, and was most
anxious I should see him.

"Then I won't: not till a decent hour," I snorted.
It was already past nine, but I had been up very late at a
great ball, where I had danced the cotillon with "my best
girl," and had walked home long after sunrise.

"Won't go, sir. Says you'll be sorry if you don't see him;
he's got some great information for you wot you won't like to
miss."

"Bother him and his information. Tell him to write."
It was a phrase I had picked up at the War Office—that particular branch of it known as the Intelligence Department—
where we found it useful in keeping off undesirable visitors.

Savory carried out the message, and there was something
like an altercation in my little sitting-room. I could hear a
nasal voice raised in loud protest, and it was evident that the
man would not go willingly. This was too much, so I set my
dog Roy at the intruder, a handsome but aggressive collie,
my nearly inseparable companion, who was now lying at the
foot of the bed. I heard a great scurry and flurry, angry barks
and affrighted cries, so I jumped out of bed, not wishing the
fellow to be quite torn limb from limb. I ran into the other
room, where I saw a gentleman—well dressed in frock-coat,
with lemon-coloured gloves, and a tall hat—flying round the
big table, with Roy at his heels. As I appeared the poor
chap dashed out of the door, flinging behind him a few
disjointed words.

"Call off that dog, will you? Cussed beast. I'd shoot
him if I'd got my Colt. Won't see me here again in a hurry.
Guess he'll be considerable sorry, will Captain Wood."

What had brought the fellow? I was half inclined to
call him back, for just then I was deeply interested in the
country from which he hailed. America—the United States,
the Great Republic—was very much on my mind; to study its
resources, its capabilities for attack and defence, its armaments,
military and naval, its preparedness or otherwise for war,
was the business of my daily life. In other words, I was
attached to the "American Section" of our Intelligence
office, and passing events were giving unusual prominence
and importance to our branch. One of those family squabbles
that so often cause friction between mother and daughter
was threatening to expand into a serious quarrel between
England and America. It was all about a disputed frontier
line, a vexed question of the reading of maps and old time
delineations. I need not be more particular; it will suffice
to say that I was very closely concerned in it all. I had been
serving with my regiment in the West Indies, and being
something of an expert in such matters, thanks to my Staff
College training, I had been sent across to the mainland to
look into the facts on the spot. Then they brought me home,
and posted me to the house in Queen Anne's Gate to advise
and draw up a full report.

But all this was purely and strictly confidential. The
public knew no more than the vaguest rumours of possible
difficulties between the two countries. No one, as I believed,
thought of connecting my name with an affair which was still
in the early stages of diplomatic conflict. I was only a subordinate, a Staff Captain, one of the lesser wheels of a machine
that was itself but little known; for great and all-important
as are its functions, the Intelligence Department works so
mysteriously and secretly that its power and usefulness are
but little appreciated outside official circles. I could not for
one moment imagine that this importunate Yankee had the
slightest inkling of what I was at. He could know nothing,
legitimately, of the duties entrusted to me, of the line on which
I was engaged; and yet he might, in which case his object in
forcing himself in on me was plain. I lay there (for I had
gone back to bed, hoping for a little longer rest) puzzling over
the reason that had brought him. I could not sleep again,
although I may have dozed. My mind was busy in that half-
dreamy unconsciousness when the brain is still active, reasoning
clearly and with an ease that does not always accompany
sober wakefulness.

Had he come for a good or bad purpose? Meaning really
to help me or to play the spy? What if, under the specious
pretence of seeking to do me a service, he had sought admission in order to worm out valuable information? Then I took
quite the opposite view, and feared I had been wrong in sending him away. He might have had something really important to say.

It worried me greatly, this last idea. I was ambitious.
What young soldier worth his salt is not eager to get on, to
stand well with his chiefs, to gain credit for good work done,
and to earn the claim of fresh chances of distinction? But I
had still stronger reasons for seeking advancement. It was
my only chance—and but a sorry one at best—of succeeding
in another ambition, high placed, and almost hopeless, as I
feared.

For like an ass I had fallen desperately in love with a girl
I seemed as unlikely to win as a princess of the royal blood.
There was a great gulf fixed between us; between Frida
Wolstenholme, rightly esteemed one of the belles of the
season, the sole representative of a proud old family, and
William Wood, captain in the Royal Fencibles, with little
beyond his pay and the somewhat remote prospect offered by
a changeful and often disappointing career.

Even now, at this very moment while I was a prey to the
blackest and most despairing thoughts, a marvellous change
in my fortunes was near at hand. It was a *coup de théâtre*, a
complete transformation scene, as sudden, as startling, as
dazzling as the most brilliant fairy *divertissement*.

Once more Savory came in, this time with a letter, which
he gave me, saying simply, "The gentleman's a-waiting, sir,"
and which I read twice, without understanding it in the very
least.

Could it be a hoax? To satisfy myself, I sat up in bed,
rubbed my astonished and still half sleepy eyes, and read it
again. It ran as follows:—

GRAY AND QUINLAN,            101, Lincoln's Inn,
Solicitors.                              July 11th, 189—

DEAR SIR,—
        It is our pleasing duty to inform you, at the request of our New York
agents, Messrs. Smiddy and Dann, of 57, Chambers Street, New York
City, that they have now definitely and conclusively established your
claim as the sole surviving relative and general heir-at-law of their late

esteemed client, Mr. Aretas McFaught, of Church Place and Fifth Avenue, New York.

As the amount of your inheritance is very considerable, and is estimated approximately at between fourteen and fifteen millions of dollars, say three millions of sterling money, we have thought it right to apprise you of your good fortune without delay. Our Mr. Richard Quinlan will hand you this letter in person, and will be pleased to take your instructions.

We are, Sir, your obedient Servants,
GRAY AND QUINLAN.

Captain William Aretas Wood, D.S.O.,
21, Clarges Street, Piccadilly.

### CHAPTER II.

"HERE, Savory! who brought this? Do you say he is waiting? I'll see him in half a minute"; and, sluicing my head in cold water, I put on a favourite old dressing-gown, and passed into the next room, followed by Roy, who began at once to sniff suspiciously at my visitor's legs.

I found there a prim little old-young gentleman, who scanned me curiously through his gold-rimmed pince-nez. Although, no doubt, greatly surprised—for he did not quite expect to see an arch-millionaire in an old ulster with a ragged collar of catskin, with damp, unkempt locks, and unshorn chin at that time of day—he addressed me with much formality and respect.

"I must apologise for this intrusion, Captain Wood— you *are* Captain Wood?"

"Undoubtedly."

"I am Mr. Quinlan; very much at your service. Pardon me—is this your dog? Is he quite to be trusted?"

"Perfectly, if you don't speak to him. Lie down, Roy. I fear I am very late—a ball last night. Do you ever go to balls, Mr Quinlan?"

"Not often, Captain Wood. But if I have come too early, I can call later on."

"By no means. I am dying to hear more. But, first of all, this letter—it's all *bonâ fide*, I suppose?"

"Without question. It is from our firm. There can be no possible mistake. We have made it our business to verify all the facts—indeed, this is not the first we had heard of the affair, but we did not think it right to speak to you too soon. This morning, however, the mail has brought a full acknowledgment of your claims, so we came on at once to see you."

"How did you find me out, pray?"

"We have had our eye on you for some time past, Captain Wood," said the little lawyer, smilingly. "While we were enquiring—you understand? We were anxious to do the best for you———"

"I'm sure I'm infinitely obliged to you. But, still, I can't believe it, quite. I should like to be convinced of the reality of my good luck. You see, I haven't thoroughly taken it in."

"Read this letter from our New York agents, Captain Wood. It gives more details," and he handed me a typewritten communication on two quarto sheets of tissue paper, also a number of cuttings from the New York press.

The early part of the letter referred to the search and discovery of the heir-at-law (myself) and stated frankly that there could be no sort of doubt that my case was clear, and that they would be pleased, when called upon, to put me in full possession of my estate.

From that they passed on to a brief enumeration of the assets, which comprised real estate in town lots, lands, houses;

"How would you like it paid, Captain Wood?"

stocks, shares, well-placed investments of all kinds; part ownership of a lucrative "road," or railway; the controlling power in shipping companies, coal companies, cable companies, and mining companies in all parts of the United States.

"It will be seen that the estate is of some magnitude," wrote Messrs. Smiddy and Dann, "and we earnestly hope that Captain William A. Wood will take an early opportunity of coming over to look into things for himself. We shall then be ready to give a full account of our stewardship, and to explain any details.

"Meanwhile, to meet any small immediate needs, we have thought it advisable to remit a first bill of exchange for 50,000 dollars—say £10,217 17s. 6d., at current rates— negotiable at sight, and duly charged by us to the estate."

"The last part of the letter is convincing enough," I said, with a little laugh, as I returned it to Mr. Quinlan. "Always supposing that it is real money and will not turn to withered leaves."

"How would you like it paid, Captain Wood? Into your bankers?"

"If you please. Messrs. Sykes and Sarsfield, the Army agents, of Pall Mall."

"It shall be done at once. I will call there, if you will permit me, on my way back to Lincoln's Inn. Is there anything more? As to your affairs generally. If you have no other lawyers, we are supposed to be good men of business, and, perhaps—of course we advance no claims— you may consider that we have served you well already, and may entrust us further with your confidence."

"My dear sir, I fully and freely admit your claims. I should be most ungrateful if I did not. Pray consider yourselves installed as my confidential legal advisers from this time forth."

"Thank you sincerely, Captain Wood. I can only express a hope that, as our acquaintance grows, you will have no reason to regret this decision. I will now—unless you have any further commands—wish you a very good morning."

With a stiff, studied bow he bent before me, and was gone. He left me a prey to many emotions, surprise, bewilderment, still predominating, but withal a sense of pleasurable excitement. It was indeed a change, a revolution in my affairs. I could hardly rise to it, realise it, or the new, almost limitless, horizon it opened. Should I stay in the Service; leave, marry, run a yacht, own a grouse moor, possess a palace, have a racing stable, a string of hunters? What could I not command with a rent-roll that was nearly royal, having as yet no ties and responsibilities but those I chose to assume?

Hitherto, like most men of my cloth, I had been constantly hard up; of late, all but in "Queer Street," for I had yielded only too readily to the fascinations of London. After many years of service abroad, this spell at home, in the heart and centre of life, was enough to turn anyone's head. People were very kind; shoals of invitations came in, and I accepted everything—balls, dinners, routs. I went everywhere on the chance of meeting Frida Wolstenholme, at whose feet I had fallen the very first day we met. I worked hard at the office, but I played hard, too, making the most of my time, of my means, which, unhappily, did not go far. Four or five hundred a year is not exactly affluence for a careless young soldier aping the ways of a finished man about town. Gloves, button-holes, and cab fares swallowed up half of it, and with the other half I had hardly been able to keep out of debt.

That, at least, and without looking further, was all over now.

Savory had suffered more than once from the narrowness of my budget, but he had been very good and patient, and I was glad to think he would be the first to benefit by my good fortune.

"Would you like your money?" I asked, as I buttoned up my coat and made ready to start for the office, a little late in the day.

"Well, sir, I *am* rather pressed. The quarter's rent is overdue, and the landlord called twice yesterday. If you could make it convenient——"

"How much do I owe you?"

"Seventeen pounds eleven for the rooms, and Mrs. Savory's bill is nine pounds."

I had taken out my cheque-book while he spoke, and wrote him a cheque for £50.

"A little cheque? Do you remember Digby Grant in 'Two Roses'? Keep what's over after you've bought a nice bit of jewellery for Mrs. S. You've been long-suffering with me, and shall be the first to share my luck."

"My gracious, captain, 'ave they raised your screw, or 'ave you backed a winner, or wot?" cried Savory after me, too much taken aback to think of thanks.

Out in the streets, along King Street, down Pall Mall, I trod the pavement with the conscious air of a man who had heard good news. Friends I passed saw it plainly on my face, and rallied me on my beaming looks and buoyant demeanour. They had not left me when I walked through the swinging doors of Sykes and Sarsfield's bank. I was no longer the humble suppliant for a pitiful over-draft, but the possessor of a fine balance who could hold his head high. Roy usually waited patiently outside, but to-day I encouraged him to enter at my heels.

I knew the good news had reached the bank by the way I was received. One of the junior partners, Algernon Sarsfield, who rode a fine horse in the Row and lived in Park Lane, used to cut me dead out of business hours, and frown coldly when he caught my eye at the other side of the bank counter. Now he came round from where he was busy among the ledgers to greet me warmly and shake hands.

"Won't you come into the parlour, Captain Wood? Mr. Sykes and my uncle are there. What can we do for you to-day?"

"Has that—ahem—small amount been paid to my credit?" I asked, indifferently.

"Yes, yes, an hour ago. Do you wish to draw against it? Is it for investment? We can recommend our brokers, Legrand and Gunning; or shall we place it on deposit?"

"I shall probably want to use it, or a part of it. I have come into a little money, you understand——"

"So your lawyer told us. Pray accept our congratulations. But do come inside."

He led the way into the glazed central compartment where the senior partners sat always "high withdrawn," and into which any favoured clients were shown.

"This is Captain Wood," said Algernon Sarsfield, and the two seniors, who had never acknowledged my existence before, got up and bowed graciously before me.

"You wish to see us about—ahem?" began Mr. Sykes, looking interrogatively at his junior.

"Captain Wood has just paid in a sum of £10,000 odd to his account—the first instalment, I believe, of a legacy. Is it not so?"

"It is, exactly so. But I'm not quite clear whether or not I shall pay in the rest here. I may have to change, or, at least, to take other bankers."

"You have, I trust, no reason to be dissatisfied with us?" said the elder Sarsfield, adding severely, "Algernon, surely you have shown Captain Wood every attention? I should be deeply grieved if we had displeased or not satisfied you. Is there *anything* we can do for you, Captain Wood?"

"May I ask one question, gentlemen?" I said, interrupting their apologies. "Is the name of McFaught known to you—an American, Aretas McFaught, of New York?"

"Why, of course; the great millionaire. But he is dead. It was all in the papers some months ago. Died intestate, I think—unless—can it be possible that you——"

I nodded my head, carelessly.

"That's where it comes from; and now, if you would be so kind, I shall be glad of another cheque book and a little ready cash to go on with."

"Most certainly. How much? Who keeps your account? Mr. Elphick? Step out into the bank, Algernon, and see Captain Wood gets all he wants. Oh, good morning," said the senior partner. "Do, please, look in if you are passing. We are always so pleased to meet our friends."

## CHAPTER III.

As I left the bank, with my sovereign purse full and the nice crisp notes for £250 carefully put by in my pocket book, I began at last to believe in my fortune. There is a solid, unmistakable reality in the chink of good gold, while the supple civility of the great financiers, who had so lately looked black at my overdrawn account, proved how completely my position was changed.

Changed, indeed, and in more ways than I thought for now at the very outset of my altered conditions I was abruptly and unpleasantly reminded that wealth has its cares, its burthens, its dangers. The latter now rose above the surface in a strange and grotesque, yet disquieting fashion.

The morning's adventures and surprises had occupied much time, and it was now getting late, past noon, in fact. We members of the Intelligence made it a point of honour to be in good time at the office—an hour or more earlier than this. It had hardly occurred to me that I need not go to the office at all. You see, I had been some thirteen years under discipline, and not many hours an archmillionaire. Besides, there is such a thing as *esprit de corps*. I was a public servant, engaged in responsible work, and I could not, would not, have neglected it willingly; no, not for the wealth of the Indies.

So I stepped briskly down the steps below the Duke of York's Column, and crossed the park at my very best pace. For all that, I was overtaken near Birdcage Walk by someone who hailed me without coming quite close.

"Captain Wood! Captain Wood!" and, turning, I saw the man who had made such an untimely call and such an abrupt exit. He still remembered Roy, and held aloof.

"One word, sir, I pray, in your own best interests. But, sakes alive, keep back that cussed hound. He is a fine beast, I make no doubt, but I'd rather he didn't smell my pants."

"Quiet, Roy. My dog will not harm you, sir. But, indeed, I owe you some apology," I said, civilly. "Only at this moment I am very much pressed——"

"If you will allow me to walk with you a few yards, no more, I reckon I could make it plain to you that I have a good excuse for intruding upon your valuable time."

The park was as open to me, and when he ranged himself alongside I made no objections. I confess I too was curious to hear what he had to say.

"You have enemies, sir," he began abruptly; and he looked so comical as he said this that I was rude enough to laugh. He was a broad-shouldered, square-faced, weather-beaten-looking man, with a florid complexion and a bulgy nose: irreproachably dressed in the very height of the fashion, but he had rather the air of a second-class tragedian, with his long, black, curly hair, and his voice so deep and so solemn as he conjured me to be serious.

"I reckon this is no laughing matter, captain; guess your enemies will soon fix that. They mean mischief."

He spoke it like a sentence of death, and seemed very much in earnest, yet I could hardly take it seriously.

"Such a threat scarcely affects me. You see, it is my business to risk my life. The Queen has sometimes enemies, and her's are mine."

"These I speak of are altogether your own, captain—people who grudge you your new wealth."

"You have heard then?"

"Heard!" he cried, with great scorn. "There is nothing I do not know about you, captain. How did you enjoy the summer on the Cuyuni River, and were the maps you got at Angostura very useful to you?"

"Hush, man, hush. Who and what are you? What the mischief are you driving at?"

By this time we had entered Queen Anne's Gate, and were at the door of the office.

"Is this your bureau?" he now asked. "May I not go inside with you, only for one moment? The matter is urgent. It affects you very closely. Your danger is imminent. They are bound, these enemies, to do you an injury—a terrible injury."

"Oh, well then, it must keep," I said, petulantly. "I cannot give you any more time now; I am expected here. I suppose Sir Charles has arrived?" I asked of the office messenger, old Sergeant Major Peachey.

"Yes, sir, he has been here these three hours. He came—on his bicycle—soon after 9 a.m., and he has asked for you, I think, twice."

"There, your business must keep, Mr.——?"

"Snuyzer. I bow to your decision, but if you will permit me I will call in Clarges Street this evening at——?"

"If you must come, come about five. Good day," and I passed into the office.

*(To be continued).*

Photo. MAYALL & CO.                                                    Piccadilly.

## BRIGADIER-GENERAL W. H. MEIKLEJOHN, C.B., C.M.G.

THIS highly distinguished officer was in command of the Malakand Garrison when the camp was attacked by tribesmen some four months ago. This was the first indication of anything like a serious rising; and in the interval which has elapsed, the name of Brigadier-General Meiklejohn has been constantly before the public. On the formation of the Malakand Field Force, Colonel Meiklejohn was given command of the 1st Brigade, and in the important action of Landikai, when Sir Bindon Blood dispersed 3,000 tribesmen, bringing at one blow the Upper Swatis into subjection, General Meiklejohn successfully carried out the turning movement which completed the enemy's discomfiture. General Meiklejohn entered the Bengal Infantry in 1861, and had seen service in six campaigns prior to his present employment with the Malakand Field Force, to wit, the Black Mountain Campaign of 1868, the Jowaki Expedition of 1877-78, the Afghan War of 1878-80, the Mahsud Waziri Expedition of 1881, the Egyptian Expedition of 1882, and the Waziristan Expedition of 1894-95. He has been six times mentioned in despatches, and was employed from 1884 to 1896 with the Afghan Boundary Commission.

# THE INDIAN FRONTIER RISINGS.

*SHABKADR FORT, FROM THE NORTH-EAST.*

THE photographs on this and the two succeeding pages have reference chiefly to the column formed at Peshawar in connection with Sir William Lockhart's operations against the Afridis.

It will be remembered that, broadly speaking, the idea of the campaign was that, while Sir William Lockhart advanced with the bulk of the expedition directly against Tirah, one separate column should cover Kohat, another move out from Kurram on the left, and a third advance from Peshawar on the right. This Peshawar column is under the command of Brig.-Gen. Hammond, V.C., a most distinguished officer, formerly of the Guides. Its composition is as follows:—1st Battalion Somersetshire Light Infantry, 2nd Battalion Oxfordshire Light Infantry, 9th Ghoorkas, 38th Dogras, No. 57 Field Battery, No. 3 Mountain Battery, the 9th Bengal Lancers, and a company of Sappers.

In addition to photographs of some of these, we give pictures taken at the same time of the troops at Jamrud and other camps within easy

*The Peshawar Column in Camp at Bara.*

distance of Peshawar. These troops are of cognate interest, as it is upon them that the duty will probably devolve of re-opening the Khyber Pass, and thus finally terminating this eventful and deadly war.

At the time of writing, the Peshawar column is still awaiting orders at Bara, which was occupied as far back as October 21st. Great masses of tribesmen are in the immediate vicinity, and their numbers will doubtless increase as Sir William Lockhart forces his way up the Bara Valley. Eventually it would seem that, as the Afridis begin to realise that they are between two fires, some heavy fighting or else complete submission will ensue.

Our first picture is of Fort Shabkadr, which lies some fifteen miles north of Peshawar, on the road into the Mohmand country. It was upon Shabkadr that the Mohmands "irrupted" at a very early stage of the risings, being promptly driven back by Brigadier-General Elles, who subsequently, in connection

*Photos. W. Rahn.*     *Colonel Woodhouse and Officers, 9th Ghoorkas, at Bara.*     *Peshawar.*

with Sir Bindon Blood, conducted a set campaign against this tribe, and brought them into entire subjection.

The next photograph, showing the Peshawar column in camp at Bara, as seen from Bara Fort, is interesting as giving an excellent idea of a Frontier camping ground and a bastion of a Frontier fort. It will be readily imagined that, even in November, tent life on an almost treeless plain like this is scarcely luxurious, and that the process of waiting on week after week in anxious expectation of orders to attack an enemy known to be in the neighbourhood, is not devoid of monotony and even irritation.

*Brigadier-Gen. Macgregor and the Officers of the 2nd Batt. Oxfordshire L.I., at Bara.*

We now come to three regimental groups, all of great individual interest, and, collectively, highly representative of the magnificent material which these Frontier risings have called into the field. The first group shows the officers and native officers of the 9th Ghoorkas, which, as previously noted, forms part of General Hammond's column. Twenty years ago the Ghoorka was comparatively little known to the average Briton who had never been to India, but nowadays there is scarcely a man in the street who has not heard or read nearly all there is to say about this warlike product of the Nepal Valley, who, for all his short stature, is one of the finest soldiers in the world, and an object of very considerable respect even to the truculent and much more stalwart fighting hillmen of the North-West Frontier.

The group of officers of the Patiala Imperial Service Infantry is one to which particular attention may well be paid. These Imperial Service Troops are the outcome of a combined desire on the part of the principal Native Princes to show their loyalty in a tangible shape, and of anxiety on the part of the Indian Government to only accept from these chiefs such military service as would be of real utility in the field. The troops are armed, paid, and equipped by the various Native Princes, and in time of peace are commanded by their own Native officers. But they are trained under the superintendence of British officers, and British officers are attached to them when they are sent on service. The Patiala contingent is a particularly fine one, enjoying the distinction of being the first Imperial Service Troops who have worked with a British force in any considerable campaign. The only other contingent which has seen service is that of Kashmir, which took part in the operations on the Gilgit side in the Chitral Expedition. The British officer in the centre of the group is Brigadier-General Macgregor, and the officer to his left, Captain Cox, in temporary command of the contingent. This photograph was taken at Fort Bara, on October 21st.

General Macgregor again appears in the group of officers of the 2nd Battalion Oxfordshire Light Infantry, he having had them under his command in the operations against the Mohmands. The Oxfords—this battalion was the old 52nd—are now with the Peshawar column, and, by their participation in this campaign, will doubtless add another battle honour to an already long regimental roll, which starts with Quebec, 1859, and includes the Peninsula and Waterloo, South Africa, the Indian Mutiny, and the New Zealand War of 1863-66.

The picture of the camp at Hari Singh Burj, which lies between Jamrud and Peshawar, has a very warlike interest attached to it. It was taken

*Patiala Imperial Service Infantry, now with the Peshawar Column.*

*Photos. W. RAHN.*  *CAMP GROUP, HARI SINGH BURJ, NEAR PESHAWAR.*  *Peshawar.*

on October 26th, and early on the following morning a party of the enemy attempted to "rush" the camp, which had previously undergone a good deal of vexatious "sniping." The attack was made on a picket of the 8th Bengal Infantry, the sentry on which challenged, but was immediately shot. The picket turned out, and the tribesmen fired a volley at them, killing and wounding several. The enemy then rushed clean through the picket, and secured a number of rifles and some ammunition. The picket was promptly reinforced, and, under the gallant leadership of Jemadar Ram Sari Khan, drove off the assailants, who were fighting hand-to-hand with the Bengal men.

*Block House, between Forts Hari Singh and Jamrud, Garrisoned by Khyber Rifles.*

The block house on the Khyber road is one situated between Fort Hari Singh Burj and Jamrud, and is fairly typical of this class of structure—not very impressive, maybe, from the standpoint of higher Western military engineering, but not unsuited to local requirements. The fort is garrisoned by the Khyber Rifles, one of whom is seen in the foreground of the photograph. The Khyber Rifles are largely recruited from the Afridis, and, though in some cases the pressure brought upon them by their countrymen to desert and join the insurgents has been too great to be withstood, there have been many instances of conspicuous fidelity, several men of the corps having been killed in defending posts in the Khyber itself.

The photograph of the 4th Dragoon Guards in camp in the "serai" under the fort at Jamrud, gives a vivid picture of camp life on service, and, in addition, affords a capital view of a very important Frontier post. It will be noted that the regiment has thatched its tents, a plan often resorted to in these parts when the stay in any one camp is of considerable duration.

Our last picture shows the 57th Field Battery at "stables" under the walls of Fort Bara. The battery belongs to the Peshawar column, and it is more than likely that, by the time these lines are in print, it will have been heavily engaged. Incidentally it may be remarked that among the most striking features of these Frontier operations has been the free use of field artillery. In most of our little Indian wars it has been the fashion to use mountain guns, which, although able to climb the most difficult hills and to come into action from apparently impossible nooks and crannies, have not, of course, the range of the beautiful 12-pr., and only half the explosive effect. On several occasions during the past four months, field batteries have been employed, with brilliant results, and, in addition to pulverising the enemy, have, by covering the infantry attack, rendered our own losses much less heavy than they might have been.

*The 4th Dragoon Guards in Camp under Fort Jamrud.*

Photos. W. Rahn.          The 57th Field Battery, R.A., at "Stables" in Camp at Bara.          Peshawar.

Photo. GREGORY        *DRUM HORSE AND KETTLE DRUMMER—3rd DRAGOON GUARDS.*        Copyright - H. & A.

ONE of the most notable features of the Military Procession of June last, for the general public, was the sight of the drum horses and kettle drummers of the cavalry regiments that preceded Her Majesty's carriage. Among these was the subject of our illustration, the kettle drummer and drum horse of the 3rd (Prince of Wales's) Dragoon Guards. The kettle drummers in our Dragoon Guard regiments are an old institution, and go back over two centuries, when the regiments themselves were first raised under the title of "Regiments of Horse." Dragoon Guard was a much later name, invented, in place of the older one, by George II. Regiments of horse alone of our cavalry were allowed kettle drums, the light cavalry regiments, or dragoons, raised at the same time, having only ordinary side drums such as the infantry had.

Photo. F. G. O. S. GREGORY & CO., *Military Opticians, 51, Strand.*                    Copyright.—*HUDSON & KEARNS.*

## TWO MILITARY MEN OF THE YEAR.

F EW, if any, of the readers of THE NAVY AND ARMY ILLUSTRATED will fail to recognise at a glance the two officers whose portraits we give here. The tall officer in Life Guardsman's uniform is Captain Oswald Ames, of the 2nd Life Guards, the tallest officer in the British Army, who, at the Prince of Wales's special request, was selected, together with four of the tallest troopers of his regiment, the 2nd Life Guards, to form the escort to the bluejackets who, with their guns, headed the Jubilee State Procession. Captain Ames entered the Army in 1884, becoming captain in 1892. The other officer shown is Captain the Hon. Maurice Gifford, of the Rhodesian Horse, who, as he rode among the Colonial Contingent at the head of his smart-looking group of cavalrymen in their khaki uniform and "smasher" hats, received a welcome from all London that was in heartiness second to none. Captain Gifford distinguished himself by special and repeated gallantry at the head of his men in several desperate close quarter fights, while engaged in putting down the Mashona rebellion, and received from the Queen for his services the Distinguished Service Order, looking at the star of which Captain Ames is shown in our photograph. Captain Gifford lost his arm in action in the Mashona Campaign, and his empty sleeve, as he passed at the head of his comrades in arms through the streets, was greeted by excited people everywhere with shouts of "Nelson."

# MAKING THE MOST OF ARMY SERVICE.

THE difficulty experienced by so many soldiers in obtaining suitable employment after transfer to the Army Reserve, should induce those serving to make the best possible use of their time. In every branch of the Service there are open to men of good character appointments more or less lucrative, and those who are willing are often afforded the opportunity of continuing their former trade, or of pursuing some new calling, while still remaining effective as fighting men.

Every body of troops in barracks is practically independent of tradesmen outside the precincts of the barrack square. Grocers, bootmakers, tailors, publicans (or, to be strictly correct, the canteen steward and his men), are to be found in their various shops. These all furnish occupation for a number of soldiers, who are all the time qualifying themselves for employment on return to civil life. In addition, there are other billets open to soldiers, which, although not classified as trades, are of such a nature that a man who has filled one of them has added greatly to his chances of success.

There are also one or two pastimes which may afterwards be turned to account, though producing no revenue while the soldier continues to serve.

*Kit Inspection.*

*The Viewers at Work.*

Among these are football and cricket. Photography, too, is a subject worthy of attention, and may well be made a source of income. The excellency which it is possible to reach in a comparatively short space of time, may be judged from the fact that all the photographs on this page are the work of a soldier—Sergeant Easden, of the Oxfordshire Light Infantry—who has studied the art for barely two years. The first picture is a sight common in barracks once a month, when the commanding officer inspects the kits of the battalion. Then everything must be laid out according to regulation. The badges of the soldier here depicted show him to have over six years' service, and the crossed rifles convey to us the fact that he has been returned as a marksman. This photograph, by order of the commanding officer, has been hung up in every barrack-room in the regiment, in order to show the men what is expected of them. They can by this means lay out their kit according to order, and satisfy the commanding officer, without continually applying to the colour-sergeant for a "kit plate."

In the second picture the viewers from the Small Arms Factory, Birmingham, are seen making their yearly inspection of rifles—the precursor of much wailing and gnashing of teeth among those who have neglected the care of their weapons, for damaged rifles must be paid for.

The Gymnasium Staff of the Oxfordshire Light Infantry form the subject of the last picture. They are six men of whose physical bearing any battalion might be proud. They too, while serving, have trained themselves in manly exercises which may assist them in obtaining posts as instructors in schools or public gymnasiums.

*Regimental Gymnasium Staff, Oxfordshire Light Infantry.*

# ATHLETICS IN THE SERVICE.

ATHLETICS and sport in general have at all times, when, of course, no more serious and pressing business in the way of duty is in hand, had particular attractions for British officers, as well as for their men. Whether it be in some small and lonely frontier garrison or outpost of the Empire, or in some large camp or fortified place of arms, the spirit of our officers and men always shows itself in the ardour with which, one and all, they embrace every opportunity when off duty for athletic recreation, thus obtaining, in one form or another, that physical training which is of such vital importance to all who follow the profession of arms. It is the same with our officers and men quartered at home in England as abroad, whatever may be the circumstances and surroundings of the stations where for the time being the soldiers of the Queen find themselves located. At home, for example, Army athletic meetings, regimental sports of every kind, polo, cricket, football—what you will—interest and occupy the leisure hours of all ranks, with notable advantage, both as inducing a strong feeling of *camaraderie* between all ranks, and tending to raise the official standard of bodily efficiency and smartness all round.

Abroad, alike in India and at the Cape, in our garrisons and cantonments everywhere, the same source of useful recreation is sought at all times, with the added advantage, to those partaking there, that the country affords for sport with the gun and rifle after large and lesser game.

*Royal Artillery Football Team.*

Where these facilities are not to be procured, others will be found, in one form or another. For one, in the way shown in our illustrations—on the water, a favourite form of exercise and recreation with those whom duty has stationed at places like Gibraltar and the island fortress of Malta. It was at the last-named place that the photographs that we publish here were taken, and they show pictures of the Royal Artillery officers and men quartered there—a pulling team of officers of the Royal Artillery in their racing boat in Malta Harbour; a portrait of the officers comprising the pulling team shown in the boat, with a cup won by them in the race; and also a portrait group of men comprising the Royal Artillery champion football team at the same station. They show, for one thing, how all ranks exert themselves to keep in training, under circumstances by no means favourable and in a climate where, to the average man, a *dolce far niente* existence is preferable to violent exertion of any kind.

In no branch of the Service, indeed, are physical exercise and hard manual training of more account and more attended to than in the Royal Artillery. For one thing, of course, the constant handling of heavy weights forms part of their calling, as it were—especially among garrison battery gunners—and an everyday occupation.

The Royal Artillery, both officers and men, are perhaps more severely trained in this direction than their comrades in any other branch of the Service, beginning, for officers, with the stiff gymnastic course which every cadet goes through at the Royal Military Academy, Woolwich.

*Royal Artillery Officers' Pulling Team, with Trophy.*

*Photos. R. ELLIS, Malta.*

*ROYAL ARTILLERY OFFICERS' PULLING TEAM IN THEIR BOAT.*

# THE NAVY & ARMY ILLUSTRATED.

VOL. V.—No. 54.]    FRIDAY, JANUARY 7th, 1898.

Photo. ELLIOTT & FRY, Baker Street.

## ADMIRAL SIR LEOPOLD G. HEATH, K.C.B.

ADMIRAL HEATH entered the Service in 1830, was promoted lieutenant by prize commission in 1840, captain in 1854, and rear-admiral in 1871, being placed on the retired list in 1873, and has since risen to full admiral on the retired list. As commander of the "Niger" he saw active service in the attack on Lagos in 1850, also in the "Niger" and "Sans Pareil" during the Russian War; he was principal agent of transports at Balaclava, for which he was promoted and received the C.B.; he was also commodore in command of the East Indian Station in the "Octavia" during the Abyssinian War of 1868, receiving the thanks of Parliament for his services, and was made a K.C.B.; he also holds the Crimean and Turkish medals, Sebastopol clasp, the Medjidie 4th Class, and the Abyssinian medal. In 1836 he gained the 1st medal at the Royal Naval College.

## THE NEW AUSTRALIAN FLAG-SHIP, "ROYAL ARTHUR."

THE first-class battle-ship "Hannibal" is one of the last to be completed of the "Majestic" and "Magnificent" set of battle-ships, with certain later improvements. She has been built under the Naval Programme of 1895, was launched at Pembroke Dockyard, and finally completed at Portsmouth. At her recent official speed trials in the Channel, the "Hannibal" developed a speed of 16·3 knots with natural draught, and 18 knots with forced draught. The "Hannibal" will be ready to hoist the pennant in March next, when she will replace the "Repulse" or the "Resolution,"

one of the two remaining "Sovereigns" in the Channel Squadron. The "Royal Arthur" was named by Her Majesty the Queen, in honour of the Duke of Connaught, when she christened the ship on February 26th, 1891, and is one of our very successful first-class cruisers laid down under the Naval Defence Act of 1889. She came home last year from serving as flag-ship on the Pacific station, under the flag of Sir Henry Stephenson, and has recently left England to relieve the "Orlando," as flag-ship of Rear-Admiral Hugo L. Pearson, new Commander-in-Chief on the Australian station.

Photo. CRIBB.

## THE "HANNIBAL" ON HER TRIAL TRIP.

Southsea

# The Bicycle Afloat for Pleasure and Business.

WE have already at various times made note of how readily the Navy, both officers and men, avail themselves of the cycle for runs on shore whenever opportunity offers, and for racing at Squadron and Fleet gymkhanas. At Naval athletic meetings, from Esquimault to Malta, there is never a gathering on shore at which the bicycle is not seen—more particularly at Malta, the scene of the gathering shown in one of our photographs to-day.

The bicycle has been in the highest popularity with all ranks and ratings of the Mediterranean Fleet for years past, its popularity in no small degree being due to the example set by the late Commander-in-Chief in the Mediterranean, now Port Admiral at Portsmouth, Sir Michael Culme-Seymour, himself a first-rate athlete and keen cyclist. Whenever his Fleet was at Malta, Sir Michael was constantly to be seen having a spin along the roads of the island with his officers, and the example had a very great deal to do with the enthusiasm with which the Mediterranean Fleet went in for the new pastime. Our photograph of a group of cyclists belonging to the "Nile," of the Mediterranean Fleet, is in point here. Out of a total ship's company of 560 men, there are no fewer than 60 accomplished riders among the warrant and petty officers, bluejackets, and marines of the "Nile," all of whom have representatives in our group. "We 'Niles,'" says the correspondent who sends us the photograph from Malta, "have been scouring the island lately, and are looking forward to taking similar pleasure at home in our towns and villages, when in a few weeks the ship returns to England to pay off."

Our photograph of a midshipman of the "Jupiter," in the Channel Squadron, shows the business application of the bicycle in the Navy, the young officer being seen equipped to act as A.D.C. to the officer commanding a landing party.

*From a Photo.*　　*By a Naval Officer.*

*A Cyclist A.D.C. of the "Jupiter."*

When the Channel Squadron was at Gibraltar recently, a general landing of the brigade of seamen was organised, and the day before a signal was made ordering all midshipmen having bicycles to report themselves, that they might be attached to the different battalion leaders. There were in all some twelve or more, and very useful they proved themselves in taking messages—no sinecure, seeing that there were 3,500 men landed, and the line of march alone covered considerably more than a mile. The officer shown in our illustration formed one of this party, and his smart, workmanlike turn-out should satisfy the most critical of the military bicycle experts at home, whether Army or volunteer, as to what the Royal Navy can do in this line of business when occasion arises. Elsewhere, it may be added, in one of our East Africa coast expeditions, two or three years ago, other Naval cyclists have done good work on the line of communications with the front.

*Photo. Ellis, Malta.*　　*Good Men at the Wheel from the "Nile."*　　*Copyright.—H. & K*

# IN MEMORIAM:—The "Serpent."

AN officer of the Channel Squadron sends us the accompanying photograph of the memorial erected near Villagarcia, Arosa Bay, on the north-western Spanish coast, to the memory of the ill-fated crew of the British cruiser "Serpent," which was wrecked near by in a storm on the night of November 10th, 1890.

The memorial is erected on an isolated peak near the sea, on the summit of a natural cairn of gigantic boulders, visible from a great distance all round. There are really here two memorials of the "Serpent." One is the tablet of marble with gilt lettering, setting forth how the "Serpent" was lost, with between 100 and 200 men drowned, and the date of the disaster, erected at the instance of the British Admiralty. This is the large tablet shown apart from the others, to the left of the photograph as you look at it. The second memorial comprises the tall cross set up on the railed-off top of the large projecting boulder in the centre of the photograph. It was erected as a special mark of sympathy by the Spanish Government, and the cross bears an inscription, "To the victims of the sea." The remaining tablets are Spanish memorials of other wrecks.

*From a Photo.*　　*The "Serpent" Memorial.*　　*By a Naval Officer.*

# H.M. Coastguard and Royal Naval Reserve.

THE accompanying pictures to a great extent explain themselves. They represent some of the scenes at a recent inspection of the coastguard station and Royal Naval Reserve men and their battery at King's Lynn, by Commander R. E. Berkeley, the inspecting commander of the division.

Commander Berkeley is a firm believer in the possibility of forming a thoroughly reliable Naval Reserve under Mr. Goschen's statesmanlike scheme, especially from the hardy fishermen and coasting seamen who surround our islands, if only they can be induced to submit themselves to a course of six months' training on board a man-of-war. Most of their gunnery instruction can be, and is, imparted to them at their batteries on shore, which are built to resemble the fighting deck of a ship; but it is all-important that they should spend at least six months on board' a thoroughly up-to-

*The Inspecting Commander Homeward Bound.*

*Rallying Round the Flag.*

From Photos          *Heavy Gun Drill.*          By a Naval Officer

date man-of-war to "find their way about," "to rub shoulders with the long-service bluejackets," and, above all, to obtain that perfect confidence in and prompt obedience to the orders of their officers which distinguish the man-of-war's man of to-day.

Many of the drill batteries of the Royal Naval Reserve are being brought up to date by having modern quick-firing and breech-loading guns substituted for the old-fashioned muzzle-loaders. It will be seen that Lynn still possesses one of the latter type, but it is to be shortly removed, and will probably be replaced by a 6-in. quick-firing gun. A 3-pounder Hotchkiss gun is also to be mounted in this battery.

The question is sometimes asked, Can six months' training, however good, make these men competent to perform all the duties of our highly-trained seamen-gunners and torpedo-men?

The answer, of course, is no, not *all* the duties; but there are numbers of these highly-trained men besides Royal Marines who in time of peace are employed in the magazines, shell-rooms, at machine guns, and other duties which could be perfectly well carried out by men of the Royal Naval Reserve, who should be prepared, on the order being given for general mobilisation for war, to assume them at once, thus freeing hundreds of seamen-gunners, torpedo-men, and Royal Marine gunners to attend to the more scientific duties connected with hydraulic machinery for working heavy guns and turrets, torpedoes, etc., which they, and they alone, could efficiently perform on board the newly-commissioned ships that we should have to man on the slightest prospect of war. The appearance of the smart, intelligent coastguards is well known to all those who go down to our coasts in the summer for a whiff of the briny; but it is not so generally known that these men are composed of the cream of our Navy, and that their high state of efficiency is maintained by one-half of them being embarked every year for the Naval Manœuvres and the other half going to their district ships for a month's drill. This is done alternately by sections.

From a Photo.    *"Ready."*    By a Naval Officer.

From a Photo.    *Using the Breeches Buoy.*    By a Naval Officer

The force consists of 4,245 officers and men. If it were only 20,000 our next Trafalgar would be won already. One of our illustrations shows a group of coastguards with their officers and Royal Naval Reserve men shoulder to shoulder, as, no doubt, they will be when the day of trial comes.

## "CLEANLINESS IS NEXT TO GODLINESS."

"CLEANLINESS is next to Godliness" is an old adage, but on visiting a war-ship you would feel inclined to think that the maxim was reversed, for if there is a place on the earth that is absolutely and spotlessly clean, it is a British war-ship. This, however, is provided that she is not undergoing the process of coaling, and even then her griminess is only of the passing moment.

The Navy have laid to heart the maxim, "Satan finds some mischief still for idle hands to do," and to this probably is due the great cleanliness of the war-ship. Satan, in fact, is—to use an Americanism—"euchred" every time, for the idle man can always be put on to a cleaning job, that is, of course, if he is idling in the time for which Her Majesty is paying him to work.

Photo. GREGORY.    *DID HE HAVE HIS PAW IN THE PAINT POT?*    Copyright.—H. & K.

# THE "RENOWN" AND HER OFFICERS.

*VICE-ADMIRAL SIR JOHN FISHER AND OFFICERS.*

THE "Renown" is a first-class battle-ship, of 12,350 tons. She is armed with four 10-in. breech-loading guns, ten 6-in., eight 12-pounder and twelve 3-pounder quick-firing guns, and eight Maxims, has a total complement of 674 officers and men, and can steam 18 knots with forced draught. There is no other vessel at present exactly resembling her. She recently left England for the North American station, as flag-ship to Sir John Fisher, the Commander-in-chief, making an excellent passage in weather which proved her to be a splendid sea-boat.

A good view is herewith presented of the quarter-deck and the after barbette. The steel covers for the skylights, which appear to screen the guns, are, of course, shut down in action, and every object is removed which could in any way

Photos. SYMONDS & CO., Portsmouth

*INTERIOR OF ADMIRAL'S CABIN.*

interfere with an all-round fire. The two midshipmen of the watch, it will be observed, are decidedly in evidence near the barbette.

In the group of officers, Sir John Fisher naturally occupies a central position. His flag-captain sits on his right, while the flag-lieutenant and secretary stand behind, all three being distinguished by the gold aiguillettes, which is the badge of the admiral's staff. The midshipmen occupy a humble but conspicuous position in front, one of them, towards the right, gazing into the camera with a most engaging smile.

The interior of the admiral's cabin presents a pleasing picture of comfort and refinement, though, if the truth be told, admirals were considerably better off in the old line-of-battle-ships than in a modern ironclad, in spite of the huge disproportion in tonnage. However, there is a good deal to be said for the modern luxuries of electric lighting and so forth, and perhaps the authorities nowadays make a more liberal allowance than formerly for furniture, etc., beyond bare necessities, though an officer's cabin must always be more or less characteristic of himself—or possibly of his wife.

Sir John is distinctly *en famille* in this picture, for Lady Fisher sits by the piano, and one of their daughters on the right. A very interesting object is a large portrait of the Queen, presented to Sir John Fisher by Her Majesty, with whom the admiral is decidedly in favour, being both an efficient officer and a good courtier, with a ready wit. He has attained his present position by sheer force of character and unwearied energy, and has always had the capacity in a marked degree of obtaining a maximum amount of work from his subordinates. When quite a young gunnery lieutenant, the men knew well that when "Jack" came on the scene, something had to be done, and done quickly. He was in command of the "Inflexible" at the bombardment of Alexandria, and afterwards devised and commanded the "ironclad train," which was used with such excellent results in reconnoitring and skirmishing. As Director of Naval Ordnance, and subsequently Comptroller of the Navy, he has displayed characteristic zeal and ability.

Captain Daniel M. Riddel entered the Service in 1861, and attained his present rank in 1892. He passed rather a long period on the lieutenants' list, but was only seven years a commander. He wears the Zulu medal, 1877-79, and is a popular and efficient officer.

*Captain Daniel M. Riddel.*

*THE QUARTER-DECK.*

Photos. SYMONDS & CO., Portsmouth.

# BLUEJACKETS EQUIPPED FOR LANDING.

THE four illustrations of bluejackets in landing rig will be of interest, as showing the latest developments in this respect. Though seamen have, from an early date, been

*Landing Rig.*

frequently called upon to take part in operations on shore, their outfit was, until recent years, by no means as complete or well-contrived as could be desired. Here, however, there appears to be nothing omitted, from a water-bottle to a

Photos. Russell & Sons.      *Landing Rig.*      Southsea.

*" Ready"—In Kneeling Position.*

formidable string of cartridges. The blanket, with certain articles of clothing rolled in it, is securely strapped up behind, while the canvas knapsack contains a day's rations. The general effect is, perhaps, somewhat lumbered up, as compared with the popular idea of the looseness and freedom of limb which is always associated with the seaman; but when Jack goes a-soldiering he must do as the soldiers do, and, indeed, he looks much more free and "portable," so to speak, than his friend Tommy does in heavy marching order.

In firing with the sword fixed, as when surprised by cavalry, or before the final rush to capture a position, the

Photos. Russell & Sons.      *A Standing Shot—Sword Fixed.*      Southsea.

modern short sword-bayonet has a very decided advantage over the old heavy one, which was, in fact, a cutlass, and rendered it almost impossible to hold the rifle absolutely steady with the great leverage it exerted. The "ready" position on the knee is, of course, a far more advantageous one for steady aim, the left elbow resting firmly on the knee when firing.

# THE NAVY & ARMY ILLUSTRATED.

## NOTES & QUERIES of SERVICE AFLOAT & ASHORE

"AFRICANDER" asks whether the officers of the Household Cavalry have to undergo competitive examination the same as the cavalry of the Line, and whether they have a regular mess when in London. A candidate who presents himself for entry to the Royal Military College, Sandhurst, must be successful in a competitive examination, unless he be a Queen's cadet or Queen's Indian cadet. It matters not whether he intends entering the Household Cavalry or not, as far as the examination is concerned. He must, however, before being gazetted to his regiment, receive a nomination from the colonel—in the case of the 1st Life Guards, 2nd Life Guards, and the "Blues," the Prince of Wales. The regiments mentioned have a regular mess when stationed in London.

* * * *

IN reply to "Fish," there are in Her Majesty's Fleet several torpedo destroyers whose speed exceeds thirty knots. Only recently the "Panther," built by Messrs. Laird Brothers, Birkenhead, underwent a series of trials on the Clyde, when, in six runs over the Greenock measured mile, she attained a speed of 30·5 knots, with an I.H.P. of 6,000. In the subsequent three hours' full-power trial—compulsory before being approved for Her Majesty's Service—the average speed worked out at 30·14. The "Bat" (Palmers, Jarrow) is the third of a series, which may be also included in this category. On her late trials at Portsmouth the mean of six runs over the measured mile was 30·053, although on her three hours' test she only attained an average speed of 29·78. In the former case the mean I.H.P. was 6,167, the engines working at 391 revolutions starboard and 400 port, the steam pressure being 230-lb., with air pressure of 3·3-in.

* * * *

THE above are by no means the fastest of this type of vessel we possess, and I merely quote them, as in your letter you contrast "recent" additions to foreign Navies with the older style of torpedo destroyer in our own Service. One instance alone will be sufficient to show we are not behind in respect to really speedy craft. The "Desperate," contracted for by Messrs. Thornycroft for thirty knots, when making her preliminary trial last spring exceeded that speed by a full knot; and on her official three hours' test she realised thirty knots, although a heavy sea was running at the time and the wind was high. But this and other performances, creditable though they be, stand in jeopardy of being—more than put in the shade—totally eclipsed, if the turbine principle adopted in the "Turbiana" is successfully extended to larger vessels. During the recent Review at Spithead this hundred-foot torpedo-boat might have been seen "strolling about" at a speed which occasionally approached close upon thirty-three knots.

* * * *

"IT is, of course, well known," writes a correspondent, "that in Napoleon's time a large number of French and Dutch prisoners of war were confined in Portchester Castle. The Spanish captives as a rule went to Plymouth. But at Portchester Castle I made another discovery the other day in the shape of mementos of an earlier occupation of the place by French prisoners—the poor fellows taken in the Seven Years' War. Of these memorials there are quite a number still existing, in the shape of names and words rudely scratched and cut on the stones of the rough grey walls of the keep at Portchester As, for instance—' D'Auril, 1756,' ' P. Caborit de Marseille, 1757,' 'Jean Hercy,' 'Joseph Cochet,' 'J. Gergaud de Cognac au Xaintonge,' 'F. Marcy,' 'N. S. Botreau,' all of 1759, to recall a few names at random, with here and there, in addition, the name of a ship or a catch-phrase scribbled down—a 'Vive le flette!' or a 'Vive le vaisseau—"le Foudroyant!"' as in one instance. Yet more curious indeed are two inscriptions of the same period—a roughly scratched ' A bas l'amiral Hawke,' and a 'Vive l'amiral de Gallissonière'— the man who defeated Byng off Minorca, to whose flag-ship,

the before-mentioned ' Le Foudroyant,' the unfortunate prisoner who wrote the scrawl apparently belonged. There are a hundred and more French prisoners' names of the Napoleonic wartime inscribed on the walls at Portchester."

* * * *

THE Carabiniers, or 6th Dragoon Guards, unlike other regiments of Dragoon Guards, wear a blue tunic with white collar and cuffs. A double white stripe is worn on the overalls (trousers). The helmet is of brass, with white metal ornaments, and surmounted by a white plume of horsehair. In undress, the forage cap is surrounded, in the case of the rank and file, with a white stripe; in the case of the officers, warrant and non-commissioned officers, the stripe is gold. The officers of the Carabiniers wear, in undress, a gold cross belt (unlike other regiments of Dragoons and Dragoon Guards, who wear a buff cross belt, except in full dress), with silver buckle, tip, and slide. This latter distinction is also peculiar to the 6th Dragoon Guards. The lambskin over the saddles of officers' horses is black, edged with white cloth in place of scarlet. The Carabiniers are at present stationed at Aldershot. The regiment stationed at Norwich is the 7th (Princess Royal) Dragoon Guards—there is no regiment known as the 7th (*King's*) Dragoon Guards. The 1st Dragoon Guards are the "King's," and usually known as the "K.D.G.'s." The latter wear a scarlet tunic with blue facings, blue overalls with yellow stripe, and helmet with red plume, in full dress. In undress, the forage cap is surrounded with yellow braid. The "K.D.G.'s" are stationed at Colchester. The 7th Dragoon Guards wear a similar uniform with black facings, and helmet with black and white plume.

* * * *

ALTHOUGH lightly-armed horsemen, called "Hobiliers," existed during the feudal period, the present regular Army, established after the Restoration, had no light cavalry till 1756, when each regiment of dragoons received the addition of a "light troop." The practice then seems to have been to detach these troops from their regiments as necessity arose, forming them for the occasion into a light brigade. The first regiment of light dragoons was the 15th, raised in 1759, now the 15th Hussars. The men carried short carbines slung to their sides, light curved swords, and pistols, the dragoons at that time carrying a long musket and bayonet.

* * * *

THE rules governing the interchange of official visits between Naval and Military officers are somewhat complicated. On the arrival of a British or foreign man-of-war at a station where there is a Military garrison, an officer is sent on board with a view to arranging with the senior Naval officer as to the exchange of visits. As soon as possible after the arrival of a ship, the officer commanding the forces must visit the Naval officer in command, if the latter be senior to him. If not, he awaits the advent of the Naval officer, and must return his call within twenty-four hours. If the Naval officer be senior, he must come ashore and return the call within the same time. If there be no general officer commanding, the senior officer takes his place. When the Naval officer is below the rank of captain, the aide-de-camp of the general, or some staff officer, is "told off" to repay the call. If the general officer commanding is also a governor or lieutenant-governor of one of the Channel Islands, he is held to represent the Queen, and is, therefore, on all occasions entitled to receive the first official visit.

* * * *

THIS "Accompt of the English Army as it was 1st April, 1689," will interest most of my readers.

The English Army, the first of April last, consisted as followeth :—

| | |
|---|---|
| Three troops of Guards with three troops of Grenadiers to them, making together | 768 men |
| One troop of Scotts Guards consisting of | 118 ,, |
| Ten Regts. of Horse in 66 troops, each troop of 50, making together | 3,300 ,, |
| Four Regts. of Dragoons in 21 troops, whereof 20 have 60 men and the other six 49 each, making together | 1,494 ,, |
| Two Regts. of Foot Guards in 45 Companies of 80 each, making together | 3,600 ,, |
| Twenty-six Regts. of Foot, whereof one has 26 Companies of 60 each, another has 14 Companies of 79 each, and the remaining 24 regts. have 13 Companies of 60 each, making together | 21,386 ,, |
| Four Independent Companies of 50 men each | 200 ,, |

So that the above particulars, which are all computed without reckoning the officers, make up 4,186 horse, 1,494 dragoons, and 25,186 foot ; in all, 30,866 men.

* * * *

THE 20th and 21st Hussars, the latter of which have recently been changed into a regiment of Lancers, were transferred from the East India Company's service to the British Establishment on that Company ceasing to exist. Owing to their diminutive stature they were familiarly known as the "Dumpy

Pice." Notwithstanding their want of inches, few regiments can show a better record, but on their first arrival in England they were a source of mirth to the better halves of our long-legged Dragoons, who found a never-failing method of raising the ire of the Hussars' wives in the question. "Does yer man use the same ladder to kiss you as he does to mount his horse?"

* * * *

REVEILLE, Retreat, and Tattoo are three most important items in the soldier's day. The first (pronounced by Tommy Atkins *revally*) is sounded at times varying between five a.m. in summer and seven a.m. in winter, and is the signal for the men and non-commissioned officers to rise and clean the barrack-rooms. It is usually sounded on a trumpet or bugle in barracks. In camp it is played by the fifes and drums, or in Scottish regiments by the pipes. In connection with the latter, "Hey, Johnny Cope" is the regulation air. Retreat is a recognised bugle call, but at important stations the various drum and fife bands take their turn in "playing retreat," as it is called. By this is meant marching up and down the barrack-square once or twice playing some air on the fifes or pipes. Retreat is sounded at sunset, and usually finds the private soldier, after the labours of the day, enjoying himself in town or preparing to go thither. Tattoo is usually sounded at ten p.m., and may also be played in the same manner as the two mentioned above. By this hour all soldiers not on pass must answer to their names in barracks. Tattoo is also known as "last post," and half-an-hour earlier it is preceded by "first post"—a signal for all to return to barracks. Both are exceptionally striking when played on the bugle. At 10.15 "lights out" is sounded, and no other bugle sound is heard till réveille next morning, except in case of alarm.

* * * *

IN answer to various enquiries I have had as to the qualifications of an engine-room artificer for the Royal Navy, the first and most important is that he must have served in some respectable firm for at least four years. If with an engineering firm, so much the better, but at any rate it must be one engaged in some cognate business, where the candidate will have learned that dexterity with a hammer and chisel and file which will be necessary for him in his new career. At the same time, though not absolutely essential, it will be well if he can use a lathe. His proficiency in these elements of his trade will be judged by the fleet engineer of the floating workshop, who, in general, is not difficult to please. Besides this, however, he must satisfy an engineer of the Steam Reserve of his capacity to read and write well, and of his knowledge of such of the ordinary rules of arithmetic as will enable him to work out some simple questions on the steam-engine.

* * * *

SUPPOSING him to have passed all these tests, together with a somewhat severe medical examination, he will now be transferred to the care of the officer previously named in the floating workshop, where he will be employed at such work as he is fit for, and to a certain extent learn the ways of the Service, for about three months at least, probably longer. He will receive pay at the rate of £95 16s. 3d. a year on appointment, and if he arrives at the post of chief engine-room artificer, he will be paid at the rate of £136 17s. a year. There are greater advantages in prospect for him, however. Mr. Goschen has promised that a certain number of engine-room artificers shall be promoted to the rank of warrant officer, of course with extra pay. Besides this, an artificer, of whom there are many, in charge of a small vessel in commission gets the same charge pay as an engineer officer, viz., 1s. a day.

* * * *

STOKERS are admitted into the Royal Navy with much less fuss being made about them and their antecedents than is the case with an engine-room artificer. And considering the difference of their positions, this is only reasonable. Anybody with the requisite power of limb and muscle can become a stoker. It is a hard life, no doubt, but I think the average age of stokers will compare favourably with that of more fortunate bluejackets. A stoker, supposing him to have a good character, is admitted without parley, provided he pass the medical examination. He is not required even to read or write, though in these days there are few indeed who cannot do both, but he ought to be of strong physique. When he first joins, he will be retained in the Reserve for a considerable period, perhaps a year, until he has learned the ways of the Service, and the use of a cutlass and rifle. He gets 1s. 8d. a day till he is "rated," and then gets 2s. a day till he rises to a possible 5s. a day, with 3d. a day extra if he happens to be a stoker-mechanic. Thus a man who has no trade ready to his fingers may do a great deal worse for himself than become a stoker in the Navy.

THE EDITOR.

YOU may see by what good and gallant service the British Empire is built, and what manner of men are the builders, if you will but read two recent books on the Benin Expedition. I warrant they are as interesting as romances. The hideous massacre of the expedition of Acting Consul-General Phillips is still fresh in memory. His purpose was to open Benin city to the influences of civilisation, and to break for ever the nightmare of blood that rested on that blighted land. In such work there must be sacrifices. Two men only escaped. They were Captain Alan Boisragon, commandant of the Niger Coast Protectorate Force, and Mr. Locke, a District Commissioner. How they escaped is told by Captain Boisragon in his "Benin Massacre" (Methuen, 3s. 6d.), a book which has reached a second edition. It is a breathless story of adventure. The two men, in the dense bush, were wounded, and were consumed with a horrible thirst, but they escaped to tell the story; and to them the reparation that followed must have been sweet.

How that reparation was brought about is told by Commander R. H. Bacon, in his "Benin, the City of Blood" (Arnold, 7s. 6d.), who recounts, with dramatic force, the progress of Admiral Rawson's punitive expedition. There is most practical value in the book, and all those likely to engage in "small wars" in West Africa will do well to read it. The advance of the several columns, and, in particular, of the column which proceeded by way of Ologbo, and captured the town of Benin after long fighting, rushing the royal compound, is vividly described. "The place stinks of human blood; sacrifices and corpses everywhere," was the grim report of Admiral Rawson. It was a terribly trying march, and the loss was considerable, but the blue-jackets and others engaged showed endless fortitude, and qualities that are never failing in our countrymen. The special value of Commander Bacon's volume is that it describes the method of the advance, the dealing with ambuscades, the system of precautionary volleys and rushes, and a multitude of other details of bush warfare.

I have lately seen it often remarked in the foreign press that Englishmen have fallen into a habit—no new one, however—of extolling themselves, and, as it is a pernicious tendency, leading to a disposition to under-value others, I would by no means encourage it, notwithstanding what precedes. Yet it is interesting to find that Captain Stenzel, of the German Navy, has just thought it well to write an exhaustive account of the British Navy, the chief instrument of our power, in his "Grossbritannien und Irland: Die Flotte" (Schall und Grund, Berlin). Now Captain Stenzel is a veteran officer, of open mind and without prejudice, who is constantly working with his pen, and who deserves to be better known in this country. It is truly astonishing to find what an intimate knowledge he possesses of the constitution of the Admiralty, our Naval policy, the various stations and dockyards, the personnel and material of the Navy, organisation, training, discipline, uniform, flags, marks of rank, and an abundance of other matters. In short, he has given a complete view of the British Navy at the present day, and the plates and plans that accompany his book are all that could be desired. Indeed, in the coloured pictures of uniform, Germans have now access to better information than is easily available to Englishmen. The volume is a section of a work which is to treat also of the Army, this latter section being by a British officer whose name I will not now mention, and it belongs to a series described as "Die Heere und Flotten der Gegenwart."

Two little books have been sent to me which deserve mention, if only for their varied character, in relation to what I have been saying. "These Sixty Years, 1837 to 1897," by E. M. Holmes and other writers (Religious Tract Society, 2s. 6d.), is a model of what such a volume should be—a brief, well-balanced, and sufficient account of the Queen's private and public life, and of the intellectual and material progress made during her reign. "Our Island Home," by G. H. F. Nye (Bemrose), with good intentions, is an example of a curiously distorted treatment of history. Children who read it cannot but be possessed with the idea that our history is mostly concerned with church government, monks and reformers, the preaching of Wesley, "Tract 90," and so forth, but of constitutional history, material progress, or the relation of the island to the Empire they can scarcely be made aware. In short, as Carlyle might have said, much that should have been distilled to a drop almost fills the author's somewhat meagre measure, to the exclusion of more important things.

If you want a book of pulse-stirring quality to read at this season, get Conan Doyle's "Exploits of Brigadier Gerard" (Newnes, 6s.). It is as good and as vivid as Defoe. That famous old favourite, "The Swiss Family Robinson," newly and beautifully illustrated, is another charming volume; and, if you want marvellous pictures, procure "All About Animals," or "The Thames Illustrated," which takes you from Richmond to Oxford. These three are from the same publisher (10s. 6d. each).

Two other books before me deserve more than a word of praise. "The Leisure Hour" volume (Religious Tract Society, 7s. 6d.) is a mine of good things, and has a particularly excellent series of articles on "The United States Navy." "Butterfly Ballads and Songs in Rhyme," by Helen Atteridge (John Milne), with illustrations by Gordon Browne, Louis Wain, and others, is simply charming for children and their elders, both dainty and fascinating. The ballad of "The Boy who went to Sea" is really delightful.

Other books to be read:—

"The Flags of the World, their History, Blazonry, and Associations," by F. Edward Hulme. (Warne, 6s.)

"The Way of the World at Sea," by W. J. Gordon. (Religious Tract Society.)

"English and Russian Military Vocabulary," by Lieutenant A. Mears. (Nutt, 3s. 6d.)　　　　"SEARCH-LIGHT."

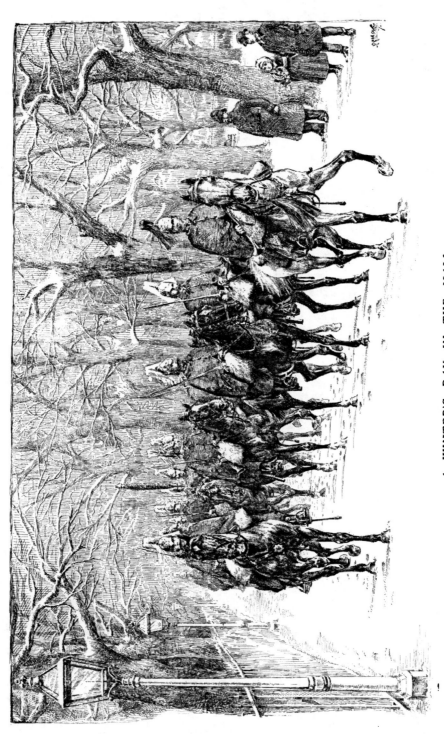

*A WINTER'S DAY IN THE MALL.*

# The Royal Irish Constabulary

## BY JAS. F. MACNAMARA.

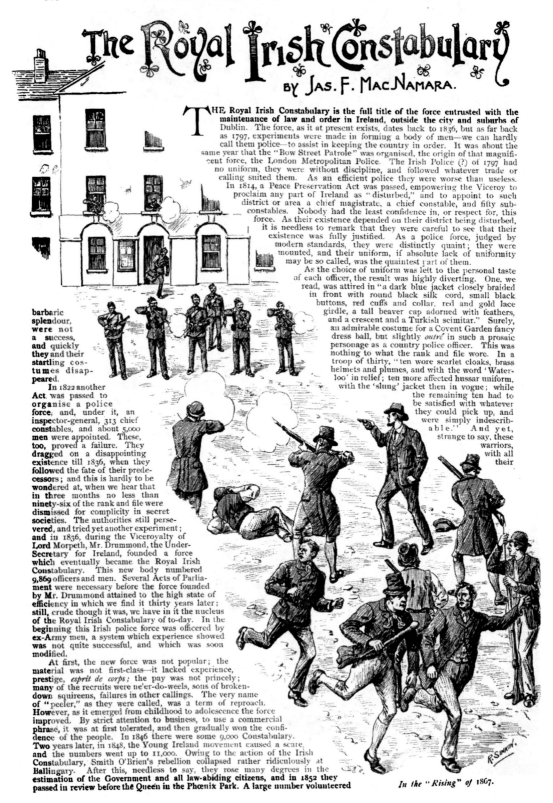

THE Royal Irish Constabulary is the full title of the force entrusted with the maintenance of law and order in Ireland, outside the city and suburbs of Dublin. The force, as it at present exists, dates back to 1836, but as far back as 1797, experiments were made in forming a body of men—we can hardly call them police—to assist in keeping the country in order. It was about the same year that the "Bow Street Patrole" was organised, the origin of that magnificent force, the London Metropolitan Police. The Irish Police (?) of 1797 had no uniform, they were without discipline, and followed whatever trade or calling suited them. As an efficient police they were worse than useless. In 1814, a Peace Preservation Act was passed, empowering the Viceroy to proclaim any part of Ireland as "disturbed," and to appoint to such district or area a chief magistrate, a chief constable, and fifty sub-constables. Nobody had the least confidence in, or respect for, this force. As their existence depended on their district being disturbed, it is needless to remark that they were careful to see that their existence was fully justified. As a police force, judged by modern standards, they were distinctly quaint; they were mounted, and their uniform, if absolute lack of uniformity may be so called, was the quaintest part of them.

As the choice of uniform was left to the personal taste of each officer, the result was highly diverting. One, we read, was attired in "a dark blue jacket closely braided in front with round black silk cord, small black buttons, red cuffs and collar, red and gold lace girdle, a tall beaver cap adorned with feathers, and a crescent and a Turkish scimitar." Surely, an admirable costume for a Covent Garden fancy dress ball, but slightly *outré* in such a prosaic personage as a country police officer. This was nothing to what the rank and file wore. In a troop of thirty, "ten wore scarlet cloaks, brass helmets and plumes, and with the word 'Waterloo' in relief; ten more affected hussar uniform, with the 'slung' jacket then in vogue; while the remaining ten had to be satisfied with whatever they could pick up, and were simply indescribable." And yet, strange to say, these warriors, with all their barbaric splendour, were not a success, and quickly they and their startling costumes disappeared.

In 1822 another Act was passed to organise a police force, and, under it, an inspector-general, 313 chief constables, and about 5,000 men were appointed. These, too, proved a failure. They dragged on a disappointing existence till 1836, when they followed the fate of their predecessors; and this is hardly to be wondered at, when we hear that in three months no less than ninety-six of the rank and file were dismissed for complicity in secret societies. The authorities still persevered, and tried yet another experiment; and in 1836, during the Viceroyalty of Lord Morpeth, Mr. Drummond, the Under-Secretary for Ireland, founded a force which eventually became the Royal Irish Constabulary. This new body numbered 9,869 officers and men. Several Acts of Parliament were necessary before the force founded by Mr. Drummond attained to the high state of efficiency in which we find it thirty years later; still, crude though it was, we have in it the nucleus of the Royal Irish Constabulary of to-day. In the beginning this Irish police force was officered by ex-Army men, a system which experience showed was not quite successful, and which was soon modified.

At first, the new force was not popular; the material was not first-class—it lacked experience, prestige, *esprit de corps*; the pay was not princely; many of the recruits were ne'er-do-weels, sons of broken-down squireens, failures in other callings. The very name of "peeler," as they were called, was a term of reproach. However, as it emerged from childhood to adolescence the force improved. By strict attention to business, to use a commercial phrase, it was at first tolerated, and then gradually won the confidence of the people. In 1846 there were some 9,000 Constabulary. Two years later, in 1848, the Young Ireland movement caused a scare, and the numbers went up to 11,000. Owing to the action of the Irish Constabulary, Smith O'Brien's rebellion collapsed rather ridiculously at Ballingary. After this, needless to say, they rose many degrees in the estimation of the Government and all law-abiding citizens, and in 1852 they passed in review before the Queen in the Phœnix Park. A large number volunteered

*In the "Rising" of 1867.*

for the Crimea in 1854, and many were employed in the Commissariat.

In 1857 the Revenue Police were abolished, and the duty of "still-hunting" and suppressing the manufacture and sale of "poteen," or illicit whisky, devolved upon the regular police

Some years after the close of the American Civil War, Fenianism, which had been for some time smouldering, burst into flame. Large numbers of disbanded soldiers, federals, and confederates, full of revolutionary ideas and burning with hatred for England, began to pour into Ireland from America. Drilling was secretly carried on all over the country, and for a while the I.R.B.—the Irish Republican Brotherhood—with James Stephens for head centre, caused something approaching a panic. No one knew what was going to happen, and the most exaggerated rumours of a rising circulated in all directions. Amid the snows of March, 1867, the "rising" took place. Everyone knows the result. Owing to that stock character in Ireland, the informer, matters were precipitated. No one was ready. Things were not ripe, and preconcerted action was impossible. The police knew as much about the doings of the rebels as the head centre himself. At Kilmallock, in County Limerick, the Police Barrack sustained a siege, and a good deal of powder and shot was expended; but the Fenians had quickly to raise it and fly on the approach of a handful of police. At Drogheda, a Sub-Inspector and the local force put to flight the insurgents at the "Battle of the Potatoe Market," without firing a shot, and at Tallaght, County Dublin, Sub-Inspector Burke and a small body of police routed the Dublin and Wicklow Fenians; and when the Dragoons, under Sir Hugh Rose, arrived at full gallop from Dublin there was nothing left for them to do but go home again. The loyalty and courage of the Irish Constabulary was not forgotten; their brave conduct evoked general praise; Parliament unanimously voted them its thanks; rewards and honours were bestowed on those who had particularly distinguished themselves; their pay was raised, and Her Most Gracious Majesty was pleased to bestow on them the title of Royal, hence they have ever since styled the Royal Irish Constabulary, or, as they are called in Ireland for brevity sake, the R.I.C. Meantime the *mauvais sujets* were gradually eliminated from its ranks, recruits of good education, respectability, and splendid physique crowded the depôt, and the whole tone of the force improved.

In 1878 came the potatoe blight and starvation, with the usual concomitant agitation. The Land League was started in County Mayo, and rapidly spread all over Ireland. The work of the R.I.C. literally increased a hundred-fold. Recruiting was pushed forward as it had never been pushed before. In 1880, 1,000 recruits were taken on; in 1881, 2,000; in 1882, 2,000; in 1883, 1,000; and yet more were wanted. The Government fell back on the Army Reserve, and several hundreds of that body who had first-rate discharges were enrolled, mostly for protection duty, but they could not stand the rigid discipline of the Constabulary, and in twelve months scarcely an Army Reserve man remained. In many instances the military were sent to aid the Constabulary, and in every case cheerfully afforded the greatest possible assistance. By degrees the agitation subsided, the high pressure was removed, recruiting once more assumed normal proportions, and, at the present moment, it is completely suspended. So much for the history of the Royal Irish Constabulary.

The force at present numbers, roughly speaking, about 11,000 men. The various ranks are as follows: One inspector-general, which position has been held since 1885 by Sir Andrew Reed, C.B., LL.D., B.L.; one deputy and three assistant inspectors-general (one of whom is commandant of the depôt), one Commissioner of Belfast City; 36 county inspectors and about 226 district inspectors, divided into three classes, according to seniority. The rank and file are made up of some 260 head constables, 2,000 sergeants, and between 8,000 and 9,000 constables. The first five officers, called the superior officers, are, with one exception, at the headquarters in Dublin, while the others are posted all over Ireland, from the Giant's Causeway to Cape Clear. A county inspector has charge of a county, and is responsible for its peace and for the discipline and effectiveness of the county force. He can punish for minor offences, such as petty breaches of discipline; the more serious cases, such as drunkenness, are invariably dealt with at headquarters. Should a man deny the charge preferred against him, he is tried by a court of enquiry, usually consisting of two district inspectors, whose verdict, however, must be confirmed by a superior officer.

A district inspector, formerly sub-inspector, has charge of a district or part of a county, consisting of ten or twelve sub-districts, each under a sergeant, and from 50 to 100 constables. The duties of a district inspector are, like Sam Weller's knowledge of London, "extensive and peculiar." He must know something of everything and be able to do most things. If His Excellency the Lord Lieutenant should honour the D.I.'s district with a visit, he must take charge of the mounted escort; if Biddy Branagan's goat has been done to death he must track the assassin to his lair. He must know as much law as the smartest local attorney; he must be able to intelligently examine the medical witnesses at coroners' inquests, and show that he knows the difference between a compound comminuted fracture of the *tibia* and an abrasion of the occipital bone. He must report eruditely on the crops and the price of land, and he must not hesitate to give his opinion, if called for, on the Financial Relations Question, bi-metallism, or cremation. A day in the life of a busy district inspector is in itself a liberal education. He revels in hard work—patrolling, protecting sheriffs and process servers against crowds thirsting for their blood, dispersing mobs, often at the point of the bayonet, at elections or party riots, these are all in the day's work; but what brings his grey hairs in sorrow to the grave is making out "Returns." An interview with a supposed mad dog, or escaped lunatic, is recreation in comparison. As regards pay and allowances, a county inspector receives about £700 a year; a district inspector, £250 to £450; a head constable, £104; a sergeant, £80; and a constable from £54 to £72; the last three ranks also getting allowances for lodging, boots, bedding, &c. The uniform of county and district inspectors corresponds so closely to that of officers in the Rifle Brigade, that few, except experts, could see the difference. All R.I.C. officers, however, are mounted. The men wear helmet, black tunic and trousers, with gaiters, valise, and great coat rolled, Snider rifle (with buckshot and ball ammunition), and sword-bayonet, in marching order; forage cap, tunic or frock, sword-bayonet or truncheon, for undress; fatigue cap and knickers for cycling.

To become a district inspector, a nomination from the Chief Secretary for Ireland must first be obtained. About ten candidates are nominated for each vacancy—sometimes even more. The age for admission is from twenty-one to twenty-six, and in the case of naval or military officers, twenty-eight. The candidate must be at least 5-ft. 8-in. in height, and pass a strict medical examination; the subjects for examination are not difficult, but the exceedingly keen competition renders success no easy task. The successful candidate spends some six or eight months at the depôt; he joins as a cadet, and when a vacancy occurs among district inspectors, he is appointed to the third class of that rank. While in the depôt he learns drill, police duties, Constabulary office work generally, equitation and musketry. When he has passed satisfactorily in all these subjects he is sent out to the country to fill a vacancy and to take charge of a district.

Half the number of vacancies for district inspectors are now given to head constables, who display special aptitude and ability, on passing a very searching literary and technical examination; while a smaller proportion are reserved for sons of Constabulary officers whose names are on the Inspector-General's list. In the ranks promotion is given either—firstly, on the recommendation of a constable's county and district inspectors, or, as rarely happens, for some extraordinarily good police work; secondly, on passing a literary examination before the Civil Service Commissioners and a technical examination before a board of officers. The second method has been only adopted of late years, and has been the means not only of bringing smart, intelligent young policemen rapidly to the front, but also of attracting young men to join who possess very high abilities and superior education. In addition to the ordinary police, there are 150 R.I.C. cavalry. They are employed mostly on escort duty, and armed with swords and revolvers.

In order to join as a constable a man must be at least 5-ft. 9-in. in height, between eighteen and twenty-seven years of age, of good education and undoubted respectability, well-developed, and perfectly sound in every respect. Latterly, several men of the R.I.C. have received good appointments in the Jamaica, Trinidad, and British Guiana police forces.

Among the district inspectors, promotion is very slow; as a rule it takes twenty-five years to become a county inspector, but other good appointments are open to district inspectors. A good many are appointed to the position of resident magistrate in Ireland, one vacancy in every three falling to them. A number of chief constables in English police forces were formerly R.I.C. officers, among the number being the chief constables of Devonshire, Cornwall, Bristol, and Liverpool, as well as the Deputy of Liverpool; while such prominent people as the Governor-General of Jamaica (Sir Henry Blake), the Under-Secretary for Ireland (Sir David Harrel), the Commissioner of the Dublin Police, the Chairman of the Irish Prisons Board, the Consul-General of the Niger Protectorate (Mr. Ralph R. Moor), etc., have at one time worn the uniform of an Irish Constabulary officer.

FOREWARNED
a Story of the Intelligence Department

By Major Arthur Griffiths
AUTHOR OF
"The Queen's Shilling," "The Rome Express," "The Wellington Memorial," etc., etc.

## SYNOPSIS OF PREVIOUS CHAPTERS.

Captain Wood is an officer on the staff of the Intelligence Department of the War Office engaged with certain confidential questions pending with the United States Government. It is the height of the London season, and he is sleeping late after a ball, when he is roused to hear some startling news. A lawyer, Mr. Quinlan, has called to tell him that an unknown relative, an American millionaire, has left him a colossal fortune. Almost at the same moment an American detective warns him that he has enemies plotting against him and his fortune, and that he goes in imminent danger of his life.

## CHAPTER IV.

I SHARED my room at the Intelligence with a colleague, Swete Thornhill, of the Artillery, a lively youth out of hours, but who stuck to his work manfully—more so than any of us; and we were by no means idle men.

"Thought you were dead," he said, shortly, and without looking up from his papers. "Wonder you took the trouble to come at all."

"I was detained by something special. Important business. Anyhow, it's no affair of your's," I answered, rather nettled.

"Yes it is, when it throws me out of my stride. I wish you'd make up your mind either to come or to stay away altogether. There has been a regular hue and cry for you all the morning, and I've been disturbed abominably. I have those calculations of the comparative penetration of the new projectiles in hand, and they take some doing."

"Well, keep your hair on. I don't want to disturb you. But who was it, anyhow?"

"The boss chief himself, Collingham, Sir Charles. He has sent three times for you, and came in twice. Wanted you for something pressing. Now, I believe, he is doing the job himself. Wise man. Do it a d——d sight better than you or any man-Jack of us."

At this moment an office messenger came in with a huge bundle of papers, which he placed before me on my desk. They were enveloped in the usual green "jacket" which meant extreme urgency, and on the outside was written, in a big, bold hand, "Captain Wood—speak."

"He'll do most of the talking, I expect," went on Swete Thornhill, maliciously. "He's fit to be tied. Go in, man, at once, and take your punishment."

The distinguished officer at that time head and chief of our department was Major-General Sir Charles Collingham, V.C., K.C.B., one of the most notable soldiers of the day, ardent, fearless, highly skilled, strong in counsel, foremost in the field, who had served almost everywhere, in all the wars, great and small, of recent years, and had made a close study of the science of his profession as well. He had travelled far and wide, knew men and many cities, was as much at home at Court as in camp; popular in Society, which he cultivated in his spare moments, although he allowed nothing to stand in the way of his work. The Service came first, and first in the Service was the all-important, transcendently useful department, as he thought it, over which he presided.

Sir Charles expected, nay, exacted, a like devotion from us, his staff officers, whom in all matters of duty he ruled with a rod of iron. None of us liked to face him when he was put out, which, it may be said, was not seldom, for he was choleric, although not cross-grained. Under a stern face and rough manner he had a kindly nature, far down, for he did not wear his heart upon his sleeve, certainly not for an erring subordinate, as he considered me just then.

I felt rather sheepish and uncomfortable as I appeared before the great man. The General was tall in stature, very thin and straight, with a still young, neat figure and defiant pose, as he stood erect and well poised on thin dapper legs and small, natty feet, while his strong, weather-beaten face—the deep bronze contrasting sharply with the bristling white moustachios, and long, projecting eyebrows, over fierce, steely-blue eyes—commanded respect. He had a deep thrilling voice, too, especially when roused; and at such times his expressions were not very choice. Indeed, Sir Charles's language encouraged his enemies and detractors to declare that he had served with the army that had learned to swear in Flanders.

He began on me at once. "By the Lord Harry, this won't do, Wood," he cried, with amazing volubility and force. "I can't stand it, I won't stand it. I'll be something ——d if I stand it. What have you got to say for yourself? Slept late? Of course you will sleep late if you waste the night flirting and philandering with that little madcap devil, Frida Wolstenholme—ta, ta, don't tell me, I saw you. But that's not the point. You may spoon till you're sick, and dance till you're silly, and make up to every heiress in England—counting on your good looks, I suppose, for I don't see what else there is to recommend you. But I won't have the business of this office neglected. Now you are late for parade, and you know I insist upon punctuality. And I practice what I preach. I was here as the clock struck ten this morning, and I'd already been to Hounslow and back on my 'bike.' But there, you'll end by putting me out of temper. Don't do it again."

"I won't, Sir Charles," I said, meekly hardly, wondering why I, a man of millions, submitted to such slavery, and I turned to go.

"Ah! by the way, Wood. Bring me that report of yours, will you, on the defence of the Canadian frontier? It is ready, I presume?"

"Well, no, Sir Charles, not quite. I have been delayed by——"

"Great Scott!" he roared, instantly blazing up again into white heat. "You lazy, idle young villain. I believe you want to drive me mad. You know as well as I do that the Foreign Office is pressing for the paper, that I promised it to Lord Salisbury within a week, and here you, you—oh! go away—I want none of your excuses. I've had enough of you. You shan't stay here, bringing discredit on the office. I'll have none of it. You shall go back to your grovelling, grabby, guard-mounting routine, and when you are grizzling your soul out in that beastly tropical hole, Bermuda, you may be sorry for the chance you've lost. Go away, I say. I've done with you. I hate the very sight of you."

And I went; meaning in my rage—for I, too, had become furiously angry—to take him at his word and walk straight out of the house. But custom is strong—the spirit of subordination, of obedience, the soldierly sense of duty, when once imbibed, are not to be shaken off in a second. When I regained my desk and saw the papers there, I remembered that I was bound in honour to fulfil my obligations. My chief had, no doubt, gone too far; but that did not release me. Before I took any further steps I must first do my tale of bricks.

"Nasty, was he?" laughed Swete Thornhill, who had his hat on, and was clearly prepared to go out to lunch. "No? Don't try any of your humbug with me. Why, we could hear him all over the house. Serve you right."

"Look here, Thornhill——"

"Leave it, man. You've had a wigging—not the first. Drop that ruler, will you." But he thought it better to make for the door. "Not coming to the N. and W., I take it? Mustn't go out till you've done your oakum. Oh, naughty, naughty——"

With that I fired off the ruler, which banged against the hastily-closed door as Thornhill ran for his life.

But he was right. Although not really "kept in," I meant to stay in and give all my energies to the work I had to do. There was not much wanting to finish my report on the Canadian frontier, and I did it out of hand. Then I sent it in to the chief, and prepared to tackle the second set of papers, which proved to be a scheme, marked "strictly confidential," for a combined attack upon New York by sea and land. But now I noticed the word "speak," and I knew that I must take verbal instructions before I set to work. I must face my irascible chief again, and I had no great fancy for it. However, it must come sooner or later, so I scribbled a few words on a sheet of foolscap, and went in.

The General was at his standing desk (he seldom sat down) poring over my other report, but he looked round as I entered, and nodded pleasantly. Bright sunshine had already succeeded the always fugitive storms in his hasty temperament.

"This will do first rate, Wood. There are only one or two points that need amplification," and we went over the items together.

Then I asked him about the other matter, and soon heard all I wanted to know. I can set down nothing of this here, for the whole affair was very secret and particular—of vital interest to two great countries—and Sir Charles impressed it on me very earnestly that the paper and plans must on no account pass out of my possession.

"You may have to work on the scheme at your own diggings, for it must go in by the end of the week; but pray be most careful. Lock up the papers in your despatch-box at night, and keep the thing entirely private."

"Do you imply that I need protection"

"It is just possible that you may wish to give the job to someone else, General, as I shall hardly be here to complete it," I said, rather stiffly, and with that I handed him the sheet of foolscap which contained my resignation.

"Why, Wood, d——n it all, you don't mean this, surely!" cried Sir Charles, aghast. "You can't have taken offence at what I said this morning? I was a trifle put out, perhaps, but I never meant it seriously. No, no, take this beastly thing back, or let me tear it up. We cannot part with you. I like you, so do the rest of us, and you are d——d useful. I will admit that frankly, heartily. This will never do. Forgive and forget, my boy. There's my hand on it. I beg your pardon, and—I know you won't be late again."

I was greatly touched by his kindness, and I told him so, but then I hastened to explain that my resignation was in no way the result of pique, and that I was on the point of sending in my papers to retire from the Service altogether.

"The simple fact is that I have come in to money, sir—a good bit of money," I explained.

"How much, if it is a fair question? I ask, because you may have a good enough income, a devilish fine income, and yet it would be wiser for you to stay here. The discipline of any regular routine work is good for independent men. Believe me, you'd soon sicken of being entirely your own master. Take to drink, or cards, or petticoats, and go to the devil hands down. What is it—two, three, four thousand a year? A very comfortable sum, no doubt, but with it you'll enjoy soldiering all the more. It will give you a good status, too, over there," pointing towards Pall Mall. "They like monied men, I think, at the War Office; at any rate, they are monstrous civil to them."

"But it is far more than what you say, Sir Charles," I went on. "I believe I am a millionaire two or three times over. Will you please read that?" and I handed him my lawyers' letter.

"Whew!" He whistled several bars of a popular street melody (very much out of tune), folded up the letter, handed it back, and then, looking me straight in the face, said, with slow, kindly emphasis:

"By George, Wood, I pity you."

It was not quite what I expected from this experienced, long-headed man of the world, and he read my disappointment in my face.

"Doesn't please you, eh? You think yourself the most fortunate chap alive? But you're all wrong. Vast riches are a nuisance—they are worse."

He threw up both his hands, and began to slowly pace up and down the room.

"A nuisance! A tyranny indeed. They will weigh you down and worry you perpetually. Lord, Lord. The care of all this money, the use of it, the defence of it! The whole world, Wood, is made up of two classes—those who have money, and those who want to take it from them. You will soon have a much poorer opinion of human nature, with their continual cry of 'Give, give.' But, there, that'll come fast enough. Let's talk about yourself. What do you mean to do?"

"Honestly, Sir Charles, I hardly know. I am still too much bewildered and taken aback by what has happened. Will you advise me, sir?"

"It's not so easy, my lad. It depends so much upon yourself—upon your principles, your tastes, and predilections. Everything is open to you. Public life—do you care for politics? Not very keenly, I daresay, and, frankly, I don't recommend it. You're too late to start on a great career, and nothing less is worth the trouble and annoyance—the incessant slavery to your constituents and the House of Commons. Of course you will marry, and I've a shrewd notion which way your fancy lies. I know her well—Frida Wolstenholme, that little minx. Miss Frida will lead you a fine dance."

"But, Sir Charles, I have never spoken to her. I have no reason to suppose that, if I did, she would accept me."

"Try her," said the General, drily. "You have three millions and odd—new and strangely eloquent reasons for convincing her of your worth."

"She is not that sort at all, Sir Charles."

"Then Eve wasn't her ancestor. I've known her from a child. She's pretty enough, I'll admit, and she's well tochered, but, by the living Jingo, I'd rather you married her than I. By George, she'll be a handful. Just look at the way she bullies her dear mother. Square it at once, my boy. Square it if you can. It may be the making of you. At any rate, it will give you plenty to do. Miss Frida will set the money moving, and you too. So much the better, perhaps."

"Then you advise me to leave the Service, sir?"

"Of course you must leave," he roared, with sudden fury. "What, a captain in the army, with a hundred and fifty thousand a year! It's out of the question. But don't be in too great a hurry, Wood. Suppose this windfall proves a fraud, where are you? You can have leave—although I don't know how I can spare you with all this going on——"

Leave was a weak point with Sir Charles. He hated to let anyone go away.

"I should like a few days, sir, soon. I may have things to settle——"

"Oh, if you must, you must, but not for a day or two, please. And, Wood, my dear chap, don't neglect this New York business. I am relying so much on you for it; you've been out there, and know all the ropes. You'll work on these papers, won't you, now, and to-morrow, and whenever you have a chance?"

So I stuck to the papers for the rest of the afternoon, and, when I left, desired the messenger to send them on in a despatch-box to Clarges Street.

## CHAPTER V.

"THAT same American gentleman has been here several times," Savory said, when I reached my rooms. "Would have it he'd got an appointment with you. Told him I didn't know when you'd be home."

"Well, show him up when he calls. I'll see him."

Presently he brought up a card with the name "Erastus K. Snuyzer" on it in gold letters, and the man himself quickly followed. He was dressed in the same irreproachable fashion as when I had seen him in the morning—good new clothes, well cut, a glossy hat, a gardenia, and the shiniest of shoes with big bows.

"Take anything?" I asked, as I offered him a chair. "Cigar, sherry, whisky?"

"Cigar, sir, yes; and, thank you, a glass of water, hot. I am an abstainer, and I follow the precepts, sir, of Dr. Saunderson, of Poughkeepsie. My constitution is frail. I suffer greatly at times."

"Well, now?" I asked, after satisfying his modest wants.

"It's this way," he replied. "My people have calculated that you might like to secure their services."

"One moment, pray; who and what are your people?"

"Saraband and Sons. You have surely heard of them? The great firm of private detectives. Successors of the Pinkertons. I was with Allen Pinkerton, myself, for years, and he reckoned I was one of his smartest pupils."

"What on earth should I do with a private detective?" I cried, with a great laugh.

"I may venture to remind you that you have just succeeded to a vast fortune; the heirship of the McFaught property must be worth several millions to you, and—and—so Sarabands desired me to call."

"Is it part of a rich man's duty or business to keep a private detective?" I was still laughing, but I found no response on the portentously solemn face of my visitor.

"That's as may be, Captain Wood. Some do and some don't. Those who didn't have come to wish they had; so might you."

"And what would happen if I were so foolish as to refuse the obliging offer of 'your people'?" I asked, smilingly.

"I beg of you to be serious, Mr. Wood. Take us, or leave us. But employ someone. Do not, for heaven's sake, attempt to run alone."

He spoke with such evident earnestness and good faith that I began to feel a little uncomfortable.

"Do you imply that I need protection, that I am in any danger, any personal danger? That unless I am taken care of I shall fall a victim to some—what shall I say?—some plot?"

"All that and more. I cannot at this stage be more explicit in my warnings. It would be giving away our business. But there are ample grounds for what I say. I indicated something of the sort of thing when I spoke to you this morning. There are those who grudge you your newly-acquired fortune, who deny your right to it, or even the testator's right to it. They are ready to employ any means—secret, insidious, even violent means, to wrest it from you. Let me tell you, sir, that even now, at this moment, you may be, I believe you are, in imminent peril—you and your life."

"But this is a matter for the police, I cried, hotly, springing to my feet. What! Was I, the owner of three or four millions, to be thus robbed and plundered, possibly murdered, in law-abiding, well-guarded London?

"Your police cannot help you in this. It is too private and particular, and they are of little good till after the event. What you want is prevention, anticipation. You must meet guile with guile, plot with counterplot, always supposing there is time."

"Where is the hurry?"

"We have reason to know that everything was planned some time since."

"Why! the news is not a day old yet!"

"It has long been expected that the McFaught millions would come to England, but the name of the real heir was only disclosed a week ago. Everything was ready, and the campaign was to commence directly it was known who should be attacked."

I looked at this heavy-featured, slow-speaking Yankee, wondering whether he was in earnest or only thought me a fool. I knew, of course, that I had now become fair game for the blackmailers, and I was inclined to imagine that Mr. Snuyzer's solicitude was only a transparent attempt to extort money.

"And what would it cost me to secure the good offices of Messrs. Saraband and Sons?" I asked, seeking enlightenment as to his probable demands.

"Our charges, sir, are no more than out-of-pocket expenses and a small retaining fee, say five-and-twenty dollars a week. After that a *pro rata* premium, according to the risks."

"Risks? I do not quite understand."

"The perils, sir, from which you are saved, whether by premonition, guardianship, or actual rescue. We have a graduated scale. I shall be happy to leave the 'skedool' with you. Here are some of the items: Divorce proceedings—either side, sequestration, false charges, wounding, loss of limb, death——"

"Murder, in short?" I still spoke in a flippant tone. "What is the rate of insurance against that?"

His face did not relax, and he answered gravely:

"From £10,000 up to any sum, according to the nearness of the risk."

"Well, I will think over your obliging offer. Possibly, if I find I cannot take care of myself, I may come to you. For the present I shall trust to Scotland Yard and my own endeavours."

"You are wrong, sir, entirely wrong, believe that," said my visitor, darkly, as he rose to take his leave. "You are in considerable danger, sir, and it will increase hourly. And you have given points against you. The chief aim of these big 'bunco steerers' is, of course, to pouch your dollars, but it is known that you are concerned with the differences between our two great countries. It is supposed that you hold important military information, State secrets that might be got out of you, squeezed out of you, if they put you in a tight place. You may decline our offer—that is your own affair. But, sir, let me conjure you to carry a six-shooter on all occasions; go nowhere—well, to no strange or unusual places—alone."

"I trust it is not quite so bad as all that, Mr. Snuyzer. Still, I am grateful, and I shall certainly remember you if, if——"

"You survive? Yes, *sir*, but do not leave it too late. You have been marked down, captain, and they will strike at you, somehow, soon. To-day, to-morrow, at any time. They contend that the McFaught millions were acquired by spoliation and sharp practice."

"Is there any truth in that?" I broke in, hurriedly.

"Bully McFaught was a smart man, and struck some close things. But he was no more entitled to States' prison than those he fought with on Wall Street. Any stick is good enough to beat a dog with, and your enemies will talk tall about surrendering ill-gotten gains, because it is a good show-card. I do not think you need lie awake wondering whether you should make restitution to the widow and the fatherless—anyway, not till it's forced upon you, as it may be."

"And you can save me from that?"

"Or worse. We think you will be well advised to consider our offer. If we can be of any service to you, remember our telephone number is 287,356, and I shall reply personally or by proxy at any time, day or night. You have, also, my address, 39, Norfolk Street, Strand. I reside there, on the premises. I shall be proud to receive your instructions, and—if it is not too late—to come to your assistance on the shortest notice. Good day, captain. Think well of what I say."

How was I to take all this? Seriously? I had read in every school book of the snares and pitfalls of great wealth, but had never dreamt—who could?—of dangers so strange and terrible as those that now menaced me, if I were to give credence to this extraordinary tale.

It was surely preposterous, the wildest, most extravagant and impossible story. What! A man's life and property in hourly imminent danger here in London, under the ægis of the law, surrounded by one's friends, protected by all the safeguards of civilised existence? It was not to be credited. I, at least, would not believe it—not till I had more direct, unmistakable evidence. I could not accept the mere hints and vague threats of a confidential agent, obviously on the look-out for a new and wealthy client.

Perhaps this conclusion did not entirely satisfy me. I felt in my secret heart that I should be wrong to quite neglect his strange and far-fetched, yet most impressive warning.

But all that would surely keep. Sufficient unto the day was its evil. Five minutes later, with my faithful Roy at my heels, I had set forth to stroll into the park. It was the hour when I was almost certain to meet with Frida Wolstenholme, and I was dying to tell her the great news.

*(To be continued).*

*Photo. MAULL & FOX.*                                                    *Piccadilly.*

## *LIEUT.-GENERAL FREDERICK WILLIAM TRAILL BURROUGHS, C.B.*

LIEUTENANT-GENERAL FREDERICK WILLIAM TRAILL BURROUGHS, C.B., Colonel of the Warwickshire Regiment, is a veteran of the Crimea and Indian Mutiny. In these campaigns, and afterwards in the Sittana Campaign, he served in the 93rd Sutherland Highlanders, to the command of which he eventually succeeded. One of the most gallant officers in the British Army, he fully earned the Victoria Cross, but did not get it. At the Secunderbagh he was one of the first, if not the very first, to enter the hole in the wall which stood for a breach, and was wounded in the head by a cut from a tulwar. At the capture of Lucknow his leg was broken at the blowing up of some buildings. For some years he commanded the 93rd Highlanders, and on retiring from the Army, with the honorary rank of Lieutenant-General, accepted the command of the 1st Orkney Artillery Volunteers, which he resigned only some two years ago. General Burroughs is the proprietor of Rousay, one of the Orkney Islands. He is in his 67th year, and is in possession of many medals and decorations.

# OUR CAVALRY REGIMENTS.

Photo. G. H. THWAITES. *Private 17th Lancers.* York.

THE 5th trace their descent from a regiment of dragoons that served under William of Orange in Ireland, and were formerly styled the 6th (Royal Irish) Dragoons. At Blenheim the regiment was recognised by Marlborough, for the execution it wrought in the ranks of the enemy, and was permitted to carry the captured kettle-drums.

The 5th were present at Ramillies, Oudenarde, and Malplaquet. At the first-named battle, in co-operation with the Scots Greys, they played havoc with the French Grenadiers of Picardy. The regiment was disbanded in 1799, but was revived in 1858 under its present title. As such it was employed at Suakin in 1885. The uniform is blue, the facings, plastron, and collar scarlet, and the plume green.

The 9th were raised in 1715, and fought against Prince James Edward Stuart, in his unsuccessful attempt to gain the throne.

In 1783 the regiment was constituted Light Dragoons. In 1816 they were converted into Lancers, and in 1830 obtained the title of "Queen's," having been noticed by William IV. when on duty at Kensington.

The regiment distinguished itself at Sobraon in the first Sikh War, and in the second at Chillianwalla and Goojerat. In the Indian Mutiny, too, the 9th Lancers were noted for their bravery, both at Delhi and Lucknow. They made the Afghan Campaigns of 1878-80, and took part in the march to Candahar. The uniform is blue, the facings, plastron, and collar scarlet, and the plume black and white.

The 17th Lancers, familiarly known as the "Death or Glory Boys," on account of their badge—a death's head—and their motto—"Or Glory," were raised in 1759. On the outbreak of war with America, the 17th were ordered to the front, and were the first cavalry regiment on that occasion to cross the Atlantic. They were present at Bunker's Hill, and returned to Ireland in 1781. Four troops were employed in the Maroon War, some of them as Marines on board the "Hermione," and five troops served at San Domingo, 1796-97. The regiment was present at Monte Video and Buenos Ayres. It was distinguished in Cutch, 1815, and in the Pindaree War, 1816-18. The 17th embarked for the Crimea in 1854, and were present at the Alma, Inkerman, and Balaclava, in the last battle forming part of the Light Brigade. They served in India towards the end of the Mutiny, and in Zululand, notably at Ulundi. The uniform is blue, the facings, plastron, collar, and plume white.

Photos. GREGORY. *Corporal 5th Lancers.*

*Private 9th Lancers.*

# HOMES OF THE ARMY.

LANCASTER enjoys, in common with a very few English towns, the distinction of being represented by a territorial regiment of its very own. This, too, notwithstanding the fact that Lancashire contributes five other regiments to our Army, namely, the East and South Lancashire, the Lancashire Fusiliers, the Manchester, and the King's (Liverpool) Regiment. As the depôt of the Royal Lancaster Regiment and the headquarters of a regimental district, Lancaster Barracks have a typical importance, which is well illustrated by the eight photographs on these two pages, for, although it has been the policy of the War Office, ever since the introduction of the Territorial System in 1881, to keep the regimental district and the depôt at rather a low standard of vitality, with the result that even in the Service itself their functions are often imperfectly understood, there is no getting over the fact that these two institutions represent the true inwardness of territorialisation, and, further, in time of war would have a

*Officers' Quarters.*

strain put upon them which in not a few cases they would have great difficulty in sustaining.

Looking, for instance, at the peace and order which characterise these pictures of Lancaster Barracks, one can have little idea of the trouble and turmoil that would reign assuming that we were in the throes of a great war in which the Royal Lancasters were taking, as they assuredly would take, a gallant and glorious part. The only indication of the altered functions of the depôt under such circumstances is the photograph of the interior of the armoury, showing rifles for the Army Reserve. Here we have a reminder of the fact that in any general mobilisation the first thing a depôt has to do is to call in all the first-class Army Reserve men belonging to the territorial regiment, sending each man a passage warrant and the comfortable sum of three shillings per postal order, with a view to expediting his arrival as much as possible. As the men arrive—there are only about 80,000 of them dotted over the country, an average of some hundreds to each regiment—they have to be lodged, boarded, clothed, and

*The Armoury.*

*Photo.* R. SMALLEY.     *Ante-Room, Officers' Mess.*

*Dining-Room, Officers' Mess.*     *Morecambe*

*Interior of Armoury.*

*In the Store-Room.*

*Men's Quarters and Armoury.*

armed, and, after they have picked up their drill on the depôt square, sent on to one or another battalion to bring up to war strength, replace war wastage, and so on. Assuming that the war was a protracted one, there would be other developments at the depôt, such as the formation of a " second provisional battalion," into which, however, we need not go further here. What has been said already is sufficient to show that, although it is possible for a depôt to become something rather resembling a "Sleepy Hollow" in the piping times of peace—of course, this is not the rule—the moment a great war takes place all these depôt barracks will suddenly become hotbeds of activity, and, let us confidently anticipate, serious mainstays of our fighting strength.

In peace time the main business of the regimental district and depôt is recruiting. The recruit comes in with more or less hay-seed in his hair, he is provided with accommodation, given rations and uniform, and at once started on his military duties, in which he is fairly well grounded before he is allowed to join a service battalion. To accomplish all this a permanent staff is, of course, necessary, and this constitutes the only stable element in a depôt barracks, all the remaining o cupants, including the Militia, who do their preliminary training at this centre, being birds of passage merely. The command of the district and depôt is vested in an officer who holds rank as a colonel on the staff, and who, as a rule, has commanded one of the Line battalions of the territorial regiment. He is assisted, generally speaking, by four officers between the ranks of major and second lieutenant, one of whom acts as adjutant; and as the commanding officer usually lives apart, and one, at least, of the others is married, the depôt mess is sometimes not a very lively institution. But this need not prevent the officer on duty at the depôt from leading a very pleasant life so far as social amenities go.

Reverting to our illustrations, these, it will be noted, give a singularly complete idea of depôt life, whether as regards the commissioned or non-commissioned ranks.

The officers' mess, is a neat structure of some architectural pretensions, and, as will be noted from the two pictures representing respectively the dining and ante rooms of the officers' mess, with distinct claims to interior comfort. The remaining photographs are of special interest to those interested in the details of barrack life from the time when the recruit, attracted by the posters on the gate, enters the square to the proud moment when he is given a rifle from the armoury, and, after spending a good many hours per diem in learning how to carry it, seeks well-earned rest on the comfortable bed provided for his use by a grateful country.

*Photos. R. SMALLEY.*          *Interior of Men's Quarters, " D " Company.*          *Morecambe.*

MAXIM GUNS 2nd BATTALION WORCESTERSHIRE REGIMENT ON THE MARCH.

*Photo. R. ELLIS, Malta.*

MAXIM GUNS IN ACTION.

*Copyright.—HUDSON & KEARNS.*

IN almost every recent campaign, whether great or small, machine guns have played an important part. They have been conspicuous both on account of their extreme mobility and alarming destructive power. As an adjunct to infantry they are invaluable, and one or two may now be found attached to almost every battalion. That their worth is fully appreciated by the Authorities may be gathered from the fact that at the recent Royal Review at Aldershot, battalions armed with these deadly weapons appeared with them on parade. Unlike artillery, however (with which machine guns must not be confused), the Maxim, now king of machine guns, can be drawn a considerable distance by the machine-gun detachment, without the assistance of a mule or horse. On any field day it may be seen careering over hill and dale at "the double," drawn by draft animals of the human species, coming into action belching forth a shower of lead, and then moving on to another position of vantage. Such work is trying at home, but it is even more so in Malta and other tropical climates, where the British soldier at his best is not too energetic.

# Miss Daniell's Soldiers' Homes at Aldershot and London.

THIRTY-FIVE years ago our great training camp was a new institution, but even then the town of Aldershot had commenced to replace the original village of 600 inhabitants on the site of which it stands. The new town offered attractions to the soldiers in the shape of public-houses, dancing saloons, and other places of resort; but the encouragements to well-doing by which the men are now surrounded were entirely wanting. In point of fact, it was extremely difficult for a well-disposed and well-conducted young soldier to pursue a straight course, the temptations being many and the aids to self-restraint few and feeble.

In these circumstances, a Christian lady, the widow of an officer, was moved with compassion for the brave lads and men whose best interests were so much neglected. That lady was Mrs. Daniell, the founder of the Aldershot Mission Hall and Soldiers' Home, a place to which soldiers of all ranks look back with the most grateful and affectionate regard. Assisted by another officer's widow

*The Aldershot " Soldiers' Home."*

*Ready for " Fifty Up."*

*Photos.* WYRALL   *An Hour with a Book*   Aldershot.

and some like-minded ladies, Mrs. Daniell opened a house as a temporary home where soldiers might enjoy harmless recreation, attend religious meetings, if so inclined, and be at all times welcome. It was little more than a year later that the present building was erected, Mrs. Daniell having, in the meantime, secured land and collected a sum of £3,000 for her object.

The saying is attributed to the Duke of Wellington, that "in every barrack there should be a place where a man could read his Bible and write to his mother." This is merely the concise expression of the root idea which has been developed and amplified by Mrs. Daniell and her ladies. The Aldershot Home contains dining, reading, billiard, and smoking rooms, bedrooms, lending library, class-room, a hall that holds about 500, and a drawing-room for officers' meetings. Any soldier can have access to books, games, and writing materials; there are classes for reading, writing, and singing; and a religious meeting, attendance at which is optional, is held for an hour every evening. At the bar, good refreshments, but no intoxicants, are provided. Add to all this the kind, pervading presence of ladies who devote their lives and their talents to the promotion of the soldier's welfare, and who are always ready to advise and sympathise with him in trouble or adversity, and it must be realised how vastly we are indebted to the wise heads and tender hearts that pioneered so beneficent a movement.

Mrs. Daniell died in 1871, having been spared to see the Aldershot Home solidly established, and to make plans for branch homes at other places. The care of the parent establishment, and the extension of the good work, devolved on her daughter, the late Miss Daniell, on whom descended a "double portion" of her mother's spirit, and whose name will long be held in high honour by officers and men, as that of an unfailing and unselfish friend of the British soldier.

Miss Daniell and her fellow-labourers have always been careful to maintain the unsectarian position which was at the outset taken up by Mrs. Daniell. All soldiers, of whatsoever persuasion, are received with equal cordiality, and no attempt is made to obtrude dogma or make proselytes. In connection with the Homes there are temperance agencies, savings banks, needlework societies for employing soldiers' wives, and other arrangements for the benefit of the men and their families; but the ruling principle and motive of the whole are supplied by the Christian faith. The furnishing and general management of the several Homes are as nearly alike as possible, so that men who have frequented one have the agreeable impression of being among old associations when they enter another.

After the death of Miss Daniell, Miss Kate Hanson was entrusted with the charge of the Homes, and it is gratifying to know that their value is as much as ever appreciated by the men.

The London Soldiers' Home, in James Street, Buckingham Gate, is the most recently-formed branch of the parent establishment at Aldershot, but the great demand for accommodation has already proved the necessity for additional room. So many soldiers pass through London and stop at the Home, that the sleeping space has been found quite inadequate, although additions have more than once been made to it. Miss Hanson has been telling her wants, and it is to be hoped that they will be promptly and liberally supplied, for it is out of character to refuse a bed to a wearied soldier who comes seeking a "home," and expecting the comforts which the name implies. This is especially so in the case of married soldiers, who are sometimes obliged to find other and inferior lodgings at what is, for their pockets, a heavy additional expense. Miss Hanson says, in a published statement, that "only a

*Photo. ROUCH.*          The London "Soldiers' Home."          *Strand.*

short time since, thirty-seven men from one Highland regiment had to bivouac downstairs," and it is a not uncommon thing for men to sleep on tables and settees, all the beds being occupied by previous arrivals.

The proposed alterations in the London Home will not cost much, and will certainly be an improvement, although it would have been more satisfactory if there had not been a diminution of the cubic air space. This, however, seems inevitable, because no adjoining ground is available for further building. The incalculable influence for the good of the Army which is put forth by these Homes should commend them to the favour of all who have it in their power to assist. In an unostentatious and inexpensive way they tend to popularise the Service, and to make it a training school for the thousands who annually return into civil life.

Miss Daniell's Homes are likewise established at Chatham, Plymouth, Colchester, and Windsor; but the most important of the branches is that of London. All these agencies should be looked upon with a friendly eye; but Miss Daniell's Homes are viewed by many with special favour because they offer an equal welcome to all soldiers, and do not bear the label of any one denomination. Another fact to their credit is that they were the first in the field. This should not be forgotten when help is required in the admirable and many-sided work of which they are the centres.

*Photo. ROUCH.*          A Quiet Game of Chess.          *Strand.*

## On Guard on the Thibet Frontier.

WE show here the quarter guard of a detachment of the 2nd Manchester Regiment—the old 96th—at Fort Graham, Gnatong, Sikkim, as equipped for their special duty in Balaclava caps, snow goggles, thick lined greatcoats and warm gloves, blue serge trousers, khaki putties, and ammunition boots. Fort Graham is the highest post in the world occupied by British troops, and its altitude above the sea is 12,300-ft. It is situated at the foot of the Jalap La (Pass) into Thibet, about seventy miles by road from the Indian hill station of Darjeeling. The men liked the change there, from the baked plains of Bengal, very much, and profited greatly while in the hills in health, as their exceedingly robust and healthy appearance on being visited at the post testified. Fort Graham was first occupied after the Sikkim Expedition of 1888. Since our photograph was taken, the European garrison there has been withdrawn and a police outpost established instead.

The fort itself, it should be observed in connection with the uniform that the men are shown wearing, lies no great distance below the snow line of the Upper Himalayas, and during its occupation by the 2nd Manchesters the snowfall was abundant all round. It is just nine miles within the frontier line between British India and Thibet.

*From a Photo.*          *By a Military Officer.*

*At Fort Graham, 12,300-ft. above Sea Level.*

# MAKING THE SOLDIER.

Photo. GREGORY.     *BAYONET EXERCISE AT ALDERSHOT.*

THE modern infantry soldier is armed with two weapons—the rifle to use at long ranges, and the bayonet for hand to hand fighting. Against the bullets of the enemy he can make use of natural and artificial cover, but when attacked at close quarters he must defend himself and try to disable his assailant with the bayonet. It is, therefore, important that he should know how to use it. Such a scene as the above may be witnessed daily in any military gymnasium.

# THE GORDON BOYS' ORPHANAGE.

THE Gordon Boys' Orphanage at Dover is one of the two excellent institutions founded in memory of the great Christian soldier who fell at Khartoum. It was founded by its present honorary manager, Mr. T. Blackman, with the full consent and approval of the hero's sisters, who have never ceased to take the greatest interest in its welfare. The little kilted lads are well cared for and well brought up, with good manners, being in consequence, universally popular. At the recent review of the Dover garrison, in honour of Her Majesty's Jubilee, the boys, at the invitation of the general officer commanding the district, had the distinguished honour of parading and marching past with the troops. This photograph was taken in July last, by permission of the officers of the Royal Engineers, in front of the statue erected by them to the memory of General Gordon, who, it is well known, was a devoted friend to boys.

From a Photo.     *Pipers and Drums Under the Statue of General Gordon at Chatham.*     By a Military Officer

King Charles II at a Board of Admiralty

## THE STORY OF THE BRITANNIAS In War and Peace
by Edward Fraser & John Leyland.

**THE KING DECIDING TO BUILD OUR FIRST "BRITANNIA," 1676.**

IN the autumn of the year 1676 there was a great scare in England. Public opinion suddenly took alarm at the startling progress that the French Navy, under Colbert's able administration, was making, and in view of hostilities with France that seemed imminent, pressure was put on the King's advisers to see to the condition of the Fleet. The general feeling of alarm found voice in Parliament in the form of an urgent demand for the immediate laying down of a number of new ships. It was represented that a large proportion of the ships of the Fleet were old vessels, dating back to before Cromwell's time, while of those built since many had been severely knocked about during the recent Dutch wars, and very little care had been taken as to repairs. The upshot of it all was that a sum of £600,000, in the money of those days, was unanimously voted by Parliament, and the King in Council announced that thirty new ships—one first-rate man-of-war of 100 guns, nine second-rates of ninety guns, and twenty third-rates of seventy guns—would at once be laid down, and pushed on with as rapidly as it was possible to build the ships. For these the money was to be found by monthly assessments of £35,000, raised by a general levy on every parish throughout the kingdom. The levy was acceded to with enthusiasm all over the country. As has always been the case with us whenever the necessity for the strengthening of the Fleet has been brought home to the nation, all came forward to make ungrudging response to the appeal. King Charles then, as if to mark with special emphasis the national character of the movement, announced his intention to appoint to the most important ship of the thirty, the proposed first-rate, the name "Britannia." Surely our Sovereign Lord King Charles, when he fixed on and placed such a name on the roll of the Royal Navy, for once, at any rate, both said a wise thing and did one.

The "Britannia," so added to the Fleet and so named, was laid down in Chatham Dockyard, and launched on the 28th June, 1682. She was at all points the finest and most powerful war-ship of the time, and every effort was made to make her worthy of her name. Here are the principal details of our first "Britannia": She was a three-decker of 1,739 tons, carrying 100 guns in all; 167-ft. 5-in. along her lower or gun deck, 48-ft. 8-in. broad amidships, and, fully equipped for sea, drew 22-ft. of water. Sir Phineas Pett, the great master shipwright of the day in England, a member of the famous family of Petts, master builders of the Navy since the time of Edward VI., the grandson of the Phineas Pett who built Charles I.'s famous "Sovereign of the Seas," designed and built our first "Britannia."

The "Britannia's" active career opens with the order for her to fit for sea as flag-ship to the Commander-in-Chief designate of the "Grand" or Channel Fleet, Admiral Edward Russell, in December, 1690, the year of the battle of Beachy Head. It was just after the court-martial on Torrington. An hour of grave national peril was at hand, and the Government were about to make a supreme effort to recover our lost supremacy in Home waters. It was, indeed, time. The French were openly announcing their intention to carry matters with a high hand, and talking of having at sea next summer no fewer than 130 ships, 86 of which were to be of the Line. The effective strength of the British Fleet at this time was no more than 80 of the Line. Spies and reports from Brest, Rochfort, and Toulon told also that they were working night and day in the French dockyards, while every man who had been afloat in the previous summer was still kept on board ship, in order that the Fleet might sail again at the earliest moment—the end of March or, at latest, early in April. Fuller confirmation of the French designs then came to hand from one of Sir Cloudesley Shovell's cruisers stationed off Scilly, which brought in a despatch captured on board a French frigate known to be specially attached to the Brest Fleet as tender to Tourville's flag-ship. The captured papers gave a detailed account of the proposed mobilisation of the French Fleet, and supplied a complete list of the ships that the French intended to fit out.

In consequence of the news there were repeated sittings of the Council of State, the King being present in person on each occasion, while the Admiralty Commissioners met day after day—at their new home in St. James's Park, formerly the mansion of the infamous Judge Jeffreys. Every available ship was ordered into commission, and thirty thousand men, the largest Naval levy yet known, Admiral Russell, as has been said, being designated to the chief command, with, for his Captain of the Fleet, the most experienced and trusted officer below flag rank in all the King's service, Sir Cloudesley Shovell.

To encourage seamen to come forward, it was announced that every man joining would be clothed at the cost of the State. "Gentlemen's sons up to the age of eighteen years" were invited to enter on board ship as "volunteers," with special pay of £24 a year. Public spirit ran high on every side. The City Fathers, asked to advance £200,000 towards the fitting out of the Fleet, met the appeal by holding a special sitting in the Council Chamber at the Guildhall, and in addition to agreeing *nem. con.* to the request, subscribed £50,000 towards it on the spot, with a further formal undertaking that the balance of the money would be lodged at the Treasury within a week. The Town Council of Plymouth in formal session resolved to present a new man-of-war forthwith to the King, a loyal determination carried out by the immediate purchase of a fine vessel of 600 tons, which was converted into a 42-gun ship and handed over to the Admiralty. In these circumstances our first "Britannia" fitted out for her initial blue water cruise, in which she opened her career with the Union at the main.

The Naval events of 1691 consisted of a long Channel cruise, during which the French Fleet, from first to last, kept out of reach of Admiral Russell, and we may pass at once to the next year—1692—when the "Britannia" underwent her baptism of fire at the great battle off Cape Barfleur.

Emboldened by their success in avoiding a general action during 1691, and recalling the good fortune that had befallen them off Beachy Head in the year before that, the French, for their campaign of 1692, planned a stroke of still greater daring. They openly spoke of throwing an Army into England to seize London and reinstate the deposed King James by force of arms. Their Fleet, they said, would force its way across the Channel regardless of what the British Navy might attempt against them. As for Admiral Russell's Fleet, they said, if the English ships, after what had happened at Beachy Head, should actually meet them at sea, Russell's men would prove shy of trying to stop them. Indeed, if the English captains did not actually declare against King William, they would make common cause with the French captains on behalf of the restoration of King James. The ex-King of England, James himself, as a fact, went about openly declaring as much, and he even said that he had positive assurance that this was what Russell's Fleet intended to do. As Duke of York, James had been Lord High Admiral of England, and had always shown lively interest in everything connected with the Sea Service, on behalf of which as King, during his short three years of reign, he had done all in his power, and he also had at that moment among the captains in Russell's Fleet a large number of personal friends, whose dislike of the recent doings of the new Government was notorious.

That, however, was not all. Not a few people in England, with opportunities for knowing something of the situation, held similar views, and helped to spread a wide-felt suspicion of the loyalty of the Channel Fleet to the new *régime.* "At all the coffee-houses admirals and captains," says Macaulay, "were mentioned by name as traitors who ought to be instantly cashiered, if not shot. It was even confidently affirmed that some of the guilty had been put under arrest and others turned out of the Service." The means by which Queen Mary and her Council (the King being in Flanders) met the dilemma with which they had to deal, constitutes the first public appearance on the pages of our history of the "Britannia."

"On the 15th of May," to tell the story, as begun, in the words of Lord Macaulay, "a great assembly of officers was convoked at St. Helen's on board of the 'Britannia,' on which Russell's flag was flying. The admiral told them that he had received a despatch which he was charged to read to them. It was from Nottingham. 'The Queen,' the Secretary wrote, 'had been informed that stories deeply affecting the character of the Navy were in circulation. It had been affirmed that she had found herself under the necessity of dismissing many officers. But Her Majesty was determined to believe nothing against those brave servants of the State. The gentlemen who had been so foully slandered might be assured that she placed entire reliance in them.' The letter was admirably calculated to work on those to whom it was addressed. Very few of them probably had been guilty of any worse offence than rash and angry talk over their wine. They were as yet only grumblers. If they had fancied that they were marked men they might in self-defence have become traitors. They became enthusiastically loyal as soon as they were assured that the Queen reposed entire confidence in their loyalty. They eagerly signed an address in which they entreated her to believe that they would, with the utmost resolution and alacrity, venture their lives in defence of her rights, of English freedom, and of the Protestant religion, against all foreign and Popish invaders. God," they added. "preserve your person, direct your counsels, and prosper your arms, and let all your people say 'Amen.'" Four days later came the great battle off Barfleur—

"When Tourville
o'er the main tri-
umphant rolled
To meet the gal-
lant Russell, in
action ship to
ship"—

in which the "Britannia's" officers and men showed to the world in gallant style that they for their part meant and knew how to keep their word.

Photo. W. M. Crockett.                    Copyright.—H. & K.
*CAPTAIN THE HON. ASSHETON G. CURZON-HOWE, C.B., C.M.G.,*
Commanding H.M.S. "Britannia."

Getting trustworthy news that the French Fleet, which had left Brest some time before, had been sighted off the Dorset coast, Admiral Russell, on the forenoon of the 18th of May, with the wind light from the south-west, sailed from his anchorage off Cuiver Cliff, Isle of Wight, standing over towards Cape Barfleur on a course to take him directly across the line of the approaching enemy. It proved exactly the right thing. At daybreak next morning, when Russell was in sight of Barfleur, just seven leagues off, the van ships of the French Fleet were sighted heading directly up Channel. Their intention, as the English admiral had judged, was to double Cape Barfleur and join hands with the transports with the

invading French Army on board, now collected in the Bay of La Hogue, and ready
for the enterprise. The English line was
formed close to the wind (light from the
west), heading in a general direction
southwardly. Our Dutch allies, twenty-
two ships, who had joined Russell a few
days before, formed the van squadron;
then came the English Red Squadron,
under the immediate orders of Russell
himself in the "Britannia"; and in the
rear the English Blue Squadron, headed
by the "Victory," the flag-ship of Admiral
Sir John Ashby. The English numbered
fifty-seven ships in all, but the Blue
Squadron was for the time separated from
the main body and to leeward, unable to
get into station owing to the wind falling
light. "I bore away with my own ship,"
wrote Russell, describing his movements
to the Earl of Nottingham, Secretary of
State, "so far to leeward as I judged each
ship in the Fleet might fetch my wake or
grain, then brought-to again, lying by
with my foretopsail to the mast to give
the ships in the Fleet the better opportunity of placing themselves as they had been directed."

While this was being carried out slowly—for during
the night the Fleet had straggled a good deal—the

THE COMPANY OF THE "BRITANNIA."

WARRANT OFFICERS AND SEAMEN INSTRUCTORS.

French, were nearing us boldly, rapidly forming line as
they advanced, finally coming to the wind on the same
tack as ourselves, just within musket shot. The enemy numbered in all fifty ships, against forty which
comprised Russell's own squadron, on
which the French attack was concentrated.
The Blue Squadron, of twenty-nine sail,
were too far to leeward to be for the time
of any account, and the Dutch van becalmed. So Russell himself explains in
a letter written just after the battle. "The
enemy's ships," says the admiral, "did
not exceed fifty ships of war, of which
number eighteen of them had three decks,
and but two so small as fifty-six guns.
Though their number was inferior to ours,
yet I positively affirm that the ships of
their Majesties which beat them did not
exceed forty, for, the weather being so
thick and quite calm, the Dutch, who led
the van, could not come to fight, and the
Blue, who were in the rear, could not
come up except in the night about eight
o'clock."

Tourville, who had the white flag at
the main in the big "Soleil Royal," of
100 guns, commanded the French Fleet.
He acted with a skill worthy of his reputation as the most *rusé* Naval officer of the

OFFICERS AND TEACHING STAFF OF THE "BRITANNIA."

day, and at the outset took prompt advantage of the situation. Concentrating his force to attack Russell's centre, he threw his full weight—his centre and rear squadrons together with half his van squadron—on Russell's squadron by itself, holding the Dutch van meanwhile in check with the other half of his own van, about half the Dutch strength. There was no need to trouble about the Blue Squadron. It was a skilful piece of tactics on the part of the French commander, and gave him a fair chance of snatching a victory. There seemed for the time more than a chance that Tourville might be able to crush his antagonist's centre by a sudden concentrated attack with overpowering numbers in a situation where the rest of the British Fleet could render their admiral no aid.

The brunt of the fighting thus fell on the "Britannia" and the ships nearest her, and they made a defence against heroic odds worthy of the nation whose ensign they bore, the "Britannia" for more than an hour and a-half closely engaging the French admiral's flag-ship, the big three-decker "Soleil Royal," at close quarters. "The French admiral," as Russell puts it, "plied his guns very warmly, though our men fired their guns faster." Until, in fact, the French had had more than enough of it. "After that time," continues Admiral Russell, "I did not find his guns were fired with that vigour as before, and I could see him in great disorder; his rigging, sails, and topsail yards being shot, and nobody endeavouring to make them serviceable, and his boats towing of him to windward, gave me reason to think he was much galled."

It was at this time, somewhere about two o'clock in the afternoon, that the favourable shift of the wind occurred which altered the fortunes of the fight. The wind freshening suddenly and veering four points, enabled the rear division of our Red Squadron, hitherto unable to help their chief during Tourville's attack, to lay up and weather the French. It likewise enabled the Dutch van to assist, and also brought up to windward of the enemy the whole of the English Blue Squadron. The tables were turned on the French, suddenly placing the entire French Fleet in serious jeopardy. But at the critical moment, just as the shift of wind had saved our Red Squadron, a fog came on to save the French—a fog so thick "that we could not see a ship of the enemy's, which occasioned our leaving off firing for a little time."

The fog lasted long enough to enable the French Commander-in-Chief to realise his dangerous position and prepare to make for port as the only course left him.

"When the fog cleared up," wrote Admiral Russell from the "Britannia," "we could see Monsieur Tourville towing away with his boats to the northward from us, upon which I did the same, and ordered all my Division to do the like; and about half-an-hour after five we had a small breeze of wind easterly. I then made the signal for the Fleet to chase, sending notice to all the ships about me that the enemy were running. . . . I sent all the ships that I could think were near me to chase to the westward all night, telling them I designed to follow the enemy to Brest; and sometimes we could see a French ship, or two or three, standing away with all the sail they could make to the westward. About eight I heard guns firing to the westward, which lasted about half-an-hour, it being some of our Blue fallen in with some of the ships of the enemy in the fog. 'Twas foggy and very little wind all night."

The battle was now over, as far as the "Britannia" was concerned, for in the subsequent boat work in the Bay of La Hogue, which completed the destruction of the enemy, though her men distinguished themselves in the "Britannia's" boats, the ship herself could take but little active part. Nor did she get another opportunity that year, her commission terminating at the end of August, at which time it was customary to lay up all first and second rates. "A man who kept the Capital ships out after September," wrote Sir Cloudesley Shovell, "would deserve to be shot."

The year following Barfleur is of note in the "Britannia's" story for the special circumstance that she had three admirals together on board her, jointly in command of the Channel Fleet, by a special commission, and flying one flag between them. Suspicious and uneasy, the Government, by way of showing their gratitude to Admiral Russell after his victory at Barfleur, ordered him to strike his flag, the command of the Channel Fleet being placed in commission under three "joint admirals," as they were called—Henry Killigrew, Sir Ralph Delaval, and Sir Cloudesley Shovell. The experiment, however—it had been tried once before, in 1690, immediately on Torrington's arrest after the battle of Beachy Head, when three joint admirals commanded the Channel Fleet by special commission, with their common flag in the

*ADMIRAL RUSSELL READING THE DESPATCH FROM THE QUEEN, MAY 15, 1692.*

*THE "BRITANNIA" ENGAGING THE "SOLEIL ROYAL" OFF CAPE BARFLEUR, MAY 19, 1692.*

"Royal Sovereign"—proved a failure, and has not been since repeated.

A better time came for the "Britannia" in 1694, when she again hoisted the flag of her old chief, Admiral Russell, for service at the head of one of, perhaps, the very finest fleets that England, up to that time, had ever sent to sea. The Mediterranean was now her destination, the French having recently transferred their Brest Fleet round to Toulon to carry on a series of operations against Spain, which country was at that time allied with England. For two years the "Britannia" and her fleet remained in the Mediterranean watching the coast of Spain, and making the French Fleet keep close in port. If there was little fighting going, owing to the shyness of the enemy, there was plenty of useful work done in other ways by the presence of so powerful a British Fleet in the Western Mediterranean, and it would seem also plenty of fun and entertainment for Admiral Russell and his officers in the way of banquets and conviviality at the various places where the Fleet cast anchor. Witness the story of the wonderful bowl of punch—the like of which was probably never seen before, nor is likely to be seen again—which Admiral Russell is said to have had brewed for a great entertainment that he gave to the Spanish authorities at Alicante. The tables for the banquet, we are told, were laid in an orange grove in four walks converging to a centre, where a marble fountain that stood there was, for the occasion, turned into a punch bowl. Into that punch bowl then went (the figures are on record):—Four hogsheads of brandy, one pipe of Malaga wine, twenty gallons of lime juice, 2,500 lemons, thirteen hundredweight of fine white sugar, five pounds of grated nutmeg, 300 toasted biscuits, and eight hogsheads of water. The gallant admiral, we are finally told, got a tiny boat built to float on his lake of punch, in which was put a sailor boy, who kept rowing round the fountain, and continually filling the glasses of the 6,000 guests that assembled on the festive occasion.

Returning to England with Admiral Russell on board towards the end of 1695, the "Britannia" then for two years served off the coast of France as flag-ship to the Channel Fleet—flying the flag of, among others, the famous Admiral Sir George Rooke—until, in October, 1697, on the Peace of Ryswick being signed, she paid off and was taken in hand at Chatham Dockyard to be refitted. There is a fine model of the "Britannia" of this time in the Naval Museum at Greenwich.

Having been the flag-ship of Russell and Rooke during the last decade of the seventeenth century, it next fell to the "Britannia" to be flag-ship to the third of our three great admirals of the period, Sir Cloudesley Shovell, in the first decade of the eighteenth century, and at the same time to be nominal flag-ship to one of the most extraordinary characters in history, the celebrated Earl of Peterborough. This was in 1705, during the war of the Spanish Succession, in Queen Anne's reign, when the "Britannia," with Sir Cloudesley Shovell's flag at the main, made her second appearance in the Mediterranean as Commander-in-Chief's ship at the head of a British Fleet. Lord Peterborough was associated with Sir Cloudesley on the special service that the Fleet was designed to perform off the coast of Spain, with, although Peterborough was a purely military officer, special powers as supreme commander over both sea and land forces. It was a curious arrangement, and one that, as might have been expected, worked curiously. Peterborough, it is told, would sometimes at the Council of War with his land officers favour certain courses, which he would immediately afterwards, in his Naval capacity in Council of War with his associated sea officers, find fault with and condemn. On one occasion, at the siege of Barcelona, for example, the Earl and his Military Council demanded from the Fleet 1,500 men to man the guns in the siege batteries, together with a contingent of 1,200 Marines. Next day Lord Peterborough, in council with the flag officers of the Fleet, took a Naval view of the situation, and formally overruled the demand as quite out of the question.

In the great event of the expedition, the bombardment and final reduction of Barcelona, the "Britannia"—both with her men on shore and by firing on the sea forts—took a prominent part, after which, towards the end of the year 1705, she returned to England. Sir Cloudesley again hoisted his flag in the ship, indeed, in the following year, as flag-ship to the Channel Fleet for a projected attack on the French coast, but owing to delays and bad management on shore, the expedition was stopped at the last moment, and the "Britannia" returned to her moorings in the Medway, never to put to sea again. Eight years later, on the great overhaul of our men-of-war that took place at the close of Queen Anne's war, on George I. coming to the throne, our first "Britannia" was taken to pieces, to be rebuilt into a new and larger ship, and so her story closes.

The new "Britannia," which came into existence in this way out of the timbers of the old, is reckoned as our second ship of the name. Her story, however, is a short one. Though on several occasions at sea, as flag-ship of the Channel Fleet, during her thirty years of existence, from 1719 to 1749, she never had occasion to fire an angry gun. Her career closes finally in the terms of an Admiralty Minute dated September 14th, 1749:— "'Britannia' to be taken to pieces and her useful remains applied to new structures."

Photo. W. M. Crockett.        THE "BRITANNIA"—MIDDLE DECK.        Copyright.—H. & K.

Much more famous a ship was our third "Britannia," a three-decker of 2,000 odd tons, launched at Portsmouth Dockyard in 1762—exactly eighty years from the sending afloat of our first "Britannia."

Photo. W. M. Crockett.        THE MESS-ROOM IN THE "BRITANNIA."        Copyright.—H. & K

It was just at the close of the Seven Years' War, when the French flag had been practically swept from the seas, and our other enemy, Spain, was *in extremis*, consequent on which state of things there proved to be no need even to commission the new three-decker. Nor, indeed, was the "Britannia's" pennant hoisted for upwards of sixteen years afterwards, during the spell of peace that followed the triumphs of Hawke and Boscawen. Our ancestors of the days when "George III. was king" managed their sea affairs on other lines than those which find favour with us. Instead of as now, when the finest ships of the day are found in commission and at sea forming part of our cruising fleets in the Channel or the Mediterranean, our ancestors preferred to keep their best and biggest ships at home, employing instead as few and as small ships in the cruising squadrons as possible.

So we come, in due course, to the outbreak of the war with France and Spain, in 1779, when first France and then Spain made common cause with England's revolted American colonies The "Britannia" now hoisted her first pennant, and in March, 1779, was appointed flag-ship to Vice-Admiral George Darby second in command of the Channel Fleet. With this force, flying Admiral Darby's flag for the greater part of the time, the "Britannia" served during three years— memorable insomuch that one would like to blot the record of them, as far as the Channel Fleet is concerned, from our Naval annals.

It was the unfortunate period in our history when, owing to downright negligence on the part of those responsible for our Naval administration, year after year a hostile combination, arrogant in the assurance of overpowering numerical preponderance, held the command of the English Channel, insulting our coasts, and defying the British Channel Fleet, though every available ship in our home ports was in the Channel, to interfere with it.

Great interest attaches to the "Britannia's" share in

Photo. W. M. Crockett.        Copyright.—H. & K.
A LESSON IN SEAMANSHIP—THE "WHISKERS" OF THE "BRITANNIA."

Kempenfelt's brilliant action with the French admiral, De Guichen, to the westward of Ushant, in December, 1781. Kempenfelt, with twelve ships, in the grey of a winter's morning met De Guichen with nineteen ships in charge of a very important convoy of store vessels on the way out from Brest to join De Grasse's Fleet, then facing Rodney and Hood in the West Indies. It chanced that the French ships of war, when fallen in with, were to leeward of their convoy. Kempenfelt saw that, and, keeping his squadron well in hand, with skill equal to his daring, dashed in between the escort and the convoy, and carried off nineteen of the pick of the French store-ships as prizes, in the face of the enemy's superior force, before the chagrined De Guichen could do anything to save them.

In 1782 a very distinguished seaman of the old school had his flag in the "Britannia" — Admiral Barrington. With him in April

*THE CHURCH IN THE "HINDOSTAN."*

of that year the "Britannia" was present in the running fight with a French squadron in the Channel, when Jervis's "Foudroyant" captured the French "Pègase." As Barrington's flag-ship, also, the "Britannia," in the following autumn, led the van squadron of Lord Howe's Fleet at the final relief of Gibraltar, taking part, in addition, in the long-range skirmishing encounter with the Franco-Spanish Armada off Cape Spartel, on which occasion the "Britannia" had twenty casualties, killed and wounded.

The breaking out of the Great War with the French Republic, in 1793, introduced the "Britannia" to her second campaign, on which she entered with the Mediterranean Fleet under Lord Hood as flag-ship of Vice-Admiral Hotham, second in command, to take throughout a prominent part in the Naval operations in that quarter which the British Government had in view. With Hood's Fleet the "Britannia" was present at Toulon in all our proceedings there, from the seizure of the port and the French Toulon Fleet with it by Lord Hood, down to the final evacuation of Toulon under fire after the successful attack of the French Republican Army on the land defences of the place in December, 1793. Although, as in the case of the other ships of the British Fleet, there was

comparatively little that the guns of our ships could effect on the occasion, the boats of the "Britannia" took an active part in rescuing the refugee Royalists of Toulon and in assisting to bring out those of the captured French men-of-war that Lord Hood was able to secure and remove.

After that, in the course of 1794, while Lord Hood and part of the Fleet were engaged in the off-shore operations round Corsica, the "Britannia," as commanding officer's flag-ship, was continuously employed, with the rest of the Fleet, watching the resuscitated French Fleet in Toulon, and later, after a successful sortie of the French, in blockading the enemy in Gourjean Bay. The French, however, knew better than to risk a battle, and there is in consequence no fighting to record in the "Britannia's" story for 1794. The year that followed, 1795, when Admiral Hotham was in chief command of the Mediterranean Fleet during Lord Hood's absence on leave at home, saw two partial engagements off Genoa and Hyères. In the first of these, the action of the 13th of March, the "Britannia" had one man killed and eighteen wounded. In the second, owing to her slow sailing, the "Britannia" was unable to get within gunshot of the enemy before Admiral Hotham, anxious lest the leaders of his

*MORNING PRAYERS ON THE POOP OF THE "BRITANNIA."*

Fleet — Nelson's "Agamemnon," the "Victory," and one or two others—should run ashore while closing with the French, signalled to the van ships to discontinue action and haul off.

The "Britannia" next records her presence at the battle of "Glorious St. Valentine" off Cape St. Vincent, on the 14th February, 1797, on which occasion she flew the flag of Vice-Admiral Thompson, Sir John Jervis's second in command. At St. Vincent, however, luck was decidedly against the "Britannia," the brunt of the fighting—it is a matter of history—falling to the share of not more than five ships out of Sir John Jervis's total fleet of fifteen:—Nelson's "Captain," Troubridge's "Culloden," Collingwood's "Excellent," with the "Blenheim" and "Prince George." The "Victory" herself, Jervis's flag-ship, only lost one man killed and five men wounded, and the "Britannia" had only one man wounded. Shortly after this the "Britannia" returned home, to lie up in Portsmouth Harbour on duty as seamen's convalescent ship.

On the war with Napoleon breaking out in May, 1803, the "Britannia" once more hoisted the pennant for active service. She was by now, except for one ship—the "Blenheim," built in 1761—the oldest war-ship on the effective list of the British Navy, and indeed on any other as well, but she was still strong and stout enough for active work. "Old Ironsides," her pet name in the Fleet at that time, serves to show the general favour and affection with which the old veteran of the sea was regarded. The "Britannia's" most notable battle-day was, however, yet to be—the day of Trafalgar—just two years later, to which "field of fame" the "Britannia" came from the blockade of Brest. Off Brest with the Channel Fleet she had served since 1803, watching an enemy who never ventured to put to sea, down to August, 1805, when the "Britannia," detached with Sir Robert Calder's squadron to reinforce Collingwood, arrived off Cadiz, to seal up Villeneuve's combined Franco-Spanish Fleet, after its return to Europe from the West Indies, until the arrival of Lord Nelson. The "Britannia" was at this time flying the flag of Rear-Admiral Lord Northesk. Calder, with Northesk as his second in command, arrived off Cadiz on the 30th August, and remained

there until Lord Nelson's arrival in the "Victory," on which followed, in due course, the fateful morning of the 21st October, 1805. At Trafalgar, as one of the ships of the weather column, Lord Nelson's line, the "Britannia" went into action sixth ship astern of the "Victory."

She broke through the enemy at the fourteenth ship from their van, firing both broadsides as she passed the line, and then joined in the general mêlée, engaging ship after ship of the enemy as each came under her guns. "It is impossible," says Professor Laughton of Trafalgar, "to describe the action of each ship in detail, for the smoke and the confusion of the lines was so great that, even at the time, individual ships had not a very clear idea of what ships they were engaged with, and still less of what other ships were doing. . . . Each made the best of her way towards the enemy's line, and fell on such of the enemy's ships as she happened to meet with." An extract from the journal of one of the "Britannia's" officers, Lieutenant John Barclay, may, however, help a little in gaining something of the "Britannia's" share in the battle. "About 12.45," says Lieutenant Barclay "Lord Nelson . . . opened both sides of the 'Victory' on the headmost ships of their centre division. He was closely followed by the 'Téméraire,' 'Neptune,' 'Conqueror,' 'Leviathan,' and this ship pushed through their line. . . . Here began the din of war! It became impossible to trace anything further, except at intervals when the smoke cleared away a little. At 1.30 the masts of the ship we were most particularly engaging on the larboard side fell by the board; supposed to be the 'Bucentaure,' but without any flag observed flying. Continued edging on slowly, for there was very little wind, and our main topsail in particular was shot almost entirely from the yard. At 3 got to leeward of their line, and led up a little on the larboard tack." Here, to supplement the story, is an extract from the "Britannia's" official log, signed by Captain Bullen, of the ship :—"12.50—We began to engage, three of the enemy's ships having opened fire upon

ON THE QUARTER-DECK OF THE "BRITANNIA" AT TRAFALGAR—REAR-ADMIRAL LORD NORTHESK RECEIVING THE NEWS OF NELSON'S DEATH.

us while edging down    1.10—Observed the ship we were engaging on our larboard quarter totally dismasted; continued our course in order to break through the enemy's line, engaging on both sides in passing between their ships.    At 3— Passed through the line.   4.30—Hauled to the wind on the larboard tack, per signal.   5.30—Ceased firing."

Yet another account of the "Britannia's" proceedings relates that, after breaking through the enemy, she dismasted a French 80-gun ship, from which a white handkerchief was soon after waved in token of submission.    Leaving a frigate to take possession, however, the "Britannia" passed on to attack other ships, and was constantly engaged, sometimes with two or three ships of the enemy at once, and fighting on both broadsides.

In honour of the part that the "Britannia" took at Trafalgar, Lord Northesk was created a Knight of the Bath, and was further granted by King George III. the right to place the name "Trafalgar" on his coat of arms, with other special heraldic augmentations, in special honour of the battle.    The two supporters of the heraldic shield of the Earls of Northesk have also ever since 1805 each borne a staff, a Rear-Admiral of the White's flag bearing the inscription, "Britannia Victrix."

The "Britannia" returned to England in May, 1806, escorting home three of the four Trafalgar prizes that we had been able to save after the storm that followed the battle, and she was paid off in June of that year.    It was her last service.    After remaining laid up at Plymouth in the Hamoaze for some years, the grand old three-decker in 1812 was renamed "St. George" (a new "Britannia" being now on the stocks), and, under the name of "St. George," the old Trafalgar "Britannia" finally passed out of existence some time later.

In the same year that the "Old Ironsides" "Britannia" had her name so arbitrarily, as it would seem, taken from her, a successor to the name was laid down at Plymouth as a 120-gun three-decker of 2,602 tons.    Launched in 1820, this, our fourth "Britannia," for several years served as flagship at Plymouth to a number of distinguished sea officers of the old war time, among them Admiral Sir Alexander Cochrane—the officer who had charge of the arrangements for deporting Napoleon to St. Helena—and Admiral the Earl of

Northesk, the same officer who had had his flag in the former "Britannia" as third in command at Trafalgar. After that the "Britannia" went round to Portsmouth to serve for some years as flag-ship there. In 1837, the year of Her Majesty's accession to the throne, the "Britannia" was flying the flag of Admiral Sir Philip Durham (another Trafalgar officer, by the way) at Portsmouth, but, as it happened, owing to Admiral Durham's absence on leave on the 21st June, the honour of firing the first Naval salute to Her Majesty fell to another man-of-war, the flag-ship of the Admiral Superintendent.

It was in a great degree owing to the fact of the "Britannia" being flag-ship at Portsmouth in 1837 that a representation of that vessel was selected for one of the two silver models made for the Naval Service Jubilee Presentation to Her Majesty in 1887.

After 1840 the "Britannia" went out as flag-ship to the Mediterranean, one of the midshipmen on board, it may be recalled by the way, being the late Admiral Lord Alcester. Returning to England, she was again flagship in the Mediterranean from 1852 to 1855,

*STAFF-SURGEON PORTER AND THE NURSING STAFF.*

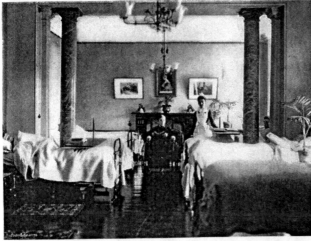

*IN THE HOSPITAL—WELL CARED FOR.*

*THE "BRITANNIA"—HOSPITAL AND CONVALESCENTS*

flying the flags of Admiral Sir William Parker, "the last of Nelson's captains," and Admiral Deans Dundas. There is a curious story told in Sir William Parker's memoirs of how the "Britannia" came to go out for her second commission to the Mediterranean. The 120-gun ship "Waterloo" had been selected as our flag-ship on the station, and had been completely fitted out for that duty, when suddenly, at the last moment, the Government, in surely a weak spirit for Englishmen, apparently fearing lest the name should give offence to the new ruler of France, Louis Napoleon, requested the Admiralty to keep back the "Waterloo" and substitute some ship with another name. That choice was the "Britannia." It was, indeed, good for the "Britannia's" fame that she went to the Mediterranean just then, for she was thus able to take part as Commander-in-Chief's ship in the Black Sea operations of the Russian War of 1854, particularly as Commander-in-Chief's flag-ship at the bombardment of Sebastopol on the memorable 17th October. It is told of Admiral Dundas and his flag-ship on this day that when the line of battle-ships of the Fleet were being drawn up before the attack, some-one pointed out to the admiral one station in particular, nearly in the centre of the allied line as it faced the Russian forts, which would most likely prove fatal to the ship occupying it.

It was explained that it was one that no ship could occupy without standing in grave peril of being sunk by the enemy's fire. Dundas looked at the chart and made a mark on it. "This," he said, "is the station that I reserve for myself, for the 'Britannia,'" and there it was that the gallant old admiral placed his flag-ship. So, at any rate, an old yarn goes.

It was in 1859 that the "Britannia" was first fitted up as a training-ship, on which service she was stationed at Portsmouth, in the berth where our first regular training-ship, the old "Illustrious," had been lying; then at Portland, whence in 1863 she was moved westward again, to take up her final moorings at Dartmouth.

For six years after this the old "Britannia" of the Russian War remained at Dartmouth, down to 1869, in which year she was sent to the ship-breaker, and a larger and newer ship, the 131-gun ship "Prince of Wales" (built in 1860 but never sent to sea), replaced her.

The newer ship was re-named the "Britannia," and is our "Britannia" of to-day.

THE history of the old "Britannias" has been a fighting history. They have carried the flag or the pennant, as the preceding account of their service has shown, on many an occasion before the enemy, and the ship which now lies, with the "Hindostan," in the land-locked harbour of Dartmouth, wears herself the appearance of a former time. Though reduced to the condition of a hulk, and bearing upon her timber walls and decks many an excrescence of present-day utility, she carries back our minds to the days of wood, hemp, and canvas. But we have now to regard the "Britannia" as a training-ship—as the school or college through which all executive officers enter the Naval service—to see where and how Naval officers are made, and we do so at a time when the surroundings of their training are about to be changed. In her—for the "Britannia," with the "Hindostan" and her tenders, are spoken of as a single establishment—they learn the first principles of discipline, imbibe the traditions of the Fleet, develop the qualities of resourcefulness, self-confidence, decision, alacrity, and all that is implied by the word "smartness," and are brought into relationship with one another, awakening youthful friendships that often continue through life. It is in the old ship here depicted that nearly every officer in the Navy, excepting those on the flag list, has been trained, and thus, for a great number of years, she has been the true nursery of the qualities they display. The "Britannia" is not a school of science. In her the cadets learn, indeed, the scientific conditions and environment of their profession, but she is devoted to the essential work of fitting them to become seamen first of all. The function of the "Britannia" is thus

*THE CADET CAPTAINS.*

one of high importance, and, amid all the discussions to which she has given rise, it is evident that she has done her work well in giving us youths developed and trained for the making of all-round, capable officers. Naval officers look back to their old training-ship with affection, begotten of the happy days they have spent in her; and, when the new Naval College is built upon the hill above Dartmouth to replace her, they will regard her disappearance with deep regret.

The building of that college has been determined mainly by considerations of convenience, accommodation, and health; but it is certain that, when the establishment has been moved ashore, advantages will not have been secured without loss. The Naval environment will no longer be quite the same; the sense of being afloat in a commissioned ship will be wanting; and, much as boat work may be resorted to, it will not be so constantly necessary as now.

But to move the "Britannia" establishment away from Dartmouth has scarcely been seriously considered. The neighbourhood is rich in natural beauties, and offers abundant opportunities for healthful exercise. It is near the sea, upon a land-locked tidal estuary, and affords ready access to Portsmouth or Plymouth at need, without bringing the youths under the unhealthy influences of port-towns.

In former times, officers were accustomed to enter the Service in what appears to us a very extraordinary fashion. Some of them, it is true, came in with the "King's Letter," and were reckoned as "volunteers by order," though they are constantly referred to, in the time of Charles II.—for it was he who made this regulation of entry—as "King's Letter boys," because they came in with royal warrant. The change was made in 1676, with the purpose of inducing many of better quality "to breed up their younger sons to the art and practice of navigation," and was in encouragement of a class of young officers whom the King had already favoured. To begin with, the qualifying service, for a lieutenant, was three years, of which one should have been passed as a midshipman; but this period was subsequently doubled. In 1728 the "King's Letter" was abolished, the examination was taken over by the Navy Board, and the Naval Academy was instituted at Portsmouth, the system continuing much the same until the college was closed in 1837. Nevertheless, singular practices continued in the Service, and, even when the entry was apparently regular, it is evident that the examination was often of a very perfunctory character, while the curious in such matters have discovered how qualifying "sea service" was sometimes passed by children ashore. If some, indeed, came in with the "King's Letter," many more entered the Service as the "servants" of admirals, captains, lieutenants, pursers, and others. The man who wished his son to join the Fleet, placed him under the patronage of a friend in some authority afloat, and this friend would enter him upon the ship's books in the manner described, and sometimes even long before he left the nursery. Thus, the rating gave no indication whatever of social grade, and it is interesting to note that in this way came Sir Cloudesley Shovell, the Earl of Peterborough, Sir Edward Whitaker, and many other men of note, into the Service.

The system continued until 1794. It unquestionably led to very grave abuses at times, but the practice of entering youths as "servants" became established, and was fully recognised. The last surviving officer so entered was the late Admiral of the Fleet, Sir Provo Parry Wallis. Nelson

*THE CADETS OF THE "BRITANNIA" AT THE PLAYING FIELD.*

himself was an example of an apparently irregular entry. He joined the "Raisonnable" as a midshipman at the age of twelve, then became a "captain's servant," afterwards coxswain, then a midshipman again in the "Seahorse," and for three years, in the East Indies, both worked aloft in the fore-top and walked the quarter-deck as an officer.

After the "servants" had been abolished, except as true domestics, by the regulation of 1794, we find boys entering the Fleet as "first-class volunteers." From these it would appear that no greater preliminary ordeal was required than jumping a chair, receiving a thump in the ribs from the doctor, the doing of some simple sums in the four

Photo W. M. Crockett.          GYMNASTICS—INSTRUCTORS AND INSTRUCTED.          Copyright.—H & K.

Photo W. M Crockett          THE GYMNASIUM—FENCING DRILL.          Copyright.—H & K

Photo W M Crockett          IN THE GYMNASIUM.—A BOUT WITH THE FOILS.          Copyright.—H. & K

rules of arithmetic, and the writing of an easy piece of dictation. It was a time when the elaborate system of competitive examinations, and the complex machinery of modern education, had not been created In 1843, young officers entered for the first time as "Naval cadets," their training being conducted, side by side with that of bluejackets, in the "Illustrious." The training began to make an approach towards its present form in 1859, when the late "Britannia," Admiral Dundas's flag-ship at Sebastopol, was commissioned at Portsmouth as a training-ship, to be brought, a couple of years later, to Portland.

It was not until 1863 that the ship was taken to Dartmouth, where she soon showed signs of decay, and the present "Britannia" replaced her in 1869.

The system of training is even now undergoing progressive change, and finality has not been reached. The period of service in the training-ship grew from nine months to two years in 1869, but latterly the boys have been entered later, and the period has again been curtailed. The short period in the ship, though necessary at present for the needs of the Service, is generally regarded as temporary and insufficient, since it hardly gives the cadets time to develop. At the same time, owing to the excellent system which now prevails on board, more is known of the youths by the officers in fifteen months, in these days, than was formerly the case in two years. This beneficent change has been wrought by alterations in the system made within a comparatively recent period.

Many hold that seamanship is likely to suffer more than any other department through the shortened period, since this important matter has come to be regarded simply as a minor subject, such as Euclid or algebra.

But, perhaps more interesting to many than discussions

*ADMIRAL DUNDAS SELECTING A POSITION FOR THE "BRITANNIA" TO TAKE AT THE BOMBARDMENT OF SEBASTOPOL, OCTOBER 17., 1854.*

concerning the policy of Naval education will be a description of the "Britannia" and her belongings, followed by an account of life on board. So, at least, we shall find where and how our young officers begin. Let us suppose, then, that a youngster who is about to enter the Service has run the gauntlet of the medical examiner, and escaped the pitfalls set before him by the Civil Service Commissioners. He has thus made good use of the nomination which he probably received from the Admiralty, has done a sufficiency of preparatory work, is furnished with his outfit, and now arrives by rail—from Paddington or Waterloo generally—preceded by his chest, at Kingswear, which is on the left bank of the Dart, facing Dartmouth. What does he find? In the first place he receives the impression, afterwards confirmed, that the "Britannia," in this land-locked harbour, with wooded hills rising on every hand, lies in a very pleasant place, against which nothing, indeed, can be alleged, save the dampness that inevitably clings to the valley in the winter.

The old three-decker is moored by chain cables in the middle of the lake-like expanse, and just ahead of her is the "Hindostan," a ship built of teak, on two decks, for seventy-four guns, at Bombay. He sees that a light covered bridge has

the middle deck of the ship, which is clear on the starboard side from the ward-room bulkheads aft to the bows, and is the place where the cadets muster, and in leisure moments indulge in skylarking or dancing, though often they may be seen snugly ensconced in the gun-ports, engrossed in volumes from their library. The cadets spend four terms on board, the two junior terms, described as "News" and "Threes," being berthed in the "Hindostan," and forbidden, by an unwritten law, to wear their caps on the backs of their heads, or to swing the lanyards to which their keys are attached, etc.; the two senior terms, known as "Nines" and "Passers-out," have their hammocks slung in the "Britannia."

The newcomer, therefore, makes his way across the bridge on to the main deck of the "Hindostan," where he also finds the starboard side is clear. Let us first descend to the sleeping deck, where the cadets' chests are ranged, and, at an appointed hour in the evening, their hammocks are slung. The space is restricted, but each cadet has "a good clear swinging billet," and every arrangement is made for his comfort, though there is no pampering on board. Cleanliness is the mark of the whole place. In both ships it is absolutely perfect, and even in the hold below the orlop deck,

*THE "BRITANNIA" ENGAGING THE FRANCO-SPANISH FLEET OFF GIBRALTAR, 1782.*

been thrown from ship to ship, beneath which is a floating swimming bath, heated by steam, and used for teaching swimming in the winter. Both the ships are housed in over their upper decks, the roofs covering, as he afterwards finds, a fine large space for prize-giving functions, concerts, and recreation on the poop, in the "Britannia," and a new church in the "Hindostan." But the larger ship still retains her foremast, bowsprit, and "whiskers"—useful relics of her former state. Somewhat astern of her is seen at anchor, when the tender is in harbour, the "Racer," a screw sloop of 970 tons, used for seamanship and navigation instruction, and constant spar and sail drill with the ship under way. The "Racer's" predecessor in this service, the "Wave," a smaller sloop of 380 tons, now lies abreast of the "Hindostan." She has had her screw removed, and is devoted to instruction in steam and some sail drill. Just ahead of the larger ship floats a pontoon, carrying the dynamos and accumulators from which electricity is supplied to the whole establishment. The river is seen to be dotted, besides, with skiffs, dinghies, yachts, and sailing cutters for the use of the cadets, and, on the Dartmouth side of the river, many establishments, which will presently be described, are visible ashore.

But it is now time to go on board the "Britannia" herself; and surely few things can be more interesting than to see in what manner of place the Nelsons and Howes of the future are living. The entry-port brings the newcomer to

where the ballast, tanks, and store-rooms are, everything is perfectly dry, and wholly fresh and sweet. Ascending to the main deck at which we entered, we go still higher to the upper deck, where are six good-sized rooms devoted to the purpose of study, under the poop of the old ship, which was raised and lengthened for the purpose. They are now empty, but we shall presently find the cadets at work in them. A few years ago it was the custom to take down the divisions of these studies every Saturday, so that the place might be used for service on the following day, but, through the liberality of the Admiralty, and of many officers and parents of cadets, an airy chapel has been built above the studies, very tastefully decorated, and fitted with an excellent organ. The forecastle of the ship, which is roofed over, is devoted to a workshop, and each deck has been fitted with great care for the accommodation of the first and second term cadets.

Returning now to the "Britannia," where the third and fourth terms are berthed, we may visit first the cadets' mess-room, which occupies a large part of the lower deck, and affords accommodation for 300 cadets, who can sit down together without crowding. The furniture is plain, but sufficient, and the room is in close communication with the pantries, galleys, etc., which are just ahead of it, and separated by a bulkhead from the mess-room and cabins of the ship's company, which are in the forward part of the vessel.

"BRITANNIA" SPORTS—SACK RACING: "READY."

"BRITANNIA" SPORTS—SACK RACING: THE FINISH.

Copyright.—Hudson & Kearns.

Photos. W. M. Crockett, Plymouth.

Descending a ladder to the orlop deck, we reach the "seamanship room," which is immediately under the mess-room, and is fitted with excellent working models of ships, anchor-gear, torpedo-booms, and everything that is necessary for the training of cadets in these matters. We return now to the middle deck, where are the cadets' library, sick bay, and sundry cabins, and ascend to the sleeping deck of the two senior terms, which is arranged exactly as in the "Hindostan," with one large bathing tank at the forward end. Here, too, are the studies, in the fitting and arrangement of which great care has been expended. Ascending next to the upper deck, we reach the poop and the large covered recreation space which has been alluded to, and in which entertainments are often contrived, the boys looking forward to them with keen pleasure. From this place there is access to the forecastle, which is the only uncovered part of the deck, where the mast is, about which the boys clamber a good deal at certain times.

But it would, perhaps, be tedious to describe further the internal fittings of the two training-ships, and, therefore, before describing the occupations, studies, and enjoyments of our young cadet, let us consider a moment the principle upon which his training is conducted. As soon as the boy joins the "Britannia," he is made to realise that, with his uniform, he has one foot in the Service, and is no longer a mere schoolboy. Then he is quickly inducted into the meaning of the word discipline, and is imbued with a knowledge of what is implied by being "on" and "off" duty. The distinction between the two is sharp and rigid. "On" duty the boy sticks closely to his work, and rare cases of shirking are sternly repressed; "off" duty, he is encouraged to display his boyish energy and spirit in every healthy form. He learns to look upon his superiors as friends interested in his welfare.

The main feature of the organisation for training is that the cadets, being divided into four terms, are also separated into starboard and port watches, these alternating their work week by week, as will presently be explained, under the distinctions of "in study" and "out of study." There are four lieutenants, assisted by chief petty officers (chief gunner's mates) under a gunner, who are responsible for discipline to the commander, who, in turn, is responsible to the captain. These officers are selected with great care, and largely on the ground of their aptitude for entering into the occupations of boys. One of them takes a "term" right

through the ship, and the cadet learns to regard him as an adviser in Service matters, a hearty companion in games, and a good friend in private affairs, from whom he can always seek counsel at need. In this way the lieutenants speedily learn the capabilities and failings of the boys, and are able to assist them in those first impressions of the Service which are never forgotten.

A minor order is also kept in the ships by the admirable institution of the "cadet captains," who are strongly supported by the officers when they do their duty, and severely dealt with when they fail. These are chosen from among the older boys, and are proud of the confidence reposed in them, and of the stripe that indicates their responsibility, and they enjoy some encouraging privileges in the ship. The conditions under which they work are well known to the cadets, and, although all are much of an age, still, duty in this sense is fully recognised. The whole large establishment is conducted by a hard and fast rule being drawn between the routine of the cadets and the work of the ship's company—there are some 270 bluejackets, marines, servants, artificers, and others—and it is interesting to see how the two departments work together.

Let us now suppose that we are on board the "Britannia" when the bugle, "Cadets turn out," sounds through the ships, winter and summer, except on Sundays, at half-past six in the morning. The bluejacket petty officers are alert to see that there is no laziness, but it is observed that stentorian shouts of, "Rouse out, rouse out! tumble out, tumble out! show a leg, show a leg!" are not now heard, for the majority of the boys are only too eager to spring from their hammocks and to tumble into the baths. Their animal spirits are extraordinary, and the splashing is proportionate. A few years ago the cadets were roused out by ship's corporals, a body of men who have been replaced by bluejackets, who can be regarded more as friends. Generally there is little need for defaulters to be called upon to "Fall in on the aft deck, sir, please," for report to the officer of the day that they were not dressed by the second warning, which is sounded at five minutes to seven. At seven o'clock the bugle sounds the "fall in," and the cadets are mustered on deck for inspection. They are then sent to their morning preparation or drills, and it may here be observed, incidentally, that every movement on board the "Britannia" is done at the "double," so that the decks and ladders present a bustling scene indeed as the cadets hasten to their occupations. You say to yourself that neither

Photo. W. M. Crockett, Plymouth.                                                      Copyright—Hudson & Kearns.

*THE "BRITANNIA" BEAGLES—COMMANDER CRADOCK AND HIS WHIPS AT THE KENNELS.*

Photo. W. M. Crockett, Plymouth

Copyright—Hudson & Kearns.

*AT THE BATHING STAGE—READY FOR THE PLUNGE.*

slackness nor skulking is possible here, and you soon discover that the boys fly with almost as much alacrity to their duties as with zest and appetite to their meals. Cheerfulness is the order of the day.

It has already been explained that half the boys are "in study," and the other half "out of study." In the morning preparation of these two classes, as again in the evening, there is a distinction. The boys "in study" work for an hour at mathematics, but those "out of study" have various duties as arranged. Some are engaged, it may be, in preparing their Scripture history or French, others are marched off to drill aloft in the tender, or are away pulling in boats. Every morning in the week—if the weather admits—parties go ashore, and are put through fencing exercises, physical drill, and gymnastic work. The physical drill, which is under the care of a lieutenant, is excellent. The instructors are from the school at Aldershot, and the results are quite surprising. Special trick work in gymnastics has been abandoned, except for a few boys, and the improvement has been marked. Cadets who had been in the ship eighteen months in August, 1897, had increased 4·4-in. in height, and 3·7-in. in chest measurement, these being considerably higher averages than during the two years' course under the old system.

At eight o'clock the "disperse" is sounded, the boys are dismissed from their studies and recalled from their drill, and they proceed to the mess-room for breakfast. Nowhere are boys better fed. The diet is plain, plentiful, and whole-some. A breakfast, according to the day of the week, they have tea, coffee, or cocoa, always rolls and butter, twice in the week oatmeal porridge, sometimes hash or curry, cold meat, bacon, or fish, or, if it be Tuesday or Friday, fried eggs and bacon, and boiled eggs and cold ham, or, if it be Thursday, sausages. It is scarcely necessary to say that outdoor occupations, and youthful energies, bring huge appetites to the breakfast table. For those boys who go afloat in the "Racer" for special seamanship instruction, particular arrangements are made.

At ten minutes to nine the "assembly" is sounded, and the cadets muster, and proceed to the covered space on the upper deck, where they fall in and are inspected, as is also the ship's company, and the chaplain then reads prayers. Then the boys gather up their books, and are marched by the cadet captains to their appointed studies, of which, however, no very full account can be given here. The chief Naval instructor has assistants for special subjects, and, generally speaking, it may be said that the four "terms" are all engaged in the same work, but in stages more or less

advanced. Fourteen hours each week are given up by the first term to algebra and plain trigonometry, theoretical and practical. In the second term the time devoted to these is reduced, and practical spherical trigonometry and navigation are added. In the third and fourth terms algebra is dropped, but nautical astronomy assumes an important place. These are the subjects taken by the Naval instructors; but there are extra subjects, which together absorb, like the others, fourteen hours in each week. These subjects are :—Charts and instruments, French, drawing, seamanship, steam, and Euclid, but in the last two terms Euclid is displaced by theoretical spherical trigonometry. It must be confessed that the very short time spent on board renders the efficient teaching of some subjects very difficult, and it is only by a closely-jointed system that this becomes possible.

Thus it happens that the very important subject of seamanship receives only three hours per week in every term but the first, and this is much regretted, although to allow more time appears impossible. The "Racer," which lies at her moorings under the stern of the "Britannia," is devoted to the practical instruction. She takes detachments of the cadets out of harbour to learn manœuvring under sail, and to grapple with the problems of sea-sickness. They are trained, to begin with, in laying in and out on the yards, then in making, shortening, and furling sails, and afterwards in crossing and sending down upper yards and top-gallant masts. In the "Racer," too, they learn pilotage with her captain, and are practised in taking sights and lifeboat work, and are generally familiarised with practical duties at sea. Their whole course in seamanship gives them a knowledge of the descriptions, fitting and rigging of ships, knotting and splicing, in which they become familiar, among other things, with "Matthew Walker" and "Turk's Head," the rule of the road, signalling in every form, working cables and letting go and weighing bower anchors, the compass, heaving log and lead, duties as midshipmen in charge of boats, working service cutters, and the steering and management of steam-boats—all this, in addition to working upper yards and masts, making and shortening sail, reefing topsails, and working ship.

We may suppose now that, while we have thus been describing the work of the cadets, they have been dispersed for an interval of ten minutes in their studies at eleven o'clock, and that the dinner bugle is now sounding at five minutes past one. Excellent appetites are brought to the dinner table. On four days in the week there is soup, always roast beef and mutton, sometimes stewed and corned beef, occasionally lamb

*JUBILEE DAY—" SPLICING THE MAIN BRACE."*

FROM PORTSMOUTH TO PORTLAND, JANUARY, 1869.—THE "BRITANNIA" UNDER SAIL OFF ST. CATHERINE'S, ISLE OF WIGHT.

or pork, veal and bacon, or meat pies or puddings, with two vegetables, and often two sweets. On Wednesdays and Saturdays, which are half-holidays, buns are served to the boys in the field. All the feeding arrangements are under a mess committee, consisting of the commander, paymaster, and chief instructor, and the officer of the day attends in the mess-room to see that everything provided is good and palatable.

But now, again, the cadets are mustered on deck, after a warning bugle, and once more hasten to their studies at two o'clock. These occupy them until half-past three, when the studies are dismissed, and the boys are away, with extraordinary celerity, to shift into flannels, and very soon are tumbling down the ladder into the boats, which they pull ashore. Here every variety of amusement is provided for them. In the boat-shed are about twenty skiffs and gigs, for boat exercise, as well as sailing cutters, which the boys of the two senior terms may use. During the summer many a bowsprit is broken and many a boat sticks in the mud, but, before the cadets leave the ship, they have learned to handle these craft very skilfully. Then, close by the shore, too, are the racquet and fives courts, the gymnasium, and the photographic dark room, for the boys are encouraged by prizes to become proficient photographers.

But the immediate purpose of coming ashore is bathing,

place, and is played under Association and Rugby rules; and here, as at cricket, lacrosse, racquets, hockey, and other games, the commander and officers share all the enjoyments of the boys, warmly supported by the captain, who is keenly interested in their occupations. It is in this way that the spirit of good-fellowship and friendly rivalry are encouraged, and it is impossible to over-estimate the advantage that results. A fine pavilion, with every convenience, is on the field, to which is attached a canteen organised by the ship, where cadets can buy their "stodge" at moderate prices.

The "recall" is hoisted at a quarter-past six in the summer, but much earlier in the winter months, and is hauled down about half-an-hour later, when the cadets are on board once more, to change their boots, shift again into blue clothing, and muster for tea.

On the half-holidays, the arrangements are a little different. On such occasions, while some of the cadets are playing football or other games, a large party will be hunting with the beagles. The commander is now master of the pack, assisted by one lieutenant, and selected cadets are his whips. The "Britannia" beagles, and the merry boys who follow them, are popular all through the country thereabout, and the farmers enter into the enjoyment and afford every facility for it. The district is well adapted for the work, and good sport is rarely wanting. Sometimes the meet may be at Stoke

*A CUTTER'S CREW AT EXERCISE: TOSSING OARS.*

which is preparatory to all other diversions in the summer time. There is good deep water at the shore, and an excellent place to dive from, and, as soon as the bugle "sounds in," the boys plunge with extraordinary splashing, and the whole river seems alive with them. The time is short, and the bugle sounds the "retire," which many hear reluctantly, but instantly obey. All are soon ashore, dressed again, and either manning the boats which have been alluded to, playing in the racquet court, or climbing the hill to the field. It is a steep ascent, approached by a staircase under a rustic archway, flanked by two figures from the stern of the old "Britannia." The climb is exhilarating, and brings the visitor to the site chosen for the new college, and the kennels, where the beagles welcome him loudly. Of this pack something shall be said presently. On the top of the hill, passing certain tennis courts, we come to the playing fields, which are in a splendid situation, affording a fine view of the harbour and the country. Here in the summer time there is constant play at the practice nets, and generally there are three "foreign" matches, always two being played on the half-holidays. The cricket is very good, for two professionals are attached to the ground, and competing elevens come from Plymouth, Torquay, and elsewhere. As the winter approaches football takes its

Fleming, or, again, on the hills above Dittisham, a pretty river-side village, to which the steam launch 'Osprey' conveys the master and his whips, towing a large boat full of boys and another of beagles. Many of the officers take part in these delightful excursions, and ladies often grace the meet. Such is the enjoyment got out of a half-holiday. Who shall say what are the unspeakable pleasures of a "whole"? Then, in the summer time, there are wandering in the woods, picnicking, bird-nesting, and black-berrying, to afford occupation for the boys. Bounds, except for the towns, there are none, and certain farmhouses are indicated to which the boys may resort for "stodge."

But the cadets are now on board again, sitting down with hearty appetites to tea, to which they have bread and butter, cold meat, water-cress, and so forth, and on certain days, of note in the memory of boys, jam and clotted cream. Tea over, they proceed to their evening preparation, which occupies an hour, during which certain of them hear lectures on winds and currents, ship-construction, etc., while others are attentively engaged at their work, with a cadet captain in each room, and it is astonishing to see the close attention the boys pay to their study. The distinction, in short, between being "on" duty and "off" is clear and well understood, and cases of skylarking in preparation time are very rare. The cadet captain has a roll of the boys under his supervision, and to him they have to report their occupations throughout the day, which they well understand must have been of an active character, and the ominous letter "L," which indicates loafing, does not often appear against them.

At half-past eight in the summer, and half-an-hour earlier in the winter, the evening preparation is over, and then the cadets gather on the middle deck, where a good band, which is composed of their servants, discourses dance music. It is a most entertaining and pleasing sight to see the boys dancing together. They enter into the amusement with great vigour and delight, though, curiously enough, the waltz is said to be unpopular with them. In this occupation the evening passes merrily away, until the strains of "God save the Queen" betoken its close. There is a warning bugle, the cadets assemble, prayers are said, and they retire and turn in, at a quarter-past nine in summer and nine o'clock in winter. The drowsy god is not long in overtaking them, for a long and well-filled day never fails to bring healthy sleep. The stranger privileged to pass along the sleeping decks half-an-hour after they have retired, when the rounds go, is astonished at the silence and absolute state of rest that so soon succeed the busy occupations of the day.

Such is the routine on board the "Britannia." There are times and seasons when it is broken by special events, and some on board look forward with trepidation to the examinations, and particularly to the final test, which is to exclude the unfit. Some boys more fortunate than the rest win dirks, prizes, or the Queen's medals, and, what is of vastly more importance to them, some few gain time by their sound work and good conduct, and, when they are drafted to ships, don at once the white patch on the collar which betokens that they are midshipmen, while the majority of the boys continue some months longer as cadets.

But we have seen that the life on board the "Britannia" is well calculated to produce youths sound of wind and limb, fruitful in resource, swift in decision, and ready in action. Sickness of a mild type has sometimes passed through the ship, due in part, perhaps, to the dampness of the situation

*THE "BRITANNIA'S" LAUNCH, "OTTER"*

in the winter, but the sanitary arrangements are under highly-skilled supervision. Facilities exist for the instant isolation of boys, and nothing can be imagined more perfect than the arrangement of the new hospital and convalescent quarters, which are beautifully situated ashore, at distances from one another. It is a well-disciplined life that the cadets pass on board, full of the character of boyhood, but of qualities always under control. Bullying has been repressed in the ship, and now prevails in no objectionable degree. Bad language is almost unknown, happiness sits on every countenance, work and relaxation go hand in hand, and the boy enters the Naval Service able to cope with its difficulties. But, of course, the training is not completed on board the ship. It goes on afloat, and is continued in the special colleges at Portsmouth and Greenwich. But the cadet is not to be pursued in this place beyond the "Britannia." His life and occupations have been described at a time when the whole subject of the training of Naval officers is under discussion, and when the system may not improbably be modified. None, however, can know the work that goes on in the "Britannia" without being convinced that it is of the very best, and that, within the limits allowed, it is extremely doubtful whether results so good are attained by any public school in the land.

*THE "RACER" SLOOP—TENDER TO THE "BRITANNIA."*

Photo. W. M. Crockett, Plymouth.

*THE "BRITANNIA" AND THE "HINDOSTAN" IN DARTMOUTH HARBOUR.*

# THE NAVY & ARMY ILLUSTRATED.

VOL. V.—No. 55.]    *FRIDAY, JANUARY 21st, 1898.*

Photo, Elliott & Fry                                          Baker Street.

### *VICE-ADMIRAL PHILIP H. COLOMB.*

HARDLY another Naval officer of our day has deserved better of the Service than Vice-Admiral Colomb. To him we owe the present system of flashing signals, the present system of Naval tactics, the adopted system of interior lighting of ships of war, and the present system of communication on board ship by voice tubes. His writings and essays on Naval defence and the possibilities open to the modern war-ships place Admiral Colomb in the forefront among those who have brought the Fleet to its present-day state of efficiency. The Navy at large also owes him a special debt for his unceasing and unsparing efforts to induce the authorities to adopt a more satisfactory scheme of Naval retirement. Admiral Colomb has seen service in China, Burma, and in the Baltic during the Russian War, to which last-named campaign he came after taking part in the Arctic Expedition of 1854. As a captain, he commanded the flag-ship on the China station, and the Portsmouth Steam Reserve, which was reorganised under his direction in 1881, being, also, Sir Geoffrey Hornby's flag-captain at Portsmouth in 1884-85. Admiral Colomb is a gold medallist of the Royal United Service Institution, and a Younger Brother of Trinity House.

# SIGNALLING IN THE NAVY.

*SEMAPHORE INSTRUCTION.*

IT is not easy to overrate the importance of the part which is played by the signal staff on board a man-of-war. It constitutes the ears and the voice of each vessel, and is the means of conveying commands or reports of the most momentous as well as of the most trivial import, from an invitation to dinner with the admiral to an order to engage the enemy.

There are, of course, various means and codes by which messages are conveyed, each being adapted to different circumstances; and at each of our principal Naval depôts there are always classes under efficient instruction in this important subject. Five of our illustrations represent some phases of this process at the Naval Barracks at Devonport, the first being a class at semaphore. The pupils are arranged in pairs, after having mastered the signification of the various positions of the wooden arms, and one man reads off the

Photos W. M. Crockett, Plymouth,     *PACKING UP AFTER INSTRUCTION.*

LEARNING THE FLAGS.

signal made by the instructor, while the other writes it on the slate. It is easy enough to learn the semaphore—every letter, etc., is indicated by one or both arms, in positions which follow a regular sequence, and are readily recollected; but to "take in" a signal rapidly requires considerable practice, and, no doubt, some of the pupils will be non-plussel if the signal is made quickly, more especially if some of the signs are employed which have more than one signification. S and Z, for instance, are represented by one combination, U, V, and W by another, I and J by a third, and Q and X by a fourth. It is easy to concoct a sentence which includes some of these letters, and reduces the beginner to a despairing condition, though to a practised hand it presents no difficulty. Semaphore signals can very readily be made with the arms, when no proper wooden apparatus is available; and it is no uncommon occurrence to see a seaman or officer standing up in the stern sheets of a boat and waving his arms about in an apparently insane fashion, which, however, conveys a perfectly intelligible meaning to the signalman on board the ship. The semaphore is used for what may be termed "conversational" signalling, and is in very constant use in the squadron.

The hours of instruction being over, we find the men packing up in the second picture, and rolling up flags into those neat little bundles, which are secured in a cunning fashion, so that they can be hoisted in that form and suddenly liberated by a sharp pull on the halliards; and woe to the signalman if the flags will not "break"!

Flags are, of course, the oldest medium of communication, and are invariably used for evolutionary, routine, and similar classes of signals. With the letters of the alphabet, and a complete set of numerals, an immense number of combinations can be made, varied by distinguishing pendants, and the men have plenty to learn in this class. The hoisting of flags, though it may appear a simple matter, has also its points and difficulties, and it is interesting to note how an expert signalman will run up a string of flags in a few seconds, and have them all blowing out clear, while a tyro will get them hopelessly entangled.

The fifth illustration depicts the use of a very pretty method of signalling, more adapted, perhaps, for other climes than ours where the sun is frequently obscured. The heliograph is nothing else than a small circular mirror, so mounted that it can be caused, by a motion of the finger, to flash the sun's rays on a given point in the distance. The well-known Morse code, composed of various combinations of dots and dashes, lends itself readily

*THE ART OF HOISTING FLAGS.*

to this mode of communication, and it can be used at great distances; a short flash being a dot, and a long one a dash. The heliograph has rendered invaluable services in modern warfare, notably in the Frontier wars in India.

In the next picture a signalman on board the "Edinburgh" is making a semaphore to some ship away to the

*THE USE OF THE HELIOGRAPH.*

*MAKING A SEMAPHORE FROM THE "EDINBURGH."*

left. The short stationary arm below the others is the "indicator," which shows from which side the motions of the long arms are to be read. The letter being made at the moment is M; but if it were read the other way it would be S.

On the signal-bridge of the "Renown," two men are taking in and writing down a signal, while a third repairs a flag.

The important science of telegraphy is not neglected, as may be seen in the last illustration, where a class of seamen are being exercised. Those on the left are sending messages to the men seated in front of the instruments on the right, who, pencil in hand, write down the words spelt out by the various deflections of the needle. As with the semaphore, it is far easier to send a message than to take one in readily and accurately.

*TAKING IN A SEMAPHORE IN THE "RENOWN"*

Photo W. M. Crockett, Plymouth.

*LEARNING TELEGRAPHY AT SHORT RANGE.*

# SNAP-SHOTS ON BOARD A BATTLE-SHIP.

*INSPECTING A BLUEJACKET SMALL ARM PARTY.*

HERE we give some snap-shot views of certain of the routine duties carried on afloat, such as come in the day's work of the modern man-of-war's man and his shipmate, the jolly Marine. They were taken on board one of the battle-ships of the Channel Squadron during its recent cruise off the coast of Spain and up the Straits.

One of the set of photographs represents the inspection of a small arm party of bluejackets on the quarter-deck by the gunnery lieutenant. The gunnery lieutenant on board a battle-ship or cruiser is the officer specially charged with the arrangements for the serving out of small arms

*MARINES PREPARING FOR INSPECTION.*

to the bluejackets, and their distribution and maintenance and good order, as well as the selection of the small arm men to the various services for which they are told off. To him, for one thing, is committed the task of the selection and supervision, when under arms on board, of the men appointed to form landing parties, the small arm companies of blue-jackets, field-piece crews, pioneers, stretcher parties, ammunition guards, and boat guards at points of disembarkation.

In this illustration we see the gunnery lieutenant passing down the ranks of a small-arm company of blue-jackets—such as would be utilised for a landing party—to

*HEAVY MARCHING ORDER FOR MARINES.*

inspect the men and their arms, as they stand with rifles at the slope and bayonets fixed, on parade. The rifles, of course, used in the Fleet on all stations are now magazine rifles, the Lee-Metford—exactly the same weapon as is used by the Army on shore.

Other of our illustrations show a party of Royal Marine Light Infantry in their full shore-going kit, or, as it is officially termed, "Heavy Marching Order." They, too, are in the rig that they would wear on going ashore to take part with their bluejacket shipmates in landing party operations, or for infantry drill, or at some review on shore. In ordinary circumstances on board ship the Marine, of course, does his duty in the much more free and easy garb of serge jumper and forage or field service cap. The brass-bound spiked helmet and cloth tunic only appear at Divisions and on

*BLUEJACKET SMALL ARM PARTY AT DRILL.*

occasions of State, such as Royal reviews and Admiral's inspections.

Another photograph shows a squad of bluejackets being drilled on board ship in their white working rig. Doubling along an unsteady deck is by no means as easy as it looks here.

Torpedoes being tested before firing is the subject of our fifth illustration, a routine practice that is necessary in the interests of efficiency and economy.

With regard to efficiency, a torpedo must naturally follow exactly its intended course until it has effected its errand, and a torpedo incapable of floating at the depth below the surface for which it is set, or that dives to the bottom and sinks when fired, is not wanted. From the point of view of the taxpayer it is necessary also that torpedoes fired for practice

*TESTING TORPEDOES ALONGSIDE.*

should come to the surface after their run and discover themselves. If they dive and are seen no more, it means a loss to the country of anything between five hundred and a thousand pounds.

To make sure that torpedoes about to be run are in trustworthy condition, as a preliminary before their run they are all brought up on deck and slung over the side, under control, in order to test their floating powers. After that they are sent down for use in the submerged torpedo-tube rooms, or where required. Every month all circuits, batteries, and instruments throughout the ship are tested, and every quarter Whitehead torpedoes are run from ships in harbour—two runs from each tube. Quarterly, also, two runs are made from each tube with the ship under way.

# THE MARINES AT BERMUDA.

THE subjects of our three illustrations are provided by the Royal Marine Detachment stationed at Commissioner's House, Bermuda. The illustrations are interesting in two ways. One for the men themselves and their billet at Bermuda, as a means of representing to the good folks at home how universally handy and useful a man the jolly Marine is, and how satisfactorily he is provided for. One reason, indeed, this, why the Royal Marines are so popular a corps from the recruiting point of view. The Marines of the Bermuda Detachment that we see here are practically all men who have done active service afloat or with the Home Divisions, and are employed under the Works Department of the Admiralty. All are men selected for character, good service, and special proficiency in various trades—as carpenters, masons, smiths, plumbers, painters, sawyers, and so on. By them a great part of the work that is done on Ireland Island, Bermuda, is performed, from the construction and maintenance of houses and official buildings, skilled labour in the various shops in the dockyard, and the repair of roads and rifle ranges,

*TYPICAL GROUP OF THE MARINES AT BERMUDA.*

down to weekly attendance at infantry and gunnery drills, and the breeding and fattening of ducks and chickens for home consumption and the market.

Our first photograph shows a group of the detachment, with three officers in the centre, and non-commissioned officers, all of the same corps, on either side. The two plain clothes men shown are members of the corps who hold the positions of foreman of works and leading hand of smiths.

Our second illustration shows the commanding officer of the Royal Marines at Bermuda, and sergeants of Marines serving there.

Our third illustration shows the canteen committee of the Bermuda Marine Detachment, with the donkey and cart that is a special care of the drummer of the detachment; also one of the canteen cows, a special care of the cook, who is seen standing just behind her.

At Bermuda island a cow is apparently an object of interest and attention that would pleasantly surprise the bovine denizens of our fields at home.

A second way in which our illustrations are of interest is more general, and, if we may so say, national. Bermuda is one of our strongest fortresses, and the principal base for the British America squadron. The island group of the Bermudas, in addition to its magnificent strategical position in mid-ocean, is peculiarly fitted by Nature as an impregnable fortress.

It is noteworthy that quite recently special measures have been taken to add to the defences of Bermuda, and at the present time the island group has been fortified with modern guns, and by means of approved scientific appliances, until its impregnability is said to be assured.

The Naval forces at the island have also been added to, and an iron-clad ram, the "Hotspur," rearmed and refitted up-to-date, has been recently placed as guard-ship there, with a flotilla of torpedo-boats and two destroyers, and measures are at this moment in progress for adding to the dockyard accommodation at Bermuda on a large scale.

*THE COMMANDANT, ROYAL MARINES, BERMUDA, AND SERGEANTS.*

Photos. Wilson & Cahill.　　　　　　　　　　　　　Bermuda.

*THE ROYAL MARINE CANTEEN COMMITTEE AT BERMUDA.*

THE readers of the NAVY AND ARMY ILLUSTRATED will learn with interest that shortly a new series of works will be produced in connection with this magazine, entitled "Stories of Our National Heroes." The Proprietors of the NAVY AND ARMY have been encouraged to take this step by the marvellous success of the illustrated Life of Nelson, which was recently produced as one of our special numbers. Each of the new works, which will form the "'Navy and Army Illustrated' Library," will be completed in twelve sixpenny, fortnightly, parts, and each part will contain twenty-four pages profusely illustrated. An immense amount of labour and care has been expended in selecting the illustrations from every possible source, both public and private, and the greater number of them are extremely rare, and quite unknown to the general public. The collection of caricatures especially is very full. The author of each work, chosen specially for his knowledge of the person and period dealt with, will take as his central figure some distinguished sailor or soldier representative of the time, and will describe the incidents of his life, his companions in arms, and the scenes in which his life's labour was passed.

* * * *

THE first volume of the series will be entitled "Wellington and Waterloo." It will be written by Major Arthur Griffiths, the author of "The Wellington Memorial," and Lord Wolseley has promised to write an introduction to the book. This will be followed by "Drake and the Beginning of Empire," by Mr. John Leyland, the well-known writer on Naval subjects, and editor of one of the Navy Records Society's works. In his life of Drake he will tell the story of the exercise of Sea Power in the great circumnavigator's time, and the wonderful story of how he and the English seafarers of the period unconsciously, but not less surely, laid the foundations of the Empire. To this work Lord Charles Beresford will write an introduction. Other volumes are in preparation, and it is intended that, as regards the paper on which these works will be printed, and the character of the reproductions, a standard shall be attained which will surpass anything of the kind ever before attempted; so that, when completed, each work cannot fail to be of special literary, artistic, and historical value. With each volume will be presented a magnificent coloured print as a frontispiece

* * * *

A MELANCHOLY interest attaches to the article on the "Queen's Keys," which appears elsewhere in this number. I regret to say that Mr. Penrose, the chief warder, whose picture appears in the drawing, has died suddenly after a short illness, and when it was too late to make any alteration in the letterpress. The vacant post of chief warder has been filled by the appointment of Mr. Middleton, late sergeant-major of the Gordon Highlanders' Depôt, and he will now therefore execute the quaint duty which falls to the lot of the incumbent of that post.

* * * *

IN reply to various correspondents who are anxious to learn something as to the duties and position of a chaplain on board one of Her Majesty's ships, I would say that both these are entirely what he chooses to make them. I do not mean that the chaplain is altogether independent of his captain, but I do say that there are very few captains who will interfere with the way in which the chaplain does his work. Thus he may, if he likes—and there are, unfortunately, a great many who do like, though much fewer than in times past—confine himself to reading the morning prayers every morning, or at least such of them as are customary in the Navy, which will occupy from five to seven minutes each day, and conducting a morning service of about an hour's duration every Sunday. Such a chaplain is often not seen in the ship except at meal times, and frequently not then. I, of course, speak of harbour only.

ON the other hand, there are plenty of good men who are always striving for the benefit of their parishioners, as they consider the crew to be. They take an interest in their sports and pastimes, know something of the private affairs of everyone who seeks their help, and so have many opportunities of putting in a word in season. In a great many instances, the idleness of the chaplain may be traced to his having little or nothing to do. But when the chaplain is a double-barrelled man, as it is called—that is, one who combines the office of Naval Instructor with his own—there is no excuse of this kind. His duties pleasantly occupy about half his time. His qualifications need not be very grand, but at any rate he is allowed a certain time for study at the Royal Naval College, Greenwich, which assuredly will not be the most disagreeable to look back upon in after years. Lastly, he commences with the pay of £219 a year, or, if he is double-barrelled, at least £350, which is more in these days than many pious and hard-working clergymen get all their lives long.

* * * *

IN reply to "Enniskillen's" question as to the identity of the present 6th Dragoons with Colonel William Wolseley's Regiment of Inniskilling Horse, I am enabled to state that no connection exists. In 1689 various troops of horse were raised in Enniskillen under the Governor, Gustavus Hamilton. These troops were regimented as (1) Wolseley's Regiment of Inniskilling Horse, which did splendid service in Ireland before, at, and after the Battle of the Boyne, and was disbanded in 1697; (2) Colonel James Wynne's Regiment of Inniskilling Dragoons, afterwards known as the Royal Irish Dragoons, disbanded in 1799, and re-raised as the 5th Royal Irish Lancers in 1858; and (3) Sir Albert Conyngham's Regiment of Inniskilling Dragoons—the 6th Dragoons of the present day.

* * * *

OFFICERS, warrant officers, non-commissioned officers, and drummers of infantry who have served eight years at home may, if they wish, register their names with a view to their being posted to the battalion abroad, and those who have served abroad for the same period may apply for transfer to the battalion at home. This privilege also applies to privates, gunners, drivers, and sappers re-engaged while serving abroad, and to warrant and non-commissioned officers of the Royal Engineers not serving in India. The names of those who are desirous of a change under the above rule are submitted once a year to the adjutant-general, through the general officer commanding, with a full statement of the applicants' service. A man is not, however, permitted to apply until he has actually completed eight years' continuous service at home and abroad. These transfers are granted whenever possible, or,·in the official language of the regulations, "whenever the exigencies of the Service admit." This phrase is often met with in official books, and is at all times a safe covering or saving clause, for, after all, the "exigencies of the Service" may be construed to mean almost anything.

* * * *

WHEN on manœuvres, or if a big field day is about to take place, réveille is often sounded earlier than would be the case otherwise, and after a night march or hard field day the general or other officer at times so far relaxes the rule as to allow of an extra half-hour or hour in bed. This indulgence, however, might be granted oftener with advantage, and without detriment to the Service. At small stations (where, perhaps, only a battalion is stationed and the voices of the general and his satellites are not heard every day) a considerate commanding officer may allow some latitude on the first day of the week, but where there are large bodies of troops this is practically unknown. At stations abroad the general officer may vary the hours for réveille, retreat, and tattoo at his discretion, according to the position of the station, but the hours laid down are adhered to as far as possible. When on active service réveille is sounded at daybreak as a general rule, and tattoo at any hour ordered by the officer commanding the forces.

* * * *

TWO little errors have crept into recent numbers, which I should like to correct. The group of officers shown on page 100 of the Indian number is described as belonging to the 8th Bengal Infantry. This is a misprint. It should have been 1st Bengal Infantry. The correspondent to whom we are indebted for the correction remarks: "The picture is an excellent one, the likenesses being very good indeed." In No. 53, in the note on the services of the Hon. Maurice Gifford, it is stated that he received the Distinguished Service Order, which is a mistake, and should have been the C.M.G., an equally valued honour, but one more directly connected with the colonies than the D.S.O.

THE EDITOR.

**E**NGLISHMEN, though slow to act on many occasions, are prone to sing aloud their song of empire. Lest they should glory too much in the present, Mr. Charles Gleig is resolved that they shall peer into a gloomy future. We all know how the late Laureate wrote of "the wild mob's million feet," and of the statesmen who should be kicked too late from their places. "When All Men Starve" (John Lane, 3s. 6d.) is the title of Mr. Gleig's book. It is a new "Battle of Dorking," well done and without the invasion. Trouble in the Transvaal, not the occupation of Kiao-Chau, is at the root of the business, Germany being aggressive, and France and Russia demanding the evacuation of Egypt. Our state is one of "splendid isolation." I do not like Mr. Gleig's implications that we should court alliances. If we have allies, self-interest must drive them to us; we never can afford to depend upon them. But to return to the story. Disaster in the Mediterranean and the Channel bring inevitable consequence. The mob, which has broken the windows of the military commander-in-chief, because we had no army, clamours for bread. Anarchy follows, and Buckingham Palace is burned. The concluding scenes are particularly well managed. There is a sound warning in the book, amid all the exaggeration, and perhaps its best feature is the recognition of the conditions, apart from absolute cutting off of food supplies, that might make "all men starve."

Prince Louis of Battenberg has broken new ground in his "Men-of-War Names, their Meaning and Origin" (Stanford, 6s.). The time has long gone by when a First Lord of the Admiralty could name ships after favourite dogs or horses ; and keen critics now scan, not always, it is true, with full satisfaction, the lists of names selected. There can now be no excuse for forgetfulness, for Prince Louis' book happily contains a list of all names formerly borne by English men-of-war. His catalogue of extant ships indicates the reason for the naming of each, and gives her class and date. I have looked through his foreign lists with equal interest. Often I had wondered who or what Osliabia and Peresviet might be that they should give names to the new Russian battle-ships. Now I know that these are the names of a couple of heroic monks who, with Dmitri Donskoi, defeated the Tartars in 1380. In such information the little book positively abounds, and no one who had not read it would suspect how much of history, biography, topography, mythology, and natural science is bound up with the names of men-of-war. Every Naval officer should have the book on his shelf.

I can do little more than draw attention to one complex book of portentous proportions. It is "Lord Cochrane's Trial before Lord Ellenborough" (Smith, Elder, and Co., 18s.), which Mr. J. B. Atlay, a barrister of Lincoln's Inn, has written for Commander E. D. Law, R.N This officer is the grandson of the great Lord Chief Justice, and the present Earl of Dundonald is the grandson of the great seaman who made that celebrated cruise in the "Speedy" in which the Spanish frigate "Gamo" was captured, and who used his fire-ships so effectively in the Basque Roads in 1809. The Commander and the Earl are at loggerheads in extolling the merits of their several grandsires, for to vindicate Cochrane you must demolish Ellenborough, and to vindicate the seaman you must deal mighty blows at the judge. How Cochrane and his friends are said to have jockeyed the market in 1814, by extraordinary rumours of the defeat of the French, what profit they made, and how they were condemned to fine, imprisonment, and the pillory, with the dramatic sequel which ended with Cochrane's restoration to rank and honours, and his burial in Westminster Abbey, will be discovered in this book. The beginning of it reads like a romance, but it soon, by its very nature, grows dull, and is in truth a book for students who will find it sound and instructive. A strong case is made out for Ellenborough, though I believe few readers will lose their liking for Cochrane.

A book to be treasured is "Renaud of Montauban" (Allen, 7s. 6d.), for its old-world quaintness, its heroic subject, and its external charms of good typography and illustrations, such as Caxton would have delighted in. It was he who did the dim romance into English, and now Mr. Robert Steele, who is learned in the lore of old France, has abridged and retouched it. In his "Story of Alexander" you could hear the distant horn of Oberon ringing through the woods of Outremer, and now the doughty deeds of Roland and Renaud, the clattering hoofs of Bayard, and the enchantments of Maugis, arouse romantic imaginings. It is a tale drawn from the old legend of the Four Sons of Aymon, who are often figured sitting astride their single horse, on the inn signs of France, and in its new form would make an excellent present.

"Nights with an Old Gunner," by C. J. Cornish (Seeley, 6s.), is simply a delight for sportsmen who love Nature as they should. Mr. Cornish and the "Son of the Marshes" know more of the natural history of sport than ninety-nine out of every hundred men who carry a rod or a gun. The former knows how to spin a fascinating yarn about his wanderings. He is equally at home, I think, on the moor or in the covert, apparently expert in setting geese on the sands, can bolt rabbits by the "crab and candle" trick, knows where to find sand eels, delights in the ebb tide, and has a pretty wit withal, and an eye open to observe all that is curious in living things and all that is odd in human kind

Messrs. Kegan Paul, Trench, Trübner, and Co. will publish early in the year "Twelve Naval Captains," by Molly Elliot Seawell, being a record of certain Americans who have attained distinction in the Navy The various articles which compose the book are both biographical and critical, and each is preceded by a portrait.

Other books to be read :—

"Famous Frigate Actions," by Charles Rathbone Low. (Virtue, 3s. 6d.)

"Four Hundred Animal Stories," by Robert Cochrane. (Chambers, 2s. 6d.)

"Miss Bobbie" (a child's story), by Ethel Turner. (Ward, Lock, 3s. 6d.)     "SEARCH-LIGHT."

---

# "Queen Victoria's Keys."

## An Ancient Military Ceremony.

### By W. SIDNEY RANDALL, B.A., Chaplain to the Forces.

**T**HOUSANDS of people visit the Tower of London every year. The popularity of this old fortress never seems to wane. Week after week the Tower is used as a practical lesson in English history, when schools are taken round the old familiar sights, not for the sake of amusement, but in order to give our young children a keen interest in the ancient records of the country.

No place in the world is more carefully guarded than the Tower of London. Since the date of the dynamite explosion these precautions have been more strict than they were before that abominable attempt. So none of the visitors ever see the quaint old ceremony, which takes place every night at eleven o'clock, known now as "The Queen's Keys."

During the day the large gates at the two entrance towers are kept open. These are the gates of the first entrance, known as the Middle Tower, and those of the second entrance, called the Byward Tower. Just within the gates of this building is the the Warders' Hall, and here the warder on duty for the night remains to open the wicket for those who are allowed to remain out and enter the Tower after twelve o'clock at night. But those who do enter the gates at this time must have the countersign, which is generally the name of a well-known town in the United Kingdom.

The old gates, which still exist beneath the Bloody Tower, are never closed now, but remain open all night. But a sentry walks just in front of them, under the walls of St. Thomas's Tower, and just beyond, at the main guard, another sentry is posted. Both these sentries challenge anyone who enters the Tower after twelve o'clock, and demand the countersign.

Those of our readers who are not familiar with these military forms, may be interested to know how the challenge is made. As soon as a sentry hears the sound of approaching footsteps, he calls out : "Halt ! Who goes there ?" The reply is given, "Friend !" The sentry replies, "Advance, friend, and give the countersign !" He places his bayonet at the charge, and when the word is given, says, "Pass, friend, all's well !" Should any person not give the countersign the sentry will call for the sergeant of the guard.

The rule is as follows :—" Her Majesty's Regulations for the Tower. No. 8.—The warder of the watch takes that duty in regular turn. He is to wear his uniform, but may lie down in the Warders' Hall. He is on duty from nine o'clock at night 'till ten in the morning. If applied to in case of accident or illness within the Tower during the night, it will be his duty to call the yeoman porter, in order to get the key of the wickets for the summoning and admission of a medical man. It is to him that the sergeant of the spur guard applies in the event of anyone demanding admission after the wickets are locked, and it is his duty to decide, according to the standing regulations of the Tower, whether admission is to be given or no. If refusal is necessary, it must be done respectfully, and with the explanation that it would be contrary to the standing regulations of the Tower. A list of the officers of the garrison who wish to enter the Tower after midnight up to three o'clock in the morning, is sent by the commanding officer of the battalion in the Tower daily to the major, and this list is given to the warder on watch for his guidance. He marks the hour on the list as they enter the Tower, up to three o'clock, when the wicket is finally closed, and the key delivered to the yeoman porter in his quarters. Should no officer's name be on the leave list, the warder on watch will deliver the wicket key to the yeoman porter at midnight."

The most interesting ceremony in connection with these gates takes place at eleven o'clock at night. "The Queen's Keys," as the ceremony is called, has often been described ; but, as a rule, the description has been written more or less inaccurately.

The following account can be relied upon to be absolutely correct : About five minutes before the hour of " locking the gates," that is, just before eleven o'clock, the yeoman porter applies to the sergeant of the guard for the escort for the "Queen's Keys." The sergeant acquaints the officer that the escort is called for, who furnishes a sergeant and six men for this duty, at the same time placing his guard under arms.

The yeoman porter, accompanied with a guard, bearing an old-fashioned lantern with a candle in it, locks the outer gate, and then shuts the gate of the Middle Tower. He then proceeds with the escort to the Byward Tower and locks the gates there. The yeoman porter then marches to the Bloody Tower with the escort, and halts under the arch of the tower. The sentry at the guard-room challenges, "Halt! Who comes there?" The yeoman porter answers, "The keys." The sentry calls, "Whose keys?" And the answer being given, "Queen Victoria's Keys," the yeoman porter places himself, with the escort, in front of and facing the guard, and then the officer of the guard gives the word, "Present arms," in which the escort joins. The yeoman porter then says in an audible voice, "God preserve Queen Victoria!" and the whole guard answer, "Amen." The keys are then carried by the yeoman porter to the Queen's House.

This quaint old ceremony is a survival of bygone days; but it must be seen to be properly understood. The yeoman porter, Mr. Penrose, comes to the gates, in his long red over-coat, and he has embroidered on his right arm the "keys," as the emblem of his post. He is the chief warder, and is the only warder who has the "keys" on his uniform. By the Queen's Regulations he is "answerable for the discipline of the warders, and reports any irregularity in their conduct to the major. He has charge of the gates, wickets, drawbridges, and entrance. He has the care of the warders' uniforms, accoutrements, and arms. He inspects the warders' quarters quarterly, and examines the cisterns, drains, roofs, and general condition of their houses, and is responsible that none but warders inhabit them. On these occasions he requires from each warder a return of every person living in his house, which return he lays before the major. He makes out all requisitions for repairs or articles required from Her Majesty's Office of Works for the Queen's House and warders' quarters. All applications from the warders must come through his hands. He inspects the boundary marks of the Tower Liberties once a year, and reports their condition to the major. He closes the iron bars in Postern Row and George Street for one hour on the first working day in August yearly He acts as clerk in the constable's office, and has charge of the books and papers therein."

The origin of this curious ceremony is lost in the mists of antiquity. There is an old record of the Tower, in which the keys are mentioned, and that is in "The Chronicle of Queen Jane," from which we take the following extract:—

"The xvjth daye of July (1553) the lorde highe treasurer was going to hes howse in London at night, and about vij of the clocke the gates of the Tower upon a sudden was shut, and the keys caryed up to the Quene Jane; but what was the cause I knowe not."

It does not much matter what the cause was, but the incident clearly shows that it was the custom at that time to take the Tower keys to the person of the highest rank within the Tower.

There are also other old records which mention "the upper porter of the Tower," who carried "the keys" and saw that the gates were duly locked.

In the reign of King Edward III. there was "one, John of London (an handy crafts man and an armourer), that had the custody of the gates, portcullises, and drawbridges of the Tower, with the wages of iiijd. per diem, and ijd. for a varlet to carry his keys after him, and also ijd. a day during the time that he should be employed in scouring the harness in the armoury, and had the same clothes and a rugg gown and a halbert allowed him, as the rest of the Yeomen had. He had to see the main gates of the Tower daily opened and locked at the usual hours, and to shake the bars and search the locks at the shutting in of the same, and then, in his own person, to bring up the keys with the rest of the warders who waited at the gates and deliver them to the lieutenant and, at night, to receive the watchword from the lieutenant and deliver it to the warders that are to watch. By his oath he was not to depart from the Tower without the license of the lieutenant being first had."

This record contains no mention of the ceremony used at the closing of the gates.

"In the first year of King Edward the IV., Richard ap Price was porter of the Tower. Next after ap Price was one Hugh Armory, the porter. In the 19th year of King Edward the IV., Richard Edwards, a page of the bedchamber, was porter for a year. Then one Lee had it. In the 22nd year of King Edward's reign, John Gervose was the porter, and he was the first who had the words 'chief porter' inserted in his patent, and he had a mansion (*sic*) in the Tower. In the reign of Richard the III., Thomas Redhead, a servant of the King, was the chief porter, with the wages of 6d. a day and a little house near the bulwark.

"Never any man of greater rank than a page of the chamber or yeoman had the place of chief porter of the Tower, until the 29th year of Queen Elizabeth's reign, and then one Sir William Gorges (a decayed and poor knight) obtained this yeoman's place, who, after his blunt manner, gave the Queen thanks for it, telling her that, being a gentle-man, she had made him a yeoman! To which the Queen answered (with a curious oath) she was sorry she had done his fellows so much wrong! He was the first that had 'Gentleman Porter' in his patent inserted. He had the wages of 1s. a day."

In the time of King James, it was ordered that, "after the great gate of the bywarde is shutt in the night tyme," people coming in and out should use "onely the little wickett." This rule is in force now, and those who have to use the "little wickett" often wish that it could be made somewhat larger.

This year the ceremony of closing these old Tower gates becomes a record one. In all its long history, never before have the keys been given up so long in the name of one King or Queen. Long may the keys of the Tower be called out as "Queen Victoria's Keys."

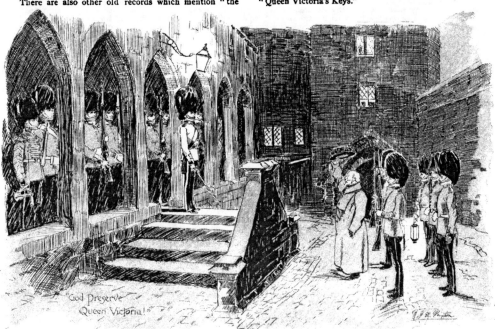

"God preserve Queen Victoria!"

# THE COAST BLOCKADE, AN EXTINCT NAVAL DEPARTMENT

by Commander Hon. Henry N. Shore R.N.

*An affray with smugglers near Kingsgate on the Kentish Coast.*

"THE Coast-blockade! What is that? I never even heard of it!" will most likely be the reader's exclamation on observing the above title. And such a confession of ignorance would be quite excusable, seeing that the writer must himself admit that he passed through the whole of his Naval career—to say nothing of several years in the Coastguard service, the lineal descendant of the Coast-blockade—without so much as hearing even a remote allusion to that once important department. And yet for fifteen years it was a power in the land, and assuredly played a part in the domestic economy of the kingdom which has never been adequately recognised or appreciated. So completely, indeed, has all recollection of it faded from the memory of man that the writer will wager that, at the present time, there is not one Naval officer in a hundred who would be able to give a satisfactory reply to the question which the non-professional reader will almost certainly ask. The following particulars may, therefore, do something towards supplying the desired information.

In a previous number of this publication, when treating of the history and origin of the Coastguard, the writer gave a brief explanation of the *raison d'être* of the Coast-blockade. It will suffice, therefore, to repeat here that this department was the outward and visible expression of an inward and fixed determination on the part of Government to combat, and eventually suppress, the gigantic system of "free trade" which had sprung up during our long wars with France, and by which the revenue was defrauded to the tune of several millions annually. The exhausting struggle in which the country had been engaged had so severely taxed its resources, that neither the leisure nor the means for combating the illicit trade had been available; but, with the advent of peace, the services of a large number of officers and men could now be utilised, and the authorities very wisely resolved to employ these in the suppression of smuggling, a task for which, by reason of their training, they were eminently fitted. The Coast-blockade was the outcome of this determination.

To whom is due the credit of having originated this particular scheme cannot now be affirmed with any certainty. A great many projects were submitted to the authorities; amongst others, one from Captain Renwick, R.N., in March, 1815, which was said to have formed the basis of the present Coastguard system. But while many of these were impracticable by reason of their expense and vexatious interference with the liberty of the subject, others again would have required more time for their development than could well be spared. The matter was pressing, the leakage of revenue enormous, and as an earnest of good intentions, the "Ganymede" frigate was commissioned by Captain McCulloch in the summer of 1816, and stationed in the Downs, for the purpose of establishing a provisional blockade of the Thames mouth, pending the development of more efficacious measures. The duties consisted in maintaining a sort of watch over the coast by means of boat patrols, and as some valuable captures were soon effected, it may be assumed that the monotony of the work brought its own reward.

Meanwhile, a much more effective scheme was in course of incubation, and this was nothing less than the blockade of the entire coast of Kent, a portion of the kingdom which, from its proximity to the Continent, had, at an early period, become the headquarters of the illicit trade, and where, on that account, the most telling blow could be struck at the enterprising gentry who conducted it. To maintain, however, a really effective blockade, something very much more was required than the patrol of the coast by boats.

It was, therefore, decided to extend the sphere of activity of the Navy from the sea to the shore. Steps were immediately taken to provide accommodation for the force to be employed. The Martello towers, erected by Pitt during the invasion scares—Pitt's follies, as they have sometimes been called—were now utilised for the first time, and in places where no such accommodation offered, a sort of barracks were erected—the modern Coastguard stations, and in December, 1816, we find Captain McCulloch reporting "the guard-houses" ready for the reception of "the officers and men to be employed on shore," amongst whom it seems was a force of marines, whom, it was suggested, should "be supplied with pistols and cutlasses."

The "Severn," 50, now took the place of the "Ganymede," the number of men borne on her books being largely augmented by entries of landsmen to meet the requirements of the new scheme, and her crew was at once landed and distributed along the coast. The stations were placed under the charge of lieutenants—of whom close on four thousand were borne on the Navy List for 1819—while one or more midshipmen or mates were placed under them. The entire force was under Naval discipline, as represented by the officer commanding the guard-ship in the Downs, Captain William McCulloch, a most able and energetic officer.

When the system was in full swing, a complete cordon of sentries encircled the coast during the hours of darkness, the men being within hail of each other, and stationed on the brink of the tide. To ensure a vigilant look-out being kept, they were visited at frequent intervals by the lieutenant or his midshipmen, while, as a further precaution against collusion, the sentries were shifted at uncertain times, so that the smugglers could never be sure of the position of any individual.

As regards the internal economy of the new force, the quarters—whether towers or barracks—were assimilated as much as possible to ship life. The men slept in hammocks, and lived in what were called "long-rooms," some tradition of which still lingers about the Coastguard stations on the South Coast. The married quarters—for some of the men had partners—consisted of a corner of the long-room screened off from the rest, where the men with their families enjoyed such privacy as a strip of Navy canvas could afford.

The discipline was extremely severe; nay, if tradition, as well as the unanimous testimony of old men who remember the blockade, are to be relied on, it was almost brutal. In consonance with the opinion which widely obtained throughout the Navy in those days, that no body of men could be kept in subjection without a lavish use of the "cat," flogging was frequent. For very slight offences the men were sent off to the guard-ship to be "dusted down" as a means of checking any disposition to kick over the traces, as well as of intensifying their zeal for the interests of the revenue.

The effects of these drastic measures were not long in manifesting themselves, especially in the neighbourhood of Deal, which village—for it merited no higher appellation at that time—had always been at the head and front of the offending. Consequently the blow fell here with greater severity than on any other part of the coast, and so keen was the pinch that within a year of the establishment of the blockade a large number of the once well-to-do inhabitants were reduced to the verge of beggary: the economic conditions of the place having been absolutely revolutionised.

Naturally, all this caused a very bitter feeling to spring up against the officers and men of the blockade—" base tools of a despotic Government"—who had brought about all this misery, and signs were not wanting of an impending storm. Certainly the smugglers would not have been free Britons had they sat quietly down and submitted without protest to what they regarded as an unwarrantable attack on their rights and vested interests. But a brief interval elapsed ere they gave a display of the spirit in which the struggle was to be conducted. From passive obstruction the transition was easy and natural to acts of violence and outrage, and in a short time the whole coast was in a blaze of rebellion against the blockade. The particular form which this outbreak assumed and the story of its suppression constitute one of the most singular, not to say sensational, chapters of our social history during the present century. Space forbids more than a brief allusion to it here. Suffice it to say that the more fiery spirits amongst the smugglers had foreseen from an early period that the trade was at stake, that the iron grip of the blockade system was tightening its hold every year, and that unless a determined and organised attempt was made to break through, and so effectually to terrorise the instruments by which the system was enforced that any further opposition on their part would not be offered to the trade, their occupation was doomed. Perceiving the necessity of immediate action, the more daring amongst the smugglers of Kent and Sussex, to which latter county the blockade had by this time been extended, organised themselves into armed

*Revenue Cutter in Chase of Smugglers' Boat, Evening Time.*

gangs for the more effectual prosecution of their business, and at once commenced operations.

The story of the "thirty years' war" that ensued is a long and interesting one, and reads more like a romance—the compilation of some sensation-loving penman—than a sober narrative of fact; indeed, were not the circumstances well authenticated, a certain amount of scepticism as to such things being possible in civilised England during the present century would be quite excusable; for during the whole of the period above mentioned the coast of Kent and Sussex was the frequent scene of bloody and murderous affrays, in which many lives were lost on both sides.

In addition to the attacks by bands of "hired assassins," the officers and men employed on this harassing service were subjected to a most vexatious persecution at the hands of parties whose profits had been seriously interfered with, while every device that the malice and ingenuity of man could conceive was resorted to, in the hope of making their position intolerable. The law was constantly put in motion against them, and the inventive powers of unprincipled attorneys were taxed to the utmost in the desire to embarrass them in their work.

Never before, in a time of profound peace, were Naval officers called on to perform more invidious duties. For, in addition to the risk to life and limb to which they were constantly exposed, the duties they were entrusted to execute required the utmost tact and temper, *vis-à-vis* to a bitterly

hostile populace, often miles from any superior officer, and deprived by the sympathies of the people of that legal assistance of which they stood so much in need; and when, too, the least false step might involve them in endless litigation and ruinous costs.

The "butcher's bill" resulting from the combats with smugglers which now constantly occurred exceeded that of many of our "small wars"; and acts of daring and gallantry were performed that nowadays would lead to something more than being "mentioned in despatches." But there was neither honour nor glory to be gained in such warfare, and the nation has shown its gratitude for the services that were rendered to it in the hour of need by consigning all recollection of them to the oblivion of official dust-heaps —the very designation of the force has been forgotten!

As years rolled by, the harsh system of discipline, combined with the irksomeness of the duties, and constant risk of being shot or maimed, caused increasing difficulty in getting men to join the Service; besides which many serious defects discovered themselves in the force itself. Bribery and corruption were rife; the men had no heart for their work; indeed, with armed smugglers in front and the "cat" behind they found themselves "between the devil and the deep sea," and chose what they considered the lesser evil, by making terms with the foe. In later times the force bore a somewhat equivocal reputation. "I always understood they were a lot of rogues," said one who knew a good deal of the "goings on" to the present writer. "It was well known that most of the men would take bribes," said another. "I always understood that was the reason why the blockade was done away with."

The only contemporary Naval writer who has thought it worth while to place on record any observations concerning the constitution of the Coast-blockade tells us that "seamen or petty officers of men-of-war rarely enter. The roll is thus filled for the most part by 'waisters' from discharged crews or, which is more frequent, by unskilled, though hardy Irish landsmen, whose estrangement from the sentiments, habits, and religion of those placed under their surveillance, seems to point them out as peculiarly adapted for a service whose basis consists in an insidious watchfulness over others, and a hostile segregation from their fellow men." (" The Naval Sketch-book," by Captain Glascock.)

In the meantime a totally distinct force for the protection of the revenue was growing up outside the sphere of the blockade, thus enabling comparisons to be instituted between the two systems and the relative advantages of each to be considered, with the result that the disestablishment of the blockade was at last determined on; and in April, 1831, the men were gradually withdrawn from the stations, their places being simultaneously taken by others belonging to the rival force, which now assumed the title of Coastguard, and was then, and for many years subsequently, under the control of the Customs.

And thus was abolished a department which, in spite of its defects and the somewhat doubtful reputation for probity it has left behind, played a most important *rôle* in the economic history of the country, and undoubtedly broke the neck of the gigantic system of smuggling which was in full swing after the Napoleonic wars.

The valuable services the force rendered to the State have, as I before remarked, never been recognised or adequately appreciated; for the reason, chiefly, that the Coast-blockade never had a historian. The very name is now forgotten. So fleeting is earthly fame!

FOREWARNED a Story of the Intelligence Department

By Major Arthur Griffiths AUTHOR OF "The Queen's Shilling" "The Rome Express" "The Wellington Memorial" etc., etc.

### SYNOPSIS OF PREVIOUS CHAPTERS.

Captain Wood is an officer on the staff of the Intelligence Department of the War Office engaged with certain confidential questions pending with the United States Government. It is the height of the London season, and he is sleeping late after a ball, when he is roused to hear some startling news. A lawyer, Mr. Quinlan, has called to tell him that an unknown relative, an American millionaire, has left him a colossal fortune. Almost at the same moment an American detective warns him that he has enemies plotting against him and his fortune, and that he goes in imminent danger of his life. Arrived at the Intelligence Office, where he is late, he is sharply reprimanded, but explains, and is given some especially confidential work to carry through connected with an attack on New York. Returning to his chambers, he again meets the American detective, who details the nature of the plot against his fortune and the military secrets he possesses. He is strongly urged to put himself under police protection, but he cannot credit the extraordinary story.

### CHAPTER VI.

SOMEONE hailed me as I passed down Piccadilly, and, turning, I recognised a man I knew, Lawford by name, a big, burly, fat-voiced man, with jet black beard, so unmistakably dyed that it increased his years and gave an unwholesome tinge to his pallid complexion. He had greasy, fawning manners—an assumption of *bonhomie* that I instinctively distrust. I never cared for him much, but he always pretended to be devilish fond of me.

I had met this Lawford on the other side of the Atlantic, in the South American city where I had spent some time in my recent mission. He gave it out that he was prospecting for gold in those parts, but many believed that he was a spy and secret agent of the American Government. It was more than likely, and explained why he had attached himself to me, trying to curry favour, and offering to put me up to many good things. He knew that I was a British officer. I had never concealed it, and I always suspected that his attentions were inspired by his desire to know what I was doing. He made nothing by it, I am happy to say.

Then we came home together in the same steamer, and I was much thrown with him on board. He was on his way to England to make his and everyone's fortune, mine included. I confess the fellow amused me, his schemes were so tremendous. He had such a profound belief in himself and in the simplicity of the British public.

"Yes, sir, I shall spoil them; stick them up, and carry off a pile of plunder. You'll do well to cut in with me, captain. You'd strike it rich; yes, sir. I can dispose of 75,000 acres of real estate which is just honeycombed with gold. The greater part belongs to me, Rufus Lawford, but I won't part till your darned capitalists are unbuttoned. But they will that when they've seen my prospectuses and heard my witching tongue."

Lawford had not found the innocents of the city so easy to beguile. He passed through many phases of good and evil fortune in the months that followed his arrival. I saw him from time to time, now gorgeous, now looking like a sweep. Sometimes he was on the eve of pulling off some gigantic operation; at others he was in the depths of despair, and borrowed a sovereign "on account" of the great fortune he meant some day to force on me. He evidently did not prosper in his schemes of promotion. But he still hung upon the frontiers of finance, in the neutral, debatable ground where every man's hand is against his fellows, and frank brigandage is more or less the rule.

I was surprised to find him in the West End, and told him so, as he overtook me with the "fifth" *Globe* in his hand.

"Halloa! Halloa! I'm taking a holiday. Those galoots eastward won't bite, and I thought I'd give myself an airing in the Park. Never expected to see you," which was a deliberate lie, for I had reason to know, later, that he had come out for that very purpose. "See your name in the papers. Presume it's you? They've got the whole story. Fine fortune, young sir, fine. Wish you joy."

I thanked him, not over-cordially, perhaps, for the man bored me, and I guessed that his was only an early attack upon my new found millions.

"Now, Captain Wood, I am delighted to have met you, for I may be able to give you a little advice. You will be assailed on all sides—you capitalists are the natural game of the promoters. Give them a wide berth. There's a mass of villainy about. Don't trust 'em—not a man of them. If you're in any difficulty, if you've got a few thousands to play with at any time, you come straight to me. I shall be delighted to serve you, for yourself, mind, and for the sake of old times. For I knew Bully McFaught well."

"Ah! indeed. Tell me about him. You knew him?" I was eager to hear more of the man from whom my strangely unexpected fortune had come.

"I knew old McFaught. No fear—knew him well, and did business with him, but not so much as I could have liked—worse luck. If I could have gotten upon his shoulders, I should have waltzed into unbounded wealth. But you had to be with him, not against him. He made *some* men; but he ruined more—stock, lock, and barrel. It don't matter to you, anyhow, whether he piled up the dollars on dead men's bones or robbed the saints. Guess you can freeze on to what he gathered."

I laughed a little uneasily, but, after all, who was this Lawford, and why should I care for what he said? It was probably untrue.

"Will you be going over to God's country, any time soon, Captain Wood? Wish you'd take me with you. You'll want a sheepdog, and I guess I'm pretty fly."

"You're very good. I shall remember; but I doubt my going just at present. Now I think I'll turn in here." We were passing the portals of my club, the Nelson and Wellington, commonly called the N. and W.

"This your shanty? Pretty smart place, I take it. Can they fling a Manhattan cocktail, any?"

But the hint was lost on me. I had had enough of Mr. Lawford, and wished to be well rid of him.

"Well, good day," he said. "If you change your mind about crossing the pond, be sure you send for me. But I suppose London's good enough for you. It's a pleasant place, I reckon, with the spondulicks to spend, and I guess you can have the best it holds, now, if it's worth the buying. See you next time."

Could I? There was one thing I hungered for keenly, and was by no means certain of securing. Lawford's chance words brought it home to me with much emphasis. My chief object at this time was to try how far one fortune would favour me with another

How would Frida Wolstenholme be affected by the news of my great good luck? I had been asking myself this momentous question ever since I had seen Mr. Quinlan. At one time I hoped for the best, next minute I was as greatly cast down. She was far above most of us, and, so far, of me especially. I counted myself the very least of all her followers, and their name was legion. She flouted us all, in turn; in turn threw everyone his crumb of comfort; laughed, chaffed, encouraged every man that pleased her and paid her court, making no distinction, with her broad catholic taste, between young and old, titled and commoner, the richest *parti* and the worst detrimental. But woe to the silly fool who permitted his hopes to blossom under her sunny smile. Next day he was certain to be in despair at her frowns. Unquestionably she was an arrant and unconscionable flirt.

I got on better, perhaps, than some of the others. Our first meeting had been in the hunting field. A few of us had clubbed together to keep a couple of horses within reach of the shires, and took it in turns to ride their tails off. Wolstenholme Hall, of which Miss Frida was the sole undisputed heiress, for her father was dead, lay at no great distance. She came to all the meets, and rode like a bird, leaving her chaperon many fields behind, and giving her mother at home much anxiety when the run was away from Wolstenholme and it took her hours to get back. They were very good to us soldiers at the Hall, and we were asked there constantly. It was in that way that I fell into Miss Frida's toils.

Some people, those especially who were jealous of her, called her a very modern girl; and so she was, to the extent of claiming complete independence and freedom from all control. Her mother had spoilt her from a child, and was now a child in her wilful, wayward daughter's hands. Frida, in truth, accepted no rule or guidance but that of her own sweet will. She chose to go her own road, but still it was the straightest of the roads. For all her caprices she walked always erect, fearless, outspoken, strong in her own purity, blamelessly self-reliant and self-possessed. It was all conceit, her enemies said, unmitigated and intolerable conceit—of her good looks, of her birth, of her broad lands. A girl so happily placed might well be forgiven for holding her head so high. To me she was simply perfect.

We often talked confidentially together, she and I, for she was good enough to say she felt perfectly safe with me. I had accepted the situation a little ruefully. Still, it gave me many opportunities denied to others. She would sit out with me at a ball for an hour at a time, and openly honour me with a preference that made other men thirst for my blood.

"There can be no nonsense between us," she would say, as coolly cutting me off from all hope as if she was a surgeon using his knife. "You haven't got sixpence. I couldn't marry you, even if I wanted to do so, which I don't—any more than you want to marry me?"

There was a note of interrogation in her soft voice, and her laughing eyes asked mine plainly what she would not say.

"Oh, of course not," I would answer, lying bravely. "I don't like you well enough."

"I thought not, and, you see, it would never do for a man to be quite dependent on his wife. Now if you were a Duke or an American millionaire, or if you had even a decent fortune and a country place or two, and, say, a baronetcy, although I do not insist upon the title ——"

She would look at me so sweetly that I half believed she was in earnest, and I had been tempted once to take her hand and hold it without any protest from her.

"You might?" I asked, hungering for the next word.

"I might put you on the list. But you are only a pauper, and a foolish one to boot, not to say an impudent one, and you mustn't do that, although we are such old friends." With that she would draw away her hand, but so slowly that I fondly thought she really liked me, until presently some rank ill-usage warned me not to be deceived by her cozening ways.

Now I leant against the railings in the Row, in my best hat and frock-coat, with a brand-new flower in my buttonhole, hoping she might see me, and that I might get the chance of a word.

How would she meet me, now that the great obstacle was removed? I was in the very category she herself had made. I could speak to her from the standpoint of her own creating. I was an American millionaire, an arch-millionaire. Her inheritance was but a drop in the ocean compared to my new-found wealth. I could buy up her acres, her Hall, the whole of Wolstenholme, everything but the ancient name; buy them ten times over, and not be at the end of my means.

The gulf between us was bridged over, and yet—without her consent I could never win across to her side.

Should I gain that consent? I asked myself the momentous question again and again as I stood there waiting, answering it with increasing hopefulness as I thought over the many pleasant passages in our long acquaintanceship.

Then the whole edifice crumbled suddenly into the dust. The Wolstenholmes' carriage was driven swiftly past. I caught Frida's look full and fair. She saw me, I knew, and the friendly, familiar bow I made her; but her only response was a blank, stony stare. It was the plainest and most direct "cut," emphasised, to show there could be no shadow of a mistake, by the shifting of her sunshade so as to quite shut me out of her vision.

What had happened? What could it mean? I was nearly beside myself as I hastily turned on my heel to leave the park. Men came up to me with friendly greetings and congratulations, for the evening papers, as Lawford had first shown me, had made my story public property; but I put them abruptly on one side. They did not take it very kindly.

*"It was the plainest and most direct cut."*

I heard one chap mutter, "*He* can't stand coin," and another declare that "Of all the stuck-up, purse-proud prigs——" But I went my way regardless, thinking only of Frida. It was the same at the club, where I looked in on my way to Clarges Street. I found everybody insufferable; all toadies and sycophants, as I thought them, and I would gladly have surrendered every McFaught dollar then and there to have had a better opinion of my fellow-creatures—at least of one of them.

## CHAPTER VII.

RETURNING to my rooms to dress for dinner, someone pushed past me just as I was letting myself in with my key. A man meanly dressed, one of the poor waifs, as I thought, who so often infest street corners ready for any job.

The incident made no particular impression on me at the time, but it was brought home to me as one link in a chain of singular events that were near at hand.

Directly I was inside the house, Savory handed me a letter, from Lawford.

"DEAR CAPTAIN WOOD" (it said)—

"When I left you in Piccadilly I ran up against some friends who are much set upon making your acquaintance  They are the Duke and Duchess of Tierra Sagrada.  He is a Spanish don, she an American beauty, Susette Bywater they called her in New York, where she and her family were well acquainted with your uncle, Mr. McFaught.

"Won't you come to the opera to-night to be introduced to the Duchess?  They beg me to say that their box is No. 27A upon the pit tier, where they will be entirely delighted to receive you.  Send back a line at your early convenience, and oblige,

"Yours very faithfully,

"RUFUS W. LAWFORD."

I had no engagements that night but a couple of balls, for neither of which, after my snub in the park, I was now very keen.  Besides, I had no wish to be very late that night.  I saw on my table an official "box" straight from the office, and knew that it contained the great scheme for the attack on New York, which was referred to me for examination and report.  I meant to give it my best attention in the early morning hours next day, and so promised myself to get to bed betimes.  A little good music would soothe me, I thought, so I wrote a few lines accepting the invitation, and proceeded to dress.

It was then, as I stood before the glass in the window that gave upon the street, I caught a glimpse of the same forlorn creature looking up at my house.  Was it mere accident?  After all I had heard that day the smallest matter still unexplained assumed a certain importance.

But it went out of my head completely when I entered the N. and W. and ran up against Swete Thornhill, with a number of other cronies, all full of my "great good luck."

"Well, young Dives," began the first, "so that's what made you so late this morning.  Shan't see you there any more, I take it?  Don't you want to adopt a poor lonely orphan?  I'm your man."

"What has Crœsus ordered for dinner?" said another, snatching at my bill.  "What!  Nothing but the joint and a pint of Medoc!  Fie, fie, Crœsus, don't be mean."

"Not many crumbs will drop from your rich table, Willie Wood.  When will you ask us to dine?"

A dozen suggestions were quickly shot off at me.  "We shall expect you to take a deer forest" and a "grouse moor," "start a coach," "a steam yacht," and it was with difficulty that I escaped to a quiet corner where I could eat my frugal meal in peace.  After that, avoiding the smoking-room, I swallowed my coffee, and went out on to the doorstep to hail a cab.

My "shadow" was still there.  He slunk slowly, and, as I thought, reluctantly, out of sight when I entered the hansom and told the cabby to drive to Covent Garden.  Remembering Mr. Snuyzer's communication a few hours before, this espionage caused me some uneasiness.  Yet it was done so clumsily that I half believed the fellow wished rather to attract than escape my notice.  Of this I had soon a clear proof.

When I alighted from the cab just short of the colonnade approach of the opera house I saw him, heard him, just at my elbow, having transferred himself there by the same mysterious process that brings a tout all the way from a railway station to your front door to unload the luggage.

"Don't take no more cabs, guv'nor," he whispered hoarsely in my ear, and next moment he was gone.  Who had sent him in such a roundabout way to tell me this?  Who, indeed, had set him on to watch me?  It must have been a friend, of course, and I gave the credit to Mr. Snuyzer.  They were evidently smart people, Messrs. Saraband and Sons, when there was a chance of business coming their way.

The night was not over yet, a night of dark doings and unexplained mysteries, all of which seemed to centre in me.  I could not quite believe—why should I?—that the scraps of conversation I was now to overhear referred to me, and yet, had I been gifted with second sight, had I, indeed, been more alive to the warnings I had received, I might have been spared much misery.  But I am anticipating.

When I reached the opera the act drop was down, and I thought to cast a look on the house before I made my way to the box where I was bidden.  My hosts were strangers, and I rather wished to see Lawford first, that he might present me to them in due form.  So I entered by one of the side ways into the stalls, and stood there watching the audience for a time.

It was a full house.  Every box was occupied with the smartest and prettiest people in town.  Among the latter was Miss Wolstenholme, on the grand tier, and, as usual, a centre of attraction.  Men came and went in constant succession; that no one stayed was proof enough to me that she was in no encouraging mood.  Should I try my luck, and, braving her seeming ill-will, seek some explanation of her treatment of me in the park?  So I studied her beautiful face long and closely through my glasses, and hesitated.  There was a hard, stony look in her beautiful eyes, her brow was clouded, her lips set firmly together.  Something had put her out, that was certain.  I knew her too well to doubt

it, knew, also, that it was unwise to approach her now, if I wished to regain her good graces.  That I myself could be in any way associated with her present captiousness never for a moment occurred to me.  At any rate, I did not attempt to attract her attention.  Indeed, as she sat there, motionless and *distrait*, I fancied she did not know I was in the house.

In the midst of this I became suddenly aware that a pair of bright eyes were fixed upon me from another direction, and I saw that I was an object of interest, more of a passing interest, perhaps, to a well-dressed, charming woman in a box on the pit tier.

Then, suddenly, Lawford touched me on the back, saying:

"Oho, so you are here.  Come right along.  Let me present you to the Duchess.  She's mightily set upon seeing you," and he led the way along the corridor to the box No. 27A.

As we got close to it I saw the door was ajar, and I was attracted by the sound of voices talking Spanish, which I knew.  Lawford held me back, possibly fearing to be indiscreet and to intrude upon some family quarrel.  What was said did not impress him, perhaps, for I think he did not understand Spanish.  The voices were raised high enough to be plainly audible to anyone outside—a man's, coarse, harsh, and menacing; a woman's, in reply, pleading softly, yet firmly.

"You know the conditions, and you are bound to assist.  The man has been handed over to us.  He is our game, our quarry.  What he has must be ours, all of it, the whole vast fortune."

"I would much rather be left out of the business.  I despise myself so.  I hate and detest the part you would have me play.  I will not go against him."

"*Sanctissima Virgen!*  Defend me from a woman's scruples.  I tell you you must—there is no alternative.  Captivate him, win his devotion.  Why not?  He is a comely youth (*guapo chico*); you have made eyes at worse.  You must and shall.  By heaven, if I thought you meant to play me false——"

He checked himself abruptly, and with a sudden, peremptory "h—sh," and came out to invite us most cordially to enter the box.  There was nothing to show that any difference of opinion had but just agitated its occupants.  Both husband and wife were smiling sweetly; the Duke's voice (he was a small, spare man with gleaming eyes and glistening teeth in his dark olive face) was now so smooth and silky that I could not imagine that it was the same I had heard in such harsh and rasping, angry tones.  His manner, too, was full of that punctilious formality that goes with the highest breeding in the blue-blooded don.

The lady (it was she who had been staring at me) sat now perfectly quiet and self-controlled.  There was no trace of emotion about her as she welcomed me, with marked anxiety to be pleasant and make me feel at home.

The *entr'acte* was not yet ended, and the Duchess swept her soft draperies aside to give me room by her side in the front of her box, where I was in full view of the whole house, Frida Wolstenholme included.

"Why, Captain Wood, this is real kind of you," she began, "to take us in this informal way.  Directly I read of your accession to old Mr. McFaught's fortune, I was most anxious to meet you.  We knew your uncle—no?—well, your relative.  Mr. McFaught was a friend of our family in the old days.  I never knew him myself; but I have often heard my father speak of him, and of his great wealth.  Will you let me congratulate you—and, Pepe"—this was to the Duke—"have you congratulated Captain Wood?  Of course you have."

"*Es claro*—of course—I know that Captain Wood is one of the chief of fortune's favourites.  But, believe me, *Señor mio*, you have also come into great trouble.  Vast wealth is a terrible burthen; to use it aright is a grave responsibility.  Especially so when—you will pardon me, Captain Wood—it has come undeserved."

"But, Pepe, it is not fair to say that.  Captain Wood was a relation—he had a right to inherit."

"I only mean that Captain Wood does not know, probably will never know, whether there were not others with greater claims—moral claims, I mean—on Mr. McFaught.  That thought would always rankle with me.  *Vaya*, I would rather it was you than me."

"Do not let him disturb you, my dear Captain Wood.  The Duke has rather extreme views in theory; but he knows that wealth is wealth.  Although we have no vast store, he would be sorry to surrender it."

We got very friendly, quite confidential, together, she and I, as we talked on, *tête-à-tête*, the Duke having gone off somewhere with Lawford.

"Of course, you have not yet tasted the joys of possession.  It is all very new to you still."

"I hardly realise it, indeed, or what I shall do with it."

*(To be continued).*

*COLONEL TEMPLER, SUPERINTENDENT R.E. BALLOON FACTORY, ALDERSHOT.*

LIEUTENANT-COLONEL J. L. B. TEMPLER is a well-known Militia officer belonging to the 7th Battalion King's Royal Rifles. He has since 1877 been attached to the Royal Engineers for ballooning work. He joined the School of Military Ballooning on its first foundation at Woolwich, twenty years ago, accompanied it on its removal to Chatham, and after that proceeded in charge of the establishment to Aldershot, whither he came with the title of Superintendent, and the honorary rank of Major. At Aldershot, on the removal there of the Chatham ballooning manufactory and experimental works, Major Templer had the great advantage of coming under the general direction of a man of such wide views and long experience as Colonel Bruce Brine, brother of the distinguished aeronaut. Colonel Templer, who was formerly a civil engineer, has ever been an enthusiastic balloonist, and has spent large sums out of his own pocket in connection with the formation and organisation of the school. He has also had the experience—as one reward of his labours—of being court-martialled, on a charge of giving away to a foreign Government secrets of his own discovery, the charge being based on evidence that was laughed out of court before the time came for the opening of Colonel Templer's defence.

# MILITARY BALLOONING.

THE idea of employing balloons in warfare dates from a time almost coeval with their invention, but no serious attempt was made to put the project into execution until the Revolutionary War of 1794.

To Coutelle, a young Frenchman, is due the credit of introducing balloons into the Army of France. Soon after the commencement of hostilities he sought out General Jourdan at Naubeuge, and, after much trouble, succeeded in gaining an interview. Jourdan looked on the suggestion favourably, and directed him to make further experiments, and to report the result. Coutelle hastened to comply with the General's wishes, and in particular to ascertain the most advantageous method of transmitting intelligence from the balloon to those below.

He decided on the plan of enclosing written notes or sketches in little bags and dropping them on the ground. Finding this method practicable, he returned to communicate the result of his observations. Jourdan was satisfied that great advantage was to be gained from the use of balloons, and forthwith commissioned the young Frenchman to raise and command, with the rank of brevet-captain, a company designated "Les Aérostiers," consisting of a lieutenant, sublieutenant, several non-commissioned officers, and thirty rank and file.

Before the battle of Fleurus, Coutelle made two reconnaissances of the enemy's position in his balloon, and on the first occasion was accompanied by the General.

*MAKING SMALL BALLOONS.*

The information gained by this means proved of considerable value, and the victory of the French over the Austrians is in great measure traceable to the way in which the captain of "Aérostiers" supplied his General with reports of the Austrian dispositions. The balloon used was filled with hydrogen gas.

During the war an improved means of communicating from the balloon was devised. The note or drawing was attached to a narrow stick, like an arrow, which was loaded and pointed to ensure its striking the ground and remaining fixed. That it might be the more easily visible, a small piece of coloured silk was fixed to the upper end of the stick. The advantage of this miniature flag is apparent—at least to every player of golf.

The plans, too, of the enemy's dispositions were drawn in different colours, each colour having a special signification, and known only to the French. Balloons continued to be used throughout

*DRESSING SKINS.*

the campaign, and at the close of hostilities Coutelle was ordered, with his friend Conté, to form a school of ballooning at Meudon. The latter soon established a system of visual signalling which was founded on the use of coloured flags, and was employed in working captive balloons.

Balloons were used with good results at the siege of Erenbritstein, for without their aid it would have been impossible for the besiegers to reconnoitre the fortress, situated as it is on a high and precipitous rock.

Bonaparte organised a ballooning corps to accompany him during his second campaign in Egypt, but before it could be employed the waggons carrying the various accessories fell into the hands of the British, and the action of the balloonists commanded by Conté was consequently paralysed. During the remainder of the campaign the aëronauts were destined to employ their superior knowledge of things heavenly in amusing the soldiers and the native Egyptians, and it is not surprising to learn that Napoleon regarded balloons as "of no strategical importance." Consequently, at the termination of the campaign, the school at Meudon was closed.

Captive balloons were used for reconnoitring by Carnot when besieged at Antwerp, in 1815. The suggestion of dropping explosives from balloons on to an enemy had its origin in Russia so early as 1812, but does not appear to have been tested until 1849, when the Austrians besieged Venice. The besiegers attached shells to a number of small balloons,

*THE STEAM SAPPER.*

Photos. F.G.O.S Gregory & Co.    *TESTING THE QUALITY OF GAS.*    Copyright.—H. & K

The fuses were ignited before the ascent, and the shells, according to the engineers, were calculated to burst over the town. The Austrian professors of aëronautics, however, appear to have totally disregarded the action of the wind, with the result that the shells burst over the Austrian lines, inflicting considerable loss. In 1854 large captive balloons were employed in conjunction with explosives, but without success. In the French campaign against Italy (1859) reconnaissance was effected by means of balloons, but there was no corps specially told off to do duty with them. The arrangements were entirely entrusted to two engineers—the brothers Godard, who made numerous ascents in fire balloons. One was made just previous to the battle of Solferino.

During the American War of 1861 a balloon staff, consisting of some fifty men and two officers, was formed and used by General McClellan. Especially during the siege of Richmond captive balloons were employed, and intelligence was transmitted to the headquarters staff by means of the electric telegraph. The train of the balloon staff comprised two balloons drawn by four horses each, an acid cart drawn by two horses, and two generators drawn by four horses each. This corps was employed throughout the war, but appears to have furnished little information. Hydrogen was used on all occasions.

While foreign nations were all more or less engaged in attempting to put to the test this new addition to the munitions of war, Britain alone seems to have viewed the experiments with cynical indifference, and it is not until 1862 that we hear of trials being instituted at Aldershot, then in its infancy, for the purpose of determining whether or not the balloon could be relied on in time of war. It was proposed, in event of the experiments proving satisfactory, to found at Aldershot a school similar to that formerly existing at Meudon in France. It may be concluded that the efforts of the British aëronauts were not crowned with unqualified success, for the project of forming a school of ballooning was not at that time carried out.

During the siege of Paris balloons were used, not to reconnoitre the enemy, but as a means of communication with the outer world. They carried with them a number of pigeons, and when the latter were liberated they returned to the besieged city bearing tidings of events in the provinces. During the siege as many as sixty-four balloons were despatched. Several were captured by the

IN MID AIR.

Prussians, and many fired at without injury; but the majority completed the journey in safety.

In 1871 the French School at Meudon was reopened, and everything was done in France to bring the new military science to perfection. The application of photography to this means of reconnoitring was looked upon with favour by the French military authorities, and gradually photography became an almost indispensable adjunct to military aëronautics. Some experiments were made at Rouen in 1880, and several satisfactory photographs were obtained at a distance of 1,100 mètres above the ground.

The attachment of search lights to balloons is, perhaps, one of the latest acquisitions to military ballooning. Search lights have been repeatedly used by German aëronauts during manœuvres, and are looked upon as being invaluable for reconnaissance by night.

During the manœuvres of 1892 several were seen hovering over the frontier by the Russian outposts, who did not hesitate to fire on the "uncanny" apparitions. Their ammunition was, however, expended to no purpose, as none of the balloons were struck. A balloon detachment, under the present commandant of the Aldershot School, was successfully employed at Suakin in 1885. This is the latest example of the kind in time of war.

*       *       *

The Military School of Ballooning at Aldershot is wholly responsible both for the theory and practice of military aëronautics in the British Army. This institution, though unknown to civilians in general, and, indeed, to the majority of soldiers, has a most important work to perform in constructing and testing every balloon destined to be used in the Service. To it is further entrusted the imparting of instruction to all those whose province it is to play the part of an aëronaut or to facilitate in some manner the effective employment of balloons in time of war.

First among these is the Balloon Section Royal Engineers, which (with the exception of preparing and fitting the skins) constructs all the appliances employed in conjunction with aërial navigation.

Several classes, too, are formed at Aldershot every year for the benefit of officers desirous of adding to their military knowledge such information as may be obtained at the school. That the courses are interesting and instructive is evident from the zeal displayed at all times by those undergoing instruction and their

FILLING ROOM.

MAKING GAS.

Photo. F.G.O.S. Gregory & Co.    *DISCUSSING THE ROUTE.*

apparent desire to amass as much knowledge on the subject as the limited time at their disposal will permit. The school is not open to the general public, nor is it possible to enter its precincts without first having obtained official sanction. He who would unceremoniously seek admission into the Holy of Holies is ruthlessly forced to beat a retreat by the sapper on sentry at the entrance. It may, therefore, be well to describe, for the benefit of all who are not within reach of obtaining the necessary passport, some of the scenes enacted beyond the barrier. The inflated part of a balloon is formed from the membrane of bullocks. The latter is, of course, received in its natural state, and a considerable amount of preparation is rendered necessary before it is ready for use. The skins are first thoroughly washed and scraped. They are then fitted together and stretched out on long tables. When thoroughly dry they are peeled off in long strips. These are in their turn fitted together, and form the large balloons. All waste material in this process is utilised in the construction of small balloons. For work such as this, including repairs, a number of female hands are employed, and are represented engaged in cleaning the skins and in making small balloons. At the School of Ballooning there are several rooms sufficiently

*WAGGONS CARRYING BALLOONS AND GAS.*

*CROWNING THE BALLOON.*

Photos. F.G.O.S.Gregory & Co.        *BALLOON PARTLY FULL.*        Copyright.— Hudson & Kearns.

large to admit of a balloon being fully inflated in them. They are fitted with large doors, which can be opened to allow of the balloon being taken out while still inflated, and it is in these rooms that repairs are executed. The mode of manufacturing gas for inflating is illustrated on a former page. Three vessels are used for the purpose. That on the shelf is filled with diluted sulphuric acid, and connected to the next, which contains a quantity of granulated zinc. The hydrogen thus generated is caused to pass through a third vessel filled with water to ensure its purification, and thence by a pipe to the gasometer. The zinc is received in sheets; it is then melted and dropped from a height into a barrel of water, and assumes fantastic formations, which are the more easily acted upon by the acid. The hydrogen passes from the gasometer through a pipe to the filling room, shown in the second picture on the same page. Here it is transferred as required to steel tubes intended for transport. Before being filled they are laid on the sockets, shown on the left of the picture, and connected to the machine (Brotherhood compressor) on the right. The supply of gas is then turned on, passes through the compressor, and fills the tubes. Each tube before being placed in this room is subjected to a severe test. It is placed in some vessel to prevent any injurious result should

*BALLOON THREE PARTS FULL.*

Photos. F.G.O.S.Gregory & Co.    *TESTING A TUBE.*    Copyright.—Hudson & Kearns

it burst, and is then filled with water. The amount of pressure is registered by the gauge, and the tube, if sufficiently strong to carry the necessary quantity of hydrogen, must be capable of standing a pressure equivalent to 3,000-lb. per square inch. Before being used for inflating, the gas is also tested. This operation is depicted taking place in presence of a group of officers. A small balloon is first weighed and then filled with gas by means of an india-rubber pipe passing through the testing instrument. A car is attached to the balloon, and the latter is filled with weights until it attains its equilibrium. When the weight of the balloon, the car, and its contents are deducted from the total, the weight of the gas is obtained. When an ascent is intended the gas in tubes is conveyed by waggons drawn by six horses or by the steam sapper to the scene of operations. The balloon itself is placed on a waggon drawn by four horses. The former are visible in the foreground, and the latter in the background of the first picture on the opposite page, in which also two men are seen fixing the valve. When this is done the balloon is crowned by the men, as shown in the second picture, and after the mouth of it has been connected to the waggons by means of three pipes joined together, the process of filling is commenced. The balloon is depicted in the following pictures when partially full and when inflated to three-quarters of its size.

In the background of the latter picture is a waggon to which a captive balloon can be attached. The amount of cable necessary is regulated by the windlass in rear.

On this page it is shown after having ascended some little distance. The officer (Captain Ward, R.E.) is in the act of taking an observation. His attendant, a sapper, is comfortably seated in the net—a position which the ordinary mortal would consider a trifle precarious. In this picture the places where the skins are joined are plainly visible. The same balloon is shown at a considerable distance above the ground in the picture entitled "In Mid Air." From the full-page illustration opposite the latter picture one can obtain some estimate of the usual size of the car attached to a balloon. In it a Quartermaster-Sergeant and Sergeant of the Ballooning Staff, Aldershot, are seen discussing the route to be taken. On the left is a limelight projector, which can be used in conjunction with the gas used for filling the balloons. The two round discs are valves, to which allusion has already been made. Those, together with grapnels, hoops, nets, etc., form articles of store, and are kept at the school in the store rooms ready for use when required. Not the least interesting part of the building is that devoted to workshops, where one's attention is easily absorbed while watching the sappers (all of whom are tradesmen or mechanics)

*TAKING AN OBSERVATION.*

Military ballooning is not yet, by any means, perfect, but giant strides are being made in that particular branch of warfare, and in the race for supremacy the school at Aldershot is well to the front among all the principal nations of Europe.

What the future of military ballooning will be it is impossible to say. All the nations of Europe are at present busily engaged in attempting to reach perfection in the science of aërial navigation, and though it cannot be ascertained what each nation has accomplished in this direction, there is reason to believe that France—the originator of military ballooning—has manufactured a balloon capable of being navigated through the air at the rate of some twenty or thirty miles an hour. Germany and Russia are also engaged in manufacturing balloons fitted with the latest scientific appliances, but the results obtained remain to be seen. Certain it is that the great Powers regard military aëronautics as an important factor in future warfare, and if the difficulty of steering can be surpassed once and for all, we may expect to find perfect batteries in the air in the event of a European war.

The principal *rôle* of the aërial machine will probably be that of dropping explosives on fortifications, ships, and buildings, which, if carried out successfully, will entirely revolutionise the science of fortification, for it will become necessary to devise some means of protection from vertical fire.

Lieut. B. Baden-Powell, writing of aërial warfare recently in the *United Service Magazine*, says, "Once we get to machines capable of going twenty to thirty miles an hour the conquest of the air may almost be said to be complete, for the apparatus could then stem any ordinary breeze and be able to go 'where it listeth.' . . . What will the good citizens of London say when they see a hostile dynamite-carrying aërostat hovering over St. Paul's? Our Naval supremacy would be comparatively useless if we had no aërial defence."

The idea that such a state of things is possible is startling in the extreme; but while we trust that London may never be bombarded from above, or, indeed, from any quarter whatever, it behoves us as a nation to keep pace with our Continental neighbours in the science of military ballooning.

turning or moulding some of the metal fittings required for employment with the balloons. On every important field-day the balloon is a familiar sight. It is usually connected with the ground by telephone, in order that intelligence of the enemy's movements may be quickly transmitted to the General in command. During manœuvres, too, the aëronauts are always in evidence, and valuable photographs are frequently reproduced from the car of the balloon at a considerable height above the ground, showing plainly not only the country below, but the exact disposition of the enemy's forces. Some particularly good specimens were obtained during the Berkshire manœuvres of 1893.

# THE
# NAVY & ARMY
## ILLUSTRATED.

Vol. V.—No. 56.]  *FRIDAY, FEBRUARY 4th, 1898.*

Photo Maull & Fox

Piccadilly.

*VICE-ADMIRAL W. R. ROLLAND, C.B.*

THE veteran Naval officer whose portrait is here shown, Vice-Admiral W. R. Rolland, dates his entry into the Royal Navy from 1832, five years before the Queen came to the throne. His Service career has been full of fighting from within a very few months of his first donning his midshipman's jacket. Admiral Rolland saw a great deal of hard service in the Far East, and also in the first China War of 1841, in which he was present in nearly every fight that took place. Fourteen years later, in the Russian War, he was first lieutenant of the "Agamemnon," and in that capacity is one of the dwindling band of heroes of the in-shore squadron at the bombardment of Sebastopol on October 17th, 1854. He took part in the second China War, and retired in 1872, being promoted Rear and Vice Admiral on the retired list in 1875 and 1879 respectively. He was made a C.B. in 1871.

# THE COMMISSION OF THE "ST. GEORGE."

FEW are the parts of the world in which the White Ensign is not seen, and many are the ships that leave England for service abroad, but of these none—certainly within recent years—has had a more eventful commission than the "St. George."

Space permits us but brief reference to the many events in which the "St. George's" company have played their part, events which are prominent in the history of the development of Africa—East, West, and South.

On October 25, 1894, Captain Forsyth hoisted his pennant in the "St. George." On December 3 the ship arrived at her future headquarters, Simon's Town, and relieved the obsolete "Raleigh" as flag-ship on the Cape station. That a new first-class cruiser had relieved the "Raleigh," to which the colonials had for some years been accustomed, was an event in the Naval history of the Cape—an event not lost upon the colonials, to judge by the keenness they evinced to see the ship. A month later the commander-in-chief, then Rear-Admiral Sir Frederick Bedford, K.C.B., commenced his annual West Coast cruise. January and February are the best months, or rather the least worst, to visit the fever-haunted places of that malarious coast. That an expedition would take place at this time was extremely unlikely. News travels fast in Africa, and the lesson taught by Admiral Bedford's expedition against Nana had not been forgotten. At Sierra Leone, however, the first intimation of the rising of the Brassmen and the looting of Akassa reached the admiral. Consequent on this the ship proceeded with all despatch to the Niger, arriving there on February 8.

African expeditions are numerous and soon forgotten, save, perhaps, by those who serve in them. The fighting consisted chiefly of boat attacks on stockades in the narrow winding creeks of the Brass River. These stockades were invariably armed with smooth-bore ordnance, varying from 3-pounders to 9-pounders. The final advance on the King's capital was made literally through a swamp. The losses sustained by the "St. George" were the first lieutenant (Lieutenant George John Taylor) and two men killed. By a curious coincidence, Lieutenant Taylor fell on February 22, 1895, and his predecessor, Lieutenant Arnold, of the "Raleigh," was killed in the Gambia Expedition on

February 22, 1894. On the completion of the Brass River Expedition the "St. George" returned to the Cape, arriving there on March 9.

Few of those who witnessed the "St. George's" farewell

*THE "ST. GEORGE," LATE FLAG-SHIP AT THE CAPE STATION.*
Photo. Symonds.

to Admiral Bedford were likely to soon forget it, the splendid cruiser, after her salute, circling the mail ship, the "Tantallon Castle," and her whole ship's company cheering.

On June 5 Rear-Admiral Rawson arrived and hoisted his flag as commander-in-chief. His staff were Captain Egerton, flag-captain, Lieutenant England, flag-lieutenant, and Mr. Rowe, secretary.

The next event was the East Coast cruise. An invitation had been issued by the Transvaal Government for the admiral, his staff, and five other officers to visit the festivities in connection with the opening of the Pretoria-Delagoa Bay Railway. Accordingly, directly on arrival in Delagoa Bay, the admiral and several officers proceeded to Pretoria by an official train. It had been arranged for the guests to visit the Eldorado of Africa, Johannesburg. Throughout the "St. George's" commission, however, it was always the unexpected that happened. A telegram arrived informing the admiral of the rising in East Africa. This necessitated his immediate return, and the ship proceeded with all despatch to Zanzibar, arriving there on July 12. The state of affairs was then learned. An Arab sheik called 'Mbaruk, one of the most powerful chiefs in the territory of the East African Company, had conspired against British rule and caused his people to rise. Consequent on this a punitive expeditionary force was landed from the fleet.

After an arduous march through an almost unknown country, the Naval Brigade attacked and captured 'Mbaruk's forest stronghold, 'Mwele, on August 17, 1895. This place was an ideal stronghold, being situated on the top of a steep forest-clad hill and stockaded all round. It was attacked and successfully stormed in three columns. Unfortunately, 'Mbaruk himself escaped and gave trouble for some time afterwards, until he finally surrendered in German territory.

On the completion of the

From a Photo. By a Naval Officer.
*ADMIRAL RAWSON AND OFFICERS ON THE MARCH TO 'MWELE.*

Mwele Expedition the flag-ship proceeded to the Cape, and arrived there on September 7. Three months later the flag-ship left Simon's Bay for Cape Coast Castle, to take part, as it was supposed, in the Ashanti Expedition. And when, after the ship had dropped her anchor off the quaint, dismal, fever-haunted town, it was announced that there would be no Naval Brigade in the expedition, the keenest disappointment was felt. However, there was a surprise in store.

During the afternoon of New Year's Day a telegram arrived for the admiral. Immediately steam was ordered for full speed in the flag-ship and "Philomel," and both these ships left for an unknown destination a few hours afterwards. The sudden and quite unexpected departure caused considerable excitement, and speculation was only allayed on arrival at the Cape, where the mystery was elucidated. It was the Jameson raid. Owing to the unsettled state of affairs in South Africa, many months were spent at the Cape, and not until August 14, 1896, did the admiral obtain permission

*INTERIOR OF STOCKADE, 'MWELE.*

to go up the East Coast. On the morning of August 26, when going up the Zanzibar channel, a steam cutter was sighted approaching the ship, manned and armed. When the latter arrived alongside and an officer boarded the flag-ship display-ing a revolver in his belt, eager questions were asked. It was then discovered that one more *coup d'état* had been attempted to gain the throne of Zanzibar. Upon the death

of Mohamud bin Thwain, Sayid Khalid, one of his nephews, had seized the palace and proclaimed himself Sultan. The admiral at once issued an ultimatum commanding the rebel's unconditional surrender, failing which he would bombard the palace. At nine o'clock next morning, the time allowed Sayid Khalid by the admiral's ultimatum had expired. Scarcely had the hour pealed from the clock in the palace

From Photo　　　　　*CAMP OF THE NAVAL BRIGADE.*　　　　By a Naval Officer

*'MWELE, AFTER ITS CAPTURE*

tower, when the signal "open fire" was struck in the flag-ship. The guns of the cruisers "Philomel," "Racoon," and the gun-boats "Thrush" and "Sparrow" boomed forth simultaneously. The reply from the palace was equally prompt. For the next few minutes there was the roar of artillery, the whirr of Maxims, and the rattle of musketry, and heavy smoke clouds hung over the palace and ships. Then the guns of the palace were silenced. The attitude of the Sultan's ship was at first doubtful, but suddenly she discharged a broadside at the "St. George," thus throwing down the gauntlet to our cruisers. The answer was a 6-in. shell crashing through her bottom, and she sank amidst a cloud of coal dust and smoke.

After the bombardment the admiral continued his cruise to the North, and early in October commenced his return voyage to the Cape. On arriving at Durban orders were again received to return to Zanzibar, and it was not until after a stay of a month there that the flag-ship returned to the Cape, where the last few weeks of 1896 were spent in peace.

Early in January, 1897, news arrived of the Benin massacre, and on the 20th of that month the ship proceeded to Brass. Space forbids us even the briefest account of the Benin Expedition. When one, however, considers that nearly all the

stores, ammunition, provisions, etc., were prepared and supplied by the flag-ship, some idea of the work that fell on the "St. George" may be gleaned. On Captain Egerton, as chief of the staff, fell the work of organising the expedition. Benin was, roughly, sixty miles inland. A native village called Warrigi, in

From Photos.                                                    By a Naval Officer.

*DESTRUCTION OF THE PALACE, ZANZIBAR.*

friendly country, and situated on the Benin River, was selected as a base. From here Benin was about thirty miles in a north-easterly direction. From Warrigi to Benin, through the dark, dense forest, the advance was continued for days and days, the men constantly under fire from an unseen foe. The final advance on the city was practically a running fight of two days' duration. Among those of the "St. George" who fell were Surgeon Fyfe, than whom no one could have been more popular, and Sydney Ansell, torpedo instructor. Two flanking columns were employed to divert the attention of the Beni from the main column. That on the west at Gwato and on the east at Sapobar. "C" Company of the "St. George" was employed in the former, under Lieutenant Frazer. The capture of Benin meant the removal from the ken of humanity of the vilest den of fetichism, where cruelties and atrocities were perpetrated unparalleled even in the story of Africa.

On the completion of the Benin Expedition the "St. George" returned to the Cape, where she arrived early

*GAZI, AFTER ITS OCCUPATION.*

in March. None too soon did she leave the fever-haunted coast, for soon the effects of climate and hardship began to tell. On the voyage to the Cape the ship was practically a floating hospital. Every nook and corner was taken to accommodate the sick.

What might be called the last act in the drama of an eventful commission was the Naval demonstration at Delagoa Bay in April, 1897.

On the 16th the flag-ship left Simon's Bay under sealed orders. When at sea it was announced that Durban was her destination.

On the morning of Sunday, April 18, a surprise was in store for the people of Durban. Early in the morning ships of war could be seen approaching from all directions. The black hulls of the ships from the Mediterranean loomed in the distance to the northward. A squadron of eight ships from three different stations, three different quarters of the globe, had been concentrated on this particular day at Durban without a soul outside the authorities knowing that such an idea was ever in contemplation until the ships hove in sight at Durban. The squadron then proceeded to Delagoa Bay, and remained for about a month.

Towards the end of 1897 news came that the "Doris" would relieve the "St. George," and orders were issued for the latter to leave for home on December 30. None of those who had the honour of serving under Admiral Rawson's flag are likely to forget him. In a short time the "St. George's" ship's company will be scattered on the four quarters of the globe, but in their hearts will live the memory of those they left behind them 'neath the sod in Western Africa.

*THE BRITISH CAMP AT CERI.*

From Photos    By a Naval Officer.

*THE NAVAL HOSPITAL AT OLOGBO.*

# CROSSING THE LINE IN THE "POWERFUL."

SEA life, and the Naval Service in particular, is proverbially conservative, but Jack must follow the times to some extent, and change his ways to suit the introduction of steam, iron, electricity, etc. The long service system in the Navy will do much to keep up the traditions and customs of the Service, and to prevent him from altering his ways too rapidly. Jack is still light-hearted and generous, smart, active, and clean, ever ready to volunteer in time of danger.

Many little customs relating to Christmas Day on board, crossing the line, ships paying off, etc., have been religiously observed and handed down for goodness knows how long. Any youngster who commands a boat's crew goes through many of Midshipman Easy's experiences; but the mastless ships, with their complicated compartments and new fashions of all sorts, have been the death warrant to many of the old sea customs in the Navy.

It was the custom, when crossing the line for the first time in the commission of a ship, to receive a visit from Neptune, upon which occasion all those who had not crossed before were introduced, and had to pass through a somewhat rough ordeal. This custom is still kept up in some ships, as the following description will show. It is a proceeding which necessarily entails a certain amount of licence, and commanding officers, doubtful of the propriety of so far relaxing the discipline in their particular ships, might be chary of granting permission. For instance, if the number of novices is considerable and they are not willing to go through the ceremony for the amusement of their shipmates, it may end in a free fight; also, a petty officer who, through any cause, whether good or bad, has made himself obnoxious to the ship's company, may be retaliated upon, and cases have occurred where such a one has been roughly handled. As a rule, the young seaman is not averse to the time-honoured initiation, and does not think the less of himself for having passed through it.

The necessary permission having been given, the ceremony of crossing the line was lately observed on board the "Powerful," outward bound. Neptune and his party appeared on board, were very courteously received by Captain the Honourable H. Lambton and the officers, and,

*A DUCKING BY THE SEA-BEARS.*

after a few appropriate introductory remarks, marched round the ship, Amphitrite and her daughter sitting on a

From Photos

*NEPTUNE'S MYRMIDONS SHAVING A VICTIM.*

By a Naval Officer

gun carriage drawn by the suite. After that Neptune was established on a throne prepared on the forecastle, and the work of shaving, ducking, etc., the young hands who had not crossed the line before commenced. The day was spent very pleasantly, and wound up with a concert in the evening given by the ship's amateur theatrical company, under the able management of the gunner, Mr. Sims, in honour of its being the anniversary of the battle of Trafalgar. One of the illustrations shows Neptune, with Amphitrite on his right and his daughter on his left. In front are the barbers with razor and brush, the others being the doctor, policemen, sea-bears, etc.

Another illustration shows a youngster undergoing the operation of shaving, and again he is seen in the canvas bath being ducked by the sea-bears.

From a Photo.    *NEPTUNE AND HIS COURT.*    By a Naval Officer.

# A NOTABLE GROUP OF NAVAL OFFICERS.

Photo. Mullins.    *ON BOARD THE ROYAL YACHT AT THE NAVAL REVIEW.*    Ryde.

THE photograph here reproduced possesses several points of special interest, both as regards the persons whose pictures are presented and the circumstances in which it was taken. We have here what might be called three generations of Naval officers, save that the relationship between them is that of uncle and nephews, and between the eldest and the youngest lies a period, which scarcely comes within the meaning of the phrase.

In both Services, and by many other people, the personality of the central figure will be at once recognised. Nearly everybody knows Sir Harry Keppel, the veteran Admiral of the Fleet and the oldest officer on the active list of the Navy. He was born in 1809. Standing a little behind Sir Harry is Vice-Admiral Sir Henry Stephenson, now in command of the Channel Squadron, but perhaps even better known as the genial and popular equerry to the Prince of Wales.

The third person in the picture is the Hon. Arthur Coke, who is at present a cadet in the "Britannia" at Dartmouth. Lady Anne Keppel, Sir Harry's sister, married the present Lord Leicester's father, therefore Sir Harry is Lord Leicester's uncle, Lord Coke's great-uncle and the great-great-uncle of the Naval cadet. The relationship between Sir Harry Keppel and Sir Henry Stephenson is that of uncle and nephew, the latter's mother being the former's other sister, Lady Mary Keppel. The photograph was taken on board the Royal yacht "Victoria and Albert" at Cowes last year

Photo. F.G.O.S. Gregory & Co.                                        Copyright.—Hudson & Kearns

*A COASTGUARDSMAN OFF DUTY.*

HERE we see one of those who keep watch and ward round our shores, a man of the Coastguard Service, which would supply the first Reserve for the Fleet in the event of war. He is shown off duty, on board one of the vessels of the First Reserve Squadron, one of the eleven coastguard ships which are stationed at certain ports in various parts of Great Britain and Ireland. Our force of coastguards has been styled by high authority " the cream of the Navy," and the phrase is strictly accurate. It is a strictly-selected body of men, a large proportion of whom, indeed, have held petty officers' ratings on board ship in the Channel, Mediterranean, and elsewhere. That our coast-guardsmen are the very pick of the Naval Service is shown by the stringency of the terms on which men are admitted. No petty officer or man of doubtful or indifferent character can get transferred to shore duty, the Admiralty requiring that every man must have the recommendation of his commanding officer, and must be fully trained either as a gunner or as a torpedo-man, and he must also possess at least one good conduct badge. Our coastguardsmen at present number 4,200; if they were three times that strength it would undoubtedly be better for the Naval position which we now hold.

# THE NAVY & ARMY ILLUSTRATED
## NOTES & QUERIES OF SERVICE AFLOAT & ASHORE

A VERY interesting relic, which, it is hoped, will before long find a resting place in the Royal United Service Institution, exists at Sligo, in the form of a figure-head, which is believed on good authority to have been that of "El Gran Grifon, Capitana," a 650 ton ship that formed part of the Spanish Armada, and which, with two others, was wrecked in Sligo Bay on the return voyage. The figure-head, which is in excellent preservation with the exception of the shield, is traditionally reported to have come ashore about one mile from Sligo on a strand now known as Gibraltar. It was formerly in the possession of Mr. Phibbs, of Seafield, County Sligo, where it had been protected from the weather by a niche or canopy specially erected in the grounds. It now stands in the garden of the widow of Simon Cullen, J.P., of Sligo. If acquired by the United Service Institution, it will meet an old acquaintance in the Spanish anchor recovered near the same spot in 1853, and presented by Admiral Sir Erasmus Ommanney to the Institution.

* * * *

MENTION of this relic reminds me that in a reprint of the "Adventures of Captain Cuellar in Connaught and Ulster," published by Elliot Stock, Mr. Hugh Allingham gives many valuable details relative to the sufferings and adventures of the unfortunate Spaniards who were cast ashore among the so-called "savages" of Ireland—a term, by the way, which the inhabitants of Connaught and Ulster seem to have done their best to deserve at that period—which Mr. Robert Crawford supplements by an admirable translation of Captain Cuellar's narrative. Captain Cuellar was in command of the "San Pedro," a galleon of 24 guns, but, unfortunately, incurred the displeasure of his Admiral by parting company without permission in order to repair damages. Although Cuellar himself was below at the time, the Admiral sentenced both him and the officer of the watch to be hanged at the yardarm, a sentence which was subsequently modified at the intercession of the Judge Advocate. Cuellar soon had an opportunity of proving his gratitude, for, being transferred to the ship commanded by his preserver, he stood side by side with him when the vessel was cast ashore on the Streedagh Strand. The Judge Advocate was in despair, but Cuellar worked strenuously to save him, by sending him ashore on a hatch. Unluckily, a heavy wave swamped the impromptu raft. Cuellar got through by the skin of his teeth, but his companion was drowned.

* * * *

EVEN a worse fate befell other Spanish officers, notably Don Diego Enriquez, the captain of the "San Juan de Sicilia," the Count de Villa Franca, and two others, who, hoping to carry ashore some of the treasure with which the ship was laden, shut themselves up in the hold of the captain's boat, ordering the hatches to be securely fastened. As the boat left the wreck, however, some seventy panic-stricken wretches jumped on to her deck and their weight caused her to capsize, those in the hold perishing miserably, the "savages," who stripped the bodies and secured the treasure, denying them even decent burial.

* * * *

"F. F." (Edinburgh).—To obtain a commission in a Highland Militia battalion you must be of recognised social position. For a first commission a nomination is necessary. This is usually in the hands of the Lord Lieutenant of the county or in that of the commanding officer. In most cases it is sufficient to be known to the commanding officer, who will arrange things for you. You will have to fill up a paper answering numerous personal questions. To this is attached a certificate of medical fitness and of moral character. If well equipped, your outfit would cost about £100, perhaps more. It is impossible to say what the annual training of twenty-eight days would cost. If you intend entering the Indian Army, you are foolish to choose a Highland Militia. Very little of the kit will be of use to you afterwards, and Highland regiments are usually expensive. You should enter some English Militia battalion. This plan would save you money. It is *possible* for a subaltern to live on his pay in the Indian Staff Corps, but it would be a struggle for the first few years.

* * * *

THERE is at present no training-ship stationed in Canada, though the statement has been made that the Admiralty and the Canadian authorities are in communication on the subject at the present moment. George Read, of Brantford, Ontario, Canada, who sends a query on the subject, as "a lad of fourteen years of age and interested in the British Navy," had best write to the captain of H.M.S. "Renown," Halifax, Nova Scotia, stating his wishes and asking what means are open to him as a Canadian boy of getting into the Royal Navy. The age limits for entry into Her Majesty's Fleet for boys are from fifteen years and three months to sixteen years and nine months old, so that he has ample time to carry out his praiseworthy intention. An irreproachable character, borne testimony to by someone who knows him at home, the written consent of a parent or guardian, and the passing of a stringent medical examination that he is sound in wind and limb, and in every way healthy, are the required qualifications. As to his prospects, they are entirely in his own hands. With smartness and good conduct he will have every chance of becoming a chief gunner or boatswain, at 9s. a day (there are between eight and nine hundred berths in the Service), or he may even in the end attain warrant officer's rank, with larger pay and a larger retiring pension.

THE name of Major-General Wolfe, who died victorious at Quebec, is one that will never be forgotten while there are men to read the history of the British Empire. Many monuments have been erected to perpetuate his fame, and various are the inscriptions which they bear, but that which stands in the "Abbey Church" tells us much in few and well-chosen words. They are as follows:—To the memory of James Wolfe, Major-General and Commander-in-Chief of the British Land Forces on an expedition against Quebec, who after surmounting by ability and valour all obstacles of art and nature, was slain in the moment of victory, on the 13th of September, 1759, the King and Parliament of Great Britain dedicate this monument." General Wolfe was born at Westerham, on the 2nd of January, 1727, and was therefore only thirty-two years of age when, by a decisive action, he broke the power of our enemies in Canada, and died on the field of battle. He was the son of a colonel in the Army, and obtained a commission in an infantry regiment at the age of fifteen. He saw much service on the Continent and in Scotland, and took part in the expedition to Rochefort. His tact in the management of men was conspicuous at an early stage, for when a mere boy he was appointed adjutant of his regiment, in consequence of displaying that quality at the battle of Dettingen. But his last exploit was his most daring and skilful, when with 4,826 men he climbed an almost precipitous cliff, under cover of the night, and on the Plains of Abraham defeated an enemy superior in number, and commanded by Montcalm, a brave and generous soldier like himself.

* * * *

I SHOULD think I am consulted about as many subjects as anyone. I am, however, heartily glad if I can perchance be of any use to my enquirers. I am asked now what is the status and general position of a bandsman on board ship. He must be a fairly good musician, and, if possible, should play more than one instrument, that is, if he ever expects to rise in the Service. His lowest pay on first joining is £24 6s. 8d. a year, and he may rise—mind, I do not say he will—to the pay of a chief bandmaster, which is £62 7s. 1d. a year. Of course, this is in addition to his rations, and there is generally a subscription among the officers to provide him with his uniform, added to which his instrument is always found him. His duties will not be very arduous—sweeping and keeping his mess clean, and, of course, practising when required by the bandmaster. He may either enlist as a continuous service man, or he may not. It will make no difference in his pay, but it will to his pension.

* * * *

"K. T." wants to know (1) what educational tests are applied to candidates for the Army Medical Staff Corps, (2) where thoroughly reliable information can be obtained respecting the Cape Mounted Rifles? Taking the last question first, "K. T." should write to the Under-Secretary of State, Colonial Office, Downing Street, Whitehall. A recruit for the M.S.C must be able to read and write, and must produce a certificate of good character from his previous employer. He must be from 18 to 28 years of age, from 5-ft. 3-in. to 5-ft. 5-in. in height (minimum), and of minimum chest measurement and weight of 33-in. and 115-lb. respectively. Enlistment is for seven years' Army and five years' Reserve service, or three years' Army and nine years' Reserve service, at the option of the recruit.

* * * *

"J. C."—Under the new recruiting regulations, the Royal Scots Greys belong to the "Corps of Dragoons of the Line," and a recruit, when he joins that corps, may be sent to the "Greys" if he so elect and the regiment is at the time open for recruiting, but he is liable to be transferred to any of the different regiments of the Corps of Dragoons. This Corps consists of the 1st, 2nd, 3rd, 4th, 5th, 6th, and 7th Dragoon Guards, the 1st (Royal) Dragoons, 2nd Dragoons (Royal Scots Greys), and the 6th (Inniskilling) Dragoons. For men under twenty years of age, the height is from 5-ft. 6-in. to 5-ft. 8-in.; over twenty years, 5-ft. 8-in. to 5-ft. 9-in.; chest measurement, 34-in., age eighteen to twenty-five. The undress uniform is a red frock, with blue facings, and forage cap, with white zigzag round the rim. A broad yellow stripe is worn on the overalls (trousers). The headdress, in full dress, is a busby with a white hackle (or plume). The terms of service are seven years with the regiment, and five with the reserve. A non-commissioned officer, after one year's probation as such, not below the rank of corporal, may extend his service to twelve instead of seven years, without reserve service. Sergeants, after completing nine years' service, *have the right* to re-engage to complete twenty-one years, and corporals may be allowed to do so. A private, provided he be a thoroughly efficient soldier, and in possession of the good conduct badge, may, after three years' service, extend his service to twelve years, and after eleven years' service may re-engage to complete twenty-one years, if he be in possession of two good conduct badges, or if specially recommended by his commanding officer.

* * * *

THE ship that brought Princess Charlotte of Mecklenburg-Strelitz over to England, before her marriage to George III., was one of the Royal yachts, the yacht formerly known as the "Princess Caroline." In honour of her illustrious passenger on the auspicious occasion, the yacht's name was changed to that of "Royal Charlotte." The command of the "Royal Charlotte" for the special service, was conferred on Captain Peter Denis (one of Anson's lieutenants during his cruise round the world in the "Centurion"), while Lord Anson, himself First Lord of the Admiralty, flew the Union Flag at the main on board, as Admiral of the Fleet and the officer specially charged with bringing the Princess over. The "Royal Charlotte" was escorted from Harwich to Stade and back by all the other Royal yachts in the Navy and six men-of-war—the "Winchester," 50 guns, "Nottingham," 60, "Minerva," 32, "Tartar," 28, and two sloops. On Princess Charlotte coming on board at Stade, the Royal Standard was hoisted at the main, and the Admiralty flag at the fore, Anson's Union Flag being shifted from the main to the mizen. The "Royal Charlotte," which as the "Royal Caroline" had been built in 1749, remained in existence until after the year of Waterlo

* * * *

THOSE who take an interest in the history of Naval uniform will be interested by the following note of the uniform worn by the crew of the "Royal Charlotte" on the foregoing occasion. An entry in the *Gentleman's Magazine*, Vol. XXXI., p. 376, under date "Tuesday, 4th August, 1761," states: "The crew of the 'Charlotte' are cloathed at His Majesty's private expence in a red uniform, with gold-laced hats, light grey stockings, buckles and pumps."

THE EDITOR.

IT is just possible that some readers of this paper may never even have heard the name of Captain Sir John Glover. I have met one educated man who confessed with shame his ignorance. But good Englishmen, who deserve well of their country, must never be so forgotten, and, for that reason, the "Life of Sir John Hawley Glover" (Smith, Elder, 14s.) is peculiarly acceptable. Lady Glover, who has written it, assisted by Sir Richard Temple, claims, very naively, that her volume possesses "living force" such as no one else could give, and I think she is right. For twenty years Glover served afloat in the Navy, gaining there the resource, readiness, enterprise, and aptitude he afterwards displayed to such good purpose ashore on the West Coast of Africa. The Foreign Office chose him for the survey of the Niger in 1857, and, six years later, he resigned active service in the Navy upon being made administrator—afterwards governor—of Lagos. Rarely has any man exercised such sway over native races. Glover created Lagos: he devoted his years, in the malarial climate that killed him, to the promotion of British interests; he played a great part in the turning movement of the Ashanti War, and was a born leader and a man among men. Therefore, I say, let this life of a downright Englishman be read by many.

"How Tom Jeffrey Saw the World" (Simpkin) has upon its exterior a three-decker speeding along under studding-sails, to give it a nautical aspect, as a taste of its character. Tom Jeffrey was a Devonshire lad, sound in wind and limb, though wooden legs and crutches had run in his family. He determined to go afloat, and went to sea as an "idler"—by no means, be it observed, a man given to ease—in the "Rattlesnake." I hope many a man, puzzled to know what to do with his boys, will read this story of fact. He will then see what a healthy, profitable, and satisfying life is that in the Fleet. Patriotism and health seem to move in the book. It is an artless story of good purpose simply and well told.

Another Devonshire story—this time all fiction, except for its extraordinarily graphic pictures of village life—is "The Lordship the Passen and We" (Innes, 6s.), by that versatile artist, well known to Naval men, and whimsical writer, Fred T. Jane. The "Lordship" is Lord Borrocombe, the "Passen" is the village vicar, and the "We" are the village caucus, grotesquely setting themselves to vex their betters and outwit themselves. There is, besides, a captain, who paints his house in black and white stripes, for all the world like a man-o'-war, and hoists all his bunting on Trafalgar Day, with a pretty daughter, who marries a young Naval officer. Mr. Jane has dealt unkindly with his rustics. Such a sordid set surely never breathed. But their language, their superstitions, and their customs, are instinct with fidelity to life. You cannot but laugh at their oddities, and such things as the song of "Old Varmer Jan" are excellent. The author is a past master in what Mrs. Malaprop would call "delusive epitaphs." His hero—save the mark!—meeting the girl he is to marry, flinging something about, and crying "Hemp zeed I zow," accosts her thus: "Thee fool! What true-love doth a mommety, flat-chested, platter-footed mally wallops of a maiden like these expect to be behold?" It is excellent fooling, but too long drawn out. The half would have been greater than the whole.

While the fame of the gallant deed of Dargai is still ringing in our ears, Mr. James Milne rushes forth with the "story of those bonnie fighters," the old "Gordon Highlanders" (Macqueen, 1s.). The history of the brave "Ninety-Twas" has been many a time told, but it would bear telling again, and here we have it in very popular form. We may now pipe the "Cock o' the North" at home—but should it have been "The Haughs o' Cromdale," as some say?—if we will. There are portraits, too, of Colonel Mathias, who led the charge, and of Sir George White, as well as of the Duchess of Gordon, with a picture of the coquettish bonnet she wore when she kissed the "braw laddies" into the ranks.

The purpose of "Deeds that Won the Empire" (Smith, Elder, and Co., 6s.), by the Rev. W. H. Fitchett, whose *nom de guerre* has been "Vedette," is not to glorify war, but to nourish patriotism. The heroes are Nelson, St. Vincent, and Hawke, Wolfe, Picton, and Wellington, and many more; the incidents are battles, sieges, the storming of citadels, fighting in mountains and passes, "bludgeon work" of many kinds, fleet engagements at sea, great sea duels, bombardments, cutting-out expeditions, night attacks, and much else of the kind. All is very well and very seriously told, with maps, plans, and a most admirable series of plates. I grieve that the author, with all his enthusiasm and understanding, has not thrown a stronger thread through his work—that he should have put "King-making Waterloo" before Trafalgar, for example. The reader should be set thinking whether Waterloo could have ever made a king—not, by the way, that king-making was the chiefest work—without Trafalgar before it to secure command of the sea. One is inclined to question, too, as something of a student in these matters, whether the admirals at the Trafalgar time did, in fact, quite so well as Mr. Fitchett thinks, guess "all Napoleon's profound and carefully-hidden strategy." But, at the same time, the book is exceedingly good, and I would recommend it as a very suitable present for thinking boys.

Other books to be read:—

"Indian Frontier Warfare," by Major G. J. Younghusband. "Wolseley Series" (Kegan Paul, 10s. 6d.)

"The Campaign of Sedan: the Downfall of the Second Empire. August—September, 1870," by George Hooper. New edition in "Bohn's Standard Library." (Bell, 3s. 6d.)

"Military Law, its Procedure and Practice," by Lieutenant-Colonel Sisson C. Pratt. Twelfth edition. (Kegan Paul, 4s. 6d.)

"SEARCH-LIGHT."

## Salt-Horse and Such-like.

By Lieut. STUART D. GORDON, R N

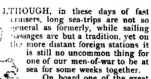

ALTHOUGH, in these days of fast cruisers, long sea-trips are not so general as formerly, while sailing passages are but a tradition, yet on the more distant foreign stations it is still no uncommon thing for one of our men-of-war to be at sea for some weeks together.

On board one of the great "liners," such a condition of things produces no appreciable alteration in the *carte de jour*. As the many meal-hours come round, you will still be seated at the saloon table, ready to do justice to the numerous delicacies which will be placed before you, on the last, as on the first, day of the longest voyage. The only difference in the state of affairs may be in your appetite, and that is mainly dependable upon your powers to resist the onslaughts of that dread malady sea-sickness.

But in a war-vessel it is very different. There, no milch-cow supplies fresh milk with which to dilute "the cup that cheers, but does not inebriate," but, instead, one's tea has to be discoloured with condensed milk. The ice-room holds no Scotch salmon, trout, or other such luxuries, for the very sufficient reason that there is no refrigerating-room on board.

Fresh butter might have been (and probably was) fresh when it was originally sealed up in the tin canisters in which we get it, but to see one of these opened in a hot climate leaves but little effort to the imagination of the seeker after knowledge to determine why this commodity is called "train-oil."

The contrast between these two phases of "a life on the ocean wave" could be extended indefinitely, but comparisons are always odious; especially are they so in this case, and particularly to the Naval officer.

On a man-of-war putting to sea, the ship's company have to unaccustom themselves to living on the fat of the land—said "fat" consisting of one pound of fresh beef (including lean and bone), and one and a half pounds of vegetables for each man *per diem*—and instead of eating baker's bread ("soft tack"), they crack and crunch ship's biscuit ("hard tack"). The days are happily well-nigh past when the only fresh meat our sailors ever tasted for weeks and weeks together was that which was found in the last-mentioned article of food.

With regard to the meat and vegetable portion of the dietary, however, it is not unusual for a ship to take a day's provision to sea with her. Also, the carrying of livestock—to the extent of two, or even three, small beasts—is not an unknown occurrence, notably on the East Coast of Africa and Arabia, where the chief or the wali of a town wishes to make a present to the ship.

These cattle are not only small, but have horns which in most cases are rudimentary. Therefore, the approved method of hoisting them in, by the horns, cannot be followed; and in slinging them with an ordinary pair of "bale slings" everything goes well until the beast feels his feet on the deck. Then, if the precaution has not been taken to tie a check-line to one of his legs, or some other part of his body, afterwards reeving it through a ring-bolt, he as often as not goes for a cruise around the upper deck, on his own account, before he is finally secured.

This was the case on board a ship on the East African station. A fine young heifer had been sent alongside as a present from the chief of the town. Although his horns were somewhat longer than is usual, still they did not seem sufficiently strong to bear his weight; consequently he was slung and hoisted inboard. Directly his feet touched the deck, he rushed aft amongst the ship's company, scattering those whom he did not actually knock down. Marines, as well as bluejackets, might be seen making frantic jumps at the nettings, or rushing for the rigging, in their anxiety to avoid the pointed horns of the beast; and it was not until he had done considerable damage to the first lieutenant's beautiful paintwork, and slightly gored a couple of men, that he was lassoed by a seedie-boy.

But the commotion occasioned by this animal was not to be compared to that caused on board another of Her Majesty's ships by—of all things in the world—a pig. The vessel in question was lying at Diego Garcia, which island—as everyone who has been there is aware—grows cocoa-nuts and pigs, and naught else. It being make-and-mend clothes day, and excessively hot, pretty nearly every soul in the ship was asleep, the men lying down about the deck in the shade of the awnings.

Presently a large "porker," forcing a gap between the gratings by which he had been penned in on the fo'c's'le, came strolling aft, indifferently treading upon, or pushing aside with his snout, the sleeping forms of the men. Thus rudely disturbed from their slumbers, the bluejackets up and gave chase. Pigs are no fools, and this one at least did not intend relinquishing his liberty without a struggle; so rushing headlong aft on to the quarter-deck, he passed between the legs of the sentry on the captain's cabin, compelling that marine warrior to assume a position of sedentary reflection rather than of "attention."

Doubling for'ard, well-nigh all hands were now in hot pursuit—in full cry after him. Returning once more to the quarter-deck, the sentry, intent on revenge, had prepared a running noose in a rope's-end, wherewith to catch him. But the animal, seeing the intention, swerved sharply to the right, when, not being aware of its proximity, he fell headlong down the skylight, landing upon the ward-room table. The doctor, who was sitting there, received a fright he declared he would never, till his dying day, recover from. Nevertheless, he did his best to expel the intruder; but the pig, adding insult to injury, retired more or less gracefully into the doctor's own cabin, and there laid himself down to rest after his unwonted exertions. By this time the Marine servants had entered the ward-room, and they, with the assistance of some bluejackets, secured the beast, and, bearing him in triumph back to the upper deck, once more penned him in on the fo'c's'le.

But to return. As has been said, the general dietary at sea on which our bluejackets have to get fat (if they can) is that provided by a generous country, apportioned on a liberal scale by a beneficent Admiralty.

Here is the "routine" of the bill of fare. First day, pickled pork; second day, salt beef; third, pickled pork; fourth, Australian mutton; fifth, pickled pork; and so on. Thus it will be seen there is pork for dinner every other day. Nor is this to be regretted, as included in the ration is a supply of split peas, which, with the addition of a small portion of celery seed (also issued), make a remarkably tasty and nutritious soup, everything being cooked together in the ship's copper.

It happened once that the ship's company of a certain vessel had an un-looked-for condiment in their pease-soup. On its being served out, several small dark objects could be seen floating on the surface. Complaint to the ship's cook elicited the explanation that it was mint. As a matter of fact, it was the tea-leaves left in the copper through the neglect of the cook's mate in not cleaning it out after making the men's tea the previous evening. Be that as it may, the bluejackets, ultra-conservative in all things, resented the innovation.

The officers necessarily mess a little less plainly than the men; yet there is a circumscribed limit to, and a sameness about, even their *menu*. Certainly a limited number of live sheep can always be taken to sea; but then mutton, mutton, mutton every day becomes, to say the least, extremely monotonous, especially when it is not prime Welsh, or even English, mutton that is usually shipped to feed the officers of a man-of-war. Indeed, many of the animals one sees coming on board, in some parts of the world, are worthy of a place in a "penny-gaff show" at a country fair, so nearly do they approach to the "living skeleton" stage.

But it cannot be expected they will keep their condition, huddled together in a pen, with nought to eat but dry fodder. Moreover, it is no uncommon thing to see sheep on board ship varying their diet with holy-stones, or stray lumps of coal.

Yet, it may be urged, do we not take fowls to sea with us, and do they not lay eggs? To the first question, the reply

is, certainly; so much so, that after being at sea for some little time, the aversion a Naval officer feels for mutton is only equalled by the feeling of repulsion he experiences at the all too familiar sight of fowl for dinner, breakfast, and lunch.

As to whether they lay eggs or not, is a question which most Naval officers will answer in the negative. But a different tale could be told by those who have made it their business to search the hen-coops (when but a few occupants remain) early in the morning. It is then by no means an uncommon occurrence to collect several new-laid eggs from the dozen or so hen-coops usually found on board a man-of-war.

The stewards will never gather these eggs so long as the bluejackets scrub the decks before they themselves are "turned out." The mate of the fo'c's'le of the morning watch, also, may occasionally have an unwonted delicacy for his breakfast, if he does not allow others to forestall him. It goes without saying that the hens will not lay when the coops are crowded, but undoubtedly they do as their numbers are thinned out, leaving the survivors more room.

In bad weather, with seas continually breaking over the fo'c's'le, it is only to be expected that some of the unfortunate birds die from exposure and cramp. The difference between the mortality among the fowls belonging to the gun-room officers and those of the captain and ward-room is striking.

A solution of the mystery may be found in the circumstance—nothing extraordinary in itself—that the individual alluded to above as "the mate of the fo'c's'le of the morning watch" is invariably a gun-room officer; also, it is very rarely that the hen-coops are locked — and even the everlasting fowl is better than "salt-horse."

In conjunction with the fare provided when making a sea passage, perhaps the greatest hardship one has to put up with is in the matter of bread. Few cooks on board ship are good bakers, consequently it is frequently the case that what they call bread is more fitted for dumb-bells or paper weights, and one has to revert to the hard, but honest, ship's biscuit. This substitute for the staff of life, being now unoccupied by its tenants of former days, is both palatable and nourishing to those who have a good set of teeth.

From the foregoing it will be seen that those employed afloat in the British Fleet (both officers and men) will probably not be delayed in responding to the call to arms through over-indulgence in the good things of this life. On the other hand, it may be said with all truth that, notwithstanding the undoubted hardships and discomforts Naval men must perforce endure, the sound and wholesome—if not luxurious—food issued as rations goes a long way to keep them in the fit state of health and vigour for which, as a class, they are distinguished; and should (which God forbid) the days of cheeseparing reform ever return, it will be an unfortunate day for the nation, as well as the sailor, that sees an inferior class of provisions supplied to our Fleet.

Even as coal is an indispensable adjunct to our war vessels, so is it imperative that the rations on which our men are fed should be of the best, and sufficient in quantity.

Thus, though not by any means an Elysium for epicures, our Navy will still be the best training school in the world for producing the fine fighting men of whom it was well said, "They don't know when they're beaten!"

# "Sport in the Army"

## By Col. F. T. Pollok

"No sport can hold a candle to pigsticking"

THERE is no doubt that, owing to our vast possessions, the British officer has greater opportunities of enjoying sport than the soldiers of other nations. The Navy has, in a measure, even better opportunities than the Army, because our vessels visit every part of the world. But the soldier need not grumble, because if he cannot roam all the world over, yet, if quartered in India or Burma, he has facilities of sport which are denied to his brethren of the Navy. The field of action is not as extended as it was half a century ago, for since several of our colonies have become self-governing, our troops are no longer sent there; but still, there is a vast field open to the military sportsman.

Of late years sport has been somewhat circumscribed even in India, for very many of the native potentates have taken to hunting in earnest, and have preserved vast tracts. Again, the Forest Department occupies many thousand acres in some of the very best localities for the *feræ naturæ*, which tracts are strictly guarded, and where it is hard to obtain permission even for a few days' shooting. Yet, with all these hindrances, there are still many localities where wild beasts abound, and which can be followed by the patient hunter without hindrance.

In Southern India there are the Wynaad jungles, Neilgherry-Annimullies, Sheveroy Hills, and Travancore, where I believe a permit is necessary, but not difficult to obtain; the Western Ghats, and Central India. In Bengal, Tirhoot and Assam especially, there is the finest pig sticking and tiger shooting in the world. Portions of the Terai are also good, and everybody knows of the varied sport obtainable in the Himalayas and borders of Thibet. Portions of Burma are especially good for big game; but well-trained elephants are a *sine quâ non*. In Assam, too, the game is varied—rhinoceros, buffaloes, gaur, mithun or gyal, tigers, bears, sambur, marsh deer, hog deer, kakur, or barking deer, are numerous; elephants are also plentiful, but are preserved.

In Lower Burma there are wild cattle, in sufficient numbers to satisfy the most ardent Nimrod. In the Nizam's country numerous bears exist in ground on which they can be ridden. The late Geoffry Nightingale killed several hundreds with the spear. In Ceylon there are elephants, principally mucknas or tushless ones, buffaloes, sambur, leopards, pig, spotted deer, and hog deer. Again, most people stationed at Aden would imagine they would not have a chance of firing off a gun during the time they were quartered there; but the enterprising sportsman, having obtained the Resident's permit, has only to cross over to Berbera and penetrate into Somaliland and he will meet with the king of beasts, the lordly elephant, wart hog, and other African game. Between Mombasa and Uganda there is plenty of game, though not as numerous now as before the rinderpest decimated the buffaloes. In the Soudan, but for its insecurity, excellent sport can be had. All sportsmen have read, I presume, the late Sir Samuel Baker's account of his sport when in search of the sources of the Nile, but, unfortunately, this field has

been closed for many a year, but it is to be hoped, when we drive out the Dervishes, that our garrisons in Egypt will be again able to visit those Elysium fields of sport.

Even in the Andamans there is fair fishing, and, if anyone likes to take the trouble, wild pig abound in the larger islands, but to get at them dense jungles full of abominable ticks have to be negotiated, and the sport is scarcely worth its difficulties.

In the Straits Settlements there is no lack of big game, but the forests and jungles are very dense, and small game shooting is very fair all over the East.

Even those quartered in Cyprus can have excellent sport. In one day I killed two bustard, over a hundred brace of cock, a couple of geese, several duck and teal, five or six hares, besides francolins, partridge, quail, and one sand grouse. There are gazelles too, but they are very wild, and hardly repay the trouble one has to circumvent them. There are boars, too, but as they lie in the very densest bush—all a mass of thorns—it is not easy to move them. The country there is far safer than in Albania, as I always found the natives, especially the Ansaries, most friendly. They are a very handsome race, reminding me of the best of the Afghans.

With the exception of snipe and duck, there is very little to be got in Lower Egypt. From Natal, where we still have troops, expeditions can be made into the interior, and one has only to read Mr. Selous' two books to realise what a paradise for game many parts of South Africa, bordering on the Zambesi, are.

For the followers of Izaak Walton there is much sport to be obtained in India. Some people like tank fishing, where the rhoé, a sort of carp, attains vast proportions. I have seen a native catch murrel by the dozen, but I, fishing close by with the best of tackle, failed to lure a single fish. In Upper India there is good mahseer fishing—this is often called the Indian salmon; it is in reality a barbel, but affords excellent sport, as it is a game fish and will fight for an hour or two or more. The late Colonel Nightingale was on to one, I believe, in the Gorge of the Godavery, the whole night. I have killed many in Assam and the Cossyah and Jynteah hills. The largest I ever landed weighed 44-lb., but I have known them caught up to 60-lb., and a Lascar on board a steamer off Gowhatty caught one over 80-lb. with a ball of rice. In the Manass, in Baghdooar, this fish is plentiful, and grows to a large size. The best lure for them is a spoon, of the size of a gravy spoon—gold on the outside and silver on the inside. It is as well to have strong tackle and about 100 yards of line.

In Malta there is very little game, and at Gibraltar the game is nil, or next to it; but by crossing over to Tangiers, which for some years was ours, excellent sport can be had. Thanks to the late Sir Drummond Hay there is very good pig sticking, and further inland there is plenty of small game.

In our possessions on the West Coast of Africa game is not plentiful, but by going down the coast to Cape Lopez the West Coast buffaloes roam in herds, and there are hippopotami in the rivers. The formidable South Africa buffalo is met with in Mossamedes, but not further north. Even in the island of St. Helena there is, I believe, now some game.

Our protectorate now extends up the Niger beyond Bida. I spent some months there and searched for game, but beyond shooting a few partridges, francolins, and guinea fowl, I found nothing. But at Lakoja there are plenty of buffaloes and antelope, and thousands of guinea fowl. Elephants come close to Lakoja at certain seasons, and they are plentiful along the right bank of the Binue.

We used to have troops at Labuan, and very good sport is to be had in Borneo, but I think our forces have been withdrawn. That excellent sportsman, Douglas Hamilton, killed a wild boar there forty-two inches high. Beyond birds of paradise there is very little to kill in New Guinea worth powder and shot.

In Australia there are kangaroos and duck and black swans, but no large game. In New Zealand it is different. Red deer and pheasants and wild pigs have been introduced, and have multiplied fairly. In Tasmania trout up to thirty pounds' weight have been captured, but it is a disputed point whether the salmon has become acclimatised, although the fry have been successfully reared and put into the rivers. In Nova Scotia, Newfoundland, and Canada there is still good sport; but very few military men can get at it without taking long leave, for our garrisons have, I think, been withdrawn. Vancouver Island is a well-known locality for game, but no troops there now. From Hong Kong, by taking leave, good pheasant and snipe shooting is to be had in China, while Japan can easily be reached. There is much to interest the visitor there, and there are also some rare pheasants and other game, but no big bags need be expected. Admiral Kennedy, one of our most popular Admirals, and second to none as a shikarie, had good sport in Mauritius and other adjacent islands, which he has so well described in various papers. But in the first island the shooting is all in the hands of a few residents of French extraction, and can only be indulged in by invitation. Socotra, a large island under our protectorate, not far from Cape Guardafui, ought to have game in it, but I do not think it has ever been visited by a sportsman, so its capabilities or otherwise are unknown. From Perim, I believe, several officers crossed over to the mainland and had fair sport, but of late the country has been too disturbed to allow of Europeans going there hunting.

I do not think there is much sport in any of our West Indian islands, or in the Bahamas, but as the latter are not far from Florida, it is not difficult to cross over on short leave, and if you do nothing else, endeavour to catch a 200-lb. tarpon, and eat oranges.

I do not purpose in this article to give records of such sport as I have indulged in either alone or in company. But during all but fifty years' service and wanderings in exceptionally favourable localities for sport, and having indulged in them all, from slaying the mighty behemoth to the tiny rain quail, I may say that there is no sport in the world that can hold a candle to pig sticking. Before the Anicuts were built and the land irrigated to the extent it is now, there used to be excellent pig sticking at Omsul Davy, about eighteen miles from Masulipatam, at Guntoor, in the Churs (islands), and along the banks of the Kistna and Godavery rivers; but now it is a thing of the past in those localities. There is still good hunting to be got at Ellichpoor and near Kamptee, and the meets from Meerut are generally very successful. But in the Indigo districts the Bengal Tent Club has the best sport. Simson, probably the best pig sticker India has produced, would find a pig and ride him where nobody else would look for one, and he is equally as good to hounds in England as he was to pig in India; a better all-round sportsman never lived.

After pig sticking, tiger shooting off elephants in the vast plains of Bengal, Assam, and Burma is the most exciting.

I never did see much sport in sitting up in a machan, or a tree over a kill, or ensconced in a mart (a circular pit dug near water), and bagging, or far oftener missing, your tiger. I'd rather shoot six on foot or a dozen off elephants than a hundred from a coign of vantage, where you sit night after night devoured by mosquitoes and inhaling malaria, in perfect safety to yourself, as far as the beast is concerned, but with a great deal of discomfort.

It is true that a man mounted in a howdah on a staunch elephant runs very little risk, but there is risk for all that. On foot the chances are not equal. A tiger will hide in a bush where one would think a hare could scarcely conceal himself, and bide his time to pounce upon the shikarie. Only those who have nerves of steel and have acquired knowledge by a long pursuit of large game should indulge in shooting tigers on foot.

Elephants may rank as next. I never could see the sense of shooting hundreds of tushless pachyderms, as many noted men have done in Ceylon. There is the same danger, of course, as when following a tusher, but there is no trophy; and is it worth while to kill these useful slaves to man just to say you have killed so many elephants?

Then comes buffalo shooting—the most dangerous animal, whether in India or Africa, and also the most treacherous and tenacious of life. I have shot so many of them I lost all count, but latterly I left them severely alone unless they were pugnaciously inclined or carried an extraordinary head. The largest are feral in Assam and Burma—those in parts of India are tame ones become feral—but all are equally savage, and take a lot of killing.

Rhinoceros, though pachydermatous, are far easier to kill, for the hide on the living beast is easily penetrated, and only hardens when taken off and dried in the sun. Yet for all that heavy charges are requisite, not on account of the hide, but because between it and the heart and lungs there is an immense mass of blubber, muscle and bone. The animal is inoffensive as a rule, and will run sooner than fight, but if its dander is risen it charges viciously, and does not use its horn, but tushes, and slashes with them. I have seen an elephant's leg cut to the bone, and as they fight amongst themselves, they are often scored all over.

There is just sufficient danger in bear shooting to make it very attractive. The noise a bear makes after being wounded is enough to upset the nerves of an old sportsman, to say nothing of the novice.

Gaur are well worth shooting, as they are grand beasts, some being as high as seven feet at the shoulder. They are not very dangerous. A few will charge, but the greater part seek safety in flight. Tsine, a wild bull found in Burma and some of the islands lower down, are very handsome cattle, but very difficult to get at, as they graze in open quins; they are not wanting in pluck either. The gyal much resembles the gaur at a distance, and the Assames call both varieties "mithun," but if pressed, they say the gaur is the "Asseel mithun," and the other, "mithun" only.

I need not here attempt to describe the chase of the numerous deer and the few antelope found in parts of India from the Himalayas down to Ceylon. There is a great charm in stalking a sambur or a spotted buck. To mountaineers the makhoor, ibex, the various wild sheep, the wild yak, and the numerous deer afford grand sport, but it is one I have never indulged in, so will say nothing further about it. I trust I have shown that to the Army officer there is grand sport to be obtained in our possessions. To enable a man to be an efficient officer he should be inured to hardships, to be able to stand the sun and various changes of climate. Who gets inured so soon as the shikarie?

Good sport on an Indian Tank

**FOREWARNED**
a Story
of the
Intelligence
Department

By Major Arthur Griffiths
AUTHOR OF
"The Queen's Shilling,"
"The Rome Express"
"The Wellington Memorial."
etc. etc.,

## SYNOPSIS OF PREVIOUS CHAPTERS.

Captain Wood is an officer on the staff of the Intelligence Department of the War Office engaged with certain confidential questions pending with the United States Government. It is the height of the London season, and he is sleeping late after a ball, when he is roused to hear some startling news. A lawyer, Mr. Quinlan, has called to tell him that an unknown relative, an American millionaire, has left him a colossal fortune. Almost at the same moment an American detective warns him that he has enemies plotting against him and his fortune, and that he goes in imminent danger of his life. Arrived at the Intelligence Office, where he is late, he is sharply reprimanded, but explains, and is giv.n some especially confidential work to carry through connected with an attack on New York. Returning to his chambers, he again meets the American detective, who details the nature of the plot against his fortune and the military secrets he possesses. He is strongly urged to put himself under police protection, but he cannot credit the extraordinary story. After office hours he starts for the Park in quest of the young lady with whom he is in love. He sees her in the Row, but she cuts him dead. Returning disconsolate to his club he is invited by an American acquaintance, Lawford, to join a party at the opera, where he meets the Duke and Duchess of Tierra Sagrada.

### CHAPTER VII. *(continued).*

"YOUR first business, Captain Wood, believe me, will be to keep your fortune." She spoke very gravely, looking at me intently over her fan. "Half the world will be in league to rob you. Ah, but yes, I am in earnest! You men fall naturally into three classes—rogues, fools, and policemen."

"And to which, pray, do I belong?" I asked lightly, not taking this bitter remark at all seriously.

"Not the first, I am sure; it would be a bad compliment to say the second; but if you were wise you would certainly become the third. A whole police force in your pay would not be too many to protect you."

"Are you in earnest?" I said, suddenly struck with something in her eyes.

"Very much so, Captain Wood. If I were a friend, an old friend let us say, I would counsel you, strongly urge you, to be constantly on your guard. Very much on your guard."

As she spoke a deadly pallor overspread her face, which was high coloured, as is often seen in very fair-haired women, even when still quite young. Her husband had returned silently, I might have said stealthily, and she first had caught sight of him standing there behind me. Why was she thus terrified? Because the Duke had heard her last words?

---

### CHAPTER VIII.

WHETHER or not the Duke of Tierra Sagrada had even heard his wife when so earnestly counselling me to be upon my guard I was unable to judge, at least, he made no sign. His manner was perfectly quiet and natural, and he spoke in an unconcerned tone when he pressed me to keep my seat in the front of the box.

At the next interval he said very courteously: "Do you propose to stay for the Cavalleria Rusticana? We are going on to a reception—Madame Bonaventura's, at the Dos Rios Ministry. Would you care to accompany us? Our carriage is here. Susette will be very pleased to present you."

"You are very good," I said, "I should like to go very much if I may run away early. I have a couple of balls to-night."

The Duke laughed pleasantly. "No doubt you are in great request. We also have engagements. I wonder if they are the sam. as yours?"

"One ball is at Mrs. Collingham Smith's, the other at Lady Delane's. I shall, perhaps, go to the second, but quite late. It will be the best, I think, and everyone will come on there. Shall you?"

Now the Duquesa interposed.

"No, we do not know the Delane's, and if I were you I should go home like a good boy after the reception. You young men are too much given to late hours."

By this time we were in the outer hall, where there was already a crush of people, all like ourselves, bound for other entertainments.

Frida Wolstenholme, with her mother, was there among the rest. I stood close by her, but she would not acknowledge my existence. Perhaps there was hardly time, for the Duquesa's carriage was soon announced, and we moved towards it directly.

Looking back, as I was about to follow the Duchess, I caught Frida's cold contemptuous face. She was watching me with immeasureable disdain.

It was a curious and not unimportant circumstance, when viewed by the light of later events, that the three houses I was to visit that night were within a stone's throw of each other.

The first, that of the Dos Rios minister, to which I was introduced by the Duke and Duchess of Tierra Sagrada, was in Rutland Gate. The next, Mrs. Collingham Smith's, was in Prince's Gardens; and the last, Lady Delane's, in Prince's Gate.

This near neighbourhood was remarked on by the Duke, when, observing that the reception did not greatly amuse me, he asked if I was not dying to get to my dancing, and where, exactly, I was going.

"You must let us send you on to Prince's Gardens in the carriage," he said very civilly. "We have brought you out of your way to a not very bright entertainment, and now we ought to speed your departure. We must stay on here for an hour or so more, but there is no reason why you should."

I protested that Prince's Gardens was only a few yards off; round the corner, in fact, and I really preferred to walk. Besides, I only meant to look in for a moment, my real destination was Lady Delane's, which was also quite close at hand.

"To be sure, yes, certainly I know. Well, well, if you will not be persuaded. But the carriage is entirely at your disposition. Is that not so, Susette?"

The Duchess acquiesced smilingly, but said nothing. It occurred to me that she was not altogether pleased at this off-hand disposal of her carriage. But she bade me good-night very cordially, and warmly endorsed the Duke's kind invitation to call and see them. I left them with the pleasurable sensation of having made a couple of charming new acquaintances.

There was another acquaintance, if I might so call him, whether friend or foe, waiting for me outside. The same shuffling, slip-shod creature whom I had seen so often that evening. Directly I went out I saw him emerge from the portico of an unfurnished house and follow me to the very door in Prince's Gardens.

He was still on the watch when I left Mrs. Collingham Smith's, having found nothing to detain me there, no sign of Frida Wolstenholme, whom I had hoped to run down. I would now have confronted this pertinacious "shadow," calling him to account for thus dogging my footsteps, and if he gave no satisfaction handing him over to the police, but it would have taken time, and I felt I had none to lose.

It was already long past midnight, I might miss Frida, and that was not to be borne. My mood had changed. Now the desire to see her, speak to her, have some explanation with her, had gradually taken possession of me, to the exclusion of all other thought. So strongly did it hold me, indeed, that when I entered the ballroom I could hardly make my bow to Lady Delane.

I looked eagerly round for Miss Wolstenholme and saw her nowhere. I realised, however, that she must be at the ball, for there sat her mother in one corner with the stony-faced resignation of a much-enduring chaperon. She was now a rather faded, though still comely, woman, of an age to prefer her snug fireside to the racket of society. Only her solicitude for her frolicsome daughter dragged her out night after night. Certainly she would not be at Lady Delane's if Frida had stayed at home.

Mrs. Wolstenholme could give me no news of her charge. "Yes; Frida is here; somewhere. That is all I know," she answered, in a weary far off semi-somnolent voice, as, no doubt, she had answered a dozen similar queries. Then she woke up sufficiently to recognise me and to show a sudden deep interest in me, new to my experience. Mrs. Wolstenholme must have heard of my rise in the world.

"But I have not seen Frida for an hour or more. I do wish, Mr. Wood, you would find her and bring her to me," she said, plaintively.

"That may not please her, Mrs. Wolstenholme," I said, rather dejectedly. But I went off on my search, but I should have failed altogether in my quest had not the first overtures come, strange to say, from Frida herself.

"Captain Wood, Miss Wolstenholme wants to speak to you," said a voice, and I saw a hated rival, with no friendliness in his face, pointing to where Frida sat behind a great mass of flowering azaleas.

She was as gracious a sight as ever: one of the fairest and brightest of a sex created for the delight and torment of mankind. Her dress is beyond my powers of description. I think it was a pale blue satin with pink roses, but that is all I can say, except that from the feathery aigrette that crowned her sunny hair to the tip of a tiny shoe pushed a little out, but working fretfully upon the carpet, she was the most absolutely charming woman I had ever seen.

I stood humbly before her, but she took no notice of me for a time. It was to the other man she spoke.

"Thank you, Captain Paget, so much. Now will you find mother and say I shall be ready in a few minutes, and perhaps you will order up the carriage?" But then directly we were alone, she turned on me with flashing eyes and cold bitter tongue.

"I have only one word to say to you, Mr. Wood. I sent for you to tell you—I want you to understand clearly—that after this we are strangers. I do not mean to speak to you or to see you again. You have behaved abominably."

I was utterly taken aback and could hardly falter out, "But why, what have I done?"

"Its what you have not done. Is it true that—but do not look at me in that hopelessly abject, idiotic way—I see it is true. Don't deny it."

She paused for a moment, then burst into a laugh, that had I been more experienced I should have known to be perilously near hysterics. Her nerves, tense, over strung, were on the point of giving way, but for some reason still mysterious and unknown to my obtuse male intellect.

"True, of course it is if you say so, that and everything else; although what you mean, or why you are so cross with me, passes my comprehension."

"True that you have come into a great fortune? That everyone knows it and talks about it, and yet we—I—we are the last to hear of it. Is that all true?"

I nodded "yes."

"Then cannot you see that you have deceived me shamefully? You led me to suppose that you were a harmless, insignificant non-entity; I have tolerated you, confided in you, treated you as a perfectly safe friend, and all the time you were one of the other sort——"

"Eligible, in fact? I begin to see," I said, with joy reviving in my heart. Would she make all this fuss unless she cared for me a little? The scales were falling from my eyes.

"But I wasn't," I went on. "Not till this morning, when I heard the news for the first time. I wanted you to hear it, too, from my lips the very first, and I went to the Park on purpose, but the gossip ran quicker."

"Another thing, Mr. Wood," she said, deftly shifting her ground, as she felt it yielding beneath her. "Why did you not come and speak to me at the opera?"

"After you had cut me dead in the Park!"

"That was because I was so disappointed in you, so annoyed. But I know why you did not come—you had other attractions, of course. Who was she? I don't think I know her by sight. Not quite pretty, but her diamonds were splendid."

"Some American woman," I said, carelessly, "married to a Spaniard. A new acquaintance. What does it matter about her? I want to be friends with you. Won't you make room for me there."

She drew just an inch or two, grudgingly, on one side.

"But no, Captain Wood, the whole situation is now so completely changed," she said, protesting feebly, and looking fixedly at her fan. "We can never be quite on the old familiar terms. You have come within the other category."

"In fact, I am entitled now to say what I should have never have dared to do before. Come Miss Wolstenholme, let us end all this squabbling and skirmishing. Frida, my darling, you know that in all things my first thought was you, my first hope that you would consent to share my good fortune!"

"No, no, Mr. Wood, just think what people would say; I should be called a mercenary wretch, accused of selling myself for your millions."

"They shall be yours. I will make them all over to you at once. I do not care for them one bit, except that they give me the right to ask you for this."

I took her gloved hand and kissed it, but she herself, turning her blushing face up to mine, offered me her lips.

"You have been summoned before this tribunal to hear its fiat."

## CHAPTER IX.

WHEN I left Prince's Gate I seemed to tread on. air. We had been among the last. Frida and I had lingered on among the azaleas till Mrs. Wolstenholme's patience was fairly exhausted, and she came herself to end the *tête-à-tête*. I think she saw enough in our conscious faces to comfort her with the hope that the pains of her chaperonage were approaching their term, and she heartily endorsed Frida's invitation to "come to lunch, and come early."

Then I saw them into their carriage, refusing their proffered seat, for I wished to be alone with my new found happiness.

The night was fine, the air soft, under the pale sky, for dawn was near at hand, and I stepped out gaily with all the buoyancy of one with whom the world went well.

I was brought up shortly and sharply to the realities of life by running up, plump, against my "shadow." The man who had stuck to my heels so pertinaciously all the evening was still on the watch.

But he was not lurking in the recesses of a house porch. I met him face to face upon the pavement, and he could not escape me.

"Look here, my fine fellow," I cried, tackling him at once. "This has gone a little too far. Take yourself off, now, or I shall give you in charge. Come—walk."

Then I caught sight of his face under the gas lamp, and instantly recognised it.

"What? you! Mr Snuyzer!" I laughed aloud. "Upon my word I am infinitely obliged to you. But really you might have saved yourself the trouble. And—pardon my saying so—I don't think you do it very well."

He would not own up at all. "Easy, guv'nor, easy," he answered, with a well-assumed snuffling voice. "Wot are you a-driving at? I've as good a right to be 'ere as you 'ev. Wot's amiss?"

"I tell you plainly, Mr. Snuyzer, it won't do," I continued. "I don't want you; and I won't have you dogging my footsteps wherever I go. Its not the way to get round me, and you'll have to drop it. Begin at once. Go your own road—that way—and I'll take this."

I pointed him down the Exhibition Road, and I myself turned into Knightsbridge and walking eastward, half disposed to do the whole distance on foot. But a hansom came up out of somewhere, a mews, or a side street, or overtook me on the road, and the driver, after the custom of his class, began at once to pester me with "Cab! Cab, sir! Cab!" pulling up to my pace, and sticking to me most pertinaciously.

At last, out of sheer disgust, and to end his importunity, I jumped into the cab and gave my address in Clarges Street.

I had barely lighted a cigar and leant back to ponder over the many surprising and mainly pleasurable events of the day, when I realised that the cab was taking the wrong direction. For some strange and incomprehensible reason the driver had turned round and was heading westward.

"Here, hi! hi!" I shouted, lifting the flap. "Where are you going?"

"Wot's up!" answered the cabby insolently, as he pulled up short. "Think I don't know my way about? Stow it, or——"

The alternative I never heard. For at that moment two men jumped up on the front tread of the cab, and opening the doors threw themselves upon me. Their weight alone would have sufficed to overpower me, to silence me, and crush out all resistance. I could do no more than give voice to one frantic yell for help, for now the strong, pungent smell of chloroform under my nostrils, and the vain struggle I made with fast increasing torpor, told plainly that they had called in another dread ally, and that I was absolutely helpless in their hands.

\* \* \* \* \* \*

How long I remained unconscious I could not say. The numbing, paralysing effect of an anæsthetic may seem to cover a century and yet no more than a short half-hour may have elapsed between the application of the drug and recovery. When I came to myself I was so stiff and sore, so dazed and stupid that I might have been dead and buried for years.

I found myself now in some sort of underground or basement room, as I judged it from the position of the windows. I was not alone. Three people, masked, sat at one end of a long table, I was at the other, seated, but tied into a chair; my hands were securely fastened with cords behind to a chair, and an iron chain was across my chest; cords also bound my legs tightly to the legs of the chair.

"Has he recovered sense and speech?" asked a deep, high-pitched voice coming from the masked man opposite me, who seemed to preside at the table.

"Answer. Do you understand?" This question was put by someone behind me, accompanied by a rude shake.

"What is the meaning of this outrage?" I cried, finding strength in the sense of my foul ill-usage.

"Silence. It is for us to speak, to question. Yours to hear, reply, obey."

"William Aretas Wood, you have been summoned before this tribunal to hear its fiats, to execute and abide by them. Chance has put into your hands the means of working infinite mischief or of doing infinite good. We do not trust you to choose aright between these different courses. It is our intention to interpose and guide you. We shall control the expenditure of your fortune—of Mr. McFaught's fortune, that is to say. It must be applied in restitution to those he wronged."

"Who and what are you who dare to dictate such terms?" I asked, protesting angrily, in spite of my bonds and abject condition.

"To neither. question need we reply, but you, who must become one of us, may learn that this is the 'Guild of Universal Excellence,' and we are its supreme council. We are an all-powerful far-reaching organisation, as you will find when you are affiliated to us, and we dare do what we choose."

"Psha! Organisation! A parcel of banded thieves, who would cover up your evil doing in high-sounding terms."

"Check your tongue, William Wood. Do not insult this council, or it will strike back. Remind him."

At this order some fiendish tormentor touched me lightly on the left shoulder, and I was thrilled through and through with such exquisite agony that the veins on my forehead stood out like whipcord and my eyes filled with tears. It was, no doubt, some cunning application of electricity.

"Let that teach you not to trifle with or oppose the Guild."

There was a long, solemn pause, then the president continued,

"William Aretas Wood, this council having fully weighed and considered the facts connected with your case have willed and do now decree as follows:—

"First. That you henceforth hold yourself and your whole fortune at the absolute incontestable disposal of the Guild. You must meet cheerfully and unhesitatingly all and every demand made upon you, whether in person or goods, freely accepting all physical labours, however onerous or irksome, and promptly liquidating all claims for cash that be presented to you by the authority of the Guild.

"Secondly. You must never divulge by word or act the reasons that oblige you to obey the behests of the Guild. If your conduct seems extravagant, your outlay wasteful or inexplicable, you must accept the odium or inconvenience thereof, and leave the world to believe, if needs be, that you are one more millionaire gone mad.

"Thirdly. In order to effectually seal your tongue and secure your unquestioning und :viating loyalty to the Guild, you must enter it, take the oaths, accept the obligations, bear its honourable brand, and hold yourself for ever its most humble and obedient servant.

"Fourthly and lastly. Understand that every affiliated servant and member of the Guild, who, having surrendered himself and its possessions under the first condition, shall dare to resist the commands of the council acting for the Guild, refuse service or payments when duly called upon, be guilty of any breach of trust, or betray one tittle of the affairs and secrets of the Guild, shall suffer death in such form and in such time as the council may decree.

"I have spoken, William Wood. Answer. Will you do all this—yea or nay?"

How was I to meet this dastardly, infamous attempt at extortion? My spirit revolted against concession, my blood boiled with rage, my indignation quite over-mastered any feeling of fear. But, indeed, I had as yet no sense of it, and I say so without bombast or pretension. I could not quite believe that these ruffians were in real earnest, and I still buoyed myself with the hope that a ransom something far short of their preposterous demands would in the end secure my release.

"Speak, William Wood. The council awaits your reply. Do you yield to its supremacy?"

"Never," I replied, stoutly, forgetting my bonds and my helplessness. "I will pay you a price--anything in reason. But not your whole demands—they are too preposterous. Name a sum, and how it shall be paid; then let this mummery cease."

"Let him be reminded," said the president, coldly, and again the sharp pang thrilled through my shoulder, inflicting intolerable anguish.

"I would strongly urge you, William Wood, to refrain from angering this august tribunal. Our patience has its limits. We shall not brook insolence, and we shall overcome defiance. We are too strong for you. I say again, will you perform our bidding?"

"What is it you ask? Tell me exactly." I was not weakening, but I wanted to try them.

*(To be continued).*

Photo. Russell & Sons.   Southsea.

*MAJOR-GENERAL STUART JAMES NICHOLSON, C.B.*

MAJOR-GENERAL STUART JAMES NICHOLSON, C.B., entered the Royal Artillery in 1855. Exactly thirty years later he saw his first war service as a lieutenant-colonel, for in 1885 he was serving in the Soudan, and saw some hard fighting, being present in the engagements at Hasheen, the tough fight at Tofrek, and the destruction of Tamai. His reward was mention in despatches and the brevet rank of colonel. He has held, also, important Artillery appointments. As a captain he was aide-de-camp to the Inspector-General of Artillery. For five years he was instructor in gunnery at the Gunnery School at Shoeburyness. After that he was assistant to the Director of Artillery at the War Office, a member of the Ordnance Committee, and finally, from March, 1887, to March, 1892, he was commandant and superintendent of the School of Gunnery. He has also held the command of the Royal Artillery at Malta, and has recently vacated the command of the Royal Artillery in the Southern District. A glance at our photograph will show that he carries his years well, for to look at him one would not think that he was born a year before Her Majesty ascended the throne, on the celebration of whose Diamond Jubilee he was made a C.B.

# THE ROSS-SHIRE BUFFS.

THE 1st Seaforth Highlanders, who but a day or two ago were in Crete, have now moved on to Egypt, where it is probable that they may add fresh honours to the glorious roll that already adorns their colours. The "Wild Macraes," as the 72nd were in old times called, are well illustrated in the typical group shown around the colours. The officer on the left, with his breast glittering with medals, is Colonel Murray, who, now in command, was adjutant of the regiment when it served with such distinction in the last Afghan War. His medals are worthy of notice, for they comprise, reading from the left, the C.B., the Afghan medal, with four clasps—the four-clasp medal was given only to men of the 72nd—the Cabul to Candahar star, the Egyptian medal, with clasps for Tel-el-Kebir and Tamai, the Order of the Osmanieh, and the Khedive's bronze star. Next is the pipe-major of the regiment, and then two sergeants on guard over the colours. The elaborate

*THE COLOURS WELL GUARDED.*

bâton of the drum-major was, if the writer's memory is not at fault, presented to the battalion by the Ghoorka regiment with which they were brigaded in Roberts's famous march. The officer on the right of the picture is Captain Egerton, who was dangerously wounded in the fighting round Cabul, was their adjutant at Tel-el-Kebir, and who wears the four Afghan and Egyptian medals won by the corps. Our other illustration depicts the regiment in the Palace Square in Malta, when the Chitral medals, their last-earned honour, were presented to them recently by Lady Fremantle, the wife of the Governor.

This is the last honour of the Seaforths, but it is preceded by a goodly roll—Mysore, Hindostan, Assaye, Cape of Good Hope, 1806, Maida, Java, South Africa, 1835, Sebastopol, Persia, Kooshab, Lucknow, Central India, Peiwar Kotal, Charasiab, Cabul, Candahar, 1880, Afghanistan, 1878-80, Egypt, 1882, Tel-el-Kebir. And the honours are practically

entirely Eastern, and fairly and curiously divided between the two battalions, the old 72nd, now in Egypt, and the old 78th, now at Dover. Both were in India in the hard fighting at the commencement of this century that gained us our Indian Empire. To the 78th, for their stubborn valour at Assaye, the East India Company made the grant of a third or honorary colour, and from this they derive their badge of the elephant, with the legend subscribed "Assaye." While the 72nd were at the Cape, the 78th were adding to their honours Maida.

The 72nd shared in the Crimea, but it was the 78th that added Persia to their laurels. Both were in the Indian Mutiny, but in this campaign the 78th saw the bulk of the hard fighting. In Afghanistan, however, the tables were turned, for there the 72nd came in for all the fun. The Egyptian honours are also with the 72nd, and they now have again the chance of adding fresh ones.

Photos. R. Ellis, Malta

*WELL-EARNED REWARDS.*

Photo. R. Ellis, Malta.

*A PEACE PARADE OF "THE SPRINGERS."*

Copyright.—Hudson & Kearns.

THE first of the regiments to push on up the Nile to help thrust the Khalifa to his downfall is the 1st Lincolnshire. The Lincolns have a roll of honours the very enumeration of which recalls the greatest glories of the British Army: Blenheim, Ramillies, Oudenarde, Malplaquet, Egypt (with the emblem of the Sphinx), Peninsula, Sobraon, Punjab, Mooltan, Goojerat, and Lucknow are their heritage of glory. This regiment is one of the oldest corps in the Service, dating its origin from 1685, and its first colonel was a Sir John Grenville, the great-grandson of that grand old Naval hero Sir Richard Grenville, who, in the "Revenge," held the Power and glory of Spain so cheap, that "he dared her with one little ship and his English few." Our illustration, taken shortly before they left for Egypt, depicts the regiment opposite the main guard at Malta, engaged in that most picturesque of military ceremonies, the "trooping of the colours"

# GOING ON ACTIVE SERVICE.

THE 1st Warwickshire, which left for Malta in 1895, went last year to Egypt, and now forms part of the force being sent up the Nile to strengthen the army under Sir Herbert Kitchener. The embarkation of a regiment –and especially if it is moving to a region where its employment on active service is probable—is always a picturesque scene, full of life and animation, and the accompanying illustrations well depict it. In the first we see the regiment mustering, in preparation for embarkation, on the grass-clad slope that underlies the frowning walls of a Malta fortress. The men are clad in marching order,

*FALLING IN FOR EMBARKATION.*

with their white haversacks, felt-covered water-bottles, and rolled great coats. Their uniform is the well-known "khaki," which, first adopted from the Indian Army as an ideal fighting colour, has now completely superseded the scarlet as the uniform of the British soldier when battling under a tropical sun. And here it may be noted that "khaki" is a colour and not a cloth, for it may be either white American drill dyed to the "khaki" or brown colour, or a warm serge similarly treated.

In another illustration we see the regiment on its march to the place of embarkation, headed by the band. The

*ON THE MARCH TO THE SEA.*

photograph gives an excellent idea of the serviceable fighting "rig" of Tommy when in the East. The regulation leather gaiters are still worn, but now, on their way up the Nile, these will have been replaced by the far more serviceable "putties," or soft gaiter bandages, which have also been adopted from our brethren of the Indian Army.

In our final scene we are shown the great transport "Britannia"—one of the finest steamers of the P. & O. Line now utilised by Government as a troop-ship—ready for the men to march in-board. Although the Warwicks have not seen service in any of the recent Egyptian and Soudan campaigns, they fought in South Africa against the Kaffirs in 1847-48 and 1851-53.

Away back nearly two hundred years ago they also were encountering African foes, for tradition has it that the antelope, which is their proud badge, was taken from the standard of a Moorish regiment in Spanish pay which they captured during the war of the Spanish Succession. The 6th won glory both at Almanza and Saragossa, and after the latter battle their colonel, Harrison, took home to lay at Queen Anne's feet thirty standards that day captured.

Photos. R. Ellis, Malta.

*THE TROOP-SHIP ON THE TIDE.*

Copyright.—Hudson & Kearns.

# PHARAOH'S ARMY.

"Said England unto Pharaoh, 'I must make a man of you,
　That will stand upon his feet and play the game;
　That will Maxim his oppressor as a Christian ought to do,'
　And she sent old Pharaoh Sergeant Whatsisname.

"Said England unto Pharaoh, 'You've had miracles before,
　When Aaron struck your rivers into blood;
　But if you watch the sergeant he can show you something more,
　He's a charm for making riflemen from mud.'"

From a Photo.　　　　　　　　By a Military Officer.

*OFFICER OF THE KHEDIVE'S CAMEL CORPS.*

WHAT the English officer, and that backbone of the Army, the non-commissioned man, have done for the "Gippy" Army is sufficiently evidenced by the advance of Sir Herbert Kitchener's force throughout the last twelve months. The compact little force that has done such magnificent service against the Dervishes is the growth of just fifteen years, for it was in 1882 that Sir Evelyn Wood and his assistants first undertook the contract of "making riflemen from mud." The Egyptian Army, then intended to consist of some 6,000 men, who were to be practically a military police, has now swollen to triple the number. The cavalry of the force, some eight or ten squadrons, are Egyptians, and are reinforced by a camel corps of seven companies, of which all but two are Soudanese. Our illustrations depict an officer of this latter, together with a group of a sergeant's command, who are taking a rest while on picquet duty in the desert. Always to the front on their much-enduring steeds, the "Khedive's Camel Corps" are the eyes and ears of the Sirdar's Army. The artillery comprise some four or five batteries, one being horse and one garrison, and the remainder mountain. The excellent illustration of a gun mule and his leader is worthy of study, for

ON PICQUET DUTY.

it shows that the Egyptian gunner can turn out as fit and smart as those of our Indian Army, and that is giving him no mean praise. Note the spick and span smartness of the whole turn-out, and remember that troops who are clean and smart in barracks and on parade have the pride of the soldier ingrained in them, and will always do well in the field.

One of our other illustrations depicts the men of the 4th Garrison Battery engaged on bridge building. Fine stalwart fellows they look, like men who, under good leadership, could do a day's hard fighting as well as a day's hard work. That the Egyptian soldier, if properly superintended, is excellent

for the hard drudgery of a campaign lacking the spur of hard fighting, is evidenced by the rapidity with which the railway across the great loop of the Nile, between Korosko and Abou Hamed, has been completed.

The remaining pictures illustrate the various types of, and life in, the infantry, of which the bulk of the Egyptian Army is composed. Prior to the advance on Dongola, the infantry comprised thirteen battalions, of which eight were Egyptian (Nos. 1 to 8) and five Soudanese (Nos. 9 to 13). Of these, Nos. 1 to 4 have each four British officers, the company officers being Egyptian, while Nos. 5 to 8 are entirely

From Photos.  By a Military Officer.

"ALONG O' MY OLD BROWN MULE."

officered by natives All the Soudanese battalions have British field and native company officers, much the same as in our Indian Army. In one picture are shown various types, both Egyptian and Soudanese, and in both summer and winter uniform. An interesting group of Soudanese are the sergeant and three men taking a stand-easy in a typical Soudan landscape. Note, moreover, that every man in the group is smiling, for the Soudanese, like most Africans, is nothing if not cheery. The group of drummers and buglers shown belong to the 12th Soudanese, a battalion that through this campaign has done yeoman's service, and is under the command of Major Townsend, of Chitral fame.

In another illustration an Egyptian barrack-room is shown, and though the accommodation is but scant, it amply meets the requirements of its hardy occupants, and in neatness and cleanliness would do credit to a smart company in a British regiment. At the outset of last year's

*TYPES OF PHARAOH'S ARMY.*

campaign the Egyptian Army was considerably increased. A 14th Battalion was formed from Soudanese recruits, taken from the battalions of the five existing Soudanese regiments, and two battalions of Egyptian reservists, now numbered 15 and 16, were also brought into being. Moreover, there were added ten transport companies of 200 men each, as well as a railway battalion numbering 600. This compact little force is officered by what may almost be styled the pick of the British Army, and in equipment and armament is of the best. The guns used by the artillery are of Krupp make, but the arm of the remainder of the force is the Martini-Henry. The cavalry, in addition to swords and Martini carbines, have also the front rank armed with lances, that ideal weapon for cavalry. Nor will this fine force be long without a strong leavening of British troops. The Lincolnshire and Warwickshire Regiments are already on their way up the Nile. The Cameron Highlanders and the 21st Lancers are also in Egypt, while the place of the Warwick and Lincoln Regiments pushed to the front is being filled by the Seaforth Highlanders from Malta, the Northumberland Fusiliers from Gibraltar, and by the Royal Irish Fusiliers

*A "STAND EASY" IN THE DESERT.*

*A CRACK CORPS—THE 12TH SOUDANESE.*

now *en route* from Burma. Moreover, detachments of Army Service and Army Hospital Corps have been sent out, and the ubiquitous British Navy is also taking its share of the fun in the gun-boats now on the Nile.

From Photos.

*"HOME, SWEET HOME."*

By a Military Officer.

# THE
# NAVY & ARMY
## ILLUSTRATED.

VOL. V.—No. 57.]     *FRIDAY, FEBRUARY 18th, 1898.*

Photo. Russell & Sons.                           Southsea.

### REAR-ADMIRAL C. C. P. FITZ-GERALD.

THE new second in command of the China station, Rear-Admiral Charles Cooper Penrose Fitz-Gerald, who is relieving Rear-Admiral Oxley in China, is one of the best known of our junior flag officers, and a man of marked ability and distinguished merit. He was born in 1841, and entered the Royal Navy in May, 1854, on the eve of the Russian War, in which Admiral Fitz-Gerald saw service in the Baltic, as a midshipman of the old "Colossus." He saw active service after that, in the same waters where he is now to fly his flag, in the second China War in 1858, as a midshipman in the celebrated old paddle frigate "Retribution." He was promoted to captain in 1880, and two years later took part in the Egyptian War, as flag-captain to Sir Francis Sullivan, in the "Inconstant." From 1883 to 1885 Admiral Penrose Fitz-Gerald had charge of the Royal Naval College at Greenwich, as captain of that institution. He received his flag in February, 1895. The gallant admiral is the author of the admirable life of the late Sir George Tryon which met with such success a few months ago. He holds views of his own in regard to modern Naval tactics, on which he is an admitted authority; and the nation is to be congratulated on the appointment of so able an officer as a second in command to Sir Edward Seymour in the Far East.

# THE MAKING OF ADMIRALTY CHARTS.

THE surveying work of the Navy is carried out almost entirely by a small group of vessels, mostly old sloops and gun-boats, specially fitted out for the duty. They number eight in all, and are scattered for the carrying out of their work all over the world—in the Mediterranean, in the Pacific, in Australasian waters, in the West Indies. The ships are mostly at the disposal of Rear-Admiral Sir William Wharton, K.C.B., F.R.S., the Hydrographer to the Admiralty, who presides over the special department charged with the issue, revision, and correction of Admiralty charts, sailing directions, and general information for mariners in the matter of lights, beacons, and so forth. There are upwards of 3,000 Admiralty charts published, and the work of keeping them up to date is the main duty of those employed on the marine survey service. As anyone who has ever seen an Admiralty chart must allow, the work entails on all concerned enormous labour and care, and the closest attention to every detail. Of course much assistance is rendered by men-of-war on the different stations whenever any discovery, such

*THE "EGERIA" AT ANCHOR IN BURGOYNE BAY, SMYTH'S CHANNEL.*

as the shifting of a shoal, or the finding of some hitherto unobserved pinnacle rock in deep water, is made, and a large amount of odd information also comes to hand through the medium of merchant vessels; but these methods of getting information are subsidiary, reliance being principally placed on the work done by the special survey ships.

Our first photograph shows the "Egeria" on survey duty off the coast of South America. The "Egeria" is one of our oldest sloops at present in commission, and the duty on which she is for the time being specially employed is in carrying out the survey of Magellan's Straits, Smyth's Channel, the coast of Chili, and, to conclude the programme of work allotted within the "Egeria's" commission, a survey of the waters of British Columbia. Our photograph shows the "Egeria" at anchor in Burgoyne Bay, Smyth's Channel, on a day when her boats are away taking soundings in the Bay.

Our second photograph shows the winding in of a sounding wire from a depth of 2,300 fathoms after bottom has been reached. Great care has to be exercised to prevent the wire being jerked or kinked, in either of which cases it may snap and the operation have to be gone through again—a big business, considering the length of wire run out. A bluejacket is seen leaning over the side to lubricate and guide the wire.

*WINDING IN THE SOUNDING WIRE IN 2,300 FATHOMS.*

Our third photograph shows the officers of the "Egeria" taking "magnetic sights," to check the ship's compasses and note any local deviation due to the earth's magnetic attraction. This operation has to be constantly seen to, and is carried out by a party landed from the ship for the purpose. The compasses are placed on tripods, and the bearings of certain well-known points and hills are taken, by means of which the extent of any deviation there may be between the direction of the magnetic North point, as shown by the ship's instruments, and the true North, as mathematically calculated, can be worked out.

From Photos.          *CORRECTING COMPASSES AT SANTA CATALINA.*          By a Naval Officer.

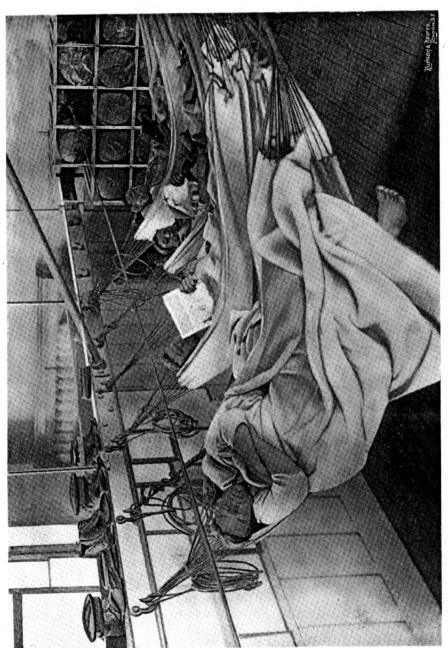

Photo: W. M. Crockett, Plymouth.

*JACK'S FOUR-POSTER.*

Copyright.—Hudson & Kearns.

A HAMMOCK is a very comfortable kind of bed, when one gets used to it. At first it is often liable to induce cramp, which naturally "murders sleep." There is, moreover, a certain art in getting into a hammock, and a lack of knowledge in this respect may entail a hasty and involuntary exit on the other side. The men in the illustration look very much at home in their swinging beds. Note the nearest, who appears to be half in and half out, but is sleeping peacefully, in spite of his apparently precarious position. Three are regaling themselves with light literature, a proceeding which is very materially facilitated in modern vessels by the substitution of the electric light for the old "police" lanterns, as they were called, which always seemed to possess a remarkable capacity for casting the light in the wrong place. One man is the happy possessor of a copy of *Tit-Bits*, a very suitable and handy journal for the hammock. In rough weather at sea a hammock is an admirable institution, the motion being scarcely felt.

# A SUB-LIEUTENANT'S UNIFORM.

A GOOD many years ago, but well within the recollection of many officers now serving, there was an extraordinary diversity of opinion in the Navy regarding the interpretation of the regulations as to uniform. Certain broad rules were universally adhered to, but for social functions and the ordinary work on board there was apparently an unlimited field for the exercise of private judgment. Thus, at an entertainment on shore, some officers might be seen in

*SUNDAY MORNING INSPECTION.*

white and others in blue trousers, and so on; and a visitor passing from one ship to another might find one officer of the watch in the severe propriety of a frock-coat and sword-belt, and another in an old monkey jacket. It began to be per

Photos. Russell & Sons.                    Southsea.
*SEMI-TROPICAL DRESS.*

*MESS DRESS.*

ceived, however, that it was not creditable that officers should appear on shore in a diversity of costumes, and so it became the custom for the admiral to indicate by signal the dress to be worn—a custom which is still continued, though greatly simplified by the introduction of minute instructions As an instance of the laxity which formerly prevailed, a signalman

Photos. Russell & Sons.          *A COLD MORNING.*          Southsea.

has been heard to read out to the ward-room officers a communication to this effect:—"Dress for entertainment this afternoon, frock-coats, trousers optional," which admitted of a very whimsical interpretation, though none of the officers were bold enough to appear in Highland costume!

All this is changed nowadays, and there is a special dress minutely prescribed for all occasions, while a suitable dress for the tropics has been legalised. Our illustrations show some variations in a sub-lieutenant's uniform, but the same rules prevail throughout all ranks The frock-coat and cap, with sword, is a sort of Sunday morning dress, and used also for such occasions as an admiral's inspection, or a visit on duty to another ship, etc The semi-tropical dress shows the comfortable monkey jacket now very properly legalised as the ordinary dress on board one's own ship; a white tunic is substituted in full tropical dress. For mess dress the gold-

*BALL DRESS.*

braided vest, which was used, quite illegally, in some ships for a number of years, is now made compulsory, and forms with the mess jacket, a very pretty and suitable costume. The great coat is a most consoling garment in a north-easter. The distinction lace, as will be noticed, appears on the shoulder

Photos. Russell & Sons.                    Southsea.

*READY FOR BATTALION DRILL.*

*GOING TO A COURT-MARTIAL.*

strap instead of on the cuff. In the ball dress the epaulettes— or scales in the case of a sub-lieutenant—first appear. These same scales are somewhat unfinished-looking articles. Why not give the sub-lieutenant a little supplementary gold fringe? The landing dress in the sixth picture is in every respect a thoroughly workmanlike and suitable costume for its purpose. The combination of frock-coat with cocked hat and epaulettes

Photos. Russell & Sons.                    Southsea.

*THE QUEEN'S BIRTHDAY.*

is of comparatively recent introduction. It is used for court-martial, etc., and is a great improvement on the old arrange-ment of undress tail coat.

In the last illustration we see the sub-lieutenant in "full canonicals," so to speak, or, as he would put it, in "war paint." The Naval full dress, more especially that of the higher ranks, with gold-laced trousers and heavy gold fringe to the epaulettes, is universally acknowledged to be an exceed ingly handsome and becoming ceremonial costume. It is used when doing honour to Royalty.

# THE MACHINERY OF THE "RENOWN."

THE North America and West Indies station has of late years been remarkably lucky in the matter of its flag-ships. In February, 1892, the "Blake," then with her sister the "Blenheim" undoubtedly two of the finest cruisers we had ever possessed in our Navy, went out with Sir John Hopkins as Commander-in-Chief. The "Blake," however, was considered rather too large for a first-class cruiser, and so the next ship that went to carry the flag was the "Crescent." Both of these ships were gazed on with feelings of admiration by the loyal colonists, who thronged on board them whenever opportunity offered. But the Admiralty conceived that they had not done enough for North America, and so Sir John Fisher had orders to hoist his flag in the "Renown" and proceed to that station last August. The photos of machinery shown here were taken on board that vessel.

In the first of the four reproductions of photographs, which were all taken by electric light, and are wonderful specimens of the photographer's art, we see the steering engines of the ship. Ships are invariably steered by steam nowadays, though, as invariably, there is always an alternative handgear provided in case of a breakdown. We all know how important the steering gear of a ship is, and it is usually operated from down below, being connected by telegraph with many stations in the ship. Formerly it was rather untrustworthy, and constantly gave trouble by refusing to act, but of late years it has been so much improved that it rarely becomes inoperative.

We have in the second picture a representation of part of one of the stokeholds, in fact, the forward end. Of course, when fires are extinguished and there is no steam, cleanliness is carried to its utmost limits; but, if there are no fires in this particular stokehold, depend upon it there are plenty somewhere else, for what with perpetually distilling fresh water, running ventilating fans, working the dynamos for the electric light, and the numberless other duties that have to

*THE STEERING ENGINES.*

be performed as much when a ship is in harbour as when she is at sea, in a modern man-of-war steam is always up, and its services are required.

The third and fourth of our pictures give us views of the "Renown's" mighty machinery, as depicted in her main engines and the starting platform. The engines consist of two complete sets, one to each screw. There are four cylinders to each set, one high-pressure, one intermediate, and two low-pressure cylinders, because if there were only one it would be of too unwieldy a size. The starting platform is that part of the engine-room from which the engineer on duty must never be far away, as it is from there that the engines are started, stopped, and sent astern.

Photos. Symonds & Co.    *IN THE STOKEHOLDS.*    Portsmouth.

ON THE STARTING PLATFORM.

Portsmouth.

THE MAIN ENGINES.

Photos Symonds & Co.

SMALL REPAIRS.

HERE we have represented the chief gunner, with his mates and armourers, overhauling a breech-loading gun and effecting such small adjustments as may be necessary in the mechanism. A far higher standard of efficiency is demanded of the modern armourer than of his predecessor of muzzle-loading days, and some improvement or elaboration of the machinery for loading and working the guns is being constantly introduced, so that he has to be very much up to date. The mechanism of a quick-firing gun, taken apart and laid about the deck, looks rather like the component parts of a gigantic and eccentric watch, and the problem, to the uninitiated, is how it is all going to be put together again in the right fashion. The method of securing the breech-block, by means of the intercepted screw, is plainly shown in the picture—a very ingenious and effective arrangement.

THE
NAVY & ARMY
ILLUSTRATED.
NOTES & QUERIES
OF
SERVICE AFLOAT & ASHORE

As advances are made in the sciences, it is now possible for the public to keep in close touch with the same by means of pictorial reproductions shown by the latest improvements in photography. One instance is a new and most destructive weapon, the invention of Hiram Maxim, of Maxim gun fame. This inventor has just completed a Naval or coast defence automatic rapid-firing gun, which projects a shell weighing 9-lb. a distance of over three miles, and it is claimed for this weapon that it has a rapidity of fire more than double any other gun of its size. One of the latest pictures of the up-to-date Biograph shows the inventor, Mr. Hiram Maxim, firing this gun in full view of the audience. As a matter of fact, a boy of ten years could go through that performance, which is simply pressing the trigger—the gun automatically firing and ejecting and reloading—as long as ammunition is within reach.

* * * *

"C. W.," a young joiner who is anxious to get a berth in the Royal Navy in connection with his trade, had better write, giving particulars of his age, experience, and trade qualifications, to the senior officer in charge of the Dockyard Reserve at Chatham, Portsmouth, or Devonport, or the captain of the port guard-ship at Pembroke, whichever place may be nearest to him and most convenient. Of course he would have to produce proofs of his general conduct and of his abilities as a workman, or indentures to the satisfaction of the authorities.

* * * *

The magnificent fighting qualities and consistent loyalty of the Gurkhas may be said to be "familiar in men's mouths as household words." There is, therefore, small need to do more than give publicity to the existence of a Gurkha Association, which has been formed for the purpose of providing for and educating (1) the orphan sons of Gurkha soldiers who have died in the Service or been killed in action, and (2) the sons of Gurkha pensioners of good and deserving character, residing in India, who are in destitute circumstances. The central idea of the association is the foundation of a Gurkha Asylum, which, once started, would be kept up by subscriptions from the fifteen Gurkha battalions. Already a considerable sum has been collected, and it would be strange indeed if such a project lacked the support of the British public. If only out of gratitude for the glorious services which the Gurkhas have rendered, not to speak of the desirableness of encouraging such an aid to Gurkha recruiting, the Gurkha Asylum should receive many English contributions, which can be sent either to Lieutenant Alban Wilson, the adjutant of the 44th Gurkha Rifles, or to Messrs. Grindlay and Co., 55, Parliament Street, S.W., marked "Gurkha Asylum."

* * * *

"W."—The preparation of pemmican requires great skill and care. When it became necessary, in 1874, to manufacture supplies at Deptford for the Arctic expedition then fitting out, recourse was had to the experience gained in 1852, when large quantities of the preparation were made at Gosport under the supervision of the captain-superintendent, Sir Edward Parry, and Dr. Nicholson, C.B., the inspector-general in charge of Haslar Hospital. The process, as then described, consisted in the purchase of rounds of beef divested of all fat and skin. These, after the bone had been extracted, were cut into thin, uniform slices, and placed on hurdles over a kiln, where they remained until the experience of the men in charge judged them to be sufficiently dried, the minimum time being, on an average, twelve hours. The slices were then cut into small pieces and carried to a mill, where they were ground into powder—an improvement on the old process of pounding in a mortar. The meat thus ground was mixed with suet—which had been carefully chopped, melted, and strained—currants, and sugar, after which it was packed into canisters. The process of manufacture was very slow, averaging about 70-lb. of meat per diem, or, after the admixture of ingredients, about 140-lb. of pemmican.

* * * *

This process was closely followed in the preparation of the supplies for the Arctic expedition of 1875-76, two kinds, plain and sweet, being made, the former, of course, containing neither currants nor sugar. The meat purchased was the finest Aberdeen beef procurable, even the wood for firing the kilns being specially selected oak free from tar. The only alteration in the recipe seems to have been the addition, to the plain pemmican, of cayenne pepper and preserved potato, the latter addition being made on the recommendation of the late Sir G. H. Richards. Cayenne seems first to have been used in 1860, in the preparation of some 2,000-lb. of pemmican, at Gosport, for the Swedish and Norwegian Government. The quantity supplied was 14,400-lb. The other articles specially prepared at Deptford for the expedition comprised corned beef, corned pork, and boiled bacon. The biscuit was also specially baked, and the rum supplied undiluted, and in as highly concentrated a form as possible. Meat biscuits, consisting of one-third pemmican and two-thirds biscuit meal, were also prepared on the suggestion of Sir George Narrs. The whole of the supplies were regulated by a committee specially appointed for that purpose, and composed of officers possessing Arctic experience. In addition to the articles already enumerated, large quantities of exceptional articles were supplied by contractors, such as cavendish and shag tobacco, Welsh wigs, down shirts, sealskin and box-cloth suits, mocassins, etc.

I am asked by a correspondent to describe the colours of a cavalry regiment. Strictly speaking, cavalry have no colours at all. Regiments of Dragoon Guards carry standards, and of Dragoons, guidons. The former are of silk damask, embroidered and fringed with gold, the latter of silk. The standard or guidon of each regiment is of a crimson colour, and bears (unless otherwise authorised) the royal or other title in letters of gold on a red ground in a circle, and the rank of the regiment in gold Roman characters on a crimson ground in the centre, the whole within a wreath of roses, thistles, and shamrocks on the same stalk, ensigned with the Imperial Crown. The white horse, on a green mount on a crimson ground, is in the first and fourth compartments, within a scroll, and the rose, thistle, and shamrock conjoined, on a ground of the colour of the facings of the regiment, within a scroll, in the second and third corners. In the case of regiments having particular badges, such badges are embroidered in the centre, and the rank of the regiment put in the second and third corners, within a wreath of roses, thistles, and shamrocks. The standard or guidon also bears the devices, distinctions, and mottoes which have been conferred by royal authority—the motto under the wreath in the centre. The tassels are of crimson silk and gold mixed, and the lance, including the royal crest which surmounts it, is 8-ft. 6-in. long. Standards and guidons, which are not borne in either Hussar or Lancer regiments, are carried by squadron sergeant-majors.

* * * *

Several correspondents ask questions about the guard and Reserve ships at the various ports and harbours round our coasts, whose presence there often arouses the curiosity of summer-time and other visitors. The answer is simple—they comprise the first Reserve squadron of the Fleet, and are kept ready to put to sea within forty-eight hours of war being declared or a mobilisation for any purpose ordered. The ships would collect at some appointed rendezvous, being manned, on the order to mobilise being given, up to fighting strength by the coastguardsmen of the district where each ship is stationed, and the merchant service Naval Reserve men living in or attached to the district. The whereabouts and addresses of these men are at all times known to the captains of the ships, and a telegram would bring the men on board at short notice. Meanwhile, all the year round a ship's company of bluejackets, with officers amounting to something under a third of each ship's sea-going complement, are ordinarily kept on duty on board. The first Reserve fleet comprises the harbour guard-ships at Portsmouth, Plymouth, and Chatham, and the coast guard-ships elsewhere from Bantry Bay to the Clyde and Queensferry, with certain small sea-going cruisers used as Royal Naval Reserve drill-ships, the whole providing a fleet of some sixteen to twenty vessels which would be available to support the Channel fleet or take its place in home waters. Comprising as it does ships like the "Trafalgar," "Nile," "Rodney," and "Howe," with the additions of the "Camperdown" and "Anson" to be made next April, the Reserve fleet should be a match, after a few days' shaking down at sea, for any fleet likely to come into Northern waters.

* * * *

Hospital attendants or orderlies are taken, as a rule, from the Medical Staff Corps, and are trained in all the duties connected with the sick and wounded. It is, however, usual to employ patients who are sufficiently strong on light duties, such as carrying round the medicines to the men in their ward, and generally assisting the nursing sister in charge, if there be one. It is sometimes found necessary to supplement the number of orderlies furnished by the Medical Staff Corps, in which case the medical officer in charge makes an application to the officer commanding the garrison or station, who takes the necessary steps for providing the men required from the troops in the garrison. When employed in this capacity a man is excused all regimental parades and duties, and usually continues to fill the billet as long as he is required by the medical officer. If the man, under any exceptional circumstances, be required to join his regiment or corps, the regulations demand that due notice be given to the medical officer.

* * * *

My answer to "X.," who asks me whether I would advise an officer to qualify as an interpreter in the Navy, considering the extreme likelihood of never being employed as such, is, decidedly, Yes. I am well aware that out of the 114 officers who have qualified as interpreters in all the languages under the sun there are just six employed, and these fortunate ones are professors of Hindoo or Swahili for the most part; but I look forward to a great change for the better. In the case of war, which is always threatened, though everybody believes it to be still afar off, it is certain that interpreters will be sought after and rewarded in a manner little thought of now. In these circumstances I consider that it would be the height of bad judgment for an officer who has the ability to neglect to get himself placed on the list of qualified interpreters, for it is always something to be known as having passed. It is always desirable in the Navy—or indeed elsewhere—for an officer to have a reputation as a specialist, if only in such an everyday subject as French.

* * * *

Lest we forget, amid the heroic deeds of modern times, the services of such men as Sir Thomas Picton, I may remind my readers that there stands in St. Paul's a monument bearing the following inscription:—"Erected at the public expense to Lieutenant-General Sir Thomas Picton, K.G.C.B., who, after distinguishing himself in the victories of Busacos, Fuentes de Onoro, Ciudad Rodrigo, Badajoz, Vittoria, the Pyrenees, Orthes, and Toulouse, terminated his long and glorious military services in the ever memorable battle of Waterloo, to the splendid success of which his genius and valour eminently contributed, on the 18th of June, 1815." There is also a column to his memory at Carmarthen, near which his home was situated. This brave soldier, who "had never known defeat" in the whole course of his service, was born at Poyston, near Haverfordwest, in August, 1758. He joined his uncle's regiment, the 12th Foot, at Gibraltar, when fifteen years of age, and was from the first devoted to the study of his profession. He served in the West Indies, and was for some time Governor of Trinidad. In that capacity he was accused of harshness and cruelty by the malice of a personal enemy; and although these accusations were disproved, they were gladly believed and retailed by evil-minded and thoughtless people. They were, however, forgotten in the brilliancy of his Peninsular career. He has been described by a not too friendly historian as a man of "stern countenance, robust frame, saturnine complexion, caustic speech, and austere demeanour," but he was also kind-hearted, absolutely truthful, an ardent patriot, and a splendid soldier.

The Editor.

O UR relations with Afghanistan and the tribes are very much a question of the day, and I, therefore, took up Sir John Adye's "Indian Frontier Policy" (Smith, Elder, 3s. 6d.) with considerable interest. The conclusion was foregone, because the General has freely expressed his opinion on many an occasion. He is all for a backward policy. Because we foolishly attempted to set Shah Soojah on the Afghan throne in 1839, and paid for our rashness with disaster, and because forward steps have continually embroiled us, we are to withdraw our isolated posts from turbulent districts, and devote ourselves to promoting the "welfare of the millions under our sway." All this is very interesting. But I do not think it will prevail with Englishmen. We still remember how those who feared a Russian advance to Merv were jeered at by a distinguished statesman as victims of "Mervousness." Since that time the Transcaspian railway has been built—an excellent line of communication, *pace* Sir West Ridgeway, and is now being extended to the Afghan frontier. We have guaranteed the integrity of Afghanistan. Is that guarantee consistent with a backward policy? Are we to suffer the tribes to become Russianised? There is more than a spice of the marauder in them. The rich plains of India are below. It needs but a Muscovite bidding to throw them on the quarry.

So many statesmen make or mar. I take up a book dedicated to one "ever reliable, never knowing when he is beaten, saving his country in many a crisis when statesmen have failed." Who is that but the British soldier, Tommy Atkins? And the book, you say? It is a new edition of "Scenes Through the Battle Smoke," by the Rev. Arthur Male (Dean). Now Mr. Male has seen as much fighting as any parson living. He was determined to see it, and so found himself at Peshawar on the eve of the Afghan War. To dissuade him was that odd inscription to another clergyman, who "translated the Scriptures into the Afghan tongue, and was shot by his own chowkeydar—Well done, thou good and faithful servant!" But Mr. Male was not to be deterred. Where fighting was going on, there he tried to be in the midst. You hold your breath when he tells you how he "walked" the gauntlet of a frenzied crowd outside the Jellalabad gate, egged on to murder him by a couple of armed Ghazis. The incident is described to the very life, with all the sights and sounds and smells of the war, humour breaking out here and there. "Oh those dead camels! Words fail utterly to describe one's feelings under the circumstances of such a meeting. It is *one* thing to pass Rimmel's shop in the Strand, but another thing to pass a defunct camel! Quite!" But I have said enough. The story of the Egyptian Campaign is as good.

When you take up "Our Troubles in Poona and the Deccan," by Arthur T. Crawford, C.M.G. (Constable, 14s.), you expect a sober, solid treatment of a weighty question, but you soon find yourself laughing at the whimsicalities of the author. As to Poona, that is all right. No general disaffection prevails, and only firm government is needed, with a reformed police to crush the Hindoo criminals. We have pampered and petted the pestilential sections of the Brahmins, and it is an imperious necessity to set up the Mahommedan aristocracy by the side of the "twice-born." This is sound policy. To establish a balance of power between native races or castes was the guiding principle of Warren Hastings. Then there is the native pass to control, and here a humorous "temperature chart" is given. The patient, Dushtec (treacherous) Rao Pájee (bad character), B.A., J.P., was at fever heat under the treatment of Lord Reay (Government House alcohol in large doses, with rancid butter) and Lord Sandhurst (Leg. Council draught), but Inspector-General John Bull approves the proposed treatment of cautery, with perhaps an operation, and anti-Congress pills. Although Mr. Crawford is thoroughly serious, he chooses thus to laugh with his reader, and to crack jokes and hit off characters as he goes along.

I like "Great Warriors—Nelson, Wellington, Napoleon " (Chambers, 2s.) for the spirit and vigour that pervade it. The worst fault of a "popular" volume is to be dull, and nothing of the kind is the case here. But greater accuracy might have been striven for. We all know how, in the song, "our Nelson led the van," but that meaningless statement should not have been repeated. "Heroic Lives"—Livingstone, Stanley, Gordon, and Dundonald—is a brother-volume.

And now your "Search-Light" must direct a beam to things of *outremer*, and with particular pleasure to the "final edition" of a work by that good seaman and admirer of England, Signor A. V. Vecchj, who calls himself playfully "Jack la Bolina." His "Bozzetti di Vita di Bordo," or "Sketches of Life on Board" (hemporad, Florence, 3 lire) are capital. Here we have the Italian bluejacket and his superiors to the life in their daily occupations and amusements, with a happy mixture of wit, drollery, and romance. I observe that Signor Biagi, who has evidently been to an English dinner, and has an echo in his ears of something he heard there, amusingly addresses Jack la Bolina, in a preface, as "You merry fellow!" We do not often hear much of the Swedish Navy, and I was therefore glad to receive little pictorial work of folding plates, "Fran Svenska Flottan " ("From Sweden's Fleet"). It includes portraits of Royal personages, pictures of ships, and scenes of life afloat, indicating popular interest in the Service.

Before it is too late, let me signal the appearance of a few articles worth reading in the January magazines—"The French Invasion of Ireland " in *Macmillan* ; "Sir John Moore at Corunna," being another "Deed that Won the Empire," by the Rev. W. H Fitchett, in the *Cornhill* ; "Turtle Catching," by Admiral Fitzgerald, in the *Badminton* ; the beginning of Mr. Seton Merriman's military story, Roden's Corner," in *Harper* ; excellent contributions on "Portraits of General Wolfe," "Washington," and "A Myth of Waterloo" in the *Century* ; and a very full account of the "Kaiser Wilhelm der Grosse," as the "largest steam-ship afloat," in *Cassier's Magazine.*　　　"SEARCH-LIGHT."

## A Glance at the Royal Dockyards.

### By CHARLES GLEIG.

HERE are, doubtless, many millions of English men and women who have enjoyed no opportunity of visiting any one of the great dockyards administered by the Admiralty. These can have but little conception of the importance of the shipbuilding and repairing work which goes steadily on at these great centres of industry ; still less, perhaps, of the splendid system of organisation under which many thousands of skilled and unskilled workmen are employed in the construction of ships of war. Yet the gates of the Government dockyards are ever open to visitors. Policemen, stout of build but courteous in manner, stand at the portals, ready, and even willing, to conduct the enquiring "tripper" over the cobble-stones leading to the docks, building slips, and workshops ; and do not, it is said, disdain to accept in return for these civilities the smallest silver coin of the realm. Those who can afford a day's excursion to Portsmouth, Plymouth, or Chatham, should not fail to pay a visit to one of these national shipyards.

To begin with, it is an extremely interesting fact that all the employés of the Royal dockyards enjoy the privilege of an eight hours' day. They have many other privileges denied to the bulk of British workmen, but this limitation of the hours of labour is of sufficient importance to interest all classes of readers. It is curious to note, too, that the experiment of instituting the eight hours' day was not the outcome of agitation on the part of the workmen employed in these dockyards, but that it is actually a State experiment, which was introduced as a concession to public opinion, and with the object of officially testing the results.

Trade Unionism has obtained no foothold in the State dockyards, for the employés are fully alive to the advantages of continuity of employment, and will embark upon no agitation likely to hazard their prospective pensions. The total number of hands usually employed at the five dockyards is about 22,000, and one of the aims of the system is to avert wholesale discharges.

Of the five dockyards, Chatham and Portsmouth are of almost equal importance as ship-building centres, each employing about 7,000 hands ; and it is at these two ports that a majority of our battle-ships have been built. Devonport is next in importance, but has hitherto lacked plant for the construction of modern battle-ships, and has been more extensively utilised for cruiser building and as a refitting yard. At Pembroke we have a much smaller dockyard, but one which has long been supplied with plant for battle-ship construction. The establishment is controlled by a captain-superintendent, instead of a rear-admiral, but there are no facilities for docking or repairing ships at the Western yard. The fifth and least important of the Royal dockyards is at Sheerness, and is chiefly utilised for the building of small cruisers.

A dockyard, as the name suggests, is not merely a building site, but also a site for docks and basins. These will be found in abundance at Chatham, Portsmouth, and Devonport ; but, unfortunately, our modern battle-ships and cruisers have outgrown the majority of the docks constructed in the old days of convict labour, and new and larger ones have had to be designed to accommodate the "Majestics" and "Powerfuls" of the present day. Most of the older dockyard buildings, as well as the existing docks, were the outcome of convict labour.

Contract work, too, is responsible for the construction of many of our battle-ships and cruisers, besides having the monopoly of torpedo craft ; but the Admiralty regard it as imperative that the Government yards should always secure their fair share of construction. The reason of this is tolerably obvious. Strikes might at any time paralyse the ship-building industry, and have ere now delayed seriously the completion of battle-ships and cruisers. But, under present conditions, and with over 20,000 workmen in its own employ, Government can at all times continue ship-building, and Trade Union agitations surge harmlessly against the dockyard gates. So, too, in time of war, it would be still more imperative to have State dockyards available for rapid ship-building and the repair of shot-ridden hulls.

# TOMMY ATKINS AFLOAT.

## *By ONE WHO HAS SAILED WITH HIM.*

THE figure of Tommy Atkins ashore is a familiar one enough to all of us. Whether it be associated with a stirring brass band, which booms out a catchy air as he marches with his regiment through the village street, followed by all the juvenile population, and by the admiring eyes of half the country wenches in the neighbourhood, or, as a beatified creature, in all the glory of a red well-padded jacket, "doing the park" with a nursemaid, his presence in our midst somehow inspires us with a sense of security. We feel an interest in him, too; indeed, we almost regard him as part and parcel of our own personal belongings—a kind of romantic servant that we keep knocking around to do our unpleasant work across the seas, and keep the Czar, the German Emperor, and other troublesome potentates duly impressed with the might and dignity of the British nation.

We never see a regiment, or a component part of a regiment, without this almost unconscious feeling of proprietorship coming over us. They are "Our Soldiers"; and when we read of their glorious services abroad, their forced marches, and their invariable success, we begin to feel quite proud they belong to us, and duly expand our chests and talk of England's greatness, as if we were individually responsible for it.

Yes, ashore, Tommy Atkins is as familiar to us as the appears, from experience of both, that the hired transports are far cheaper and otherwise preferable to the regular troopers, only about two of which are in commission at the present time.

The ships are—man-of-war fashion—all painted white, both outside and on deck, when once they are chartered by the Government; the house flag is hauled down, and replaced by the transport ensign (somewhat resembling the R.N.R. flag, with the addition of a large yellow anchor), and special fittings are introduced below. These fittings are all stocked at Southampton and carefully marked, so that the regular passenger accommodation can be altered to that required for the troops in two or three days. As a matter of fact, some months ago one of the transports came in from Australia full of cargo and left again within eight days with 1,000 troops for Malta and the Cape. During this time all her cargo was discharged, over 600 men being daily employed, and by the time she was gazetted to sail everything was as ship-shape as if the process of altering her interior arrangements had occupied as many weeks as it did days.

The departure of a transport is an interesting event, and many sightseers, besides his relatives and the girl he is going to leave behind him, assemble at the wharf at Southampton to see the last of Tommy who has been ordered to India or the Cape.

That he does not look forward, with particularly pleasurable anticipations, to his seven years' exile, goes without saying. Stories told by time-expired soldiers of the agonies of sea-sickness, the life among the "niggers" —as they invariably call every coloured race, be they real

Troops Embarking

postman or the tax-collector, but it is with Tommy as a sailor that I propose to deal in this article.

The moment he leaves the train at Southampton and gets his accoutrements aboard the transport, all the glamour with which we are accustomed to surround him fades away. He becomes quite an ordinary person, and his admirers who could see him doing fatigue duty on deck would scarcely recognise in him the dashing son of Mars who marched with such a brave step and upright carriage to the strains of martial music a few days before.

It was in 1894 that the Government decided to do away by degrees with the five Indian troopers so well known in the Service—the ships of the General Trooping Service are now almost forgotten—and replace them by hired transports. These were chartered from the three largest shipping companies —the P. and O., Cunard, and British India Companies—who between them placed five vessels, viz., the "Victoria" and "Britannia" (P. and O.), the "Pavonia" (Cunard), and the "Dilwara" and "Jumna" (British India), at the disposal of the Imperial authorities during the trooping season.

They are all fitted as armed cruisers, and are invariably manned with European crews, most of the officers and many of the men belonging to the Royal Naval Reserve.

Thus the Government have reverted to the old-time method for the conveyance of troops, and it

West India negroes or high caste Hindoos—the heat of the climate, and the thought that he will not taste good, honest roast beef and bitter beer until his return, all tend to damp his ardour, which up to his embarkation has been artificially stimulated by the farewell glasses of well-meaning friends. He flies up the gangway with his gear and accoutrements, with a long face, roundly cursing, beneath his breath, the land of the coral strand and the nigger aforesaid; for him he has, of course, the most supreme contempt.

Having left their belongings on board, the soldiers go ashore again to be told off to messes, each of which consists of from sixteen to eighteen men. Once on board again, they are given a good square meal that would bring water to the mouth of a deep-sea sailor, every man sitting down to his food at the same time. Then an inspection of the ship is undertaken by the captain, a Naval officer, a staff officer, and the colonel commanding, and the men are told off to fire and boat quarters. The arrangements in this particular have been so perfected by constant practice that the whole performance is gone through, for the first time, in half-an-hour. Armed men are stationed at the boats, to prevent any rushing in case of emergency, and the strictest discipline is maintained throughout.

After this has been performed to the satisfaction of the officers, the bedding is served out, and so careless is Tommy of his belongings, that frequent inspection is found to be necessary to prevent him losing his blankets. Neatly-fitted racks are made in the hammock-room

At the sound of the bugle.

for the storing of the bedding during the day, and in addition to the non-commissioned officer in charge, a ship's officer and a military officer are always present at the issuing and the taking in. A hammock and two blankets are served to the unmarried of the rank and file, while the sergeants and their wives and families are accommodated with beds.

When all the more important duties have been assigned to the twelve or fourteen hundred men who form the complement of a large transport, the fatigue duties are given out, which consist in cleaning the ship, on deck and down below, and other matters which Tommy, however industrious he may be ashore, simply abhors afloat.

The "blanky" fatigues are the bane of his existence on ship board, and it is amusing to see the forty soldiers told off to wash decks go about their work for the first few mornings. Everything is new to them, and their eyes and minds are occupied upon anything but their work, and I fear very little weight is put into the broom until they get used to the strange scenes going on around them.

Holystone is a thing Tommy never takes to kindly. He looks upon dragging a stone over the deck as a wicked waste of an hour, that could be so much better employed in his hammock, and retains a firm conviction that a housemaid's scrubber and some soft soap would have the desired effect in half the time. He settles down to things better after a few days, and begins to feel more at home—that is, if he happens to be a good sailor. If he doesn't, he finds new and elaborate swear words appropriate to the "boat" (as he calls it), which, as his vocabulary of invective has been very liberally drawn upon for other occasions, requires no mean inventive capacity.

Sentries are posted about various parts of the ship, to prevent irregularities; and though Tommy is well accustomed to performing this kind of duty on shore, he often makes rather an awkward fist at it, at first, on board ship.

Most of the recruits who are sent to India have never been aboard a ship before in their lives—many of them have never even seen one; and the names they give the various parts of the vessel and the rigging are calculated to make a sailor roar in derision. A sailor, by the way, for some reason, has anything but a high regard for Tommy, and so his duties are not appreciably lessened by Jack, who delights in the muddles he gets in, and slaps his thigh as he relates the latest "bull" made by "one of them militia blokes"—Jack calls them all militiamen—to his pals in the fo'c's'le, a portion of the ship from which Tommy is rigidly excluded. Tommy invariably calls the funnel the "chimney," the gangway the "stairs," and the deck the "floor," and distinguishes the for'ard and aft of the ship by calling them the "thin" and the "thick" end respectively He never gets quite used to sailor terms, and, even at the end of the voyage, speaks of the "heaving of the boat," or the "blooming colonel on the bridge."

He is sorely puzzled as to how the ship's officers rank, and why they wear so little gold lace.

I overheard a fellow, who spoke as one having authority and not as the scribes, explaining the matter to his mate one day. "You see, Fred, it's like this. The (cuss word) bloke with the stripe on his shoulder—he's the (swear word) ship's capting. All the other blanketty blokes wot goes upstairs to the turret place—them's the — lieutenants." "And who's that there joker?" asked Fred, pointing to the chief engineer, who was certainly more than seven; "'e never goes upstairs, and 'e aint no steward." "Why, you blanky galoot, that's a middy." "A pretty old middy, aint 'e?" hazarded Fred, somewhat dubiously. "Lord love yer," replied his instructor, "there's tons of 'em as old as him; 'e's got as far as 'e can; 'e's been plucked, and 'e'll never get no further."

The lifebelt parade is, perhaps, the only portion of the ship's routine that Tommy

really takes any interest in. Besides being a novelty to him, it affords excellent material for chaff; and the comic artist (and there is often one among the men) invariably chooses the moment of "lifebelts" for his most scathing work. At the sound of the bugle the men fall in, as if for parade. The

belts are passed up by those stationed in the ladders, and within fourteen minutes every Tommy on board has his belt on securely. Everyone in the ship, with the exception of the officers' wives and invalids, is bound to have a belt on when the captain and colonel go round on their tour of inspection, and a sufficient number of belts are taken to the hospital and their use explained to the patients.

At 10.30 every morning an inspection of the ship is made by the captain, the colonel, adjutant, and military officer of the watch, during which every nook and cranny of the vessel, and all the mess utensils, are overhauled. This over, the troop—who have been paraded on the upper deck the while—are dismissed, and, with the exception of those on guard, are at liberty to kill time as they please. And Tommy can kill time better than anyone I know. To most persons a long sea voyage, even relieved by the various distractions provided, is more or less monotonous, but it is by no means so to Tommy. As a general rule there is nothing he loves better than to loll about the deck. He has made up his mind for a good steady loaf when he gets on board, and manfully he sticks to his determination during the voyage.

Some few regiments engage largely in calisthenic exercise. The adjutant of one regiment I sailed with used to rise every morning at six o'clock and make a number of his men go through all sorts of Sandow exercises until nine. These men landed in the pink of condition.

During the fine weather concerts are occasionally organised among the men, and on some of these occasions it happens that exceptional talent is displayed.

All sorts of amusements are supplied by the Government for the use of the troops, though the game that Tommy loves best is "lotto," or, as he calls it, "ouse"—meaning, I suppose, "house." This game, which requires very little skill, is, as most of my readers are doubtless aware, played with numbered cards and counters. Twelve cards, with various numbers printed in squares, are served to as many men, while a thirteenth man, acting as "bank," shouts out (much louder than is at all necessary) various numbers corresponding to those on the cards, which he reads from counters, one by one extracted from a bag. The man claiming the number covers the corresponding square with something—usually a piece of ship's biscuit—and the one who first fills his card is declared the winner. As Tommy always makes a strictly gambling game out of this, it is interdicted by Government, which is, I suppose, one of the reasons why he is so partial to it. He has a gamble whenever possible, quite content to risk the chance of punishment for his little bit of sport.

Talking of punishment reminds me that very little is generally required, and, although cells are fitted up in all the transports, they are rarely used. Extra fatigues, the stoppage of their "baccy," or the compulsory answering to their names every hour, when the bugle sounds, for "defaulters" are usually found quite sufficient punishments for the petty

offences that the newly-fledged soldiers commit on the outward voyage.

Of course homeward-bound men "doing time" for various offences are closely confined, except for a short time daily, when they are escorted for exercise on the fo'c's'le. The colonel of the regiment is, of course, the judge and jury, and justice is dispensed in a manner that would make some of our legal luminaries open their eyes.

One of the reasons for the orderly conduct of the troops during the voyage is the fact that no intoxicants are sold on board, except on

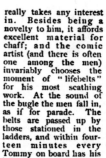

The Bathing Parade.

the return trip, when a tot of rum is allowed the time-expired men at a penny a head. On arrival at the various ports of call, also, the troops are kept strictly to the ship, except at places like Cape Town, where they are marched for a few hours daily, if the ship remains more than three days in port.

The outward-bound canteen is what Tommy calls a "dry" one, though lemonade, sherbet, etc., are sold, in addition to "extras," i.e., jam and other dainties, which are all of the very best quality. Pickles, which seem to take Tommy's fancy as a cure for sea sickness, are retailed at one penny a small bottle.

The hours for meals on a transport will strike most late diners as peculiar. Breakfast is served at seven a.m., dinner at noon, and supper at four p.m. In cold weather all the men are in bed by eight p.m., and asleep by nine. They seem to be capable of putting in a good eight hours' sleep, despite their snoozes during the day, and then turn out at réveille looking as if they had only had a few hours' repose.

The warrant officers—the bandmasters, regimental sergeants, and schoolmasters—are entitled to second-class fare, while the non-commissioned officers, the next in rank, are given what is termed class sixteen. The wives of the non-commissioned officers are berthed and messed in the class next to class sixteen. This accommodation is excellent. Certain portions of the poop deck are marked out, and allotted to the various grades, and I have seen more squabbles over these little squares than over anything else on board. Mrs. Tommy Atkins, in class sixteen, observes that Bandmaster Burns's wife is taking up about 2-in. of her room space, so, instead of condescending to remonstrate with the trespasser, she immediately informs her husband, who at once proceeds to lodge a complaint against these irregular proceedings. It is always the unfortunate husband who is hauled over the coals if anything is wrong, whether in such cases as that alluded to, or in the event of a cabin not being clean or tidy. In the majority of cases, Tommy has to submit to the strictest petticoat government, for soldiers' wives have but few hobbies outside their babies—which are numerous—and, like their husbands, evidently make up their minds to "stand easy" during the voyage. If Tommy ever considers abstruse questions at all, the vexed problem as to whether marriage is, or is not, a failure, is certain to be definitely decided by him on his first sea trip. As a rule, in most regiments, there are one or two gentlemen in the ranks, and if they are pushing sort of fellows they generally get easy jobs given them on board, which carry with them a little saloon fare. Then, again, the regimental cooks, bakers, and the pantry hands, told off to assist the ship's company, are envied by their comrades as persons who revel in pickings and easy times. In many things soldiers are very like children, and "a good square feed" of dainties will send them into the seventh heaven of contentment.

Although it was not considered necessary during the first season, all the transports now carry a permanent military staff, consisting of four deck-sergeants, one quartermaster-sergeant, and six medical staff, who remain in the ship during the trooping season. They render excellent service to the ship's company, as they soon learn the ropes, and become quite sailor-like at the end of their term of service.

Each transport carries a Roman Catholic and a Protestant chaplain, who are considered sufficient to attend to the spiritual welfare of the troops, all of whom—with the exception of those sick or on duty—are compelled to attend the two services held on Sundays, and the prayers which are delivered at 9.45 a.m. daily. It is no use Tommy declaring himself an Atheist. He would not be excused if he worshipped the sun, or pinned his faith to a spook. Whether the religious instruction he receives at the hands of his official teachers does him much lasting good is, perhaps, a matter open to doubt; but a country bent on Christianising the benighted savage could consistently do no less than look after the spiritual well-being of its own servants, even though rum and

opium do not form part of the process in the latter case, as they too often do in the former.

Nearly every regiment possesses a private pet, which has very often to be left behind on embarkation, as the regulations on this subject are very strict.

In India Tommy keeps any number of pets, and on his return loves to bring a parrot with him. The regulations allow twenty-five per cent. of the men to bring home parrots, and I have seen as many as 300 or more of these birds distributed about the troop-deck.

During the hot weather large sail baths are rigged up in each well deck for the use of the troops. Regiments returning home make good use of these baths, though the outward-bound men are not very partial to too much cold water. It is, indeed, surprising what a difference there is between the outward and homeward bound soldiers, both as regards cleanliness and general capability. One year in India does them more good than four years' service at home.

Tommy's great delight is to get a little information from one of the ship's officers as to the speed of the vessel, the probable time of her arrival at the port, or, better still, something about the weather. Possessed of this knowledge, he will inform his pals "that according to his judgment" the ship ought to be going at such and such a speed, or, "the sea will increase as we round the next point," at which latter piece of information he has the satisfaction of seeing his hearers making tracks for more pickles, and feels bound to back his opinion by following suit.

Almost every voyage the outward-bound transport passes the homeward-bound one in the Suez Canal, and then there is a free exchange of compliments, the returning warriors generally, by virtue of their undoubtedly sounder premises, getting the better of the good-humoured wordy warfare.

Waiting to disembark.

"You're going the wrong way," "'Ow's yer liver?" and enquiries as to whether their respective mothers are aware they have left home, greet the India-bound troops, who reply with similar sallies, the while the bands on both vessels attempt to drown each other, and continue to play lively, and more or less appropriate, airs, until they eventually steam out of hearing.

No cavalry regiments, with the exception of those bound for the Cape, carry their horses with them, and only the chargers of the colonel, the senior major, and the adjutant, besides the Government stud horses, accompany the soldiers on their outward voyage. For these, special grooms are carried, and one of these men is in attendance on his four-footed charges night and day.

The transports generally arrive at their destination between the hours of six and eight a.m. On such occasions the troops have to turn out at four a.m., return all the ship's gear, pay for deficiencies, and prepare themselves for disembarkation.

Naturally the greatest bustle prevails, but it is remarkable how quickly each soldier procures his own rifle, bayonet, and valise. At Bombay huge baskets of helmets are sent off to be fitted on the troops before they land, for during the voyage those who use them at all wear helmets supplied by the ship. At some of the ports there are no wharves at which the ships can come alongside. At Durban, for instance, they lie in the open roadstead, and here the troops have to be landed in baskets accommodating four at a time.

Once on land again, Tommy quickly becomes the smart, dapper fellow we know so well; and, in the novelties of colonial experience, soon forgets the trials and pleasures of the trip across, and settles down into the admirable fighting machine that Rudyard Kipling has immortalised, on whose glorious deeds no Briton is ever tired of expatiating.

FOREWARNED
a Story
of the
Intelligence
Department

By Major Arthur Griffiths
AUTHOR OF
"The Queen's Shilling,"
"The Rome Express,"
"The Wellington Memorial,"
etc., etc.

## SYNOPSIS OF PREVIOUS CHAPTERS.

Captain Wood is an officer on the staff of the Intelligence Department of the War Office engaged with certain confidential questions pending with the United States Government. It is the height of the London season, and he is sleeping late after a ball, when he is roused to hear some startling news. A lawyer, Mr. Quinlan, has called to tell him that an unknown relative, an American millionaire, has left him a colossal fortune. Almost at the same moment an American detective warns him that he has enemies plotting against him and his fortune, and that he goes in imminent danger of his life. Arrived at the Intelligence Office, where he is late, he is sharply reprimanded, but explains, and is given some especially confidential work to carry through connected with an attack on New York. Returning to his chambers, he again meets the American detective, who details the nature of the plot against his fortune and the military secrets he possesses. After office hours he starts for the Park in quest of the young lady with whom he is in love. He sees her in the Row, but she cuts him dead. Returning disconsolate to his club, he is invited by an American acquaintance, Lawford, to join a party at the opera, where he meets the Duke and Duchess of Tierra Sagrada. At the opera, Wood's suspicions of foul play are strengthened, but he goes on with his new friends to other entertainments and, at last, meets Frida Wolstenholme at a ball, where he makes his peace, proposes, and is accepted. He picks up a cab, and scarcely settles into it when he is attacked, hocussed, and loses consciousness. Recovering at length, he finds himself tied and bound, and subjected to a cruel and painful ordeal.

## CHAPTER IX. *(continued).*

"YOUR signature to certain papers—deeds of gift, surrender, and assignment—legal documents by which you transfer, of your own free will, the bulk of your fortune to this Guild."

"I will sign nothing of the kind," I said without hesitation, hotly

"That we shall see. Bring the documents; place them on the table before him; loosen his right arm."

In obedience to this order an outstretched hand thrust several parchments under my eyes. I was struck by this hand. It was a well-shaped, well-cared-for hand, rather dark-skinned, but scrupulously clean—the hand of a gentleman, or, at least, of one who had done and did no hard work.

Another point caught my attention and fixed it just for one moment, something that I quickly realised might prove of great importance by-and-bye, if I won out of my present trouble. I saw what might, if committed to memory, afford a clue to identity at some future time.

The hand was margined by the conventional white shirt cuff, but this, in the movement with the papers, had been caught and drawn back so as to bare the wrist and expose the forearm some way up.

On this fleshy part there was a mark, a tattoo mark, a curious device rather less than an inch square, which is here figured:—

G

U ❖ E

G

"Once more!" The cold, hard voice recalled me to my situation. "Think well how you will act. Put your hand to those papers, and you shall be molested no further. You shall be escorted to your rooms in Clarges Street and left in peace. There will be no outward change in your situation; you may still pose as a rich man. We do not grudge you a fine income and an ample expenditure. But that will be dependent on our good will. What we may grant you we may also withdraw. You will hold everything—your whole fortune, your very life—at our disposal, if occasion should arise. Should you fail us—well, you have heard the penalties of treachery or disobedience visited upon the brethren of the Guild——"

"I am not a member, and will never become one."

"We shall see. But be advised. Come in freely and without coercion. You shall be warmly accepted by us, you may take a leading part then among us, become—who knows?—a member of the council and dictate terms to others as we are now putting pressure on you."

"I tell you it is useless. I will sign nothing under compulsion."

"Think, Wood. Consider the alternative. You must choose between life and death."

"You mean to murder me?"

"Ah! Does that touch you? You cling to life, perhaps? Now, in the heyday of your youth, with all to make life joyous—health, wealth, the love of woman."

The vision of my darling rose before me to intensify the bitterness of my trial.

"But we shall not kill you, Wood—not outright. That were too merciful, too easy a restitution for your obstinate contumacy. We would rather you lived as the slave and servant of the Guild, which prefers to work through you rather than after you. For that reason we demand your submission, and if you will not make it of your own accord we must force and compel you—we have the means."

I laughed aloud, daring them to do their worst; but my heart sank within me as, in the same metallic, passionless voice, the president unfolded their plans.

"We shall hold you here, or elsewhere, a close prisoner in our hands until you yield. The place is remote—secret; it has been specially prepared for your reception. No one will seek you here, or, indeed, anywhere, for the world shall be made to believe that your disappearance has been voluntary. What say you? Will you sign?"

"I would rather die."

"You shall not die—you shall live, I tell you, live to suffer daily, hourly, a living death, without mercy or compunction, until you sign We shall starve you, flog you, torture you continually. Lay all this well to heart——"

"Fiends! Hell hounds!" I cried, goaded nearly to madness, but still without a thought of surrender. "I dare and defy you."

"This has gone far enough. We will bandy words no longer with you. The tribunal leaves you to ponder over its warnings, to weigh well the alternative of resisting it or accepting its clemency. But that you may fully realise its power and the dread weapons it wields, there shall be now administered one touch of our quality."

At these words I was overwhelmed with a new spasm of pain. The stab of a thousand knife points, the scathing torture of fire, made me scream aloud. Then a horror of black darkness fell upon me. I seemed to be swallowed up in a vast bottomless abyss, and lost all sense of being in absolute annihilation.

## CHAPTER X.

### From Saul J. Snuyzer, of Messrs. Saraband and Sons, of New York City and Chicago, Ill.

In my earnest desire to further the wishes and interests of your firm, I visited the gentleman named in your last pleasure, and put before him briefly and with much circumspection the reasons why he should secure the services of Messrs. Saraband and Sons. Captain Wood did not respond very cordially to my proposal, which he guessed was not serious. It is my settled conviction now that he would give the earth to reconsider that hasty and mistaken reply.

As I was satisfied he would yet be glad to put himself under your protection, I proceeded to set a private watch on him at once. This has led to rather unforeseen and, I regret to add, unfortunate results. I must mail this letter to-day, and, so far, I can do no more than report my proceedings.

I was fully conscious, from the outline you forwarded of the nefarious designs projected against Captain Wood, that he was likely to soon find himself fixed up in a tight corner, but I was not exactly prepared for the promptitude with which his enemies would operate.

I shadowed him the evening of the first day, now just forty-eight hours ago, following him to the Hyde Park, to his club, to his house. I was at first in my own clothes, but I changed to the disguise of a street rough, and as such was much interfered with, I may state, by the London police. In this dead-gone country a man is judged by the coat he wears.

In Hyde Park only one person spoke to Mr. Wood. I knew him by sight and name—a half American, Jimmy Lawford—having crossed with him once in the same Cunarder and taken a hand in the same game of poker in the smoking saloon. He passed then as an ocean drummer, although some said he was engaged in the Secret Service of the Federal Government; now, I take it, he just loafs around. Just the sort of chap to be in this crowd against Wood.

I did not hear what he said to Wood, but when leaving by the Park gates I noticed Jimmy in close talk with a hansom cabman, who had got off his perch, and was very particular to hear what Lawford said.

I only caught the last word or two: "Any time to-night or to-morrow night. You'll get the office, mind you're on the *quee vee*."

Something told me that this talk between Lawford and the hackman might have to do with Captain Wood. I just made the lucky shot, and when I got the chance I warned my gentleman not to trust himself in strange cabs.

He did not cotton to my advice much, as you will see. I thought at first he had, for he left the Opera in a smart carriage with friends. I got behind. We travelled west, and at Rutland Gate I learnt that the carriage was that of some Spanish Duke; but it meant nothing to me. Only as an agent I am bound to place that Duke, and I propose to make some enquiries concerning him to-day or to-morrow.

After Rutland Gate Captain Wood made two calls; the second was a late one, in Prince's Gate, and it was nigh on 3 a.m. before he came out.

I was still hanging about, although dog tired, and just by his elbow when he saw two ladies into their carriage. I heard him say plainly:

"Good night, Mrs. Wolstenholme; good night, Frida. I shall be round in Hill Street before lunch."

Then he must have caught sight of me, for he turned in a tantrum, and I was hard put to it to face him.

"See here, my friend," he says very sharply, "what's your game? You've been at my heels all day. What d'ye mean by it? Speak up, or I'll hand you over to the first policeman."

All at once the tone of his voice changed, and he burst out into a great laugh.

"Oh, good Lord!" he cried. "It it's not that blessed Yankee detective. Why, you garden idiot, if you can't do it better than that, who do you suppose would employ you?"

"Easy, guv'nor, easy," I answered, as bold as possible. "I don't know yer, and yer don't know me. Cab or carriage, sir? What name, sir?"

He was not to be humbugged that way, and he told me so. "I see it, see it all; but it's not good enough, Mr. Snuyzer. Now, be pleased to clear out. You go one way, I go the other. Walk right away."

I felt uncommonly foolish, but he was not to be gainsaid; and we parted, taking opposite directions.

It was not for long, however. I turned as soon as I thought it safe, and again made after Mr. Wood.

I could see nothing of him, although the road ran straight as far as the Knightsbridge Barracks. But I pressed on, expecting to overtake him. Then a cab passed, and I was for taking it, but the man would not answer my hail. It rolled on ahead, and I thought I had lost it till I saw it stop quite short in the street.

"Got a fare after all," that was my idea, until I heard a couple of short, sharp shouts, and back comes the cab ten miles an hour, cabbie standing up and flogging his horse like mad.

It was so near daylight that I got a view inside the hansom as it passed me full tilt. I caught sight in that short moment of a muss of people inside the cab, two or more men struggling and fighting with someone underneath them.

Of course, Captain Wood was being hocussed and carried off. I reckoned that up on the spot, and gathered myself together then and there to give chase to the cab.

I followed it steadily down the Kensington Road, losing my distance, of course, very fast. By the time I reached the High Street I had lost the cab.

But a man at an early coffee stall had seen it pass holding straight on the main road towards Holland House. I heard of it again at St. Mary Abbott's Terrace, and was told that it had turned up Addison Road. I traced it by Holland Road to Shepherd's Bush Green, and there a herring was drawn across the scent.

I was on the track now of two cabs, one going by the Shepherd's Bush or Uxbridge Road, the other by the Starch Green Road.

I followed the first, and drew blank. It was a night hawk working home to his stables, and where, by-and-bye, I caught the chap settling into his crib. He swore he hadn't had a fare for the last two hours, and I could see he was speaking truth, for his horse had not turned a hair.

I harked back then to the Starch Green Road, asking all and several for my galloping hansom cab. There were very few people about at this early hour, only the policemen, and they looked very shy at my tramp's clothes, giving no answer. A loafer I met winked when I spoke, suggested that the cab was "on the cross," and bid me mind my eye. At last a couple of decent farm folk bringing in milk told me they had passed a hansom with a worn horse on the far side of Hammersmith Bridge, in the district of Barnes.

By the time I reached the Strathallan Road it was broad daylight. I found a long road of detached villa houses, each in its own garden, many with stables adjoining. I figured it out, as I walked up and down this road twice, that one of these cottages was just suited for the purpose of sequestrating Captain Wood, if he could be gotten to it. He could be driven straight into the stable-yard; the cab would be no more seen when the coach-house door closed behind him, and no one neither the neighbours nor the police, would be a bit the wiser as to what mischief was being worked inside.

It took me just two hours to examine the entrance gates of every villa house with stables in that road. In three of

"Watch it, young squire, with both your eyes"

them there were the new tracks of wheels marked plainly in the thick-lying summer dust. I could not discover which were the most recent, but I carefully noted the numbers of these houses, meaning to put a watch upon them all.

I called up the boy Joseph Vialls—a very smart young squire, too—from the office in Norfolk Street, as soon as I could get a telegram through. By the time he arrived, I had narrowed my investigations to a single point for further observation

The day had so far advanced that the business of life was well begun. I saw the blinds drawn up in two of the houses, the front doors opened, the women helps busy shaking the mats and washing down the stoops. Presently some of the young folks ran out into the gardens, and I could see the family gatherings round the breakfast tables, from which on the early morning air came the smell of hot coffee and Eng ish breakfast bacon, with the temptation of Tantalus for a starving man who had been out all night.

All this while the third house remained closed, hermetically sealed. It was closed up, tight shuttered, not a sign of life in it.

If there was a mystery in any part of this Strathallan Road, it was surely in there behind those silent walls. This third house I especially recommended to Joseph's attention when he joined me.

"Watch it, young squire, with both your eyes, and if you see anything strange, anyone come out or go in, just wire me to Norfolk Street and to Dumbleton, and I will come right to you ; only be careful you're not seen yourself."

As soon as I was certain he quite understood his orders, I made the best of my way back to the town.

For, you see, gentlemen, although I had a strong presumption that Captain Wood had been carried off in this cab, I was by no means certain. The fact of his disappearance must be verified, if I was to act with any assurance on the strange information I thought had come within my knowledge.

### CHAPTER XI.

WHEN I reached my lodgings in Norfolk Street I was pretty well washed out. After a long day I had been on the track the whole night through, without a wink of sleep or a scrap of food. A detective needs to have a robust constitution, and mine is tricksy, in spite of the care I take of myself. But let that pass. I know my duty, and I do not shrink from it.

But I turned in for an hour after treating myself with two meat extract capsules in boiling water, with a "pacifying pastille." It is a Philadelphia patent, and I can strongly recommend it as a tonic and pick-me-up.

At 10 a.m. I woke much refreshed, and dressed myself with care, having regard to my self-respect, my high place in your confidence, and the probable requirements of the business in hand.

As I dressed I pondered deeply over this business, and the course that I should adopt. My first and most urgent duty was to secure the release of Mr. Wood, always supposing that my gentleman was the person actually carried off in the cab.

At present I had no certainty of this, only a bit more than strong suspicion. Yet if I could ascertain that he had not returned home I should be justified in taking surmise for fact.

Before going out I called in Dumbleton, the second assistant, from the office, which, as you have been informed, is *en suite* with my own rooms, and desired him to remain on duty until he saw me again. He was not to quit the place for all the earth, to attend to the telephone, and receive all telegrams. I was expecting to hear from Joseph Vialls at the Strathallan Road.

Then I went to Clarges Street. The man there remembered me, but looked strangely when I inquired for Captain Wood.

"You have not heard the news, then?" he said.

"What in thunder is there to hear more than I have to tell you?" I asked, nettled at thinking someone was before me.

"Why, that the Captain has met with an accident."

"What sort? When? Where? Isn't he at home?"

"At home, bless your heart ! Of course not. He slipped up somehow last night, or early this morning, and hurt himself badly."

"Who told you that story? Do you believe it?"

"I believe the Captain's own hand-writing."

"What did he say, exactly?" I was quite taken aback, as you may suppose, but did not want to show it too much.

"Here, read it for yourself. It's not all his own, of course, and you will understand why. But that's his name at the bottom there, sure enough."

It was written on good grey note-paper, in a fair running hand, and it said

"Savory, I've come to grief driving home. Horse slipped up on the curb, and I was thrown out of the cab. Some kind people picked me up and are taking good care of me. But I shan't be able to move hand or foot for some days. Send me by bearer portmanteau of things, shirts, dressing gown, dittoes, cheque-book, letters, papers, and the rest.
　　　　　　　　　　　　　　　　　　Yours,
　　　　　　　　　　　　　　　　　　　　"W. A. WOOD.

"17A, Laburnum Street, Harrow Road."

"And you sent them—how?"

"By the cab that brought the letter."

"Why didn't you go with them yourself?"

"I thought of it, certainly, and I wish I had."

"You may well wish that. And now if you will be guided by me you'll go and find out 17A, Laburnum Street right away, if there's any such place at all."

"Oh, but there is. It's in the directory."

"Is that so? Well, if you come across Mr. Wood there I'll run you for next President of the United States. You've got just the face for a postage stamp."

"What in the name of conscience d'ye mean? What's 'appened to him, then?"

"It's my opinion that Captain Wood has fallen among thieves, brigands, worse—ruffians, who'll hold him to ransom for blackmail, rob, murder him, God knows what, unless some of us can circumvent their blackguard manœuvres. And I am going to try. I don't believe in cab accidents and Laburnum Streets. You may, so you'd better go and judge for yourself."

"I'm going now at once." With that he set to whistling, and the Captain's dog, a beast with whom I had a fierce encounter the day before and was beaten badly, came bounding down the stairs.

"The Captain 'll be glad to see Roy. I wonder he didn't ask for him. They can't bear to be parted long, dog least of all. Wherever Captain Wood is, Roy wants to be there too. He'd find him any day in the thickest crowd."

He was not going to find him in Laburnum Street, I was pretty sure of that, but it was right to look there, on the off chance that this story was true. For myself, I was more than ever persuaded of foul play, and I considered I was bound to lay the whole matter before the London police.

I was not very well received at Scotland Yard. I never thought they'd go back on one of their own sort, but they wouldn't allow I was a partner at all, and the head man I saw—an inspector only, for the colonels, and captains, and commissioners were as invisible as the editor of a New York daily—looked me up and down with a jeer and a sneer.

"Oh, you're one of them brilliant private detecs," he said, "that puts us professionals straight, and wipes all our eyes, eh? Such bloomin' clever people want no help or advice from us. You play your own game, your own way."

They put my back up, still I talked to them fairly and civilly. There was too much in the business to risk failure by getting mad. But I couldn't work it at all.

"We don't know who you are," said the inspector at last. "That's the plain straight tip for you. Bring us proper credentials ; that card of Sarabands is no good. Anyone can show a card. Get a certificate from your Consul. If he'll warrant and support you, we'll take the thing up. Can't do it on your own simple statement—not such a tale as that ; no, not by no means. Good day."

I was terribly riled, but, not to waste time, I took a cab straight to Great St. Helen's, where, of course, I was perfectly well known. One of the senior clerks came to me directly.

"What can we do for you, Mr. Snuyzer? Want an introduction to the Metropolitan Police? Why, certainly. Reckon it's no use asking what you're after? Big case?"

He was a friend, and had often given me information in a small way. I thought perhaps he might help me now, for I'd heard from you they were mostly Americans working this conspiracy, and it was likely enough they'd know at the Consulate whether any big "toughs" and "bunco men" were in London just then.

"It's something to do with the McFaught millions," I said. "You've heard, no doubt, of that young Englishman's luck?"

"Scissors ! why, yes. He was here this very morning, only an hour ago." (It was then about one o'clock.) "Captain William Aretas Wood, they called him. Is he your client?"

It hit me like a blow this news, for I saw at once what it meant. Captain Wood could not be lying injured in a street off the Harrow Road and walking about Great St. Helen's. I wanted no more proof of foul play.

"We are acting for Captain Wood. Case of attempted fraud. They've soon found he's fair game. But what brought him here, if I may ask?"

*(To be continued).*

Photo. Russell & Sons.     Baker Street.

*LIEUTENANT-GENERAL SIR F. W. E. F FORESTIER-WALKER.*

L IEUTENANT-GENERAL SIR F. W. E. F. FORESTIER-WALKER has the distinction of being the
youngest lieutenant-general on the effective list, and is not yet fifty-four.  He is a Scots Guardsman,
having joined that regiment, as an ensign, in 1862, and left it, as lieutenant-colonel, in 1886.  His main
foreign and war service has been in South Africa, where he was for several years assistant military secretary.
He served in the Kaffir War of 1878, for which he received the C.B., and his conduct also earned him mention in
despatches.  During the Zulu War of 1879 he was the principal staff officer to No. 1 column, was present at the
action of Inyeyane, and formed one of the force shut up in Ekowe.  After the relief, he served on the line of
communications, and was in command of Fort Pearson and the Lower Tugela district.  He next accompanied
the Bechuanaland Expedition, 1884-85, in the capacity of assistant adjutant and quartermaster-general, and for
his services therein received the C.M.G.  He commanded in Egypt from 1890-95, and is now in command
of the Western District.  His well-earned promotion to K.C.B. came to him in 1894.

# OLD BATTLE-FIELDS—HASTINGS.

OF all the characteristics of the English race, none is more permanent and striking than their intense hatred of any foreign rule. It was to this feeling that Harold, son of Earl Godwin, owed his support from the nation on his succeeding to the throne of Edward the Confessor. And he needed all the support obtainable, for he was soon beset with troubles on all sides. The first blow was struck by his brother Tostig, formerly Earl of Northumberland, who had fled the country after the Northumbrians' revolt, and had entered into negotiations with Harold Hardrada, King of Norway. Thereupon a Norwegian fleet ravaged the Yorkshire coast, Scarborough was taken and burned, and a decisive victory gained at Fulford. Harold immediately hastened with his household troops to the North, and engaged the Norwegians in a desperate engagement at Stamford Bridge, in which Harold Hardrada and Tostig were killed.

Harold had no time to rejoice over this victory before he heard the news that William had landed at Pevensey, and was ravaging the country all along the coast. To put an end to this, he was forced to hurry South, and to give battle without delay. Arriving in London, he hastily summoned his subjects to arms, and then determined to have at least the advantage of choosing his own ground. Arriving at Senlac, a "low spur of the Sussex Downs," there Harold arrayed his somewhat motley army—in one long line, extending to almost a mile in length, facing the South, and defended all

Photo. Valentine & Sons.        Dundee.

*THE HILL OF TELHAM.*

along the front by a rough trench and a strong palisade. The land sloped gently down to marshy ground on the right, to the centre it sloped more steeply, while again to the left the approach was comparatively easy. In the centre, round the Royal Standard and the Golden Dragon of Wessex, were ranged Harold's bodyguard, or *hus-carls*, clad in full armour, and wielding heavy axes; the English having learnt the art of military equipment from the Danes, who had settled in the country after their numerous incursions. On the flanks were the less heavily armed troops, and the masses of untrained men who had flocked to obey Harold's summons to fight against the invader.

*THE SCENE OF HAROLD'S DEATH.*

From the mound of Telham, William surveyed the English position. He had no alternative but to fight. To remain on the defensive meant starvation; to march to London without fighting, even if it were possible, would have led to his being cut off from his ships. He posted his men in three rows—archers in front, next the armed men on foot, then the armed horsemen.

Under cover of a deadly shower of arrows from the first line, a general advance was made, followed by a charge on the centre of the English position by the knights, while the mercenaries gathered from Brittany and Maine attacked their flanks. But determined and furious as the charge was, it made no impression on the stockade. The Normans fell back disheartened, and became entangled in the marshy ground on their left. A rumour was spread that William was killed. Something very like a panic ensued, and if it had not been for his decision and resolution in rallying his troops, the battle would have been lost. Gathering his men together once again, he led another furious charge which broke down the English defences, though it could not shatter the steady row of warriors, who remained almost unmoved by the shock.

William now saw that his only hope of victory was to make another charge from the left and then to draw the English from their position by feint of flight.

This he did with great success. Then, ordering his men to turn on their enemies, they made another charge, and the hill seemed almost won. At six in the evening the issue of the battle was still in doubt.

The High Altar of Battle Abbey now marks the position of the Royal Standard, round which the struggle was longest and fiercest, Harold's bodyguard showing the utmost determination never to yield, but to fight, if need be, till not a man should be left.

At last, ordering his archers forward to shoot into the air, so that the arrows should fall on the heads of the English, and at the same time leading another charge, William soon completed the victory. One of the first victims of the arrows was Harold himself, who fell shot through the eye, and the battle ended in a desperate hand-to-hand fight over his dead body. Night coming on, the Conqueror pitched his tent on the exact spot where Harold fell, and "sate down to eat and drink among the dead."

Photos Bradshaw        Hastings.

*SENLAC.*

Photo: F. G. O. S. Gregory & Co., 51, Strand.

Copyright.—Hudson & Kearns.

## YEOMEN OF THE GUARD.

H ER MAJESTY'S Body Guard of the Yeomen of the Guard was instituted by King Henry VII., and did duty for the first time at the coronation of that monarch on the 30th October, 1485. Since that date it has invariably been on duty on all occasions of State or Royal ceremony. The corps consists of 140 yeomen, all of whom have been non-commissioned officers in the Army and are decorated for service in the field. It is commanded by a captain, who is always a peer, but not necessarily a military officer. The appointment is purely political. The other officers are the lieutenant, the ensign, the clerk of the cheque and adjutant, and four Exons, all of whom must have held commissions in the Army or Royal Marines, and have seen service. The first captain was John de Vere Earl of Oxford. Earl Waldegrave, the well-known rifle shot and enthusiastic volunteer, now fills the office.

# FOOTBALL IN THE ARMY

FOR some years the authorities have encouraged the pursuit of football in the Army. Nor can the value of such an excellent sport be over-rated. It develops not only the physical but the mental faculties of the soldier, and is productive of courage, self-reliance, and dash.

Each company in a battalion has its own team, and strives to eclipse the others by systematic training and constant practice. The best players in the battalion are, of course, chosen to play for the regimental team. On no occasion are men of all ranks so excited as when an inter-regimental match is being played. Indeed, a contest for the Army Cup is considered an event of much graver moment than a royal review or gigantic field-day. As is befitting, this

TEAM OF 51—65 REGIMENTAL DISTRICT.

Photo. Wheeldon.

TEAM OF "F" COMPANY 2nd BATTALION ROYAL IRISH FUSILIERS.

Photo Raftery

TEAM OF 2nd BATTALION NORTH STAFFORDSHIRE REGIMENT.

healthy rivalry is fostered by the officers, who themselves frequently are pillars of the regimental team.

The last photograph on this page is that of the team of the 2nd Battalion North Stafford-shire Regiment. It is among those teams which compete this season for the Army Cup, and beat that of the Argyll and Sutherland Highlanders by two goals to one. At the time of going to press it has yet to play the team of the Black Watch—or Royal Highlanders, to use their more modern title. A tough battle between the two may reasonably be expected. Colonel Williams, who evinces a strong interest in the game, appears on the right, and the Quartermaster, Lieutenant Burrage, on the left.

Colonel Clark, the officer commanding the 51—65 Regimental District, is another officer who encourages football among his men. He has presented a shield to be competed for yearly by the depôts of the Yorkshire Light Infantry and the York and Lancaster Regiment at Pontefract. If a team wins two out of three times, its name is engraved on the shield. The first match took place on the 16th December, 1897, and was won by the team of the depôt King's Own Yorkshire Light Infantry by three goals to two. A representation of the shield is seen between the two teams in the upper photograph, taken by Colour-Sergeant Hewes, of the 3rd Battalion King's Own Yorkshire Light Infantry.

Not only are regiments accustomed to compete. There exists a healthy rivalry between companies of the same battalion. The remaining photograph shows the team of "F" Company 2nd Batt. Royal Irish Fusiliers as composed last season. It was successful against "B" "E" and "G" Companies, and won the company challenge shield, which is shown in the centre of the group. Such enviable trophies have combined to make football the most popular pastime in the Army.

# THE AFRIDI WAR.

WE are able in this issue to place before our readers a very interesting series of photographs, which not only illustrate the life of our troops now fighting on the North-West Frontier, but also bring vividly before us the difficult nature of the country for military operations. The first group of officers are those of the 9th Bengal Infantry, one of those glorious Ghoorka rifle regiments whose name is now as well known and loved in England as it is in India. In another photograph the regiment is shown fallen in and prepared to man the breastworks of the entrenched encampment at Bara.

The 9th Ghoorka Rifles inherit the battle honours of Bhurtpore and Sobraon, served through the last war in Afghanistan, and are now again doing yeomen's service in the same wild country. The group of turbaned officers wearing the steel chain shoulder straps are those of the 9th Bengal Cavalry. This is the corps with whose fame India rang in the Mutiny days, when it was the celebrated Hodson's Horse, and since the Mutiny it has seen service in Egypt and Chitral, but was not employed in the last Afghan War. The group well illustrates what lots of opportunities for seeing service fall in the way of the Indian officer, for it will be noted that out of the ten officers only three fail to sport a medal ribbon. In another group are depicted the officers and non-commissioned officers of the commissariat and transport staff of the Peshawar column. Behind them

*OFFICERS OF THE 9th GHOORKAS.*

*COLONEL GARSTON AND OFFICERS, 9th BENGAL LANCERS.*

From Photos.                                    By a Military Officer.
*OFFICERS of the COMMISSARIAT and TRANSPORT, PESHAWAR COLUMN.*

a group of fine bearded Lancers represent the Bengal cavalry attached to them for escort and orderly duties. Not much glory or honour is to be won out of the work that these men have to do, but none the less is it true that the safety of the Army and the whole success of operations are in a very great measure in their hands. It would be impossible to overrate the difficulties in the way of organising and transporting supplies in a country such as the troops have of late been campaigning in. The public, therefore, should remember that in every campaign a very large portion of the credit for any successful operation should go to the commissariat and transport staff.

From our photographs a very good idea of the nature of the country is to be obtained, and they show well the stony character of the level ground and the sparseness of the vegetation, with, for a background, the bare rugged hills through whose defiles the troops have to fight, and over which the long miles of supply train have to be unwearyingly and unceasingly guarded. The men in the curious costumes are not, as might be imagined, some sort of foreign miners, but our own sturdy lads of the Oxfordshire Light Infantry, clad in the Balaclava caps and warm winter jackets served out to them, for it can be cold, and bitter, deadly cold in the Tirah uplands.

In another photograph—that of the group in which the front rank are kneeling with their rifles at the ready—a section of "F" Company of the Oxfordshire is shown, and illustrates excellently the Service kit worn under ordinary weather conditions in India. A not unimportant function of camp life is shown in the photograph of the officers of the Inniskilling Fusiliers at breakfast in the camp at Bara. No man can either fight or march well on an empty stomach, and, judging from the well-supplied tables, the officers of the Inniskillings don't mean to.

In camp at Bara a meal in the open may be enjoyed in peace and comfort, but when the wily sniper was about, it was not at all improbable that the meal a man was sitting down to would be his last, and, moreover, that he would not live to finish it. More than once during the campaign officers were shot by snipers while actually at meals.

In the large photograph the lines of the Inniskilling Fusiliers in camp at Bara are depicted, the time being high noon. It will be noted that in the foreground of the picture there are associated with the British soldiers a number of native soldiers, who, from the quoit in their turbans, evidently belong to a Sikh regiment. They seem on excellent terms with their white comrades, and are, probably, a native regiment brigaded with them. No more speaking testimony to the excellent morale of the Indian Army exists than the cordial *camaraderie* that so often springs up between a British and a native regiment.

The photograph which represents General Hammond and his staff reconnoitring the Gandao Pass on November 5th is another one that very interestingly illustrates the hill scenery in this part of the world. In certain places thick pine forest is to be found; but hills bare of vegetation, desolate boulder-strewn plains, are generally the distinctive features of the landscape.

One of the smaller pictures gives us a very good idea of the sort of accommo-

*THE OXFORDS IN BALACLAVA CAPS AND WINTER SERVICE JACKETS.*

dation the officer has to put up with when campaigning under these conditions. The small tent is his abode, and protection from the heat of the mid-day sun and the bitter cold of the winter night. This officer, however, fares fairly well, for the men of his company have turned to and considerably improved the protection by surrounding the hut with a stone wall and roofing the enclosure in with brush-wood—a proceeding that will cause its occupant to sleep considerably warmer than before.

The two other landscape scenes are of very special interest, as they illustrate the celebrated position of Dargai, the storming of which aroused such keen enthusiasm at home.

The first photograph shows the position as seen from the Chagru Kotal. The Chagru Kotal was the position held by the guns under the support of whose fire the infantry advanced to the attack. A glance at the position is enough to show how, held by brave and determined men armed with weapons of precision, magnificently defensible it was, and to explain the great loss of life that was involved by its capture.

In the other landscape we see in the centre the village of

*OFFICERS OF THE INNISKILLINGS AT BREAKFAST.*

From Photos.                                                                                    By a Military Officer.

*THE OXFORDSHIRE LIGHT INFANTRY IN SERVICE KIT.*

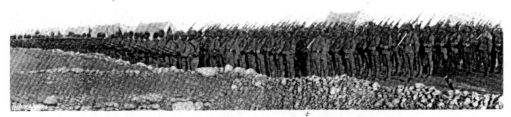

*THE 9TH GHOORKAS MANNING THE BREASTWORKS AT BARA.*

Dargai, now burned by our soldiers. In the foreground the portion of the encampment shown consists of the quarter-guard and hospital. In the background the mighty Dargai hill, Narikh Suk as it is generally called, stands out against

Finally, of the greatest interest are the two groups of Afridis, showing in the one an Afridi company of the 27th Punjab Infantry, the other the same men, dressed not in uniform, but in their own tribal costumes. But few

*GENERAL HAMMOND AND STAFF RECONNOITRING GANDAO PASS.*

the sky-line. This hill was, after the engagement, occupied, and became the principal heliographing or signalling station between Shinawari and the front.

regiments of the Indian Army are entitled to enlist Afridis, and of these the 27th is one, and magnificent soldiers they make ; for though proud, fierce, and vindictive, they can, by

From Photos.     By a Military Officer

*THE INNISKILLING FUSILIERS IN CAMP AT BARA.*

judicious handling, be subordinated to discipline, and are never deficient in those qualities of courage, endurance, and hardihood which go to make a good soldier. And hardly ever have these men proved untrue to their salt, but have

AN OFFICER'S SLEEPING QUARTERS.

always been faithful and loyal, with but rare exceptions. It is true that there have been exceptions, but they are so few that they ought not to give rise to a suspicion of the fidelity of the frontiersmen actually enlisted into our own Army. When Lord Roberts's force was storming the Peiwar Kotal, an Afridi of one of the regiments fired a shot to give the alarm to

DARGAI, FROM CHAGRU KOTAL.

From Photos.　　　　By a Military Officer.

AFRIDI COMPANY 27th PUNJAB INFANTRY IN UNIFORM.

Afridis 27th Punjab Infantry in Oriental Costume.

the enemy, and was immediately bayoneted. Again, during a recent frontier campaign, two shots were fired during a night advance. Isolated cases of this kind are all that can be brought against the Pathan in our ranks, though over and over again, in frontier campaigns, he has fought for us against his

From Photos.　　　　By a Military Officer.

THE SCENE OF THE FAMOUS CHARGE.

own or kindred races. Of the men here shown many have their homes, relatives, and families in Tirah. Those homes have been burned to the ground, their relatives, friends, and families are now homeless and foodless, and exposed to all the rigours of a severe winter in the higher ranges of the Tirah mountains; and yet, though many Afridis are with different regiments at the front, there have been scarcely any desertions. In truth, the anger of the men seems to have been bitterly aroused against their fellow clansmen. They consider them foolish and blameworthy for having taken up arms against a Government that has always treated them with justice and fairness, and deem that the punishment that has been meted out to them has been fully deserved. The Afridis, as a tribe, are one of the largest and most important of all the frontier tribes, and their geographical position renders them doubly of importance, for it is this tribe which controls the Khyber Pass, practically the main trade channel between India and Cabul. The groups shown in our illustrations represent all the important sub-sections of this great tribe, such as the Malikdeen Kheyls, Kuki Kheyls, Zakka Kheyls, Orukzais, etc., etc. Though bitterly fanatical and revengeful, the Pathan has his good points, and many a border thief is a gentleman at heart, as witness Kamal in Kipling's fine ballad "East and West." Moreover, he is a fighting man born and bred, and, when the British officer has had his way with him, makes a trooper, or a rifleman, not easy to beat.

# THE
# NAVY & ARMY
## ILLUSTRATED.

*FRIDAY, FEBRUARY 25th, 1898.*

# Our Citizen Army.—III.

## By CALLUM BEG.

Photo. Payre & Gard.    *SERGEANT, WEST KENT YEOMANRY, 1897.*    Catford.

THE past year of Jubilee has done much to bring Our Citizen Army into close touch with the Regular Forces. During the time of rejoicing in the Capital all branches of the Service were to be seen marching together, living together, and, when off duty, fraternising freely. Nor did this happy state of comradeship exist only among our troops at home. Greater Britain was not behind the Mother Country in patriotism. From every part of the globe Colonial volunteers and men of the permanent forces willingly came to do honour to the Queen. These, too, were welcomed by civilians and soldiers alike, and formed strong links in the chain of universal brotherhood which binds us to our Colonies.

In 1897 the nation learned more of those who are ready to defend its rights than it could have done at any previous period. Indeed, one could learn much as to the appearance of different regiments, both at that time and in the past, by viewing the pageant as it passed on its way to St. Paul's. The occasion was one that invited a retrospect—a comparison between our troops of to-day and those that marched under the British flag in 1837. Even during the reign of Queen Victoria every branch of the Service has undergone innumerable changes.

It is, perhaps, in the matter of dress that these are most apparent to the civilian, in so far as a gay uniform has stronger attractions for the majority than dry statistics or voluminous military history.

The events of last year are still fresh in the memory of all. The first illustration is, therefore, one that may well demand some share of our attention. If less serviceable, the uniform is more picturesque than that of the present day. The old coatee somewhat resembles the uniform of the modern lancer, though the scales or epaulettes—a useful protection to the shoulders—have long vanished into oblivion. The horse

TROOPER, DRILL ORDER, WEST KENT YEOMANRY, 1897.

instead of being attached to the belt of the rider as in 1837, is fastened to the saddle. This, in itself, has a military significance. If the hussar parts company with his charger, he is deprived both of his sword and carbine, which is carried in a bucket on the off side of the horse. Unless his sword were drawn when he was unhorsed, the dismounted cavalryman would probably be conveyed to the lines of the enemy.

During the reign of William IV., the Chislehurst troop, raised by the late Earl Sydney, formed an escort to His Majesty when he visited Bromley. On this occasion a royal postillion was overtaken by illness, whereupon a trooper promptly volunteered to fill his place. King William was pleased to accept the man's services, and the royal carriage proceeded with its two postillions—one in uniform and the other in the royal livery. The regiment was originally equipped as light dragoons, but the uniform at present, as shown in the illustrations, is blue with scarlet facings and busby bag. The plume is red and white. Within the last few years it has twice taken part in the manœuvres in the South-Eastern District. With the Royal East Kent the regiment forms the Kent Yeomanry Brigade.

The Queen's Own Worcestershire Hussars form, with the Shropshire Yeomanry, the 5th Brigade, with headquarters at Worcester. Last year the regiment made an important change in the mode of its annual training. Instead of taking up billets as in previous years, the hussars spent the time under canvas. Each man groomed and fed his horse and cleaned his kit and, in short, performed all the duties falling to the lot of a cavalry soldier in camp. No doubt this system is more productive of efficiency than that usually resorted to, and, in the case of the regiment in question, was attended with excellent results. The camp was pitched in Witley Park, the seat of the Earl of Dudley, who is a major in the Worcestershire Hussars. The first illustration shows a squadron drawn up in review order in front of the palatial building. The

Photo. Payne & Baird. Catford.
SERGEANT, DRILL ORDER, WEST KENT YEOMANRY, 1855.

furniture, as well as the head-dress, are more ornamental than those now sanctioned by regulation, and the carbine is carried in what appears to be a somewhat uncomfortable position. A picture on this page represents a sergeant of the same period, dismounted, in drill order. The cap will hardly bear comparison with that of the present day, and the sabre is a much more clumsy weapon. The two other illustrations depict the West Kent yeoman as he is now equipped. 'The uniform is similar to that of an hussar. As may be noticed, the sword,

Photos. Payne & Baird. Catford.
TROOPER, REVIEW ORDER, WEST KENT YEOMANRY 1897.

second depicts another parading outside the temporary stable in a more serviceable attire, before proceeding to drill. The junior officer is in the act of inspecting the ranks before reporting to the officer in command.

In the third is seen the mode of watering horses in camp. The water is conveyed from the stream to the trough by means of an hydraulic engine on the left of the picture. The last photograph of two non-commissioned officers and two troopers shows how closely the uniform resembles that of the

Photo. McIsaac & Riddle.                                          Oban.

### ASCENDING BEN NEVIS.

hussars of the regular Army. It is blue, with facings, busby bag, and plume of scarlet.

The Hertfordshire forms with the Suffolk Yeomanry the 7th Yeomanry Brigade, with headquarters at St. Albans. It is partly recruited in London, and took part in the Lord Mayor's Show of 1896. As may be seen from the illustration, the uniform is similar to that of dragoons or dragoon guards. It is scarlet with white facings, and the plume is black.

Sergeant-Major Parrott is the central figure of the group. He is one of the oldest—if not the oldest—yeomen in the Service. He joined in 1842, and has been forty-five years efficient. The trumpeter, on the other hand, must be one of the youngest in the Yeomanry. He enlisted in the Hertfordshire Regiment in 1895, at the age of thirteen. Four of the group, including the two non-commissioned officers on either side of the mounted men, are wearing the old stable jacket which by a recent order has ceased to be worn in the regular cavalry. The commanding officer is the Earl of Clarendon.

The Staffordshire Yeomanry—The Queen's Own Royal Regiment—was formed in 1794, when a sum of over £8,000 was subscribed towards it by the inhabitants of the county. The original articles of the corps are interesting, as showing the conditions on which the patriots of Staffordshire offered themselves for service.

### "SHOULD AULD ACQUAINTANCE BE FORGOT."

Photos. from *                                                                    Volunteer Officer.

### INSPECTION, SCOTTISH BORDER BRIGADE.

*SQUADRON WORCESTERSHIRE HUSSARS (REVIEW ORDER).*

*SQUADRON WORCESTERSHIRE HUSSARS (DRILL ORDER).*

Photos Bennett & Sons

*WATERING HORSES, WORCESTERSHIRE HUSSARS.*

SERGEANT-MAJOR, WORCESTERSHIRE HUSSARS.

Worcester

Photo. Bennett & Sons

All pay received from Government was to be divided equally among the corps, and all pay allowed to officers was to be put "into one general Stock Purse." The document stated that in this way "the daily allowance to every person serving in the ranks will be augmented considerably beyond the pay allowed by Government to Light Dragoons, and . . . . persons enrolling themselves will not be liable to any other expense than the maintenance of themselves and their horses during the few hours they are called together for exercise."

The regiment at first consisted of five troops, but afterwards six troops were added, and in 1819 the strength of the corps was 838 of all ranks. The first commanding officer was Earl Gower, and the present commanding officer is the Duke of Sutherland. The first illustration represents the Wolverhampton troop on parade. The uniform, which is blue, is similar to that worn by hussars. The facings and busby bag are scarlet, and the plume white. The Staffordshire Yeomanry,

Photo. Bennett & Sons.                        Worcester.

*NON-COMMISSIONED OFFICERS AND MEN, WORCESTERSHIRE HUSSARS.*

Photo. Draycott.     *OFFICER, WORCESTERSHIRE HUSSARS.*     Walsall.

with the Warwickshire, forms the 8th Yeomanry Brigade, with headquarters at Lichfield.

The West Somerset, with the North Somerset Yeomanry, forms the 4th Brigade, with headquarters at Taunton. The total strength is 250 of all ranks, divided into three squadrons. Viscount Portman is honorary colonel, and the regiment is commanded by Lieutenant-Colonel F. W. Forester. The uniform, of hussar pattern, is blue with scarlet facings. Red is the colour of the busby bag, and white that of the plume.

As observed in a former number, scouting forms an important part of the duties of yeomanry. A reference to our illustrations will show that the yeomen of West Somerset are instructed theoretically in a somewhat novel and interesting way. Tapes of various breadths are used to represent roads and rivers. Other objects on a table depict buildings, woods, trees, etc., and miniature horsemen guided by the instructor take the place of scouts. By means of such an excellent system the troopers become thoroughly conversant with their duties in the field.

The Duke of Lancaster's Own Yeomanry Cavalry has its headquarters at Worsley. The honorary colonel is the Earl of Ellesmere, and the commanding officer Colonel C. M. Royds. The uniform is scarlet with blue facings. The plume of the head-dress is white. This regiment, linked with the Westmoreland and Cumberland Yeomanry, constitutes the 14th Brigade.

Photo. Curtis & Co.                        Harlesden.

*GROUP, HERTFORDSHIRE YEOMANRY.*

THE 1st Volunteer Battalion Cameron Highlanders has its headquarters at Inverness. It is clothed in much the same way as the regular battalions to which it is attached, except as regards the facings, which are buff instead of blue. The photograph shows "E" Company (Fort William) ascending Ben Nevis, under Lieutenant J. Cameron, on the 22nd June, 1897. The parade was held in honour of Her Majesty's Jubilee. On reaching the summit of the highest mountain in Great Britain the troops fired a *feu de joie*.

The road by which the ascent was made is zigzag in form, and the photograph was taken as the men were rounding one of the angles. A piper is a necessary adjunct to every Highland company; one appears in the picture leading on his comrades. Strange as it may seem to the Southerner, the mere fact of climbing does not necessitate any cessation in the music.

This particular company is recruited and quartered in the Cameron or Lochiel country, where in 1793 the 79th Cameron Highlanders were raised by Cameron of Erracht.

Photo. Whitlock Bros.  Wolverhampton.

*OFFICERS, 1st VOLUNTEER BATTALION WARWICKSHIRE REGIMENT.*

The battalion is commanded by Colonel Macdonald, and is 950 strong.

Another distinguished Scottish corps is the 1st Roxburgh and Selkirk, popularly known as the Border Rifles. The regiment has its home on the Border, with headquarters at Newtown St. Boswells. That there are veterans in the ranks cannot be doubted. The three seen in the first photograph are Quartermaster-Sergeant Turnbull on the right, Band-Sergeant Gray in the centre, and Private Robson on the left; all three are in possession of the long service medal. The picture is specially interesting as showing the old blue bonnet, formerly the undress cap of the Border Rifles. Last year two teams of the battalion were respectively first and second in the competition for the Minto Cup, presented by the Earl of Minto, commanding the Scottish Border Volunteer Brigade. The teams consisted of an officer, a sergeant, and fourteen rank and file. They marched eleven miles and at the conclusion fired a succession of volleys at various distances. There were nineteen teams in all, five of which were furnished by the Border Rifles. Notwithstanding the intense heat, not one man of the battalion fell out. It may be mentioned that the corps instituted competitions in volley firing thirty years ago. In 1867 the Border Rifles acted as bodyguard to Her Majesty when she visited the Border. The commanding officer is Sir R. Waldie Griffith, and the corps is 963 strong, only seven of whom are non-efficient. It forms part of the Scottish Border Infantry Brigade, consisting of six battalions. The following photograph depicts the brigade marching past when in camp at Minto. The brigadier, the Earl of Minto, is riding a white Arab He has taken up his position on the right of the inspecting officer after having marched past at the head of his brigade.

The 1st Volunteer Battalion Warwickshire Regiment had its origin in Birmingham in 1859, when seventy gentlemen were enrolled before the Lord Lieutenant.

That the Volunteer movement found favour in Warwickshire from the outset may be inferred from the fact

Phot. from a  Volunteer Office

*OFFICERS, 1st VOLUNTEER BATTALION THE KING'S OWN.*

Photo. Lambert Weston.  Dover.

*PERMANENT STAFF, 1st VOLUNTEER BATTALION THE BUFFS.*

that before the end of 1860 twelve companies had been raised.

The first uniform adopted was grey with green facings, but in 1863 a uniform similar to that of the 60th Rifles was chosen, and is still worn. The battalion was present at the Review held in Hyde Park in 1864, and again in 1866. On both occasions its smart appearance called forth the appreciation of the Press. The foundation stone of the present palatial headquarters in Birmingham was laid in 1881. The building was erected at a cost of £16,000, and claims to be the most commodious headquarters in Great Britain. The drill hall is 220-ft. long and 90-ft. wide. Besides regimental offices, there are a company mess-room, officers' mess and ante-room, sergeants' mess, canteen, lecture-rooms, band-rooms, and dressing-rooms.

In 1889 Viscount Wolseley visited Birmingham to distribute the prizes of the year to the battalion. On this occasion the report of the general officer commanding the district was read, and stated that in the 1st Volunteer Battalion Warwickshire Regiment things were done throughout in a workman-like manner. The following year the battalion had the honour of finding the Queen's Prizeman — Sergeant Bates, who had long been known as

*LONDON ENGINEERS ERECTING STOCKADE.*

*MAKING GABIONS AND FASCINES.*

*DIGGING A SHELTER TRENCH.*

Photos. Bard.          Catford.

*DRAWING STORES FOR BRIDGE BUILDING.*

a first-class shot. The War Office, after frequent application, granted in 1891 permission to augment the battalion by four companies. The authorities proposed that four of the existing companies should be detached to form a second battalion. This suggestion was not well received in Birmingham, and in the end it was arranged that the corps should be divided into two battalions for drill, etc., with separate adjutants and staff, but that it should continue to be regarded as one battalion officially. This arrangement has worked well, and the strength of the corps is now sixteen companies.

In 1892 the regiment encamped on Cove Plateau, Aldershot, 1,486 strong, and in 1894 with the South Midland Brigade at Great Yarmouth. Under the new system it is now customary to train in brigade. The regiment was one of the first to form an ambulance corps, and has also signalling and cycling detachments. The commanding officer is Colonel W. S. Jervis, who saw service in the Mutiny at Delhi and Lucknow.

The 1st Volunteer Battalion East Kent Regiment (The Buffs), with headquarters at Canterbury, is the oldest body of volunteers in Kent, and was formed in 1859. It now consists of ten companies, stationed at different places throughout the county. The corps is commanded by Colonel E. W. Knocker, C.B., V.D. The former distinction was conferred on that officer last year, in recognition of thirty-eight years spent in the cause of volunteering. Under his command the regiment has reached a high state of efficiency. When encamped at Lydd, the 1st Volunteer Battalion East Kent Regiment was highly complimented by Sir William Butler, commanding the South-Eastern District, on its splendid appearance and efficiency. The strength of the battalion is between 900 and 1,000 men. The uniform is green with scarlet facings.

No branch of the Service is more useful in the time of war than the Royal Engineers. On them depend, to a large extent, the building of bridges and throwing up of earthworks. The four illustrations of the London Engineers serve to show how advanced our volunteer corps are in their military duties.

In the first picture the men are shown constructing a portion of a stockade. To make this a number of planks are placed together and secured above and below by ribands. A trench is excavated, in which the

OFFICERS, 2nd *YORKSHIRE ROYAL ENGINEERS (VOLUNTEERS).*

lower part of the planks is placed, and it is then filled again. Another trench is dug in front, in which various obstacles are placed, and the earth is utilised to strengthen the structure. It will be noticed that every third plank is a short one; this admits of rifles being brought into action. Head cover can be obtained by means of sand bags. Stockades can be made of another pattern by cutting loopholes in the logs. To save interior space in a fieldwork, and for other reasons, earth is often built up at a steeper slope than it could stand of itself. To insure this a revetment or wall is constructed. Revetments are made of various materials, sand bags, gabions, fascines, etc. The gabion is manufactured, as may be seen in the second picture, by placing

COMBINATION FLOATING AND FRAME BRIDGE.

Photos. Garratt.                SUSPENSION BRIDGE.                Leeds.

a number of stakes in the ground and working "withies" of pliable brushwood round them until some 3ft. of basket work is finished. These are then placed at the required slope and filled with earth.

A fascine is a long brushwood faggot. It is put together in a "cradle," composed of stakes crossed as shown on the right of the second picture.

A revetment of fascines is made by placing one row above another and pegging them together by means of pickets.

In the third illustration a shelter trench is shown in course of construction.

The fourth picture represents a scene of daily occurrence before the work of the day is commenced. A Service waggon is attending at the stores to draw the necessary materials for the building of a bridge. The headquarters of the London Engineers are at Islington, and the uniform is similar to that worn by the Royal Engineers of the regular Service.

The work performed by the 2nd Yorkshire Engineers, of which there are two illustrations, is, if anything, more interesting. The first bridge is made by combining two different methods. The right half is supported by floating piers made of barrels, the left half maintained by means of frames or trestles touching the bottom of the stream, and securely fastened together. The number of men standing on the bridge proves it to be no ornament but a useful structure.

The bridge in the background of the next picture is a single sling bridge combined with trestles. As before, the latter rest on the bed of the stream. That in the foreground is a cable suspension bridge of 139-ft. span.

There are no piers between the banks. The structure, as its name implies, is suspended by cables. Though apparently very flexible, it is capable of bearing infantry in file, or field guns passed over by hand. Bridges of the same pattern were used in the Chitral Campaign. These bridges were built in ten hours—a most creditable performance. The headquarters of the corps are at Leeds.

*OFFICERS, 1st VOLUNTEER BATTALION ROYAL FUSILIERS.*

Photos. McKenzie.                                          Alice Street, London.

*1st VOLUNTEER BATTALION ROYAL FUSILIERS AWAITING ORDERS.*

Photo. W. M. Crockett, Plymouth.                     Copyright.—Hudson & Kearns.

*MOUNTED COMPANY, 2nd VOLUNTEER BATTALION DEVONSHIRE REGIMENT.*

Photo. Whitlock Bros.　　　　　　　　　　　　　　　　　　　　　Wolverhampton.

*COLONEL HON. F. C. BRIDGEMAN, COMMANDING STAFFORDSHIRE BRIGADE.*

COLONEL HON. F. C. BRIDGEMAN, whose photograph appears on this page, is brigadier of the Staffordshire Brigade. He was formerly in the Scots Guards. From 1875 to 1876 he acted as aide-de-camp to General H.S.H. Prince Edward of Saxe-Weimar, and two years later was attached to the special mission to Spain. He afterwards served in the Suakin Expedition, was present at Hasheen and Tamai, and wears the medal and Khedive's star.

On another page will be found the staff of the East Yorkshire Brigade. The central figure is the brigadier, Colonel Legard, formerly of the Royal Artillery. He served in the Zulu Campaign, and was acting Deputy Assistant Quartermaster-General of the 1st Division. On his left is Major-General Thynne, C.B., commanding the North-Eastern District, who is well-known among volunteers as a strong advocate of Brigade Camps.

The photograph of the 1st Volunteer Battalion the King's Own (Royal Lancaster Regiment) was taken when the corps was in camp. The central figure is Colonel Strongitharm, the commanding officer. On his left is that distinguished soldier Sir Baker Russell, formerly in command of the North-Western District. The officer on the right of the Colonel is Major-General Eccles, commanding the Northern Counties' Brigade. He took part in the Crimean Campaign, 1854-55, and was present at Alma, Inkerman, and Sebastopol. He wears the medal with three clasps and Turkish medal. On the right of Sir Baker is Colonel Cargill, formerly brigade-major. The uniform of the 1st Volunteer Battalion Lancaster Regiment is scarlet with blue facings, similar to the Line battalions. The well-known badges, the lion and rose, are easily observable on the officers' caps.

The 1st Volunteer Battalion Royal Fusiliers traces its origin to a company raised at the Working Men's College, and known as the 19th Middlesex. To this were added two more companies, the whole under command of Captain Hughes, Q.C.

The headquarters were afterwards moved to Queen Square, and the strength of the corps was soon raised to ten companies. Lieutenant-Colonel Bathurst, of the Coldstream Guards, became commanding officer of the new battalion in 1860, and was followed in March, 1864, by Major Hughes. The latter is perhaps better known to the public as the author of that charming book, "Tom Brown's Schooldays," than as a military officer. That such a man was a popular commanding officer is no matter for surprise, and when he resigned the command five years later, he was gazetted honorary colonel of the battalion. The first uniform was grey, and the regiment then formed part of the well-known Grey Brigade, to which the Queen's Westminster, Inns of Court, and London Scottish belonged. In 1878 a scarlet uniform was adopted.

The headquarters were removed in 1863 to the Apollonican Hall, St. Martin's Lane, and again in 1871 to Fitzroy Square. The battalion parade is the playground of University College School, Gower Street.

In 1883 the corps became the 1st Volunteer Battalion of

OFFICERS, 2nd VOLUNTEER BATTALION NORTH STAFFORDSHIRE REGIMENT.

the Royal Fusiliers (City of London Regiment). It then assumed the uniform of that regiment and the busby as a head-dress. The corps has from an early date turned out in force for manœuvres and camps of exercise. The shooting of the battalion has always been satisfactory. Once at least it was first on the list of all corps in the Home District—a decidedly enviable honour. Like the majority of regiments in London, it has good cycling and ambulance detachments.

One of our illustrations represents the men of the battalion taking part in a field-day. Such a scene is common when outposts are being practised. To the picquets fall all the primary work of delaying the enemy.

Supports are therefore not required to come into action till ordered, and are placed at convenient places in rear of the picquet line. While still remaining alert, ready to advance or make a stand when required, the men are allowed to pile arms and lie down, reserving their strength till the crucial moment arrives. The officers are always vigilant, as they here appear, looking for signals from the front, but with the exception of the sentry on duty the men are allowed to take their ease.

One of the smartest battalions in the Plymouth Brigade is the 2nd Volunteer Battalion

OFFICERS, 1st VOLUNTEER BATTALION SOUTH STAFFORDSHIRE REGIMENT.

Photos. Whitlock Bros.                                                                                           Wolverhampton.

OFFICERS, 3rd VOLUNTEER BATTALION SOUTH STAFFORDSHIRE REGIMENT.

Photo. Dean

*RUGBY SCHOOL RIFLE CORPS.*

Rugby.

*"C" COMPANY, HARROW CADETS.*

Devon Regiment, with headquarters at Plymouth. There are ten companies, one of which is commanded by H.R.H. Prince Alfred of Edinburgh.

The appearance of the mounted company reflects great credit on the corps, especially when we consider that the photograph was taken after a week's marching through the county. The officer in command is Lieutenant Woollcombe. The men are armed with revolvers as well as rifles. The latter are carried slung over the right and the cartridge-belt over the left shoulder. The cyclists, who are only second in importance to mounted infantry, are drawn up on the left. The uniform is green with scarlet facings.

The photograph of Major-General Mackay Heriot appears

*VOLLEY FIRING—PRESENT!*

on another page. This officer was formerly in the Royal Marine Light Infantry, and now commands the Plymouth Volunteer Infantry Brigade. He served in the China Expedition of 1857-58, including the blockade of the Canton River, the landing before, storming and capture of the city. He was wounded at the attack on the forts at Peiho, 25th June, 1859. In 1860 he served with the Chinese Coolie Corps, took part in the expedition to the North, and was present at Sinho, the storming of Tangku and of Taku Forts. For his services he received the medal with three clasps. General Heriot has always been a popular officer and a keen soldier.

The 2nd Volunteer Battalion of the North Staffordshire Regiment has its headquarters at Burton-on-Trent. The corps, which consists of eight companies, was formerly known as the 5th Staffordshire. Like the 1st and 3rd Battalions South Staffordshire Regiment, it forms part of the Staffordshire Brigade. The uniform is scarlet and the facings blue.

The nucleus of the 1st Volunteer Battalion South Staffordshire Regiment was formed (about 1859, in the early days of independent companies), in the shape of the Handsworth Company of Rifle Volunteers. This, it is said, was the first company of volunteers to be raised in the Midlands. The late Mr. Henry Elwell was the first captain, Sir Francis Scott the lieutenant, and Mr. Richard Mole the ensign. The headquarters were at the Bowling Alley, New Inn, Handsworth.

The uniform was grey with green facings and brown belts. This was found by members, who were also obliged to provide their own rifles and side-arms. An administrative battalion was soon formed from this and other companies, and the battalion claims the distinction of being the first battalion in the Midlands to train in camp. As early as 1865 it encamped in Sandwell Park, the seat of the late Earl of Dartmouth. That nobleman was captain of the Patshull Company, and gave a site for one of the best shooting ranges in the district at Sandwell. Since 1865 the battalion has encamped regularly at Aldershot, Strensall, Cannock Chase, Lowestoft, and other places. The corps has always occupied an honourable place in the musketry returns. There is no lack of recruits. Indeed, the battalion could be increased in strength if such increase were sanctioned by the War Office.

About 1876 the uniform was changed to scarlet with white facings, and the men are to-day similarly clothed to the regular battalions of the same regiment. The headquarters are at Handsworth, near Birmingham.

Photos. J. T. Newman.          *BEDFORD CADETS BEFORE THE BATTLE.*          Berkhampstad.

*RUGBY CADETS ON THE MARCH.*

The 3rd Volunteer Battalion South Staffordshire Regiment was formed from the old 5th Corps of Staffordshire Rifle Volunteers, raised in 1860, and was composed of twelve companies. These were afterwards known as the 4th Staffordshire Rifle Volunteers until 1881, when the corps received its present title. The battalion has since 1879 trained annually in camp, and represented the county at the Royal Review at Aldershot last year. It forms part of the Staffordshire Volunteer Infantry Brigade, for which it furnishes a Brigade Bearer Company (sixty-four of all ranks), fully equipped, and ready to take the field on the shortest notice.

The strength of the battalion is 1,173, of which no fewer than 820 encamped at Aldershot last year. This speaks volumes for the *esprit de corps* of the battalion. The honorary colonel is S. S. Tudor, V.D., and the commanding officer J. B. Morgan, V.D. The uniform is scarlet with blue facings. On the last page but one the encampment of the Staffordshire Brigade at Lowestoft may be seen. The way in which the "lines" are laid out speaks for the training of the brigade, and it would be hard to find a more regularly planned camp than the one in the picture referred to.

During the early days of volunteering a battalion which was fortunate enough to form a camp in summer was usually dependent on its own resources. Seldom did more than one corps encamp on the same ground

Photo. Elliott & Fry.   Baker Street.
*COLONEL LEGARD AND OFFICERS, EAST YORKSHIRE BRIGADE.*

simultaneously. Under these circumstances, however zealous the volunteer might have been, his knowledge of things military was confined to the routine of regimental life. He returned to his calling in civil life without having learned much of the "game of war."

With such a small force as a battalion it is practically impossible for one to learn anything of the developments of the battle-field. Of late years the War Office has been fully alive to the importance of bringing together for manœuvres as great a number of battalions as may be ably handled by one competent brigadier.

The outcome of modern military ideas is the excellent brigade system now enjoyed by the volunteer force at large.

Seldom, if ever, are corps now permitted to form regimental camps. Manœuvres on a large scale are "the order the day." To dwell on the advantages of the new as compared with the old system would be idle.

*NON-COMMISSIONED OFFICERS, DUKE OF LANCASTER'S OWN YEOMANRY.*

By associating with other corps a battalion gains in efficiency, and becomes familiar with the movement of large bodies in the field. When, too, the volunteers are quartered and exercised with their brethren of the Line, the increased advantage is obvious. Every year Aldershot is the scene of mimic warfare on a gigantic scale, in which our citizen soldiers take the field and play no unimportant part. It is to be hoped that this year the authorities will see their way to arrange for the mobilisation of an adequate force of volunteers on Salisbury Plain, in addition to Regular and Militia troops. The recent purchase by Government of so large a tract of land in Wiltshire cannot fail to prove of inestimable value in future years.

The 1st Cinque Ports Volunteers had their origin in a Rifle Club that flourished in the year 1852, though there are records of a volunteer

Photos. Martin.   *OFFICERS, DUKE OF LANCASTER'S OWN YEOMANRY.*   Prestwich.

*TROOP, STAFFORDSHIRE YEOMANRY.*

corps existing in Hastings as early as 1794, to which was added in 1803 yet another company. The uniform as depicted in the illustration of the officers in 1857 is in strong contrast to that worn at the present day. It was managed by a committee and drilled with "various kinds of fowling-pieces." Two companies are stationed at Hastings, and the remaining six companies have their headquarters at various towns in Sussex.

"B" Company is stationed at Battle, "C" at Ticehurst, "D" at Lewes, "E" at Rye, "G" at Rotherfield, "H" at Ore, and the cadets at the College, Eastbourne.

There is, therefore, little opportunity for drilling in battalion. Since 1880, however, they have sent a large detachment to camp annually. Last year the corps took part in the manœuvres near Worthing, when about 600 men joined in the operations.

The Cinque Ports were present at the Review before the Queen and the Prince Consort in 1860. Reference to the first picture will show the type of uniform worn at this period.

The second illustration represents the occupants of a tent during the manœuvres in the uniform now worn. From the bottles it would appear that the six warriors

Photos. Whitlock Bros.                                                          Wolverhampton.
*OFFICERS, STAFFORDSHIRE YEOMANRY.*

have declared in favour of non-intoxicating liquor. When in camp for the short space of a week the work is invariably hard, and dinner then becomes a much more important item than at other times.

To the orderly man falls the lot of carving, or, rather, of dividing the rations equally among his comrades. The regiment is commanded by Colonel H. M. Brookfield, M.P., formerly of the 13th Hussars.

The Lords Warden of the period are said to have been honorary colonels of the old corps in 1794 and 1803. The Marquess of Salisbury, K.G., now honorary colonel. This position has been held by the Wardens of the Cinque Ports in succession since 1863. The uniform is grey with blue facings.

Photo. W. H. Jacob.          *OFFICERS, 4th MIDDLESEX.*          Sandgate

IN a former part of " Our Citizen Army" the cadet corps of public schools were noticed at some length. They are not dependent on the annual public school field-day at Aldershot for their tactical instruction. One or two rehearsals invariably take place before the event of the year in the vicinity or within easy reach of the principal public schools. The four photographs on another page were taken during a field-day at Ashbridge, Hertfordshire, where detachments from Rugby, Harrow, Bedford, and other schools assembled. On the common adjoining the park of Earl Brownlow the troops engaged found ample opportunity for manœuvring under active service conditions In the third picture the young soldiers are seen

Photo. from a

*"THE DAYS THAT ARE NO MORE."*

Volunteer Officer.

Photo. Pearson.

*IN CAMP—TEETOTAL TENT.*

Hastings.

Sorotype Company.

*COLONEL A. M. BROOKFIELD, M.P.*

Lewes.

drawn up on the road before marching off to the rendezvous. That the event is regarded as interesting to the natives would seem apparent from the number of spectators who accompany troops, mounted and dismounted.

Older volunteers have every reason to be proud of their younger comrades. They evince the strongest interest in the operations, and are, of course, thoroughly well disciplined. The companies as seen here have a smart and soldierly-like appearance. A company from Harrow forms the subject of the first illustration. The boys have just arrived at the appointed place, and look, without exception, smart in the extreme. An old-fashioned soldier, however, would be struck by the fact that the tall and small men are mixed, and that no attempt has been made to "size" the company. Nowadays, every company of infantry is divided into four sections, each under a section commander—a non-commissioned officer. To foster comradeship and *esprit de corps* it is laid down that men of each section should as far as possible work together under their own section commander. Such an excellent system requires but little explanation. It is obvious that those who are accustomed to act together will be able to give a better account of themselves than if they were continually being changed from one place in the ranks to another and placed under a different non-commissioned officer. On that account a company about to take the field is not "sized," in order that the "section system," as it is termed, may be given full play. Doubtless a company properly sized is more "fair to look upon," but in the battle-field usefulness must be considered before artistic sentiment.

The last scene on the same page is one to be witnessed frequently just before forming for attack. The commanding officer, naturally anxious to husband the strength of his troops, permits them to fall out as they here appear before advancing to the attack. Meanwhile the officers are busy attending to the instructions of their chief. One of the pictures represents a " hot corner" in the battle-field. The men are firing volleys by sections as they advance to storm the position. While Nos. 2 and 4 sections fire Nos. 1 and 3 advance to their next position. Then, under their fire, Nos. 2 and 4 advance and align themselves with Nos. 1 and 3.

The advances may be carried out in quick time or by rushes. The mode adopted depends on the amount of cover available and on the fire of the enemy.

The 4th Middlesex (West London Rifles), which was raised in 1859, was first commanded by Lord Truro. This corps originally had its headquarters at Islington. From there the corps moved to South Street, Park Lane, and in 1880 to Swallow Street, Piccadilly. Neither of these places, however, were found suitable, and the battalion eventually in 1885 took up its abode in Kensington, where headquarters were built at a cost of £3,000. This sum was raised through the liberality of Colonel Lewis, the officers, and their friends, without asking the rank and file to subscribe.

Colonel Lewis, who succeeded Lord Truro as commanding officer in 1879, served in the Royal Marine Light Infantry, and saw active service in Japan in 1864. He was present at Simonoseki and the capture and destruction of Japanese works from the 5th to 8th September of the same year. In 1893 a team belonging to the corps succeeded in bringing home the *Daily Telegraph* Cup, competed for by eighteen volunteer corps and five battalions of Guards. The 4th Middlesex are justly proud of their band, which is mostly composed of old soldiers of the Line, and of their ambulance and signalling sections. The uniform is grey with scarlet facings.

The 3rd Volunteer Battalion Welsh Fusiliers was formed in May, 1897, from the 2nd Battalion, and was placed under the command of Colonel C. H. Rees, V.D., with headquarters at Carnarvon.

Already the new battalion has won distinction in musketry. Out of forty-five battalions quartered in the North-Western District in 1897 it took ninth place in "individual" and fourth in "sectional" practices. Although individual firing has been encouraged to a great extent in the past, the modern tendency is to stimulate sectional volley firing. The reason is apparent to every student of tactics, for the modern battle can never be won by independent riflemen, but rather by bodies of men firing together under control and subject to perfect fire-discipline. In September, 1897, the battalion held its first annual rifle competition, which proved a great success.

Photo. from a                                    Volunteer Officer.

*OFFICERS, 3rd VOLUNTEER BATTALION WELSH REGIMENT, AND GOAT.*

Photo. Heath & Bullingham.                    Plymouth.

*MAJOR-GENERAL MACKAY HERIOT,*
**Commanding Plymouth Brigade.**

Cups to the value of 200 guineas were offered for competition, and to these were added a hundred guineas as prize-money. The Royal Welsh Fusiliers have the privilege of marching past in review preceded by a goat. In order that the newly-formed battalion might uphold the ancient tradition, the Marquess of Anglesey, honorary colonel, presented it with the animal seen in the photograph of the officers. Several officers in this illustration are wearing the new mess-jacket with rolled collar.

The 3rd (Blythswood) Volunteer Battalion Highland Light Infantry took its origin from six companies of Lanarkshire volunteers which in 1860 became the 4th (Central) Administrative Battalion. In the following year the regiment became the 2nd Battalion. In 1867 Colonel Campbell, of Blythswood—now Lord Blythswood—was appointed to the command, and held that position till he retired in 1896. In 1865 the title of the corps was again changed to that of the 31st Lanarkshire Volunteers. In September, 1873, the corps was joined by the old 5th Lanark Volunteers, known as the "Glasgow Eastern Rifles," and in 1877 the battalion registered an enrolled strength of twelve companies. Some two and a-half years later its title was changed again, and it became the "8th Lanark." Under the command of Colonel Campbell the battalion became very popular and efficient, and on that account the War Office sanctioned the title "Blythswood," which it has borne ever since.

The uniform was at first green. It was afterwards changed to scarlet, and in 1886 the uniform of the Highland Light Infantry was adopted. In 1888 the corps was known by its present title. Colonel William Clarke, V.D., is now the commanding officer. He is known as a keen soldier and supporter of the Scottish Rifle Association, of which he is a past president. The present strength of the battalion is 940, of which 922 are efficient. The uniform as seen in our illustration is decidedly picturesque, and is similar to that worn by the old 71st and 74th

Photo. W. M. Crockett, Plymouth.                    Copyright.—H. & K.

*INSTRUCTION IN SCOUTING, WEST SOMERSET YEOMANRY.*

CAMP OF STAFFORDSHIRE BRIGADE—LOWESTOFT.

Photo. Whitlock Bros.

Photo. Lafayette.

OFFICERS, 3rd (BLYTHSWOOD) VOLUNTEER BATTALION HIGHLAND LIGHT INFANTRY.

Regiments. The old-fashioned shako is now worn only by two regular regiments, and by few corps of the reserve forces.

With eight other battalions the 3rd Volunteer Battalion Highland Light Infantry forms the Glasgow Brigade.

The 1st Dumbartonshire Rifle Volunteers form a battalion of Princess Louise's (Argyll and Sutherland Highlanders), although, as yet, they have not assumed the territorial title. Among the seven battalions attached to the 91st Regimental District, this corps is the only one which is known by its old title only. With six other battalions the 1st Dumbarton-shire forms the Clyde Brigade, under Colonel Sir Donald Matheson, K.C.B., a well-known officer in Scottish volunteer circles. The total strength of the battalion is 1,183, of which only 16 are non-efficient. In musketry, too, it holds its own, claiming 241 marksmen, 226 first-class shots, and 496 second-class shots. The corps takes the field with qualified detach-ments of mounted infantry and cyclists. All the officers are proficient, and about half the number have qualified in tactics. It is a remarkable fact that the 1st Dumbartonshire claims no fewer than nine acting chaplains. The corps is commanded by Colonel Denny, and the uniform, which is somewhat similar to the Line battalion, is scarlet with yellow facings. Its headquarters are at Helensburgh.

Such information on the Volunteer Force as the foregoing should prove of especial interest in 1898, when, as most mili-tary critics opine, we are on the eve of important changes. During the coming Session of Parliament the regular Army will no doubt come in for a large share of the attention of the Legislature. It is, therefore, only reasonable to infer that in any scheme of military reform sanctioned by the authorities our volunteer forces will play an important part.

Step by step, in organisation and equipment, they have steadily but surely become more and more like professional soldiers. In short, Our Citizen Army has now reached such a pitch of military proficiency that without it any plan for the defence of Great Britain would be incomplete. Doubt-less there are weak spots in its constitution, but one by one these are disappearing, and there seems no reason why, under wise legislation, the force should not become even a stronger factor than it at present is in the welfare of the Empire.

Photo. from a

Volunteer Officer

OFFICERS, 1st DUMBARTONSHIRE RIFLES.

# THE
# NAVY & ARMY
## ILLUSTRATED.

VOL. V.—No. 58.]    *FRIDAY, MARCH 4th, 1898.*

Photo. West & Son    Southsea.

## THE COMMANDER-IN-CHIEF ON THE AUSTRALIAN STATION.

REAR-ADMIRAL HUGO LEWIS PEARSON, who has just relieved Rear-Admiral Cyprian Bridge as Commander-in-Chief in Australasian waters, was born in 1843, and joined the Royal Navy in December, 1855, towards the close of the Russian War. He became sub-lieutenant in 1862, lieutenant in 1863, commander in 1872, and captain in December, 1879, being posted to that rank from the Royal Yacht. He was promoted to flag rank in the New Year's *Gazette* of 1895. Rear-Admiral Pearson first hoisted his flag in the Naval Manœuvres of 1896 in the "Warspite" cruiser, as second in command under Sir Edward Seymour. He was again second in command of the reserve squadron during the manœuvres of last year, with his flag in the "Sans Pareil." Rear-Admiral Pearson was, on November 1st last, appointed to his present post, and hoisted his flag at Portsmouth in the "Royal Arthur," in which ship he, in January of the present year, relieved Admiral Bridge in Australia.

# ON THE SOUTH-EAST COAST OF AMERICA.

THE " Flora " is the new Commodore's ship on the South-East Coast of America station. She has relieved the " Retribution " there, which ship is returning home to pay off.

Captain Arthur Prothero, who took the " Flora " out, handed the ship over to the captain of the " Retribution," Captain Charles Norcock, the senior officer on the station. With the arrival of the " Flora " Captain Norcock hoisted the broad pennant of a Commodore of the second class in her, thus making the South-East Coast of America station not only a completely independent charge, but raising the status of the senior officer. The " Flora " was commissioned at Devonport by Captain Prothero on January 13th of the present year, and left England some days later—on January 24th.

The " Flora " is a second-class cruiser of the 1889 Naval Defence Act programme, and is one of the later batch (the " Astræa " class) of these vessels which were laid down on somewhat larger dimensions than the earlier ships of the Admiralty 1888 programme—the " Apollo " and " Æolus " classes, to the latter of which the ship the " Flora " has relieved belongs. Thus, while the " Retribution," which was launched in August, 1891, is of 3,600 tons displacement, and carries seventeen quick-firers, with a complement of 273, the " Flora "—launched in November,

SIGNAL STAFF OF THE "FLORA."

THE COMMANDER, 1st LIEUTENANT, AND PETTY OFFICERS OF THE "FLORA."

Photos. W. M. Crockett, Plymouth.                    Copyright.—H. & K.

CAPTAIN PROTHERO AND OFFICERS OF THE "FLORA."

1893—is of 4,360 tons displacement, and carries nineteen quick-firers, in addition to a boat or field gun, and has a complement of 318 of all ratings. Altogether, therefore, the replacing of the " Retribution " by the " Flora " is a decided gain all round for the British force on the station. The " Flora " is a twin-screw cruiser, constructed of steel, and sheathed and coppered, her engines and vitals being protected by a horizontal armoured steel deck from one to two inches thick.

The northern limits of the South-East Coast of America station extend from Cape Orange, the extreme northernmost point of Brazil, four degrees north of the Equator, straight out eastwards to a point about the centre of the South Atlantic. Southward of this imaginary limiting point, the eastern limit of the station stretches right away down to the Antarctic Circle, following a parallel course to the South-East Coast of America as far as Cape Horn. In the South Atlantic the eastern limits of the command fringe on and march with the western limits of the Cape station, while northward of the northern imaginary line of demarcation the North America and West Indies station extends. At Cape Horn the extreme limits of the Pacific station come into touch.

There is thus, as will be seen, an immense area of water to be patrolled by the British ships of the station, and all our trade passing round Cape Horn from Chili, Peru, and California, comes within its care and guardianship.

The squadron comprises one second-class cruiser as Commodore's ship (the " Flora ") and three sloops (the " Basilisk," " Beagle," and " Swallow "), and while their usual anchorages are at Rio Janeiro, Monte Video, and Stanley Harbour in the Falkland Islands, they periodically visit all the ports on the coast.

*THE COMPANY OF THE "FLORA."*

# GUN-ROOMS, PAST AND PRESENT.

From a Photo.                                    By a Naval Officer.

*THE GUN-ROOM OF THE "RENOWN."*

TO those whose recollection takes them back some thirty or forty years in the Service, this picture of the pleasing and refined, not to say luxurious, gun-room of the "Renown" will suggest comparisons, not odious in this instance, but agreeable, as contrasting the pleasant lot of the junior officers of to-day with that of their predecessors. Indeed, the term gun-room as applied to their mess place is of comparatively recent adoption, for in the early days of the present century the subordinate officers' habitation was known only as the midshipmen's berth, though it contained others of mature age. The furnishing and embellishments of these dreary apartments were of the scantiest, and the mode of life in them could, in most instances, be very fittingly described as " pigging it." True, the old line of battle-ship's gun-room was large and roomy enough, and in some cases a determined effort was made at having things done respectably ; out the dark and gloomy dens of small frigates, and, worse still, of corvettes and sloops, might well discourage any such attempts.

The "Renown's" gun-room affords a good example of the radical change which has taken place. The tastefully-decorated luncheon table, handsomely-framed pictures, and general air of refinement, all combine to testify to the fact that the junior officers of the present day are afforded every opportunity of living like gentlemen, and gladly avail themselves of it ; the piano adds a finishing touch to this pleasant interior.

# A DISTINGUISHED SEAMAN.

THE Albert Medal of the First Class is the very rarest of all decorations awarded by Her Majesty, and it is conferred only for exceptional personal bravery and daring in saving life. It was publicly bestowed on Stoker Lynch on January 22nd, by Admiral Sir E. Fremantle, at the Royal Naval Barracks, Devonport, before a large assemblage, with every mark of honour that could accompany the ceremony, the Admiral recounting the story of Lynch's heroism and " in the name of the Queen " making the presentation of the medal, which Lady Fremantle fastened on Lynch's jacket.

Here is the story of heroism as told by the London *Gazette* in notifying the award of the decoration to Stoker Lynch :

"The torpedo destroyer 'Thrasher,' with the 'Lynx' and 'Sunfish' in company, left St. Ives on passage to Falmouth. In thick and foggy weather, the 'Thrasher,' followed by the 'Lynx,' grounded at Dodman's Point, causing serious injury to the boilers and the bursting of the main feed-pipe. The ship's company was landed on the rocks The starboard hatchway became distorted by the doubling up of the deck, preventing egress, and Stokers Edward Lynch and James H. Paul were compelled to escape by the port hatchway, close to a break in the steam pipe. This was partially closed up, and Paul was unable to follow Lynch, who then, lying on the deck, reached down into the escaping steam and drew Paul up on to the upper deck. Lynch was shortly afterwards observed to be badly scalded about the head, arms, and upper portion of the body in this rescue, the skin hanging off his hands and arms. Oil and wool were applied to alleviate the pain, but Lynch called attention to Paul, whom he wished attended to first, saying that he himself was not much hurt, but Paul was very bad. 'I am all right ; look after my chum,' said he. The manly conduct of Lynch induced the surgeon to make inquiries concerning the rescue of Paul from the stokehold, and he found that Lynch with difficulty released himself from the hatchway, lay down, and leaning into scalding steam, caught Paul and dragged him up through the hatchway, and in this way received his own injuries, which are such as to show that in rescuing his comrade he must have plunged the forepart of his own body into what was practically a boiling cauldron It appeared also that Lynch, in a most heroic manner, had previously sacrificed his own opportunity of quitting the stokehold in order to aid his comrade Paul in escaping."

Photo. W. M. Crockett, Plymouth.                              Copyright.—H. & K.

*STOKER LYNCH OF THE "THRASHER."*

# THE GERMANS IN CHINA.

THE planting of the German eagle, inscribed with the "gospel" of the Emperor's "hallowed person," on Chinese soil, and the injunction to Prince Henry to "up and at" the unwilling with "mailed fist," together with the resolution of the Prince to preach the gospel indicated both to those who would bear it and "those who would not," have created no small stir among the nations looking on. England was foremost among these spectators, and therefore the illustrations which we give to-day of the German squadron in Chinese waters should interest our countrymen.

Here you may see the whole of the fleet which has been charged with the important duty of first making manifest what the Kaiser calls the newly-united and newly-arisen German Empire in its transmarine mission.

It is a fleet composed both of old vessels and new, not at all homogeneous, but including some modern ships of power and speed.

When Admiral von Diederichs made his demonstration in Kiao-Chau Bay, he had his flag in the old "Kaiser," and with him were the cruisers "Irene," "Prinzess Wilhelm," "Arcona," and "Cormoran."

The "Kaiserin Augusta" followed, reaching the Bay from Hong Kong on December 30th, and Prince Henry of Prussia, leaving Kiel on December 15th, with his flag in the "Deutschland," and having the "Geñon" in company, made

*THE "STITCH" IN TIME.*

such leisurely progress eastward to place himself under Admiral von Diederichs' orders that he did not reach Aden until exactly a month later.

The two flag-ships "Kaiser" and "Deutschland" are very much like one another. They are old iron ships built in 1874 at Poplar, in the days before the Germans had made up their minds to build only in Germany. But, though the ships are old, they have been modernised, and have acquired a new lease of life before being assigned to harbour service or the ship-breaker. The "Kaiser" is the larger of the two,

Photos. Schmidt & Wegener.    Kiel.

*PREPARING THE MID-DAY MEAL.*

*Photo. Frank Meares.* THE PROTECTED CRUISER "GEFION." Kiel.

*Photo. Schmidt & Wegner.* THE THIRD-CLASS CRUISER "ARCONA." Kiel.

*Photos. Schmidt & Wegner.* THE PROTECTED CRUISER "IRENE."

*Photo. Symonds & Co.* THE BATTLE-SHIP "KAISER." FLAG-SHIP. Portsmouth.

THE PROTECTED CRUISER "PRINZESS WILHELM."

THE BATTLE-SHIP "DEUTSCHLAND," FLAG-SHIP.

*Photo. Schmidt & Wegener.*
THE PROTECTED CRUISER "KAISERIN AUGUSTA."

THE PROTECTED CRUISER "CORMORAN."    Kiel.

displacing 7,531 tons, as compared with 7,319 tons, and her length (292-ft.) is some feet more than that of her sister. In general disposition of armament the two ships resemble our own "Alexandra." There is a 10-in. end-to-end belt, and the same armouring on the central citadel, which has two 10.2-in. guns well above the water-line on each of its sides, and one at each angle, making eight in all. Then there is a 6-in. gun projecting from the stern, and six others are on the superstructure, with nine small quick-firers and some machine guns. The engines are of 5,700 horse-power, and the ships are credited with a doubtful 14½ knots. If the two flag-ships are of respectable age, the cruisers are nearly all of modern character. The "Kaiserin Augusta" is an especially fine ship, built at the Germania yard in Kiel in 1892, and displaces 6,331 tons. She has a steel deck, and, for armament, eight 6-in. guns on her broadsides and two in the bows in sponsons, as well as a couple more aft, eight 3.4-in. quick-firers, and smaller pieces. The special feature is her propelling machinery, which drives three screws, the midmost one projecting much further aft than the others. This arrangement has both advantages and disadvantages. The total power in the "Prinzess Wilhelm." is a sister of the "Kaiserin Augusta" is 14,000 horses, and the speed being 22½ knots, she should have the heels of a good many other ships in Chinese waters. The "Irene" is a sister of the "Prinzess Wilhelm." These are also the produce of German private yards—second-class cruisers of 4,400 tons—launched in 1887. They have steel decks, and are fairly well armed, with four 6-in. breech-loaders, ten quick-firers, and light and machine guns. They should steam at nearly 19 knots. The "Gefion" is a little smaller (4,207 tons), but armed with eight 6-in. guns, and sixteen quick-firers behind shields. Her speed is 20 knots. The "Arcona" and "Cormoran," third-class cruisers, of 2,373 and 1,640 tons, call for no special description. German seamen have many good qualities, and may be trusted for hardihood. Here are types of them—a bluejacket sentry, with men repairing a boat, and a party smoking and telling yarns as they pare the potatoes for their midday meal.

# OUR NEW CRUISERS.

THE "Powerful" is one of the two mighty cruisers which are among the latest additions to the Navy in their class. She and her sister, the "Terrible," have been referred to before in these pages, and an illustration of their external appearance has been given.

They embody all the most recent improvements in mechanism, etc., including water-tube boilers and electrically-worked training gear for the two heavy guns. As cruisers they are of portentous dimensions, measuring 538-ft. in extreme length, and 71-ft. beam, with a displacement of 14,200 tons. These are large figures, but in order to combine high speed with sufficient coal-carrying capacity and good sea-going qualities it is found necessary to construct big ships.

The view is taken from the bow, and shows one of the two 9·2-in. guns, with its long muzzle projecting from the protecting shield. The turn-tables on which these guns are mounted, with their complicated mechanism, are specially protected by 6-in. steel armour.

Photo. Russell & Sons.

*THE UPPER DECK OF THE "POWERFUL."*

Southsea.

# OUR NEWEST BATTLE-SHIP.

Photo. Cribb.

*THE "CÆSAR."*

Southsea.

THE "Cæsar" represents the latest type of first-class battle-ship in the Royal Navy. She belongs, nominally, to the "Majestic" class of battle-ship, but she is in many respects as great an improvement as a fighting craft on her prototype as the "Majestic" herself is on the "Royal Sovereign." The dimensions of the "Cæsar" are: 14,900 tons displacement; 390-ft. between perpendiculars; 75-ft. extreme breadth; 27-ft. 6-in. mean draught. Her guns are four 12-in. 46-ton breech-loading wire guns; twelve 6-in., sixteen 12-pr., twelve 3-pr., and eight ·45 Maxims, all quick-firing. She carries twenty-two torpedoes, to be fired from four submerged tubes and one stern above-water tube.

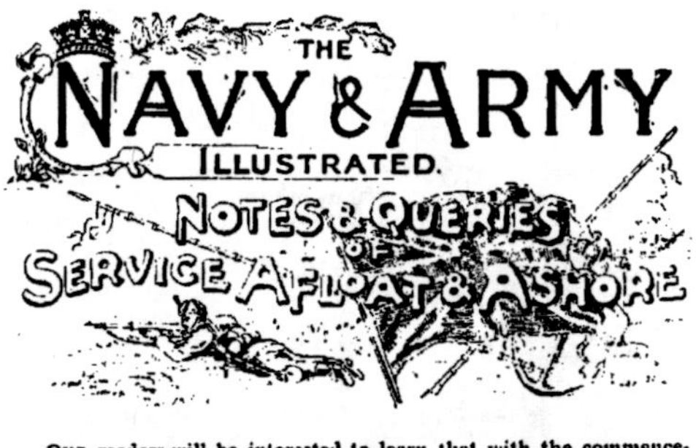
THE
NAVY & ARMY
ILLUSTRATED.
NOTES & QUERIES
OF
SERVICE AFLOAT & ASHORE

OUR readers will be interested to learn that with the commencement of our sixth volume the NAVY AND ARMY will appear weekly instead of fortnightly, as has hitherto been the case. The proprietors are taking this course owing to the continued popularity and increasing demand for this now well-established periodical. It will not only enable us to give a larger number of illustrations, but permit of the NAVY AND ARMY assuming a more up-to-date character. I am receiving daily numbers of photographs from the frontier in India, from Egypt, and from many other places, particularly in the Colonies, a large proportion of which, owing to the pressure on our space, I have yet been unable to show. I have had to continually ask for the patience of my numerous friendly correspondents, but I trust that, now the paper is to appear weekly, they will shortly be gratified by the reproduction of the illustrations they have so kindly sent me. I should like also to thank very heartily the officers and men of our land and sea forces for their cordial co-operation in my work. The manner in which so many of them, in various parts of the world, have taken the opportunity to obtain photographs of occurrences intensely interesting to the readers of the NAVY AND ARMY is proved by our circulation to have been much appreciated by the British public. It will assist me much if in sending me photographs my correspondents will also give short descriptive accounts of the events or persons depicted. I hope when the paper appears weekly that it will be registered, and thus lessen the postage.

* * * *

THERE is little mystery about ships' bells at sea. The sailor divides his time into four-hour spells from midnight to noon; and into one four-hour spell, two two-hour spells, and one four-hour spell, from noon to midnight. The four-hour spells are called "watches," and the two-hour spells, "dog-watches." The latter are from 4 p.m. to 6 p.m., and from 6 p.m. to 8 p.m., and serve to divide the twenty-four hours of the day and night into any unequal number of parts, with the idea of alternating the men on duty during the same hours on successive days. The bells are struck at every half-hour during each watch, "eight bells" at noon, 4 p.m., 6 p.m., 8 p.m., midnight, 4 a.m., and 8 a.m. Thus 12.30, 4.30, and 8.30 are on board ship "one bell"; 1 o'clock, 5 o'clock, and 9 o'clock, "two bells"; 1.30, 5.30, and 9.30 o'clock, "three bells," and so on.

* * * *

IN answer to "G. E. C.," there is no regiment in the British Service which demands that its recruits shall be 6-ft. In the Household Cavalry men are taken from 5-ft. 11-in. to 6-ft. 1-in. in height, and, of course, many grow to 6-ft. 2-in. after enlistment. The minimum chest measurement is 36-in. The maximum standard for dragoons, dragoon guards, and lancers, is 5-ft. 9-in., and for hussars, 5-ft. 8-in., but these measurements are liable to change. In the foot guards the minimum is fixed at 5-ft. 8-in. The other branches of the Service accept recruits much smaller. Your second question ("If the Victoria Cross is made of bronze, why does it present a white appearance on the wearers, and in your photographs?") is hard to answer. I have never seen a Victoria Cross which looked white. The Khedive's Star is often so much polished that the browning is rubbed off, and it then appears bright, but this is not the case with the "V.C.," which is entirely composed of bronze.

* * * *

IN the celebrated Whitaker collection of medals, there is to be found a Naval General Service Medal with four clasps, to which an interesting story attaches. It was won by Francis Patterson, a native of Limerick, who was pressed into the Service in 1793. He was discharged after twenty-two years' service in 1815, and when the medal was issued in 1848 he received it, with clasps for, Hotham's action of 14th March, 1795, Camperdown, Copenhagen 1801, and St. Domingo. As a matter of fact, however, the old sailor was entitled to many more, for he was present in thirteen actions, amongst them being the Nile and Trafalgar, and for the latter he held the bronze medal given to all those therein engaged by Mr. Boulton. For some reason, however, his services were not substantiated, and he only received the four clasps. On his receiving his medal without the Nile and Trafalgar clasps, so angry was he that he dashed it on the ground, and the mark can be to-day seen on the rim. This burst of passion is the more extraordinary as he was a small, quiet, inoffensive little man. He died in Limerick nearly forty years ago, at the extreme age of 101, and, as his biographer quaintly remarks, "temperate to the last."

* * * *

WHEN Lieutenant-General Sir John Moore fell at Corunna, on the 16th January, 1809, the Commander-in-Chief recalled to the troops "the military career of that illustrious officer for their instruction and imitation." May it not be recalled for the same purposes now? Throughout the whole course of his life Moore proved himself eminently capable. He combined kindness with firmness, and added to the highest professional attainments a cool and unruffled intrepidity. He was born at Glasgow in 1761, learned drill and languages on the Continent as a boy, and joined the 51st Regiment, at Minorca, in 1777. As stated in the Army Order above quoted, "he felt that a perfect knowledge and an exact performance of the humble but important duties of a subaltern officer are the best foundation for subsequent military fame." That fame he had fully earned before it was enhanced by the historical retreat which "terminated a career of distinguished honour."

WHO was Tom Cox? I might indeed say, Who is Tom Cox? For I am afraid this personage, who is supposed to be more legendary than real, is still to be found in the Service, though rarely, it may be hoped. Tom Cox is—not was—a gentleman who may occupy any rank in Her Majesty's Navy, and who is more noted for his "jaw" than for his actual work. He is an artful dodger, who knows how to elude duty, although he usually boasts of being the only man on board who does anything. Jack says that when he comes up on deck "he comes up one hatchway and pops down the other." He also accuses him of "taking three turns round the long boat and a pull at the scuttle." In short, Tom Cox is not a favourite on board any vessel, and it is right that he should not be.

* * * *

THE Standing Army of England dates from the 7th January, 1661. Prior to that year there was no permanent military establishment under the monarchy. In the event of invasion—for instance, the Spanish Armada in 1588—or internal rebellion, such as the Irish Rebellion of 1599, the Sovereigns had, before Charles I. ascended the throne, found no difficulty in raising and calling out Militia levies, at very short notice, to perform the military services required of an army. These "occasional soldiers," as Macaulay styles them, upheld the honour of England on many notable occasions, and earned the admiration of one of our greatest soldier historians, Sir Walter Raleigh. No better illustration of the value which an English Sovereign set on the Militia can be cited than by quoting an answer given by Charles I. to the Earl of Pembroke, when the latter, as spokesman of the Parliamentary deputation which waited on the King at Newmarket, 9th March, 1642, asked His Majesty to grant the Militia to Parliament for a time. "Not for *an hour*," exclaimed the King.

* * * *

APROPOS of the recent decision of the Admiralty to condemn the cruiser "Shannon" as unfit for further service as a fighting ship, a correspondent asks for information about the vessel. In 1875, when the "Shannon" was launched as a cruiser, the Admiralty had not made up their mind as to the type of ship actually required, with the result that the "Shannon" has always been more or less of a compromise, with resultant defects. The "Shannon" was intended to be not only a cruiser, but also a ship capable, at a pinch, of taking part in the line of battle; and, in consequence, she has remained a hybrid sort of vessel, a craft, in the words of the old saw, "neither fish, flesh, nor good red herring." She is, indeed, a compound of odd peculiarities. A single screw ship, her propeller is of the early type, made to lift out of the water when the ship is under sail, the "Shannon" being fully masted and rigged as a sailing vessel. Another curious feature is her "shifting" ram, designed to unship in ordinary times, and be stowed away on board until wanted—a curious notion adopted in view of the disaster to the "Vanguard" from the ram of the "Iron Duke," which happened just when the "Shannon" was on the stocks. Another peculiarity is the "Shannon's" armouring with a belt extending along the water-line only as far forward as abreast the foremast, where it turns inwards right across, as a transverse bulkhead, leaving the bows bare of side armour, with only the protection of a horizontal armoured deck and the coal bunkers. This was the first experiment in the under-water system of protection, carried further in the "Citadel" ships of the "Inflexible" and "Admiral" classes, which appears in a modified form in some of our recent ships. A final peculiarity of the "Shannon" is the mounting of her stern chase 12-ton gun on a travelling platform amidships, with the idea of its being fought at the after port on either side of the ship.

* * * *

HUSSARS were first introduced by Matthias, King of Hungary, 1458-90, and were so called from the Hungarian word "Husz," which means "twenty," for the King, in order to raise regiments of Light Horse to serve on his Ottoman frontier, decreed that every twenty houses should furnish one soldier for that particular service. The term was afterwards applied to all Light Cavalry troops. The 7th is, perhaps, the crack hussar regiment of the British Army. They were the first of the light dragoon regiments to be converted into hussars in 1807, even as they were the senior of the old dragoons converted into light dragoons in 1784. At Warburg, in 1760, their boots became completely worn out, and the troopers were obliged to swathe their feet in haybands, from which circumstance the regiment received its nickname of "Strawboots," or "Old Straws." Hussar regiments carry no standards. By the way, there is a difference between standards and guidons. The former are carried by dragoon guards, and the latter by dragoons. The officers of the 7th Hussars in undress uniform are permitted to wear white collars and cuffs, a privilege shared by the officers of the Oxfordshire Light Infantry.

* * * *

A CORRESPONDENT finds fault with the rank of Admiral of the Fleet as a cumbrous and unwieldy title not understood by the public. He instances how the newspapers talk of Admiral Sir Henry Keppel and Admiral Commerell, where they mean, of course, the Admirals of the Fleet of those names. One never, he says, sees the papers mixing up Field-Marshals with Generals in this way. The error is, of course, one of ignorance. It is probably helped by the fact that in modern times the rank of Admiral of the Fleet has been extended so as to include a number of officers under that designation. For a century and more, until the first year of George IV.'s reign, there was only one Admiral of the Fleet, the title and rank being a special designation and official distinction of the senior officer on the active list of the Navy, who was thus elevated into a special rank by himself, apart from and above all other admirals. The custom by virtue of which there was only one Admiral of the Fleet was, in fact, first broken through in 1821, when Earl St. Vincent was specially raised to that rank, and so posted jointly with the Duke of Clarence, who had been sole Admiral of the Fleet since 1811. Lord Melville, First Lord of the Admiralty, in his letter to Lord St. Vincent, appointing him a second Admiral of the Fleet, pointed out that enquiry had been made, and there being found no legal impediment to the Board of Admiralty conferring the rank on more than one flag-officer, Lord St. Vincent would be promoted to the rank. When Her Majesty came to the throne, the establishment comprised two Admirals of the Fleet. At the present time it comprises three, with the Duke of Edinburgh and Sir Henry Keppel, our "Father of the Fleet," as additional, under a special Order in Council. The Prince of Wales and the German Emperor are Honorary Admirals of the Fleet.

THE EDITOR.

THE Prince of Wales is most closely identified with the public and social life of the country, and possesses in a marked degree the breezy personality that is dear to Englishmen, so that I suppose the number of those who will like to read a brightly-penned narrative of his career must be considerable. Knowing how difficult it is to write the life of a person in an exalted station while he is still alive, I took up "H.R.H. the Prince of Wales, an Account of his Career" (Grant Richards) with fear of disappointment, but I was agreeably surprised. The anonymous writer's merit is that he has flung away ambition, and chosen the modest *rôle* of a simple chronicler. His narrative flows pleasantly along, dealing first with the Prince's youth and education, his marriage and married life, his several tours, and his serious illness. I think there is nothing here that a diligent student of the papers might not have discovered for himself—if the author had not spared him the trouble, and there is no trace of inspiration. An amusing story is told of a visitor to Cambridge, who expressed doubt of the Prince's intellectual abilities, being confounded by the librarian, who exhibited his name immediately after that of a Senior Wrangler in the entry book! The latter half of the volume narrates chiefly the Prince's good service to a multitude of public works in the country. The series of pictures is, perhaps, the most interesting feature of the book. Here we have the Prince as a sailor and a soldier, and at every period and in every aspect of his life. The charming personality of the Princess, too, is depicted in a delightful set of pictures, and the writer renders his tribute to all the good qualities of that gracious lady.

I must crave some indulgence for writing of "Eighty Years Ago, or the Recollections of an Old Army Doctor" (Redway, 5s.). But, as one of the old dramatists says, "What can a man before he be born?" Your "Search-Light" had no beams when this volume was published in 1896. And yet, though an old book, as the world goes now, you would do well to read it. The author was the late Dr. Gibney, of Cheltenham, and his son, Major R. D. Gibney, has edited the story. It is one of the easiest and freshest narratives you can imagine. After describing in most amusing fashion the life and education of medical students in Edinburgh, Dublin, and London, in the early years of the century, it shows you the author gazetted to a cavalry regiment in country quarters in Ireland. Then it carries you by road and canal towards Waterloo. You are present at an inspection by Wellington, who "did not look well," and old Blucher—"Marshal Vorwärts." Then, by Nivelles, you go on to Quatre Bras, meeting many wounded by the way, reach the battle-field at midnight, retire to Genappe, where the French lancers attack, and so to Mont St. Jean, where you sit through the night up to the hips in muddy water, warm your shivering bones by a camp fire in the grey dawn of the memorable 18th of June, and witness many events of the battle. A very dramatic picture of active service.

With some curiosity I took up "Republics North and South" (Beale Brothers, 5s.), because it is by "One who does not believe in them." The book has no literary merit, and is a somewhat free attack upon American institutions, if not upon the American people. The author traces every blot to the introduction of universal suffrage.

Mr. Oppenheim is our greatest authority on the history of Naval administration, and his article in the *English Historical Review* (Longmans, 5s.) is every whit as interesting as its predecessors. He is dealing with the period from 1673 to 1679, and chiefly with victualling and the pass. The victualling scale was liberal, but there were constant frauds by the pursers. In this matter Pepys showed himself a very vigilant official, and though not always above corruption himself, proved he was ever jealous of the honour of the Service. The beef and pork were to be up to weight, and there were to be no such pieces as "leg bones, shins of oxen, or the cheeks of hogs, or ox-hearts." In the Mediterranean, instead of a gallon of beer, the men received a quart of good "beverage wine, so strong that when three times its measure of water were added, it should preserve the water from stinking." We learn, too, that Narborough found his lieutenants defective in seamanship, and Mr. Oppenheim suggests that many breaches in discipline afloat were due to the practice of appointing "gentlemen captains." A very instructive article.

Some things in the February magazines claim mention. In *Chambers' Journal* a clever story is woven about the man who fired the fatal shot at Trafalgar, and there is an amusing gossip about ships' names. The Rev. W. H. Fitchett continues his "Fights for the Flag" with a capital "Blake and the Dutchmen," a noble tribute to the great seaman, in the *Cornhill*. It is good to read of such deeds. You may laugh heartily at a yarn concerning "A Lunch for the General," by Lieutenant Dallas, in *Belgravia*, or experience the *dolce far niente* of "The Sublime of Boating" in *Longmans'*. I am heartily glad to see that the old *Brigade of Guards' Magazine* has got a new lease of life as the *Household Brigade Magazine*, and makes a prosperous appearance under favourable auspices.

While the smoke curls upward as you discuss some of the things I have spoken of, you may care to have by you "Gossip for Smokers" (Redway, 1s.), which is full of good things from the land of Nicotia. Hence there floats an ode by C. S. Calverly, of which I will venture to quote a verse, and so conclude:

> "Thou who, when fears attack,
> Bidst them avaunt, and black
> Care, at the horseman's back
> Perching, unseatest,
> Sweet when the morn is grey;
> Sweet, when they've clear'd away
> Lunch; and at close of day
> Possibly sweetest."
>
> "SEARCH-LIGHT."

# Twice Round the Clock.

### Being Twenty-four Hours of a Cavalryman's Life.

#### By G. H. RAYNER.

A FINE, sharp winter morning. The hands of the guard-room clock are nearly straight up and down the dial; and the orderly trumpeter has already disappeared to "knock up" the others of his fraternity and their chief, the trumpet-major, who will shortly dispel the dreams of the barrack with the stirring notes of réveille.

The men of the night guard are preparing to dismiss, and the day guard are discarding forage caps for full dress headgear, and doffing the cloaks worn by them during the night. Six strikes as the trumpet-major marches on the "fiddlers," as the regimental trumpeters are affectionately termed. "Rise, soldiers, rise, and get your highlows on," sings the brass, and in a moment the erstwhile silent, darkling buildings burst into light and life. No lagging or loafing in bed of a morning for Tommy. If he does not jump lively at the last note, his cot is carefully capsized by his room-corporal, or he is seized by the legs and lugged on to the floor with no gentle bump. Meantime the men of the night guard have lounged into their troop-rooms, and, in no happy frame of mind, are changing their overalls and jackets for the "slacks" and "serges" that constitute working stable dress. Here it must be explained that the night guard consists of men who mount guard from 6 p.m. to 6 a.m. They are principally posted on the stables, but are armed, and have the same duties as ordinary sentries. The day guard is usually mounted at 3 p.m., and remains on duty for the next twenty-four hours. The day guard finds the sentry at the gate, on the guard-room, and supplies an orderly for the orderly-room. The day guard is picked from trained soldiers, whilst the night guard is drawn from recruits and "casuals," as officers' batmen, staff assistants, such as orderly-room and quartermaster's stores' men, and the men in the young horse and remount stables. The night guard on coming off at 6 a.m. do not retire to rest, as might be innocently supposed; but, after changing dress, go straight to another full day's work. The day guard, on dismissal, are off duty till réveille next morning.

At 6.15 the trumpeter on duty sounds the "dress," or regimental call, and every duty man by this should be at stables. The lucky casuals can "stick it out" in bed until 7.30 or 8; but officers' servants and young horsemen are supposed to be at stables at the ordinary time. The orderly sergeants of troops are calling the roll in front of the troop stables, and as each man answers to his name, he enters his stable and proceeds to remove the litter from his horse's stall. All hands sweep out the stable, shake up the litter, and stack it outside, and then proceed with their respective charges to the watering troughs. Horses should be watered and back in their stalls before, or by the time, the full strength of the trumpets sounds "stables."

The orderly troop sergeant-major for the day makes his appearance and parades the length of the stables, and is shortly reinforced by the arrival of the officer for the day. Troop sergeant-majors and sergeants are presumed to be at their posts when "stables" sounds, but, as a rule, are not exactly punctual. Sometimes a young and enthusiastic subaltern puts in an appearance early, but I am bound to say this is the exception. Every man is busily employed grooming his charger, and here we will leave them for a moment to look at those whose duty does not lie at stables.

Officers we can dismiss as being snugly between blankets, but their servants are either at their stables or busy with the domestic duties at their masters' quarters. The troop cooks are busy boiling the water for breakfast, and the quartermaster-sergeant and his aides are weighing out the meat and counting the tale of loaves that make up a soldier's daily free rations. Soon after 7 there will remain but few sleepers throughout the barracks, save, perhaps, the married quarters; but there our story does not take us. At 7.30 troop officers begin to appear, and make a tour of inspection through their troop stables. The quartermaster is now at the barn superintending the weighing of forage, straw for bedding, and hay and oats for the horses' feed. A certain proportion is allowed for each horse, and each troop receives its allowance in bulk. A certain number of men from the troop proceed to the barn with a large net, which is filled with hay and then weighed. If somewhere near the proper weight it is passed, and borne off to the verandah outside the stables. The requisite number of sacks of corn are also carried there and deposited in an immense barrel, the lid of which is secured by a padlock, of which the troop sergeant-major keeps the key.

The orderly trumpeter has for the last few minutes been trotting—at a respectful distance—behind the orderly officer, and now that gentleman, observing the clock denoting 7.45 a.m., nods to his satellite, who, lifting his instrument to his lips, pours forth the welcome "feed." And don't the horses recognise it! A chorus of neighing greets the first note, and the man who delays emptying the nosebag into his charger's manger occasionally risks an awkward reminder from his charge in the shape of a kick in that portion of his anatomy nearest to the hungry animal. Each horse in the troop stables is entitled to three feeds of corn per diem, and also has its rack filled the same number of times with hay. The nosebag holds exactly three feeds, and is filled every morning by a non-commissioned officer, whose duty it is to see that the allotted portion is not exceeded. The horses in the "sick lines," that is, under treatment by the veterinary surgeon, are on such food as that officer decides, and are attended by the farrier-major and his assistants, the farriers and shoeing smiths, in stables situated so as to be completely isolated from the troop stables.

The "feed" is immediately followed by the regimental call, a signal for the orderly men to rush off to draw rations and bring up breakfast. A quarter of an hour later "dismiss" sounds, and then "breakfast up." Tommy does not dally over tea and toast and the morning paper. Within fifteen minutes the remorseless trumpeter sounds the "dress," and recruits prepare for riding school, whilst dismissed men (older soldiers) go on various duties, exercise and the like. Another quarter of an hour, and riding school "fall in" sounds. The "mob" of recruits, for the next two hours, we will leave to the tender mercies of the riding-masters and

An inspection by the orderly officer.

"roughs," as the gentlemen who are "branded with a blasted worsted spur" are familiarly termed—not without grim humour. The exercise party, leading spare horses, go out for the morning constitutional of an hour and a-half or two hours. They will return about 11 a.m., at which time the recruits are gladly leaving the riding school and *manèges.* "Orderly-room" sounds at this hour, and the colonel and officers put in an appearance, the guard turning out at the approach of the chief. Recruits and all duty men rapidly change into working dress, and at 11.15 "stables" sounds. Every soul about barracks will be busily employed at his work, whatever it may be, until 1 p.m. Men are at work in office, stables, cook-house, hospital. Even the sentries on the guard-room and gate assume—if possible—a smarter, straighter carriage during the two busiest hours of the day. The veterinary is going round his "sick lines"; troop officers are visiting their stables; in the orderly-room the discipline of the corps is being upheld by the trial of minor offences—if there are any defaulters; and horses and saddlery are having a polish put on them that obtains nowhere outside a cavalry regiment.

"Feed" sounds at 12.45, being followed at the usual interval by "dismiss" and "dinner up." The soldier has now the longest period of rest he gets during the working day. At 2 "dress" sounds; "fall in" for foot parade for recruits goes at 2.15; and "general parade" is at 2.30. For an hour to an hour and a-half the recruit learns the mysteries of dismounted drill, the sword exercise, and "how to walk and where to put his feet." Dismissed men, if not on fatigue

duty, have the afternoon till evening stables at liberty, but cannot leave barracks without special permission.

Defaulters are being drilled in heavy marching order by the orderly sergeant, or are on various fatigues. At 2.45 p.m. "dress for guard," and at 3 the day guard, resplendent in full dress, and burnished to their glove buttons, fall in in front of the guard-room. The orderly officer inspects them, and chooses the smartest, cleanest man for the orderly (this lucky individual, who has no sentry duty to perform, and gets a night in bed, is said to have "got the stick," in soldier parlance), and the old guard turns out and duly hands over the charge of the barracks to the new comers.

The canteen begins to wear a busy appearance now. At 3.45 foot parade is dismissed, and the trumpet sounds for "school" and "fencing" classes, both of which every man must attend till proficient. At 5 p.m. "tea" is announced, followed in the usual fifteen minutes by "dress," and at 5.30 "stables" sounds for the last time. All duty men attend stables, those who are going on night guard leaving at 6 p.m., when "dress for guard" sounds. At 6.15 "feed," followed by "fall in for night guard," and at 6.30 the welcome "dismiss" is the sign to leave work for the day. The night guard is posted to its different points, and the other men are free to occupy the rest of their evening as they think best. There is plenty of work for most of them. Arms and accoutrements have to be prepared for the morrow, and most soldiers put in two hours' solid work in the barrack-room. The canteen is lit up, and the piano is going now. Here until 9.30 will be the "sound of revelry by night."

If a mess night, the band will play for officers' mess, in summer this popular function taking place in the barrack square. Defaulters are at drill, on fatigue, or have to report themselves at the guard-room every half-hour until 9.30 at the sound of the never-tiring trumpet. Many men, having got passes, are going out of barracks, every man so

doing having to look in at the guard-room, that the sergeant may see each man is properly dressed. After dark the sentries commence to challenge everyone approaching their posts, and the night is startled with their "Halt! who goes there?" and the necessary reply. At 9.15 the "first post," or warning, sounds, and at 9.30 the full strength of trumpeters sound the wild but beautiful strains of the "last post." The canteen closes to the strains of "God save the Queen," and men return to their respective rooms. Just before 10 p.m. orderly sergeants go round their troop-rooms, receiving the reports of corporals in charge, who have to account for every man under their charge, and at 10 they hand in their reports to the orderly troop-sergeant-major at the guard-room Names of all men absent without leave are noted, and the same are "made prisoners" on their return to barracks. The barrack gate is ceremoniously locked, and no man can go out that way, at any rate until it is opened at réveille to-morrow morning. Men returning to barracks are admitted, and report themselves at the guard-room, where their passes are verified; if they have been absent without leave they go into the "clink." At 10.15 "lights out" sounds, and the whole barracks, excepting officers' and sergeants' quarters, are plunged in darkness. The orderly officer may make his tour of inspection, turning out the guard and visiting the sentries, any hour of night or morning, and a few belated non-commissioned officers may struggle home to the married quarters; but with these exceptions no soul stirs within the barrack walls save the alert sentry, rousing the slumbering midnight with his melancholy hourly note, "All's well."

A foreign draft

THE SEA REGIMENT PART III
BY ONE OF ITS UNITS

"FORM fours—r-r-right! To 'Ongkong, Ascension, an' 'Alifax—quick mar-r-r-ch!" bellowed Sergeant-Major Hollingsworth of the Sea Regiment; and the last thing the "military details" heard, as they stepped with shouldered arms past the guard at the barrack gates to the dockyard and the great world beyond, was a hoarse injunction from the same source to hold their 'eads up and look straight to the front.

"Solomon's homilies to youth in a nutshell," commented Bronzeface, a captain of the regiment, to his visitor, a subaltern of the Loyal Mid-Wessex. They were sitting on the flower-bordered terrace before the officers' mess, and had been watching the inspection of the white-helmeted foreign drafts by the adjutant.

"From the casual way in which that detachment was marched off parade," mused the visitor, "one would suppose that China and North America were at the bottom of the High Street. In my regiment the whole battalion would have turned out, and the bands in garrison would have played the draft away. Yet your own band is fiddling at Wagner's 'Walküre' in the practice-room. I call it positively indecent!"

Bronzeface laughed. "My dear Makee-learn," said he—for our old friend it was, at present on leave from his regiment—"the two cases are hardly analogous. The Loyal Mid-Wessex is seven hundred strong, the Sea Regiment seventeen thousand. With you the coming or going of a foreign service draft is an event. Considerable preparation is made for it, and the whole battalion is interested in it. With us it is an incident of daily routine that in no way affects the usual drills and parades. Many of those men who have just marched through the gates were only requisitioned by the Admiralty late last night. They were warned off at once, medically examined, marched to the quartermaster's stores and fitted with their tropical clothing, paraded at the pay-office for payment up to date and explanation of accounts, mustered their kits for inspection by the company captains, and are now, at nine o'clock in the morning, on their way to three different foreign stations."

"With more than half the regiment stretched round the globe on patrol work," said the Makee-learn, "you must need a wonderfully elaborate system at your various headquarters in England."

"The need is well supplied, sonny," returned Bronzeface, complacently. "The present system is the outcome of two hundred and thirty years' experience!"

"And yet, of course, mistakes must sometimes occur. When you have so many thousands of men scattered about the oceans and islands of the planet, it must be difficult for the orderly-room people at headquarters to keep touch with them all—to relieve each man at his proper time, for instance."

"I believe that a man *was* once overlooked," admitted Bronzeface. "It was in the dusk of a Christmas afternoon that the colour-sergeant on the barrack gate was confronted, so he says, by a tall private in heavy marching order of an obsolete pattern. He wore knee breeches and a weird conical hat with the monogram 'A.R.' in the centre.

"'What in the devil's name are you?' asked the sergeant, falling back a pace.

"'I was fugleman o' the grenadier company the day we marched out o' barracks a-singin' "Lillibullero!"' returned the man in a dismal, far-away voice, staring hard meanwhile at the guard-room arm-rack; 'and you may lay to it that wasn't yesterday neither. Three months arterwards we Marines took Gibraltar, and I was the first—and last—sentry posted in the cavern that goeth under the straits to Africa. 'Tis true, look you, that I have not yet been relieved by the sergeant of the guard; but when Queen Anne—whom God long preserve!—hears that he hath forgot me all these years, I make little doubt that he, and not I, will suffer. But'—he swore a quaint oath, and pointed at the Lee-Metfords in the rack—'what manner of platoon exercise, prithee, is a man expected to do with new-fangled muskets like those?' Then the gleam of the gate lamp caught his face for the first time, and the colour-sergeant fell backwards into the guard-room as though he had been shot."

"What became of the private?" asked the Makee-learn, suspiciously.

"I never heard," said Bronzeface, rubbing his chin, "but the N.C.O. went before the colonel in the morning. Being Christmas time he was let off with a severe reprimand. Some day I shall write a temperance tract. Its title will be, 'The Forgotten Fugleman, or the Colour-Sergeant's Conversion.'"

The Makee-learn made haste to change the conversation. "Under certain conditions," he asked, "could an officer of the Royal Marines ever assume command of a man-of-war?"

"Under no conditions whatever," replied Bronzeface, promptly. "One of our fellows, it is true, commanded a gun-boat up the Nile the other day, but that is hardly what you mean. With the exception of the additional subject of Naval gunnery—and a very big addition it is—our training is purely military, and precisely the same as yours. The executive officers of the Navy, on the other hand, being professional sailors, are specialists afloat, and as such, of course, always 'run the show.'"

"Well," said the Makee-learn with emphasis, "it is a good thing, anyhow, that our Naval brigades when landed on active service are commanded by highly-trained, professional soldiers!"

"I never said so," corrected Bronzeface.

"How modest we are! But, at least, you cannot deny that *you* are the specialists when it comes to placing an outpost line, building a bridge, or making the dispositions for a defence."

"I don't wish to deny it. What I meant was that I never said we commanded Naval brigades. We are only licensed, as it were, to run military ones. I fancy you are confounding the British with the American Navy. It is in the latter Service that the sea-soldiers direct the military operations of the sailors. In ours the sea-soldiers, in common with the rest of the brigade, are generalled by a Naval officer."

The Makee-learn whistled softly to himself. Fearful and wonderful, indeed, was this sister Service, whose officers found themselves equally competent to manœuvre fleets and to brigadier the very flower of the British infantry !

"Makee-learn," said Bronzeface presently, standing up, " you have seen a battalion of the Sea Regiment land from the Mediterranean fleet and drill on the Corradino parade at Malta. You have been to sea with us in heavy weather, and watched us at target practice with the great guns, and you have just had a glimpse of the red stream which perpetually flows through our barrack gates into the Seven Seas."

" 'Rar, 'ear ! " cried the Makee-learn, applauding with his stick upon the terrace.

" ' Who the devil *are* the Marines ? ' you once asked in the dining-room of the Malta club, and from that moment I felt it was my mission in life to enlighten one fellow-creature, at all events, as to who the devil they are."

"You have proved yourself a born missionary," testified the Makee-learn. "Though I must admit," he added, "that the strength of your convictions has occasionally betrayed you into the use of—er—somewhat lay language ! "

"Nevertheless, it's child's talk to what I *think*," said Bronzeface, viciously decapitating a geranium with his cane. "Now, get up. I am going to complete my lectures on the Sea Regiment—such as they have been—with a final object-lesson. You have got to come round these barracks with me and see something of the working of one of the five great divisions of the regiment in England. They are at Plymouth, Gosport, Eastney (Portsmouth), Deal, and Chatham, and they ——"

"May I have a drink before we begin ? " interrupted the Makee-learn, plaintively.

"The sun—God forgive me for talking sea jargon under the Army Act—isn't over the foreyard yet," said Bronzeface, piously, "which means that the conventional hour for the day's first drink hasn't yet arrived. However, I suppose we may as well do the officers' mess first as last."

As the long whisky and soda hissed down the Makee-learn's throat, the tail of his eye caught a framed and faded document hanging on the wall of the great glass-roofed entrance hall. It was a table of the sea-soldiers' pay in the reign of Queen Anne, when the regiment had already attained the staid age of half a century, and—O! shade of Tobias Smollett!—the Makee-learn gathered from it that drummers and chirurgeons' mates in those far-off days were of about equal value in the eye of the State. Trophies of arms and shields (some of them still blood-stained), brought home from every quarter of the globe by dead and gone generations of sea-soldiers ; water-colour drawings of the various uniforms worn by the regiment since the days of Pepys and Charles II.; quaint old prints of sea and land fights in which it had been engaged, from La Hogue to Alexandria, from Bunker's Hill to Tel-el-Kebir ; a rare old "breeches" Bible; brass guns and gongs, to say nothing of idols, captured in China ; the head-dress worn by the grenadier company of the Marines during the American War of Independence ; a drum taken at the battle of Copenhagen, and a suit of Japanese armour at the bombardment of Simonoseki—with these and a hundred other tokens of the regiment's antiquity and valour the hall and ante-rooms were crowded.

But it was the grand old mess-room itself—the *sanctum sanctorum*, where the ancient colours drooped above the doorway, and the great gold eagle of a French frigate spread its wings over the opposite window—which caused the Makee-learn to cock his chest and hold his head the higher. For, boy as he was, as an officer of the British Army was he not also co-inheritor with these bronzed and weather-beaten sea-soldiers to the glorious legacy bequeathed them by their

predecessors ? On the walls around him were some of those very men, gazing from shadowy canvases at their reflections in the identical table—black and polished now by time and a thousand hands—at which they had so often drunk "The King." And, facing each other from opposite ends of the great room were two of those self-same Kings—stately, full-length portraits ; one, a Lawrence, of William IV., "General of Marines"; the other, so said Bronzeface, the only equestrian picture of George III. in existence.

"Almost," whispered the Makee-learn, for the tattered colours and the subdued light from the tall windows gave him a sense of being in church, "thou persuadest me to be a Marine."

Bronzeface took him into the plate-room and showed him the unique collection of gold and silver snuff-boxes, the salt-cellars presented to " ye Marine mess" by some periwigged sea-soldier of William and Mary ; into the china closet with its priceless sets, out of which the posturing, beruffled officers and the simpering, curtseying ladies of the early Georges had sipped their " China tay," until presently the pair stood again upon the shady flower-fringed terrace.

The Makee-learn gasped. "I should not be in the least surprised," he said, "to see Mr. Secretary Pepys mincing across the parade in his ' new camelott suit,' or General Wolfe, of Quebec fame, coming to call on his old regiment."

"You would never persuade them," said Bronzeface, pointing to the parade, "that those fellows yonder were practising ' the attack of a position.' "

Two companies in extended order were advancing by short rushes, and dropping on the knee to fire, while their instructor made day hideous with the shrillest of whistles. The Makee-learn's mind reverted to the compact formations of Marlborough's time.

"If the morals of the brutal and licentious soldiery have become stricter since the ' good old days,' " he observed, "the drill has certainly grown looser."

Then Bronzeface took his visitor round the great, airy barrack-rooms of his company, where order and cleanliness reigned supreme ; into the sergeants' mess—a second and cheaper edition of the officers'; from the men's recreation-room through the shooting gallery, bowling alley, theatre, racquet court, canteens, and cook-houses to the quartermaster's stores, and the tailors' and shoemakers' shops, each with its busy crowd of stitching, hammering soldiers. In one room a lecture on explosives, shells, and fuses was going on, while in another a detachment was being initiated into the mysteries of knotting and splicing, lashing and stowing hammocks. In the main battery, which was an exact reproduction of a man-of-war's fighting deck with its double row of 6-in. quick-firing guns, a young " makee-learn" sea-soldier officer was drilling the quarters; while outside upon the creek a cutter's crew were learning from a weather-beaten corporal "how to pull an oar." In addition to all this, the major-instructor was conducting an examination of officers, and yet another party were away in a gun-boat at target practice under his subaltern-assistant.

"They make you Johnnies earn your pay," was the Makee-learn's comment. "Although you are a light infantry regiment, you are a devilish fine artillery brigade as well ! "

"You are beating up for another whisky and soda," laughed Bronzeface.

"I don't mind if I do have another when we get back to the mess, but I mean what I say, all the same. My dear fellow, how on earth have you managed to survive it all these years ? Serving under the Army Act one day and under the Naval Discipline Act the next, infantry soldier, artilleryman, sailor. If I were to stay here a whole year I don't believe at the end of it I should quite know what Marines are."

"I don't believe you would," said Bronzeface, quietly, " for with all my seventeen years' experience of them, I'm hanged if *I* do ! "

The Guard Sergeant and the Fusileman.

*The two previous Articles entitled " The Sea Regiment" appeared in our issues for October 30th, 1896, and May 28th, 1897.*

### CHAPTER XI. *(continued).*

"SOME question of legal powers. Granting attorney to representatives in New York, assigning certain properties by deed to trustees. Legal business. The law, you know, requires the signature to be given in the presence of the United States Consul."

"You saw Captain Wood, did you, yourself?"

"Why, certainly. A man worth millions; he interested us all. Took it quietly enough, though. Rather ordinary sort of sportsman. Tall enough, but no show about him. For so rich a man he went very plainly dressed—only a Derby hat and a business suit."

What, as you know, gentlemen, they call in this country a suit of "dittoes"; the same clothes, no doubt, as those sent from Clarges Street.

"Handsome young man, eh? Tall, fair, holds himself well?" I suggested.

"Why, no! Rather mean, I should say. Fair, yes; thick-set, coarse-looking; but I had no talk with him. He and his friends were in the inner room with the Consul himself."

"His friends?" I hazarded.

"I suppose so, but he might have found better. There was that Lawford—Jimmy they call him. I don't know much about him—no good, anyway. And there was Colonel McQuay, who ran the Cyclostoma swindle out West, and a little black-faced Spanish chap, who looked hungry enough to eat him, clothes and all. If you're a friend of Captain Wood's, Snuyzer, I'd warn him against being too thick with that crowd."

"Warn him!" I said to myself as I walked away from the Consulate. "If he'd listened to me he would have never got into this fix."

Much as I had been surprised by the promptitude with which these unscrupulous foes had got him into their toils, I was now amazed with the breadth, the boldness of their scheme.

It was as clear to me as if I had seen it all in print. To seize, sequestrate, securely hold their prisoner, with heaven knows what added ill usage, it might be make away with him utterly, while his double, some cleverly set up second self, their puppet or confederate, personated him, acted for him, making ducks and drakes of his fortune, acquiring every red cent that was movable and within reach, without fear of interference or retribution, provided only they kept fast hold of their prey.

How far was it in my power to meet and frustrate these felonious but astutely-planned measures? At least I had one or two threads, one or two clues, in my hand.

I believed that I could exactly locate the present place of Captain Wood's detention. I knew the very house or its out-buildings in which he was imprisoned. To get him out must be my next job. If he were once free, much mischief, the worst certainly, might be prevented. But whether he were immediately released or not, it was of little less importance to follow up his persecutors to ascertain what they were doing, and work to counteract and defeat them.

Three of them, at least, I had heard of, thanks to my friend at the Consulate, two by name and clear identity; the third should be discovered through the other two.

My next moves were clearly and imperatively marked out for me.

As I passed along the Strand I called in at Norfolk Street. Young Dumbleton was there at his post. No sign from Joseph, so all was presumably without change in the Strathallan Road.

But time was getting on. Close on 3 p.m., and nothing done as yet in Mr. Wood's behalf. I was impatient, eager to act for him, and yet I knew I must proceed regularly.

First, while Dumbleton rang up a messenger boy, I wrote a brief letter to Messrs. Knight and Rider, your agents and correspondents in London, instructing them to forthwith find Jimmy Lawford and Colonel McQuay, then "shadow" them and all associated with them closely, especially the little Spaniard and the fair-haired double of Mr. Wood. I gave the Leviathan Hotel as Lawford's usual place of resort, described him fully, also the Colonel, but could add no more than a vague indication of the others.

Then, filling my comfit box with the Bighorn digestive meat lozenges, a most excellent and sustaining food for people who have no time for regular meals, and eating one or two as I went along, I drove to Clarges Street.

The man Savory had returned, and I knew by his face that he had drawn blank in Laburnum Street.

Of course, no Mr. Wood was there. I did not require to be told that. Savory was also satisfied now, a good deal on the evidence of the collie dog.

"Master Willie was nowhere on the premises. Roy will answer for that. I told him to 'go look,' although the woman of the place—it was a sort of second-rate lodging-house—called him a dreadful dog and tried to stop him. Roy's teeth helped him to quest right through the house."

"Fine fellow! We'll take him with us to look for Mr Wood—eh, Roy?"

He was like a Christian, that dog, for he made friends at once, wagged his tail, and put his nose in my hand. When Savory added on some gibberish with "ulloolooloo, go search, Roy," he first howled and yelped, then ran up and down the hall entry like a mad thing.

"Where are we going, sir?" asked Savory, growing respectful as he recognised my authority. That's the way with Englishmen helps, I have observed—either stand-off or servile, according as they think you a poor critter or some pumpkins.

"To Scotland Yard straight. They wouldn't listen to me this morning. Now, perhaps——what have you got there?"

"It's a letter, sir, brought by hand half-an-hour ago, for Mr Wood. Marked 'Very immediate,' d'ye see? But—you wouldn't, surely?"

This was in alarmed protest as I was about to break the seal.

"Wouldn't I, though! Why, it's a question of life and death with Captain Wood. Anything and everything that is likely to help us must be made use of. I stand on that; and here goes."

But just as I was about to open the letter we were interrupted by the arrival of a tall, military-looking old gentleman, with a fierce face and a very hectoring, over-bearing manner.

---

## CHAPTER XII.

WE were standing in the hallway, the man Savory and I, for although he knew what my business was he did not trust me enough to let me go upstairs. The front door was just ajar, he inside and I still on the stoop, when this high falutin', masterful sort of gentleman came up and said to both of us:

"Is this where Captain Wood lives? Look sharp, I want to know."

There was a shortness in his tone and manner which, being a free born American, I could not stomach at all. He might have been a nigger-driver talking to black Africans, and I looked at him in a way to warn him not to raise my dander.

"Come, speak out; which is the man of the house? Is Captain Wood in? I must see him at once. I am Sir Charles Collingham."

At this Savory bowed low. They are a mean, lick-spittle lot, these Britishers, when there's any talk of titles or big toads in their puddles.

"Yes, yes, Sir Charles: quite so, I know you now. But Captain Wood is not in."

"Where shall I find him? I must see him at once. It is a matter of duty. Where is he?"

"That's just what we want to know," I put in. "It puzzles us entirely. He has got into some mess somewhere, and we can't tell for certain what has happened to him, or where to find him."

"And who the devil are you, pray?" asked my gentleman, insolently. "And what in G——'s name have you to do with Captain Wood? You are an American, I perceive."

"Wal, that's so, and what difference does that make? Aint I good enough to know Captain Wood or for you to talk to?" He had pretty well raised my dander this time.

"Pshaw, I've nothing to say to you. I don't know you, and I don't want to know you, and you may go to the devil your own road as soon as you please."

And without waiting for more, he brushed past me, pushing Savory aside, and saying:

"I must go up to his rooms; there are some papers up there I want. Show the way, please," and he ran upstairs.

Of course, I followed. I was as much concerned about Captain Wood as he was. Besides, I felt it due to my self-

respect and position, as one of your most trusted agents, to call this over-bearing Britisher to account.

The new visitor, General Sir Charles Collingham, as I presently heard he was called, was the first in the room; and he went straight to the bureau or escritoire, at which I expect Captain Wood did his writing business. The General fell upon the papers and turned them over with much haste and excitement. Then he turned to Savory, and said in the same peremptory tone, "Where is the despatch-box from my office, sent here last night? I don't see it; fetch it, will you."

"But it went to the Captain this morning, Sir Charles, with his portmanteau and other things."

"Great powers, how could it, when you don't know where he is?"

"If you will permit me to explain," I here put in, although I wonder I went on, for I saw clearly on his face that he thought me an interfering nonentity, altogether beneath his contempt. But as I told my story, his manner changed, his look of utter incredulity and amazement gave way to one of absorbed interest; and by the time I had finished he had thrown himself into the nearest armchair with a loud and prolonged whistle, an evident let-off to his disturbed feelings.

Then he sprang to his feet, and walked up and down the room like a madman, talking to himself aloud:

"It's not possible. It's too preposterous. I cannot, ought not, to believe it. But yet, by the Lord Harry, strange things do happen."

Then he pulled up short and faced me as if I were a criminal and a tough.

"I suppose you are to be trusted? Who and what do you call yourself? You haven't dreamt all this? You weren't drunk last night?"

"I am a water-drinker, Sir Charles Collingham, and take it, for choice, hot — according to my physician's rule," I replied, severely. "You, I conclude, from your title, are a British Army officer; but I do not consider you are a gentleman to make such aspersions."

"Come, come, don't lose your temper. I never do—it's a mistake—in business; and you haven't told me yet who you are, and what you have to do with Captain Wood."

The shortest way was to give him one of my cards. He was not unacquainted with the name of Saraband, and said so, courteously enough, now so civil that, judging him to importance, I gave him a brief outline of the plot to which we believed Captain Wood had fallen a victim.

*"Of course, you are from Capt Wood"*

Indeed, he became really a person of had fallen a victim.

"You think it is the money, do you? Nothing else?" he asked, sharply.

"Why, what else could there be?"

He hesitated for a moment, but said at last:

"I'm not at liberty to tell you exactly. They are confidential matters connected with the Service. But there might be reasons to induce designing people to carry off Captain Wood and hide him for a time. He possesses certain information of the highest value to——Well, I must not tell you. But the disappearance of these papers, of the despatch-box in short, supports me in that view."

"There are public grounds, then, for instituting a keen search for Captain Wood?"

"Very much so indeed; and we must instantly call in the police. I shall go at once to Scotland Yard and set the detectives in motion."

"Guess I've been there already, and they only laughed at me."

"By George, they will not laugh at me! Why this might

become a Cabinet question. If those papers have fallen into the wrong hands there may be the devil of a row. Wood or no Wood, I must have them back this very day; and I can't stop talking here."

"One moment, Sir Charles, my—our interest in Captain Wood is hardly second to yours. Anyway they are identical. It would be best, I submit, to work together."

"Quite so. That is very sensible. Have you any plans? What would you propose?" He was as sweet as milk by this time.

"Well, obviously one thing presses urgently. A descent should be made by a posse of police upon that house in the Strathallan Road. If I had had my way—if those darned dunder-headed devils in Scotland Yard had accepted my story—it would have been made hours and hours ago. Now it is quite on the cards that the birds have flown; although, if that were so, I think I should have heard something from my assistant on the spot, young Joseph Vialls."

"In any case there shall be no more delay. Here you, sir"—this was to Savory—"hail the first cab. I'm off to Scotland Yard. Will you come with me?"

"I'd rather meet you, Sir Charles, out yonder; for I suppose you'll go yourself with the police?"

"Certainly I shall, possibly ahead of them; so *au revoir.*"

"Stay, Sir Charles. I had forgotten this letter, which came an hour ago. It is addressed to Captain Wood, and it might throw some light on this mysterious affair. To be sure it is in a woman's hand; but I was just about to open it when you appeared. Do you think I dare?"

"By all means. Every scrap of intelligence is of the utmost importance now. I'll do it. I can settle afterwards, if necessary, with Captain Wood."

So he broke the seal, opened the letter, and instantly burst into a loud cheery laugh.

"Oho! Miss Frida, so you have not been long in coming to an understanding with our man of many millions. Read it," he said, and he handed me the letter. It was headed "273, Hill Street," and was signed "Frida." There were only a few lines:

"*What has become of you? I thought we were to see you early, before luncheon. I have been simply furious; now I am frightened; something must have happened. It cannot be that you have already forgotten —— last night?*"

"Reckon I know what she means by 'last night,' for I heard their parting at the door of the house in Prince's Gate."

"Where, no doubt, they had been billing and cooing," added the General. "Well, she is his 'mash,' and she is entitled to know what has happened. You had better go round by Hill Street, on your way to Barnes. Enough said—I'm off."

We soon started, Savory and I in a second hansom; and, at the man's suggestion, took the dog.

"He'll surely find the Captain," said Savory, "if there is any sort of scent"; and the dog seemed to understand his business, for directly we reached Hill Street he was the first inside the house, and raced upstairs in a business-like way, and evidently quite at home in the place.

By-and-bye he came down again, followed by about the brightest, smartest, and sweetest young creature I had seen since my last Sunday walk on Fifth Avenue after church.

It's not in my line to say what she wore, but I think it was a tailor-made garment, and it fitted her like a glove. All I could see were her flashing eyes, and the red lips apart as she tackled me sharply.

"Of course you are from Captain Wood? This is his dog. What have you got to tell me? Quick. Explain. Where is he himself?"

"I wish, madam, I could tell you that for certain, but I cannot. The fact is, the Captain is——"

"Here! Step in here." She opened the door of a room, showed me a chair, then took her stand on the hearthrug, with her arms behind her back and a look on her face that made me—old as I am and in such poor health—feel very envious of Captain Wood.

"Go on, please. The worst first. He is ill, injured?"

"He may be both or neither, but there is no saying till we find him. He is missing. Well, not exactly that, for I have a strong hope that I know where he is. But he has been carried off and is in durance, a close prisoner, I believe."

Her eyes opened wider and wider with terror, surprise, and indignation; the last, I think, the strongest of the three.

"Let me have the whole story, or as much as you know of it. Make haste, please."

She still stood erect and fearless, showing great mastery over herself as I told briefly and quickly all I knew. Except that the colour came and went, that her cheek was now crimson, now blanched a creamy white, that her eyes glittered with the tears she still resolutely kept back, this brave child suffered no sign of emotion to escape her at the peril of her lover.

"Well, what have you done?" she asked, imperiously. "What do the police say?"

I began to explain.

"Tut, tut. Let us have no excuses, no beating about the bush. You have known this—let me see—more than twelve hours, and yet my, my—friend, Captain Wood, is still there where you say they took him."

"Where I *believe* they took him."

"This won't do at all, Mr. ——. I don't know who you are or what you call yourself——Snuyzer, an American detective? Ah! well, Mr. Snuyzer, I shall now take this matter in hand. We've got to find Captain Wood—at least I have, whether you come into the business or not."

"I shall be sorry to be left out, miss; but there are others besides us have taken it up now. I've seen a British General, Collingham by name."

"Yes, yes, I know. Willie's—I mean Captain Wood's chief at the Intelligence. I was just going to send to him. He is a man of great influence and importance. A man of the world, who knows his way about. He has been told then? What is he doing?"

"Working the police. He will take a mob of them down to where I traced the Captain. I am going on to meet them there."

"Then I'll go too. Wait here, please, while I put on my hat," and she rang the bell. "When the man comes, tell him to bring my bike round. No; I'd better take you with me. Order my pony cart. Say it must be at the door in ten minutes from now."

She fairly took my breath away with her promptitude and self-possession, and I could have gone down on my knees to her then and there to ask her to be my partner for life. The two of us together would have beat creation in our business.

By-and-bye, no, much sooner, in less than ten minutes, she came downstairs dressed for driving, and buttoning on her gloves.

"Come, sir," she said, brisker and sharper than ever. "I cannot easily forgive your previous dilatoriness, but we must try and make up for lost time. Here is the pony cart, and we will take the dog."

Under any other circumstances it would have been a rare treat to be out riding with this pretty creature in her own private buggy, to be driven through Hyde Park at the brightest time of the day. But I had barely time to thank my stars I was in my best frock-coat and hat, for as she flogged her trotting pony into its best pace she insisted upon hearing the whole story over again.

"What have they done to him, d'ye suppose?" she asked, bravely, but I saw that it cost her a good deal to say it. "They would not harm him, surely?"

"I guess he's worth more to them alive than dead. Money's what they're after, I believe, although this General has another idea. I reckon they'll try first to make some terms with him. If he resists, refuses to accept——"

"As I certainly believe he will," she put in, quickly.

"They will hold him fast, somewhere apart and hidden, while they help themselves to his pile. You can see what they're manœuvring after by setting up this puppet."

"It was not he himself, of course, who was at the Consulate this morning?"

"Could not have been. I had thought of that, but it don't fit either way. If he was hurt he couldn't have gone, nor yet if he was a prisoner, as I firmly judge him to be, still; and if neither, why should he play hide and seek with a crowd of crooks? Besides, you would have heard of him or from him, miss, during the day."

"I suppose so. No." She corrected herself at once, stifling any possible doubt of his loyalty. "Of course I should have heard of him, have seen him, before this. And their plan will be to hurry over to the United States, some of them, all of them, perhaps, with this sham Mr. Wood, and use him in laying hands on what they can?"

"Precisely, miss." Her smartness did me good to see, and I told her so admiringly. "They'll try to put the power of attorney and the assignments into force and wreck the property."

"That, of course, must be prevented. Captain Wood's lawyers, some person with authority, must warn the American agents or bankers, put them upon their guard."

"Why, certainly. Only it must be done in person by someone who is well acquainted with the real Captain Wood and can expose the impostor. They have the start of us, and no time must be lost. We have to find the emissary. If it was so agreed I myself could go by the very first steamer."

She looked at me as I said this just for one moment, but it was through and through me. Did she distrust me? The whole story was my own. It was unsubstantiated. Nothing was proved, not even that harm had come to Captain Wood. Then, she knew nothing of me. I might be an impostor, one of the very lot hostile to Captain Wood.

"Of course someone will have to go. More than one probably. There are many who would be willing to; but at this moment we have still more urgent business, and that is to find Captain Wood."

*(To be continued).*

Photo. Elliott & Fry.                                                                              Baker Street.

### *GENERAL SIR WILLIAM OLPHERTS, K.C.B., V.C.*

SIR WILLIAM OLPHERTS is one of the surviving veterans of Lucknow, at the head of which heroic band as chairman he has presided on several occasions at the annual Lucknow banquet in memory of the heroic defence and equally heroic relief of the great mutineer stronghold of the North-West Provinces in 1857. It was at Lucknow in the Mutiny that Sir William won his V.C., with the C.B. and brevet of major, and the sobriquet by which he is best known to the Service, "Hell-Fire" Olpherts. At that time he was a captain of Bengal Artillery, and his V.C. was awarded him in particular, in the words of Havelock's Field Force Orders, "for highly distinguished conduct on the 25th September, 1857, when the troops penetrated into the City of Lucknow, in having charged on horseback with Her Majesty's 90th Regiment when . . . . it c ptured two guns in the heavy fire of grape, and having afterwards returned under a severe fire of musketry to bring up limbers and horses to carry off the captured ordnance, which he accomplished." The Mutiny though, in which Sir William distinguished himself by his fiery valour repeatedly, in innumerable actions with the Pandies, is only an incident of a long and brilliant career—in Burma in 1841, at Gwalior in 1843, with Sir Charles Napier in Scinde in 1845, with Sir Colin Campbell on the Peshawar Frontier in 1852, in the Crimea throughout the Russian War. He became general in 1883.

# HER MAJESTY'S VISIT TO NETLEY.

*NETLEY HOSPITAL, FROM THE SOLENT.*

WE are able in this number to give some photographs of the Queen's late visit to the Royal Victoria Hospital at Netley. In the main, no doubt the visit was intended as a token of esteem for those of her soldiers who were wounded or rendered ill in her service in the Tirah Campaign, but the whole hospital was inspected; and a visit to Netley well

Photos. F.G.O.S. Gregory & Co., 51, Strand.        *THE ARRIVAL OF THE QUEEN.*        Copyright.—Hudson & Kearns

*MEDICAL STAFF CORPS BRINGING IN INVALIDS.*

repays one. As will be seen from the photograph, it is a lovely building, beautifully situated on Southampton Water, and, seen from the Solent, forms one of the most picturesque views on that very picturesque piece of ocean. Not only is it the finest military hospital, probably in the world, but it is also the school where our Army surgeons go through their military training. One of our illustrations shows the arrival of the Queen at Netley Hospital, where she was received by a guard of honour of the King's (Shropshire Light Infantry). It was arranged that Her Majesty should first visit the surgical wards, which are situated on the top floor of the building. Then a descent was made to the second floor, and the medical wards

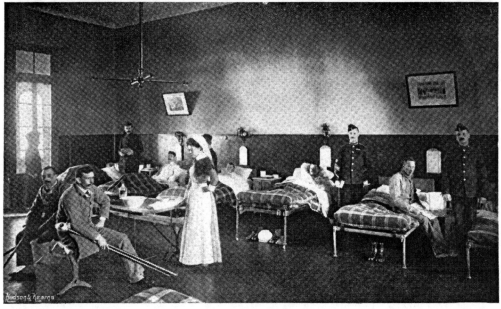

*A WARD IN THE HOSPITAL.*

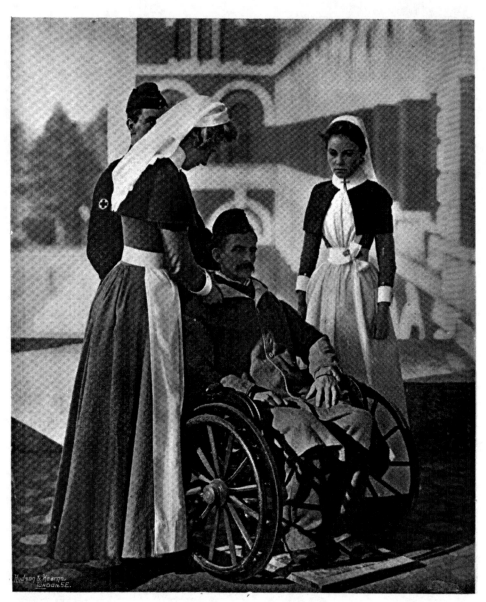

Photo. F.G.O.S. Gregory & Co., 51, Strand
### TAKING THE AIR IN THE GROUNDS.

visited, and finally the Queen passed through the convalescent wards, which are situated on the ground floor of the building. There is, to our mind, something different about the ward of a military hospital to a ward in any civil institution of the kind. A ward of any kind in any first-class hospital is always, of course, kept exquisitely neat, spotlessly clean, and beautifully ventilated. Then, again, a ward is on the whole rather a cheerful place than otherwise, though, of course, the atmosphere of suffering always surrounds one. But so cheery and bright are both nurses and patients, that the feeling of depression soon leaves one. This of course applies to Netley as to any other hospital, but at Netley there is something more. The uniforms of the doctors and attendants give a colour to the scene, while the white aprons and caps of the good sisters and nurses are also in evidence. But, above all, we are intensely interested in the patients, for we remember that in every case they are men suffering from wounds and illness contracted in the service of their country in some out-of-the-way corner of the globe. We look down the ward, and we see in imagination the great British Empire stretching out North, East, South, and West. It is like having a map before us. That poor fellow in the corner contracted his illness in Barbados. The man in the bed next him was injured in an accidental explosion at Halifax. The cripple in the wheeled chair in the verandah lost his leg by a charge of "pot-leg" fired into it at close quarters by a nigger in the African bush. That stalwart trooper turning over the leaves of a book at the table owes his empty sleeve to an Afghan Snider bullet he got in the Khyber Pass; while the man sitting opposite him is just pulling round after bad dysentery that he got dacoit hunting in a Burman jungle. And so they come from all quarters of the globe, some to be more or less invalids for life, some to become once more hale and sound, some to have paid to them the only honours we can give to the dead brave—the roll of the muffled drums and the sharp report of the volley firing.

# ENGLAND'S VETERANS.

TO-DAY, the oldest in-pensioner of that historical institution, the Royal Chelsea Hospital, is Thomas Cross, who
was admitted on December 1st, 1887.  Born at Morden,
in Kent, he is 94 years of age, a fine old man with a face
like a ripe brown hazel-nut, with merry eyes, and in full possession of his faculties.  He joined the 40th Foot in 1825,
has four war medals, and was never wounded.  He saw service
in New South Wales, Van Diemen's Land, India, Afghanistan,
at the defence of Candahar, and is one of those who defeated
the Mahrattas at Marahjpore.

In another room in the hospital is an invalid, a comparatively young man, for he is but 66 years of age.  For 23 years
has this man lain bedridden, a martyr to the most acute form
of rheumatic arthritis.  Readers of Kinglake's " Invasion of

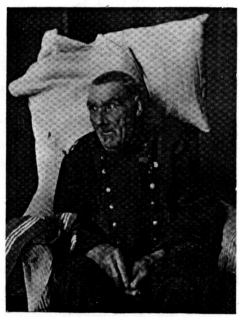

*THOMAS CROSS, AGED 94.*

*SERGEANT CONWAY, AGED 66.*

the Crimea " will recall Sergeant Conway, of Turner's battery,
who saved Captain Henry, R.A., V.C., when the latter was
about to be bayoneted unto death.  Conway was born at
Charlemont, County Armagh, on St. Patrick's Day.  His has
been an adventurous career.  At the close of the Russian
War he went to Canada, and took his discharge at Hamilton,
Ontario.  Some years later, while at Perth in Western
Australia, he was appointed veterinary surgeon to the Government.  He received the French eagle for bravery.  He missed
getting the V.C., because those who could have recommended
him passed away ere they could see justice done.

# THE 3rd BATTALION PRINCE OF WALES'S OWN
### (WEST YORKSHIRE REGIMENT).

*THE COMMANDING OFFICER, ADJUTANT, AND SERGEANT-MAJOR.*

FEW battalions belonging to the Militia
Forces can boast of such a record of
service as the 3rd Battalion The Prince
of Wales's Own (West Yorkshire Regiment).
It was raised at York in 1759, where have
been its headquarters ever since that date.
The battalion was continuously on service
for twenty-three years (excepting an interval
of twelve months after the Peace of Amiens
in 1802), and has done in all no fewer than
thirty-four years of embodied duty.

When the Gordon Riots convulsed the
Metropolis the battalion formed part of the
military force stationed in London, and was
encamped in the gardens of the British
Museum.  It was actively engaged in the
arrest of Parker, the ringleader of the mutiny
at the Nore, and saw service in Ireland
during the Rebellion, in 1814 and in 1816.
When the Russian War broke out it had
the honour of being included among the
militia regiments selected to garrison the
Mediterranean.  In recognition of this service the 3rd Battalion West Yorkshire
Regiment bears on its colours the word
Mediterranean.  This privilege was granted
by Her Majesty in 1856, and is shared by
but few other militia battalions.  When doing
duty in "the sunny South" the regiment

volunteered for active service, and would have journeyed to the seat of war had the disastrous campaign continued. Such a creditable record justifies us in considering the battalion a worthy ornament to the "Old Constitutional Force."

The White Rose of York was sanctioned in 1811 as the regimental badge. The badges now worn in the cap, as may be seen in the photograph of the permanent staff, are the Prince of Wales's plume and the White Horse.

In 1892 H.R.H. the Duke of York became honorary colonel, and still continues to fill that appointment. The uniform is, like that of the Line battalions (the old 14th Foot), scarlet with white facings.

The first photograph depicts Colonel G. T. Hay, C.B., the commanding officer, with the adjutant, Captain H. B. C. Trevor, and Sergeant - Major Pincombe.

The second picture represents the officers, all dressed in what is generally known as "fatigue kit."

In the third are seen the non-commissioned officers and drummers of the permanent staff who during the non-training period do duty at the Depôt, York. The seven drummers in front are distinguishable by the "wings" on the shoulders of their tunics, and it is a fact worthy of notice that the third man from the left is wearing no fewer than *nine* good conduct badges on his left arm. It is hardly suffi-

THE OFFICERS.

THE PERMANENT STAFF.

THE REGIMENTAL GUARD.

cient to say that such a proof of long service is seldom to be met with, for the number of chevrons convey to the military man the fact that the drummer in question has served for thirty years in an exemplary manner. It is therefore unlikely that any private soldier now serving can surpass this record, if indeed he can equal it.

The following illustration is that of the regimental guard. It is commanded by a sergeant, and occupies the guard tent. A private detailed for guard duty does two hours' sentry-go, followed by four hours' rest, and so on. The strength of the guard is therefore based on this consideration and governed by the number of sentry posts which it is required to furnish. A guard of this description, as well as taking care of Government property placed in its charge, is also entrusted with the care of prisoners awaiting disposal by court-martial or the commanding officer. Unlike volunteers, the militia are subject to military law when called out for training, whether attached to regulars or not.

Such a scene as that following is an every-day sight in a militia camp. A considerable portion of the battalion has just returned from musketry practice at the rifle ranges, and the men are now busy cleaning their rifles and accoutrements for the morrow's parade.

From Photos     SCENE IN CAMP.     By a Military Officer.

Very stringent rules for sanitation obtain in camp. Early every morning the "curtains" of the tents are rolled up, as they appear in the photograph, to admit of a free supply of fresh air. In fine weather, too, the wooden floors and bedding are placed outside the tents, and round these the men are accustomed to congregate. The rifles of each tent are neatly stacked at the entrance, to admit of more room in the tent during the day. In camp there are usually to be found no permanent cook-houses, and on that account the meals are cooked in the open, or in a covered-in wooden shed, as in the last illustration. On the left is shown a temporary contrivance for baking bread, known as the "Aldershot oven." The photographs were all taken at Strensall during the annual training of the battalion.

From a Photo. *A FIELD KITCHEN.* By a Military Officer.

# THE SOUDAN CAMPAIGN.

IN the present number we are able to produce some more photographs illustrative of the recent military developments in Egypt. In one we see the Cameron Highlanders

*SIDI GOBER STATION—WAITING FOR THE TROOPS.*

drawn up on parade preparatory to leaving barracks for the front, where they by now have arrived. They are one of the

*THE ARRIVAL AT THE STATION.*

finest and best disciplined corps in the Service, and until the other day, when a second battalion was—or rather is now in

From Photos By a Military Officer.
*GENERAL HENDERSON PUTS IN AN APPEARANCE.*

From Photo. By a Military Officer.
*CROSSING THE LINE TO THE TRAIN.*

process of being—raised, they had the distinction of being the only one-battalion corps in the Army. Raised in 1783 by Cameron of Erracht, afterwards Sir Alan Cameron, K.C.B., they served in Holland, North America, and with Abercromby in Egypt. They went to Copenhagen in 1807, and in 1809 were in Spain. During the retreat on Corunna the regiment lost 90 officers and men, though as they were not actually in action on the 18th of January, 1809, Corunna is not one amongst the actual record of their regimental honours. But the roll is a goodly one, nevertheless, for it comprises : Egmont-op-zee, Egypt, Fuentes d'Onor, Salamanca, Pyrenees, Nivelle, Nive, Toulouse, Peninsula, Waterloo, Alma, Sebastopol, Lucknow, Egypt, 1882, Tel-el-Kebir, Nile, 1884-85.

In the desperate fighting at Fuentes d'Onor the Camerons found themselves opposed to the French Imperial Guard, and there they lost their commanding officer, the gallant Colonel Phillips Cameron, the eldest son of the Cameron who originally raised the regiment. The latter's story is a most romantic one. He was born in "the '45," and so inhaled the warlike spirit with the first breath that filled his infant lungs. As a youth he had to flee to America, having killed a kinsman in a duel, and there he served as a volunteer with a regiment disbanded in 1784—the 84th Royal Highland Emigrants. The first battalion of this regiment was raised in Canada in 1763, from the families of old soldiers of the 42nd, 77th, and 78th Highlanders who had settled in Canada

*OFF TO THE SOUDAN.*

after the peace of 1763. The second battalion was similarly raised from settlers in Nova Scotia. Old Sir Alan, who was immensely popular with his Highlanders, was always known as "Old Cia mar tha," as he always acknowledged his men's salutations with the Gaelic greeting of "Cia mar tha thu?" ("How are you?").

In another photograph we have depicted the pipe-major of the Camerons instructing some Soudanese bandsmen in the manipulation of his national instrument of harmony—or discord, if you so wish to consider it. The tall pupil on the left of the picture, and wearing the Zouave costume, belongs to the 9th Soudanese. This, one of the smartest corps in the Egyptian Army, was brigaded with the Camerons in the 1884-85 campaign on the Nile, and the two regiments became what Tommy Atkins would call "thick chums." So much so, indeed, that the 9th were known as the "2nd Battalion Cameron Highlanders." They defended Kosheh, near Wady Halfa, during a thirty-one days' investment by the Dervishes in the winter of 1885, and fought together at the battle of Ginniss on the 29th of December in that year.

*TEACHING THE "2nd BATTALION" THE BAGPIPES.*

The other photographs give us pictures of a regiment entraining at Alexandria on departure for the front. One shows us the railway station at Ramleh, near Alexandria, where the troops commence their journey frontierwards. In another we see Major-General Henderson, who commands the garrison at Alexandria, snap-shotted with his wife as he has driven down to the station to see the regiment off.

In another snap-shot the regiment is shown entering the station, with a heavy background of the palm trees which line the road from Alexandria to Ramleh.

In another we see the troops crossing the line to the up platform for Cairo. The heavy marching order, and the khaki-covered helmets of the men, show that they are meant for real work, and not playful manœuvres.

Finally, in the troop train on the siding, the regiment is at last "off to the front." That they may soon meet the Khalifa and his men is the earnest wish of every soul in the closely-packed train.

From Photos.     *LEAVING FOR THE FRONT.*     By a Military Officer.

# The Glories and Traditions of the British Army
## THE*RIFLE*BRIGADE.*
### By Lieut. Col. Percy Groves. R.G.A.

*THEIR FIRST AFFAIR—THE EXPERIMENTAL RIFLE CORPS AT FERROL, AUGUST 25th, 1800.*

"What more can I say to you, Riflemen, than that wherever there has been fighting you have been employed; and wherever you have been employed you have distinguished yourselves."—*Speech of H.R.H. the Duke of Clarence to the Rifle Brigade at Plymouth, 29th July,* 1828.

TOWARDS the close of the 18th century, Colonel Coote Manningham and Lieut.-Colonel the Hon. William Stewart represented to the Government the advantage of adding to the establishment of the British Army a special corps, the men of which should be furnished with arms of precision and carefully trained in the duties of riflemen. Their suggestions met with approval, and in January, 1800, H.R.H. the Commander-in-Chief issued orders for the formation of an Experimental Corps of Riflemen, to be composed of detachments specially selected from fourteen Line regiments, which were mentioned in the Orders. These picked detachments assembled at Horsham, under Manningham and Stewart, and the first parade of the Experimental Corps was held on the 1st April, 1800. The sergeants and rank and file of the several detachments had left their pikes and muskets with their regiments, and were now armed with a 7-grooved rifle, sighted to 200-yds., the invention of Ezekiel Baker, a London gunsmith.

After a few months' training at Swinley Camp, near Windsor, the officers and men attached to the corps were ordered to rejoin their regiments, except three detachments (Travers' 79th, Gardner's 2nd—1st, and Hamilton's 27th), which, at Stewart's request, were permitted to accompany Pulteney's expedition against Ferrol. In a smart encounter with the Spaniards, on the 25th August, the three detachments had four officers (including Stewart) and eight men wounded. "Of this, the first affair in which the regiment was engaged," writes Sir W Cope, "it may be observed that it has the high honour of having shed its first blood before its actual embodiment, and while it only con-

*AN OFFICER OF THE RIFLES, 1801.*

sisted of detachments experimentally assembled for instruction." Though successful in his attack, General Pulteney made no further attempt on Ferrol, but re-embarked his troops, and sailed for Gibraltar. Stewart and two other officers of the corps returned home, the rest accompanied their men to Gibraltar.

Meanwhile Colonel Manningham had received orders to re-form the Rifle Corps, of which he was appointed colonel, by commission dated the 25th August, 1800. At the same time Stewart was gazetted lieutenant-colonel, and the officers who had served with the late Experimental Corps were transferred to the Rifle Corps now permanently established.

The Rifle Corps was formed chiefly of volunteers from Fencible regiments on the Irish establishment, who began to assemble at Blatchington about the end of August, and continued to join throughout the autumn of 1800. At this time the corps was popularly known as "Manningham's Sharpshooters."

The uniform of the Rifle officers consisted of a dark green jacket, with collar and cuffs of black velvet, trimmed with black cord and silver buttons; dark green pantaloons, and hessians. A crimson barrel sash, with cords and tassels, was worn round the waist; the pouch and sword belts were of black leather, the former furnished with silver whistle and chain; the headdress was a helmet (light dragoon pattern), black, with silver mountings, bearskin crest, a turban, and a green feather. The Riflemen wore a plain jacket with short skirts looped up in front; pantaloons and half boots; and a tall, peakless cap, slightly bell-topped, with a green feather. "The privates," says the *British Military Journal* for February, 1801, "are armed with a rifle-gun; a sword, which may be used as such, or as a bayonet; a pouch for cartridges, and a powder horn suspended from a cord slung over the shoulder. The sergeants are distinguished by a whistle on the pouch belt."

In 1801, Captain Sidney Beckwith's company of the Rifle Corps was distributed amongst Nelson's squadron which, on the 2nd April, captured the Danish Fleet at Copenhagen, when Lieutenant and Adjutant J. A. Grant, who had volunteered for this service, was killed whilst fighting the quarter-deck guns of the "Isis." "His head," writes Cope, "was taken off by a cannon ball as clean as if severed by a scimitar." Grant was the first officer of the regiment killed in action. Colonel W. Stewart was also present at Copenhagen, in command of the troops (49th Foot and Beckwith's Company) serving with the Fleet. Nelson, in one of the despatches he sent off, says : "The Hon. Colonel Stewart did me the favour to be on board the 'Elephant,' and himself, with every officer and soldier under his orders, shared with pleasure the toils and dangers of the day."

On the 25th December, 1802, the Rifle Corps was numbered the 95th of the Line, "and thus assumed the name (95th Rifles) under which it was long known, and which its services in Europe made famous." At this period the regiment was very popular, and recruits of a good class were readily obtained. Four ex-officers were, at one time, serving in its ranks, one of whom was actually drawing half pay, and was eventually recalled to full pay.

Early in May, 1805, a 2nd Battalion was added to the 95th, then commanded by Sidney Beckwith. This battalion was embodied at Canterbury, and the command of it given to Major Hamlet Wade —one of the original officers of the corps— who was promoted lieutenant-colonel. Many amusing stories are told of "this extraordinary dashing, gallant Irishman." Wade was an expert shot, and he and two privates, Spurry and Smeaton, used to hold up a target for each other at 150-yds. and 200 - yds. — no mean feat with the Baker rifle.

One day the Earl of Chatham, while watching the practice, remarked that the markers must run great risk. "There's no danger, sir," rejoined Wade, and bidding a Rifleman hold out a target at 200-yds., he fired and hit it. The old Earl was horrified ; whereupon Wade coolly said : "Oh ! we all do it," and,

*DEATH OF LIEUT. GRANT ON THE DECK OF THE "ISIS," APRIL 2nd, 1801.*

running out, he took his turn at holding out the target. In June, 1806, three companies (Macdonald's, Elder's, and Dickenson's) accompanied Sir Samuel Auchmuty's expedition to South America. On the 16th January, 1807, Auchmuty landed near the mouth of the La Plata ; on the 20th he occupied the suburbs of Monte Video, and—though ill provided with guns or ammunition--forthwith invested that town, which was well fortified and garrisoned. On February 2nd a breach was reported practicable, and orders were issued for an assault to take place next morning. The assaulting column paraded a full hour before dawn, under Colonel Gore Browne, of the 40th, and marched off while it

was still dark. Gardner's Riflemen headed the column, the stormers being led by Dickenson ; then came the light and grenadier battalions, followed by the 38th Foot, with the 40th and 87th in support. So silently did the men march that, favoured by the darkness, the head of the column got close up to the town before any alarm was given

Suddenly a bugle sounded, the Spaniards were on the *qui vive*, and at once opened fire. Unfortunately, the head of the column missed the breach—which during the night had been repaired with ox-hides filled with earth, so that in the dim light it was undistinguishable from the uninjured parts of the wall --and many of the stormers were shot down while searching for it. At last, Captain Renny, commanding the 40th light company, hit upon the situation of the breach, and at

his call the eager stormers raced to the spot. Ladders were reared against the earth-filled hides. Gallant Renny was the first to mount, but was instantly shot dead. Infuriated at his fall, the British soldiers dashed into the breach, and scrambled up in the teeth of a deadly fire. Dickenson and his "Green Jackets" were the first to gain the summit, but were closely followed by their comrades and the flankers of the 40th.

Side by side, officers and men mingled together; the Rifles and the old Somersetshires fought their way into the town ; cannon were planted in the streets, and for the moment their fire proved very destructive. Dickenson was killed while cheering on his men, Lieutenants Scanlan and Macnamara (of the 95th) were wounded ; but the worst was over. The British troops came pouring through the breach, the streets were cleared at the bayonet's point, and by daylight Sir Samuel Auchmuty was in full possession of the town of Monte Video. The citadel held out for a while, but surrendered in the course of the day.

The Rifles had one officer and ten men killed, two officers and nineteen men wounded. They were specially thanked in Orders, and eleven sergeants received silver medals in recognition of their gallantry.

In May, General Craufurd arrived at Monte Video with reinforcements, including a wing of the 1st—95th, under Major M'Leod. Subsequently, the eight Rifle companies took part in the disastrous attack on Buenos Ayres, where they lost, between the 2nd and 5th July, 15 officers and 278 men, killed and wounded.

On the evacuation of La Plata, all these companies returned home. Meanwhile, the headquarter wings of both battalions of the 95th saw service in Denmark with Lord Cathcart's force. The 1st Battalion wing was mentioned in despatches for its "conduct and steadiness" at Kioge, August 29th, 1807.

The year 1808 brought with it no hopes of peace. Bonaparte's insatiate ambition kept Europe in arms, and ere long led England to undertake that memorable struggle known as the Peninsular War. Appealed to by the Spaniards and Portuguese to assist them in freeing their countries from the Gallic yoke, the British Government decided, as a first step, to send an expedition, under Sir Arthur Wellesley, to expel Junot's French legions from Portugal. Four companies of the 2nd—95th, under Major Travers, were attached to this expedition, which landed in Portugal early in August. On the 15th of that month, the first shots of the campaign were fired by the Riflemen of the 2nd—95th and 5th—60th, who formed the advance of Wellesley's army, then following in the track of the French, as they fell back on Lisbon. On the evening of the 15th, the Rifles, who had just entered Caldos, were ordered to push on to Obidos and drive the French picquet out of that

After an Engraving.  *THE BATTLE OF VIMIERA.*  By C. Heath.

village. This service was quickly performed, for the enemy offered little resistance; but, unfortunately, some of the Riflemen pursued the picquet nearly a league beyond Obidos, and, when well away from their supports, were attacked by a much superior force of horse and foot. Though taken unawares, the Rifles made a determined stand, keeping their foes at bay until Spencer's brigade came to their assistance. In this affair, the 95th lost Lieutenant Ralph Bunbury and two men killed, Captain Pakenham and six men wounded. Bunbury was the first British officer who fell in the Peninsula. On August 17th, Wellesley attacked Laborde's position at Roliça. The French were posted on a plateau in front of the village —which is situated on a lofty eminence—their flanks resting on precipitous heights, while in their rear several passes afforded a retreat into the mountains. The Riflemen were to cover the advance of Wellesley's centre column, and keep up communication with his left. Dashing into the rugged glens, they attacked the enemy's light troops. The crack, crack of the Bakers was promptly replied to by the sharp report of the Voltigeurs' short muskets, the wild cheer of the Riflemen defiantly answered by the shrill war cry of those famous *tirailleurs*. The Voltigeurs fought right well, but were slowly driven from hill to hill by the Rifles, who proved themselves superior as light troops—being better trained and armed, and more under their officers' control—and, the British having been successful all along the line, the severe contest ended in the defeat of the French.

Wellesley, having received reinforcements from England (August 20th), while in position at Vimiera, resolved to advance on Lisbon, but General Burrard, who had arrived unexpectedly in Maceira Roads, vetoed the advance, though he declined to land and assume command. Wellesley was, however, destined to score another victory ere he was superseded, for on the morrow the French made a vigorous assault

on his position, and were repulsed with great loss. Had the retreating enemy been pursued, their defeat must have become a rout; unfortunately Sir Harry Burrard came ashore and forbade any forward movement until the arrival of Sir John Moore with further reinforcements. "Well, gentlemen," said Wellesley to his staff, when he heard his senior's decision, "we have nothing to do now but go and shoot red-legged partridges!" At Vimiera, the 95th were hotly engaged, and suffered severely, thirty-seven men being killed, five officers and forty-eight men wounded.

The result of this victory was the Convention of Cintra, by which Junot evacuated Portugal. Sir Arthur then returned home, and Moore assumed command of the forces in the Peninsula.

When, in November, 1808, Sir John Moore entered Spain, his forces included the four companies of the 2nd—95th which fought in the late campaign, and a wing of the 1st—95th, which had been with him to Sweden. On December 20th, he was joined by reinforcements under Sir David Baird, with whom came the left wing of the 1st, and the headquarter companies of the 2nd—95th. The entire regiment was now with Moore near Sahagun, the 1st Battalion, under Beckwith, being posted to the reserve, the 2nd, under Wade, to Crauford's brigade.

On Christmas Eve, Moore commenced his historic retreat to Corunna. Across a country knee-deep in snow, with the enemy at their heels, his weary soldiers toiled, turning at bay and repulsing their pursuers whenever attacked, and on the last day of the year, thoroughly done up, they reached Foncevadon. Here Crauford's brigade (43rd, 52nd, and 2nd—95th) left the main body, and, marching

After an Engraving.  *THE DEATH OF SIR JOHN MOORE.*  By W. Heath.

to Vigo, embarked for England on January 21st, 1809. The 1st—95th continued with the reserve, which, under General Paget, formed the rear guard of Moore's army, and, besides suffering great hardships, was constantly engaged with the enemy. The story of Moore's retreat has been often told, so we will relate only one very spirited affair, in which the 1st—95th played the principal part. On January 3rd, the battalion, forming—with a party of the 15th Hussars—the rear guard of the reserve, halted in front of Cacabelos, on a hill sloping to the River Guia, while the other divisions of the army pushed on to Villa Franca. The hamlet of Cacabelos stands partly on the hillside, partly on the opposite bank of the Guia, which is spanned by a bridge at the foot of the village street. The road from the town of Bembibre passes over this bridge, through Cacabelos, thence to Villa Franca. Towards three p.m. on the 3rd, a strong force of Chasseurs-à-Cheval and Voltigeurs, under General Colbert, approached Cacabelos from the direction of Bembibre.

*MOORE'S RETREAT TO CORUNNA - THE DARING EXPLOIT OF TOM PLUNKETT, JANUARY,* 1899.

The alarm was given, and Moore (who constantly accompanied the reserve) seeing the Chasseurs were pricking forward, ordered the battalion to retire across the Guia, covered by Norcott's and O'Hare's companies and the Hussars. The moment the battalion quitted the hill, the Chasseurs, putting spurs to their horses, came tearing down the road, and, on nearing the two companies, they dismounted, linked horses, and advanced à *la tirailleur.* Sharp skirmishing ensued, but not for long, for the Chasseurs, finding the Rifles more than their match at this work, soon doubled back to their horses. Moore then ordered the Hussars to charge them, while the Rifles followed the battalion through the village, and took post on the far side of the bridge. Hardly had Norcott and O'Hare entered the village, when a number of French horsemen galloped up in support of the Chasseurs, and advanced so rapidly that Moore, his staff, and the Hussars were compelled to retire at racing speed. When Norcott saw the General and the Hussars careering down the road, with the French at their heels, he called to the Riflemen to open ranks and let them through, and, the moment they had passed, he formed both companies across the street, and poured such a rapid fire upon the enemy that the pursuit was instantly checked. The Rifles seized this opportunity to make good their own retreat, and, scampering through the village, they reformed on the other side of the bridge.

General Paget had, meanwhile, got the main body of the reserve into position on some heights half-a-mile from the Guia, with the two guns and the Hussars posted on the Villa Franca road, and the 95th midway between the heights and the river. As soon as Norcott and O'Hare lined the river bank, on either side of the bridge, Colonel Beckwith detached three companies, under Major M'Leod, to support them. By this time the Voltigeurs had appeared on the scene, and, fording the Guia, they attacked the detached companies in flank, while the Chasseurs dashed across the bridge. After desperate fighting the five companies—that is, Norcott's, O'Hare's, and the three under M'Leod—were forced to retire into the vineyards bordering either side of the Villa Franca road; but they had no sooner gained cover than the Chasseurs and Voltigeurs made a combined attack upon them. The Riflemen defended their position for nearly an hour. Then Moore, seeing that they could not maintain the unequal contest, ordered the reserve to retire from the heights, and, when the column was fairly in motion, he sent a message to M'Leod to withdraw from the vineyards and rejoin the battalion, which would then follow the main body. As the Riflemen quitted their position, the French, led by Colbert in person, charged the Hussars and guns. Instantly the "Green Jackets" threw themselves again into the vineyards, and opened such a deadly fire on the enemy that they reined in, and then fell back in confusion. Colbert, however, rallied his men, and once more they prepared to charge; but at this critical moment Private Tom Plunkett, a noted shot, jumped over the bank, ran some paces down the road, and, throwing himself on his back, with the sling of his rifle caught over his foot, took deliberate aim, and shot

the brave Colbert dead. Colbert's orderly-trumpeter, seeing him fall, rode straight at Plunkett; but Tom had reloaded his rifle, and the trumpeter shared his General's fate. Tom then doubled back and rejoined his comrades. M'Leod held the position until the reserve had made good its retreat. Then he withdrew from Cacabelos, leaving nineteen Riflemen dead on the snow-clad ground, and forty-eight in the hands of the French

Worn out with fatigue and hunger, constantly harassed by the enemy, Moore's army continued to retire over the Galician mountains, and on the 11th January it reached the heights above Corunna. Five days later Sir John Moore fought his last battle, when his gaunt, ragged battalions were brought to bay by Soult's veterans, upon whom they inflicted a severe defeat, thus proving that their terrible sufferings had in no wise affected their indomitable courage or fighting powers. At Corunna Beckwith's Riflemen were once more pitted against their old friends the Voltigeurs, repulsing them after a two hours' contest, and taking over 160 prisoners. That same night (16th January), their General's remains having been reverently interred, the British troops embarked for England

On returning from Spain both battalions of the 95th went into quarters at Hythe. Here their decimated ranks were soon recruited, chiefly by volunteers from the Militia; indeed, so many good men flocked to the regiment that a 3rd Battalion was raised, of which Major M'Leod (from the 1st Battalion) was appointed lieutenant-colonel.

Its establishment completed, the 1st—95th, under Beckwith, again embarked for the Peninsula, and landing in Portugal in June, 1809, was formed, with the 43rd and 52nd, into Crauford's Brigade—"the Light Brigade, whose deeds of arms in Portugal, Spain, and France, can never be forgotten while England has an army." The battalion took part in Crauford's famous forced march from Calzada to Talavera (28th-29th July), where it arrived just too late to share in Sir Arthur Wellesley's victory over Marshal Victor—the victory which gained Sir Arthur a peerage.

Meanwhile the 2nd—95th served with the Walcheren Expedition, and lost over 300 men through sickness in less than six weeks. So reduced was the battalion by the results of this disastrous campaign, that it was incapacitated for active service for some time; but as its companies were recruited, and the health of their men improved, they were sent out, one or two at a time, to the Peninsula. Early in 1810, two companies of the 2nd and three of the 3rd Battalion embarked for Cadiz, where, in the following July, they were joined by the headquarters and two companies of the 3rd, under Colonel Andrew Barnard. Cadiz was at this time closely invested by Victor, whose advanced posts were pushed up to the Sancti Petri river, except near the bridge of Zuago (the only communication with the mainland), which was so stoutly defended by the British piquets, "that," writes Ford, "it proved a *pons asinorum* to the French, for they never could get over it." The 2nd Battalion companies under Lieutenant-Colonel Norcott, and the wing of the 3rd, under Barnard, fought at the battle of Barrosa (5th March, 1811), losing, between them, 101 officers

*CAPTURE OF A FRENCH GUN BY LIEUT. FITZMAURICE AT VITTORIA, JUNE 21st, 1813.*

and men killed and wounded. A few months later they joined Lord Wellington's army, and were attached to the Light Division. To record all the services of the 95th Rifles in the Peninsular War would require far more space than we have at our disposal. Their battalions, or portions of their battalions, were present at nearly every battle, siege, and skirmish during the campaigns of 1810-14; and the fact that between the 19th March, 1810, and the 18th April, 1814 (on which day Toulouse, the final battle of the war, was fought), the regiment lost in action upwards of 120 officers and 1,300 non-commissioned officers and men, proves that the Rifles, whenever engaged, were well to the front; while the despatches and reports of the generals under whom they served bear ample testimony to their gallantry in the field and soldierly conduct in bivouac and quarters. We will relate a few of the many instances in which the Riflemen particularly distinguished themselves during the campaigns of 1810-14.

In March, 1810, a French corps, under General Ferey, occupied Santa Felice, opposite the pass of Barba del Puerco, from which it was separated by the turbulent torrent Agueda. Barba del Puerco was held by four companies of the 1st—95th, under Beckwith, three companies occupying the village, whilst the fourth was on picquet at the bridge spanning the Agueda. On the night of March 19th, General Ferey placed himself at the head of 600 Grenadiers, and, favoured by the darkness and the roar of the torrent, surprised the sentries on the bridge, who had barely time to discharge their rifles before they were overpowered. The Frenchmen then dashed across the bridge and made for the pass. Here they were confronted by the picquet (O'Hare's company), who bravely opposed them, defending the face of the hill, step by step, muzzle to muzzle, as they were forced up it by overwhelming numbers. But the Riflemen in the village had heard the alarm, and, led by Colonel Beckwith, they rushed to their comrades' aid, not waiting for regular formation, but just fighting the enemy, hand to hand, as they met them. Beckwith and his men attacked their foes with such furious daring that in half-an-hour the French Grenadiers had had enough of it, and, turning tail, they fled across the bridge, leaving two officers and seven men killed, and six prisoners in the hands of their opponents. Of the Rifles, Lieutenant Mercer and three men were killed, and seven men wounded. In a Divisional Order, dated March 25th, General Craufurd made the following remark :—"This action reflects honour on Lieutenant-Colonel Beckwith and the regiment, inasmuch as it was of a sort which the riflemen of other armies would shun. In other armies the rifle is considered ill-calculated for close action with an enemy armed with a musket and bayonet; but the 95th Regiment has proved that the rifle in the hands of a British soldier is a fully sufficient weapon to enable him to defeat the French in the closest fight, in whatever manner they may be armed."

At the storming of Ciudad Rodrigo (19th January, 1812), the 1st and 2nd—95th furnished part of the forlorn-hope, and the 1st Battalion took an active share in the assault. Here fell the gallant General Craufurd, who had since 1807 been constantly associated with the 95th ; here Captain Uniacke, of the 1st Battalion, met his death, by the explosion of an expense magazine, just as he reached the rampart.

Again, the regiment earned "immortal honour" at the assault on Badajos (6th April, 1812), in which eight companies of the 1st, two of the 2nd, and five of the 3rd Battalion took

part. "Who," writes Napier, in his graphic account of that sanguinary fight, "shall measure out the glory of O'Hare of the 95th, who perished on the breach at the head of the stormers, and with him nearly all the volunteers for that desperate service? Who shall describe the martial fury of that desperate soldier of the 95th who, in his resolution to

After a Drawing.    By J. A. Atkinson.

*THE RIFLES IN THE PENINSULAR WAR.*

win, thrust himself beneath the chained sword-blades, and there suffered the enemy to dash his head to pieces with the ends of their muskets?" The 95th lost at Badajos 9 officers and 57 men killed, 14 officers and 225 men wounded. Major O'Hare was very popular in the regiment, and his death was much regretted by all ranks.

Lieutenant FitzMaurice, of the 1st Battalion, performed a daring action at Vittoria (21st June, 1813). Having cleared the village of Arinez, the Rifles were driving the enemy before them, when FitzMaurice noticed a battery of French artillery retiring in haste. Thinking he might intercept it, FitzMaurice started off at speed, followed by his men; but they, being in heavy marching order, could not keep up, and when he reached the road only two were with him. Five guns had now passed, but FitzMaurice intercepted the sixth, and, springing at the lead horses, caught one by the head; whereupon the driver discharged a pistol at him, and sent a

From a Contemporary    Engraving.

*THE BOMBARDMENT OF BADAJOS.*

*THE FIRST SHOT AT THE BATTLE OF WATERLOO.*

ball through his cap. One of the Riflemen then shot a centre horse, thus bringing the team to a standstill, and, other men of the company running up at the moment, the gun was captured and the gunners and drivers made prisoners.

In the attack on the French position near Tarbes (20th March, 1814) the three battalions (sixteen companies in all) of the 95th took a most conspicuous part. The enemy occupied a hill, or rather a succession of heights, intersected with hedges and ditches, their front covered by clouds of light troops. The Rifles were sent to dislodge these troops, and had first to force their way through covert of considerable growth; "then they emerged at the foot of the hill, and the enemy's ranks rose 'tier above tier' on the mountain-side." In the face of a withering fire, the Riflemen attacked the French with their wonted dash. Several of their number, officers and men, were shot down; but the gallant "Green Jackets" would not be denied, and, after hard fighting, they drove the enemy from the heights. "Nothing could exceed the manner in which the 95th set about this business," says an eye-witness. "They possessed an individual boldness, a mutual understanding, and a quickness of eye in taking advantage of the ground, which I never saw equalled. They were, in fact, as much superior to the French Voltigeurs as the latter were to our skirmishers in general."

After the final struggle before Toulouse came the news of the fall of Paris, and Bonaparte's abdication. A cessation of hostilities followed, and in July, 1814, the 95th Rifles returned home. In the winter of 1813-14, detachments of the three battalions served with Sir Thomas Graham (afterwards Lord Lynedoch) in Holland, and took part in the investment of and fighting round Antwerp, including the action at Merxem, 2nd February, 1814. They subsequently joined the army in Flanders, and were present at Waterloo. During the Peninsular War, the officers substituted a tall, peakless cap for the helmet; they wore, too, a furred pelisse over their jackets. The "Belgic cap" (a low-crowned cap, with a false "stand-up collar" and cord and tassels) was issued to the men about 1810-11.

Two months after their return from the Peninsular War, five companies of the 3rd—95th, under Major Mitchell, joined the expedition against New Orleans. On December 11th, 1814, this expedition arrived off the Mississippi, and the troops were disembarked on an island in the River Pearl. On the 23rd, the Riflemen landed at the Bayou Catalan in Lake Borgne, and bivouacked in a field off the New Orleans road, parallel to the Mississippi. During the night an armed schooner dropped down the river and cannonaded the bivouac, without, however, doing much harm. At the same time, a strong force of Americans attacked Captain Hallen's company, which was on picquet about a mile to the front, while a second body advanced through a wood to turn the British right. Hallen and his Riflemen stubbornly stood their ground, and repulsed their assailants again and again; but, at length, they were

forced back by sheer weight of numbers. Hallen, however, though badly wounded, soon reformed his company, and, attacking the Americans in his turn, retook the post. While this hot encounter was going on, Major Mitchell started off with some thirty men to reinforce the picquet; but, in the dark, he marched right amongst the enemy, and was captured with all his party. This "affair of posts" cost the 95th three officers wounded and one missing, twenty-three men killed, fifty-nine wounded, and forty-one missing. Subsequently the five Rifle companies took part in the disastrous attempt to pierce the American lines before New Orleans (8th January, 1815), and in the operations against Fort Boyer. They returned home in March, 1815.

In the Waterloo campaign six companies of the 1st—95th, under Sir A. Barnard, were attached to Kempt's brigade of the 5th (Picton's) Division; six companies of the 2nd and two of the 3rd—95th, under Lieutenant-Colonels Norcott and Ross, to Adam's brigade of the 2nd (Clinton's) Division. The 1st Battalion reached Quatre Bras about three p.m. on the 16th June, and Leach's company (under Lieutenant Fitz-Maurice) was ordered to occupy a small wood, the seizure of which by the enemy (who were already in possession of the wood of Piermont) must have interrupted communications between Quatre Bras and Ligny. "While performing this task," writes Sergeant Costelloe ("Adventures of a Soldier," by Edward Costelloe, K.S.F., formerly a non-commissioned officer in the Rifle Brigade and late captain in the British Legion), "I could see the enemy emerging from a wood about a mile on our right, which was rather on a hill, with a plain between us. We had scarcely taken possession of the wood, when I beheld a French cuirassier on vedette. He was fired at by our men, and his horse shot under him. He disengaged himself as the horse was falling, waving his sword in defiance, but he was immediately dropped by another Rifleman. I can venture to assert that our company was the first of the British army who pulled a trigger at this celebrated battle." Costelloe's assertion that the 95th "opened the ball" at Quatre Bras is borne out by Siborne, who says: "Here, for the first time in this campaign, the troops of the two nations became engaged. The skirmishers who successfully checked the further advance of the French, and secured the wood, were the 1st Battalion of the 95th Rifles, whom the old campaigners of the French Army, at least those who had served in the Peninsula, had so frequently found the foremost in the fight, and of whose peculiarly effective discipline and admirable training they had had ample experience." Besides the occupation of the wood, the 1st—95th held the Namur road, lining the embankment, and pouring a smart fire upon the enemy. The French made desperate attempts to turn the left of the British line, on which the battalion was posted, and, by sheer weight of numbers, forced FitzMaurice's men from the wood; but at last the Rifles received the order to advance, and, jumping over the bank, they dashed in amongst the enemy, driving them from the road and from some buildings which they had occupied.

At the "crowning victory," on the memorable 18th June, the 95th Rifles again displayed those fighting qualities which had already made them famous. During the day each battalion had its two senior officers disabled by wounds. The 1st

*THE EXPEDITION AGAINST NEW ORLEANS—AN AFFAIR OF POSTS, DECEMBER 23rd, 1814.*

Battalion was on the left centre of the position, its right resting on the Namur road, in rear of La Haye Sainte, its left extending behind a hedge running along the ridge to the left. Immediately in front (divided from La Haye Sainte only by the road) was a small knoll, with a sandpit in its farther side, which was occupied by three companies. The battalion had not been long in position when the French guns opened fire, and their columns began to advance. "The scene was grand and imposing, and we had a few minutes to spare for observation," says Kincaid, who was adjutant of the 1st—95th at Waterloo. "The column destined as *our* particular *friends* first attracted our notice, and seemed to consist of about ten thousand infantry. . . . We saw. Bonaparte himself take post on the side of the road, immediately in our front; each regiment as they passed him rent the air with shouts of 'Vive l'Empereur' . . . it was a singular contrast to the stern silence reigning on our side. . . . Our Rifles were, in a few seconds, required to

Guard," which sent those famous veterans flying from the field. This charge "was remarkable for the order, the steadiness, the resoluteness, and the daring by which it was characterised" (Siborne). The losses of the 95th at Waterloo were: 1st Battalion—1 officer and 20 men killed; 14 officers and 124 men wounded. 2nd Battalion—34 men killed; 14 officers and 179 men wounded; 20 men missing. 3rd Battalion—1 officer and 3 men killed; 4 officers and 36 men wounded; 7 men missing.

The 95th subsequently formed part of the "army of occupation," and remained in France until the autumn of 1818. By an Order, dated 16th February, 1816, the regiment was removed from the Line, and styled the Rifle Brigade.

Towards the end of the year 1818 the 3rd Battalion was reduced, some of its men being drafted into the 1st and 2nd Battalions, while the remainder were discharged. About this time, changes were made in the uniform of the Rifle Brigade,

THE "WAR OF THE AXE," 1846-47—THE RETURN OF THE "GREEN JACKETS" TO KING WILLIAM'S TOWN.

play their parts, and opened such a fire on the advancing skirmishers as quickly brought them to a standstill; but their columns advanced steadily through them, and our post was quickly turned in both flanks, which compelled us to fall back and join our comrades behind the hedge, though not before some of our officers and theirs had been engaged in personal combat. When the heads of their columns showed over the knoll which we had just quitted, they received such a fire from our first line that they wavered; but cheered and encouraged by the gallantry of their officers, they at last advanced to the opposite side of our hedge, and began to deploy. Our first line, in the meantime, was getting so thinned, that Picton found it necessary to bring up his second, but fell in the act of doing it." Maddened at the death of their gallant general, the 5th Division poured a terrific volley into the French infantry, and drove them back in confusion. The battalion continued hotly engaged throughout the day, except between two and three p.m., when it had a brief respite, and suffered heavy losses in officers and men.

The companies of the 2nd and 3rd Battalions were at first posted between the village of Merbe-Braine and the road to Nivelles; but after the battle began they formed up, in quarter-column, on a plateau overlooking the Nivelles road, and subsequently they moved more forward, and drew up close to the road. When an attack was made on Hougoumont, they charged and drove back a crowd of French skirmishers; after which exploit they halted in a hollow extending from the ridge towards the south-east of Hougoumont. Here they were charged by the Carabiniers and Grenadiers-à-Cheval of the Imperial Guard, and during the intervals between these charges the 2nd Battalion suffered much from artillery fire. "In one of these charges Captain Eeles formed his company of the 3rd Battalion in line with the rear face of the square of the 71st, and ordered his men not to fire till he gave the word. Then allowing the Carabiniers to approach within thirty or forty yards of the angle of the front on which they were charging, he gave them such a volley as, combined with the fire of the square, brought half of them to the ground." The 2nd Battalion later on joined in the charge on the "Old

a high bell-topped shako being substituted for the "Belgic cap," while the officers adopted the "slung jacket," *à la hussarde*. With a few minor alterations, this handsome dress was worn until 1853 or 1854. The Brigade continued to use the Baker (in which some slight improvements had been made) until 1838, when the Brunswick rifle, sighted to 300-yds., was issued.

In 1842, a Reserve Battalion, consisting of six companies, was formed, and sent out to Nova Scotia.

During the "War of the Axe," 1846-47, the 1st Battalion saw much arduous service in Kaffraria. "It was," writes Mrs. Ward, in her interesting account of this war, ' the useful 'Green Jackets,' the untiring Rifle Brigade, who worried Sandilli out of his hiding-place among the mountains." On the return of the battalion to King William's Town, Sir Harry Smith (himself an old Rifleman) complimented Colonel George Buller on commanding such a corps, and warmly praised the men for "that bravery and endurance which they had displayed during the long and harassing warfare through which they had struggled."

Scarcely had the Kaffir War been brought to a successful termination, when the Dutch Boers broke out into rebellion, and assembled in great force beyond the Orange River. Two companies of the battalion formed part of a column which, under Colonel Buller, was sent against the rebels, and these companies particularly distinguished themselves at the action of Boem-Plaatz, 29th August, 1848. Here the Boers held a strong natural position, improved by a breastwork of piled stones. A flank attack by the Cape Corps having failed, the Rifles advanced in extended order, driving the Boers from ridge to ridge, until, after two hours' hard fighting, they fled in dismay. This affair ended the campaign.

The battalion returned home in 1850, and during the following year, while stationed at Dover, it was reviewed for the last time by the Duke of Wellington, the Colonel-in-Chief of the regiment. Another Kaffir outbreak necessitating the despatch of reinforcements to the Cape, the 1st Rifle Brigade was again selected for active service, and took a prominent share in the Kaffir War of 1851-52-53. The services of the battalion in the Kaffrarian Campaigns are commemorated by the honours "South Africa, 1846-47, 1851-52-53."

On September 14th, 1852, the Duke of Wellington died at Walmer, where the Depôt 1st Rifle Brigade was quartered; and until their illustrious chief's remains were removed, the Depôt companies furnished an officers' guard at Walmer Castle to watch over them. On their removal to London for interment, they were escorted to Deal, by torchlight, by the whole Depôt; while the 2nd Battalion, on the day of the funeral, headed the procession from the Horse Guards to St. Paul's.

H.R.H. the Prince Consort succeeded the great Duke as Colonel-in-Chief of the regiment, which in 1862 was granted the title the Prince Consort's Own.

We now pass on to the Russian War, in which both battalions were employed. At the battle of the Alma the 1st Battalion was not actually engaged. The 2nd was with the Light Division, and came in for the thick of the fighting. In his despatch, Lord Raglan states that the capture of the great redoubt was "materially aided by the advance of four companies of the Rifle Brigade under Major Norcott." In recommending him for the V.C., Sir George Brown adds: "Major Norcott's conduct on that occasion was not only conspicuous to the whole division, but attracted the notice of the enemy; for the officer in command of the Russian battery, who was subsequently made prisoner, informed Lord Raglan that he had laid a gun especially for the 'daring officer in the dark uniform on the black horse.'"

During the siege of Sebastopol, the Rifles were constantly on duty in the trenches, and they fought with consummate bravery and dogged determination at Inkerman; but perhaps their most notable exploit was that of the "Ovens." The French general, Canrobert, drew Lord Raglan's attention to the importance of dislodging certain Russian sharpshooters who had established themselves in some rifle-pits in front of the left attack, and greatly annoyed the allied working parties by their incessant and well-directed fire; whereupon Lord Raglan determined to occupy these rifle-pits, which were known amongst the British soldiers as the "Ovens." The attack on the "Ovens" was confided to the 1st Rifle Brigade, and on the 20th November, 1854, a party, consisting of Lieutenants Henry Tryon, Claude Bourchier, and William Cuninghame, four sergeants, and 200 rank and file, was detailed for the service. Marching down to the trenches, Tryon kept his men under cover until it was dark; then he advanced stealthily, creeping along the broken ground, which led first down an incline, then upwards to the pits. The party was divided into three columns—Tryon with the

of the advanced party, and thereby ensured the entire success of the attack. Throughout the long November night the enemy made repeated efforts to recapture the "Ovens"; but the Riflemen withstood all their attacks, and held the position until morning, when they were relieved by another party from the battalion. This feat of arms, the first of its kind during the war, was warmly eulogised by Lord Raglan; while so pleased was General Canrobert, that he, too, made it the subject of a general order—a most unusual distinction. Bourchier and Cuninghame received the V.C., Colour-Sergeant Hicks, who was by Tryon's side when he fell, the French war medal.

Lieutenant the Hon. H. H. Clifford, Captain (then Sergeant) J. S. Knox, Sergeant J. Bradshaw, and Privates R. Humpston, R. McGregor, and F. Wheatley, also won the coveted cross in the Crimea. During the war the Rifles lost upwards of 850 officers and men in killed and wounded, and nearly 700 by disease.

In 1855 another 3rd, and in 1857 a 4th Battalion, were added to the establishment of the regiment, which has consisted of four battalions ever since.

When, in 1857 the Sepoy Mutiny broke out, the 2nd and 3rd Battalions were sent to India. These battalions took a very active part in suppressing the rebellion, and were repeatedly praised in despatches and general orders; for though the single word "Lucknow" commemorates their services during these troublous times, "one battalion alone kept the field from its landing (November, 1857) until the last day of the Mutiny; marched 1,745 miles in 161 marches; often bivouacked in the open, never once in quarters; and had a fourth of its officers, and a fifth of its non-commissioned officers and men, killed, wounded, or invalided in twenty months." Captain (Sir) H. Wilmot, Corporals W. Nash and S. Shaw, and Private D. Hawkes were recipients of the V.C.

We may here mention that another V.C. was won by Private T. O'Hea, of the 1st Battalion, then stationed in Canada, under the following circumstances: On June 9th, 1866, O'Hea was one of a guard in charge of a railway van containing 2,000-lb. of ammunition. On reaching Danville, the van was found to be on fire, and was hastily pushed down the line away from the station, the inhabitants of the neigh-bouring houses flying in terror. O'Hea ran down to the van, burst open the door, tore away the covering from the ammunition, and extinguished the fire.

The 1st Battalion remained in Canada until 1870, when it returned home. It subsequently went to India, and was actively employed during the Burmese Campaign of 1886-87. The 2nd Battalion took part in the Ashanti War of 1874-75;

*THE CRIMEAN CAMPAIGN—THE ATTACK ON THE "OVENS," NOVEMBER 20th, 1854.*

"stormers," Bourchier with the "supports," and Cuninghame with the "reserve." Taken by surprise, the Russian sharp-shooters, though supported by a strong column of infantry, beat a hasty retreat; but hardly had the Rifles possessed themselves of the pits, when a Russian battery opened on them with grape and canister, and Tryon was shot dead. Bourchier now assumed command, and maintained his advantage; whilst Cuninghame, who had brought up the reserve, repulsed a determined attempt to turn the left flank

the 3rd accompanied the expedition against the Mohmunds in 1863-64; and the 4th saw service in Afghanistan (Ali Musjid) in 1878-79. In all these campaigns the officers and men of the Rifle Brigade showed themselves to possess the same undaunted spirit which animated their forbears of the famous 95th—a spirit which has ever characterised this *corps d'élite,* and which its present officers, from the Colonel-in-Chief, H.R.H. the Duke of Connaught, down to the junior subaltern, take a pride in fostering.

# The Battle Honours of the British Fleet
## The "Swiftsure" by EDWARD FRASER

*THE BATTLE OF GRAVELINES—"WHEREVER THE FIGHT WAS FIERCEST THE 'SWIFTSURE' PUSHED FORWARD."*

THE "Swiftsure" bears one of the most illustrious of the fighting man-of-war names on the roll of the British Fleet. Her record, in fact, is a tale of battle honours that hardly another man-of-war on the Navy List to-day can show.

Queen Elizabeth herself appointed the name in 1573, the year the first "Swiftsure" was built, under its original style of "Swift-suer," or "swift-pursuer"—an ideal name, surely, for a fighting craft that was to be one of the smartest fighting men-of-war of all the Great Queen's Fleet.

Our first "Swiftsure" received her baptism of fire in the fighting with the Spanish Armada in 1588, when, as one of the ships of Drake's own squadron, she followed the flag of the great captain, fighting from first to last side by side with Drake's own "little 'Revenge.'" and taking a leading part wherever the battle was hottest. In the opening fight off the Eddystone the "Swiftsure," as one of the foremost of the English van, had her part in hustling the windward wing of the Spaniards in upon the centre, compelling the galleons to jostle one another and crowd together in confusion, with bad material effect in the way of damage to hulls and masts and spars, and worse moral effect on the nerves of the Spanish captains.

Then the "Swiftsure" fought broadside to broadside in the long, desperate action off the Dorset Coast, on Tuesday, July 25th, when the Spaniards, favoured by a shift of wind, tried to overwhelm Drake's squadron in-shore under the lee of Portland Bill. In the sharp set-to off the Isle of Wight, on the day after the Portland fight, she was again among the foremost—till every powder barrel in the "Swiftsure's" magazines had been opened. Then, in the final "crowning mercy" battle off Gravelines, when the panic-stricken Spaniards, after the night of fire-ship havoc in Calais Roads, made their headlong rush northwards to try and rally in the open waters of the North Sea, no ship of all the English fleet did better service than the "Swiftsure." With the "Revenge" she headed the English attack, from the opening shots at daybreak until the afternoon had run its course, fighting most of the time so close alongside the big galleons that a shot might have been thrown by hand from one ship to another. Of all the heroes of that tremendous day none deserved better of England than the captains of Drake's squadron, and of them not one did more dashing work than sturdy Ned Fenner of the "Swiftsure." Wherever the fight was fiercest the open-jawed gilded tiger figure-head on the "Swiftsure's" long projecting prow was ever thrusting itself, gleaming in the flash of the guns, as it were showing the way to the ship, as the "Swift-

sure" pushed forward, her red and white striped upper works ablaze with musketry from bow to stern. With Drake the "Swiftsure" hung hard on the heels of the flying Spaniards to the last, and from her bow chase guns came one of the last shots fired by English man-of-war at the flying Armada.

Drake's cruise to the coast of Spain in the year after the Armada is the next episode in the "Swiftsure's" story, notable for the escapade of the Queen's boy favourite, the Earl of Essex, on board the "Swiftsure." Slipping off from Court by night, Essex and three other hotheads made a wild gallop down to Plymouth and got on board the "Swiftsure," putting to sea before their pursuers could arrive with a frantic message of recall from Whitehall.

Then we meet the "Swiftsure" in the famous St. Barnabas Day's battle in Cadiz Harbour, on June 11th, 1596, following Essex and Sir Walter Raleigh, "to take, sink, burn, and destroy" the second Armada, with which King Philip designed to exact reparation for the overthrow of 1588. At Cadiz the "Swiftsure" helped to avenge the fate of her own old Armada consort, Grenville's "Revenge." She had a principal part in destroying the great war galleon "St. Philip," the Spanish flag-ship "that saw Sir Richard Grenville die." In the "Islands Expedition" of 1597, the "Swiftsure" once more saw service against the Spaniard, again, too, following the fortunes of Essex and Sir Walter Raleigh, and in three notable war cruises after that.

Her last fight was in Lagos Bay, on October 21st, 1602, when flying the admiral's flag of the celebrated Sir William Monson, at the head of a squadron cruising off the coast of Spain to waylay a treasure fleet from the Spanish Main. The treasure ships were behind time, and Monson watched for them in vain until October 21st. On that day the "Swiftsure" sighted a strange sail and chased after her. The chase proved to be a war galleon, one of a squadron sent from Cadiz to escort the treasure ships in. The Spaniard did not show fight, but ran in for the land, finally bringing up close under the guns of a fort near Cape St. Vincent. The "Swiftsure," pushing in under all sail, followed with the intention of running her enemy alongside, grappling, and boarding. But at the critical moment blundering or want of nerve on the part of the man at the helm caused the "Swiftsure" suddenly to bear up, with the result that she exposed herself at close quarters to a terrific raking broadside that the enemy at that instant fired. The "Swiftsure" was disabled by it at one blow. In Monson's own words: "It rent the ship so that a team of oxen might have crept through her under the half-deck, and one shot killed seven men." In the end, in consequence, although for some time the fight went on, Monson was unable to close and carry out his intention, and after a desultory action with both the galleon and the fort on shore, at nightfall he worked the "Swiftsure" seaward, to return direct to England to repair damages. During the fight, curiously, the Spanish squadron of war galleons to which the "Swiftsure's" antagonist belonged came on the scene, and at the same time the "Swiftsure's" consorts of Monson's squadron. Neither side, however, attempted to interfere. Both squadrons apparently feared being hit by friend or foe, or else they were so interested in the progress of the "Swiftsure's" duel, each hoping to see his own side victorious, that they could not attend to each other.

Her fight in Lagos Bay was the Elizabethan "Swift sure's" farewell to the sea. King James re-built the "Swiftsure," but he chose to rename her the "Speedwell," under which name the old Elizabethan veteran met an untimely end by shipwreck — in the year 1624.

So fine a fighting man - of - war name, though, was not to be let die. King James had to make amends to the Navy some twelve years after he took away the Armada "Swiftsure's" name, and he did so by re-storing the name in one of the new men-of-war built under what we may call James's "Naval Defence Act" of 1618. This is the "Swift-sure" whose beha-viour before the enemy was the saving grace of the Cadiz failure of 1625.

Quarrelling with Spain over the broken-off marriage between Charles, Prince of Wales, and the Infanta, King James on his death-bed left a war with Spain as a legacy to his son, who, for his part, under Bucking-ham's influence, took up the quarrel with a light heart. A fleet was collected and sent off the coast of Spain to seize a point on the mainland as a base whence the annual Treasure Fleet from the Indies on its way home could be profit-ably attacked. The "Swiftsure" was the Vice-Admiral's ship, flying the flag of the then Earl of Essex. The charge of the whole force was given

"ESSEX, ANGRY AND DISGUSTED, BADE HIS MEN CEASE FIRING."

to Sir Edward Cecil, Viscount Wimbledon, as Admiral and General. Off Cape St. Vincent, by the advice of Sir Samuel Argall, Essex's flag-captain in the "Swiftsure," an attack on Cadiz was decided upon, the Council of War deciding on Argall's advice to anchor in Cadiz Bay, off St. Mary Port, whence the troops accompanying the fleet might march overland to attack St. Lucar and threaten Cadiz. With orders accordingly, the fleet, on Saturday, October 22nd, 1625, stood into Cadiz Bay, the "Swiftsure" leading. But a surprise awaited them at the outset. To the general astonishment as they entered the bay—nobody seems to have given a thought to the Spanish fleet—twelve Spanish war galleons with fifteen galleys appeared at anchor under the walls of the city covering a

merchantman convoy. The result was at first confusion to all—except to Essex and his captain.

The presence of the enemy was enough for Essex and Argall. Disregarding the cut and dried plan, which was simply to steer for St. Mary's and anchor off there, they put the "Swiftsure's" head straight for the enemy. Of course, they said, we shall be backed up. But not another ship of the "Swiftsure's" own squadron, nor a single one of Cecil's ships, followed. No preparations had been made for an emergency, and all stood stolidly on, to carry out their orders and anchor off St. Mary's. One and all kept their helms steady for the appointed anchorage. The "Swiftsure" might apparently go to her fate. But such, fortunately, was not the termination of so bold a venture. As surprised at seeing us as we were at seeing them, the Spaniards thought only of flying. They cut cables, and ran for the inner har-bour. The "Swift-sure" followed some distance, and then after a few long range shots she brailed up topsails to await the support which surely must come. To go further in was out of the question. Single handed no captain would thrust a ship in between forts and batteries such as barred the entrance to Cadiz Harbour. But no help came, and the fleet passed on its way unheeding. Essex in the end, after waiting some time, had to put the "Swiftsure" about and withdraw, eventually rejoining the main body of the fleet, now anchored off St. Mary's.

A second occa-sion was given the "Swiftsure" four-and - twenty hours later. She was told off to head the attack-ing squadron, which Cecil ordered to make the first move against Fort Puntal, the chief of the harbour de-fences. The attack was a second failure, this time owing to the poor support given to the "Swift-sure." A squadron of the armed mer-chantmen attached to the expedition were put under Essex's orders, but as soon as they got within long range shot of the Spanish guns the merchantmen refused to go further. Letting go their anchors on the further side of the flag-ship—with the "Swiftsure" between them and the enemy—they began blazing away at a useless distance, sending their shot ahead and astern of the "Swiftsure" and over her, but refusing to go any nearer. Finally, one vessel clumsily sent a shot right into the "Swiftsure" herself, on which Essex, angry and disgusted, bade the whole set cease firing and get away. The "Swiftsure" herself had done her best, but she, too, in the end had to withdraw, over-matched. When Puntal fell a day later, to an attack on its weak land side by the soldiers of the expedition, the first thing the Spanish Governor of the fort asked on surrendering was, "Who led the attack on the sea front batteries yesterday?" He was answered by another question. "Do you know who took Cadiz last time?" "Only too well," was the rejoinder; "the Earl of Essex." "Well, then," said the English officer, "it is the son of the Earl who is in that ship." "*Madre de Dios!*" exclaimed the Don. "I think the devil is there as well. Honour me by graciously permitting me to pay my respects in person to so brave a man."

How the soldiers were landed to take Cadiz on the isthmus side and failed, and how Cecil sailed home again after missing the treasure galleons by a day, is all that need be told more of the Cadiz affair of 1625. Nor, indeed, is there much more to tell of our second "Swiftsure" herself beyond that she took part in the various squadrons sent out to attempt the relief of Rochelle; was one of the ships paid for by the City of London in the famous Ship Money Fleet of 1635; and finally was flag-ship of the Parliamentarian Lord High Admiral, the Earl of Warwick, during the first three years of the Great Civil War, doing good service against Cavalier coast forts, also effectively preventing relief coming to King Charles from the Continent.

We last hear of our second "Swiftsure" in 1651, when she sailed for England with Admiral Penn to hunt Prince Rupert's Corsair fleet out of the Mediterranean, but when three days out at sea the old ship could keep no longer water-tight, and had to return home to go into dock and be taken to pieces and rebuilt. This is the explanation of the fact that no "Swiftsure" served with Blake in the battles of the first Dutch War.

Our third "Swiftsure's" story begins as flag-ship to Vice-elsewhere. On the memorable April 20th, 1657, when Blake achieved his heroic victory at Santa Cruz, the "Swiftsure" fought in the hottest of the fight, with Blake's own squadron, told off to deal with the Spanish forts and shore batteries. In her post as second to Blake's flag-ship, the "St. George," the "Swiftsure" took her full share in the desperate fighting.

Three years go by, and we next see the "Swiftsure" with the Royal Standard of England at the main. The wheel of fortune had gone full circle since 1657, and it was the third week of May in the Restoration year. The "Swiftsure" was one of the fleet that brought King Charles over to England, with, for her own special passenger, Prince Henry, Duke of Gloucester, the noblest in character of the second generation of our Stuart Princes, a Prince cut off before reaching his prime. He was the little Prince whom Charles the First, when on the night before his execution he bade his children farewell, took on his knee and said, "You must never let them make you King while your brothers Charles and James are alive," drawing from the tiny boy the spirited answer, "They will have to cut my head off first."

Another five years, and the "Swiftsure" was once more in battle in the first great fight of the second Dutch War, the battle off Lowestoft, on June 2nd, 1665. She was a flag-ship, flying the Red at the mizen of the gallant Sir William Berkeley, Rear-Admiral of the Duke of York's own squadron. Berkeley, who only entered the Navy in 1660 as lieutenant of this very "Swiftsure," was a young man of barely twenty-five, but he is said to have done his duty with a judgment

"*BERKELEY, FIGHTING ALMOST ALONE, KILLED SEVERAL WITH HIS OWN HAND.*"

Admiral William Penn—father of the first Quaker—in Cromwell's memorable expedition to the West Indies which gave us Jamaica. The "Swiftsure" sailed at the head of a powerful fleet, on board of which was a large army, on Christmas Day, 1654. England was at peace with Spain at the time, but Cromwell wanted to pick a quarrel, and, posing as the champion of the Protestant faith, on the plea of taking revenge for recent cruelties of the Inquisition on some unfortunate Englishmen, sent Penn to attack the Spanish settlements in the West Indies. Hispaniola was the point specially aimed at, and in April the fleet landed General Venables and his army to capture out of hand San Domingo, the fortress capital of the island. But the army failed disastrously. They marched into an ambuscade, and, after being badly beaten, had to be taken off. The withdrawal of the troops led to recriminations and squabbles between Venables and his officers at the Councils of War held in the "Swiftsure's" cabin, in which the shrewish tongue of Mrs. Venables—the general's wife, present as a guest on board—made things more unpleasant. This strong-minded lady had chosen to accompany her husband, who did not dare to say her nay. Penn in the end himself took over the responsibility, and of his own accord sailed off to make an attempt elsewhere—at Jamaica, where, as it happened, the weak Spanish garrison, taken by surprise, capitulated, almost without firing a shot, the whole island falling into the victors' hands Wednesday, May 9th, 1655, is the date of Penn's *conp*.

More exciting work, though, was in store for the "Swiftsure"

that an officer twice his years could not have bettered. The "Swiftsure," it was allowed on all hands, had a principal part in inflicting on the enemy the crushing defeat that the Dutch experienced that day. She led the whole fleet twice through the enemy, and as each side passed and repassed, "bore the first brunt which was performed on both sides." When at the end of the day the Dutch broke and ran with six ships of her squadron, Berkeley pursued, destroying with the fire-ship attached to the "Swiftsure" four of the enemy, who had run foul of one another "in a cluster."

In the second great battle of the war, the fight of June, 1666, the "Swiftsure" was again in the thickest of the fray, and with Sir William Berkeley, as before, on board, this time with the Blue at the fore, as Vice-Admiral of the Blue Squadron. It proved, at the same time, the "Swiftsure's" last fight and that of her gallant commander. The English fleet under Rupert and Monk, Duke of Albemarle, had shortly before the battle divided, a third of it going off under Rupert to meet a French squadron reported to be coming north to join the Dutch. In Rupert's absence, Albemarle, whether misled as to the real strength of the Dutch, or hoping to do better without his joint admiral, rashly attempted to bring on a general action with the ships remaining with himself. Leaving his anchorage at the Nore, he stood out to attack De Ruyter lying at anchor between Dunkirk and the Downs —with the result that he was over-matched. The Dutch were three to two of ours, and after a desperate set-to that lasted the whole of one day, Albemarle had to retreat to regain the shelter of the Thames, hard pressed at every point.

One of the first victims of Albemarle's blunder was the "Swiftsure." Leading the van of Albemarle's attack, she was cut off early in the opening fight, and then, unable to recover her consorts, she was edged off to leeward by a number of Dutch ships, that set on the "Swiftsure," and in the end, after a desperate fight, surrounded, boarded, and captured her. "Highly to be admired," says a contemporary writer, "was the resolution of Vice-Admiral Berkeley, who, though cut off from the line, surrounded by enemies, great numbers of his men killed, his ship disabled and boarded on all sides, yet continued fighting almost alone, killed several with his own hand, and would accept no quarter; till at length, being shot in the throat with a musket ball, he retired into the captain's cabin, where he was found dead, extended at his full length upon a table, and almost covered with his own blood." So the Dutch captors of the ship found the Vice-Admiral, to whose remains they paid every honour that brave men could bestow on a brave adversary. A lying report was current in England after the battle that the Dutch took the body of Sir W. Berkeley, stripped it, and paraded it from town to town set up in an empty sugar cask with a flagstaff attached bearing the "Swiftsure's" flag, until Berkeley's relatives sent money to bring the remains to England; but the story was false. The Dutch as a fact embalmed Berkeley's body, treated it with most reverent care, and placed it in the chapel of the Great Church at The Hague, sending a message by flag of truce to King Charles that they awaited his pleasure for the final disposal of the remains.

The "Swiftsure" herself the Dutch took into their own fleet. They refitted her and renamed her the "Oudehorne," after a rich burgher of Amsterdam who paid for her repair,

"Swiftsure's" capture in 1666 is still in existence. The Royal coat-of-arms shield of carved and painted oak, borne by the "Swiftsure" on her stern as an English man-of-war, was set up outside the Weigh House at Hoorn as a trophy. When in course of time it began to rot, a stone shield was carved to take its place, in exact representation of the original "Swiftsure" trophy, bearing the English arms of Charles the Second, and with for supporters the figures of two armed Dutch sailors. Any tripper to Hoorn to-day can see the stone shield on a gable of the old Staaten College or Court House there.

"In the room," as the phrase went, of Berkeley's "Swiftsure," a new ship to carry on the old name was forthwith appointed, our fourth "Swiftsure." She was sent afloat in the spring of 1673, just in time to bear a part in the two final battles of the third Dutch War, in the fight off the Dutch Coast on June 4th, and in the big action of August 11th. The first affair was a long range fight, ending in a practical "draw"; the second one of the most sanguinary encounters our Navy has ever had. On August 11th the brunt of the battle fell heavily on the van division of the Red Squadron, where the "Swiftsure" fought. De Ruyter out-manoeuvred Rupert, cut off Rupert's van and centre divisions of the Red Squadron from their rear division and from the whole of the English Blue Squadron, and threw himself with the two and a-half squadrons of the Dutch fleet furiously on the two isolated "Red" divisions. Only by sheer dogged pluck at close quarters, by standing to their guns in the true English spirit of not owning that they were beaten, did the "Swiftsure" and her consorts eventually pull through. After a terrific struggle they managed to rejoin the Red rear division and avert a disaster, the battle ending as a drawn contest, with

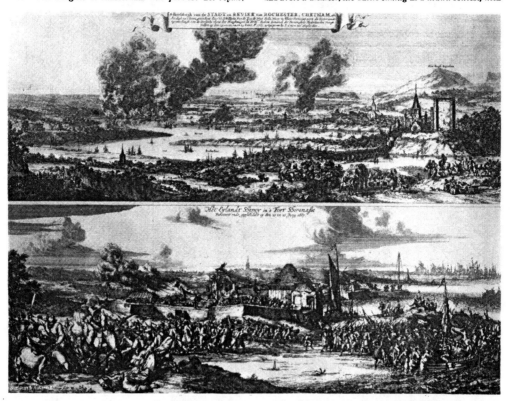

THE DUTCH IN THE MEDWAY, 1667—DESTRUCTION OF SHEERNESS AND THE SHIPS OFF ROCHESTER.

After a Contemporary Engraving Published at Amsterdam.

and under her Dutch name the ex-"Swiftsure" lived to take part in the raid up the Medway of June, 1667, in the great battle of Sole Bay in 1672, and in De Ruyter's three battles with Prince Rupert in 1673. Though in all these fights a marked ship, and her appearance well known from the reports of spies, she escaped all special efforts to sink or capture her, coming through unscathed, until in 1676 the ex-"Swiftsure" perished in the battle with the French off Sicily, when the veteran De Ruyter met his death. A memento of the

both Dutch and English exhausted and too shattered to fight to a complete finish. Upwards of fifty killed and wounded out of a ship's company of 270 odd, according to the ship's muster roll, was the "Swiftsure's" "butcher's bill"—over a sixth of all on board. In Rupert's whole fleet that day five captains were killed, and Sir Edward Spragge, the Admiral of the Blue, while the total number of casualties in the lower ranks and ratings was so appalling that the Government suppressed the despatches giving the full returns.

THE HOME-COMING OF CHARLES II.—MAY, 1660.

Incidental points in the "Swiftsure's" story, in the sixteen years of peace that followed the termination of the third Dutch War, are the posting of Charles the Second's son, the Duke of Monmouth, as captain of the ship, during a few weeks in the autumn of 1673, in order "to learn sea affairs and how to command a man-of-war," under, as dry-nurse, Captain Richard Rooth, who had commanded on board in the fighting of the summer; and the flying by the "Swiftsure," during some months in 1678, when England seemed on the point of war with France, of the pennant of Captain Edward Russell, afterwards famous as the victor at La Hogue—at which battle the "Swiftsure" made her next appearance at sea.

On May 19th, 1692, the "Swiftsure" was one of Sir Cloudesley Shovell's rear division of the Red Squadron, in which post she came in for her full share of what hard knocks were going. The "Swiftsure's" log for the battle still exists—a faded scrawl and barely legible—with but little to tell of the ship's part in the fight. There was "some firing and a good deal of fog," says the writer, and with little more he goes on to the damages his ship received:—Her masts

on, and the Governor of the town surrendered; firing till 2 when the ships ceased."

Having taken Gibraltar, Rooke had to fight the French Toulon fleet, sent out to save or relieve the fortress, to prevent the French interfering with our newly-installed garrison. The day was August 13th, 1704, off Malaga, and the French had been in sight since noon the day before. "At 5 a.m.," says our officer of the "Swiftsure" in his log, "we were almost within gunshot of the French, and at the same time both fleets drew into line-of-battle ahead. At 7 a.m. we bore down, and at 8 o'clock began to engage the admiral of the French van squadron, flying the blue and white flag." This was the big "Fier," an 80-gun ship, more powerful by ten guns than the "Swiftsure." The cannonade was hot, but the "Swiftsure" stood up well to her antagonist. "At ten," our officer's log continues, "the main topmast was struck down, and the sail set on fire had to be cut away. At eleven our mizen topmast was shot away, through which loss the 'Swiftsure' fell down towards the enemy." The French van by this time were edging off to leeward, and the "Swiftsure" escaped the rough handling they expected. The ship continued

THE CAPTURE OF THE "FOUDROYANT," FEBRUARY, 1758.

and yards, bowsprit, spritsail yard and ensign staff, with the braces, sails, and rigging, "badly cut and shattered," and "from forty to fifty people killed and wounded—severall by muskett shott." A significant entry this last, as showing that, at any rate, the ship came to close quarters with the enemy. A note in a State paper, dated six months after the battle, adds that second Lieutenant Pike, of the "Swiftsure," was court-martialled "for running into the hold during the battle, and dismissed the Service, after being carried in a boat with a halter round his neck to each ship in the Fleet, where his crime was read."

In the great boat attack in the Bay of La Hogue, so disastrous to the French fugitives from the battle, the "Swiftsure's" men had an active share, themselves burning, as the ship's log records, two French men-of-war. After La Hogue, the "Swiftsure's" story is but that of a Channel cruiser on police duty against French privateers, and at the end of the war in 1697 she went into dock, was taken to pieces, and rebuilt into our fifth ship of the name, the "Swiftsure" of what our ancestors of the last century used to call "Queen Anne's War."

Rooke's brilliant attack on the treasure galleons in Vigo Harbour was the occasion of the new "Swiftsure's" baptism of fire, the "Swiftsure" being well forward in the line-of-battle, and, after Admiral Hopsonn's "Torbay," one of the first through the boom. Her second battle was at the taking of Gibraltar, where the "Swiftsure" was one of the in-shore squadron which silenced the Spanish batteries, and with their boats stormed the Mole. "At 5 a.m.," says a log of an officer of the "Swiftsure," for July 23rd, 1704, "stood in, and anchored in four fathoms close the town. At 5.30 a.m. the Red flag was hoisted and firing began. Very hot till 11 a.m., when the enemy in the town hung out a flag to capitulate. At 12, signal made to man and arm boats. At 1, landed at the New Mole. Immediately we landed the tower blew up, destroyed our boats and wounded all the party, killing one man. Pushed

firing at whatever French ship could be seen in the smoke, till between five and six o'clock the battle ceased. Malaga cost the "Swiftsure" forty-six men in killed and wounded, and everything above the water-line badly smashed by shot, including three lower-deck guns split from muzzle to trunnion.

Captain Robert Wynn—one of the great Welsh family of Wynns—commanded the "Swiftsure" at Vigo, Gibraltar, and Malaga. He returned home in the ship, and handed her over to one of the most interesting Naval characters of the time—another gallant son of Wales, Captain Richard Griffiths. There was no better-known officer in all Queen Anne's Fleet than "Honour and Glory Griffiths," as the Fleet called him, and the story of his career can hardly be matched outside the pages of romance.

Originally the skipper of a coaster which a French privateer, at the beginning of King William's war, captured off the Isle of Wight, Griffiths owed his transfer to the Royal Navy to an act of extraordinary daring. On the very night after his capture, Skipper Griffiths, with the aid of his ship's boy, surprised the Frenchmen on watch on deck, overpowered them, and hove them overboard, after which, clapping on hatches to imprison the rest of the prize crew, he put the ship about and ran for an English port. King William gave Griffiths a gold chain and medal, with a gold medal for the boy, and made the skipper captain of the "Mary" galley, in which Griffiths had the luck to carry home Admiral Russell's despatches announcing the victory of La Hogue. After doing good work with Benbow off the French Coast, Captain Griffiths' name came later prominently before the public in connection with a court-martial, the outcome of the narrow escape of Captain Griffiths' then ship, the "Trident" 54, one dark November midnight in 1697, when ashore on the Irish Coast on the way home from Newfoundland, having previously lost her rudder in a storm, and being also disabled by the number of sick on board. "Not knowing where we were," wrote Griffiths to the Admiralty, "and having no boat or

*QUIBERON BAY, NOVEMBER 20th, 1759—THE "SWIFTSURE" ENGAGING THE "SOLEIL ROYAL."*

other way of saving a man, I thought I could not do too much to save the King's ship and all our lives; and then, with my cane in one hand, and a case knife in the other to cut down their hammocks, I did rouse up as many men as I could, and, with God's assistance, got her off, and next day into Baltimore, and after to Spithead." The "Trident's" officers, at Spithead, laid a complaint against Griffiths for, amongst other things, "beating them, the officers, among others, and running up and down the deck with a case knife in his hand," and a court-martial trial resulted, at which Griffiths was found guilty of "not carrying on a due discipline in His Majesty's ship." He was suspended until, when hard knocks were being given, and we were again at war with France, the brave old salt found himself in command on the "Swiftsure's" quarter-deck.

In the "Swiftsure,"

After a Contemporary Engraving                    Published in Holland
THE BATTLE BETWEEN BLAKE AND TROMP IN THE CHANNEL, 1653.

Captain Griffiths' career, if adventurous, was hardly fortunate. First, on February 22nd, 1707, the "Swiftsure," with the "Warspite," was convoying a fleet of merchantmen to Lisbon, when she fell in with a fleet of seventeen French men-of-war off the Scilly Islands. Griffiths ran his guns out, but to fight was hopeless, and he ordered his convoy to scatter and make off. Though some of the merchantmen were taken, most escaped, and, with the two men-of-war, reached Lisbon safely. There the British admiral in command commended Captain Griffiths and exonerated him from blame. From Lisbon the "Swiftsure" joined Sir Cloudesley Shovell in the operations, in conjunction with Prince Eugene's army, on Toulon, where she assisted to save the Prince's army from the consequences of the rashly-undertaken expedition. With Shovell the "Swiftsure" returned to England, and she was in the fleet on the terrible night of October 14th when Sir Cloudesley himself lost his life and part of the fleet was lost on the outlying reefs off Scilly. Again on March 25th, 1708, Captain Griffiths, in the "Swiftsure," with a squadron of four ships, was cruising off Dunkirk, and fell in with a French fleet of fourteen men-of-war. Old "Honour and Glory" wanted to fight, but dared not, and could only follow and watch, and then return to the Downs to report.

In 1711 the "Swiftsure" took part in Sir Hovenden Walker's expedition against the French Canadian Settlements, but the campaign completely failed, and the fleet came home—the "Swiftsure" to pay off and go into dock, and to be rebuilt under another name.

The "Swiftsure" of the Seven Years' War comes next to the "Swiftsure" of Queen Anne's War, with a gap of forty odd years between. Lord Anson, then at the Admiralty, gave the ship her name, the "Swiftsure" being one of the

first men-of-war added to the Navy after the Peace of Aix-la-Chapelle. She was a fine two-decker of 74 guns, launched on May 25th, 1750.

Her first fight was as a ship of the Mediterranean fleet, which the "Swiftsure" joined in 1757, the year following Byng's failure. The French were proposing an invasion of England by means of an army which the French Brest and Toulon fleets combined were to escort over. To prevent the two fleets joining, Hawke with the Channel fleet watched Brest, and Osborn, with the fleet to which the "Swiftsure" belonged, watched Toulon. The Toulon fleet, however, or the greater part of it, got out of port during a temporary absence of Osborn's ships, and ran for the neutral harbour of Cartagena, where Osborn again shut them in. The "Swiftsure" with the fleet was off Cartagena when, on February 28th, 1758, fresh ships from Toulon arrived to raise the blockade and reinforce their friends. The presence of the British fleet prevented the attempt, and the new-comers had to double back, pursued by part of Osborn's fleet. Three ships—the "Monmouth," the "Swiftsure," and the "Hampton Court"—went after the French admiral in the big "Foudroyant," of 80 guns. It is a famous story how the "Monmouth," outsailing her consorts, got alongside the "Foudroyant," and fought her at close quarters from seven in the evening till midnight, until the "Swiftsure" came up to finish the fight. Steering by the flash of the guns ahead, the "Swiftsure" arrived on the scene just at midnight. The Frenchmen were not yet subdued, and seeing the utterly disabled state of the "Monmouth," the "Swiftsure" hailed her to cease firing, and pushed herself in between the "Monmouth" and the big French ship. Two broadsides from the "Swiftsure" settled the "Foudroyant," who thereupon hauled down her lights and surrendered.

The "Swiftsure's" next fight was in Boscawen's battle off Lagos Bay in August, 1759. Boscawen had relieved Osborn and blockaded the French in Toulon—whither the Cartagena ships had managed to return—until compelled to fall back on Gibraltar to refit. The French seized the opportunity, slipped out, bound for Brest, and were half-way through the Straits before one of Boscawen's look-out frigates, at the last moment, saw them passing. The frigate gave the alarm, firing guns and burning flares, and the British fleet was at sea in full pursuit by midnight. At seven next morning a Swedish convoy they passed reported ships ahead, and an hour later the French

From an Engraving.                    After Francis Swaine.
THE DEFEAT OF DE LA CLUE BY BOSCAWEN, AUGUST 18th, 1759.

were in sight in the north-west. Overhauling the enemy fast, by one we were nearly within gunshot. The French had passed Gibraltar fourteen sail strong. Boscawen signalled to engage as the enemy were caught up, and, with his four leaders, the "Culloden," "America," "Swiftsure," and the "Namur" (flag-ship), stood straight at the enemy. The "Culloden" and "America" began firing on the French rear, and then the "Swiftsure" was hailed by Boscawen himself from the quarter-deck to stretch ahead and tackle the French van. Shooting forward in fine style, the "Swiftsure" passed close by the whole line of the French—five ships—giving each two or three broadsides, and receiving a like return, until, at half-past three, she was alongside the French leader. With that ship and the second French ship, for an hour and a-half the "Swiftsure" fought a brisk battle, gradually forcing the French to head off their course and towards Cape St. Vincent. The French were unable to shake the "Swiftsure" off until five o'clock, when, with her three top-gallant masts shot away and her yards and rigging shattered and cut to bits, she began to drop astern. It was not until half-past six that the "Swiftsure" ceased fire. She helped, finally, to force the enemy ashore in Lagos Bay, where Boscawen finished his work by destroying three French ships and making prize of two.

In the other great Naval battle of "the Wonderful Year"—as 1759 is known in our national annals—Hawke's splendid victory in Quiberon Bay on November 20th, it again fell to the "Swiftsure" to do distinguished service. Hawke had been blown off Brest by a gale, and the French fleet, in his absence, put to sea, but, returning quickly, Hawke caught the French up in the Bay of Biscay. Sighting the enemy between nine and ten in the morning, Hawke dashed at them, pushing a flying squadron on ahead to engage the enemy as they were caught up. The "Swiftsure" was one of these, and came into action second or third ship of the British fleet. She attacked first the big French "Formidable," of eighty guns, gave her three or four close broadsides, and then pushed on and engaged six French ships in succession. Sir Thomas Stanhope—he had been knighted for the "Swiftsure's" share at Lagos—was not a man to delay over taking possession of an enemy when others ahead were to be fought. He shoved forward, fighting his way until the "Swiftsure" came up with the "Soleil Royal," Admiral Conflans' flag-ship—reputed the finest man-of-war afloat. The "Soleil Royal" was doubling back, attended by two French seventy-fours, to aid the "Formidable" and the French rear, and the three began by setting furiously on the "Swiftsure." Stanhope and the "Swiftsure" were ready for them. Fighting both broadsides as well as possible in the raging seas, the "Swiftsure," for nearly half-an-hour, returned the three Frenchmen as good as they gave, until a sudden and unfortunate accident stopped the fight. A shot from the "Soleil Royal" cut away the tiller ropes, and before they could be replaced, the "Swiftsure" broached to in the storm, helpless for the time, while the three French ships passed on, to meet Hawke in the "Royal George." At the same instant the "Swiftsure's" main top-gallant mast was shot away, her main topmast shot two-thirds through, and the main and fore-topsail yards were rendered unserviceable. "She for some time lay muzzled," says Captain Stanhope in his journal, "by which act we were left out of further action." After

Quiberon, the "Swiftsure" was flag-ship of a squadron covering the attack on Belleisle in 1761, and was paid off in 1763—to pass, a few years later, to the ship-breaker.

The "Swiftsure" of the Nile—a seventy-four built in 1787—was the successor to the "Swiftsure" of Lagos Bay and Quiberon. She joined Nelson with the squadron that Troubridge took up the Straits to reinforce the admiral. The battle, as all the world knows, was fought at night, on August 1st, 1798. By chance when the firing began, just before seven, the "Swiftsure" and a consort, the "Alexander," were astern, having been detached during the day to look into Alexandria, but, standing direct for the flashes of the guns, both ships within an hour of the action beginning were in their stations, the "Swiftsure" in the outer line of Nelson's attack, opposite the French centre, and close to the French flag-ship "L'Orient." The berth was that vacated a few minutes before by the British "Bellerophon," which had been compelled to quit the line, overpowered by the French three-decker.

The "Swiftsure" first saluted her foe with a crashing broadside right into "L'Orient," to which the French ship replied with equal spirit, and then a stubborn ship to ship fight began, the "Alexander," which had passed through the French line and taken post opposite "L'Orient" on the in-shore side, joining in. For an hour and a-quarter the "Swiftsure" pounded at "L'Orient," until shortly after nine o'clock the French flag-ship was suddenly seen to be on fire. The "Swiftsure," on that, at first redoubled her efforts, training every gun on the quarter of the French ship where the fire was, to prevent the crew mastering the flames, while from the "Swiftsure's" poop the marines volleyed musketry at the spot. There was no alternative. The battle was as yet uncertain, whilst also the batteries of "L'Orient" herself that the fire had not reached were still fighting furiously. Soon, however, it was seen that the flag-ship was doomed, the flames spreading until from stem to stern the giant three-decker was a mass of fire.

Now arose a new peril to the "Swiftsure," in view of what might happen when the flames should reach the powder magazine. The "Swiftsure" was close to leeward of the burning ship. Orders were promptly given to cease firing and shut down ports and hatchways, while the "Swiftsure's" firemen and others with buckets of water were stationed all about the ship ready to deal with any burning wreckage that might come on board.

Then they waited, Captain Hallowell declining to move the "Swiftsure" further off, as the "Alexander" had done. "We are so near," he said, "that everything will go over us." They waited until ten o'clock, when "L'Orient" blew up with a tremendous crash that seemed to cast a stupor over the battle for some minutes after. It made the "Swiftsure" quiver from keel to masthead, opening seams and doing general damage through-out the

ship. As Hallowell had foreseen, however, most of the flaming mass drove bodily over the "Swiftsure." What fell on board the firemen were able to deal with. After the interval of deadly silence that followed on both sides for some minutes after the explosion, the "Swiftsure" recommenced action. She now, with other ships, attacked in particular the French "Franklin" and the "Tonnant," the ships ahead and astern of "L'Orient's" berth, and kept her guns on them until the "Franklin" surrendered and the "Tonnant" moved off to surrender elsewhere.

After the Nile, for three years the "Swiftsure" served off Alexandria and on the Italian Coast, until June, 1801. On the 24th of that month, while on a cruise in charge of a convoy for Malta, she fell in with a French squadron of four ships of the line, and, after making a magnificent resistance, as the French themselves admitted, the "Swiftsure" had to yield.

It was from Captain Hallowell that Nelson received the gift of the coffin in which the body of the hero now rests in St. Paul's, made out of a fragment of "L'Orient's" mainmast picked up in Aboukir Bay by the "Swiftsure's" men, with other wreckage of the ill-fated French flagship.

Hallowell had the piece of mast cut up into planks, which were put together into a coffin, iron staples and spikes from other fragments of "L'Orient" being used to fasten the whole together. The coffin thus was made entirely out of the French ship. It was presented to Nelson in 1799, off Naples, with this letter:—

"My Lord,—I have taken the liberty of presenting you a coffin made from the mainmast of 'L'Orient,' that when you have finished your military career in this world you may be buried in one of your trophies—but that that period may be far distant is the earnest wish of your sincere friend, BEN HALLOWELL."

The Trafalgar "Swiftsure," the successor to the "Swiftsure" of the Nile, and also a seventy-four, was built in 1803. At Trafalgar she was in the rear of Collingwood's line, owing

*THE "BELLEISLES" CHEERING THE "SWIFTSURE" AT THE BATTLE OF TRAFALGAR.*

"Prince," of ninety-eight guns, coming up, the "Swiftsure" left the half-beaten "Achille," and pushed ahead to join in the fight elsewhere. After the battle, the "Swiftsure" was given charge of the "Victory's" special antagonist, the "Redoutable," which ship she took in tow until the "Redoutable" sank astern of the "Swiftsure," at three in the morning of October 23rd, during the great storm that ensued after Trafalgar. At Trafalgar we recovered, as one of our prizes, the old "Swiftsure" of the Nile. On being brought to England she was renamed the "Irresistible," under which name the ship existed as a harbour hulk for several years.

*THE ARMOUR-CLAD SWIFTSURE OF 1869.*

to which fact the "Swiftsure" was one of the last of our ships to get into action. Yet the "Swiftsure" did good work at Trafalgar. She was the first ship to relieve the sorely-pressed "Belleisle" in her forlorn-hope fight with five French ships, one of which—the "Achille"—the "Swiftsure" took off as her own opponent. As the "Swiftsure" came up and passed under the "Belleisle's" stern, it is related by eye-witnesses, the men of the two ships burst into rounds of hearty cheering, the "Belleisle's" men to signify to their rescuer that, though a dismasted and shot-torn hulk, they were unconquered, waving a Jack flag from a boarding-pike, whilst the ship's ensign, just then shot away for the third or fourth time, was being nailed to the stump of the mizen mast. Taking off the "Achille," the "Swiftsure" fought her until, on the British

The British Trafalgar "Swiftsure" remained on the Navy List until 1847, when she in turn came to her end, which was to be knocked to pieces in Portsmouth Harbour as a target for shell practice by the gunners of the "Excellent."

Our present "Swiftsure," the ninth ship of her name, was launched in 1869, and has seen many years' service in the Mediterranean Fleet, with which, in 1878, she took part under Sir Geoffrey Hornby in the famous passage of the Dardanelles.

# THE
# NAVY & ARMY
## ILLUSTRATED.

Vol. V.—No. 59.]　　　*FRIDAY, MARCH 18th, 1898.*

Photo. W. M. Crockett, Plymouth.　　　　　　　　　　　Copyright.—Hudson & Kearns.

*SIR HENRY F. NORBURY, M.D., K.C.B., ETC., INSPECTOR-GENERAL OF HOSPITALS AND FLEETS.*

SIR HENRY NORBURY entered the Service in June, 1860, and attained the rank of staff-surgeon in December, 1872. He was in charge of the Naval Brigade landed from the "Active" during the Kaffir War, 1877-78, when he was mentioned in despatches and strongly recommended for promotion; was present at numerous skirmishes, at the actions of the Quorra River and Quintana in the Transkei. Subsequently he was principal medical officer of Colonel Pearson's Column, and present at the battle of Inezane and the relief of the garrison of Ekowe; several times mentioned in despatches. He afterwards joined General Crealock's Column as principal medical officer, and was twice mentioned in despatches. He was promoted to fleet-surgeon in July, 1879, and made a C.B. in November of the same year; deputy inspector-general in April, 1887; and attained his present rank in November, 1894. He was appointed to the charge of Plymouth Hospital in April, 1895, and has since received the honour of knighthood.

# THE ROYAL NAVAL HOSPITAL, PLYMOUTH.

*GENERAL VIEW OF THE HOSPITAL.*

THE hospital at Plymouth, as at our other Naval ports consists of a large range of buildings, enclosed in extensive and well-kept grounds, and our first illustration gives a good idea of the general appearance of the establishment, relieved by a group of children, probably those of one of the resident medical officers, on the smooth lawn. In the centre stands the clock tower, with a kind of bird-cage, which appears to have been considered indispensable when these buildings were erected, for they all possess it in slightly varying forms.

With the large number of seamen in port, and constantly arriving from abroad, the medical officers are usually pretty busy; and in the next picture may be seen an every-day incident—the landing of a patient from a ship's boat at the slip. This is often an unpleasant ordeal; for if a man is really very ill, or badly wounded, the process of being carried down the ship's side, or slung over it in a canvas cot, is not a soothing one, to say nothing of the bumping of the oars and the subsequent disembarkation. However, since Jack must of necessity serve afloat, the difficulty cannot well be got over, until some inventive genius perfects a process of aërial locomotion; and once in bed, in the large and airy ward, under the care of the nursing sisters, the trials of transport are speedily forgotten. It would be impossible to over-rate the

*LANDING A PATIENT IN A COT.*

value of the services of these same sisters, who have taken the place of the kindly but rough-and-ready male nurses of bygone years; and many a poor fellow, racked with the pains of malarial fever from some African swamp, or desperately injured in action, or through accident, has testified to their gentle and skilful nursing and unfailing devotion to duty.

The group of officers—with a much less effective and picturesque background than the nursing sisters—includes the inspector-general, Deputy-Inspector-General T. Browne, Fleet Surgeon H. T Cox, a staff-surgeon, and three juniors, the Rev. J. Brabazon, chaplain, and the store-keeper and clerk, both retired paymasters. The medical staff appears none too large for such an extensive establishment; but the inspector-general and his colleagues have, in addition to the nursing sisters, a numerous company of assistants in the sick berth attendants, a very valuable body of men, many of whom display great aptitude for the duties of their calling, while some have distinguished themselves signally before the enemy. Several of those in the group, it will be observed, wear a goodly row of medals, but many of those in the rear are young men who are being instructed in their duties before assuming the responsibility of nursing their shipmates afloat, where "sisters" are

THE NURSING SISTERS.

not forthcoming. The next illustration shows the interior of a ward, and presents a pleasing picture of comfort and cleanliness, with the addition of some refinements of adornment in the shape of pictures and plants, and flowers on the table—a great boon to those who are compelled to lie prostrate for days, incapable perhaps of any movement save turning their weary eyes again and again on the surrounding objects. This is a ward the name of which suggests reminiscences of some terrible tragedies, for it is devoted to accident cases. Here, on some quiet afternoon, perhaps, comes a hurried message from the chief to prepare for the victims of a sudden and unexpected disaster; the premature explosion of a charge, as in the recent case on board the "Bouncer," or, more terrible still, the bursting of a huge boiler, such as occurred years ago on board the "Thunderer" at Spithead, and soon a ghastly procession of scorched and shattered bodies is admitted, and the skill and energy of the surgeons and nurses are taxed

THE OFFICERS.

SICK BERTH ATTENDANTS.

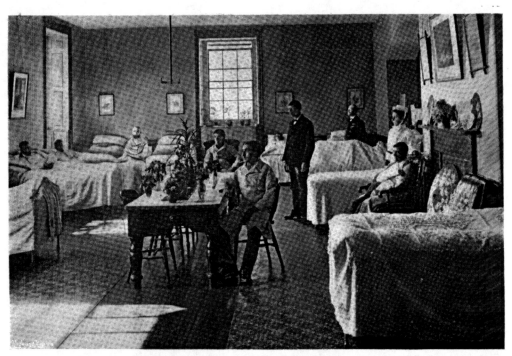

*THE ACCIDENT WARD*

to the utmost to revive the failing spark of life in some, or to assuage the last agonies of others who are past hope.

Thus, even in time of peace, the seaman carries his life in his hands ; for in spite of science and care in construction, a cartridge will sometimes go wrong, or a boiler give out, perhaps through the carelessness of some poor fellow who pays the forfeit with his life. Lastly, here is a touching picture of some veterans, whose fighting days are long since past : two of them can only get about in invalid chairs, crippled in their country's service, and now permitted to end their days peacefully in these quiet surroundings. Only a limited number can be accommodated, of course : and those who are able do a little work in sweeping up and tending the paths and lawns, or helping indoors where they can. The sun-dial seems a fitting object in their midst ; a time-worn type of bygone days. Some of these "sheer hulks" were doubtless serving when steam, iron plates, and electrical mechanism were almost unknown.

*" SHEER HULKS."*

# THE NAVY AND ASTRONOMY.

IF the weather in Norway on the morning of the 9th of August of 1896 had been fine, then it was nearly certain that the party which went up to those latitudes to observe the total eclipse of the sun would have created a

*THE INSTRUMENTS COMING ASHORE AT VIZIADRUG.*

*THE PACKING CASES AND MEN COMING FROM THE SHIP.*

record. The magnificent help of the "Volages," and the great trouble expended by both officers and men, showed what could be accomplished in a short space of time, and how well it could be done. This year, instead of travelling to Norway and leaving the warm weather of England behind one, the eclipse expeditions have had to go further afield—this time to India—to catch that fleeting shadow cast by the moon during an eclipse. The party that took up its encampment in the Varanger Fjord in 1896, and was helped by the faithful officers and men of the "Volage," this year turned southwards also, and was met at Colombo by the "Melpomene," which ship was intrusted to carry out this year what the "Volages" so gallantly attempted in 1896. With more favourable weather conditions, in fact, one could not have had better, and with also the experience of the former occasion, the party, under the direction of Sir Norman Lockyer, and composed of Mr. A. Fowler and Dr. W. J. S. Lockyer, together with Lord Graham, went out under brilliant auspices. Instruments were taken enough to occupy the attention of all the officers on the ship and as many men as would volunteer. Needless to remark, practically every man volunteered, so that the party had its work cut out to organise such a host. On the route to the station Sir Norman addressed the ship's company, and explained to them his mission and the requirements of the party.

In Naval fashion we steamed gracefully into the harbour of Viziadrug, (writes a correspondent), and dropped anchor slightly to the north of the old fort. No delay was made about going ashore and choosing a suitable site for the instruments. The old fort, which had been previously regarded as our station, was found to meet all the necessary requirements as to locality and height above sea level, so the following day the instruments were brought ashore, and work was started. Arrangements had been made that native masons and carpenters should be on the spot, and these were at once used for making the concrete bases and huts for the instruments. In two or three days the ground on which we had begun to erect huts entirely changed its appearance; in fact, quite a village of a naval character had been run up, if one judged by the majority of the people that were about. Every instrument had its complement of men, and

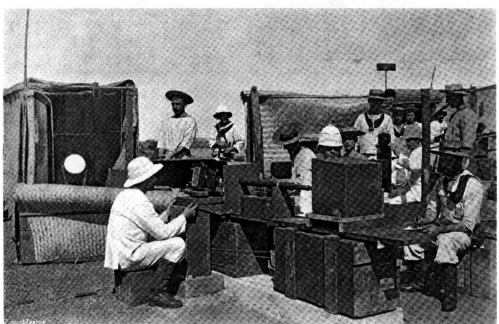

Photos. Copyright.     Hudson & Kearns.

*MR. FOWLER AND HIS ASSISTANTS AT WORK IN THE "CENTRAL HOTEL."*

several were entirely worked by the officers and men.

The immense programme which we had undertaken began now to take a working shape. Lieutenants Quayle and Colbeck had erected the discs, which occupied the attention of twenty-one men during the eclipse, the captain having undertaken to observe at one of them. The 6-in. equatorial, which was used by Sir Norman Lockyer and Professor Pedler, was erected almost entirely by Naval aid, and was housed in the "Town Hall," or "Totality Hut," as the men had named it. The 6-in. and 9-in. prismatic cameras, which were all worked by Mr. Fowler and Dr. Lockyer with their Naval assistants, were housed in matting sheds, called the "Central Hotel" and "Mainsail Hall" respectively. Another important instrument, or rather two others were located in the "Empire Palace," and were entirely intrusted to members of the ship.

A most important piece of work was the calling out of the time from the commencement of the period of totality until the end. This was done by two bluejackets, who used the eclipse clock which we took out. One illustration shows them at their stations, one calling out the time every ten seconds after the captain of the "Melpomene" had said "Go!" the other waiting to relieve him when half the period

*CAPTAIN BATTEN ADDRESSING SOME OF THE VOLUNTEERS.*

of totality was over. This was arranged so that each man had one minute in which to observe the eclipse. Captain Chisholm Batten is about to say "Go!" when all the instruments will be set in action.

Some days before the eclipse, drills were the order of the day, and it was imperative that each man should know exactly the calls that would be given by the bugler before totality commenced. For this reason the bluejackets were assembled to obtain this information, and one of the illustrations shows the captain addressing his men. In the rehearsals, which took place daily, everything went off smoothly; and another of the illustrations shows Mr. Fowler in his "Central Hotel" at work with his 6-in. prismatic camera and his Naval assistants, Lieutenant De Wet being the chief among them.

The day of the eclipse at last arrived, the sun rising in a cloudless sky. The volunteers marched up to the camp some little time before the first contact was heralded, and a "stand easy" was indulged in until the bugle called the "assemble," which meant that each man should take up his allotted position. Darker and darker it became, and weird was the scene which was presented to us. Just before the time of totality, the calls were given, as previously stated in the drills, and at the word "Go!" from Sir Norman Lockyer totality commenced. The corona shot out magnificently before our eyes, and the camp was a busy scene. Orders, such as snap, expose, sixty-seven seconds, etc., were mixed up all together, but thoroughly understood at the respective instruments. Bluejackets at that moment were sketching the corona, making temperature observations, photographing, making spectroscopic observations, and many other kinds of work to which they, a fortnight previously, had not been accustomed. Every officer was employed in some important work, and the captain was one of the disc observers.

The development of some of the photographic plates was at once proceeded with, and very satisfactory they proved.

As Sir Norman was entering the bungalow, Lieutenant Blackett stopped him, and, calling the bluejackets around, three ringing cheers were given for the chief of the expedition, and others for those of his party. In response to this display of enthusiasm, Sir Norman said:

"You have no right to cheer me, but I have the right to cheer you, and had I a hundred and fifty throats I would do it right heartily. It is you, the officers and men of H.M.S. 'Melpomene,' who have been running this camp, and we three have just stood by. . . . . A hundred and fifty British bluejackets have observed an eclipse just as perfectly as if they had been drilled for years, instead of a few days. We have been perfectly successful along all the lines of work we laid down, and we have done everything we tried to do. I do not really thank you a bit, but I congratulate you from the bottom of my heart upon the splendid success you have achieved."

Thus was brought to an end the eclipse of 1898, and "Down instruments" became now the order of the day, and "Batten Camp" presented, in a short space of time, a scene of desolation. During the next forty-eight hours not only were the parties ashore busy in repacking, and copying the negatives obtained, but those on board were making preparations for the start southwards again.

On the morning of the 25th of January everything had been safely placed on board again, and the "Melpomene" slowly steamed out of the bay, leaving the old fort, in which so many pleasant moments had been spent, far behind. One may take this opportunity of expressing our heartiest thanks to the captain and officers for the hospitable way in which the party was looked after, and for the grand service they have rendered in making the eclipse of 1898 a record eclipse.

*THE TIME-KEEPERS WITH THE CAPTAIN.*

*"MAINSAIL HALL," SHOWING THE 9-in. PRISMATIC CAMERA.*

Photo. R. Ellis, Malta.

Copyright.—Hudson & Kearns

### THE CAPTAIN OF A BATTLE-SHIP COMING ON BOARD.

DEGREES of dignity are very clearly defined on board a man-of-war, increasing in importance from the lower ranks to the captain. It is doubtful if anyone who has not lived a short time in a man-of-war could appreciate the supreme position occupied by the captain of a battle-ship. The quarter-deck, being that part of the upper deck occupied by the officers, and from which the officer of the watch and commanding officer give their orders, where also officers arriving and leaving are received, has always been treated with great respect. Anyone coming on the quarter-deck has to salute; no noise or skylarking is allowed; the seamen are only permitted to pass on one side of it, unless actually necessary to go to the other. This was all very well in the old class of vessels, but in the modern ones it is often difficult to decide where the quarter-deck should be. A bridge between the masts, well forward, is now the promenade of the captain and officers when the ship is under way; but still, in harbour, the after-part of the upper deck over the officers' accommodation is kept sacred. The accompanying illustration shows the incident of Captain Churchill, of the battle-ship " Nile," coming on board his ship. The group shown consists, on the right, of the lieutenant who is officer of the watch, next to him the midshipman of the watch, and then the boatswain's mate; Captain Churchill is in the entry on the left. The signalman having reported the captain's boat approaching the ship, those shown repair to the gangway and wait for his arrival. As the boat comes alongside the boatswain's mate gives a prolonged wail with his pipe, every-one on deck stands to " attention " and salutes, and the pipe is repeated as the captain steps on to the deck. This ceremony is performed every time the captain leaves the ship and returns. The officer of the watch then reports to him any signals that have been made, or anything of importance that has occurred during his absence.

# THE PERSONNEL OF THE FLEET.

*OFFICERS OF THE "BOXER."*

Photos. R. Ellis, Malta.     *OFFICERS OF THE "BRUIZER."*     Copyright.—Hudson & Kearns.

THESE two little groups of officers are characteristic of the type of vessel in which they are employed, and form a striking contrast with the pictures which appear from time to time in these pages of the officers of first-class battle-ships, standing rank behind rank, with a row of midshipmen seated in front—some fifty all told. And yet, in the hands of an able and daring commander, a torpedo-boat destroyer embodies immense possibilities in a very small compass. Buzzing about among the enemy's fleet at a speed of twenty-five or thirty knots, she may keep them all on the *qui vive*, and perhaps eventually compass the destruction of a vessel of fifteen or twenty times her value, or frustrate a deadly attack by torpedo-boats on her friends.

# THE NAVY & ARMY ILLUSTRATED.
## NOTES & QUERIES OF SERVICE AFLOAT & ASHORE

IN size, and very probably in speed, of first-class cruisers, those of this country are the finest owned by any Naval Power. Our "Terrible" and "Powerful" displace 14,200 tons, have a horse-power of 25,000, and can steam over 22 knots. In speed America beats us, for the "Minneapolis," with a displacement of 7,375 tons, can, with 18,509 horse-power, steam 23 knots. France hopes to do so, for her "Jeanne d'Arc," now building, of 11,270 tons, is estimated to produce 28,000 horse-power and steam at over 23 knots. None of the other Powers have any first-class cruisers as fast as these. The American "Brooklyn," their finest *armoured* cruiser—the "Minneapolis" is not armoured, and only meant for a commerce raider—displaces 9,271 tons, and steams 21 knots. The Russian "Rossia" runs to 12,000 odd tons and steams 20 knots. The new Japanese cruisers building are some 2,500 tons less, with the same speed. The German "Furst Bismarck" is of 10,650 tons, and can steam at 19 knots. Finally, the finest Italian cruiser, the "Garibaldi," is of only 6,840 tons, and estimated for a speed of 20 knots.

* * * *

THE man in the street knows that three chevrons on a soldier's arm indicate that he is a sergeant. So far he is on safe ground, but beyond this he is not so secure. For instance, the badge of the lance-corporal is one chevron, "the dog's hind leg"; but in the cavalry and foot Guards the youth who has put his foot on the first rung of the ladder which leads to a commission or a court-martial wears two. The gay squadron sergeant-major of Dragoons wears three chevrons and a crown in full dress, but when, on conquest bent, he dons his lace-bedizened stable jacket, his right arm is covered with a golden arabesque from cuff to shoulder. The Life Guardsman indicates his rank as corporal-major by *four* chevrons and a crown when in undress, but in full dress he discards these for the gorgeous gold aiguillettes. The finest badge worn by a non-commissioned officer is probably the beautiful embroidered design of globe and laurel worn by colour-sergeants of the Royal Marines.

* * * *

WERE there ever such persons as wreckers? In answer to this question I can only say that I wish, for the sake of mankind, that I could give a negative answer. Wreckers were once indeed but too common all along the coasts of Cornwall and Devonshire, and also all round the extensive and dangerous seashore of Brittany, as well as in some English colonies. It was bad enough when the wreckers only plundered the ships that storms had cast on their shores, but what shall I say of the wickedness of those fiends when they kindled fires on their shores, so placed as to lure the unwary navigators. In cases of wrecks happening through the act of God there was once a general idea that the vessels, being Godsends, were the property of the inhabitants living near the shore, and in some of the colonies wrecking was long looked upon as a perfectly legitimate practice; so much so, indeed, that there is on record an instance of a British Naval officer being threatened with legal proceedings by a colonial lawyer for having prevented wreckers from plundering a ship that had gone ashore on a reef.

* * * *

"T. A." (Inverness) asks: "Does an adjutant holding Army rank of captain take precedence of a captain of volunteers holding the *honorary* rank of major?" The regulations are very plain on this subject, and no doubt should ever arise. Honorary rank does not confer the right of any higher command than that to which the holder may be entitled by virtue of his substantive commission. Adjutants when holding Army rank not below that of captain rank *regimentally* as senior captains. It therefore follows that an adjutant who is a captain in the Army is senior to all other captains of his regiment, whether they be honorary majors or not. When employed on duties that are not regimental, an adjutant holding higher Army rank than that of captain takes precedence and command according to such higher rank. Officers of volunteers when serving with officers of the regulars, on the other hand, rank as *juniors* of their respective ranks.

* * * *

AMONG the many items which go to make up the kit of a sailor is one which appears to have particularly caught the attention of "Landsman," and to have aroused his curiosity as to its meaning. "One Housewife" is the item in question. If "Landsman" entertained fears at any time that our sailors carried with them, as part of their kit, a house wife, as the term might be understood ashore, he has been sadly mistaken. The contents of a seaman's "housewife," pronounced by Jack "hussif," are as follows: 1 tailor's thimble, 1-oz. beeswax, 16 large metal buttons for trousers, 6 small ditto for wristbands, 16 bone buttons for trousers, 1 piece of 18-yds. half-inch white tape, 2 pieces (8½-yds. each) of three-sixteenths-inch white tape, 12 short needles for sewing on shirt buttons, 4 darning needles, ¼-oz. pins, 2-oz. blue worsted, 25 skeins of white-brown thread, 25 skeins of black thread, and 2 skeins of white cotton. Perhaps it is not generally known that a sailor provides his own kit, materials for making his clothes being provided by Government, but paid for as wanted. As every sailor, too, must make his own clothes, or pay a messmate for doing so, it is evident that the "hussif" is in no sense a superfluous item in a man-of-war's man's kit.

"A LONDONER" writes to ask how the 1st and 2nd Life Guards can be distinguished one from the other when dismounted and in undress uniform. He knows that, mounted and in full dress, the 1st have black bearskin shabracques, and wear a red cord on their pouch-belts, while the 2nd use white lambskin saddle-covers, and a blue cord on the cross-belts. In undress uniform the troopers belonging to the 1st Life Guards wear a double red stripe down the outside of the overalls, whilst the men of the 2nd Lifes have only a single red stripe. Speaking of red, or, more correctly, of scarlet, King William III. issued an order in 1698 to the effect that no persons might use scarlet liveries for their servants, and that colour was to be the exclusive right of his own Guards. As regards liveries, that order is still respected, and only Royal servants wear scarlet coats.

* * * *

IN reply to a correspondent who asks how the officers of the "civil" branches of the Navy are distinguishable in uniform. First of all by the absence of the curl, or small circle formed on the uppermost ring of lace round the cuff of the sleeve, which is worn exclusively by executive officers. Each particular civil branch is known by the colour of the insertions of cloth between the rings of gold lace round the sleeve, which rings distinguish the various ranks of officers in all branches of the Navy, whether executive or civil. The narrow insertions of scarlet cloth between the gold lace rings denote officers of the medical branch of the Service; white cloth insertions denote the accountant and paymaster's branch; purple cloth denotes the engineer's branch, and light blue cloth the Naval instructor's branch. In full dress, furthermore, the epaulette device of the civil branches is a star, where the executive branch wear the anchor and cable. These notes should serve to enable anyone to identify any Naval officer's branch of the Service at sight.

* * * *

"WHAT is the oldest existing military corps in the world? I see in your number of 29th October, 'Notes and Queries,'" writes a correspondent, "the question raised as to which is the oldest regiment in the British Army? I believe the choice to lie between the Royal Scots (1st Foot) and the Buffs (3rd Foot). The former were raised in 1625 for the service of Sweden in the Thirty Years' War, passed into the service of France after the death of Gustavus Adolphus, and were presented by Louis XIV. to Charles the Second on the Restoration. The Buffs were raised for the service of the States-General of Holland to fight the Spaniards, but I do not know in what year. The service of both of these regiments in the British Army dates from 1660, and they must be almost the oldest regiments in Europe. There is an Austrian cavalry regiment, now, I think, the 8th Dragoons, formerly Dampier's Cuirassiers, which was raised in 1618, and served throughout the Thirty Years' War. I know a Saxon Grenadier regiment which dates back to 1670, and I doubt if there are many older regiments in the German Army. The oldest Russian regiment dates from the year 1700. In the old French Royal Army there were regiments of infantry raised as far back as 1556. These ancient regiments were called 'Les Vieux,' and the next senior ones 'Les Petits Vieux.' They were all disembodied at the Revolution, and incorporated in the new Republican levies. But as the Republicans could not improvise cavalry, they were obliged to leave the old Royal regiments of cavalry embodied, and these became regiments of Napoleon's *Grande Armée*, under different names and numbers. After Waterloo, however, the whole of Napoleon's Army was broken up by the Bourbons, and the identity of its regiments entirely and sedulously obliterated. The oldest French regiments now existing have thus had not more than eighty years of corporate existence.

* * * *

"THE military corporations which could boast of the longest historical record were the original companies or 'Buluks' of Turkish Janissaries, raised in 1335, and disbanded in 1826. During their existence of nearly five centuries, they retained the same organisation, the same titles, numbers, and badges, and even the same dress. They used jestingly to refer their origin to the Creation, in the same way that the Royal Scots have been nicknamed 'Pontius Pilate's Guards.' There are bodies of Palace Guards in Europe which have enjoyed a corporate existence nearly as long as the Janissaries, such as Her Most Gracious Majesty's Honourable Corps of Gentlemen at Arms and the Yeomen of the Guard, as well as the company of His Holiness the Pope's Swiss Guards, raised by Pope Julius the Second, in A.D. 1505. But these corps have no longer any military character, and only serve to adorn the pageantry of a Court."

* * * *

A BRITISH merchant ship is entitled to wear the Blue Ensign on the following conditions:—The officer commanding must be an officer on the retired list of the Royal Navy, or an officer of the Royal Naval Reserve. Ten of the crew must be officers and men of the Royal Naval Reserve—men who are "entitled to be absent on leave"; that is, who are not in arrear with their drills. In the ten men may also be included firemen, and men holding Naval Reserve deferred pension certificates. Before hoisting the Blue Ensign, the officer commanding the ship has to provide himself with an Admiralty warrant, and the fact of his holding the warrant must be noted on the ship's Articles of Agreement. The Blue Ensign, with certain "seals" or badges in the fly, is worn also by ships in the official service of the Colonies (except commissioned ships of war, which wear the White Ensign), ships employed by certain public offices, and hired transports, which last vessels wear a Blue Ensign with the yellow Admiralty anchor in the fly. Hired surveying vessels, commanded by Naval officers, also wear the Blue Ensign.

* * * *

IN the cavalry and artillery the senior non-commissioned officer of the squadron, battery, or company is only responsible for the discipline and training of the men, the pay, clothing, and interior economy generally being attended to by the quartermaster-sergeant of the unit. The sergeant-major and quartermaster-sergeant are of equal rank, and wear the same badge, three chevrons with crown above, but the former is *ex officio* the senior. This division of work was introduced in the artillery about twelve years ago, and in the cavalry when the squadron organisation was reverted to, comparatively recently. Previously the troop or battery sergeant-major had to perform all clerical duties connected with his charge. In the Departmental Corps, in which the units are large and frequently much scattered, special clerks are detailed for the work.

THE EDITOR.

# SHAKESPEARE AND HIS SOLDIERS.

*By GEORGE C. MILN.*

> "This is Monsieur Parolles, the gallant militarist,
> That had the whole theorick of war in the knot of his scarf,
> And the practice in the chape of his dagger."
> —"All's Well that Ends Well."

*"ONCE MORE INTO THE BREACH, DEAR FRIENDS; ONCE MORE."—HENRY V.*

IT is somewhat surprising that no elaborate attempt has ever been made to connect the Bard of Avon with the profession of arms. It has been a common thing to find enthusiasts of callings the most diverse claiming professional kinship with the great poet. He has been made out in turn to have been a physician, a botanist, an angler, an astronomer, a philosopher, and a politician. Only one inconspicuous attempt has ever been made—so far as the writer has been able to discover—to connect Shakespeare with the Army of his day. And yet, if facile familiarity with the terminology of a special calling be regarded as conclusive proof of expert craftsmanship in that calling, it would certainly be easy to prove that Shakespeare was indeed a soldier. His plays are, as Iago complained of Othello's reply to his advocates,

> "Horribly stuff'd with epithets of war."

He not only revels in military descriptions which almost "smell of powder," but he lapses familiarly into the slang of the canteen and the barrack-room of his day; and he has, besides, risen to some of his loftiest heights in panegyric of the art of war. Henry V., Richard III., Hotspur, and many other vivid portraits from his wonderful plays, immediately suggest themselves as affording proof of this; but there is, perhaps, in the whole range of his plays nothing more sublime, pathetic, and tender than Othello's so-called "farewell speech":—

> "O, now, for ever,
> Farewell the tranquil mind! Farewell content!
> Farewell the plumèd troop, and the big wars,
> That make ambition virtue! O, farewell!
> Farewell the neighing steed, and the shrill trump,
> The spirit-stirring drum, the ear-piercing fife,
> The royal banner; and all quality,
> Pride, pomp, and circumstance of glorious war!
> And O you mortal engines, whose rude throats
> The immortal Jove's dread clamours counterfeit,
> Farewell! Othello's occupation's gone!"

If one were to lose sight for an instant of the almost infinite sweep of Shakespeare's imagination, it would be easy to drop into the statement that only one who had personally experienced the fascinations of the battle-field could so vividly paint the misery of a great soldier looking down upon his own broken career. But we must remember that Shakespeare's imagination swept the earth, and garnered truth in

every corner of it. His genius was essentially sympathetic. He entered instantly and intimately into closest touch with every subject and every class he handled. Not only have thousands and tens of thousands felt and claimed mental and emotional consanguinity with the great poet, but, as I have already intimated, widely separated classes and professions have formally claimed him as having actually belonged to their special guilds. This is not only interesting as throwing a brilliant suggestive side-light upon Shakespeare's genius, but, so far as I know, it is quite unique. Our other poets have been allowed to rest secure and honourable among their fellows. To Shakespeare alone belongs the special distinction of being thus passionately affiliated to a dozen different professions and avocations.

The arguments which have been used to substantiate these claims prove too much. Admit the force of any of them, and you must parcel your Shakespeare up among a score of different callings; and that is absurd. It is probably true that the class lore of Shakespeare is neither so exact nor so wide as his genius is intense and sympathetic. He speaks an universal language, using the tongue of genius. Readers of Shakespeare are confounded, as were the assembled Jews on the Day of Pentecost. "The multitude came together, and were confounded, because that every man heard them speak in his own language."

Shakespeare produces the same effect. He speaks to different classes in their own "tongues." When he gives a pen picture of a type, it is founded on certain information, clothed with well-known peculiarities, and suffused with the warmth of poetic genius. Take, as an illustration, the nautical knowledge displayed by Shakespeare in "The Tempest." No doubt it is very entertaining, and discovers a generous familiarity with the wisdom of the forecastle in Shakespeare's time. Shall we, therefore, argue that Shakespeare was a sailor? Mr. Rudyard Kipling has recently published a story in which he sketches character types drawn from the cod fisheries of the North Atlantic. I venture to say that Kipling discloses wider and more exact knowledge of the modes of speech and the habits of this class than Shakespeare has ever shown of a similar class. Shall we, therefore, set it down as proven that Kipling is a sailor bold masquerading as a writer? It would be as reasonable in one case as it would be in the other. The only use we can make of these singular claims is to turn them to account as showing how diverse and enormous is Shakespeare's audience, and how potential and far-reaching is his poetic insight.

It is with no intention, therefore, of adding Shakespeare's name to the Army List that I engage in the pleasant task of emphasising his military knowledge and picking out for admiration a few of his delightful soldier types.

Before proceeding to individualise his more prominent and heroic warriors, it may, perhaps, prove interesting to the military reader to glance at the generic description of the soldier—as such—which occurs in the great speech of Jaques in "As You Like It." This speech, I take it, should be received as an outline sketch of the genus military, and not as including in some mysterious way all the possible characteristics of the warrior:—

> "Then, a soldier,
> Full of strange oaths, and bearded like the pard,
> Jealous in honour, sudden and quick in quarrel,
> Seeking the bubble reputation
> Even in the cannon's mouth."

There is such a thing as over-reading one's Shakespeare. Let us not be guilty of that careful stupidity.

In this speech of Jaques, we have simply a sketch in broad outlines of the conventional soldier of Shakespeare's day—and nothing more. It presents a generic rather than a special type; and let us be grateful

KING HENRY 4th part 1st.

Falstaff *Yea & I'll swear I killed him*

*FALSTAFF AND HOTSPUR.*

that the military type has undergone vast improvement since the time of Shakespeare.

"Full of strange oaths" is a description as little applicable to the soldier of to-day as is the succeeding one, "bearded like the pard." The beard and strange oaths have been simultaneously discarded by the better type of modern soldier—the former, perhaps, more completely than the latter. Only the most hopeless "Tommy," given over habitually to "clink," would think of cultivating either. The day when "good round oaths" were thought to be the necessary and inevitable insignia of the brave soldier is fast receding from view, and will soon be as completely lost to sight as the pike and the halberd.

The next feature of Shakespeare's portrait of the soldier is one which has characterised the profession of arms in every age, "Jealous in honour." Indeed, some of the most ludicrous scenes in literature have been drawn about this theme—the delicate, sensitive, and passionate honour of the soldier. If sometimes a strain too intense, it is, at any rate, a quality extravagance in which leans to virtue's side. "Jealous in honour" is indeed a happy phrase, as indicating the quick sensitiveness of a soldier's resentment of any imputation upon his courage or his integrity.

A pleasant but significant illustration of this is found in the colloquy between Henry V. and his sturdy follower, Fluellen, which occurred upon the field of Agincourt:—

"*K. Henry.* What think you, Captain Fluellen? Is it fit this soldier keep his oath?

*Fluellen.* He is a craven and a villain else, an 't please your Majesty, in my conscience.

*K. Henry.* It may be, his enemy is a gentleman of great sort, quite from the answer of his degree.

*Fluellen.* Though he be as goot a gentleman as the tevil is, as Lucifer and Beelzebub himself, it is necessary, look your grace, that he keep his vow and his oath: if he be perjured, see you now, his reputation is as arrant a villain, and a Jack-sauce, as ever his plack shoe trod upon Got's ground and his earth, in my conscience, la!"

"Sudden and quick in quarrel" is another phrase in this outline sketch of the soldier by Shakespeare which goes to show the very wide distance between the ancient ideal of soldiership and the modern. Discipline, steadiness, self-restraint —these are the antithetical qualities to "sudden and quick in quarrel," and these are the qualities cultivated in the modern soldier. In truth, the entire purview of military life and ideals has so changed since Shakespeare's day, that it is only when we come to those essentials, strength and courage, and the spirit of adventure, which must always characterise the soldier, that there is no change. Of the soldier of to-day—in India, in South Africa, or in the frightful swamps of Benin—it may still be said he is

"Seeking the bubble reputation even in the cannon's mouth."

In all that relates to manner, to discipline, to equipment, and to drill, the modern soldier is vastly in advance of his mediæval prototype; while in the prime essentials—the gallant heart, the adventurous and daring spirit, the inflexible purpose—the true soldier of all ages is identical.

There is, then, nothing remarkable about this summing up of the typical soldier by Shakespeare, except its lucidity of thought and its graphic phrasing. It is when we come to discriminate between this soldier and that of Shakespeare's drawing—between the brave and the cowardly, the noisy "swashbuckler" and the quiet but fearless fighter; between

"*SEEKING THE BUBBLE REPUTATION EVEN IN THE CANNON'S MOUTH.*"

the ardent and fiery and the determined though modest soldier—that we perceive how close and how inclusive must have been the observation and the study upon which the great playwright built his military characters. Shakespeare's nicety in discriminating between types is never more apparent than it is when he limns his soldiers; and in no other field does he seem to have harvested facts, fancies, and typical peculiarities with greater care and zeal.

There are so many fascinating figures upon the great poet's war canvas, that it is perplexing to select a few for close inspection. I will, however, as it were, thrust my hand into the wheel and pluck out a name by chance. Observe the splendidly heroic and romantic type presented in Henry V. We have in him at once a soldier and a king. Responsibility crystallises his character; and with the death of the weakly but ambitious Bolingbroke we see the companion of the sensuous swashbuckler, Falstaff, spring like a human Jove into the glistening armour of an ideal soldier. It is a far cry from the apron of the counterfeit "drawer," waiting upon old Falstaff in Eastcheap, to the glittering field of Agincourt; but the distance is not so great as that between the days of Prince Hal's rollicking idleness and the dauntless soldier who led the English before Harfleur.

Surely Shakespeare never more truly caught the modest daring of the English soldier than when he outlined his concept of the soldier king:—

" Once more into the breach, dear friends, once more ; Or close the wall up with our English dead ! In peace, there's nothing so becomes a man As modest stillness and humility ; But when the blast of war blows in our ears, Then imitate the action of the tiger : Stiffen the sinews, summon up the blood, Disguise fair nature with hard-favour'd rage ;

Now set the teeth, and stretch the nostril wide ; Hold hard the breath, and bend up every spirit To his full height ! . . . . . . . And you, good yeomen, Whose limbs were made in England, show us here The mettle of your pasture. . . . . I see you stand like greyhounds in the slips, Straining upon the start. The game's afoot ; Follow your spirit ; and, upon this charge, Cry—God for Harry ! England ! and Saint George !"

The day of hand-to-hand fighting has almost passed away ; and it is, perhaps, true that the success of battles depends less now than it did in those days upon the dauntless courage. and lion-hearted daring of the leader. Scientific precision has taken the place of personal magnetism. Still it is not difficult, even in these days of Maxims and long-range field guns, to imagine the effect of such a heroic spirit upon troops eager for the fray. Patriotism and personal pluck—these are the watchwords of Agincourt. They were still the watchwords of Candahar and Khartoum, of Chitral and Benin.

In Hotspur we have daring and indiscretion. In Cassio we see the conventionally brave soldier—ready to fight or to woo "at the drop of the hat," but still "a soldier fit to stand by Cæsar and give direction!" In Mercutio, the merry fire-eating soldier of fortune. In Iago, the routine fighter, fearless, but wise. In Macbeth, the barbarian chieftain who knows no weakness on the field of battle but such as proceeds from the hauntings of a blood-stained soul. In Brutus, the lofty spirit who brings the method of the Senate to the field, but who, with all his philosophy, takes no single moment's counsel of fear. In Falstaff, the braggart whose battles are those of the canteen or the mess-table. In Othello, the soldier born—whose tropical blood once aroused knows no cooling while an enemy still holds the field. And so we might run down the list, ever finding this great artist picking out some distinctive feature to differentiate his types, yet always holding true to the great basic qualities of courage, daring, and self-forgetfulness, which always have adorned, and always will ennoble, the true fighting man. It is not always with the general that Shakespeare concerns himself. There are lieutenants and privates in his army who present features as admirable and as true. It was reserved for Mr. Kipling to heroise the modern "Tommy," but Shakespeare was before him even here.

I have always been much moved in playing two *rôles* of my repertoire by the conterminous study of two comparatively insignificant characters beside me on the stage. One the delightful and devoted figure of Eros, in "Antony and Cleopatra," the other that momentary hero, "the bleeding sergeant," in "Macbeth."

So great is the charm and power of real genius, that it obliterates the present and makes us "see the future in the instant." I recall playing Antony in a long run, and being assisted by an Eros whose private character was not admirable. Yet, such was the matchless power of Shakespeare's craft that I grew upon the stage to love and weep over the person that in the street I despised. The long, long, stormy day of Antony's life is past. The shadows of night draw on apace. He has surrendered his career to the wiles of a woman—"the serpent of old Nile!" But he would neither die upon the sword of Cæsar, nor be dragged with "pleach'd arms" and "corrigible neck" by the wheel of fortunate Cæsar through the streets of Rome! So he begs his death, as earlier Brutus and Cassius had done, of his some-time slave. It is a pathetic picture.

> "*Eros.*   Turn from me then that noble countenance,
> Wherein the worship of the whole world lies.
>                                         (*Turning from him.*)
> *Ant.*   Lo thee.
> *Eros.*   My sword is drawn.
> *Ant.*   Then let it do at once
> The thing why thou hast drawn it.
> *Eros.*   My dear master,
> My captain, and my emperor, let me say,
> Before I strike this bloody stroke, farewell.
> *Ant.*   'Tis said, man—and farewell.
> *Eros.*   Farewell, great chief. Shall I strike now ?
> *Ant.*   Now, Eros.
> *Eros.*   Why there then,        (*Falls on his sword*)
> Thus do I escape the sorrow
> Of Antony's death."

Well might Antony exclaim: "Thrice nobler than myself! Thou teachest me, O valiant Eros, what I should, and thou could'st not." Of the same sort is the other instance cited. Bravery without question, duration and daring linked together. These are qualities which lie back of Balaclava, of Quebec, of Louisburg, of Gibraltar, and of Waterloo. "This is the sergeant," says young Malcolm, "who, like a good and hardy soldier, fought 'gainst my captivity!"

The sergeant—yes! and the private, too, have shared the glory with their officers of many a hard fought field; and so

many a valiant soldier, to whom fortune has not given the distinction of a commission, has won by deeds of personal daring the glory of a V.C. It has been so in ages of the past, is so now, and still will be so in ages yet unborn. To all such

*"SO! IN THE NAME OF CHESHU, SPEAK FEWER."—HENRY IV*

we may well say as said the good King Duncan to the "bleeding sergeant":—

> "So well thy words become thee as thy wounds;
> They smack of honour both."

THE next generation of Englishmen will have no excuse for not knowing what the British Empire is. The old builders thereof went at their work blindly, seeking their own ends, but impelled by a species of instinct, much, says Mr. Story, after the manner of polyiferous reef-builders. They would have marvelled much to see the nineteenth century search-lights turned on the solid structure they reared. Mr. Alfred T. Story has essayed to illuminate "The Building of the Empire" in two very handsome volumes (Chapman, 14s.), and, in my judgment, successfully. The subject is one of stupendous magnitude, but Mr. Story shows himself to have been well equipped for dealing with it. His subjects are grouped with quite remarkable skill, and the chapters are penned with such natural ease and grace as to make the perusal a real pleasure. Of course Mr. Story writes from a soundly patriotic standpoint in his demonstration of our successive Naval triumphs over the Spaniards, the Dutch, and the French. When I read his brilliant account of the defeat of the Armada in 1588, I had just laid down the newly-published third volume of Captain Fernandez Duro's "Armada Española"—published, be it noted, under the auspices of the Spanish Government—with its narrative of our failure at Corunna and Lisbon in 1589; and it is certainly not less amusing than instructive to note the disproportionate significance assigned to events by two competent writers from various patriotic standpoints. But, of course, the victory of 1588 was at least as important to us as the failure of 1589 was to the Spaniards, and Mr. Story rightly finds here the corner stone of his structure. He passes on from those sounding times, whose history is a romance, to the planting of our influence in India and America, shows the difficulties that then beset our progress, the events in which we triumphed, and, sometimes, the little wisdom with which our colonists were governed. But the revolt of the American Colonies, as Mr. Story's book explains, taught the much-needed lesson, and after a long period of neglect the pulse of the Empire quickened, the titanic contest with France was waged, and colonial expansion went on. Where there is so much to praise in Mr. Story's book the criticism of detail is ungracious. Yet I may point out that a fatality seems to have attended his writing of personal names. The great Frenchman is "Duplaix," the Spanish admiral at Trafalgar "Guarina," and even our well-known Naval writer, "Prof. Loughton." Other inaccuracies are in the book, which is accompanied by an excellent set of pictures.

While Mr. Story sings the song of Empire, Captain Francis Younghusband, in his "South Africa of To-Day" (Macmillan, 8s. 6d.), shows what difficulties confront us in that region. You will not anywhere find so luminous and dispassionate a statement of the case as in these reprinted letters from the *Times*. Captain Younghusband puts the matter in a nutshell when he says that, while the Boers went to the Transvaal chiefly to win freedom, the Uitlanders went principally to win money. The Boers love the independence they have gained, and are brave and self-reliant, with excellent personal qualities; but they shirk the competition of modern life, enjoy, from the industry of aliens, debilitating civil advantages, and show no capacity for the government of an inordinately rich and rising State like the Transvaal. Captain Younghusband came to the conclusion that they will certainly fight for their independence, and to resist the intrusion of strangers into the control of the country. Therefore the right policy for England is that of abstention from direct interference in the internal affairs of the Transvaal, while strongly enforcing our rights of free access and just treatment which the London Convention confers. The book gives a favourable picture of the outlook in Rhodesia, where Captain Younghusband found Imperial rule hated and the rule of the Company appreciated. This hatred proceeds from the idea that the needs of the colony are not appreciated in London, and that the Colonial Office is more or less swayed by ignorant public opinion and the faddists of Exeter Hall.

If you wish to know "Who's Who" in 1898, you will discover it in the well-known volume bearing that title (Black, 3s. 6d.). The energetic editor fills about 1,000 pages with his magazine of facts, and gives nearly 7,000 biographies, with the large reinforcement which stiffens his pages this year. It is enough for a man or a woman to make a mark in the world, to cause this editor to spread his net and make him or her a biographical captive. But it is not enough to be told who's who, for here, too, we find what's what, in regard to a vast number of points concerning which the busy man may desire enlightenment at his breakfast-table. In short, the book is a marvel, and a most useful companion.

I do not propose to do more—for the benefit of those who are interested (and how numerous are they!) in the fleets of the Powers—than just draw attention to Mr. Fred. T. Jane's "All the World's Fighting Ships" (Sampson Low, 10s. 6d.). Here, in oblong album form, every war-ship in the world, or nearly every one, is depicted, with the purpose of making their characteristics known, and themselves recognisable at sea. A good deal of information about them is given in four languages, and there is a special classification, with visual and nominal indices. Inexhaustible energy has been necessary for the production of such a volume. That remarkable pocket-book—apparently the original of all such—the "Marine Almanach," has also just been issued by Gerold, Pola (7m. 20pf.), as well as Durassier's "Aide-Mémoire," by Charles-Lavauzelle, in Paris (5fr.). These are invaluable companions, and herald the appearance of the library-shelf "Brassey."

I mention the *Artist* (Constable, 1s.) as a hint to all art-lovers. This charming magazine seems, in some respects, to be distancing its rivals. Variety, freshness of treatment, knowledge and taste are its merits, with illustrations of most fascinating character. I should have liked to discuss its contents, but they must speak for themselves.

"SEARCH-LIGHT."

# A SHEET ANCHOR.

### *BY COMMANDER CLAUD HARDING, R.N.*

THE "Aphrodite's" launch was aground at the entrance to the harbour of Port Royal, Jamaica, and there did not seem much probability of her being quickly floated. She had gone away with a picnic party, and had been run alongside a plateau of rock to enable the people to land for lunch, and when they re-embarked and prepared to take their departure they found that the launch was aground on a ledge of rock, and all their efforts to get her off had hitherto proved ineffectual. The water rapidly deepened to seaward, and, having no small boat, they were unable to lay out an anchor, by which means they might easily have hauled the launch off.

The party consisted of the commander of the "Aphrodite," who was giving the entertainment, Lieutenant Howard, a big, powerful man, two other officers, and four bluejackets. While on shore, sitting on the rocks amusedly watching the exertions of the crew to get the launch afloat, were four young women and one elderly one, for whose pleasure the expedition had been arranged.

Of the five ladies, it is only necessary to notice one—Miss Effie Carstairs.

She was extremely pretty, but her greatest charm was a peculiarly fascinating manner, which attracted men to her like a magnet.

Howard had been very hard hit by her, and had, in fact, made her an offer of marriage, which she declined, and she was just the least bit piqued that he took his rejection philosophically, and seemed resigned to his fate.

Miss Carstairs had of late received great attention from Captain Hon. Arthur Stoney, eldest son of Lord Soursop, aide-de-camp to the Governor of the island, and it was currently reported that they were engaged to be married.

The ladies at first were much interested in the efforts of the men to get the boat afloat, but when more than an hour had elapsed without the launch being moved an inch, they became a little depressed. The commander was full of resource; but all his plans proved ineffectual, and the boat remained fast.

"Give me your candid opinion, Mr. Howard. Is there any chance of getting the boat afloat?" asked Miss Carstairs.

"Not without laying an anchor out," he answered.

"Why don't they do that?"

"We have nothing to lay it out with. It is very stupid to have come away without a small boat, and we shall be here for the next six hours, as far as I can see."

Miss Carstairs' head drooped. "Are you very much disappointed?" Howard asked.

"More than I can say. To-night is the ball at the General's." Howard saw that she was nearly crying.

"By Jove! I forgot that; and Stoney is leaving for England next week, isn't he?" he muttered, as if thinking aloud. "It's a bit rough on me, but 'tis of no use being a dog in the manger, and I'll see what I can do."

He returned to the boat, and Miss Carstairs noticed him having a discussion with the commander. Howard seemed to be making some suggestion to which the other demurred. She overheard the commander say, "My dear fellow, I won't let you do it; if you should trip up and fall, with the anchor on top of you, nothing in the world could save you from being drowned; besides, there are too many ground sharks about."

There was some further discussion, but eventually Howard overcame the commander's objections. An anchor

*SUDDENLY THERE WAS A SHOUT OF DELIGHT.*

was brought aft and the hawser bent to it. Then, to her surprise, Howard jumped overboard, and an anchor was lowered over the side. Silently they paid out the hawser over the quarter, when suddenly there was a shout of delight as Howard reappeared floating on the water. The hawser was hove taut, and a purchase clapped on to it. With the first good haul the launch moved a few inches; with the next she shifted a foot.

"Come on board, ladies. We shall be afloat in a minute," called out the commander.

In a few more minutes the launch was afloat and riding at the anchor Howard had carried out on his shoulder, walking along the bottom of the sea.

"Was it a very dangerous thing that Mr. Howard did?" Miss Carstairs asked the commander before leaving the boat.

"If he had done it in action, he would have won the Victoria Cross," the latter replied.

\*   \*   \*   \*

The ball at the General's was in full swing. Captain Stoney and Miss Carstairs were sitting in the garden under a jasmine tree. He was holding her hand.

"Miss Carstairs, Effie, you know that I love you," he said. "I loved you from the first moment I saw you, and you care just a little bit for me, don't you, darling? You will think of me when I am away, and pity me, Effie, for I am the most miserable wretch on the face of the earth. I wrote home to my father, and told him of a certain little sorceress out here who had bewitched me. He replies that if I marry without his consent, he will stop my allowance. What am I to do? I am stone broke, and entirely dependent on my father. You will think of me sometimes when I am away, and be sorry for me, won't you, darling?"

A hard look came over Miss Carstairs' face. "Captain Stoney," she replied, in chilly accents, "I hope after this night I shall never think of you again, for any thought I should have of you would be exceedingly unpleasant. Even if I cared for you, which I do not, your speech would be most insulting. What right have you to call me by my Christian name, and in terms of endearment? What should I think of a man who, believing he has won a girl's affections, has the base insolence to ask her to pity him for his dishonourable cowardice? Let us return to the ball-room."

\*   \*   \*   \*   \*   \*

"Am I to congratulate you, Miss Carstairs?" asked Howard, later in the evening.

"Yes."

"You are going to marry Stoney, then?"

"No. You may congratulate me that I am *not* going to marry Captain Stoney."

"Why?" hesitated Howard.

"You are surprised! You think you risked your life for no purpose this afternoon? That is not the case. You did me a service I shall never forget."

"You can easily repay it if you would."

"I will repay it in any way you like," she answered, holding out her hand.

"You are grateful to me for laying out the anchor. Will you let me be your sheet anchor for life?"

"Yes, for with you to depend upon I fear neither storm nor stress."

FOREWARNED
a Story of the Intelligence Department

By Major Arthur Griffiths
AUTHOR OF "The Queen's Shilling," "The Rome Express," "The Wellington Memorial" etc. etc.

## SYNOPSIS OF PREVIOUS CHAPTERS.

Captain Wood is an officer on the staff of the Intelligence Department of the War Office engaged with certain confidential questions pending with the United States Government. It is the height of the London season, and he is sleeping late after a ball, when he is roused to hear some startling news. A lawyer, Mr. Quinlan, has called to tell him that an unknown relative, an American millionaire, has left him a colossal fortune. Almost at the same moment an American detective warns him that he has enemies plotting against him and his fortune, and that he goes in imminent danger of his life. Arrived at the Intelligence Office, he is given some confidential work to carry through connected with an attack on New York. Returning to his chambers, he again meets the American detective, who details the nature of the plot against his fortune and the military secrets he possesses. He meets Frida Wolstenholme at a ball, where he proposes, and is accepted. He picks up a cab, and scarcely settles into it when he is attacked, hocussed, and loses consciousness. Recovering at length, he finds himself tied and bound, and subjected to a cruel and painful ordeal. Snuyzer, the American detective, having shadowed Captain Wood all night, sees him carried off towards Hammersmith, follows his tracks, and believes he has run him to earth. Sets an assistant to watch the house, and returns to London. Hears at Wood's chambers that he has met with an accident; another at the American Consulate that Wood had been there. Now Sir Charles Collingham supervenes with anxious enquiries for confidential papers that are missing. Miss Wolstenholme is informed of Captain Wood's disappearance, and the whole party, with Wood's collie dog, proceed to Hammersmith.

## CHAPTER XIII.

AS we drove into the suburb of Hammersmith I thought it time to suggest some plan of action. I was for leaving the buggy with the groom this side of the bridge, a good deal short of the Strathallan Road, and that we two, Miss Wolstenholme and I, should walk forward and reconnoitre.

The young lady went one better.

"It would save time if we called at the police station as we pass and prepare them. We may have to force an entrance into that house."

The police had been warned from headquarters, and were prepared to assist us. The General, too, had called. He had come down on his bicycle, and was waiting somewhere near, they told us. A couple of men with a sergeant had been detailed for duty, and I was giving them the direction, when the young lady added in her pretty peremptory way:

"You will make haste, of course, constables? I shall drive on ahead down the Strathallan Road, slowly, and back again to meet you. We shall have the latest news."

"My boy will be there," I said, "Joseph Vialls. He has been on the watch the whole day, and he may have something interesting to report."

But to my deep chagrin, when we reached the house my boy Joseph was not there, nor was he to be seen anywhere, near or far.

Now I could have staked my life on little Joseph Vialls. He was a London lad, who had seen much in his short life, on shore and afloat; for, although I had picked him off a crossing on account of his quick tongue and bright ways, he had been to sea on Thames lighters right round the coast. Now I was training him to our business. He took to it naturally, knew what was expected of him, and was not the sort to be fooled into quitting his post or going off on fandangoes on his own account.

Miss Wolstenholme turned on me like a tiger when we drove past the house and back, still without a sign of Joe.

What did I mean? Had I told her the truth? If she found that I had deceived her I should make nothing by it, there was too much at stake, and more of the same sort.

"See here, miss," I said, taking her up rather short, "we shan't progress much if we fall out just at the start. I am as anxious to serve the gentleman as you are, although, may-be, I'm not so sweet on him."

"Don't dare to speak in that way to me," she answered, fiercely. "Get out of this cart, and go and ring the bell. The sooner we get inside that house the better. Make haste, please."

I tell you, gentlemen, that girl would have helped a tortoise to skip. The mere sound of her voice sent a spark through me as though she was a battery and I an electric wire.

I hammered at that door, and hung on to that bell, till I woke all the echoes of that dead-alive suburb. No one came; there was not a sign of life within, only the twang, twang, tingle, tingle of the bell, just as it sounds when you've lost your latch-key and all the family is asleep in the top back of the house.

Presently the police came up, and the General, who had been cruising about on his bicycle, joined Miss outside. They all stopped there talking to her a bit, and I judge they were hesitating to act, arguing it out with the General, who was very fierce and positive, ordering them about short and sharp, but doing little good till Missy took up the running. But she soon sent them flying in after me, and came with them. I tell you there was no hanging back or busnacking when she left her buggy and stood with the rest of us at that closed up door.

One of the constables nipped round to the back, where he found a strip of garden with a low wall. He was over that like ninepence, and in through the scullery window. Half a minute more and we heard him unchaining the front door. Then we all trooped into the entry and ran through the house, some high, some low, but none of us finding anything. There was not a scrap of furniture, nor the signs of any occupancy that we could see.

But Miss, she also hunted, halloaing on the collie dog with a "go look, Roy," worry, worry, worry, which drove the beast nearly mad. He hunted and quested through the house with a short snapping bark as if he was rounding up a sheepfold, and it was he—marvellous animal—who led us into the basement, into a sort of cellar between the front parlour and the kitchen.

Here he raced round and round like a thing possessed, yelping furiously.

The place was all black darkness; no windows, not a glint of daylight. But someone struck a match and lit a lantern or bull's-eye, and we could make out what there was there. One big long table, a kitchen table with seats on each side, and at the end a strange thing that told its own story.

It was a sort of wooden erection, something between a scaffold and a bulkhead; two great upright timbers wedged in tight between the ceiling and the stone floor—might have been a support, pillar like, for the roof or ceiling, but we could see it was meant to make someone fast to—a pair of stocks, you might say, or a whipping-post. And so it had been used, no doubt. For there was a long chain and padlock hanging between the uprights just over a low bench that served as a seat for whoever was held there a prisoner.

This was where the collie raged about most fiercely, sniffing, scenting, hunting to and fro, always under the encouraging voice of missy, who shouted "Lu-lu-lu, good dog, find him then. Where is he? Out with him, Lu-lu."

Of course, his master had been there. None of us had a doubt of that, any more than of the plain fact that he was not there now. We looked at each other blankly, after a bit, hardly knowing what to do or say next till miss stamped her pretty foot and cried, "Well?"

"I have my suspicions," began the sergeant, knocking his hands together rather jovially, till the dust flew out of his white lisle thread gloves. "It's not all fair and square. I shall make a report to that effect and await instructions."

"Psha!" interrupted miss; "and meantime Mr. Wood may be murdered. I shall offer a reward of £500 to whoever finds him, but it must be within the next twenty— four hours."

"Now you're talking," I said, heartily, "and I don't see we gain much by staying here. The cage is empty, and we've got to follow the birds wherever they've flown."

"If you'll excuse me," said the sergeant, who had got mighty eager when he heard of the reward, "the most proper course, as I see it, is to start from this here house. Whose is it? Who took it? Likewise who put up this rum apparatus, and why? When those questions is answered by the neighbours, house agents, tradesmen, and such - like, we may come to lay our fingers on them as is responsible for this here business."

"You had better do all that then," said the General, very discontented, "and I shall go to New Scotland Yard to the fountain-head. There's more in this than you duffers seem to think. We want the best man they've got, a *real* detective, to take up the case."

This was aimed at me. It was unkind, you'll say. But, after all, how much had I done? and where was boy Joe?

"It's not like him," I was saying half to myself as we stood together, miss and I, while she was taking the ribbons, and with one neat brown shoe on the step, was just getting into her cart. "Either he's been caught spying—and that's not like him—or he's hanging on to their heels like bird-lime. But—what in thunder's that?"

I saw some rough writing in white chalk upon the gate, and an arrow figured there with the point towards London:

"'Ooked it. Follerin' on.
"Joe."

They were as plain as print, so was their meaning, and I pointed out the words triumphantly to Miss Wolstenholme.

"I knew that boy wouldn't fail me. He's got grit, he has. Some day he'll be able to teach me my business——"

"I wish he would begin soon," said miss, peevishly. "It's always the same story. Some day, one day, next day, never. And all this time he—poor Captain Wood is——"

"Bear up." I was real sorry for her, you know, although she did vex me above a bit with her contemptuous way of talking. "Matters are not so black now as they looked a few moments ago. Joe will never go back on us. He's after

them like a nose-hound, and he'll do the trick yet, you bet your bottom dollar. We shall be on the inside track whenever he turns up, as he will, sooner or later, with the key to the whole conundrum."

"I'm not going to wait for that, Mr. detective. It's mere conjecture, a far-away chance at best, even if—I trusted you, which I don't entirely, and that's the plain English of it— there. Let this famous boy of yours—of whose very existence we've no distinct proof—let him bring us to Mr. Wood, and I'll hand over the reward, with an ample apology for having any doubts. Until then—good day."

With that she gave her pony a smart cut with her double thong, and the beast, nearly springing through his collar, started off like a mad thing, with the other mad beast of a dog yelping and screeching and jumping up at his muzzle or trying to bite at his heels. The General also gave me a contemptuous good day, and springing on to his "bike," like a boy went off at a real right down scorching pace after the buggy.

I expect that is the last I shall see of her, for she never took a card of mine or asked where she could find me again, and I've fully made up my mind that never so long as I live will I hunt after her. When Joe reappears, as I tell you, gentlemen, I most confidently expect he will at any moment, and with important news so that I can pick up fresh threads, I'll do the next job alone. I don't want no high - falutin' young duchesses treating one like dirt, for a true-born American citizen is as good as any Emperor, let alone a pert minx with ever so pretty a face. We shall see. If there was no better reason than the wish to humble her, I mean to see the thing right through to the very end.

I wish I could make out more before I mail this letter. But the bag closes right away, and there is nothing to hand, neither from Joe nor from Messrs. Knight and Rider, who, as I tell you, are shadowing that other crowd.

"Went off at a real right down scorching pace."

## CHAPTER XIV.

Passages from the diary of Wilfrida Evelyn Wolstenholme.

*(It is a small gilt-edged volume, bound in white vellum and richly tooled.*

*On the cover is an illuminated scroll with the words "Strictly private."*

*Under them: "Whoso reads what is written here does a dishonourable act."*

*Again below, in ink:*

*"What was begun in foolishness has been continued in sober earnestness. I have removed the pages that precede the strange and terrible adventures connected with the disappearance of W. A. W. What follows all the world may now know.")*

Steam Yacht "Morfa."

July 17th.—Although still harassed and oppressed by hideous anxiety, I want, in this my first moment of leisure, to set down clearly and fully the strange events that have occurred since that memorable evening in Prince's Gate. I have been in a whirl ever since. But I have forgotten nothing; every act, every thought is indelibly fixed in my memory from the moment that I realised my loss.

I could not do so at first. I had been so indescribably happy. Dear, downright, simple-hearted Willie Wood—to think that it should be he, he of all men—the many men, ah me!—just plain Captain William Wood, whom mother had always warned me would never, never do. Poor darling mother, I think she has changed her opinion once or twice since then. At first he was so very very nice, so good and true. Now—well now—I believe she wishes she had never heard his name. Then she might have escaped this painful experience, and I, too, should have escaped the pain and sorrow and constant anxiety that oppresses me.

Forget! I shall never forget that afternoon when the American detective brought me the news. What an odd creature he was. Not a bit of a gentleman, although he tried so hard to look it: very much over-dressed—trust a woman to notice that—with a sort of company manner voice, which didn't disguise his Yankee accent or tone down his awful Americanisms; and most outrageously, offensively polite. Ugly, horribly so, with a red spotty face, and great goggle eyes which were fixed on me wherever I went. From the way he looked at me, I might say ogled me, I could have fancied he had conceived a sudden admiration for my small self. It showed his good taste, perhaps, but did not make him more attractive. Certainly he did not inspire confidence, and when he told me the whole story I did not believe him. I could not—the thing seemed too impossible.

What! Willie, my Willie Wood, Captain Wood, an officer of Her Majesty's Army, a staff officer, too, one of the Intelligence Department, well known in London and all through the Service.

But then, where was he? Surely he did not stay away of his own accord? Not after that last night. There was no reason in it, very much the reverse, unless he was a faithless wretch, who had wanted to make a fool of me, to punish me for my treatment of him—and the rest. But no, no, honest Willie was incapable of such treachery. I was a traitor, too, to think it of him, with his voice still sweet in my ear, his kisses still wet on my lips.

I might doubt this American's extraordinary tale, but it was evident that others did not entirely distrust him. If I was to believe him, Sir Charles Collingham had taken up the business and was already gone to Hammersmith. I felt that I must go there with all possible despatch. It was the only way to make quite sure. So I had the pony-cart round, and drove this Mr. Snuyzer down.

I know now that the poor wretch was honest and straightforward, but I could not get over my repugnance to him at first. There was something in his air as he sat beside me, a sort of elation and supreme self-satisfaction that nearly maddened me, and I was all but making him get out and follow in a hansom cab. But I hardly trusted him even for that.

And so when we got to the very house, and drew quite blank, I made up my mind, that the man was an arrant impostor. Nothing fell out as he said. "His boy would be on the watch"; there was no boy. He was quite certain of the house into which Willie had been carried. The police broke in. There was no Willie Wood.

The whole thing was humbug. I felt convinced of it, and said so, only to regret it directly after. It could not be quite humbug, or, if it was, Roy, dear Willie's lovely dog, was in it too, for Roy had certainly smelt him out in the cellar where we found the awful apparatus and things, and I ought to have known that a dog's instinct is always true.

But I was very short with Mr. Snuyzer, and left him *planté là*. It was a mistake, of course, for it was losing a chance; the man might be useful, and, after all, he was the only one who, whether the right or the wrong one, had any sort of clue.

That was good old Sir Charles Collingham's opinion and Colonel Bannister's, the big official, chief constable, or assistant-commissioner, or something whom the General brought with him to Hill Street. I found them there closeted with mother, who had heard all about it from them. She was rather in a limp condition, dear mother, having quite failed to take in the situation, and unable to say or suggest anything.

The Colonel—he was rather a cross-looking, middle-aged man, with square-cut short whiskers and a bristling grey moustache—took me sharply to task for letting the American slip, and I should have been offended at his tone, but I knew I had been wrong.

"From what you tell us he had, no doubt, been in communication with Captain Wood yesterday, and he would have saved us some time and trouble if we had him under our hand now. He must be hunted up," said the Colonel.

"Your people know him at Scotland Yard. He was there to-day, and they sent him on to the United States' Consulate. He told me that himself," I said.

"They will know him at the Consulate, probably. I will send there to enquire," said the Colonel, making a short note. "And Captain Wood's man knows him. They came here together this afternoon."

"And, for the matter of that, so do I," added Sir Charles. "Not much, of course, and he's an uncommon queer-looking chap. But the fellow seems honest and straight-forward."

"Unless the whole thing is a put up job," remarked the police colonel with a meaning smile. "A scheme to throw you off the scent of these papers, which you say are so important, Sir Charles——"

"By George, they are that," the General broke in. "Don't

you see? It is probably a trumped up story about the plot against Wood, simply to cover the theft of the papers."

"But Captain Wood has gone; he has been carried off," I said.

"'Gone,' yes," sneered the Colonel. "But, 'carried off'—how do we know that? It's not the first time a young gentleman has disappeared for four-and-twenty hours or more. Who knows all the inns and outs of Captain Wood's affairs and private movements?"

At that moment Harris the butler came up with a card. "Gentleman asks if he can see you most particular. Same as came this afternoon—Mr. Snoozer, but he's got a dirty scrub of a boy with him."

"Joe," I cried. "Show them up here, Harris. Yes; bring both of them, of course. We shall hear something now."

Mr. Snuyzer came up to the drawing-room, at a run, I'm sure. He was almost at Harris's heels; the boy Joe lagged a little behind and stood abashed at the door, and Roy, who by constitution hated all boys, especially ragged ones, took this hesitation as suspicious, and gave an ugly growl with a show of his fierce teeth. The collie, I should mention, had never left me since he was brought to Hill Street.

"Look yar, what did I tell you, miss?" began the detective, coming straight at me, and talking rather excitedly. "I never thought to show myself here again, but by thunder it was too strong for me. I've got the pride of my business, and I wanted you to see I was right to believe in Joe. Now, speak out, young squire."

I must say I thought well of the boy from the very first. He was an apple-cheeked, healthy-looking, bullet-headed urchin, with clear, china blue eyes, very wide open just then, in astonishment, I think, not fear. He did not care one bit for the dog, but faced him sturdily, stooping as if to pick up a stone, with a "Would you—br-r-r, lie down, will you," that sent the collie, still growling, under the sofa.

"How was it, Joe? Won't you sit down? Let's hear what happened," I said, just to encourage him, and he asked nothing better than to tell his story, and, taking his seat at the very edge of a chair—after dusting it—he began:

"It was this way, mum—miss. When he—Mr. Snuyzer there—set me on the nark, I mean watch, this morning, I held on to the job close for a matter of three hours, and never saw nothing. Worn't no move at all in the house till about eleven o'clock, when a trap comes down the road, and pulls up at the garden gate. A carriage, but from some mews, not a private turn-out; the coachman he was in an old blue coat and silver buttons, bad hat—half-a-crown an hour business—regular fly. But inside was a dona—a real lady, you understand, dressed up to the knocker; I saw her get out——"

"Would you know her again?" we asked, all of us, in a breath.

Joe nodded his head.

"I couldn't see her face at first, she'd got a thick blue veil on. But afterwards I got my chance, as I'll tell you directly. She was a snorter, too, real jam, and no mistake; a lady, like as I've seen at the music 'alls."

"When did you see her face?" asked the Colonel, rather disdainfully.

"In the carriage, when I was a-setting right opposite her. I'll come to that. But first of all I must tell you how it was. You see, the dona, she wouldn't go right into the garden at first. She kept at the gate, spying-like, watching the house, and doubting, as I fancied, if she ought to go in. Then she made a dash forward for the front door, but before she reached the steps someone came down, a man——"

"Would you know him again?"

"Rath-er, in a thousand. He was a little black-muzzled chap, with a skin like a pickled walnut, and he came out all in a hurry, as though he had been watching for her.

"He waved her back, but she stuck to it, and they must have had words, for I see'd him take her by the wrist, and pull her out towards the carriage.

"I was crouched close under the wall, for I'd sneaked up at the back of the carriage to spot what I could, and I was just by the door when the small chap opened it, and was for forcing the dona to get in.

"'I will not go, Papir' (Pepe), she says. 'Not till I have heard what you have done to him. There was to be no violence, you promised that. And I wish to be sure; I must know,' she says, 'that he aint come to no harm,' she says.

"With that the little fellow gives her a great shove; I think he'd 'a' struck her, but just then he caught sight of me.

"'Why, in the name of'—some foreign gibberish—'where have you dropped from? What brings you 'anging about 'ere?'

"I tried to stall him off by axing for a brown, and offered to sell him a box of matches, but he cut up very rough, and wanted to lay 'old of me, saying he'd call the slops and give me in charge for loitering and all that. But I cheeked him and slipped through his fingers—'twasn't difficult—and ran up the road.

*(To be continued).*

Photo. Elliott & Fry.                                                    Baker Street

### LIEUTENANT-GENERAL SIR WILLIAM STIRLING, K.C.B.

SIR WILLIAM STIRLING is an officer of the Royal Artillery, which regiment he entered in June, 1853—just a
twelvemonth before the outbreak of the war with Russia.   As lieutenant, R.A., he had the good fortune to see
active service throughout the whole of the Crimean Campaign of 1854 and 1855, and took part in practically every
engagement that was fought, from the opening affairs of Bulganac and M'Kenzie's Farm, the battle of the Alma, the
repulse of the Russian sortie of October 26th, 1854, the battles of Balaclava and Inkerman, during the siege of
Sebastopol, and down to the final taking of the fortress.   Four years later he was in India, where he saw service at the
close of the Mutiny as Brigade-Major of Artillery with the Rajpootana Field Force.   From India Sir W. Stirling went to
China, where he served with the expeditionary force of 1860, and was present in several actions and at the final
surrender of Pekin.   Since then Sir William Stirling has seen service with Lord Roberts in the Afghan War of 1878-79,
for which campaign he was, in November, 1879, awarded the C.B.   In 1890 General Stirling was appointed Commandant
of the Royal Military Academy, Woolwich.   He was promoted to his present rank of lieutenant-general in 1892, having
been major-general since 1887.   Sir William Stirling holds the reward for distinguished and meritorious services.

# KEEPING THE PEACE AT KLONDYKE.

THE Canadian North-West Mounted Police as a force is outside the Dominion Militia and is specially maintained for service in the Western Provinces of Canada, where there is no Militia organisation. The force numbers 1,000 men, employed to patrol the thousands of miles of prairie and mountain country between Manitoba and the Klondyke gold-fields, where a number of them have just been sent to keep order among the crowds of sharps and gamesters who are swarming there. In drill, physique, and morale, there is hardly a finer force in the world, composed as the corps is of men nearly all 6-ft. high, who can ride and fight like any of the redskin heroes of Fenimore Cooper's romances. For parade their uniform is not unlike that of our Dragoon Guards :—

*MEN OF THE NORTH-WEST POLICE OFF DUTY, MACLEOD DISTRICT BARRACKS.*

Scarlet tunic, blue cloth breeches with broad yellow stripe, riding boots and spurs, white helmet with brass spike and chain, and white haversack with cross belts. An astrachan fur reefer is added in winter, while for work on the plains in summer the men turn out in dark, drab-coloured jacket, grey shirt, and brown slouched hat. The force is drilled as cavalry, but the rank and file carry no swords, each man having a Lee-Metford carbine and heavy revolver. Raised originally in 1873, when the Great Plains of the West came by treaty under the Canadian Government, the keeping of the Queen's peace throughout the North-West has been the special charge of the Mounted Police ever since, as Sitting Bull's army of "braves," after the massacre of Custer, in Wyoming, learned, and Louis Riel and his half-breeds in 1885. The force is both military and civil, and forms quite a small army, self-supporting and self-reliant, with every man trained to fight, carry despatches, cook his own dinner, bivouac in the open, drive a commissariat team or break in a prairie horse. No finer

fellows serve the Queen, in whose Royal Procession last June twenty-two men of the North-West Police took part, winning the admiration of all who saw them.

*OFFICERS, CANADIAN NORTH-WEST POLICE, MACLEOD DISTRICT HEADQUARTERS.*

Photos. W. G. Blackie.                                                                    Victoria, British Columbia

*MACLEOD DISTRICT DETACHMENT NORTH-WEST POLICE ON PARADE.*

# THE EASTERN SOUDAN.

THE photographs from the Eastern Soudan which accompany this note are, in view of present developments, of very great interest. One gives us a view of the fort at El Teb, an outpost of the Egyptian troops that are holding Suakin and Tokar and the surrounding country. This fort is close to the old battle-field, where even to-day the bleached skulls and bones show out in lines and groups according as the men fell. The troops garrisoning the fort look smart and alert, and are a detachment of the 4th Egyptian Battalion, which garrisons Tokar. The men in front belong to the Tokar Mounted Police, and formed the escort of Major-General Knowles, C.B., on his visit of inspection to the post. The group in the second photograph are the Sheikhs of the friendly tribes in the neighbourhood of Suakin and Tokar who had assembled to meet General Knowles at Fort El Teb when on his tour of inspection. It is the only photograph of these men ever taken, for the Arab, like most high-class Mahometans, has an intense aversion to being photographed, and this was only overcome by the artist, Mrs. Knowles, the General's wife, urging on them that the English General was so taken with them that he wished always to have their faces near him. This being fully understood, the chiefs sat quietly down, spread their hands on their knees, and submitted to the inevitable. The fine old fellow in uniform, seated to the left, is Abd-el-Kader, the head of the Allanga tribe, which first settled in the rich Kassala plain, and gave to the city they there founded the name of their chief, Kassa. He is of

*INTERIOR OF THE FORT AT KASSALA.*

great influence in this country, and a staunch friend of Egypt, in whose army he holds rank as honorary colonel. When the Dervishes captured Kassala, Abd-el-Kader was then in command of a battalion, but succeeded in escaping into Abyssinia, and was there appointed to a command in the Abyssinian army, in which he considerably distinguished himself in the fighting against the Dervishes. For years he had lived at Tokar, but has now returned to his old home at Kassala, since it has been handed over to Egypt by Italy. Another interesting figure in this group is the one in native costume standing next to the two in uniform at the rear of the group. This is a young Arab, by name Ahmed-a-wad, who is now head of the Tokar Mounted Police, and who distinguished himself greatly by his bravery in the 1896 campaign. When Colonel Lloyd was advancing out of Suakin with 800 men to meet Major Sidney bringing 250 men from Tokar, the two forces to unite in supporting the friendly Arabs who were being raided by Osman Digna, this hero rode twice through the Dervishes to carry communications between one force and the other. Finally, the third photo represents the fort at Kassala, and shows us an Egyptian mountain battery, which forms part of the garrison, at drill. The fort was built by the Italians shortly after their occupation of Kassala, and is a rectangular structure about 630-ft. long and half as broad. It is surrounded by a stout wall some ten or eleven feet high, and also protected by a deep moat and wire entanglements. The lofty pillar which rises in the background of the photograph is of interest, as it is a relic of the old civilisation of the Soudan, which the success of the Mahdi temporarily shattered, and which there is now every hope will very soon be restored. It is indeed the brick chimney of what was in the Egyptian days a flourishing cotton factory. The fort was built to enclose this building, and its lofty engine-rooms, etc., are now used as armoury, officers' mess-room, etc., etc., while the old boiler plates form part of the drawbridge which crosses the moat. It is pleasant to imagine the Soudan once again restored to civilisation.

*FORT EL TEB.*

From Photos.

By a Military Officer.

*A GROUP OF "FRIENDLIES."*

# SIGNALLING IN THE ARMY.

THE importance of an efficient signalling staff is fully recognised in the Army, and every regiment of cavalry and infantry has its signalling establishment. The headquarters of Army signalling is ordinarily the School of Signalling at Aldershot, under an inspector of signalling, a colonel, with an assistant inspector, a captain. Classes of instruction are formed every year, each comprising thirty officers and thirty non-commissioned officers. Aldershot supplies each unit of cavalry and infantry, and each garrison artillery station of two or more companies, with one officer instructor and two non-commissioned officers as assistant instructors, who all hold proficiency certificates. The instruction in each case is intrusted to these officers. In the infantry, classes consisting of one officer and nine rank and file are formed under their tuition during the summer months each year, from whom the battalion staff of signallers is drawn. Each battalion provides six qualified signallers, who are inspected every autumn by the Inspector of Army Signalling. Our first photo-

Photo. Evelyn & Co.                                                                   Aldershot.
*LIEUT. LAMBERT AND SIGNALLERS, 2nd EAST LANCASHIRE REGIMENT*

Photo. J. W. Gavin.                                                                   Norw.ch.
*CAPTAIN COOPER AND SIGNALLERS, 7th DRAGOON GUARDS.*

graph shows the signallers of the 2nd East Lancashire Regiment, the signalling champions for infantry since 1896.

In the cavalry special attention is similarly paid to the training of the twelve regimental signallers who form the staff of every cavalry regiment, the tuition being, as in the infantry, under Aldershot - trained officers. Our photograph shows the signallers of the 7th Dragoon Guards, who hold the second prize for cavalry signalling in the Service. The groups are shown fully equipped with heliograph and flags for day signalling, and the Begbie B.B. lamp with its limelight apparatus for night signalling, telescopes, etc.

# THE 1st BATTALION BLACK WATCH.

"THE colours of the 'Forty-twa'." What a story of valour the words suggest. No regiment has ever gained a better name for courage and dash. None has ever been more worthy of the nation's praise. It was formed in 1739 from several independent companies of Highlanders. These were clothed in the Highland dress and wore the tartans of their respective commanders. The tartan was for the most part dark, and it was this circumstance which gave rise to the name "Freicudan Du," or "Black Watch," now borne officially by the regiment. It joined the army in Flanders after the battle of Dettingen, and won distinction at Fontenoy. The Highlanders formed part of the advance guard, and were ordered to occupy the village of Vesor. Thence they advanced against

From a Photo.                                                                   By a Military Officer.
*A COMPANY OF THE BLACK WATCH.*

the French sharpshooters while the Duke of Cumberland reconnoitred the position of the enemy. When it was found necessary to retreat, the 42nd covered the retrograde movement, and, as the Earl of Crawford said, "acquired as much honour as if they had gained the battle." The regiment also took part in the Flanders Campaigns of 1746-47.

On the 3rd July, 1758, George II. ordered it to be styled the "Royal Highland Regiment of Foot," and by the title of 'Royal Highlanders' the regiment is still known. The 42nd were present in the unsuccessful attack on Ticonderoga in the same year, and a second battalion, then formed, took part in the conquest of Guadaloupe. They saw much service in America in 1759-60 and during the War of Independence, when the Highlanders fought at Long Island, Brandywine, and Fort Washington During the last-named battle they were especially conspicuous on account of their bravery.

Pyrenees, Nivelle, Orthes, and Toulouse. The 42nd formed part of the Highland Brigade in the Crimea, and were present at the Alma, Balaclava, and Sebastopol.

When the Mutiny broke out the Black Watch proceeded to India. Under Sir Colin Campbell it fought at Cawnpore, Lucknow, and the capture of Bareilly, and soon after its return home once more went on service to Ashanti.

In 1882 the 42nd proceeded to Egypt and fought at Tel-el-Kebir. They went to Suakin under Sir Gerald Graham and were present at El Teb and Tamai. Again, in 1884-85, they took part in the Nile Campaign and maintained their

THE COLOURS AND COLOUR-SERGEANTS OF THE "FORTY-TWA."     COLOUR-SERGEANT W. FOWLER.

In 1796-97 the regiment served under Sir Ralph Abercromby in the West Indies. In 1798 it was present at the capture of Minorca But it was in Egypt (1801) that the Black Watch won the admiration of all British subjects. At Alexandria it routed a demi-brigade of the French, known as the "Invincibles," and deprived it of its Standard. The 1st Battalion fought under Sir Arthur Wellesley in Portugal at Vimiera, and the 2nd at Busaco, Fuentes d'Onoro, and Ciudad Rodrigo The following year the 1st again sailed for Lisbon, and was distinguished at Salamanca, Burgos,

glorious reputation at Kirbekan. No wonder, then, that they are proud to display the honours on their colours as we see them in the illustration.

Although, as we are so often reminded, our Army at home is composed of mere boys, it is evident that abroad our soldiers have for the most part arrived at the years of discretion. The fact is amply demonstrated by the appearance of the winning team in the regimental bayonet exercise competition, and Colour-Sergeant Fowler, under whom the team was trained, is a worthy representative of the non-commissioned ranks.

From Photos.                                                                          By a Military Officer.

WINNING TEAM BAYONET EXERCISE COMPETITION.

# WITH THE FIGHTING LINE IN NORTH-WEST INDIA.

THE illustrations here given represent various phases of the operations of our troops under Sir Bindon Blood in reducing the rebellious tribes in the Swat country lying between Peshawar and Chitral.

*CAMP RUSTAM AFTER A NIGHT ALARM.*

The first picture gives a good idea of the local scenery, and shows a standing camp of the expeditionary force. Before dawn the camp had been aroused by a night alarm, and the fires then lit are still burning.

The next photo is of very great interest, for it represents the "serai" at Malakand, where the first outbreak took place, and which was so gallantly held by Colonel Meiklejohn and his garrison against the attacks of the tribesmen. The enemy

*THE "SERAI" AFTER THE FIGHT.*

were driven back at every point, but succeeded in setting fire to the "serai," which was defended by twenty-five men of the 31st Punjab Infantry, who held out gallantly as long as possible, until the fire drove them to effect their escape.

The next picture is also an especially interesting one, for it represents men actually under fire, it being a photograph taken during a skirmish in the Mahmund Valley, and

From Photos.                    By a Military Officer.

*A SKIRMISH IN THE MAHMUND VALLEY.*

*A CONVOY CROSSING THE PANJKORA.*

shows the Highland Light Infantry and the 24th Punjab Infantry extended in line. This last fine regiment is composed mostly of Sikhs, but it has also two companies of Pathans. Raised when the old Bengal Army mutinied, it has seen a fair share of frontier fighting, and in the present campaign much distinguished itself.

The next two views were taken on the Panjkora river, the first one showing a convoy of camels crossing the river,

*PANJKORA SUSPENSION BRIDGE.*

the guard being furnished by a detachment of the Highland Light Infantry; the other shows the suspension bridge with a convoy in the foreground, the bridge being a light frail structure supported by wire ropes. The next picture shows us the troops returning after an engagement. The men leading are the infantry of the Guides, while immediately behind them come the kilted pipers heading the column of the Highland Light Infantry. Note the springy step of the Guides, whose name is now as well known in England as

From Photos.                    By a Military Officer.

*RETURNING FROM A SKIRMISH.*

in India. Everyone has heard of the marvellous march of the Guides from the extreme north-west of the Punjab to Delhi during the Mutiny, and in this campaign, again, they have made a march which beats the record. They received the orders that they were to at once proceed to Malakand at 9 p.m., and in sixteen hours, in the most oppressive heat, had completed the march of thirty-two miles, ending up with a long uphill climb of seven miles.

From a Photo.                                    By a Military Officer.
*WITH THE CONVOY CAMELS.*

From a Photo.                                    By a Military Officer.
*SAPPERS MAKING A ROAD.*

In the next illustration we are again shown a convoy crossing the Panjkora river, while finally, in the last picture, we see No. 4 Company of the Bengal Sappers and Miners making a road for the passage of a field battery of the Royal Artillery.

# A FAMOUS PET.

Photo. R. Ellis, Malta.                          Copyright—Hudson & Kearns.

*THE REGIMENTAL GOAT OF THE ROYAL WELSH FUSILIERS.*

THE Royal Welsh Fusiliers have long enjoyed the privilege of leading a goat with a shield on its horns at the head of the drums. The origin of the custom is somewhat obscure, but Donkin, writing last century, mentions it as a regimental custom over a hundred years ago. It is related that at Boston, before the American War, a drummer-boy who was astride the goat was flung on the mess-table and killed. After this unfortunate accident the time-honoured if somewhat dangerous practice was discontinued. It occurred when the animal was marching round the table with the drums at the ceremony of distributing leeks on St. David's night. In the above picture the goat is seen in charge of a drummer. On the right is the sergeant-drummer, formerly known as the drum-major. For many years the goats have been presented by Her Majesty the Queen.

Photo.—F.G.O.S. Gregory & Co., 51 Strand.

Copyright.—Hudson & Kearns.

*THE TRAINING OF ARMY HORSES.*

A NYONE who has witnessed the Royal Military Tournament at the Agricultural Hall must remember to have seen an incident such as is here depicted. The horse is made to lie down at the bidding of the rider, while the latter, using the steed as a rest, engages the enemy with his carbine. To ensure the hearty response of the horse in this scene the animal must be carefully trained. This portion of its education is not always completed without trouble on the part of the tutor. Even trained horses sometimes evince a strong objection to stretch themselves on "mother earth," or become restive under fire. To a competent staff of rough-riders falls the lot of schooling the horse. The corporal of the 17th Lancers in the above illustration has just succeeded in bringing his charger to the ground. That he is a rough-rider is seen from his badge—a spur.

CPSIA information can be obtained at www.ICGtesting.com
Printed in the USA
BVOW03s2043270515

402065BV00015B/261/P